W9-CMG-135

#127

| | | | | bN | bR | bK | |
|---|---|---|---|---|---|---|---|
| bP | | | | | | bB | |
| | | | | bP | | bP | bP |
| | | | | wP | | | |
| bN | | bR | | wR | | | wP |
| | | bP | | | | | |
| | | wP | | wN | wN | wP | |
| | wP | | | | | wR | |
| | | wb | wr | | | | |

# The Chess Struggle
# In Practice \

## *Candidates Tournament*
## *Zurich 1953*

**David Bronstein** \

Translated by Oscar D. Freedman
Edited by Burt Hochberg

*David McKay Company, Inc.*
NEW YORK

286 LIB
5/9/94 E-6-3 252 CLB

794.15
B

COPYRIGHT © 1978 BY DAVID MCKAY COMPANY, INC.

All rights reserved, including the right to reproduce this book,
or parts thereof, in any form, except for the inclusion of brief
quotations in a review.

Library of Congress Catalog Card Number: 78-59140

ISBN: 0-679-130640

Manufactured in the United States of America

EUCLID PUBLIC LIBRARY

Ma '79 02815

MAY 3 1979

# Table of Contents

# Note to the Second Russian Edition

The author has set himself a difficult task: to create an original textbook on the middlegame out of the material of an international tournament of grandmasters.

Grandmaster Bronstein is well known for his profound play and for his original conception of the principles of chess. This is revealed in his avoidance of approval of grandmaster draws and in the thoroughness of his annotations.

The numerous favorable and at times even laudatory reviews of Bronstein's first literary work, as well as the testimony of readers, indicate that the author has successfully accomplished his aims.

The second edition has been slightly shortened, compared with the first, by the exclusion of outdated material. The introduction has been expanded, and errors discovered in the first edition have been eliminated.

# Translator's Note

The subject of this book, David Bronstein's first, is the candidates tournament in Neuhausen-Zurich, Switzerland, in 1953. Its theme, however, is that element of chess which we call art. Grandmaster Bronstein's intention was to freeze a moment of chess history, to say to the chess lovers of his time and of all future times: this was the state of the art at the midpoint of the twentieth century.

This translation of the second Russian edition (1960) offers the English-speaking world not only its first analysis by a grandmaster of this great and historic tournament in its entirety, but also, and more importantly, the benefits of Grandmaster Bronstein's unique insight into the very essence of chess art, that which more than any other element of the game gives us esthetic satisfaction and pleasure.

The translation was started in 1962. Oscar D. Freedman, whose first language was Russian, was then the manager of the Manhattan Chess Club in New York City, of which I was a member. On odd afternoons Oscar and I would go over games from this book, with Oscar translating aloud and I moving the pieces. We were not thinking then of translating the book, but before long we realized that this was no ordinary tournament book. Bronstein had not simply annotated games but had written about something much deeper, much more essential and valuable to the chess world. We decided to make a full translation and offer it to a publisher.

The work progressed as it had begun: with a chess set between us, Oscar would translate aloud, sentence by sentence, and I would move the pieces and write everything down. Our efforts to interest publishers in the project failed, however, in part because of the sheer size of the book, in part because of a certain clumsiness in the first-draft translation, and in part because the work was mistaken for a mere tournament book—and, at that, a tournament that had taken place a dozen years earlier.

In 1968 my friend Oscar died at the age of 75 and it somehow became important to see that his work was not wasted. A revision of the manuscript was begun, but due to the pressure of other work, it was not completed for several years. By then the popularity of chess, which was increasing dramatically in direct parallel with Bobby Fischer's successful drive toward the world championship in the early 1970s, was creating a larger market for chess books and thus a more receptive attitude on the part of publishers. And so, David McKay Company, which of all major publishers is the most active in publishing good chess books, agreed to take on the Bronstein project.

Although the translation had already been revised, I thought I should have one last look at it prior to publication. That "last look" turned into another complete revision. Again because of other work, which sometimes meant long periods without touching the translation at all, the revision took several years to complete.

Due to the effects of the economically turbulent 1970s, one of which was a fairly steep rise in the cost in book manufacturing, the English edition of Bronstein's work differs in certain respects from the original. The detailed index of openings in the original has been simplified. The summaries of the results of each round, thirty in all, have been unfortunately deleted. The text moves of some games are printed in paragraph form rather than in columns, particularly in the later rounds.

I thank Hanon D. Russell for verifying the translation and for providing much helpful advice. I thank Roger Cox for his fierce devotion to editorial principles and for listening courteously while I ranted and raved. And most of all I thank my wife, Carol, who likes David Bronstein and so decided to help, and who prepared the diagrams, and who did her very best not to make me feel guilty about leaving her alone night after night, Sunday after Sunday . . .

Burt Hochberg<br>
New York, 1977

# In Lieu of a Preface

In setting out to work on my first chess book, my thought was to put myself in the place of the reader and to remember my emotions when I opened each new book on chess, hoping to find living ideas, understandable words, accounts of the beauty of chess art. I learned much from books, and even now I remember the best of them with gratitude.

Books about chess tournaments are a distinct type of literature. The author's creative possibilities seem at first glance rather limited, for he is obliged to write about predetermined chess material not of his own making. That is not quite the case. The author can interpret the games in his own way, make generalizations, and reveal the ideas and plans actually used, as well as those which might have occurred in a given game.

A large tournament is not merely a collection of games. If the tournament participants are the strongest players in the world, the games have a definite interconnection; they are full of ideas which crystallize and develop during the course of the tournament, while the competition as a whole represents a particular stage in the development of chess thought. Hastings 1895, Petersburg 1914, New York 1924, Moscow 1935, Groningen 1946, for instance, were such tournaments. The international tournament in Switzerland unquestionably belongs among such contests.

While working on the book I proceeded on the assumption that each game was valuable, that it was a work of art produced by a creative struggle between two masters of the same class. The core of a chess game is a creative battle of plans, a struggle of chess ideas, which reaches its highest form in the middlegame.

A number of typical positions that occur as a result of the clash of plans are analyzed in the book; certain strategical concepts are examined, such as weak dark squares, the two-Bishop advantage, counterplay on various wings, the relative strengths of the pieces, overprotection, and others; and such elements of the fight as intuition, resourcefulness, determination.

The games of a grandmaster tournament take the reader into the creative sphere of the leaders of contemporary chess and show how the battle takes shape and how a work of chess art is created. The author wanted to discuss the most unexplored and most interesting stage of the chess game—the middlegame and its treatment by the grandmasters of today. That is the basic aim of the book.

The author tried not to overload the book with variations. Variations are interesting if they reveal the beauty in chess; they are useless if they go beyond what a human being is capable of calculating; they are harmful if they are substituted for the study and explanation of those positions in which intuition, imagination, and talent decide the outcome of the struggle.

At the same time I should like the chess player who reads the book to rise to a somewhat higher level of practical chess strength.

The reader will also see mistakes in the games of the tournament, but he will not condemn the masters too harshly if he appreciates the peculiarities of the chess struggle. A living human being sits at the board with the thoughts and feelings of his own day, which are sometimes far removed from chess. As he chooses a plan or even the next move he cannot help thinking about his own standing in the tournament, recalling the result of yesterday's game, watching the other participants' boards. A game is not an analysis; everything must be figured out in the mind without moving the pieces, reference books may not be consulted, advice may not be sought . . . The grandmaster gets an idea, takes a last glance at the clock—it is time to decide, to take the risk! He moves the Knight to K5. It is easy, of course, a year later, having become familiar with all the analysis and having sat for days with the position before him, for the writer to tell the reader authoritatively: "A mistake. The cautious N–K1 is to be preferred . . ."

Perhaps mistakes will be found even in my analysis and evaluations, although I have tried to reduce them to the minimum. I hope the reader will regard them with tolerance and help to correct them.

I submit my work uneasily to the judgment of the reader, and I shall consider its aims accomplished if the content of the book as a whole broadens the reader's chess horizons, increases his mastery, gives him an idea of modern chess creativity, and helps him achieve a fuller appreciation and a greater love of the full depth of chess.

# Introduction to the Second Edition

Now that the preparation of the second edition of the book has been completed, I should like to explain what I kept silent about in the introduction to the first edition four years ago. The work I submitted to the judgment of the reader was far removed from the standard commentary prevalent in chess literature. Any lack of artistic and literary qualities is especially intolerable in a chess book, which is in fact a cross between art and literature. I do not wish to speak ill of the many outstanding tournament collections and reference books, but for some years now the interest of chess players in this genre of literature has been noticeably declining, and the once unlimited demand has dwindled. In this situation, how would a literary and, regrettably, rather expensive collection be received?

I rejected the role of a collector of variations and did not want to edit a compendium of annotations. It seemed to me that the book should consist basically of the ideas and summations of the author, and the moves of all the games annotated by him. In the substance of the book I sought to reveal the richness and boundlessness of chess ideas, and to bring its form nearer a work of literature.

Judging by formal indications, the author was to some extent equal to his task: the edition sold out very quickly and approving reviews appeared. Most valuable to me, however, were the numerous letters and opinions I received from readers, not nearly all of whom were answered, I regret to say. Along with their justified individual criticisms of the book's shortcomings, they maintained their approval of its basic principles and fundamentally agreed with them. Those letters were the best reward for my work, and I take this opportunity to thank everyone who wrote to me. I must particularly thank P. A. Romanovsky for his detailed and most valuable review —for the reader and the author—in the magazine *Chess in the U.S.S.R.*

I accepted the offer to publish a second edition with pleasure, having in mind to reduce everything that was obsolete and secondary, to develop a few things further, and to supplement the introductory article to reflect the latest events in the chess world.

Thus, considerably less space is given in the second edition to the texts of games which I did not use for summarizing and explaining concepts of the art of chess. This applies especially to the games of the last rounds, when the tournament results had been determined and the intensity of the struggle had abated. Moreover, a few errors in analysis found by readers and by the author have been corrected, and the editing of the text has also been improved and some diagrams substituted.

In conclusion, I should like to express the hope that chess lovers will in future assist the author in his work with strict criticism as well as words of approval.

Inasmuch as this book is dedicated basically to the middlegame, it is appropriate to begin with a few words about the evolution of opening thought and about the modern opening repertoire.

In former times, say the second half of the last century, the game usually began with the advance of the King pawn, and in most cases Black replied P–K4. Defenses such as the Sicilian and the French were in use, of course, but were relatively rare. Not counting a few exceptions, no fewer than half of the games played in tournaments were open games, sometimes many more. At the end of the last century and the beginning of this one, a sharp increase occurred in White's preference for closed games and in Black's for semi-open games. Thus, in the Cambridge Springs tournament of 1904, the Queen's Gambit took first place among all openings, the Ruy Lopez second, and the Sicilian Defense third. Also appearing in the tournaments of the 1890s and 1900s were the Indian defenses—the first indications of a new concept.

The most outstanding tournaments of the twenties were characterized by the almost total disappearance of the open game, except for the Ruy Lopez; the prevailing openings were the Queen's Gambit and the Queen pawn openings. At the same time, White's successes with the Queen's Gambit and the Ruy Lopez gradually led to the spread of asymmetrical defensive systems—the Indian against P–Q4 and the Sicilian against P–K4. This was a very fertile period for the development of opening ideas. Victories of young grandmasters were associated with their discoveries of new openings—the Nimzovich Indian Defense, the Reti Opening, the Grünfeld Defense, the Alekhine Defense.

In the double-round tournament at Bled (1931), in which Alekhine, Bogolyubov, Nimzovich, Vidmar, Flohr, Tartakower, Spielmann, Maroczy, and others played, the Queen's Gambit and Queen pawn openings occurred seventy-seven times; of these, White won twenty-nine games and Black all of thirteen. Meanwhile, of the twenty-one games with Indian defenses, White won two games altogether, and lost . . . fourteen. Is it surprising that in the period that followed, encompassing the thirties and forties, far fewer lovers of the Queen's Gambit were to be found? The many successes of Soviet and foreign players were inseparably linked with the creation and development of new systems in the King's Indian and Sicilian defenses, as well as in the Nimzo-Indian and Grünfeld.

Today, the opening formations for White and Black can be divided into three basic groups.

Both sides, in accordance with classical principles, develop pieces, seize space, create a pawn center, avoid weaknesses, etc. This is characteristic of the struggle in most variations of the Queen's Gambit, the Ruy Lopez, and the French Defense and in some systems of the Sicilian and the Nimzo-Indian. Black realizes that the first move confers an appreciable advantage in these cases, especially in symmetrical formations, and that he has to struggle long and patiently for equality. His winning chances are slight, but a draw might, with diligence, be achieved. The result of the world championship match between J. R. Capablanca and A. A. Alekhine was typical for these openings. Thirty-three of the thirty-four games in the match opened with the Queen pawn: twenty-five of them ended in draws; six were won by White, two by Black. Today's masters refuse to go into such openings, rejecting symmetrical formations and seeking defenses with counterchances.

Thus a second group of openings appeared, in which one side is guided by classical principles while the other deliberately rejects some of them for the sake of obtaining active piece play and attacking the White pawn center, and sometimes simply for the sake of complicating the play. This group comprises the basic systems of the King's Indian Defense, the Sicilian, the Grünfeld, the Nimzo-Indian, and a few sharp, forcing variations of the Queen's Gambit.

The third group concerns openings in which White does not try to seize the central squares in the early stages but only to control them, and in the meantime he does not define the pawn structure, preserving maximum flexibility and a readiness to play a maneuvering game. Here White is willing to enter complications at a suitable moment, or to bring the game to a technical stage if he is able to obtain a positional advantage. To this group belong the Closed

Sicilian, a number of variations of the Reti Opening, the English Opening, the King's Indian Reversed, and a few others.

It must be noted that the name of an opening does not pre-determine the nature of the struggle in the opening. In the Queen's Gambit, for instance, the Orthodox System is a typical example of a struggle along classical lines, but then there are the Botvinnik System and the risky "Peruvian" variation, with their forcing play and counterchances for Black. The Queen's Indian Defense, although not among the symmetrical openings, does not give Black any real counterchances. In the Nimzo-Indian Defense, one of the most remarkable and vigorous discoveries of the "hypermodern" school of the twenties, it is possible to transpose flexibly to positional themes or to sharp variations.

The changes in opening concepts were closely correlated with the development of chess thought in general. The Queen's Gambit was most widely practiced in the period during which the principles of the positional school were dominant. With all the positive signifi-cance of those principles, one great shortcoming must be noted: the assessment of positions by their outward appearance. In the eyes of the supporters of Tarrasch, the propagandist of Steinitz's theories, such factors as backward pawns, a strong pawn center, or a superi-ority in development were decisive in the assessment of a position and the formulation of a battle plan. "One badly placed piece and the entire game is bad," said Tarrasch. To many of his contem-poraries, the principles of the positional school, clothed by Tarrasch in simple and easily understood form, seemed to be irrefutable chess wisdom.

Hence there arose the concept—which has survived to the present day—of the so-called consistent game, in which one of the players conducts his logical plan from start to finish as though he were proving a geometric theorem. In the treatment of an "ideal" game of this type, one player represents the guardian of the principles, the other the transgressor. The "good" player accumulates posi-tional advantages and puts them in a savings bank, like money to buy a motorcycle, and then, when a sufficient sum has been col-lected, throws it into a combinational attack and gives an instruc-tive mate or, even more instructively, wins the Exchange. And what, you may ask, has the other player been doing all this time? Placidly looking at his backward pawns and misplaced pieces, helplessly extending his hands, until finally—"Black resigns."

It should not be necessary to prove that such games do not occur between grandmasters of equal strength or that annotators often take the side of the winner and represent the desirable as the actual.

Chess thinking was dominated by the views of the positional school for a long time, but in the twenties its weak points were revealed. As the Queen's Gambit was being squeezed out of the repertoire, the names of Nimzovich, Reti, Tartakower, and other masters who stood absolutely opposed to the one-sided interpretation and exaggerated importance of positional principles, were appearing in first place in tournament crosstables.

The young masters of our country who were later to advance to the front rank of the world's chess players appeared in the arena around 1935, led by Botvinnik. The concerted and continual successes of Soviet players gave some the impression that the Soviet school of chess was a homogeneous totality of chess ideas and concepts. I do not think this is quite so. As a matter of fact, chess players of the most diverse styles get along well in the family of Soviet masters. For example, Spassky and Petrosian, in their manner of play and in their conception of chess, differ no less than did Spielmann and Schlechter, and Tal differs from Botvinnik no less than Lasker from Capablanca.

What, then, are the characteristic ideas of the fifties? How did the tournament in Switzerland contribute to the modern development of those ideas? What is the trend of further chess progress?

To be noted above all is the extensive knowledge that chess players have absorbed from the experience of past generations of players, which now permits them to conduct the struggle with great courage, ingenuity, imagination, and risk—all based on sober assessment of the pluses and minuses of a contemplated operation.

The understanding of positional play has grown immeasurably. Though Tarrasch taught to avoid weaknesses in one's own camp and create them in the opponent's, to accumulate small advantages, to occupy open lines, not to assume the attack until sufficient prerequisites had been met, today things are sometimes done quite differently. Weak squares and weak pawns are self-inflicted in order to mislead the opponent, open lines are ceded so as to save the Rooks for other, more promising plans, attacking plans are revealed in order to conceal one's true intentions.

The network of standard basic positions on which in one way or another every player depends has undergone extraordinary expansion. As a result, it was found that a great number of positions that had once been considered lost could be successfully, indeed actively, defended; but this required, first of all, intense calculative play, and second, the ability to leave a weak point to its fate at the critical moment and carry the fight to another region. It has only recently become clear that precisely this manner of conducting the struggle was characteristic of Emanuel Lasker's style, and, because it was not understood by any of his contemporaries, it was one of his main advantages.

Lasker, the greatest psychologist in chess, did not have only this one trait, however. He knew how to swing the pendulum of the struggle back and forth as no one else did, not exceeding the bounds of safety himself but imperceptibly pushing his opponent toward the precipice. He deliberately made second-best moves as though asking his orthodox opponent to punish him. Now even this method has been discovered and surpassed. Modern players are sometimes ready to give the opponent an apparent positional advantage as early as the first moves.

A striking example is the position that arises in the King's Indian Defense with Black's KPxQP, as well as the group of positions after 1. P–Q4 N–KB3 2. P–QB4 P–B4 3. P–Q5 P–K3 4. N–QB3 PxP 5. PxP. The Boleslavsky System in the Sicilian Defense, with the gaping hole at Black's Q4 and his hopelessly backward pawn on Q3, seems incredibly audacious, but it has withstood every trial. Some other examples will be found in the book.

The reader will also find here descriptions of the technical methods and resources used by contemporary masters in the middlegame. Technique is far more advanced today compared with a few decades ago. That which was once a rarity, a find, has today entered the public domain.

Mastery of any art is impossible without technique, as it is in chess.

However, the importance of technique in chess should not be exaggerated. At the end of a game, when we say "it is now a matter of technique," the matter often proves to be not so clear or simple. Thirty years ago, Capablanca was considered the strongest player with respect to technique, and today it is Smyslov. In analyzing the so-called technical games and endgames played by Capablanca and Smyslov, I came to the conclusion that they were based on combinational elements and long, accurate calculation, and that consequently theirs was a rare, supreme technique. In greater or lesser degree, this way of treating the endgame is used by many grandmasters. I mention here only two from the Switzerland tournament: Euwe against Stahlberg and Gligoric against Euwe.

There is one more peculiarity of contemporary practice that the reader will notice more than once in the games of the Switzerland tournament—a readiness to react quickly to a change in the opponent's plan and abruptly change one's own plan if there is a practical basis for doing so.

One of the most striking and promising tendencies brought out during the tournament was unquestionably the desire to turn to open piece play at the first opportunity. As we see, the style of Morphy seems to be irresistibly attractive to players of all times, and it is the chess player's dream—grandmasters not excepted—to bring it back and raise it to a higher style. It seems to me that we are closer to it now than at any time in the last hundred years.

The new trend, whose representatives have been insistently paving the way in U.S.S.R. championships, in the 1955 and 1958 interzonals, and in the 1959 candidates tournament, is characterized by the striving at any price to take the struggle from a logical stage to a combinational one—or, more precisely, to a calculative one. The material aspect of the question—a pawn more, an Exchange less—has no special significance here. Proof of the correctness of a combination in all variations is not an absolute requirement. Quite the contrary: in most cases it seems that the attacked side can defend himself if he can find a series of best moves. But here too the grandmaster tends to rely on himself, on his phenomenal capacity to calculate a great number of impossibly long and complex variations.

Thus the outward design of the game sometimes assumes the strangest forms. "I struggled with him [a master of the calculative style] for 32 moves and could not predict any of his replies, except once, when he had to take the Queen," said one positional master, not at all in jest.

The most outstanding representatives of the dynamic style today are undoubtedly grandmasters Mikhail Tal and Boris Spassky. Of course, complication and calculation as a method of conducting the struggle is not the only tool of these exceptionally talented and versatile chess players. They possess perfect technique in positional play, conduct the endgame brilliantly, and know the openings well: but their ability to impart a dynamic character to the game and bring it to a stage in which appraisal by external guidelines is absolutely impossible and during which, willy-nilly, one has to play move by move or even variation by variation, is just where they surpass other masters.

The time came when one of them had to test his strength and the viability of his style in single combat with the strongest player of the previous twenty years—Mikhail Moiseevich Botvinnik. The result of this contest, like those of the tournaments that preceded it, demonstrated, first of all, that in the person of Mikhail Nekhemyevich Tal we have a representative of a definite trend, and second, that the trend exists, which means that this kind of chess struggle, based both on the calculation of variations and on logic and principles, is on the rise.

The author of this book, during the twenty years of his chess life, has himself played some sharp and tense games in which he sometimes had to balance on the edge of a knife, but it would be wrong to conclude that chess is based solely on the calculation of variations. I hope that the future course of chess history will not lead to such a conclusion either, and that the new style of play will become one of the elements in the arsenal of creative and technical resources of the art of chess.

# Introduction to the English Edition
by International Grandmaster MAX EUWE
President, International Chess Federation
World Champion 1935–37

It is an honor and a pleasure for me to prepare an introduction to a book by Grandmaster David Bronstein. But this is by no means an easy task, for the world in which Bronstein lives is quite different from the one inhabited by most chess grandmasters. In reply to the often posed question whether chess is a science, a sport (that is, a struggle), or an art, Bronstein responds decisively that it is an art.

In Bronstein's view, the idea of playing chess for the sake of gaining a point or a half point will be completely outmoded in fifty or a hundred years. In his contribution to the book *Subjective Considerations About Chess*, he makes this interesting prediction of the strange future of chess:

> Chess theaters will invite grandmasters of the super class to appear as guests. Their superiority will be made manifest by the speed with which they solve problems. They will become types of intellectual magicians, performing miracles of intuition and logical brain work. Though they will bring people to ecstasy, they will suffer no particular tension because their work will be appreciated for itself, not for its results. The audience will see them as soloists with an orchestra rather than as winners or losers.

Perhaps even more remarkable in Bronstein's dream of the future is this:

> Tournaments and matches as they are known today will cease to exist; only very rarely will tournaments be organized, and then as picnics to give audiences the opportunity to return to the good old days. For the younger members of the audience

this carnival will be merely a lesson in the early days of chess history.

It is all too beautiful to be true. But, in any case, this sketch of the future identifies Bronstein as a great artist. His impressions of the Zurich Candidates Tournament of 1953 are very much his own. For one, the result of the tournament is not a matter of overriding importance to him. This illustrates not only his uniqueness as a commentator but also his modesty; for in this very strong candidates tournament Bronstein shared an honorable second place with Reshevsky and Keres, behind the winner Smyslov.

But if the result of the tournament has no significance as such, we may still ask: Do today's masters play more strongly than those who participated in the Zurich tournament twenty-five years ago? Indeed, what progress have we made since even long before that?

The level of performance in all sports improves steadily. Today the hundred meters is run in ten seconds; always heavier weights are lifted; the discus and the javelin thrown ever greater distances. Comparison in these sports is possible because we have accurate methods of measurement. Although it is not so easy to measure and compare performance in football and soccer, for instance, there is no doubt that technique in these sports has improved—as it has in chess.

What is technique? Technique is the mastery of something that can be learned. But it is more than that: it includes the ability to apply what has been learned to similar situations (although not necessarily to very complicated ones). For example, in a given position with King and pawn against King and pawn I know how to use my King to drive the enemy King away. The application of this knowledge to positions with more pawns on the board is technique. A well-known rule of Tarrasch's provides that Rooks should be placed behind passed pawns—behind the opponent's pawns to stop them, behind one's own pawns to support their advance. If I successfully apply this rule to some other Rook endings no one will call me inventive—it is merely technique. Similarly, mating the enemy King in the middlegame by virtue of superior force during an attack in which, for example, a Bishop is sacrificed on KR7 or a Knight on KN7, is more than likely a combinative sequence that has occurred very often before. The execution of this attack, then, is technique.

Technique in chess has advanced. To see this clearly, compare the situation today with that of Cambridge Springs 1904. It is hardly any wonder that we have seen so very many beautiful performances in the middlegame and endgame in these seventy-five years, for each new creative accomplishment became part of an ever-growing technical arsenal. We do not speak of technique in connection with Lasker's famous double Bishop sacrifices on KR7 and KN7 in his game with Bauer in 1889: that was a creative accomplishment, one of many by this chess genius who was to become champion of the world and hold his title longer than any of his successors. But the similar sacrificial maneuver Tarrasch used in Hamburg 1910 to defeat Nimzovich may be referred to as technique. In so far as technique is concerned, the present generation of chess players is better, much better, than their predecessors of fifty years ago, for today's players have recourse to a far larger arsenal of technical equipment. But with respect to creativity there is not much difference (with certain individual exceptions): if we compare Alekhine to Tal, Capablanca to Karpov, or Lasker to Botvinnik, I am not certain that the older generation will come out worse.

Creativity is not furthered by too much study or by uncritical imitation of precedents—indeed, overreliance on technique may be a hindrance to creativity. But many very strong players sometimes tend to be uncreative when creativity is not required; only when faced with a difficult problem do they delve more deeply into the position and use their creative abilities to find the right path.

In other words, they avoid tiring themselves by unnecessary calculation. This is an important point.

The essential difference between Bronstein, Tal, and perhaps Spassky on the one hand, and Petrosian, Smyslov, and perhaps Karpov on the other, is that Bronstein and Tal calculate continuously and extremely deeply, often without a clear result but sometimes with such success as to elicit the admiration of all chess players, whereas Smyslov and Petrosian, though capable of calculating no less profoundly than the combinational players *par excellence*, begin to calculate only if they sense that something worthwhile will come of it. Thus the latter players work in a much more economical way. Continuous analysis (calculation) is tiring, and this not only takes its toll of a player during a given game but also affects his entire career. Bronstein and Tal are clear examples of this. Though they have sparkled as no others before or since, they have done so for only five to ten years. Certainly they have not been completely extinguished, but they can no longer claim places at the very top. They have exhausted too much of their creative energy.

The economical use of creative energy is not a characteristic of a period but only of certain players between 1950 and the present. This automatically brings Fischer into the picture. Fischer's style is less pronounced than that of his contemporaries; he has an excellent grasp of all kinds of positions. He knows when a deep calculation will pay off and when it will be a waste of time. In those doubtful cases when calculation may or may not be profitable, Fischer, who dislikes uncertainty, would rather be safe than sorry. In his chess no less than in his life, he may calculate too much but never too little. The principle of chess economics thus applies to him only partially, for in his tournament play he is often clearly at odds with a rational economic distribution of effort. Even when he has been assured of first place long before the last round, he nevertheless continues to play at top strength. Although in such cases this effort is unnecessary in terms of the result of the tournament, it testifies to his qualities as a sportsman, especially with respect to the opponents he had defeated earlier, and because of this he is a great attraction to chess audiences.

Fischer and Karpov are alike in that they play with great ambition: we know that Fischer treats every game as though his life depended on it, and Karpov's ambition is demonstrated particularly by the frequency of his participation in tournaments after he obtained the world title. Having won that title by default, he has been doing everything possible to prove that he is worthy of it.

Karpov uses his resources more economically than Fischer when he has a commanding lead in a tournament. True, Karpov too sometimes wins on such occasions, but at other times he takes it easy by drawing games, especially as Black; by thus husbanding his energy economically he is laying the foundations for a long-term world championship. Karpov is primarily a positional player, but his style is not as quiet as that of Smyslov or Petrosian. However, Karpov never "forces" a position, and this accounts for the relatively large number of games he draws as Black. He has a very sound style: all his pieces participate in the struggle and it is very rare that any of them remains inactive for long. Someone wrote that Karpov's pieces seem to be linked by an invisible thread. His fine concept of positional play enables him to play intuitively much of the time, and so he can conserve energy by not using his calculative powers until they are needed.

Karpov represents the ideal balance of economy of effort and enterprising initiative. Something similar can be said of Smyslov in the 1953 Zurich tournament, but with a slightly greater emphasis on economy.

Bronstein has designated Tal and Spassky as representatives of this "dynamic" style of play, a style which he claimed would predominate in the chess of the future. At the moment it appears that Bronstein was wrong in this respect. Indeed, Tal and Spassky both made their way to the top, but their genius sparked for only a few brief years. The turning point in Tal's career is clearly marked, but in Spassky's case that point is not so clear. His style is less dynamic: in terms of combinative skill he is not a perfect representative of Bronstein's ideal, for he does not always put dynamic considerations first, preferring sometimes to rely on his extensive technical arsenal. He played best in his two encounters with Petrosian for the world championship, proving himself to be Petrosian's equal in positional play and occasionally surpassing him in combinative depth. But he lost to Fischer because he was overconfident of his capacity for dynamic play, which he was unable to use to full advantage against the American grandmaster.

Comparing the five leading players of 1953 (Botvinnik, Smyslov, Bronstein, Reshevsky, and Keres) with those of today (Karpov, Fischer, Korchnoi, Larsen or Mecking, and Spassky), I find no great difference either in strength or in style. But although the players of the 1970s are no more creative than were those of 1953, certainly their technical skill in handling the opening and the endgame is greater.

Bronstein writes admiringly of the high quality of many of the endgames played at Zurich 1953. It must be taken into consideration, however, that a great deal of home analysis was done in order to produce them—analysis of a completely different order than that done over the board with a time limit.

Here I must digress.

It is often said that the very best players are generally excellent connoisseurs of the endgame. This is true, but only when speaking of the days when the institution of seconds did not exist and when it was considered unsporting for a master to accept another master's help in analyzing a tournament or match game. But because it was difficult to know whether any such help was being used during the analysis of an adjourned game—and more difficult still to control it —the rules did not specifically forbid this practice, even though the use of such outside help obviously meant that the moves actually played did not truly represent the player's chess ability. The passage of time, however, brought seconds into the picture. The practice at that time was to play for five hours and then adjourn to the next day. So a player would spend the entire night with his seconds analyzing the multifarious possibilities of the adjourned position, which after five hours of play was usually in the endgame stage. When Lasker first heard that masters were using seconds to help with analysis, he was more indignant than surprised. "It is unheard of," he stormed, "that a third person should mix in with the analysis of my games."

Lasker was not alone in this attitude, but the chess world kept silent. Only many years later—and only in some countries—was this unavoidable evil condemned as Lasker had condemned it half a century earlier. In order to limit the amount of help a player could receive from his seconds, the United States Chess Federation proposed some years ago that the daily playing schedule be changed from simply five hours of play to five hours of play followed by two hours of rest and a further two hours of play. The two-hour rest period would certainly be insufficient for thorough and reliable analysis of a position, and, since statistics had shown that most games were concluded in less than seven hours, this proposal would considerably reduce the advantage gained by outside analysis. Thus the games would more truly represent the actual endgame skills of the players themselves. After the idea had been tested in various countries for several years, the 1976 congress of the International Chess Federation at Haifa voted overwhelmingly to adopt the five-plus-two-plus-two system. In addition to the new regulation's advantage of reducing the extent of outside analytical help, it will practically eliminate the all-night analytical session: no longer will a player's sleep be disturbed by nightmares of adjourned game positions.

While it is certainly true that endgame technique has become more refined in the twenty-five years since the tournament in Zurich 1953, this must not be taken to mean that today's players are inherently stronger in the endgame than those in 1953.

There have been interesting changes in the opening phase. As Bronstein notes, the tendency of masters to play less-known openings in tournaments and matches dates from the nineteenth century. This was due not so much to a distrust of generally accepted principles of development and center control as to a certain preference for "romantic" chess, a style that was beginning to disappear in favor of a rigid system of principles which prescribed that this or that procedure was good and another was bad.

This tendency was particularly noticeable in various new systems for Black, who until then had been shackled by the classical conception of what constituted a good opening and had thus had little opportunity to display any initiative. The enterprising player who tried an early fianchetto or tasted other forbidden fruit, hoping to present the opponent with difficult or insoluble problems in attempting to refute the new idea, did so with a guilty conscience. It was not until the 1920s that these deviations from classical precepts acquired—thanks to Reti's revolutionary *Modern Ideas in Chess*—a scientific basis, then respectability, and, finally, full acceptance.

This breakthrough in opening thought took place some thirty

years before Zurich 1953, yet the ideas expressed in Reti's historic manifesto needed still more time to take root. For example, not one pure fianchetto defense was played in this tournament, despite the certain knowledge in 1953 that the pawn center was not the only legitimate goal in the opening and that its preparation could be delayed for some time without harm. Rather, the feeling persisted that one should have at least some grip on the center. The correct answer to 1. P–Q4, therefore, was not 1. . . . P–KN3 but rather 1. . . . N–KB3 so as to control White's K4. Today 1. P–Q4 is answered by 1. . . . P–KN3 without hesitation, and 2. P–K4 is countered by 2. . . . B–N2 or 2. . . . P–Q3. These defenses did not come on the scene until the 1960s.

The handling of the Sicilian Defense has also changed. The Taimanov Variation (1. P–K4 P–QB4 2. N–KB3 P–K3 3. P–Q4 PxP 4. NxP P–QR3 5. N–B3 Q–B3) had not yet been introduced into tournament play in 1953, and the Najdorf Variation (1. P–K4 P–QB4 2. N–KB3 P–Q3 3. P–Q4 PxP 4. NxP N–KB3 5. N–B3 P–QR3) had not yet become popular. Today a great many variations of the Sicilian Defense have been analyzed very deeply, and the percentage of Sicilians played in recent tournaments is double that in Zurich 1953.

In 1953 the King's Indian and the Nimzo-Indian were very much in vogue. They are still played very often, but nowadays openings such as the Benoni, the Volga and Benko gambits, and many variations of the English Opening play prominent roles in almost every tournament. However, most well-known openings have been so thoroughly analyzed that today's masters must have a far greater knowledge of variations than their predecessors at Zurich, and it is consequently much more difficult now to spring a surprise on an opponent who is well-versed in opening theory. For this reason, some masters, notably Fischer, have gone back to an in depth study of some of the variations that had been used by Steinitz and were later abandoned as inferior.

Finally, to compare the chess scene as a whole in 1953 with that of today, and thus to answer the question posed earlier: in the twenty-five intervening years, interest in chess has doubled, material conditions for masters and grandmasters have improved considerably, and there are many more strong players today than there were then. Nonetheless, the individual player has not attained a clearly higher level of proficiency in chess.

# Round One

## Game 1

For a long time I suspected that the question of dark-square weaknesses and attacks on the dark squares that I read about in books was incomprehensible not only to me but to the writers themselves. I used to tell myself, in fact, that my opponent's dark squares were weak when his men stood on light squares and he had no dark-square Bishop. But what if he took all his pieces off the dark squares? What could I attack then?

That is how I reasoned until one day it dawned on me that a dark-square weakness meant that the pieces on the light squares were also weak. Likewise, a weakness of the light squares leads to the weakness of the men on dark squares, as in, for example, the Geller–Najdorf game in the 13th round. The key to the attack on the dark squares was to occupy them with my forces, by which I attacked my opponent's men on the light squares.

The Szabo–Geller game is one of the most graphic examples of play exploiting the dark-square weakness, and the combination possible after Black's 24th move begs to be in a textbook: it all takes place on the light squares.

## Catalan Opening

| L. Szabo | Y. Geller |
|----------|-----------|
| 1. P–QB4 | N–KB3 |
| 2. P–KN3 | P–K3 |
| 3. B–N2 | P–Q4 |
| 4. P–Q4 | PxP |
| 5. Q–R4ch | QN–Q2 |
| 6. N–KB3 | P–QR3 |
| 7. QxBP | P–QN4 |
| 8. Q–B6 | |

Szabo conceives a plan to weaken the dark squares in his opponent's camp, and he begins a subtle maneuver to bring about the exchange of dark-square Bishops in order to increase his domination of those squares.

1

| 8. . . . | QR–N1 |
|---|---|
| 9. B–B4 | N–Q4 |
| 10. B–N5 | B–K2 |
| 11. BxB | QxB |
| 12. O–O | B–N2 |
| 13. Q–B2 | P–QB4 |
| 14. PxP | NxP |
| 15. R–B1 | QR–B1 |
| 16. N–B3 | N–B3 |

An imperceptible but serious inaccuracy: Black retreats a piece from the main theater of action. The move . . . N–B3 allows a possibility based on Black's inadequate protection of his Rook on QB1: 17. NxP PxN 18. P–QN4. Szabo, however, continues to implement his plan to fix the QRP and QNP on light squares. Much better is 16. . . . N–N3, increasing Black's control of QB5 and making it difficult for White to answer P–QN4.

| 17. P–QN4 | N–R5 |
|---|---|
| 18. Q–N3 | NxN |
| 19. RxN | RxR |

| 20. QxR | O–O |
|---|---|
| 21. R–QB1 | R–Q1 |

Geller cannot contest the QB-file. After 21. . . . R–QB1 White simply takes the Rook: QxRch BxQ 23. RxBch N–K1 24. N–K5! and there is no way to prevent 25. B–B6.

**22. P–QR3      N–Q4**

Realizing that White's positional pressure will become very dangerous if he is permitted to infiltrate the seventh rank or to occupy QB5 with a Knight, Geller decides to complicate the play, at the same time preventing both threats.

| 23. Q–Q4 | P–B3 |
|---|---|
| 24. N–K1 | P–K4 |
| 25. Q–B5 | |

A consistent but rather colorless continuation of White's plan. Q–R7! is livelier, of course, maintaining control of the dark squares and attacking the opponent's men on the light squares. Black cannot eject the White Queen by 25. . . . R–R1 because of the obvious 26. BxNch, and if 25. . . . K–B1 then 26. N–Q3 R–R1 27. Q–B5, when after the exchange of Queens White's Knight occupies QB5. Finally, if 25. . . . R–Q2 an elegant little combination is possible: 26. QxB! If Black then takes the Queen, 27. BxNch followed by R–B8ch leads to the complete annihilation of the Black forces—curiously, they all die on light squares.

Perhaps Black intended to answer 25. Q–R7 with 25. . . . P–K5, and if 26. BxP then not 26. . . . N–B5? (which is refuted by the pretty 27. B–B3) but 26. . . . QxB 27. QxB QxKP, with unclear play. However, after 25. . . . P–K5 White's Bishop leaves its blocked diagonal for the adjacent one (26. B–R3), where it works well.

| 25. . . . | QxQ |
|---|---|
| 26. PxQ | |

White would keep a clear superiority in the ending by 26. RxQ, but Szabo probably thought he could force a win by combining the pin on the Knight with the threat to advance his QBP; however, Black finds the defensive maneuver R–Q2–K2–Q2.

| 26. . . . | B–B3 |
|---|---|
| 27. R–Q1 | R–Q2 |
| 28. B–R3 | R–K2 |
| 29. N–B2 | P–QR4 |
| 30. B–N2 | R–Q2 |
| 31. B–R3 | R–K2 |
| 32. K–B1 | |

Szabo refuses to repeat moves, although his position is not better. Such errors of judgment are common to all chess players, beginner to grandmaster. To lose one's objectivity toward a position is tantamount to losing the game.

| 32. . . . | K–B2 |
|---|---|
| 33. K–K1 | |

This was White's last chance to force a draw by B–N2–R3.

| 33. . . . | R–B2 |
|---|---|
| 34. R–Q3 | B–N2 |

Now White even loses his QBP.

35. N–K3 RxP 36. N–B5 B–B3 37. N–Q6ch K–B1 38. B–N2 P–N3 39. K–Q2 K–K2 40. N–K4 R–B5 41. P–B3 P–B4 42. N–B2 R–QR5 43. N–Q1 P–K5 44. PxP PxP 45. R–N3 R–Q5ch 46. K–B1 P–N5

Black's plan is simply to obtain a passed pawn and promote it to a Queen. White is unable to offer any real resistance.

47. N–K3 N–B6 48. PxP NxPch 49. K–N1 B–R5 50. R–N2 N–B6ch 51. K–B1 PxP 52. R–Q2 RxR 53. KxR K–Q3 54. N–N4 K–B4 55. P–R4 K–Q5 56. P–R5 PxP 57. N–K3 N–N8ch 58. K–K2 B–N4ch 59. K–B2 P–N6, White resigns.

# Game 2
## Nimzo-Indian Defense

| M. Najdorf | S. Reshevsky |
|---|---|
| 1. P–Q4 | N–KB3 |
| 2. P–QB4 | P–K3 |
| 3. N–QB3 | B–N5 |
| 4. P–K3 | |

The originator of this opening, Grandmaster A. Nimzovich, could hardly have imagined that thirty years later chess masters would still not have decided the basic question: whether 4. P–QR3, to force the Bishop to declare its intentions, is good or bad. If it were known to be good, then at least there would be no fruitless searching for an advantage in other variations.

| 4. . . . | P–B4 |
|---|---|
| 5. B–Q3 | O–O |
| 6. N–B3 | P–Q4 |

Nimzovich never unnecessarily occupied Black's QB4 with a pawn; he hoped that after exchanging on QB6, doubling White's pawns, he could sooner or later force White's P–Q5 and post a Knight on QB4. Much water has flowed since his day, however; modern players do not believe that in the long run it is possible to exploit the doubled pawns. One of the basic modern ideas for Black in the Nimzo-Indian Defense is immediate counterattack in the center with all available means.

| 7. O–O | N–B3 |
|---|---|
| 8. P–QR3 | BxN |
| 9. PxB | QPxP |
| 10. BxP | Q–B2 |

A position as well known and as thoroughly studied today as were the Muzio and Evans gambits a hundred years ago.

What are the principal features of this position and the main considerations that determine the plans for each side?

White's pieces and pawns seem to have a great deal of potential energy, which must be made kinetic by the advance of the center pawns and the activation of the Rooks and the tightly restricted dark-square Bishop. The most logical plan is first to play P–K4 and P–K5 to drive Black's Knight from KB3 and then to create suitable conditions for a Kingside attack.

Black, meanwhile, must prevent the advance of White's KP, or he must counterattack the White pawn center, whose stability will be reduced as soon as the KP advances to K4.

In this game Reshevsky combines both ideas for Black and obtains a favorable placement of his pieces, while Najdorf struggles in vain to realize his plans.

## 11. P–QR4

Of all the possible and usual continuations here, this one seems least logical because it solves only one part of the problem—the development of the Bishop, and even then to a poor location. Since Black's QBP can be readily supported, White's Bishop will not be very effective; moreover, the isolated pawn on QR4 does not enhance White's position.

| 11. . . . | P–QN3 |
| 12. B–R3 | B–N2 |
| 13. B–K2 | KR–Q1 |
| 14. Q–B2 | N–QR4 |
| 15. PxP | PxP |
| 16. P–B4 | B–K5 |
| 17. Q–B3 | QR–N1 |

A new weakness has appeared in White's camp: QN3 will remain under Black's control, for White cannot play QR–N1 and N–Q2 is unfavorable.

| 18. KR–Q1 | RxRch |
| 19. RxR | B–B3! |

Black begins a carefully planned siege of the QRP.

| 20. Q–B2 | P–KR3 |
| 21. P–R3 | N–N6 |

Black has no time to transfer his Knight to QN3; if 21. . . . N–Q2 22. B–N2 N–N3 then 23. Q–B3, with threats to KN7 and QR5.

| 22. B–N2 | N–Q2 |
| 23. Q–B3 | P–B3 |

Black has a strategically won game: White's QRP is lost, and his pair of Bishops cannot be put to effective use. In this difficult situation, Najdorf utilizes the vitality of his position in a desperate attempt to save the game by tactical means.

## 24. N–R2

As time pressure approaches there is less strategy and more tactics.

24. . . .             N–N3

How can White defend against the threat of . . . NxRP? He does not have to answer, for Reshevsky, with four minutes left for the remaining sixteen moves, offered a draw. Apparently he could not fully calculate the consequences of

White's combination: 25. N–N4 NxRP 26. NxBPch PxN 27. QxP.

Immediately after the game, and then in his published comments, Najdorf proved that he definitely had a draw; for instance, 27. . . . NxB 28. B–N4 and perpetual check by BxPch and B–B5ch is unavoidable. A pretty variation is 28. . . . Q–KN2 29. BxPch K–R2 30. B–B5ch K–R1 31. R–Q8ch RxR 32. QxRch Q–N1 33. Q–B6ch. If Black does not take the RP on his 25th move but plays P–K4, then 26. Q–B2 followed by Q–N6 should lead to perpetual check.

White's problem would be more difficult if Reshevsky played 24. . . . BxRP instead of N–N3, leaving the Knight to defend the Kingside. Then 25. N–N4 would not be so effective because of 25. . . . P–K4 26. Q–B2 N–B1.

Another possibility after 24. . . . N–N3 25. N–N4 is 25. . . . N–Q5 and, for instance, 26. PxN NxRP, etc. The purpose of 25. . . . N–Q5 is to close White's QB3–KB6 diagonal and thus prevent NxBPch and QxBP. It was impossible to calculate all these variations in time pressure, so Reshevsky preferred to offer a draw.

## Game 3
### English Opening

| T. Petrosian | P. Keres |
|---|---|
| 1. P–QB4 | P–QB4 |
| 2. N–KB3 | N–KB3 |
| 3. P–Q4 | PxP |
| 4. NxP | P–K3 |
| 5. P–KN3 | P–Q4 |
| 6. B–N2 | P–K4 |

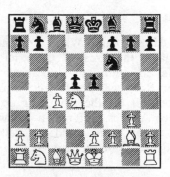

Keres's active opening play is quite unlike his opponent's slow play. Making use of the tactical possibility 7. N–KB3 P–Q5 8. NxKP Q–R4ch, Keres gets two strong central pawns which only await an opportunity to advance.

| 7. N–B2 | P–Q5 |
|---|---|
| 8. O–O | N–B3 |
| 9. N–Q2 | B–KN5 |
| 10. N–B3 | P–QR4 |

It is time to think about castling and developing the Rooks to support a pawn advance. The tempting plan to castle long—10. . . . BxN 11. BxB P–K5 12. B–N2 P–KR3

13. P–N3 Q–Q2 14. B–N2 O–O–O—does not work because on his 11th move White takes the Bishop with the pawn, which later moves to B4 and breaks up the enemy's central pawns. The text move averts White's possible P–QN4.

**11. B–N5 B–QB4**

Black creates the threat . . . P–K5, but White finds a way to keep the pawn from advancing. After . . . B–K2! the blockade would not be possible, and White would be practically forced to trade on KB6 to prevent the threatened pawn advance.

**12. P–K4 P–KR3**
**13. BxN QxB**
**14. N/2–K1 Q–K3**

White's Q4 is undoubtedly the most important point in the position; it is through this point that the action of Black's KB against the White King and of a Black Rook against the White Queen must pass. A Black Knight on that square would restrict the White Queen by taking four of its squares, and it would also strengthen the pin on White's Knight. With his next obvious move White reduces the significance of this network of communications virtually to zero. The blockaded pawn on Q5 frustrates the Bishop and the QR, which had high hopes of speeding to Q1. This knot could have been cut at the cost

of a pawn—14. . . . P–Q6— with very promising play.

**15. N–Q3 B–K2**
**16. P–KR3 BxN**

Black cannot take the RP because after 16. . . . BxP 17. BxB QxB 18. N/QxP NxN 19. NxN he loses either his QP or his right to castle. The Bishop cannot retreat to R4 because of 17. NxQP!

**17. QxB QxBP**
**18. KR–B1 Q–K3**

**19. Q–B5**

The fine concluding move of White's system of defense. It is based on combinational motifs. Black loses if he exchanges Queens and continues P–B3: 19. . . . QxQ 20. PxQ P–B3 21. RxN! PxR 22. BxPch K–B2 23. B–Q5ch! and then the QR is captured. If Black defends his KP with his Bishop, White will have a positional advantage after the exchange of Queens. On 19. . . . Q–Q3, strong is 20.

P–B4 P–KN3 21. PxP or 20.
R–B5.

**19. . . . B–Q3 20. QxQch
PxQ 21. P–R3 K–Q2 22. B–
B1 P–R5 23. N–K1 R–R4 24.
R–B2 R–QB1 25. QR–B1 N–
R2 26. RxR NxR 27. B–B4
B–K2**

A clearly drawn position has
emerged: White's Knight now
returns to Q3, and Black is unable to break through. Keres
continues the game to the 41st

move and adjourns in order to
look for some hidden chance.

**28. N–Q3 N–Q3 29. P–B3
NxB 30. RxN B–Q3 31. K–B2
R–R3 32. K–K2 P–KN4 33.
K–Q1 R–R1 34. K–K2 P–R4
35. R–B1 R–R1 36. R–KR1
P–R5 37. P–KN4 P–N4 38.
R–QB1 R–QN1 39. K–Q1 R–
N3 40. R–B2 R–N1 41. R–B1
R–QB1**

The game was agreed drawn
without resumption of play.

# Game 4
## Ruy Lopez

**Y. Averbakh**      **V. Smyslov**

| | |
|---|---|
| 1. P–K4 | P–K4 |
| 2. N–KB3 | N–QB3 |
| 3. B–N5 | P–QR3 |
| 4. B–R4 | N–B3 |
| 5. O–O | B–K2 |
| 6. R–K1 | P–QN4 |
| 7. B–N3 | P–Q3 |
| 8. P–B3 | O–O |
| 9. P–KR3 | N–QR4 |
| 10. B–B2 | P–B4 |
| 11. P–Q4 | Q–B2 |

The Tchigorin Defense of the
Ruy Lopez is usually a familiar
guest in contemporary competitions, but in the Zurich
tournament it was seen only six
times. White concentrates his
forces for a Kingside attack,
but this attack can hardly reach
its culmination because today's
grandmasters know how to set
up a solid defensive position. It

is no accident that in recent
times most games with this
variation have ended in draws.

| | |
|---|---|
| 12. QN–Q2 | B–Q2 |
| 13. N–B1 | KR–K1 |
| 14. N–K3 | B–KB1 |
| 15. B–Q2 | P–N3 |
| 16. QR–B1 | |

It is difficult to see the connection between White's last
two moves and his strategical
plan: the Bishop on Q2 and the
Rook on QB1 are no more
active than they were on their
original squares. After this loss
of two tempos White has no real
prospects on the Kingside. Having chosen piece play on this
flank, Averbakh does not want
to assume the added risk of
advancing his KNP.

| | |
|---|---|
| 16. . . . | N–B3 |
| 17. PxBP | PxP |

| 18. | N–R2 | QR–Q1 |
| 19. | Q–B3 | B–N2 |
| 20. | KR–Q1 | B–K3 |
| 21. | B–N1 | Q–K2 |

In the first round the players wrestle without much bloodshed; so far not a single soldier has crossed the border of his territory. Each opponent keeps the scene of his intended action as secret as possible.

| 22. | N/2–N4 | NxN |

| 23. | NxN |

Black was ready to answer 23. PxN with 23. . . . Q–R5.

| 23. | . . . | N–R4 |
| 24. | P–QN3 | N–B3 |
| 25. | B–K3 | RxRch |
| 26. | QxR | R–Q1 |
| 27. | Q–B3 | R–Q2 |
| 28. | R–Q1 | P–N5 |

As a result of White's slow play Black has a slight advantage. He now wants to occupy

Q5 with a Knight. A plan with . . . P–B5 deserves consideration, and to this end 28. . . . P–QR4 is not bad.

**29. RxR**

| 29. | . . . | BxR |
| 30. | N–R6ch |

Smyslov was not afraid of this check, intending simply to retreat to B1, but at the last moment he saw that this would be answered by the knife thrust 31. BxP!, and the Queen is lost. He must give up his dark-square Bishop, which in other circumstances could have been fatal.

| 30. | . . . | BxN |
| 31. | BxB | PxP |
| 32. | QxP | N–Q5 |

Drawn. The centralized Black Knight fully compensates for the strong position of the Bishop on R6.

# Game 5

It is difficult to be objective when annotating one's own games. Variations favoring the annotator always appear interesting—one talks about them willingly and in detail—but variations favoring the opponent are generally not clear. One usually looks for (and usually finds) justification for one's mistakes, but those of the opponent seem natural and therefore require no explana-tion. For this reason it is neces-sary to state, before I begin to annotate my game from the first round, that Black does not have a decisive advantage for a very long time, almost until the very end. White loses this game for a psychological reason: he fails to notice the critical moment when it is time to think about a draw. I will try to clarify the purely chess reasons in my notes.

## King's Indian Defense

| M. Taimanov | D. Bronstein |
|---|---|
| 1. P–Q4 | N–KB3 |
| 2. P–QB4 | P–B4 |
| 3. P–Q5 | P–KN3 |
| 4. N–QB3 | P–Q3 |
| 5. P–K4 | P–QN4 |

What does Black achieve by sacrificing a pawn? First, he weakens the advance-guard of the White pawn chain—the QP —and then, after Black's in-evitable P–QR3 followed by White's NPxRP, he obtains the good diagonal QR3–KB8 for his QB, which has fewer prospects on the QB1–KR6 di-agonal. Other factors that favor the sacrifice are the two open files that give Black active play against White's QNP and QRP. Black's Bishop on KN2 should not be forgotten, since in this system Black deliberately re-tains his KP on K2, and this automatically increases the Bishop's scope. An interesting strategical idea here, which is inherent in other variations of the King's Indian, is the de-velopment of the QR without moving it.

There are negative aspects of the sacrifice, of course, the main one being the loss of a pawn. If White can gradually overcome his difficulties he will clearly have winning prospects in the endgame. It is for this last rea-son that the variation was used only once in this great tourna-ment. I went into it, however, partly because I did not want to start the tournament with a long defense, to which Black is usually condemned in "normal" continuations.

| 6. PxP | B–KN2 |
|--------|-------|
| 7. N–B3 | O–O |
| 8. B–K2 | P–QR3 |

Up to this point, one might have hoped to regain the pawn; now it is a real sacrifice.

| 9. PxP | BxP |
|--------|-----|
| 10. O–O | |

I once had a similar position as White against Lundin in Stockholm 1948. I exchanged Bishops and Black recaptured with the Knight, which he then transferred to Q5 via B2 and N4. Thinking this maneuver was too slow for Black, in the present game I recapture with the Rook, intending to develop the QN via Q2–N3 to R5 and to trade it for White's QN in order to weaken the defense of the QRP and QNP.

| 10. . . . | Q–B2 |
|-----------|------|
| 11. R–K1 | QN–Q2 |
| 12. BxB | RxB |
| 13. Q–K2 | |

Taimanov intends P–K5 to break up Black's position, but

this move will not be tactically feasible. Instead of R–K1 and Q–K2, more prospects were offered White by B–KB4 and Q–Q2, followed possibly by placing the Rooks on QB1 and QN1, with the gradual evacuation of all the pieces and pawns from the Bishop's long diagonal in view. Then would be a good time to prepare P–QN4 and start the actual realization of the extra pawn. That, incidentally, is how I played against Lundin, and I think it was the correct plan.

| 13. . . . | KR–R1 |
|-----------|-------|
| 14. P–KR3 | |

Taimanov is not satisfied with the aforementioned 14. P–K5 because of 14. . . . PxP 15. NxP NxN 16. QxN QxQ 17. RxQ K–B1.

| 14. . . . | N–N3 |
|-----------|------|
| 15. B–N5 | N–K1 |
| 16. B–Q2 | |

Again 16. P–K5 PxP 17. NxP P–B3 does not work; nevertheless, it is not necessary to retreat the Bishop. Better is 16. P–R3, offering Black a pawn with the object of exchanging the dark-square Bishops: 16. . . . BxN 17. PxB RxP 18. QR–B1. Black would still be active on the Queenside, but his King would be surrounded by dangerous weaknesses on the dark squares.

| 16. . . . | N–R5 |
|---|---|
| 17. NxN | RxN |
| 18. B–B3 | BxB |

I did not want to capture on R7 because White would then reach his goal: 18. . . . RxP? 19. RxR RxR 20. P–K5, and Black has nothing to attack on the Queenside whereas White is beginning to make dangerous threats in the center.

| 19. PxB | Q–R4 |
|---|---|
| 20. Q–Q3 | Q–R3 |

Black's superiority in the ending is based on the fact that the anchor pawn on K2 is easily defended because it is still in the rear. White's pawns on QB3 and K4 make excellent targets for Black's Rooks. If White's KP advances, his QP is weakened. A few variations show this concretely: 21. QxQ R/1xQ 22. R–K2 N–B3, or 22. P–K5 N–B2, or 22. QR–N1 RxRP 23. R–N8 R–R1 24. KR–N1 R–R8. Taimanov correctly avoids exchanging Queens on R6, and he should avoid the exchange later.

| 21. Q–Q2 | RxRP |
|---|---|
| 22. RxR | QxR |
| 23. P–K5 | |

Either White is overestimating his chances in the ending or he simply does not see the strength of Black's 24th move.

| 23. . . . | QxQ |
|---|---|
| 24. NxQ | |

| 24. . . . | PxP |
|---|---|
| 25. RxP | K–B1 |

Black has a weak pawn on QB4, and all White has to do to guarantee a theoretical draw is, for example, to exchange Knights and give up both his Queenside pawns for Black's QBP, since four pawns against three on the same side in a Rook ending is usually not enough to win. However, this will not be so easy to accomplish.

**26. N–N3**

Grandmaster Taimanov is a born optimist. Having safely escaped his difficulties, does he really think he can simply win the Black pawn? Now 26. K–B1 is better for the ensuing ending, after which there would be much less danger of losing.

| 26. | . . . | P–B5 |
| 27. | N–B5 | R–R8ch |
| 28. | K–R2 | N–B3 ! |

Meeting the threat of N–Q7ch and threatening to attack White's QBP. It soon becomes clear that Black can attack the Kingside pawns, too. A Rook behind enemy lines is a formidable force.

| 29. | N–K4 | N–Q2 |
| 30. | R–N5 | R–R7 |
| 31. | R–N4 | |

White almost lost his Knight. If 31. K–N3 P–B4; or if 31. K–N1 then R–K7 32. N–N3 R–K8ch 33. K–R2 P–B4.

| 31. | . . . | P–B4 |
| 32. | R–B4 | N–N3 |
| 33. | N–N5 | NxP |
| 34. | R–Q4 | |

If White takes the pawn on his B4 he loses his KBP, and the attempt to win White's KRP is parried as follows: 34. RxP RxP 35. NxPch K–N2 36. N–N5 RxPch 37. KxR N–K6ch and the Knight ending is won for Black.

| 34. | . . . | N–N3 |
| 35. | R–Q8ch | K–N2 |
| 36. | P–B4 | P–R3 |
| 37. | N–K6ch | K–B2 |
| 38. | N–Q4 | N–R5 |
| 39. | R–QB8 | NxP |
| 40. | RxP | |

If the Knights were off the board the game would end in a draw, but Black's Knight succeeds in forking.

| 40. | . . . | N–Q4 |
| 41. | N–B3 | |

White defends the KBP, but . . .

| 41. | . . . | RxPch |
| 42. | K–R1 | R–KB7 |
| | **White resigns** | |

## Game 6
### King's Indian Defense

M. Euwe                    A. Kotov

| 1. | P–Q4 | N–KB3 |
| 2. | P–QB4 | P–B4 |
| 3. | P–Q5 | P–K3 |
| 4. | N–QB3 | PxP |
| 5. | PxP | P–Q3 |
| 6. | N–B3 | P–KN3 |
| 7. | P–KN3 | B–N2 |
| 8. | B–N2 | O–O |
| 9. | O–O | P–QR3 |

The system of development Black has chosen is not positionally ideal, but he does have a few trumps: the open K-file, good diagonals for both Bishops, and three pawns against two on the Queenside. On his part, White usually places a Knight on QB4 and organizes pressure against Black's QP—the key to the enemy fortress. In this game Euwe decides to do battle on the Queenside and strives to create weak points there which he can occupy with his pieces. The game later becomes interesting due to the aggressive play of both opponents, who do not balk at sacrifices.

| 10. P–QR4 | QN–Q2 |
|-----------|-------|
| 11. N–Q2  |       |

A typical maneuver in this position: White transfers his Knight to QB4 and plays P–R5, neutralizing his opponent's Queenside pawn majority by blockading it; if Black plays P–QN4, a White Knight gets to QR5 and QB6.

| 11. . . . | R–K1 |
|-----------|------|
| 12. P–R5  | P–QN4 |
| 13. PxP e.p. | NxNP |
| 14. N–N3  | Q–B2 |
| 15. N–R5  | B–Q2 |
| 16. P–R3  | B–N4 |
| 17. B–K3  | KN–Q2 |

Black activates his pieces. He plans to bring his Knight from Q2 to QB5 via K4, or to play P–B5 and then N–QB4.

**18. Q–N3**

Hindering Black's plan. White is not worried about the loss of his KP because of the compensating attack on the dark squares; e.g., 18. . . . BxN 19. QxB BxP 20. KR–K1 B–N4 21. B–R6 P–B3 22. R–K6, or first 22. P–N3 with the threat R–K6.

| 18. . . . | N–B3 |
|-----------|------|

Black had the strong 18. . . . QR–N1 at his disposal, emphasizing the insecure position of White's Queen; for instance, 19. NxB PxN 20. N–B6 R–N2, and 21. QxP is impossible because of 21. . . . NxP. The threat of . . . P–B5 would be even stronger with the Rook on QN1. The plan chosen by Black is less effective. He sacrifices the Exchange hoping to create complications.

| 19. KR–B1 | B–Q2 |
|-----------|------|
| 20. Q–Q1  |      |

White prepares the decisive break P–QN4, but Black prevents it by giving up his Rook for the Bishop.

| 20. . . . | RxB |
|-----------|-----|
| 21. PxR   | B–R3 |
| 22. Q–Q3  | R–K1 |
| 23. K–R2  | RxP |
| 24. QxP   |     |

24. .... R-K4 25. R-B1 B-QB1 26. Q-N5 B-Q2 27. N-B6 K-N2 (Neither now nor on the last move could White's QP be taken. If 27. .... QNxP, White exchanges twice on Q5 and checks on K7 with the Knight.) 28. R-R6 N-B1 29. Q-N8 QxQ 30. NxQ B-B4 31. R-B6 R-K1 32. P-K4 B-Q2 33. P-K5 RxP 34. NxB NxN 35. RxN R-K6 36. R-B6 N-K4 37. RxQP R-Q6 38. R-Q1 R-K6 39. R-QB6, Black resigns.

## Game 7
### King's Indian Defense

| G. Stahlberg | I. Boleslavsky |
|---|---|
| 1. P-Q4 | N-KB3 |
| 2. P-QB4 | P-KN3 |
| 3. P-KN3 | B-N2 |
| 4. B-N2 | O-O |
| 5. N-QB3 | P-Q3 |
| 6. N-B3 | QN-Q2 |
| 7. O-O | P-K4 |
| 8. P-K4 | R-K1 |
| 9. P-KR3 | PxP |
| 10. NxP | N-B4 |
| 11. R-K1 | P-QR4 |
| 12. Q-B2 | |

About fifteen years ago the King's Indian was employed in Soviet tournaments only by those few players who wanted to avoid the passive and well-known theoretical variations of the Queen's Gambit; abroad this opening was hardly played at all. It suffices to say that a very short time ago—in the Match-Tournament for the World Championship in 1948 —the King's Indian was seen in only two of the fifty games. In the Zurich tournament, however, every third game beginning with P-Q4 turned out to be a King's Indian, and now foreign chess players use it no less than we do.

The position in the diagram is well known to theory, and the move played is one of the latest. White wants to develop his Bishop to K3 but first he has to defend his KP!

It is true that the Knight on Q4 is unprotected for the moment and that Black can win the central pawn by 12. . . . KNxP 13. NxN BxN; but then it will be White's move, and he gains control of KB6 by 14. B–N5 Q–Q2 15. N–B6ch BxN 16. BxB, depriving Black of his "Indian" Bishop. But without it the whole King's Indian setup makes no sense, and the extra pawn would not ease Black's situation. The few attempts to prove otherwise all ended in Black's utter devastation. That is why no one is tempted by the KP anymore.

| 12. . . . | P–R5 |
| 13. B–K3 | P–B3 |
| 14. QR–Q1 | KN–Q2 |

The King's Indian is characterized by intense struggle along the entire front. The system White has chosen in the present game assures him of the gain of considerable territory, not only in the center but also on the Kingside.

The reader should be warned against getting the wrong impression. White's task of converting his significant spatial advantage into a material one is not an easy one. The secret of the durability of the King's Indian is that in ceding territory Black obtains some hardly noticeable but definite advantages. The main ones are

his two long-ranging Bishops, his excellently placed Knight on QB4, and his Rook on K1—all constantly aimed at White's KP. And one must not forget the pawns. The "weak" pawn on Q3 is merely waiting to advance to Q4, and White must keep a watchful eye on it. Black's outside QRP serves an important function, for it always threatens to move to R6, upsetting White's plans in that area, and this forces him to redouble his efforts to protect his QB3 and QB4. If 12. Q–B2 is White's latest theoretical accomplishment, the same can be said of Black's 14. . . . KN–Q2. Black used to play . . . Q–R4, but after 15. B–KB4 he had to place his KB or KR in an inferior position. Now the QP can be covered by N–K4.

| 15. P–B4 | Q–R4 |
| 16. B–B2 | N–N3 |
| 17. B–B1 | B–Q2 |
| 18. P–R3 | |

Stahlberg decides once and for all to safeguard his position by preventing Black's pawn from getting to R6. The square QN3 is thus deprived of its pawn protection, but the QNP and its surroundings, as well as the QRP and the Knight on B3, are strengthened.

The next phase of the game —until around the 30th move —consists of delicate maneuvering as both sides probe weak points. White prepares P–K5,

Black P–Q4 and P–KB4, and each side tries to prevent the other's breaks.

| 18. . . . | QR–Q1 |
|-----------|-------|
| 19. K–R2 | B–QB1 |
| 20. N–R2 | N/3–Q2 |
| 21. B–N2 | N–B3 |
| •22. N–QB3 | R–Q2 |
| 23. N–B3 | R/2–K2 |

The next two moves by both White and Black are not altogether customary: Black is bringing maximum force to bear against the KP, and White is trying to distract him by threatening to take the QP. In the implementation of this recent highly characteristic idea, the pride of White's position—his centralized Knight—can find no better spot than its original KN1, for otherwise it would be in the way of his other pieces.

I think now is the time to acquaint the reader with the mysteries of Black's QP in the King's Indian. Even though it is situated on an open file and is constantly exposed to attack, it is not an easy nut to crack. The simplest method for White is apparently to retreat the Knight from Q4, but Q4 is precisely where White needs the Knight to be: its jobs are to supervise QN5, QB6, K6, and KB5 and to neutralize the influence of Black's KB. Only after White has taken steps against possible Black attacks (P–R6, B–K3, P–KB4) can his Knight leave the center, but during that time Black can regroup his forces.

So the weakness of the QP proves to be imaginary. Contemporary methods of play in the opening recognize the illusory weakness of such pawns. But it was just because of the "eternal" weakness of Q3 that the King's Indian was long considered a dubious opening.

## 24. N–KN1

In five moves the Knight returns to help the KP cross the frontier. It is possible to advance the pawn immediately and give up control of KB5, which could then be occupied by Black's QB. After 24. P–K5 B–B4 White would have to resolutely sacrifice his Queen and play pawn takes Knight. This would win for White, but the simple 24. . . . PxP would give Black excellent play.

White can now win the QRP, but the dark-square Bishop, which is needed by White no less than by Black, is far too high a price.

With his 24th move Boleslavsky invites the White Rook finally to capture the long-attacked point, but after 25. . . . N–N3 Black's Knight would invade QB5. Stahlberg makes very probably the most correct decision: to lay seige to the QP and force the exchange of the "Indian" Bishop.

| 24. . . . | KN–Q2 |
|---|---|
| 25. B–Q4 | N–N3 |
| 26. BxB | KxB |
| 27. RxP | NxBP |
| • 28. R/6–Q1 | B–K3 |

Although the general contours of the position have not changed, an important event has occurred: the dark-square Bishops, White's QBP, and Black's QP have been laid to rest.

The absence of the dark-square Bishops forces each player to make appropriate adjustments in his original strategical plan. For example, Black must first consider how to protect himself from the danger on the long diagonal, as well as from the possible advance of White's KBP to B6 and his Queen to KR6. In view of the seriousness of the danger, Boleslavsky's last move was very good: his Bishop is ready for action on the KN1–QR7 diagonal, and the KBP will go to B3 to protect the King from attack on the long diagonal. The pawn's place will be taken by the Bishop. Meanwhile, White will be constantly striving to break through his opponent's new line of defense. He must resolve to spare nothing in this effort, for otherwise his opponent will seize the initiative. Then the weaknesses in White's position (QN3, the lack of pawn control of Q3, K3, and KB3, the passive role of the Bishop), hardly noticeable during the attack, will become targets for various combinations.

| • 29. Q–B2 | P–B3 |
|---|---|
| 30. N–B3 | B–B2 |
| 31. P–K5 | |

A sacrifice in the style of Stahlberg—an expert tactician and a master of the Kingside attack. White cannot be allowed to remain on K5 and so the pawn must be eliminated. But this opens the KB-file, and the Black King may find itself in a dangerous situation.

| 31. . . . | PxP |
|---|---|
| 32. NxKP | NxN |
| 33. RxN | RxR |
| 34. PxR | RxP |

**35. R–KB1  R–B4**

Boleslavsky, despite his great time pressure and the heat of the battle, refuses the sure draw he can have by the accurate retreat 35. . . . Q–B2, defending against the two threats QxBch and Q–B6ch.

His hope of exploiting his extra pawn cannot be realized in view of his exposed King. Even if Black succeeds in avoiding the many dangers and wards off the attack, White is sure to find perpetual check.

**36. Q–Q4ch**

Solving part of White's problem: the Queen occupies the long diagonal.

**36. . . .  K–N1**
**37. RxR  PxR**
**38. Q–K5**

Judging by his last two moves, Black very likely overlooked this modest move. Now his position becomes alarming.

**38. . . .  Q–N3!**

The pin on the Knight must be broken at once. The threat was not only 39. QxP but also 39. P–KN4, and if 39. . . . PxP 40. N–K4. Black's timely transfer of the Queen to N3 averts the main danger.

The attempt to hold the pawn on KB4 by 38. . . . B–N3 ends sadly because in addition to having the move P–KN4 White can set up a new pin to drive

Black's King into a mating net: 39. B–B1 Q–N3 40. B–B4ch K–B1 41. Q–B6ch K–K1 42. N–Q5. It is not possible to go into such a variation in time pressure. Now White restores the material balance while Black's King remains insecure.

**39. QxP  B–N3**
**40. Q–K5  N–Q6**

This move, made at the time control, serves to remind Black's opponent that there are targets in his camp, too. Black's Queen is ready to take the QNP or, under favorable conditions, to go to KB7 and threaten N–K8.

**41. Q–K6ch**

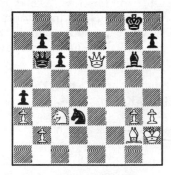

**41. . . .  K–N2?**

This move was written on the scoresheet, which was placed in an envelope and handed to the referee. Stahlberg did not know the sealed move, of course, so he had to analyze both of Black's possibilities, 41. . . . K–N2 and 41. . . . B–B2.

**42. Q–K7ch**

When adjourning, Boleslavsky was counting on 42. N–Q5 and thought that after 42. . . . QxP White would have at best perpetual check. The strong move actually played substantially changes the situation.

Retreating to KN1 is out of the question now because White continues 43. N–Q5 anyway. So the Bishop must be interposed, but now the Knight can get to Q6 via K4. Therefore, instead of 41. . . . K–N2 the preferable sealed move was 41. . . . B–B2. White could then get perpetual check or win the QRP by 42. Q–N4ch, but the invasion of White's KB7 by Black's Queen would fully compensate for this loss. The most likely outcome—a draw. Actually, the game does end in a draw, but after interesting new adventures.

| 42. . . . | B–B2 |
|-----------|------|
| 43. N–K4  | QxP  |

| 44. N–Q6  | Q–KB7 |
|-----------|-------|
| 45. N–K8ch |      |

Though far from obvious, these moves seem correct . . .

| 45. . . .  | K–N1 |
|------------|------|
| 46. N–B6ch | K–N2 |
| 47. N–R5ch | K–N3 |
| 48. P–N4   | N–B4 |

Drawn, on Stahlberg's offer. The attempt to end the game by a mating combination with a Queen sacrifice—49. P–R4 P–R3? 50. QxN!! QxQ 51. B–K4ch—would be repulsed by 49. . . . N–K3.

48. P–R4 wouldn't have won either: Black answers 48. . . . P–R3, and after 49. Q–K4ch KxN 50. K–R3, with the apparently unstoppable mate threat P–N4, Black has the counterthrust 50. . . . N–B5ch, liquidating the danger.

However, P–R4 would have won on his 45th move (instead of N–K8ch).

# Round Two

## Game 8
### Queen's Gambit Declined

| A. Kotov | G. Stahlberg |
|----------|--------------|
| 1. P–Q4 | N–KB3 |
| 2. P–QB4 | P–K3 |
| 3. N–KB3 | P–Q4 |
| 4. N–B3 | B–K2 |
| 5. PxP | PxP |

White's usual plan in the Exchange Variation of the Orthodox Defense is a minority pawn attack. He puts his Rooks on the QN- and QB-files, advances his QNP, and exchanges it on QB6, giving Black an isolated pawn. This plan is too straightforward and not dangerous for Black, as proved in many master games. Black eventually gains the K-file, which gives him active piece play on the Kingside and approximate equality.

Kotov, far from thinking of a draw in this game, exchanges pawns in the center for an entirely different reason. Following the tradition of the past masters, he plans to castle long and to attack on the Kingside

with his pawns. For the next five to seven moves White cleverly disguises this intention.

| 6. B–B4 | P–B3 |
|---------|------|
| 7. Q–B2 | P–KN3 |
| 8. P–K3 | B–KB4 |
| 9. B–Q3 | BxB |
| 10. QxB | QN–Q2 |
| 11. P–KR3 | N–B1 |

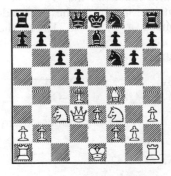

Black's last five moves were links in a single chain. Stahlberg is most likely the only contemporary grandmaster who maintains the Orthodox Defense in his repertoire, and he plays it like a virtuoso. The system with 7. . . . P–KN3 and the transfer of the Knight to K3 before castling is his invention. Neither Kotov in this game nor the author of these lines in the second half of this tournament nor even World Champion Botvinnik in Budapest 1952 were able to show the negative side of the Swedish grandmaster's favorite defense.

**12. P–KN4**

Kotov has been keeping his "military secret" for a long time, and only now reveals his true intentions.

| 12. . . . | N–K3 |
|---|---|
| 13. B–N3 | |

This move is definitely inconsistent here; it would be good if White intended to carry out a pawn attack on the Queenside, but inasmuch as he has advanced a pawn to KN4, the more provocative B–K5 is better.

| 13. . . . | Q–R4 |
|---|---|
| 14. N–Q2 | O–O |

Boldly castling under enemy fire.

**15. O–O–O**

White replies in a similar vein. The battle begins . . .

| 15. . . . | B–N5 |
|---|---|
| 16. K–N1 | BxN |
| 17. QxB | QxQ |
| 18. PxQ | |

. . . and here it ends. As a result of the exchanges, the QNP is now on QB3. Each side is satisfied with the changed situation: White has obtained a new open file and moved one of his pawns closer to the center; Black has averted the danger of the pawn storm and controls the key square K5.

| 18. . . . | N–K5 |
|---|---|
| 19. NxN | PxN |
| 20. K–B2 | QR–Q1 |
| 21. P–QR4 | |

The game has turned into an ending that is somewhat in White's favor. Black must play accurately.

Instead of 21. P–QR4, better for White is 21. R–QN1 so as to answer 21. . . . R–Q2 with 22. R–N2. Then, when the KB-file is opened he will have counterpressure on Black's QNP. The move P–QR4 is needed only if Black plays P–QN3.

| 21. . . . | P–KB4 |
|---|---|
| 22. PxP | RxBP |
| 23. P–QB4 | R–Q2 |
| 24. K–B3 | N–N2 |

| 25. R–Q2 | K–B2 |
|---|---|
| 26. B–N8 | P–N3 |
| 27. R–QR2 | R–QR4 |

As a result of his inappropriately active play, White's position has worsened.

| 28. B–K5 | N–B4 |
|---|---|
| 29. R–KN1 | P–R4 |
| 30. B–B4 | |

He should play B–N3. The exchange of minor pieces by NxB is not to be feared by White. Now the Knight penetrates to B6 via R5, after which the condition of White's Bishop becomes critical and its long diagonal becomes a short one.

| 30. . . . | N–R5 |
|---|---|
| 31. R–N5 | RxR |
| 32. BxR | N–B6 |
| 33. P–R4 | |

If 33. B–B4 then P–KN4 followed by 34. . . . N–N8.

| 33. . . . | NxB |
|---|---|
| 34. PxN | K–K3 |
| 35. P–R5 | P–R5 |
| 36. R–R1 | |

White has a lost game, since he can do nothing to stop Black's passed pawn; however, the following variation offers a practical chance for a draw: 36. PxP PxP 37. R–R1 R–KR2 38. R–R1 P–R6 39. R–R2. Pawns are still equal and White's Rook is unapproachable, and for Black to win, his King has to go for the KNP. White can use that time to attack Black's QNP and QBP: 39. . . . K–B4 40. K–N4 KxP 41. P–B5 and if PxPch White draws, but after 41. . . . P–N4 he misses the draw by one tempo: 42. P–Q5 PxP 43. KxP K–R5 44. P–B6 and if White's King were on N6 the game would be drawn. This chance was worth taking, especially since it would have been taken before adjournment.

| 36. . . . | PxP |
|---|---|
| 37. K–Q2 | P–R6 |
| 38. K–K2 | P–R7 |
| 39. P–B3 | R–R2 |
| 40. R–R1 | PxPch |
| 41. KxP | P–R5 |

**White resigns**

## Game 9

One of the best games in the tournament, and the winner of a beauty prize. White starts a strong Kingside attack by sacrificing his QBP. Geller has every chance of succeeding if Black, according to tradition, counter-attacks on the Queenside. Euwe, however, carries out two remarkable ideas: 1) he makes good use of communication with the Queenside to attack the Kingside, and 2) he lures his opponent's forces deep into his own territory in order to isolate them from the defense of their King.

It is extremely interesting to see how White's pieces dig deeper and deeper into their frontal attack on the King while Black regroups circuitously.

## Nimzo-Indian Defense

| Y. Geller | M. Euwe |
|---|---|
| 1. P–Q4 | N–KB3 |
| 2. P–QB4 | P–K3 |
| 3. N–QB3 | B–N5 |
| 4. P–K3 | P–B4 |
| 5. P–QR3 | BxNch |
| 6. PxB | P–QN3 |
| 7. B–Q3 | B–N2 |
| 8. P–B3 | |

A small but important detail in this opening: as a result of Black's substitution of P–QN3 and B–N2 for the usual N–QB3 and O–O, White, who failed to react correctly in time with N–K2, has to spend an extra tempo to prepare P–K4. Such details must never be overlooked, but they should not be overemphasized either. It is sometimes said that White's advantage consists of the first move; if he loses a tempo the advantage should go to Black. In practice, however, White's advantage is that he has a greater choice of possible plans to suit his taste; when play is in full swing the loss of a single tempo is not always of great importance.

| 8. . . . | N–B3 |
|---|---|
| 9. N–K2 | O–O |

| 10. O–O | N–QR4 |
|---|---|
| 11. P–K4 | N–K1 |

Black moves the Knight to avoid the pin B–N5 and to answer White's P–B4 with . . . P–B4, blocking the Kingside. White therefore takes control of his KB5 before moving his KBP. Defending the QBP is pointless: it was already doomed by White's 5th move.

| 12. N–N3 | PxP |
|---|---|
| 13. PxP | R–B1 |
| 14. P–B4 | NxP |
| 15. P–B5 | P–B3 |
| 16. R–B4 | |

White's attack becomes threatening. Black's last move was necessary because White intended to advance his pawn to B6 and to answer . . . NxP by pinning the Knight and attacking the King with the combined force of Queen, Rook, and three minor pieces. Now White needs only two moves to transfer his Queen and Rook to the KR-file, after which nothing, it seems, will save the Black King.

But Euwe is not easily upset. Remember that in his life he played more than seventy games against Alekhine, the most dangerous attacking player of his time.

**16. . . .          P–QN4!**

The beginning of a remarkable plan. It is clear that any defensive maneuver on the Kingside that depends on pieces without significant scope—R–KB2, Q–K2, etc.—is doomed to fail. But Black has another defensive resource—counterattack! The QB, the QR, and the Knight on QB5 occupy good launching positions, and all that remains is to activate the Queen. The basis for the counterattack is Black's preponderance on the central squares. With P–QN4 Black reinforces his Knight's position and opens the way for the Queen to N3. Nevertheless, the impression is that these operations will be too late.

**17. R–R4          Q–N3**

Pinning the White Queen to the defense of the QP, Black impedes White's plan to play Q–R5. Incidentally, if 17.

Q–R5 Q–N3 18. N–K2 N–K4, an echo variation arises: White has no time for R–KR4.

**18. P–K5          NxKP**
**19. PxP            NxB**
**20. QxN            QxP**

Each of White's moves requires careful and accurate calculation. Here, for instance, the natural 20. PxP would not have worked because of 20. . . . Q–B3.

**21. QxPch**

So, at no great cost White has been able to break through. Black's position again looks critical.

**21. . . .          K–B2**
**22. B–R6          R–KR1**

Black's 16th move, P–QN4, was the beginning of a strategical plan of counterattack, and the Rook sacrifice is its main tactical blow, aiming to divert White's Queen far from its QB2 and to use that time to attack the King.

**23. QxR            R–B7**

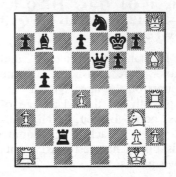

The threat is mate in a few moves: . . . RxPch, . . . Q–B5ch, etc. Careful analysis, which required no less than a week, proved that White could avoid the mate by means of a few very difficult and "only" moves. Necessary is 24. P–Q5. If 24. . . . Q–N3ch 25. K–R1 Q–B7 26. R–KN1 BxP, White is saved by 27. R–K4!. If at once 24. . . . BxP, not 25. R–Q4 but only 25. R–Q1! Then after 25. . . . RxPch 26. K–B1 PxB, neither 27. RxP nor 27. RxB is good, but again an "only" move, 27. QxP. Still, Black has a Bishop and two pawns for a Rook, which, considering the exposed position of White's King, gives him good winning chances. Needless to say, there was no practical possibility of Geller's finding all these moves over the board.

Analysts have also demonstrated that the overall idea of . . . R–KR1 was premature. R–B5 was better first. Nevertheless, it will be hard for chess lovers to agree. A move like 22. . . . R–KR1 is not easily forgotten.

| 24. | R–QB1 | RxPch |
|-----|-------|-------|
| 25. | K–B1 | Q–N6 |
| 26. | K–K1 | Q–KB6 |

**White resigns**

# Game 10
## Reti Opening

**V. Smyslov**          **L. Szabo**

1. P–QB4 N–KB3 2. P–KN3 P–B3 3. N–KB3 P–Q4 4. P–N3 P–KN3 5. B–QN2 B–N2 6. B–N2 Q–N3 7. Q–B1 O–O 8. O–O QN–Q2 9. PxP PxP 10. B–Q4 Q–Q3 11. Q–R3 N–K5 12. BxB KxB 13. QxQ NxQ

Exchanging Queens and dark-square Bishops, White counts on the open QB-file and especially on the advantage of his "good" Bishop, which, compared to Black's light-square Bishop, is not restricted by its own pawns.

14. R–B1 P–K3 15. N–B3 P–N3 16. P–Q4 B–R3 17. N–K5 NxN 18. PxN N–N4 19. NxN BxN 20. R–B2 QR–B1 21. R/1–QB1 RxR 22. RxR B–R3 23. P–B4 R–QB1 24. RxR BxR 25. K–B2 B–R3 26. K–K3 P–R3 27. B–B3 P–B4

White's plan is too inoffensive and not good enough to win. Black must keep his Bishop on the QR3–KB8 diagonal and his King on K2, and, especially, he must not move his pawns. His last two moves have helped his opponent create a passed pawn.

28. PxP e.p.ch KxP 29. K–Q4 P–KN4 30. PxP PxP 31. P–K4 PxP 32. KxP B–N4 33. P–KR4 PxP 34. PxP P–R4 35. K–Q4 P–R5 36. P–N4 P–R6

In allowing Black's pawn to get to R6 White has lost his winning chances. On his 35th move he should have put his pawn on R3.

37. B–K4 B–K1 38. B–N1 B–B2 39. K–B3 P–K4 40. P–N5 B–Q4 41. K–N4 P–K5 42. KxP P–K6 43. B–Q3 B–B6 44. K–N4 P–K7 45. BxP BxB 46. P–R4, Drawn.

## Game 11

### Nimzo-Indian Defense

**P. Keres          Y. Averbakh**

1. P–Q4 N–KB3 2. P–QB4 P–K3 3. N–QB3 B–N5 4. P–K3 O–O 5. B–Q3 P–Q4 6. N–B3 P–B4 7. O–O N–B3 8. P–QR3 BxN 9. PxB P–QN3 10. N–K5 B–N2 11. P–B4 N–QR4 12. PxQP QxP 13. Q–K2 PxP 14. KPxP N–N6 15. R–N1 NxB 16. QRxN QR–B1 17. Q–N2 Q–Q3 18. P–B5 PxP 19. BxP R–B2 20. P–B4 R–Q1 21. R–B4 P–KN4

An unexpected and correct decision. Black leaves his Knight on B3 without pawn protection and exposes his King's position in order to drive away the Rook and win a pawn. Based on his calculation of the

variations, Averbakh has concluded that the pawn cannot be won back, and in the absence of Queens Black's weaknesses do not worry him. Besides, White also has weak pawns on the Queenside.

22. R–KB2 QxQP 23. QxQ RxQ 24. QR–KB1 R–Q3 25. P–KR4 PxP 26. R–B4 R–B4 27. N–N4 NxN 28. RxNch K–B1 29. BxP B–R3 30. R/1–B4 R–R3 31. B–Q3 P–R6 32. PxP RxRP 33. R–Q4 B–B1 34. R–Q8ch K–K2 35. R/4–Q4 B–K3 36. K N2 R N4ch 37. K–B2 R–QR4 38. R–QN8 RxP 39. B–K2 R–R7ch 40. K–K1 R–QR8ch 41. R–Q1 RxBch, White resigns.

## Game 12

### Nimzo-Indian Defense

| S. Reshevsky | T. Petrosian |
|---|---|
| 1. P–Q4 | N–KB3 |
| 2. P–QB4 | P–K3 |
| 3. N–QB3 | B–N5 |
| 4. P–K3 | O–O |
| 5. B–Q3 | P–Q4 |

| 6. | N–B3 | P–B4 |
|----|------|------|
| 7. | O–O | N–B3 |
| 8. | P–QR3 | BxN |
| 9. | PxB | P–QN3 |

This move is supposed to give Black a cramped game. But if a "cramped" game is what a player likes he is bound to achieve better results with it than with a "free" game. Such general evaluations, though prevalent in the minds of theoreticians, are far less influential in a practical tournament game than they are thought to be.

| 10. | BPxP | KPxP |
|-----|------|------|
| 11. | B–N2 | |

It is basic chess strategy in all phases of the game to strive to strengthen one's position and to find the correct ideas to accomplish this goal. A great role is played also by the correct order of moves, but even though this is only a technical detail it is one upon which the success of the strategy depends. In this case White's basic idea is obvious: he must develop both Bishops well. This can be accomplished in two ways: to play P–QR3 and B–QR3 or to take the QBP and then play P–QB4. Seemingly against all logic, however, White puts his Bishop on a diagonal occupied by pawns, and for this very reason Black plays P–B5 and firmly locks it in.

What's the point? It seems that 11. P–QR4 is met by 11.

. . . PxP 12. BPxP B–N5 or 12. KPxP N–K5 attacking the QBP. And on 11. PxP PxP 12. P–B4, Black answers R–N1 and White has no B–N2.

After the preparatory B–N2 White can play P–B4 without fear, either immediately or after exchanging on QB5. Black's reply, therefore, not only serves a purpose, it is practically forced. The ensuing struggle is defined by the pawn structure thus created, which was determined much less by the wishes and tastes of the players than by the opening variation. White starts moving his KBP and KP and creates a passed QP, combining the advance of his center pawns with an attack along the KB-file. Although during this time Black has a three-to-two pawn majority on the Queenside, he cannot exploit his numerical advantage because he has to contend with White's pair of Bishops when White is superior in the center.

| 11. | . . . | P–B5 |
|-----|-------|------|
| 12. | B–B2 | B–N5 |
| 13. | Q–K1 | N–K5 |

Here Black can change the character of the fight by taking the Knight: 13. . . . BxN 14. PxB N–KR4—but he refuses because of White's two Bishops, strong pawn center, and open KN-file. But this standard formula was nothing to worry about here since one Bishop would be hemmed in by pawns and the pawn center would not be dangerous at the moment. For example, 15. P–K4 N–B5 16. K–R1 Q–R5 17. B–B1 PxP 18. PxP N–Q6 19. BxN PxB 20. Q–K3 KR–K1 21. P–B3 P–B4 22. P–K5 QR–Q1, and the pawn on White's Q3 is untouchable.

However, after 13. . . . BxN 14. PxB N–KR4 White could strengthen his position systematically with P–B4, P–B3, Q–B2, QR–Q1, B–B1, K–R1, and P–K4, in this or some other sequence according to Black's play (R–KN1, etc., might be needed). Against this plan Black could offer only a direct attack on the King, but with very little chance of success because his maneuvering possibilities would be limited: the pawn barrier would inhibit the agility of his Knights.

Petrosian continues along logical lines, believing that by making no dubious moves and not disturbing the equilibrium he cannot obtain a lost position.

| 14. | N–Q2 | NxN |
|-----|------|-----|
| 15. | QxN | B–R4 |
| 16. | P–B3 | B–N3 |
| 17. | P–K4 | Q–Q2 |
| 18. | QR–K1 | PxP |
| 19. | PxP | KR–K1 |

Now 20. P–QR4 would be followed by 20. . . . N–K4! 21. B–R3 N–Q6 22. BxN PxB 23. QxP QxRP.

| 20. | Q–B4 | P–N4 |
|-----|------|-----|

Black defends against the maneuver P–QR4 and B–R3 and at the same time reminds his opponent about Black's numerical advantage on this flank.

## 21. B–Q1

When attacking the King, we are all accustomed to posting the Bishop on Q3 or QB2, or occasionally on N1. Reshevsky undertakes a roundabout maneuver to strengthen his position and to create conditions for the as yet impossible advance of his pawns.

| 21. | . . . | R–K2 |
|-----|-------|------|
| 22. | B–N4 | Q–K1 |
| 23. | P–K5 | P–QR4 |
| 24. | R–K3 | R–Q1 |
| 25. | KR–K1 | R–K3 |

Reshevsky's clever play and Petrosian's iron logic make this game one of the gems of the tournament. Black must block the White pawns, and Petrosian immediately offers the Exchange in order to free his K2

for the transfer of his Knight to Q4. True, Black gets serious compensation: his Knight on Q4 will be exceptionally strong, as will his Bishop, which will lack a light-square opponent. Notice that now or on his last move White could have started a direct Kingside attack by P–KR4–5 and R–N3, getting good winning chances; but he counts on winning in another way.

**26. P–QR4**

Inviting 26. . . . P–N5, which would be answered by 27. P–Q5 RxQP 28. BxR PxB 29. QxBP (weak is 28. QxBP QRxP), but Petrosian consistently carries out his plan.

**26. . . .        N–K2**
**27. BxR        PxB**
**28. Q–B1**

Keeping an eye on the pawn on QB4 and preparing to return the Exchange—for a pawn. On 28. Q–B2, N–Q4 is unpleasant: 29. R–B3 P–N5.

**28. . . .        N–Q4**
**29. R–B3        B–Q6**

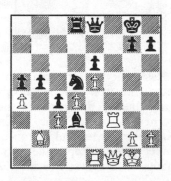

**30. RxB        PxR**
**31. QxP        P–N5**

Black has no choice, of course. Taking the RP is pointless. But White now faces a difficult psychological problem: to exchange on N4, leading to an almost certain draw, or to push the pawn and chase the Knight, getting chances to win —and to lose.

With hardly enough time to calculate the variations, it is understandable that Reshevsky chooses the simplest continuation. On 32. P–B4 N–N3 33. R–QB1 NxRP 34. B–R1 Q–B3 or 33. P–Q5 PxP 34. P–B5 NxP 35. B–Q4 R–B1 36. Q–KB3 Q–K3, White's pawns are blocked and Black has a very threatening position.

**32. PxP        PxP**

Possible is 32. . . . NxP 33. Q–QN3 N–Q4 or 33. Q–N5 QxQ 34. PxQ N–Q6 35. R–K2 R–N1 36. R–Q2 RxP 37. RxN RxB 38. P–Q5, with a draw.

**33. P–R5        R–R1**
**34. R–R1        Q–B3**
**35. B–B1**

Tempting Black into a variation with unclear consequences: 35. . . . RxP? 36. RxR QxBch 37. Q–B1 Q–K6ch 38. K–R1 P–R3 39. R–R8ch K–R2 40. Q–N1ch P–N3 41. R–R7ch K–R1 42. P–R3; but Black need not take this risk: his position is not inferior.

| 35. . . . | Q–B2 |
|-----------|------|
| 36. P–R6 | Q–N3 |
| 37. B–Q2 | P–N6 |
| 38. Q–B4 | P–R3 |
| 39. P–R3 | P–N7 |
| 40. R–N1 | K–R1 |

| 41. B–K1 | Drawn |
|----------|-------|

Black has a slight advantage but it cannot be exploited. The opponents agreed to a draw after home analysis.

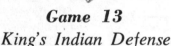

## Game 13
### King's Indian Defense

**D. Bronstein**     **M. Najdorf**

| 1. P–Q4 | N–KB3 |
|---------|-------|
| 2. P–QB4 | P–KN3 |
| 3. N–QB3 | B–N2 |
| 4. P–K4 | P–Q3 |
| 5. B–N5 | P–B4 |
| 6. P–Q5 | N–R3 |

Only six moves have been made but already much has happened. Making use of the White Bishop's being at KN5 and not at K3, where it is usually posted to participate in the struggle for Q4, Black hastened to counter-attack the White center with . . . P–QB4. White's P–Q5 prevented Black's Knight from get-

ting to QB3, so Najdorf now transfers it to B2 and plans . . . P–QR3 and . . . P–QN4. However, this takes a lot of time, and the results achieved are disproportionately small considering the effort spent. The Knight occupies a passive position at QB2 and for a long time is of no use. In the end it nearly ruins Black's game.

| 7. B–Q3 | N–B2 |
|---------|------|
| 8. KN–K2 | P–QR3 |
| 9. P–QR4 | QR–N1 |
| 10. O–O | O–O |
| 11. Q–B2 | B–Q2 |
| 12. P–R3 | P–N4 |

**13. P–B4**

The KP and KBP, provoked by the position of Black's pieces, can't help advancing. White gains more and more space, whereas Black's QNP does not compensate for his cramped position; compare the King Rooks, for instance.

| 13. . . . | N/3–K1 |
|---|---|
| 14. RPxP | PxP |
| 15. R–R7 | PxP |
| 16. BxBP | R–R1 |

White's KR–R1 cannot be allowed, but now White exchanges Black's only active piece.

| 17. RxR | NxR |
| 18. Q–N3 | P–B3 |

Since the Queen cannot constantly stand guard over the KP, Black decides to take the crucial step of closing his Bishop's diagonal.

| 19. B–R4 | Q–N3 |
| 20. Q–R3 | KN–B2 |
| 21. P–QN3 | N–N4 |
| 22. NxN | BxN |
| 23. P–B5 | |

White's gradual accumulation of small advantages has reached appreciable proportions, and the text move begins the search for the decisive strengthening of his position. The threat is now 24. N–B4 P–N4 25. N–K6 PxB 26. NxR. Furthermore, the last move helped to fix the KP and KBP on dark squares.

On the other hand, it was worth thinking about moving the QB to a new diagonal; it has done its duty here in having forced Black to play P–B3, and it would give Black a lot more trouble by moving to K1. Possible is 23. R–R1, but although Black could not play P–B4 immediately because of 24. P–K5 PxP 25. P–Q6ch K–R1 26. QPxP, etc., White would continually have to consider Black's P–B4 a possibility.

| 23. . . . | B–KR3 |
|---|---|
| 24. PxP | PxP |
| 25. P–K5 | BxB |
| 26. PxB | QPxP |
| 27. Q–Q3 | |

For whose benefit did White sacrifice a pawn? Can't Black start a counterattack? For the moment he cannot, whereas White needs two or three moves —for example, N–B3 and R–QN1—to gain complete command of the points on the Queenside, and then he can take the QBP or the KP/7. The accomplishment of this plan is aided by the unfortunate position of the Knight at QR8.

| 27. . . . | K–R2 |
| 28. N–B3 | Q–N6 |

White's last two moves were not bad, but they could have been a little better; for instance, 27. B–B2 R–B1 28. Q–Q3 K–N2 29. P–R4. Now Najdorf finds a tactical possibility to complicate the game and, most important, to exchange Queens, which facilitates the defense.

| 29. R–N1 | P–K5 |
| 30. RxQ | PxQ |
| 31. R–N7 | K–N1 |
| 32. K–B2 | |

Of course White does not take the pawn, for that would allow Black's Knight finally to get out of the corner.

| 32. . . . | B–B5 |
| 33. K–B3 | R–N1 |
| 34. RxRch | |

After the exchange of Rooks almost all of White's advantage disappears. Better is 34. RxP R–N6 35. BxP or 34. . . . B–Q3 35. R–K6 B–K4 36. BxP BxN 37. BxB R–N6 38. B–R5! White did not choose this continuation because he overestimated the strength of Black's pawn on Q6, even though his own pawn on Q5 would have become extremely dangerous.

Best was not 33. K–B3 but B–N3, offering to trade Bishops. However, White overlooked Black's reply 33. . . . R–N1.

| 34. . . . BxR 35. N–R4 |
B–Q3 36. B–B2 K–B2 37. K–K3 N–B2 38. KxP N–R3 39. K–K4 P–B4ch 40. K–B3 P–K3 41. N–N6, Drawn.

## Game 14
### Nimzo-Indian Defense

| S. Gligoric | M. Taimanov |
| 1. P–Q4 | N–KB3 |
| 2. P–QB4 | P–K3 |
| 3. N–QB3 | B–N5 |
| 4. N–B3 | |

In the overwhelming majority of the Nimzo-Indian Defenses played in this tournament White continued 4. P–K3—the fashion is so strong that I suppose it will continue long after the tournament in Switzerland. Gligoric's choice, N–B3, is also quite playable. Although in this game Black is able to equalize and even seizes the initiative, Gligoric himself is to blame for this.

| 4. | . . . | P–QN3 |
|---|---|---|
| 5. | B–N5 | P–KR3 |
| 6. | B–R4 | P–KN4 |
| 7. | B–N3 | N–K5 |
| 8. | Q–B2 | B–N2 |
| 9. | P–K3 | P–Q3 |

Isn't Taimanov losing a piece (10. Q–R4ch N–B3 11. P–Q5)? No, because the White Knight is insufficiently protected (11. . . . NxN).

| 10. | B–Q3 | BxNch |
|---|---|---|
| 11. | PxB | P–KB4 |

**12. O–O**

Gligoric is not worried about the further advance of the Black pawns, correctly believing that this would only weaken Taimanov's position. He invites Black to play P–KR4. What chess player can resist such a temptation? But Taimanov sees in time that after 12. . . . P–KR4? 13. P–KR4! he has no attack. By the quiet maneuver

QN–Q2–B3 he strengthens the pressure on White's K4, which leads to some advantage for Black.

Instead of castling, White can place Black's entire system of development in doubt by acting with more determination; namely, 12. P–Q5, breaking the communication between Black's Bishop and Knight. On 12. . . . PxP White plays 13. N–Q4 (which would follow many other answers by Black) with a very strong attack, threatening the simple P–B3, among other things. It is not possible to avoid mentioning, even though chronology is violated, that Taimonov got the same position against Keres in the 22nd U.S.S.R. Championship a year and a half after this game; the Estonian grandmaster, as he relates, had prepared the improvement 12. P–Q5! in advance. Keres and this writer agree on this idea, but here we diverge: White answered 12. . . . PxP not with 13. N–Q4 but with 13. PxP BxP and only then 14. N–Q4 N–Q2 15. P–B3 NxB 16. PxN Q–B3 17. BxP O–O–O 18. Q–R4 with a splendid position. Black was forced to lay down his arms on the 29th move.

| 12. | . . . | N–Q2 |
|---|---|---|
| 13. | N–Q2 | QN–B3 |
| 14. | NxN | BxN |
| 15. | BxB | NxB |
| 16. | P–B3 | NxB |

| 17. PxB | Q–Q2 |
|---------|------|
| 18. P–R4 | |

Taimanov has kept his octave of pawns intact while White's keyboard is slightly damaged in two places, and this is the extent of Black's positional advantage. Whereas in the previous phase of the game all the minor pieces were exchanged, in the coming phase it is the pawns' turn. In the course of the next twelve moves twelve pawns are captured! This mechanical aspect reflects White's well-known strategic idea: to expose Black's King and to create weaknesses on the opponent's Queenside by the break P–B5.

| 18. . . . | P–QR4 |
|-----------|-------|
| 19. P–B5 | NPxP |
| 20. PxP | O–O |
| 21. KR–Q1 | Q–B3 |

| 22. PxP | PxP |
|---------|-----|
| 23. P–N4 | QR–B1 |
| 24. PxP | RxP |

The pawn skirmishes have turned out in White's favor; Black has a weakness on Q3 and his King is slightly exposed.

### 25. P–K4          R–KB2

White was planning the futher advance of the KP to open a diagonal for the incursion of the Queen to N6. This does not now occur, for if 26. P–K5 Black gives a check and takes the KP with his Queen. Soon more pawns are exchanged and the game nears a draw.

| 26. R–Q3 | P–N5 |
|----------|------|
| 27. PxP | QxKP |
| 28. Q–Q2 | QxNP |
| 29. R–K1 | R–KN2 |

Black moves all his pieces to the KN-file, but this proves to be insufficient.

| 30. RxQP | RxP |
|----------|-----|
| 31. R/6xP | R–KN6 |
| 32. R/1–K2 | RxPch |

Drawn, since after 33. RxR QxR 34. RxRch KxR 35. QxP, both commanders are left almost without troops.

# Round Three

## Game 15
### Grünfeld Defense

**M. Najdorf     S. Gligoric**

1. P–Q4 N–KB3 2. P–QB4
P–KN3 3. P–KN3 P–B3 4. N–
QB3 P–Q4 5. PxP PxP

The choice of opening denotes a lack of aggressive intentions by both opponents. The almost symmetrical position, with its solid and immobile pawn center, clearly indicates how the game will end.

6. N–R3 B–N2 7. N–B4
O–O 8. B–N2 P–K3 9. O–O
N–B3 10. P–K3 P–N3 11. P–
N3 B–QR3 12. R–K1 R–B1
13. B–N2 R–K1 14. QR–B1
B–N2

Here or a move earlier White could have tried to lend the game at least the appearance of a fight by P–KN4 followed by P–KR4. There was no great risk, and Black's position could scarcely have been breached; the two captains therefore decide to let the prevailing winds guide them to a quiet harbor.

15. N–Q3 B–QR3 16. B–
QR3 B–B1 17. BxB RxB 18.
N–B4 N–K2 19. P–KR4 P–
R4 20. Q–Q2 Q–Q3, Drawn.

## Game 16
### Catalan Opening

**T. Petrosian     D. Bronstein**

1. P–Q4     N–KB3
2. P–QB4     P–K3
3. P–KN3     P–Q4
4. B–N2     PxP
5. N–KB3

The Catalan Opening only seems harmless; actually it contains many subtleties, and it is no wonder that Keres, Smyslov, and Petrosian play it so often. One of the nuances is White's

5. N–KB3. White usually gives check here and recaptures the pawn, but in that case Black's QB gets to B3 via Q2. Now White has a choice: according to circumstances he can recapture the pawn by N–K5x QBP or QN–Q2xP, or he can still play Q–R4chxBP.

If Black tries the well-known "equalizing" maneuver P–QB4, as in the Queen's Gambit, then the fianchettoed Bishop becomes very strong; for instance, 6. O–O N–B3 7. Q–R4 B–Q2 8. PxP N–QR4 9. Q–B2 BxP 10. N–K5 QR–B1 11. N–QB3 P–QN4 12. B–N5, with excellent play for White.

**5. . . .          B–N5ch**

A new continuation. Black wants to force the Bishop to Q2 to prevent the Knight from going there. On 6. QN–Q2 White fears 6. . . . P–B6 7. PxP BxP, when Black keeps his extra pawn; but the consequences of 8. B–QR3 BxR 9. QxB are interesting to examine.

**6. B–Q2          B–K2**
**7. Q–B2**

White does not check, avoiding 7. . . . B–Q2 and 8. . . . B–B3. Now if 7. . . . B–Q2

White has 8. N–K5, eliminating Black's light-square Bishop and thus strengthening his own.

**7. . . .          B–Q2**

Anyway! On 8. N–K5 Black replies 8. . . . N–B3, compromising his pawn structure. After 9. NxN BxN 10. BxBch PxB 11. QxBP Black has Q–Q4 and White must exchange Queens, which fully equalizes the game. But if 9. QxBP in this variation, then 9. NxN 10. PxN N–Q4 11. BxN PxB 12. QxQP Q–B1 13. O–O B–QB3, with a good attack for the sacrificed pawn.

**8. O–O B–B3 9. QxBP B–Q4 10. Q–B2 N–B3 11. B–B3 B–K5 12. Q–Q1 O–O 13. QN–Q2 B–N3 14. N–B4 B–K5 15. QN–Q2 B–N3 16. N–B4 B–K5 17. QN–Q2, Drawn.**

Just when the opening is becoming the middlegame, White does not want to continue the fight with an enemy piece on his K4, and Black does not want to allow his opponent's Knight to settle on K5. Unable to agree on the location of these pieces, the players repeat moves.

# Game 17
## Nimzo-Indian Defense

| Y. Averbakh | S. Reshevsky | 3. N–QB3 | B–N5 |
|---|---|---|---|
| 1. P–Q4 | N–KB3 | 4. P–K3 | P–B4 |
| 2. P–QB4 | P–K3 | 5. B–Q3 | O–O |

| 6. | N–B3 | P–Q4 |
| 7. | O–O | N–B3 |
| 8. | P–QR3 | BxN |
| 9. | PxB | PxBP |
| 10. | BxP | Q–B2 |

Having obtained a good position as Black in the first round against Najdorf, Reshevsky repeats exactly the same moves against Averbakh. Najdorf played 11. P–QR4 here, but Averbakh plays the more logical 11. R–K1, with P–K4 in view. The first skirmish begins around this advance, and in ten moves it ends in favor of White, who occupies his K4 with a piece before the Black pawn can get there.

| 11. | R–K1 | R–Q1 |
| 12. | Q–B2 | P–K4 |
| 13. | N–N5 | |

| 13. | . . . | R–B1 |
| 14. | P–Q5 | |

Black counterattacked the White pawn center and played R–Q1 so as not to allow P–Q5, but the plan did not work. The

Rook had to go back to defend KB2, and White's pawn was allowed to advance. The position permits another, sharper treatment—14. B–Q3. This move maintains the tension on QB5 and K5, forces a weakening of Black's Kingside, and prepares a piece attack; for instance, 14. . . . P–KR3 15. N–K4 NxN 16. BxN BPxP 17. BPxP PxP 18. B–N2.

| 14. | . . . | N–QR4 |
| 15. | B–R2 | P–KR3 |
| 16. | N–K4 | NxN |
| 17. | QxN | B–Q2 |

White's threat was P–KB4. Taking the pawn would have been disadvantageous because the game would have been opened in White's favor. Defending the KP by . . . P–B3 would also have been bad because of B–N1, when White's Queen gets to KR7. Black's defensive setup is based mainly on his KP. B–Q2 is needed to meet the threatened 18. P–KB4, which could now be answered by 18. . . . PxP, and if 19. PxP? QR–K1. The move also serves to control the QR5–K1 diagonal.

| 18. | P–QB4 | P–QN3 |
| 19. | Q–Q3 | QR–K1 |
| 20. | P–K4 | Q–Q3 |

On White's balance sheet for the last ten moves these activities should be noted as having completely succeeded: he has played P–K4, closed the center, and is ready to storm the Black King's position. In the event this leads to an endgame, he is assured of a protected passed pawn on Q5. The Bishop on QR2 is of course to be noted on this list as passive, but it can be transferred to Q3 via N1. And what can Black do against the coming attack on his King? He must prepare to weather the storm: he must place his pawns on dark squares, his Rooks on the K-file, and his Knight on Q3, where it will blockade the pawn and protect the light squares.

| 21. Q–KN3 | R–K2 |
| 22. B–Q2 | N–N2 |
| 23. P–B4 | KR–K1 |
| 24. B–B3 | P–B3 |

Black reinforces his K4 with all his might; by simultaneously putting pressure on K5 he provokes P–B5.

**25. P–B5**

The correct evaluation of the position! Averbakh does not take the KP even though after 25. PxP PxP 26. R–KB1 followed by doubling Rooks on the KB-file, White's advantage would be obvious because one of Black's Rooks would be temporarily chained to the defense of the KP. He refuses the pawn because Black would answer 25. PxP with 25. . . . RxP, and

Black's Knight, soon to occupy Q3, would be no weaker than White's Rook.

But now, with Black's Bishop walled up, White can transfer his Rooks and mobilize his KRP and KNP.

| 25. . . . | R–KB1 |
| 26. B–Q2 | |

It is useful to know, before launching the attack, where Black's King will go to escape the threat of BxP.

| 26. . . . | K–R1 |

White is now fully prepared for the immediate pawn storm P–KN4 and P–KR4. These moves will have to conform to his partner's play, of course, but Black has a very difficult task. With his next move, however, White loses an attacking tempo and permits Reshevsky to remind him of Black's counterchances (an extra pawn on the Queenside, the possibility of attacking the QBP, and the weakness of White's QN3).

**27. B–N1 N–R4 28. Q–Q3 B–R5 29. B–B2 BxB 30. QxB N–N2 31. P–QR4 Q–Q1 32. R–R3 N–Q3 33. R–R3 N–B2, Drawn.**

An attack by White would entail some risk, since Black has only to prepare P–QN4 to give him good counterplay on the other flank.

# Game 18
## Queen's Gambit Accepted

| L. Szabo | P. Keres |
|----------|----------|
| 1. P–Q4 | P–Q4 |
| 2. N–KB3 | N–KB3 |
| 3. P–B4 | PxP |
| 4. N–B3 | P–QR3 |
| 5. Q–R4ch | |

This is, in effect, the shortest game of the Zurich tournament. Although it continues to the 41st move, Szabo may as well resign after giving this check. It turns out that he is giving Keres pawn and move, just like the odds-play in handicap tournaments for masters against weaker players in Tchigorin's day. One can only be astounded that Szabo could drop a pawn after thinking for so long on his 5th move. Keres, by the way, was so surprised that he took fifteen minutes to answer.

| 5. . . . | P–N4 |
|----------|------|
| 6. Q–B2 | |

The whole point is that White has not played P–K3. With an open diagonal for his KB, it would be worth giving some thought to taking the pawn with the Knight and answering 6. . . . B–Q2 with 7. BxP. But now Szabo has to choose: remain a pawn down, or give up a piece by 6. NxP B–Q2 7. Nx Pch QxN 8. Q–B2, hoping eventually to take the QBP. But even in that extremely doubtful event he would get no more than two pawns for his piece.

| 6. . . . | N–B3 |
|----------|------|
| 7. P–K4 | P–K3 |
| 8. B–N5 | |

A pawn down, Szabo is nervous. Why not B–K3? His central pawns on K4 and Q4 promise White good chances to complicate the play. With B–N5 Szabo decides to give up a second pawn, figuring that if the QP is taken he will gain a few tempos for development. However, with two extra pawns Keres easily parries the attack.

8. . . . NxQP 9. NxN QxN 10. QR–Q1 Q–B4 11. B–K3 Q–B3 12. B–K2 B–N2 13. B–B3 P–K4 14. O–O B–B4 15. N–Q5 BxB 16. NxB O–O 17. P–KN4 KR–K1 18. N–B5 N–Q2 19. P–N3 N–N3 20. Q–B1

PxP 21. PxP QxQ 22. RxQ
QR–B1 23. KR–Q1 P–N3 24.
N–R6ch K–N2 25. P–N5 P–
QB4 26. B–N4 R–B2 27. R–
Q6 N–B1 (White's threats force
Keres to demonstrate his famous
alertness.) 28. R–KB6 BxP
29. R–Q1 P–B5 30. PxP PxP

31. P–B3 B–Q6 32. RxP N–
K2 33. R–Q6 N–N1 34. R–
QB1 R–N2 35. B–Q7 R–Q1
36. NxN KxN 37. B–B6 RxR
38. BxR R–N3 39. B–Q5 K–
B1 40. R–R1 P–B6 41. R–
R8ch K–K2, White resigns.

## Game 19
### Grünfeld Defense

| M. Euwe | V. Smyslov |
|---------|-----------|
| 1. P–Q4 | N–KB3 |
| 2. P–QB4 | P–KN3 |
| 3. P–KN3 | B–N2 |
| 4. B–N2 | P–Q4 |
| 5. PxP | NxP |
| 6. P–K4 | N–N3 |
| 7. N–K2 | P–QB4 |

The often-used Smyslov
System in the Grünfeld Defense.
Black attacks the central pawn
with P–QB4 and P–K3, ex-
changes on his Q4, and blockades the pawn with a Knight on
Q3. But even though White's
QP will be isolated and blockaded it will remain very strong.
Black will always have to consider its advance a possibility,
especially since it will not be so
simple to post one of his
Knights on Q3. The future
course of the struggle depends
on whether White can advance
the pawn to Q6 at the right
moment and reinforce it there.
If he can, White will have the
upper hand; if not, good counterchances will appear for
Black.

Personally, I feel that this
system favors White. Perhaps
Smyslov now shares this opinion, for despite the successful
outcome of this game he did
not use this system again in
Zurich, nor in any other tournament.

| 8. P–Q5 | P–K3 |
|---------|------|
| 9. O–O | O–O |
| 10. P–QR4 | |

Smyslov happens to be con-
tending with a great connoisseur
of the Grünfeld Defense. In
the Amsterdam tournament in
1950, Euwe played an analogous game against Pilnik and
continued N/1–B3 here. Euwe
stated in the tournament book
that his move was not good,
and he recommended 10. P–
QR4! N–R3 11. N–R3 PxP 12.
PxP N–N5 13. N–B3!. Smyslov
goes into the variation anyway,
lending the game special interest.

To fully appreciate the move 10. P–QR4, it is interesting to note that in game 129 of this tournament, in the 19th round, Euwe played 10. N/2–B3 against Keres, conceding that it is stronger than 10. P–QR4.

It seems to me that the two moves are about equal and both good enough.

| 10. . . . | N–R3 |
| 11. N–R3 | PxP |
| 12. PxP | B–B4 |
| 13. N–B3 | |

Rather more precise is 13. P–R5, but Euwe figures that in the variation 13. N–B3 N–N5 14. B–K3 N–Q2 15. Q–Q2, the Knight will have to go to Q2 anyway.

| 13. . . . | N–N5 |
| 14. B–K3 | R–B1 |

Smyslov conducts an active defense, now threatening to post a piece on Q6 to break the contact between his opponent's two flanks. The advance of the pawn to Q6 and the subsequent Exchange sacrifice is a logical culmination of White's entire setup, but it would be stronger after 15. P–R5.

| 15. P–Q6 | B–Q6 |
| 16. BxNP | |

The correct strategic idea in an inaccurate tactical setting. 16. P–R5 is now necessary to answer 16. . . . BxR 17. KxB N–Q2 18. BxNP R–N1 with 19. P–R6.

After the move in the game an interesting fight, based mainly on the calculating of variations, takes place among the pieces. Black's chances in this fight are not objectively inferior.

| 16. . . . | R–N1 |
| 17. B–N2 | BxR |

A brave decision. Many would prefer an equalizing line here, or at any rate the more easily calculable 17. . . . QxP.

| 18. KxB | N–Q2 |
| 19. N–B4 | N–K4 |
| 20. NxN | BxN |
| 21. BxP | Q–R4 |

Two pawns, one of which is passed and has already reached the sixth rank, sufficiently compensate for the Exchange. However, the maneuver begun by Smyslov underscores the insecurity of the passed pawn. 22. N–N5 is not playable now because of 22. . . . RxN, so the Bishop has to retreat.

**22. B–K3        KR–Q1**
**23. N–K4        BxQP**

The scales tip from one side to the other. Just when Black has achieved an advantage Euwe launches a complicated combination with the pretty intermediate move N–Q7.

**24. N–B6ch      K–R1**

It later becomes clear that 24. . . . K–N2 would have been better. In one of the variations it is important for the King to defend the KBP.

**25. B–Q4        B–K4**

The picture of an apparently hopeless position for White. His next move is very pretty.

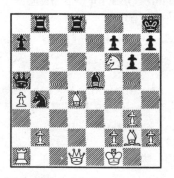

**26. N–Q7**

The idea is to lure the Rook to an undefended square. If 26. . . . RxN 27. BxBch QxB 28. QxR QxQNP 29. R–Q1, two

Black pawns arc attacked. Bad is 26. . . . BxB 27. QxBch K–N1 28. N–B6ch K–R1 29. N–Q5ch K–N1 30. N–K7ch K–B1 31. Q–R8ch KxN 32. R–K1ch.

**26. . . .        P–B3**

After 26. . . . Q–R3ch 27. K–N1 BxB 28. QxBch P–B3 or 28. . . . K–N1 29. NxR RxQ 30. NxQ, leading to an ending in White's favor.

**27. BxB         PxB**
**28. Q–Q2**

Smyslov's persistent play for complications bears fruit: Euwe does not find the best move 28. Q–Q6. The main variation is 28. . . . R–N3 29. Q–K7 N–B3 30. Q–B6ch K–N1 31. R–Q1, threatening the lethal 32. B–Q5ch. Black would therefore have to exchange Queens and seek salvation in a hard end-game a pawn down: 28. . . . Q–R3ch 29. QxQ NxQ 30. NxR RxN 31. R–K1.

**28. . . .        QR–B1**

Were his Queen on Q6 White could now continue 29. Q–B6ch and 30. B–R3, forcing Black to play Q–R3ch, and after trading Queens White would win back the Exchange and end up with an extra pawn.

**29. K–N1        Q–B4**

A brilliant resource, not fore-seen by White. Black brings his Queen into battle elegantly and with decisive effect and threatens to win the pinned Knight.

**30. B–R3            Q–K2**

**31. Q–K2**

Euwe thinks 31. R–Q1 would have been better here, but I do not see a big difference: 31. . . . R–B2 32. Q–K1 N–B3 33. P–QN4 QxP 34. NxP QxQch 35. RxQ NxN 36. RxN R–Q7 and Black should win.

**31. . . .            RxN**
**32. BxR            QxB**
**33. QxPch          K–N1**

Black's win with an extra piece is, as they say, a matter of technique. But the technique is far from simple in this case because White has two pawns as well as some chances for his piece: his King is more secure, and Black's Knight has no points of support in the center.

Black's general plan is to avoid exchanging his Queenside pawn if possible, to find a safe refuge from checks for his King, to transfer his Knight to the

Kingside, and, finally, to use his superior force to attack White's pawns on KB2 and QN2 (or QN3).

The implementation of this plan requires exceptional stamina, long calculations, and rapid evaluation of the positions that come up.

**34. Q–K4            P–QR4**
**35. P–R4            Q–Q4**
**36. Q–N4            R–KB1**
**37. R–Q1            Q–B6**
**38. Q–B4ch          Q–B2**
**39. Q–B5            Q–B4**
**40. Q–B4ch          Q–B2**
**41. Q–B5            Q–B4**
**42. Q–B4ch          K–N2**

The last moves were made in severe time pressure, and so far Black has accomplished nothing substantial except to tie down White's Queen to the defense of KB2. Now he must secure QB3 for the transfer of his Knight.

**43. Q–Q4ch          Q–B3**
**44. Q–B5            R–B2**
**45. R–Q2            Q–K2**

The threat of Q–K8ch earns Black a tempo to regroup.

**46. Q–B3ch          R–B3**
**47. R–Q4            N–B3**
**48. R–Q5**

White can get a third pawn for the piece by 48. R–KB4 Q–K4 49. RxR QxQ 50. Rx Pch KxR 51. PxQ, but the ending is still lost. Euwe gives the variation 51. . . . N–K4 52. K–

B1 K–B4 53. K–K2 K–K5 54. P–R5 P–R3, and White loses his pawns.

| 48. . . . | Q–K3 |
|---|---|
| 49. R–QB5 | P–R4 |
| 50. P–N3 | K–B2 |
| 51. R–QN5 | Q–Q2 |
| 52. K–N2 | Q–K2 |
| 53. Q–B4ch | K–N2 |
| 54. Q–Q3 | K–R3 |
| 55. R–Q5 | R–B2 |
| 56. R–Q6 | N–K4 |

The Knight gradually penetrates to KN5.

| 57. Q–K3ch | K–R2 |
|---|---|
| 58. R–N6 | |

58. R–Q5 is of no help in view of 58. . . . R–B4 59. RxP Q–N2ch 60. P–B3 N–B5. The text move loses immediately.

| 58. . . . | Q–B2 |
|---|---|

After 58. . . . N–N5 59. QxQ RxQ 60. P–N4 White could hope for salvation. But now the threat is N–N5, and if 59. P–B3, Q–B7ch is decisive. White resigns.

Smyslov displayed great mastery and an extraordinary will to win at all stages of this tense game.

## Game 20
### King's Indian Defense

| G. Stahlberg | Y. Geller |
|---|---|
| 1. P–Q4 | N–KB3 |
| 2. N–KB3 | P–KN3 |
| 3. P–KN3 | B–N2 |
| 4. B–N2 | O–O |
| 5. O–O | P–Q3 |
| 6. QN–Q2 | |

A peculiar and overly passive system that Stahlberg uses occasionally against the King's Indian. He keeps his KP in its initial position, advances his QBP only one square, and exchanges his QP, absolutely refusing a pawn center and a fight for center squares. This is often

followed by a maneuvering stage, exchanges, and a draw. In this game, however, Geller does not share his opponent's intentions, and he fights very energetically to seize space, first on the Kingside and then all over the board.

| 6. . . . | N–B3 |
|---|---|
| 7. P–B3 | P–K4 |
| 8. PxP | PxP |
| 9. N–N3 | Q–K2 |
| 10. B–K3 | R–Q1 |
| 11. Q–B1 | |

As a result of his passive strategy, White cannot put his

Queen on QB2 because of 11.
. . . B–B4.

| 11. . . . | P–K5 |
|---|---|
| 12. N–Q4 | N–K4 |
| 13. B–N5 | N–B5 |
| 14. N–B2 | P–B3 |

Stahlberg's maneuvers are guided not by strategical plans but by practical principles based on his vast tournament experience and his chess intuition. He does not move pawns or create obvious weaknesses in his position, and he does not display the slightest aggression. While he does not avoid exchanges, neither does he avoid tactical traps when the occasion demands. So now, despite a number of aimless (and harmless) White moves, his position is not bad at all. Geller displays great ingenuity and perseverance in overcoming Stahlberg's skillful and not entirely innocuous defense.

| 15. N–K3 | N–Q3 |
|---|---|
| 16. R–Q1 | P–KR3 |

Just now, when the Knight is temporarily blocking the diagonal, Black frees himself from the pin, transfers his King to R2, and then accomplishes P–KB4.

| 17. B–B4 | N/B–K1 |
|---|---|
| 18. N–B1 | K–R2 |
| 19. Q–B2 | P–KB4 |
| 20. B–K3 | B–K3 |
| 21. B–Q4 | N–B3 |

Black's advantage has crystallized somewhat: White's pieces are congested and his light-square Bishop out of play, and Black's strong little pawn chain on the Kingside stands ready to be mobilized. However, all this is not enough to win the game. Black mobilizes his Queenside pawns to increase his opponent's severe cramp, and he then exchanges White's active pieces, leaving him only the Bishop on N2 and the Knight on KB1. Stahlberg keeps his composure and continues his passive tactics, believing that he is not in danger of losing.

| 22. B–B5 | P–N3 |
|---|---|
| 23. BxN | RxB |

Even such as important piece for White in the King's Indian as his dark-square Bishop is not spared in Stahlberg's play for exchanges. This might have cost him the game.

| 24. RxR | QxR |
|---|---|
| 25. R–Q1 | Q–B2 |
| 26. N–K3 | P–B4 |

| | |
|---|---|
| 27. N–Q2 | R–Q1 |
| 28. N/2–B1 | RxR |
| 29. NxR | Q–B2 |
| 30. N/Q–K3 | |

A transparent trap. If Bishop takes pawn, White's P–QB4 cuts off its retreat.

| | |
|---|---|
| 30. . . . | P–QN4 |
| 31. P–QR3 | P–QR4 |
| 32. N–Q2 | N–Q4 |

Since Geller intends to close the position he should not exchange his last Knight. Since he exchanges it he should not close the position.

| | |
|---|---|
| 33. NxN | BxN |
| 34. P–K3 | |

Stahlberg breaks his own rule against making pawn moves without reason. Nothing forces him to weaken his Q3 and give Black's Queen an invasion point. Better is N–B1, N–K3, and Q–Q2.

| | |
|---|---|
| 34. . . . | P–QB5 |
| 35. B–B1 | P–R5 |
| 36. B–N2 | Q–Q2 |
| 37. P–KN4 | |

In order to give the Knight a way out via B1–N3, the opportunity for which soon arises, as we shall see.

| | |
|---|---|
| 37. . . . | B–K3 |
| 38. PxP | PxP |
| 39. N–B1 | |

Stahlberg tires of the boring play for a draw and wants to reach his desired goal more quickly by bringing his Knight via N3 and K2 to Q4. But just at this moment there is a chink in his defensive formation. He should continue B–B1, still not allowing Black's Queen to get to Q6.

| | |
|---|---|
| 39. . . . | Q–Q6 |
| 40. Q–B1 | P–R4 |

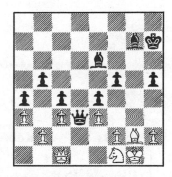

With his time-control move Geller destroys the fruits of his labors, and his deserved victory escapes. With 40. . . . P–N5 he can utilize his two Bishops to place White in an untenable position: 41. RPxP P–R6 42. PxP BxP, and Black's pawn will cost a piece, or 41. BPxP P–B6, breaking through with P–R6.

**41. N–N3    P–R5**

But now, because KB1 is available for White's Bishop, the breakthrough would be too late, and on 41. . . . P–N5 White would have time for B–B1, driving out the Queen.

One move earlier a win, one move later a draw: such is the importance of timing in chess.

42. N–R5 B–B2 43. NxB KxN 44. B–B1 Q–Q1 45. B–K2 Q–N4ch 46. K–B1 P–R6 47. Q–Q1

The game having been adjourned and analyzed, White goes bravely into the variation with a pawn sacrifice, knowing that the game will end in perpetual check anyway.

47. . . . Q–N7ch 48. K–K1 QxP 49. Q–Q4ch K–R2 50. B–B1 Q–N8 51. Q–Q7 K–N1 52. Q–Q8ch K–N2 53. Q–Q4ch K–N3 54. Q–Q6ch, Drawn.

· *Game 21*

## Queen's Gambit Accepted

| I. Boleslavsky | A. Kotov |
|---|---|
| 1. P–Q4 | P–Q4 |
| 2. P–QB4 | PxP |
| 3. N–KB3 | N–KB3 |
| 4. P–K3 | P–K3 |
| 5. BxP | P–B4 |
| 6. O–O | P–QR3 |
| 7. Q–K2 | PxP |

Usually . . . P–QN4 is played here, but Kotov deliberately delays this move until after White's N–QB3. Then, when White answers with the undermining P–QR4 Black can play P–N5 with tempo. Exchanging in the center, Black plans to develop his pieces comfortably and then post a piece on Q4. But this solves White's main difficulty in the Queen's Gambit Accepted—the development of his QB—and in addition the K-file is opened.

Boleslavsky concentrates most of his pieces in the center, and interesting complications arise, the pawn on Q4 playing the role of detonator.

| 8. PxP | B–K2 |
|---|---|
| 9. N–B3 | P–QN4 |
| 10. B–N3 | B–N2 |
| 11. B–N5 | O–O |
| 12. KR–K1 | |

A characteristic move in this opening. White attacks not only the KP but through it the KB. If, for instance, 12. . . . QN–Q2 13. QR–N1 N–N3, already possible is 14. BxP PxB 15. QxPch R–B2 16. N–K5. Kotov therefore tries to liquidate the threat of BxP as soon as possible by exchanging or driving away the Bishop on QN3.

| 12. . . . | N–B3 |
|---|---|
| 13. QR–Q1 | N–QR4 |

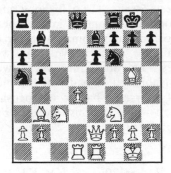

All the commentators agreed that this was a mistake because it allowed White a beautiful breakthrough which gave him active play and, thirty moves later, victory. Stahlberg, and Euwe in his first commentaries, supposed that N–QN5 was necessary. However, many years ago Rauzer showed in his analysis that 13. ... N–QN5 14. P–Q5 QNxQP 15. NxN BxN 16. BxB NxB 17. BxB QxB 18. RxN was good for White. Najdorf, therefore, recommended 13. ... N–Q4 14. NxN BxB 15. N–B3 N–N5. Euwe later concurred.

We should like to take rather a broad view of this "chess mistake." To begin with, N–QR4 is revealed as a mistake only later, by White's clever and far from obvious play. His endgame advantage—a strong Bishop against Black's Knight —is surely not simple, nor is it very much!

Besides, the outcome of the struggle after 13. ... N–Q4 is not known. White has a hidden attacking possibility in 14. NxN BxB 15. N–N6. If Black does not take the Knight but plays 15. ... R–N1, he loses the Exchange by NxB and N–Q7. On 15. ... R–R2, 16. P–Q5 is very strong. If he takes the Knight Black gets into an extremely unpleasant situation after 16. NxB. 16. ... P–KR3 loses because of the Knight sacrifice on B7 followed by QxKP. But how is he to defend against the thematic P–Q5? Unknown. 16. ... NxP does not work because of 17. Q–Q3 N–B4 18. NxKP PxN 19. Bx Pch K–R1 20. BxN or 18. ... Q–B3 19. N–B4, etc.

Had the game actually approximated this course, 13. ... N–Q4 would have been considered an error, and 13. ... N–QR4, which seems to contain no particular danger, would have been recommended.

Black's difficulties, as we shall see, have another cause. White's pieces, in contrast to Black's, are three moves ahead! —he has two Rooks on central files and his Bishop is on an attacking diagonal. If there is logic in chess, three strong developing moves should tell. The grandmaster's task is to prove White's superiority; in this case his task takes the path of complex combinations.

The uniting of logic and combinative skill is very characteristic of Boleslavsky's artistry.

**14. P–Q5        NxB**

It is easy to see that taking the QP with Bishop, Knight, or pawn would cost a piece.

**15. PxP**

**15. . . .        Q–N3**

If Bishop takes Knight, there follows 16. PxPch K–R1 17. RxQ BxQ 18. RxR RxR 19. RxB with two Black pieces under attack, one of which will fall, leaving White two pawns up. If this is not enough for White, 16. QxB N–Q5 17. Q–Q3 is possible.

**16. PxN        PxP**
**17. N–Q4**

White does not need the pawn but the square K6.

**17. . . .        B–Q3**
**18. QxPch      K–R1**
**19. N–B3       QR–Q1**
**20. B–B4**

White should be given credit for choosing this of all possible continuations. The phrase suggests itself: "Two Bishops and good development in an open position fully compensate for a missing Black pawn." As we see, he does not have two Bishops but a bad Knight, and of course he has no compensation—but all this had to be foreseen!

**20. . . .        BxN**

Bad is 20. . . . KR–K1 21. RxB RxQ 22. RxQ RxR 23. B–B7.

**21. RxB        RxR**
**22. QxR        QxQ**
**23. BxQ        R–K1**
**24. RxRch      NxR**
**25. B–K5**

Now Boleslavsky has a chance to demonstrate his skill in the endgame. White starts with a typical technical maneuver in the fight between Bishop and Knight: the Bishop should stand two squares from the Knight on a square of the opposite color. As we can see, the Knight has no moves. Going to B3 would be absolutely hopeless, for the Knight vs. Bishop endgame is an easy win for White with an extra pawn.

Boleslavsky continues by fixing the QNP and QRP on light squares and bringing his King to the center, and after a few preparatory moves he takes the QRP with his Knight.

**25. . . . B–B3 26. P–QN4 P–KR4 27. P–B3 K–R2 28.** N–K2 P–N4 **29. K–B2 P–R5 30. P–KN3 PxPch 31. PxP K–N3 32. P–N4 B–N2 33. K–K3 B–B3 34. N–B3 B–N2 35. N–K4 B–Q4 36. N–B5 K–B2 37. NxP K–K3 38. B–B3 B–R1 39. N–B5ch K–B2 40. N–K4 K–N3 41. B–K5 B–Q4 42. N–Q2 K–B2, Black resigns.**

White would continue 43. K–Q4 K–K3 44. N–K4.

# Round Four

## Game 22
### Queen's Indian Defense

| Y. Geller | I. Boleslavsky |
|---|---|
| 1. P–Q4 | P–K3 |
| 2. N–KB3 | N–KB3 |
| 3. P–B4 | P–QN3 |
| 4. N–B3 | B–N2 |
| 5. B–N5 | P–KR3 |
| 6. BxN | QxB |
| 7. P–K4 | |

Other things being equal, it always pays to place the pawns in the center. Geller did not want to lose time retreating the Bishop and decided to test in practice whether Black's two Bishops would suffice against a strong pawn center.

| 7. . . . | B–N5 |
|---|---|
| 8. B–Q3 | P–B4 |

Black opens the center to give his Bishops more freedom.

| 9. O–O | PxP |
|---|---|
| 10. N–QN5 | Q–Q1 |

The best defense against the threat of N–B7.

| 11. N/5xQP | O–O |
|---|---|
| 12. Q–K2 | N–B3 |

| 13. QR–Q1 | NxN |
|---|---|
| 14. NxN | |

In many variations of the Nimzo-Indian Defense White gets the two Bishops as a result of an exchange on his QB3. In this case it turns out that Black has the two Bishops, but White has the better position: he has left Black behind in development, and he expects to make good use of this, for Black has a backward pawn on Q2 and his Q3 is weak. Geller occupies Q6 with a Knight and then fixes Black's QP with his Rook. Boleslavsky's counterplay is based on his strong Bishop, which will get the long diagonal as soon as White advances P–K5, and on the possibility of opening the KN-file for his heavy pieces.

| 14. . . . | B–B4 |
|---|---|
| 15. B–B2 | R–B1 |
| 16. P–K5 | Q–N4 |
| 17. P–B4 | |

52

White switches completely to attacking the QP, believing that Black's QB is not dangerous. Later, however, the Bishop will avenge this snub. 17. B–K4 makes sense, to liquidate the threat on the long diagonal once and for all.

**17. ...          Q–K2**

But now 18. B–K4 would be followed by 18. ... B–R3 19. P–QN3 P–Q4 20. PxP e.p. QxP, when Black gets rid of his weak pawn and White loses his Knight.

**18. K–R1          P–B4**
**19. N–N5          P–R3**
**20. N–Q6          BxN**
**21. RxB           R–B3**
**22. KR–Q1**

Geller's decision to exchange Rooks goes against his logical play. White is pressing the pawn on Q7, for which two Rooks are clearly better than one. The retreat of the Rook followed by KR–Q1 would force one of Black's pieces to occupy a passive position—R–QB2, B–B1, or R–Q1.

**22. ...          RxR**
**23. RxR          B–B3**
**24. P–N4**

The Queenside diversion P–QN4 followed by P–QR4 and P–N5 would be good in a quieter situation, for instance if Queens were absent. This is the time to think about defense by Q–Q3 or K–N1, but Geller continues his attacking momentum, trying by violent means to force a decision in a position that is not yet ready for it. Boleslavsky now plays his trump.

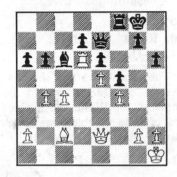

**24. ...          Q–R5**

First he attacks the KBP, taking advantage of the threat of mate on the first rank; if 25. P–N5, for instance, Black can take on N4 with the pawn and then with the Bishop.

**25. R–Q4          P–KN4**

Another pair of trumps— opening the KN-file and demonstrating that the Rook on Q4 is not defending the KBP.

**26. K–N1**

The sudden change in the weather has an effect on Geller's stamina and composure. Nevertheless, this should not cost a pawn; better is 26. Q–K3, and although White then comes under a strong attack with 26. ... PxP 27. RxBP Q–N4

28. Q–B2 K–R1, nothing forced is apparent yet.

| 26. | . . . | PxP |
| 27. | Q–B2 | Q–K2 |
| 28. | P–QR3 | Q–N2 |

A beautiful maneuver.

| 29. | RxBP | QxP |
| 30. | R–Q4 | R–B2 |
| 31. | B–Q3 | |

The ending after the exchange of Queens would be hopeless for White. Both sides are in time trouble, but Boleslavsky plays very precisely.

**31. . . .          P–B5**

The pawn's advance is the beginning of the end.

| 32. | B–B1 | Q–B3 |
| 33. | R–Q2 | P–N4 |
| 34. | P–B5 | Q–R8 |

Advancing the pawn to K6 decides at once. In time pressure Black first wants to exchange Queens.

| 35. | Q–R4 | Q–B3 |
| 36. | QxQ | RxQ |
| 37. | K–B2 | P–K4 |
| 38. | P–N3 | PxPch |

Geller, in time trouble, probably does not see that his Bishop is under fire.

**39. K–K1 R–B6 40. PxP RxNP 41. R–Q6 K–N2 42. B–Q3 P–K5 43. B–K2 RxP 44. B–N4 R–Q6, White resigns.**

## Game 23
### French Defense

| V. Smyslov | G. Stahlberg |
| --- | --- |
| 1. P–K4 | P–K3 |
| 2. P–Q4 | P–Q4 |
| 3. N–QB3 | N–KB3 |
| 4. B–N5 | PxP |
| 5. NxP | B–K2 |
| 6. BxN | BxB |
| 7. N–KB3 | N–Q2 |
| 8. B–B4 | O–O |
| 9. Q–K2 | N–N3 |
| 10. B–N3 | B–Q2 |
| 11. O–O | |

In this game the chess board becomes the arena for a battle of wills between Smyslov and Stahlberg as they repeat their game of three years earlier in Budapest. Then Stahlberg continued 11. . . . B–QR5, and after 12. NxBch it turned out that taking the Knight with the Queen was not playable because of 13. BxB NxB 14. Q–B4, winning a pawn. Now he exchanges the light-square Bishops two moves later but achieves no significant improvement.

White has a tangible superiority in space and full freedom to maneuver, whereas Black's Bishop is under attack by the Knight and requires the protection of the Queen. The advance of Black's Knight is also

impeded. In such conditions the
slightest inaccuracy by Black
can be fatal.

| 11. . . . | Q–K2 |
| 12. KR–K1 | QR–Q1 |
| 13. QR–Q1 | B–QR5 |
| 14. BxB | NxB |
| 15. Q–N5 | N–N3 |
| 16. P–B4 | P–B3 |
| 17. Q–N3 | Q–B2 |

White was threatening 18.
NxBch to force PxN, for 18.
. . . QxN would have been fol-
lowed by 19. P–B5, winning
the QNP. Stahlberg's 17. . . .
Q–B2 does not parry this threat.

Stahlberg may be censured
for not playing the more precise R–Q2, but even then White
would have many ways of increasing the pressure, if only by
18. P–QR4 or N–B5 and N–
Q3, not to mention the simple
NxBch, N–K5, R–K3–R3 with
an attack.

| 18. NxBch | PxN |
| 19. Q–K3 | K–N2 |

Smyslov's logical play makes
Black's defense more and more
difficult. Of course the QBP
cannot be taken because of Q–
R6, when Black has no time to
defend his KBP. For instance,
19. . . . NxP 20. Q–R6 Q–K2
21. N–R4, threatening N–B5
and R–Q3. There is no salvation in 19. . . . K–R1 in view
of 20. Q–R6 N–Q2 21. P–Q5,
and after the exchange of pawns
White's Rook gets to Q5 and

from there to KR5; or 20. . . .
Q–K2 21. N–R4. To continue
the attack after the text move
White needs to transfer his
Knight to KN4—but how can
it get there?

**20. N–K5**

An excellent move with a
charmingly simple idea. There
is no other way to KN4 but
through K5, so the Knight
throws itself on the bayonets.
What could be simpler! The
whole point is that eliminating
the Knight would open the way
for a mating attack by the
Queen and Rook: 20. . . . PxN
21. Q–N5ch followed by Q–
B6ch and R–K3. The beautiful
forcing maneuver to keep
Black's King in the corner is
an interesting variation of practical importance: 21. Q–N5ch
K–R1 22. Q–B6ch K–N1 23.
R–K3 KR–K1 24. Q–R6—a
quiet move—24. . . . K–R1 25.
R–KN3 threatening Q–N7
mate, and if . . . R–KN1 then
obviously 26. Q–B6ch.

| 20. . . . | Q–K2 |
|-----------|------|
| 21. N–N4  | R–KN1 |
| 22. N–R6  |      |

A little concluding combination. The Rook cannot leave because of the threat N–B5ch. Equally as good as the text move, by which White wins the Exchange and brings the game

to a technical phase, is 22. Q–R6ch, continuing the attack.

22. . . . Q–B2 23. NxR RxN 24. P–QN3 K–R1 25. Q–R6 R–N3 26. Q–R4 N–Q2 27. R–K3 Q–R4 28. R–R3 N–B1 29. R–N3 QxP 30. RxR NxR 31. QxBPch K–N1 32. Q–B3 Q–B7 33. Q–Q3, Black resigns.

## Game 24
### Nimzo-Indian Defense

| P. Keres | M. Euwe |
|----------|---------|
| 1. P–Q4  | N–KB3   |
| 2. P–QB4 | P–K3    |
| 3. N–QB3 | B–N5    |
| 4. P–K3  | P–B4    |
| 5. B–Q3  | O–O     |
| 6. N–B3  | P–Q4    |
| 7. O–O   | QN–Q2   |

A slight modification in a fashionable variation: the Knight is brought to Q2 instead of B3. In this game we see Euwe the theoretician. He wants to demonstrate that Black can draw easily by keeping the Bishop pair and forcing piece exchanges.

| 8. P–QR3 | QPxP |
|----------|------|
| 9. BxP   |      |

If White takes the Bishop Black has the good intermediate move 9. . . . PxP, attacking two White pieces. After 10. BxP PxN, neither Q–N3 nor the immediate PxP gives White any tangible advantage.

| 9. . . . | PxP     |
|----------|---------|
| 10. PxP  | B–K2    |
| 11. B–R2 | N–N3    |
| 12. N–K5 | N/N–Q4  |
| 13. Q–B3 | NxN     |
| 14. PxN  | N–Q2    |
| 15. N–N4 | N–B3    |
| 16. NxNch | BxN    |
| 17. B–B4 | B–N4    |

An amusing situation! One by one, Black methodically exchanges every White piece participating in the fight; after the two Knights comes the Bishops' turn. White cannot avoid these exchanges; he can only choose the squares on which they occur.

| 18. B–N3 | B–R5 |
|----------|------|
| 19. B–K5 | B–B3 |

As bothersome as a fly, this Bishop.

| 20. KR–K1 | BxB |
|-----------|-----|
| 21. RxB   | Q–B3 |
| 22. Q–K4  |     |

Trading Queens is pointless, for in the Rook endgame White's QRP and QBP would give him trouble.

**22. . . .          R–N1**

White has some advantage in development, but he cannot find where to apply his forces since Black has no weaknesses and there are so few pieces. In the meantime, Black plans to find a good place for his Bishop either via Q2 to B3 or P–QN3 and B–N2.

**23. P–Q5**

With many pieces on the board such pressure is always of some promise, but here it is only a reminder of what might have been.

**23. . . . PxP 24. BxP B–Q2 25. R–K1 B–B3**

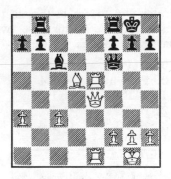

**26. P–QB4 P–KN3 27. P–N3 QR–K1 28. K–N2 RxR 29. QxR QxQ 30. RxQ BxB 31. PxB R–Q1 32. R–K7 RxP 33. RxNP R–QR4 34. R–N3, Drawn.**

The achievement of this drawn position is a victory for Euwe the theoretician, but this is not the end . . .

## Game 25
### Grünfeld Defense

| S. Reshevsky | L. Szabo |
|---|---|
| 1. P–Q4 | N–KB3 |
| 2. P–QB4 | P–KN3 |
| 3. N–QB3 | P–Q4 |
| 4. B–B4 | B–N2 |
| 5. P–K3 | O–O |

Black offers the sacrifice of a pawn by 6. PxP NxP 7. NxN QxN 8. BxP in the interest of rapid development of his pieces on the Queenside, but Reshevsky prefers a quiet continuation.

| 6. Q–N3 | P–B4 |
|---|---|
| 7. BPxP | PxP |
| 8. PxP | P–K3 |

Having started the game in gambit style, Szabo does not stop halfway but sacrifices another pawn. This gambit, invented by Grandmaster Trifunovic, is based on White's not having developed a single Kingside piece. Black strives to destroy his opponent's pawn center and to create threats to his King. But in this case two pawns is too high a price.

| 9. | PxP | N–B3 |
|----|-----|------|
| 10. | PxPch | K–R1 |
| 11. | N–B3 | NxP |
| 12. | NxN | QxN |
| 13. | B–K3 | Q–K4 |

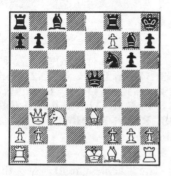

This position can be found in the book by Trifunovic, Gruber, and Bozic, *The Grün- feld Defense* (Part One, Second System, Variation 18, Con- tinuation A). It says there that for his two pawns Black has two threats, N–N5 and B–K3. It is clear that both players had pre- pared this variation in advance, and Reshevsky, as we will now see, wards off both threats with the aid of one Bishop.

| 14. | B–K2 | B–K3 |
|-----|------|------|
| 15. | B–QB4 | B–Q2 |

Szabo loses heart, and mak- ing essentially the first move of his own he immediately loses the battle. The spirit of this variation calls for exchanging Bishops and developing the QR

to QB1 with tempo. If 17. Q– N3 then 17. . . . N–N5 18. N– Q1 R–B2, and Black wins back one of the pawns. After 17. Q– Q4 Q–KR4, Black's threat of N–N5 keeps White from cas- tling and wins the pawn on Black's B2. White would prob- ably reply 17. Q–KB4, but then 17. . . . Q–K3 would be possible, giving fair counterplay.

| 16. | P–KR3 | P–QN4 |
|-----|-------|-------|
| 17. | B–K2 | B–K3 |
| 18. | QxP | N–Q4 |
| 19. | NxN | P–QR3 |
| 20. | Q–B5 | QR–B1 |
| 21. | Q–R3 | BxN |
| 22. | O–O | RxP |

Black hastens to eliminate the most annoying pawn. If he takes the QNP, then after ex- changing Queens White con- tinues 24. QR–Q1, and 24. . . . BxRP is impossible because of the elegant mate 25. R–Q2 R– QN1 26. RxB RxR 27. B–Q4 mate. Black would have to take the BP on his 24th move, leav- ing White a pawn ahead.

| 23. | KR–Q1 | B–N2 |
|-----|-------|------|
| 24. | BxP | |

A little combination: if 24. . . . R–R1 25. Q–N3, with a double threat against QN7 and KB7.

**24. . . . Q–K5 25. BxB RxB 26. QR–B1 R–K1 27. R–Q2 B–K4 28. QR–Q1 K–N1 29. P–QN3 B–B2 30. Q–R6 R–N5 31. Q–Q3 Q–K4 32. Q–Q5ch, Black resigns.**

## Game 26
### Nimzo-Indian Defense

**D. Bronstein**    **Y. Averbakh**

1. P–Q4 N–KB3 2. P–QB4 P–K3 3. N–QB3 B–N5 4. P–K3 O–O 5. N–B3 P–QN3 6. B–K2 B–N2 7. O–O P–Q4 8. PxP PxP 9. B–Q2 B–Q3 10. R–B1 P–QR3 11. N–K5 P–B4 12. N–N4 QN–Q2 13. NxNch NxN 14. PxP PxP

White's passive play, his premature exchange on Q5, and the unfortunate position of his Bishop on Q2 do not permit him to organize an attack on Black's hanging pawns.

15. B–B3 R–K1 16. N–R4 QR–B1 17. Q–N3 B–R1 18. KR–Q1 N–K5 19. B–K1 R–N1 20. Q–Q3 Q–R5 21. P–KN3 NxNP

Rather than wait for his opponent finally to decide to attack the pawns on Q4 and QB4, Black simplifies the position by a series of exchanges.

22. RPxN QxN 23. B–B3 B–K4 24. BxB RxB 25. RxP QxP 26. P–QN4 R/4–K1, Drawn.

## Game 27
### King's Indian Defense

**S. Gligoric**    **T. Petrosian**

| | |
|---|---|
| 1. P–Q4 | N–KB3 |
| 2. P–QB4 | P–B4 |
| 3. P–Q5 | P–K3 |
| 4. N–QB3 | PxP |
| 5. PxP | P–Q3 |
| 6. N–B3 | P–KN3 |
| 7. N–Q2 | |

This is a violation of the classical opening principle not to move the same piece twice. White moves the Knight not only twice but even three times to post it on QB4. Does this mean that the principle is incorrect? Of course not! The point is that Black has already deviated from classical rules twice—he has exchanged a center pawn for one on the flank, voluntarily creating a backward pawn on Q3, and his last move has created a weakness on the dark squares. If one partner plays concretely and the other believes only in following the rules, it is not difficult to guess who will win.

As an illustration, take this extreme case: 1. P–KB3? P–K3 2. P–KN4? What should Black do? Moving the Queen so early in the game is not recommended, but in view of White's mistakes 2. . . . Q–R5 is not bad.

The transfer of the KN from B3 via Q2 to QB4 was played in a similar position in the well-known Nimzovich–Marshall game at the New York tournament of 1927, and it has been popular ever since. The idea is to pin Black down by pressure against the QP and the point QN6 and to deny him his only active plan in this position, P–QR3, P–QN4, etc., while the Knight can be maintained on QB4 by P–QR4–5. Furthermore, on Q2 the Knight prepares the advance P–K4, which, combined with P–KB4 and P–K5, is basic to White's strategy in this position.

7. . . .          QN–Q2

To answer 8. N–B4 with 8. . . . N–N3.

| 8. P–KN3 | B–N2 |
| 9. B–N2 | O–O |
| 10. O–O | Q–K2 |
| 11. N–B4 | N–K4 |
| 12. NxN | QxN |
| 13. P–QR4 | P–QR3 |
| 14. P–R5 | |

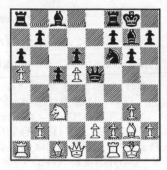

White has the better position. Black does not have the power to exploit his "extra" pawn on the Queenside, for White's RP is holding two Black pawns. Meanwhile, at his first opportunity White can start a pawn storm with P–K4, P–KB4, and P–K5, clearing the way for the pawn on Q5. The fact is that Grandmaster Gligoric would rather maneuver pieces than make hasty pawn moves, so his KP never reaches the fourth rank.

| 14. . . . | R–K1 |
| 15. B–B4 | Q–K2 |
| 16. Q–N3 | |

It is hard to win a game without moving pawns. Here 16. N–R4 N–Q2 17. R–N1 and 18. P–QN4 looks good in order to open the QN-file and approach Black's QP from the flank. Furthermore, Black's QBP might be forced to advance to QB5 where White could try to win it.

| 16. . . . | N–Q2 |
| 17. KR–K1 | N–K4 |

| 18. | N–R4 | B–Q2 |
| 19. | N–N6 | QR–N1 |
| 20. | B–Q2 | B–N4 |
| 21. | B–QB3 | |

White has kept his previous advantage. He intends to drive away Black's Knight, exchange Bishops to weaken the Black King's position, and then play P–K4–5. Sensing real danger, Petrosian resorts to tactical devices. His next moves—P–B5 and P–KB4—complicate the play but do not improve his position.

| 21. | . . . | P–B5 |
| 22. | Q–B2 | P–B4 |
| 23. | P–R3 | Q–QB2 |
| 24. | P–B4 | N–Q2 |
| 25. | NxN | BxN |
| 26. | BxB | KxB |
| 27. | Q–B3ch | K–N1 |
| 28. | K–R2 | Q–B4 |
| 29. | P–K3 | P–QN4 |
| 30. | PxP e.p. | RxNP |
| 31. | R–R5 | Q–N5 |
| 32. | R–K2 | QxQ |

The weakness of Black's QBP and QRP as well as the con-crete threat of QxQ and RxP force him to exchange Queens and go into an ending that is inferior despite his passed pawn. The next phase of the game takes place in time pressure, during which both opponents play inaccurately.

| 33. | PxQ | K–B1 |
| 34. | K–N1 | |

This allows Black to regroup and release the Rook from the defense of the RP.

| 34. | . . . | R–N8ch |
| 35. | K–B2 | B–N4 |
| 36. | P–N4 | R–B8 |

It is better to attack the pawn from the side by 36. . . . R–N6 and after 37. R–B2 to continue the plan begun by K–B1: to bring the King to the Queenside to try to increase the mobility of the passed pawn.

| 37. | R–R3 | K–B2 |

Even now . . . R–N1 intending . . . R–N3 is better. Black does not have to display such ingenuity to draw.

| 38. | B–B3 | R–K2 |
| 39. | P–R4 | R–Q8 |
| 40. | P–N5 | R–Q6 |

The Rook is badly placed here. There is only one move to make before the draw.

| 41. | P–R5 | |

The game was adjourned here. After home analysis the opponents agreed that Black could draw. Gligoric wanted only to see Black's sealed move.

Of course, Petrosian would not let the pawn get to R6.

| 41. . . . | PxP |
|---|---|

**Drawn**

## Game 28

The reader is informed in advance that this is one of the most interesting games in the tournament and the winner of a beauty prize. In both of its stages—the opening and the middlegame—Najdorf plays at such a high level of erudition and mastery that the third stage is not needed.

## King's Indian Defense

| M. Taimanov | M. Najdorf |
|---|---|
| 1. P–Q4 | N–KB3 |
| 2. P–QB4 | P–KN3 |
| 3. N–QB3 | B–N2 |
| 4. P–K4 | P–Q3 |
| 5. N–B3 | O–O |
| 6. B–K2 | P–K4 |
| 7. O–O | N–B3 |
| 8. P–Q5 | |

Shortly before the Zurich tournament Taimanov used the variation 7. . . . N–B3 8. P–Q5 twice in the 20th U.S.S.R. Championship. In both cases he succeeded with exactly the same plan: a pawn break on the QB-file, encirclement of the flank, and penetration to the rear, where all of Black's pieces were clustered on the Q-, K-, KB-, and KN-files. White left only his dark-square Bishop on guard to defend his King. The games appeared in the chess press everywhere and left the impression that they had been lost in the opening. Some players, however, continued to have success as Black with this "refuted" variation of the King's Indian. For instance, in Mar del Plata 1953 Najdorf fell victim to it as White against Gligoric and drew with difficulty against Trifunovic. But these games were not known to Taimanov when the Zurich tournament started.

So both players go through the opening with high hopes. Najdorf strictly follows what he learned from the Yugoslavian analysis, which continues for at least twenty-one moves, and Taimanov's optimism is based on his successes.

| 8. . . . | N–K2 |
|---|---|
| 9. N–K1 | N–Q2 |
| 10. B–K3 | P–KB4 |
| 11. P–B3 | P–B5 |
| 12. B–B2 | |

This system of defending the Kingside, invented by Taimanov, looks very impressive. The pawns distributed on the light squares form a toothlike fortified wall and the dark-square Bishop protects all the spaces between the teeth. But if one looks at the position without preconceptions, then it is naive to speak of any advantage for White. Can Black derive more from the opening than the development of all his pieces, the advance P–KB4–5, the seizure of the dark squares, and, consequently, real attacking chances on the Kingside? On the other hand, in view of the extreme sharpness of the situation Black has to play precisely, combining his attack with defense on the Queenside and especially Q3 and K2, and he must take advantage of every tactical opportunity.

| 12. | . . . | P–KN4 |
|-----|-------|-------|
| 13. | N–Q3 | N–KB3 |
| 14. | P–B5 | N–N3 |
| 15. | R–B1 | R–B2 |
| 16. | R–B2 | B–B1 |

This is the system used by Gligoric and Trifunovic in Mar del Plata. The pawn on Q3 is now defended, the Rook can get to the KN-file, and Black's Knights threaten the Kingside. Taimanov, however, relying on the unassailability of his position, continues his daring storm of the Queenside.

| 17. | PxP | PxP |
|-----|-----|-----|
| 18. | Q–Q2 | P–N5 |
| 19. | KR–B1 | P–N6! |

An extremely promising pawn sacrifice.

| 20. | PxP | PxP |
|-----|-----|-----|
| 21. | BxNP | N–R4 |
| 22. | B–R2 | B–K2 |
| 23. | N–N1 | B–Q2 |
| 24. | Q–K1 | B–KN4 |
| 25. | N–Q2 | B–K6ch |
| 26. | K–R1 | Q–N4 |

One after another, as if following a script, Black's pieces arrive on the battlefield. Taimanov should now get rid of the Bishop on his K3, even at the cost of the Exchange, and to that end he should play 27. N–QB4.

| 27. | B–B1 | QR–KB1 |
|-----|------|--------|
| 28. | R–Q1 | P–N4 |
| 29. | P–R4 | P–QR3 |
| 30. | PxP | PxP |
| 31. | R–B7 | R–N2 |
| 32. | N–N3 | N–R5 |
| 33. | R–B2 | B–R6 |

A picturesque position! The Queenside has become utterly deserted, seven pieces are attacking White's King, and the point KN2, now attacked four times, apparently cannot be defended. On PxB there follows mate in three, and RxP is also a threat.

| 34. | Q–K2 | NxNP |
| 35. | BxN | BxBch |
| 36. | QxB | Q–R5 |

White cannot save his Queen: if it retreats Black checks on N6.

| 37. | QxRch | KxQ |
| 38. | R–N2ch | K–R1 |
| 39. | N–K1 | N–B5 |
| 40. | R–N3 | B–B7 |
| 41. | R–N4 | Q–R6 |
| 42. | N–Q2 | P–R4 |

The game was adjourned here; White sealed 43. R–N5 and resigned without resuming. After 43. . . . . R–KN1 44. Rx Rch KxR there would be no defense to mate.

# Round Five

## Game 29
### Queen's Indian Defense

| T. Petrosian | M. Taimanov |
|---|---|
| 1. P–Q4 | N–KB3 |
| 2. P–QB4 | P–K3 |
| 3. N–KB3 | P–QN3 |
| 4. N–B3 | B–N2 |
| 5. P–K3 | P–Q4 |
| 6. PxP | PxP |
| 7. B–N5ch | |

White has to develop the Bishop anyway; without losing time and by making use of the fact that it is disadvantageous for Black to interpose a piece, he provokes . . . P–B3, blocking Black's Bishop. Therefore, it was better for Black not to hurry to advance his QP on his 5th move but first to play B–K2.

| 7. . . . | P–B3 |
|---|---|
| 8. B–Q3 | B–K2 |
| 9. O–O | O–O |
| 10. P–QN3 | QN–Q2 |
| 11. B–N2 | B–Q3 |

Not entirely logical. White will obviously want to transfer a Knight to KB5, and the Bishop will then have to leave; it is better first to prepare a place for it on KB1 with the otherwise useful move . . . R–K1.

| 12. N–KR4 | R–K1 |
|---|---|
| 13. N–B5 | B–KB1 |
| 14. R–B1 | N–K5 |

It is not quite enough to base such a decision on an evaluation of the position alone; precise long-range calculation is also needed. Sensing that his position is gradually deteriorating, and well aware of Petrosian's strength in just such positions, Taimanov shifts gears and invites his opponent on a combinational excursion. The decision is psychologically correct and very characteristic of Taimanov's style.

| 15. BxN | PxB |
|---|---|

**16. Q–N4**

The tempting 16. P–Q5 PxP 17. NxQP gives nothing after the trade of Bishop for Knight: 17. . . . BxN 18. QxB N–B4. However, 17. N–N5 would be worth trying, threatening N–B7 and N–Q6, or 16. . . . R–B1 then 17. Q–N4. But 16. P–Q5 PxP 17. NxQP N–B4 18. N–R6ch PxN 19. N–B6ch, etc., is playable. Curiously, these combinations, as well as the one actually played, are caused by the pawn on Black's QB3 that closes the Bishop's diagonal—the result of a scarcely noticeable opening inaccuracy by Black.

**16. . . .        P–N3**

The threat was N–R6ch, Nx Pch, and NxQ.

**17. NxP**

White expresses his readiness to sacrifice a piece. Now 17. . . . P–KR4 could follow, and then White's Queen would have to leave either the N-file, freeing Black's pawn to take the Knight on B5, or the fourth rank, removing the protection of the Knight on K4. However, Taimanov does not wish to undertake the risks and limits himself to trading his Rook and two pawns for two Knights. Material equality is maintained, and the struggle is rekindled with new force.

| | |
|---|---|
| **17. . . .** | **RxN** |
| **18. QxR** | **PxN** |
| **19. QxKBP** | **B–N2** |
| **20. P–K4** | |

With the idea of transferring the Rook via B3 to the attack on the Kingside.

| | |
|---|---|
| **20. . . .** | **N–B1** |
| **21. P–K5** | |

Petrosian decides to mobilize a pawn storm with his KP and KBP. Though tempting, this requires one more move than chess rules allow. It is necessary, as Najdorf suggested, to continue 21. R–B3 P–B4 22. R–N3 PxP 23. R–Q1 N–K3 24. Q–N4 or 21. . . . QxP 22. B–R1 B–B1 23. Q–B3, with a strong attack.

The text move shuts in White's Bishop and hands the long diagonal to Black, which brings the Bishop on N2 and the Queen on Q4 into harmony.

| | |
|---|---|
| **21. . . .** | **Q–Q4** |
| **22. P–B4** | **P–B4** |

Forcing White to turn to defense. Now the advantage is Black's.

| 23. | Q–R3 | PxP |
| --- | --- | --- |
| 24. | QR–Q1 | Q–K5 |
| 25. | QR–K1 | Q–Q4 |
| 26. | R–Q1 | R–B1 |
| 27. | RxP | Q–R4 |
| 28. | R–B4 | |

Due to Black's terrible threat of R–B7, White is forced to consent to the exchange of Rooks and the weakening of his Queenside pawns.

| 28. | . . . | RxR |
| --- | --- | --- |
| 29. | PxR | Q–B4ch |
| 30. | R–B2 | QxBP |
| 31. | Q–QN3 | Q–K5 |
| 32. | Q–B2 | N–K3 |
| 33. | P–B5 | |

Although the endgame would favor Black, White should exchange Queens to escape at least the direct threats to his King, which are becoming quite dangerous.

| 33. | . . . | N–B4 |
| --- | --- | --- |
| 34. | Q–Q2 | Q–N8ch |
| 35. | R–B1 | Q–Q6 |
| 36. | Q–K1 | Q–Q4 |
| 37. | Q–N3 | N–K5 |

| 38. | Q–R4 | N–B6 |
| --- | --- | --- |
| 39. | Q–N4 | P–KR4 |

Leaving only one body-guard for his King, as he usually does, Taimanov has placed all the rest of his pieces on the best squares.

White's Queen has to defend KN2 and K2 at the same time. The last move forces it to give up one of these squares, and Black carries out the decisive combination.

| 40. | Q–R3 | N–K7ch |
| --- | --- | --- |
| 41. | K–B2 | |

41. K–R1 would be followed by 41. . . . N–B5 42. Q–KB3 NxP. But now Black has 41. . . . Q–Q7. Therefore, White resigned without waiting for his opponent's reply.

## Game 30
### King's Indian Defense

| Y. Averbakh | S. Gligoric | 3. P–KN3 | B–N2 |
| --- | --- | --- | --- |
| 1. P–QB4 | N–KB3 | 4. B–N2 | O–O |
| 2. N–QB3 | P–KN3 | 5. P–Q4 | P–Q3 |

| 6. N–B3 | QN–Q2 |
| 7. O–O | P–K4 |
| 8. P–K4 | PxP |
| 9. NxP | |

This position has been so frequently encountered recently that a few words should be said about it; not about systems or mind-cluttering variations but about the ideas that guide both sides for many moves. Black exchanges in the center to open the diagonal for his Bishop and to attack Q5, and soon he will attack the KP with his Knight and Rook. A post at QB4 for his Knight will be secured by P–QR4, and that pawn may advance even farther, to R5 and R6.

So far White is not attacking anything, but he has a strong center and freedom to maneuver. Look at the board: White's men are arranged on four ranks, Black's on three, and between them lies a no-man's-land. This geometric description to some extent reflects the character of the opening: the opponents' forces have not yet come in contact. White's further plans are simple: to develop the Bishop and Queen; to connect the Rooks; to prepare an attack against the QP, which should become weak in this kind of formation; and to see to the defense of his KP. The various methods of defending this pawn determine the various systems of play. It would be nice to play

Q–B2, but then the Knight on Q4 would be defenseless, a circumstance Black could turn to account; if White starts with B–K3, Black has N–KN5. This play for tempos and various combinational possibilities, which is due to the presence of all the pieces and nearly all the pawns, constitutes the chess lover's principal attraction to the King's Indian Defense.

| 9. . . . | N–B4 |
| 10. P–B3 | |

Before leaving for the tournament in Switzerland every participant prepared certain new systems, particularly in such popular defenses as the King's Indian, the Sicilian, and the Nimzo-Indian. One of the most successful novelties in a known system is used by Averbakh in this game: P–B3, R–B2, R–Q2. White prepares an attack on the QP, but practice has shown that taking it with the Queen is unwise because the Queen is subject to attack on Q6 and soon has to leave. The invasion of the enemy camp must begin with a weaker piece. Meanwhile, P–B3 strengthens the security of the KP, and the KB's diagonal is only temporarily closed.

| 10. . . . | P–QR4 |
| 11. B–K3 | P–R5 |
| 12. R–B2 | P–B3 |
| 13. N–B2 | Q–K2 |
| 14. R–Q2 | |

White has built up a rock-solid position. Now Black can defend his QP only tactically—14. . . . R–Q1 obviously does not work because of BxN. Gligoric proves equal to the task: he has a command of all the fine points of the King's Indian Defense, not mechanically but creatively. It is hard to believe that Black does not yield his QP during the next ten moves.

**14. . . .                    KN–Q2**
**15. R–B1**

Taking the QP is met by P–R6 and if 16. NxP then BxN, winning a piece. White repulses this threat; but later . . . ?

**15. . . .                    B–K4**

This seems pointless—surely the Bishop cannot hold out here for long. But it does, nonetheless.

**16. B–B2**

If 16. P–B4 BxN 17. PxB NxP 18. BxN QxB 19. RxP, and although Black's Kingside is weakened White's is no stronger, and the pawns are even.

**16. . . .                    R–K1**
**17. N–K3**

To drive the Bishop away by N–N4.

**17. . . .                    N–B1**
**18. N–K2                    Q–B2**
**19. R–N1                    P–R6**
**20. P–N3**

If 20. P–N4 N–R5.

**20. . . .                    P–R4**
**21. Q–B2                    B–K3**
**22. N–B3                    N–R2**

The position is ripe for decisive action and White proceeds to attack on all fronts, but perhaps it is worth making just one more preparatory move: QR–Q1.

**23. P–QN4                   N–R3**
**24. P–B4                    B–N2**
**25. P–KB5**

A move like this is either very good or very bad. The shortcomings of moving the pawn to B5 are so obvious that it is playable only when a forced variation can be calculated to a clear advantage. In this case, Averbakh probably failed to correctly evaluate the position arising after Black's 33rd move.

**25. . . .                    B–Q2**
**26. Q–N3**

Somewhat slowing the tempo of the attack. Perhaps better is

26. PxP PxP 27. P–K5 RxP 28.
QxP, getting close to Black's
King and paralyzing his activity
by the threats RxP, N–B5, N–
K4, etc.

| 26. . . . | N–B3 |
| 27. PxP | |

But now this exchange is a
mistake. It is still not too late
to play QR–Q1 and on . . . B–
KB1 to continue the attack
with P–B5.

| 27. . . . | PxP |
| 28. P–B5ch | B–K3 |
| 29. PxP | BxQ |
| 30. PxQ | B–B2 |

Many weaknesses have ap-
peared in White's camp.

| 31. P–N5 | NxBP |
| 32. PxP | PxP |
| 33. R–N7 | QR–B1 |

Perhaps Averbakh thought
his Rook on the seventh rank
would give him the advantage,
but Black's QRP is so dangerous that Black's position must
be considered superior.

**34. R–B2**

The threat was . . . N–N5.

| 34. . . . | N–R3 |
| 35. B–B1 | N–B4 |
| 36. RxB | |

Averbakh's ingenuity does
not desert him even in the most
difficult circumstances. He sets
a trap for his opponent in time
pressure, but Gligoric finds the
right answer.

| 36. . . . | KxR |
| 37. B–B4ch | K–B1 |
| 38. N–B5 | |

Hoping for 38. . . . PxN 39.
BxNch.

**38. . . . N/4xP 39. NxB
KxN 40. NxN RxN 41. B–R6
R–Q1 42. P–R3 R–QN5 43.
RxP N–K5 44. R–B7ch K–R1
45. B–K3 R–N7, White re-
signs.**

## • Game 31
## King's Indian Defense

| L. Szabo | D. Bronstein |
| --- | --- |
| 1. P–Q4 | N–KB3 |
| 2. P–QB4 | P–Q3 |
| 3. N–KB3 | QN–Q2 |
| 4. P–KN3 | P–K4 |
| 5. B–N2 | P–B3 |

White's development seems
beyond reproach, but it is not
flawless: he has not taken control of his K4, and Black makes
immediate use of this to prepare P–K4 and P–Q4. Szabo
prefers to exchange on his K5,
but then Black gets easy play
and even starts thinking about
seizing the initiative.

| 6. PxP | PxP |
| 7. O–O | B–B4 |

| | |
|---|---|
| 8. N–B3 | O–O |
| 9. Q–B2 | Q–K2 |
| 10. N–KR4 | R–K1 |
| 11. N–R4 | |

One of the characteristics of modern chess is the dynamic position in which, although the chances for each side may be determined, it is difficult to decide which of them has the advantage. Each player usually thinks he stands better, although at times one thinks he is worse.

The basic factor in the present struggle is Black's KP. Supported by the Queen and Rook it might easily get to K6. To counter this, White wants to disrupt the enemy ranks by Knight raids on the flanks. Black decides not to lose time retreating the Bishop because if it is exchanged his Knight will occupy a good post on QB4 and a diagonal will be opened for his QB; furthermore, his next move prevents the Knight on KR4 from retreating to B3. All this would repay the "sacrifice" of the King's Indian Bishop with interest.

| | |
|---|---|
| 11. . . . | P–K5 |
| 12. N–B5 | Q–K4 |
| 13. B–R3 | |

With the unequivocal threat of 14. B–B4; however, now Black has time to hide his Bishop, not only opening the Queen's way to QR4 but also accentuating the unfortunate position of White's Knight on QR4. After 13. NxB NxN 14. N–K3 the game would be about even, but now the initiative goes completely over to Black. Grandmaster Szabo is not satisfied with the bird in his hand and goes after the two in the bush, which soon fly away.

| | |
|---|---|
| 13. . . . | B–B1 |
| 14. B–Q2 | Q–B2 |
| 15. B–N2 | |

Necessary because the threat to move the Knight from Q2 would have created an unpleasant pin on Black's QB1–KR6 diagonal.

| | |
|---|---|
| 15. . . . | P–KN3 |
| 16. N–K3 | Q–K4 |
| 17. P–B4 | Q–KR4 |

Also strong is 17. . . . PxP e.p. 18. PxP Q–Q5.

**18. P–KR3**

In view of Black's positional threat of N–B4, B–R6, etc., White is practically forced to sacrifice his KP.

**18. . . .          QxKP**

The Black Queen sets out on a long and dangerous journey. Five Queen moves for one pawn is obviously unprofitable arithmetic for Black. But what can White accomplish during those five moves?

| | |
|---|---|
| 19. QR–Q1 | Q–Q6 |
| 20. Q–B1 | Q–Q3 |
| 21. P–KN4 | Q–B2 |

As it turns out, White has made one usefu¹ move, QR–Q1; as for the advance of the King-side pawns, that may be called rather more double-edged than favorable for White.

It must be added that Black could have managed his pieces even better; for instance, 19. . . . N–B4 20. N–B3 and only then 20. . . . Q–Q6. In that case Black's Knight would have stood actively on B4, his QB would have had an open diagonal, and White's QB would have been temporarily deprived of QB3.

What conclusion can we draw from all this? That with good development it is not dangerous to spend a few moves to win an important pawn. It is necessary, however, to evaluate the position sensibly and to calculate all the variations exactly.

**22. B–QB3**

**22. . . .          B–N2**

Captivated by his plan to get as much advantage as possible

from the position of White's Knight on R5, Black violates both requirements just mentioned.

The obvious 22. . . . P–QN4 would force White to trade his most threatening piece, the QB. The variation 23. BxN NxB 24. PxP Q–R4 seemed not clear enough to me and I decided to make some waiting move. Now . . . P–QN4 really is a threat, but . . .

**23. P–N5          P–N4**

Alas! Black must give up a Knight so as not to fall into a mating attack—23. . . . N–R4 24. BxB NxB 25. N–N4, and then with Q–B3 White takes full command of the QR1–KR8 diagonal. Knowing Szabo's ability to conduct a direct attack, I did not doubt the outcome of the game if I entered this variation. Now Black must continue the fight with the energy of desperation.

**24. PxN          B–B1**

The Bishop returns home without glory, its horse lost on the way.

**25. PxP          PxP**
**26. N–Q5          Q–B3**
**27. P–B5**

The reason for this pawn move can be seen in the variation 27. . . . PxN 28. PxP RPxP 29. N–K7ch BxN 30. PxB RxP 31. Q–R6 N–K4 32. R–Q8ch R–K1 33. BxN!. Black's next move is directed against this threat: he connects Rooks and defends his first rank.

| 27. . . . | B–QN2 |
| 28. PxP | RPxP |
| 29. N–K7ch | BxN |
| 30. PxB | P–N5 |

At least there is a moment to deflect the horrible Bishop from the long diagonal.

**31. BxNP**

31. Q–B4 is not bad.

| 31. . . . | QxN |
| 32. B–QB3 | |

Szabo definitely wants to give mate. B–R3, preserving the pawn on K7, is good enough to win.

| 32. . . . | RxP |
| 33. Q–R6 | |

A tactical finesse: White provokes the Black Knight to K4 so that he can attack two pieces. Strangely, this move gives Black hope of defending because White's QR1–KR8 diagonal is momentarily closed. 33. Q–N5

QR–K1 34. RxN and 35. Q–B6 is stronger.

| 33. . . . | N–K4 |
| 34. Q–N5 | Q–K1 |

Black is so terrorized by White's QB that he can think only of quickly playing QR–B1xB. Q–K1 is a thoughtless move; just now it is necessary to try 34. . . . QR–K1 and to reply to Euwe's recommended 35. R–Q8 with the simple R–K3, somehow remaining suspended over the abyss.

| 35. R–B4 | R–B1 |
| 36. R–R4 | |

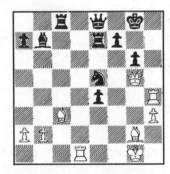

| 36. . . . | RxB |

For the first time since the 23rd move I took an easy breath, only now noticing 37. Q–B6! with mate in a few moves.

| 37. Q–R6 | P–B3 |
| 38. PxR | R–N2 |

Earlier Black wrestled with the Bishop on QB6; now he struggles with its ghost. Correct is 38. . . . K–B2, but White has enough advantage to win.

| | | |
|---|---|---|
| 39. | R–Q8 | QxR |
| 40. | Q–R8ch | K–B2 |
| 41. | QxQ | P–N4 |
| 42. | R–R6 | |

After checking the sealed move and determining that the time limit had not been exceeded, Black resigned.

## *Game 32*

### *Nimzo-Indian Defense*

| M. Euwe | | S. Reshevsky |
|---|---|---|
| 1. | P–Q4 | N–KB3 |
| 2. | P–QB4 | P–K3 |
| 3. | N–QB3 | B–N5 |
| 4. | P–K3 | P–B4 |
| 5. | B–Q3 | O–O |
| 6. | P–QR3 | BxNch |
| 7. | PxB | P–QN3 |

This continuation is appropriate in another order of moves—in game 9, Geller–Euwe, for instance, where B–Q3 had not yet been played and Black had not yet castled. In that game White was forced to spend a tempo on P–KB3, but now he can play P–K4 successfully, easily achieving an advance that in other cases requires much reinforcement. It is surprising that such an authority on the Black side of the Sämisch Variation as Reshevsky allows this possibility, and that Euwe does not take advantage of it. After 8. P–K4 the threat is B–N5, and if Black's Knight is removed to K1, then 9. Q–R5! starting an attack before castling.

The reader will see a similar development in game 77, where Reshevsky risks repeating this variation against Keres.

| | | |
|---|---|---|
| 8. | N–K2 | B–N2 |
| 9. | O–O | P–Q3 |
| 10. | Q–B2 | P–Q4 |

One might think that Reshevsky has forgotten the right of a pawn to advance two squares! However, the pawn's gradual advance has its logic. Since White has played sluggishly and omitted 10. N–N3, Reshevsky corrects his mistake of the 7th move and prevents White's P–K4 for a long time. If Black answered 10. N–N3 with P–Q4, there would follow 11. BPxP KPxP 12. N–B5. So the correct reply would be 10. . . . N–B3. Now Black answers the exchange of center pawns with a clever maneuver that is possible only with White's Queen on B2.

| | | |
|---|---|---|
| 11. | BPxP | QxP |

Black threatens no more or less than mate on KN7, and the natural P–B3 would be followed by 12. . . . P–B5; therefore, White's only move is 12. N–B4, but the Knight does not stand very well on B4. Thus the threat of mate, not so naive as it seems, leads to a significant change in the position that is definitely not in White's favor.

| 12. N–B4 | Q–B3 |
| 13. P–B4 | PxP |

Bad, of course, is 13. . . . P–KN4; after 14. P–Q5 Black's position would be completely ruined.

| 14. PxP | QN–Q2 |
| 15. B–N2 | KR–K1 |
| 16. KR–K1 | QR–B1 |
| 17. QR–B1 | N2–B1 |
| 18. B–B1 | |

A changing of the guard.

| 18. . . . | N–N3 |
| 19. NxN | |

This exchange is explained by Euwe's intention to give mate by opening the KR-file. Much

better is N–Q3, maintaining the possibilities of N–K5 and N–N4 to annoy the Black Queen and to free his KB for work on its rightful diagonal, QN1–KR7.

| 19. . . . | RPxN |
| 20. R–K3 | KR–Q1 |
| 21. Q–K2 | Q–Q3 |
| 22. R–R3 | |

It seems our guess was correct.

| 22. . . . | Q–B5 |
| 23. R–Q1 | B–R3 |
| 24. R–KB3 | Q–K5 |
| 25. R–K3 | Q–N5 |
| 26. P–B3 | |

Reshevsky, an expert in Queen maneuvers, provokes one and soon another weakening. White does not want to exchange Queens, fearing the endgame with his hanging pawns.

| 26. . . . | Q–B5 |
| 27. P–N3 | Q–R3 |
| 28. R–B3 | Q–N4 |
| 29. Q–KB2 | R–Q2 |
| 30. R/1–B1 | |

White must not fail to transfer his Bishop via QB1 to KB4 and then to K5. This is the right moment—30. B–B1 Q–QR4 31. Q–QN2 followed by 32. B–B4, and Black is not permitted N–Q4, while R–B2 is no longer possible.

| 30. . . . | R/2–B2 |
| 31. R/1–B2 | Q–QR4 |
| 32. B–B1 | |

But this is definitely not the right moment: he must defend by 32. R–B1, although White's game is now completely spoiled. Black would transfer his Knight via K1 to Q3, continuing the attack on the hanging pawns.

**32. . . .          N–Q4**

Euwe probably overlooked this winning move.

**33. PxN RxR 34. RxR QxR 35. B–N2 Q–N6 36. BxB R–B7 37. P–Q6 RxQ 38. P–Q7 Q–Q4 39. KxR, White resigns.**

## *Game 33*

The reader has of course noticed—and will notice again —that I avoid detailed description of the opening variations. The two sides go to battle by various routes and they cannot all be described. I consider this game an exception because Keres uses a defensive system that is not found in the opening manuals.

### *Queen's Gambit*

| G. Stahlberg | P. Keres |
|---|---|
| 1. P–Q4 | N–KB3 |
| 2. P–QB4 | P–K3 |
| 3. N–KB3 | P–Q4 |
| 4. N–B3 | P–B4 |
| 5. BPxP | BPxP |

Theory considers only 5. . . . NxP, and it is thought that White gets a slight advantage by continuing 6. P–K3 N–QB3 7. B–B4. The move employed by

Keres, never before seen in an important event, introduces one of the systems he prepared for this tournament. Is it a good defense? Apparently no worse than others. At any rate, Keres uses it three times, and his result of 2½ points speaks for itself.

**6. QxP**

White wins a tempo for developing his Queen but Black soon regains it by N–B3. There is no point in sacrificing a piece for three pawns by 6. PxP PxN 7. PxPch K–K2 8. QxQch KxQ 9. PxP, for the pawn on KB7 would be lost sooner or later.

| | |
|---|---|
| 6. . . . | PxP |
| 7. B–N5 | |

In later games (Nos. 155 and 210) Najdorf and Geller played 7. P–K4 against Keres; but they were already forewarned whereas Stahlberg, encountering an unknown variation for the first time, cannot risk a sharp continuation.

| | |
|---|---|
| 7. . . . | B–K2 |
| 8. P–K3 | N–B3 |
| 9. Q–Q2 | O–O |
| 10. B–K2 | B–K3 |
| 11. O–O | N–K5 |

The possibility of this liberating maneuver is a vital link in this system and was undoubtedly foreseen by Keres. If now 12. BxB QxB 13. NxP? Q–Q2, Black wins a piece.

| | |
|---|---|
| 12. NxN | PxN |
| 13. BxB | |

Danger still lies in wait for White: 13. QxQ BxQ and again White loses a piece.

| | |
|---|---|
| 13. . . . | QxB |
| 14. N–Q4 | KR–Q1 |

The last trap. If 15. NxN RxQ 16. NxQch K–B1, Black regains his piece with the better position.

| | |
|---|---|
| 15. KR–Q1 | NxN |
| 16. PxN | R–Q3 |

Keres's new system has passed its baptism by fire. The following play revolves around White's QP. It is isolated but also passed: desirable to take but necessary to blockade.

| | |
|---|---|
| 17. Q–K3 | B–Q4 |
| 18. QR–B1 | QR–Q1 |
| 19. B–B4 | P–KR3 |
| 20. P–KR3 | P–R3 |
| 21. BxB | RxB |
| 22. R–B4 | P–B4 |
| 23. P–B3 | |

Stahlberg, in turn, wants to give his opponent a weak pawn.

| | |
|---|---|
| 23. . . . | P–QN4 |
| 24. R–B6 | Q–Q2 |
| 25. RxQRP | PxP |
| 26. QxBP | RxP |
| 27. R–KB1 | R–Q7 |
| 28. R–R8 | RxR |
| 29. QxRch | K–R2 |
| 30. Q–B3 | P–N3 |

Black has a small but clear positional advantage, which is possible to explain but difficult to illustrate with specific variations. Black's King is better protected from possible checks; of particular importance is his pawn on KB4, which shields the King from checks on the diagonal. An analogous situation almost led to a loss for Keres in his game against Taimanov in the 29th round. In the present case, however, White's pieces are solidly posted, and P–KN3, which opens the seventh rank, certainly cannot increase Black's hope of winning.

**31. R–K1          RxP**
**32. Q–R3**

White seems to have some threats, too.

**32. . . .          Q–Q5ch**
**33. K–R1          P–R4**
**34. Q–K7ch**

Here White can easily play 34. Q–B8, answering Black's only move, R–K7, with 35. RxR Q–Q8ch 36. K–R2 QxR 37. Q–B7ch K–R3 38. P–KR4 with a probable draw.

**34. . . .          K–R3**
**35. Q–B8ch**

Here, as two moves earlier, White misses an easy draw: 35. P–KR4, threatening Q–N5ch and Q–K7ch.

**35. . . .          K–N4**
**36. Q–K7ch       K–R3**
**37. Q–B8ch       Q–N2**
**38. Q–B5**

The Rook endgame is lost for White if he exchanges Queens.

**38. . . .          Q–KB2**
**39. P–R3          R–N6**
**40. R–Q1          P–B5**
**41. R–KB1        P–B6**
**42. RxP           RxR**
**43. PxR           QxPch**
**44. K–R2**

The Queen endgame can be drawn by very accurate play. Keres envisions a position in which White will be unable to avoid exchanging Queens. For this his King has to get through to the Queenside. His winning method is interesting and useful to know, but he succeeds in this game only because of White's inaccuracies.

44. . . . P–R5 45. Q–K5 Q–B7ch 46. K–R1 Q–KB4 47. Q–R8ch K–N4 48. Q–Q8ch K–B5 49. Q–Q2ch K–B6 50. Q–Q1ch K–K6 51. Q–K1ch K–Q6 52. Q–N1ch K–K7 53. Q–N2ch K–K6 54. Q–B1ch

K–K5 55. Q–N1ch K–B6 56. Q–Q1ch K–B5 57. Q–Q2ch

A mistake that helps Black to establish a winning position. Correct is Q–QB1ch in order to answer K–K4 with Q–B5ch, not allowing the King to pass to the Queenside.

57. . . . K–K4 58. Q–B3ch K–Q4 59. Q–N3ch K–B3 60. Q–QB3ch K–N2 61. Q–N7ch

K–R3 62. Q–B3 Q–B8ch 63. K–R2 Q–B7ch 64. K–R1 K–N3 65. Q–B8 Q–K8ch 66. K–N2 Q–K5ch 67. K–N1 Q–Q5ch, White resigns, since Black has bases of support on the QB-file from QB2 to QB5 to exchange Queens. In fact, on 68. K–N2 there would follow 68. . . . Q–Q4ch 69. K–R2 Q–Q3ch and the exchange would be unavoidable.

## Game 34
### Queen's Gambit. Declined

**I. Boleslavsky      V. Smyslov**

1. P–Q4 P–Q4 2. P–QB4 P–QB3 3. N–KB3 N–KB3 4. N–B3 PxP 5. P–QR4 B–B4 6. P–K3 P–K3 7. BxP B–QN5

A system of defense prepared by Smyslov for the Zurich tournament. He used it four times, drawing quickly each time. I believe, nonetheless, that this variation is difficult for Black. Smyslov had to use great skill to equalize, and his opponents did not always take advantage of their opportunities. After this tournament, neither Smyslov nor any other master used this defense, and it passed out of practice.

8. O–O QN–Q2 9. Q–K2 O–O 10. P–K4 B–N3 11. P–K5 N–Q4 12. NxN BPxN 13. B–Q3 P–QR3 14. BxB BPxB 15. B–K3 Q–K2 16. QR–B1 KR–B1 17. B–Q2 P–R3, Drawn.

## Game 35
### Sicilian Defense

**A. Kotov          Y. Geller**

1. P–K4 P–QB4 2. N–KB3 N–QB3 3. P–Q4 PxP 4. NxP N–B3 5. N–QB3 P–Q3 6. B–KN5 P–K3 7. Q–Q2 B–K2 8. O–O–O O–O 9. P–B4 P–K4

A theoretical novelty, used for the first time in this game. It was further developed in Soviet championships but in the end was found to be not fully satisfactory for Black. In this game Kotov avoids risk and quickly simplifies the position.

10. NxN PxN 11. PxP PxP 12. QxQ RxQ 13. RxRch BxR 14. B-QB4 B-K2 15. P-KR3 B-Q2 16. R-Q1 B-K1 17. P-R3 K-B1 18. B-K3 N-R4 19. N-K2 N-B3 20. N-B3 N-R4 21. N-K2 N-B3 22. N-B3, Drawn.

# Round Six

## *Game 36*
### *Sicilian Defense*

| V. Smyslov | A. Kotov |
|---|---|
| 1. P–K4 | P–QB4 |
| 2. N–KB3 | P–Q3 |
| 3. P–Q4 | PxP |
| 4. NxP | N–KB3 |
| 5. N–QB3 | P–QR3 |
| 6. B–K2 | P–K4 |

The outcome of the Smyslov–Kotov game was difficult to predict, but the opening was easily guessed: Smyslov considers it his duty to open with P–K4 and Kotov always answers . . . P–QB4.

This time Kotov deviates slightly from his tradition: he usually plays the Scheveningen Variation, advancing the pawn to K3 and later, at a critical moment, to K4; here, in recognition of fashion, he plays P–K4 on the 6th move. One of the points of P–K4 is that N–B5 is not playable here in view of 7. . . . BxN and 8. . . . P–Q4.

| 7. N–N3 | B–K2 |
|---|---|
| 8. B–K3 | QN–Q2 |
| 9. O–O | O–O |
| 10. P–B3 | Q–B2 |
| 11. Q–K1 | |

Smyslov allows Black too much freedom by not playing P–QR4 here or on the previous move. Even if Black had played 10. . . . P–QN4, 11. P–QR4 would have been possible: 11. . . . P–N5 12. N–Q5, taking with the Queen after 12. . . . NxN; but now . . . P–QN4 meets with no resistance. White's only achievement in the opening is his safe and solid control of K4. This is not so little, and it will influence the course of the game, but he should have wanted more.

| 11. . . . | P–QN4 |
|---|---|
| 12. P–QR3 | N–N3 |
| 13. Q–B2 | R–N1 |
| 14. QR–N1 | |

The threat was 14. . . . N–B5 as well as N–R5. The need for a move like R–N1 denotes a certain disharmony in White's camp.

| 14. . . . | B–K3 |
|---|---|
| 15. K–R1 | N–B5 |

N–B5 has its logic, but P–Q4, demonstrating that the QP is not at all weak, seems much more attractive. Not only would Black score a moral victory by proving that he controls his Q4 better than his opponent does, but he would also obtain free piece play: 15. . . . P–Q4 16. PxP KNxP 17. NxN NxN 18. B–B5 N–B5.

| 16. BxN | PxB |
|---|---|
| 17. N–B1 | R–N2 |

Smyslov comes up with a good answer to Black's straight-forward threat of doubling Rooks and winning the QNP. 17. . . . P–Q4 is strong here, with the same idea.

| 18. N/1–R2 | P–Q4 |
|---|---|

The most inappropriate moment. 18. . . . P–QR4 is necessary now; only after 19. P–QR4 Q–N1 20. N–N5 is 20. . . . P–Q4 possible.

| 19. PxP | BxQP |
|---|---|
| 20. N–N4 | BxN |
| 21. PxB | |

| 21. . . . | Q–B3 |
|---|---|
| 22. B–N5 | |

Taking advantage of the fact that Black's Bishop is temporarily tied down, White goes over to Kingside attack. Since 22. . . . RxP is not playable now because of 23. BxN PxB 24. Q–Q2 B–K3 25. N–K4, Black's disappointed Rook leaves N2.

| 22. . . . | R–Q2 |
|---|---|
| 23. KR–K1 | R–K1 |
| 24. QR–Q1 | |

Smyslov plays simply and directly, his pieces gradually occupying better and better positions; he now threatens BxN.

| 24. . . . | N–R4 |
|---|---|
| 25. Q–R4 | P–N3 |
| 26. NxB | RxN |
| 27. RxR | QxR |
| 28. Q–K4 | |

White provoked . . . P–KN3 as though to prepare an attack, but, correctly realizing that the castled position would be very difficult to breach, he proposes to go into a better endgame based on the point K4.

**28. . . .                QxQ**

It is a mistake for Kotov to agree to exchange Queens, for his endgame chances are obviously worse due to his very weak QRP and QBP. With Queens on, he might get the chance for . . . P–KB4 and . . . P–K5.

| 29. RxQ | P–B3 |
|---------|------|
| 30. B–K3 | R–QB1 |
| 31. P–N4 | N–N2 |
| 32. P–KN5 | |

32. B–B5 does not win a pawn in view of 32. . . . P–QR4 33. RxBP PxP, and the NP cannot be taken by the Rook or the Bishop, and if 34. P–N3 N–K3 35. BxP RxR 36. PxR N–Q5, with a probably drawn endgame.

But White finds a way to exploit the weakness of Black's K4.

| 32. . . . | K–B2 |
|-----------|------|
| 33. PxP | KxP |
| 34. B–Q2 | N–B4 |
| 35. B–B3 | N–Q5 |
| 36. P–B4 | |

Nothing is gained by 36. BxN PxB 37. RxP P–B6 38. P–N3 R–K1, since the Rook invades the seventh rank and wins the QBP, drawing. Kotov takes the QBP immediately, but his

Knight gets driven to QR8 and his position becomes critical.

| 36. . . . | NxP |
|-----------|-----|
| 37. R–K2 | N–R8 |

**38. RxP**

Smyslov's subtle play has brought him a winning position, but now in time pressure he chooses the wrong way. White wins quickly by 38. PxPch K–K3 39. R–KB2. Perhaps the ideal move is not even 38. PxPch but 38. K–N2 and only then PxPch. Smyslov's plan looks strong, but it gives Black a hidden chance for a draw.

| 38. . . . | K–B2 |
|-----------|------|
| 39. R–QR5 | N–B7 |
| 40. RxP | R–QN1 |
| 41. R–B6 | NxP |
| 42. R–B7ch | |

A necessary check. If 42. RxBP immediately, then N–Q4 43. B–K5 R–N6, and Black's King gets to KB4 via K3. But now after 42. . . . K–K3 43. RxBP, N–Q4 does not work because of 44. R–K4ch, and

Black's King cannot go to B4 because he loses his Knight or to Q3 because of B–K5ch. However, even after the check a draw is obtained by

| 42. | . . . | K–K3 |
|-----|-------|------|
| 43. | RxBP  | N–Q6 |
| 44. | P–N4  | R–KB1 |

**Drawn**

## Game 37
### King's Indian Defense

P. Keres     I. Boleslavsky

| 1. | P–Q4  | N–KB3 |
|----|-------|-------|
| 2. | P–QB4 | P–Q3  |
| 3. | N–QB3 | P–K4  |

A radical remedy against the Sämisch Attack and the Four Pawns Variation. Whatever White plays now will not be part of the Sämisch formation. If 4, P–Q5, for instance, Black is not obliged to fianchetto his KB but can play 4. . . . B–B4 and answer 5. P–B3 with P–K5. If 4. P–K4, Black gains time for development with 4. . . . PxP 5. QxP N–B3, and then . . . B–K2 or . . . P–KN3. On 4. PxP PxP 5. QxQch, Black's King, though deprived of castling, will find shelter on QB2. Even so, White will still have ways to exploit his advanced KP. Keres has something else in mind: B–N5, which though seldom played is positionally one of the most solid.

| 4. | N–B3 | QN–Q2 |
|----|------|-------|
| 5. | B–N5 |       |

Since Black's P–Q3 and P–K4 have not allowed the

strongest attack in the King's Indian, White takes revenge by not allowing the usual form of the King's Indian with Black's Bishop on KN2. In fact, after 5. . . . P–KN3 6. PxP PxP 7. NxP Black loses a pawn. Of course, Black can reply 5. . . . B–K2, but this development of the Bishop is a far cry from the intentions of a King's Indian player. In that case White plans to play simply P–K3, B–K2, and O–O without fear of . . . P–K5, since his QB is already outside the pawn chain.

Boleslavsky, who continually and most successfully works on improvements for Black in the King's Indian Defense, feels a moral obligation to correct established opinions, and for this game he has prepared a headspinning variation with the sacrifice of the Rook on QR1.

| 5. | . . . | P–KR3 |
|----|-------|-------|
| 6. | B–R4  | P–KN4 |
| 7. | PxP   |       |

If the Bishop retreats farther, Black's KP rushes straight to K6 with the familiar idea of inhibiting the development of the entire flank—7. B–N3 P–K5 8. N–Q2 P–K6. Now we see the main variation of Boleslavsky's innovation.

| 7. | . . . | PxB |
|----|-------|-----|
| 8. | PxN | QxP |
| 9. | N–Q5 | QxP |

Some pieces in the King's Indian Defense are valued according to an unusual price list, on which the value of the dark-square Bishops is particularly high. Therefore, despite his shattered pawns Black has achieved something by eliminating White's QB while keeping his own KB.

Black's last move continues his prepared sharp attack with the Rook sacrifice. The possibility of this attack depends on the centrally located White Knight's going to QR8 and being taken out of play. The whole question is whether Black can create a real threat in the short time before White brings out his Bishop and gets his Knight back to the center.

Boleslavsky is counting pri-

marily on the following variation, in which his dark-square Bishop plays first violin: 10. NxPch K–Q1 11. NxR P–Q4! 12. R–B1 B–N5ch 13. N–Q2 N–B4 14. R–B2 Q–K4 15. P–K3 B–B4.

Returning the Queen to Q1, as recommended by Najdorf, is unattractive: 9. . . . Q–Q1 10. Q–Q4 N–K4 11. NxN B–N2 12. NxBP KxN 13. Q–B4ch K–N1 14. O–O–O P–B3 15. N–B3 Q–R4 only seems acceptable; in fact the sole threat of BxN is not dangerous to White, who can simply take on Q6 with the Queen; for instance, 16. QxQP BxN 17. PxB QxPch 18. K–N1 B–B4ch 19. P–K4 BxPch 20. B–Q3.

### 10. R–QN1

The simple move that Boleslavsky missed in his preliminary analysis. After 20. NxPch K–Q1, the move R–QN1 is not dangerous to Black in view of the check on White's QB3; but now, with the Knight not yet on B7, the check is unplayable and Black's entire attack is refuted.

| 10. | . . . | QxRP |
|-----|-------|------|
| 11. | NxPch | K–Q1 |
| 12. | NxR | N–B4 |

Upset by his mistake, Boleslavsky makes another one. True, 12. . . . P–Q4 is useless now, for there is no check on QN5, but 12. . . . B–N2 keeps some attack; for instance, 13.

R–B1 Q–R6 14. Q–Q2 N–B4. If Black wins back the Knight on R1 he will have a pawn for the Exchange. But now Keres forces the exchange of Queens with a series of sharp moves and liquidates the danger.

13. R–R1 Q–N7 14. Q–Q4 QxQ 15. NxQ B–N2 16. P–K3 R–K1 17. B–K2 BxN 18. PxB N–N6 19. RxP NxP 20. R–R2 P–R6 21. R–N1 R–N1 22. P–N4, Black resigns.

## Game 38
## Queen's Gambit Declined

| S. Reshevsky | G. Stahlberg |
|---|---|
| 1. P–Q4 | P–Q4 |
| 2. P–QB4 | P–K3 |
| 3. N–QB3 | P–QB4 |
| 4. BPxP | KPxP |
| 5. N–B3 | N–QB3 |
| 6. P–KN3 | P–B5 |

The Swedish Defense, often used by Stahlberg and Stoltz. With the further . . . B–QN5 Black tries to weaken the attack on his QP, and with . . . N–K2 he adds to the pawn's defense without fearing the pin on his Knight that is possible when it goes to KB3. However, 6. . . . P–B5 results in a considerable strengthening of White's QP; when it becomes passed after 9. P–K4 it will tie up the Black pieces. Black's QBP will in no way be equivalent, for it is not passed and is unlikely ever to attain that status.

| 7. B–N2 | B–QN5 |
|---|---|
| 8. O–O | KN–K2 |

| 9. P–K4 | PxP |
|---|---|
| 10. NxP | O–O |
| 11. Q–B2 | |

An innovation by Reshevsky. 11. P–QR3 B–R4 12. Q–R4 is usually played here, but with 12. . . . B–KN5 Black indirectly attacks the QP and then takes it in exchange for his QBP. The meaning of Q–B2 is not, of course, to sacrifice a pawn—which is only a secondary variation inasmuch as Black obviously cannot take it (12. . . . NxP 13. NxN QxN 14. R–Q1 Q–K4 15. B–B4, and White regains the pawn with a colossal advantage in development)—but rather by attacking the QBP to win a tempo to bring a Rook to Q1. Supported by a Rook White's QP will become very mobile, and its rush to the seventh rank will create dangerous tactical possibilities.

| 11. . . . | |
|---|---|
| 12. B–K3 | Q–Q4 |

Allowing Black to post his QB on B4, and after 13. N–R4 NxP 14. BxN QxB 15. NxB NxN 16. KR–Q1 Q–K4 17. R–Q5 QxR 18. N–B6ch or 16. . . . Q–N3 17. P–QR3 B–R4 18. QxP, White's pieces are much more comfortably placed than Black's; the threat is 19. P–QN4, and taking the pawn on QN7 is not good because of 19. Q–Q5, attacking the Knight on B5 and the Bishop on QR5.

| 12. . . . | N–N3 |
| 13. N–R4 | Q–QN4 |
| 14. NxN | RPxN |
| 15. P–QR3 | B–K2 |
| 16. P–Q5 | N–R4 |
| 17. P–Q6 | |

Reshevsky's forceful, concrete play literally does not let his opponent make one move of his own choosing. Black is continually forced to meet threats without a moment's respite. This game is very characteristic of Reshevsky and is undoubtedly one of his best in the tournament.

| 17. . . . | B–Q1 |
| 18. N–B3 | Q–R3 |
| 19. QR–Q1 | B–N5 |
| 20. R–Q4 | B–B4 |
| 21. Q–R4 | R–N1 |

Obviously intending . . . P–QN4 to free himself at least a little; but White does not give him the chance.

| 22. R–Q5 | B–K3 |
| 23. R–K5! | P–QN3 |

The pawn on Q6 is not defended, and although the Rook can be attacked in four ways each leads to material loss for Black. Stahlberg limits himself to the modest P–QN3 to defend the Knight and transfer his Queen to QB1.

Here I would not refrain from 24. RxB, since Black's Queen and Knight are far from his King and his pawns weak, and since White's pair of Bishops control the entire board. Of course the variations would have to be worked out, but I am convinced that the chances would not be bad. I recommend that the reader investigate 25. N–N5 as well as 25. Q–B2 and 25. B–R3.

**24. P–Q7**

Reshevsky's move is also strong, though partly dictated by time pressure. With no time for thought, he prefers to bring the game to its technical stage, where he has an unquestionable advantage.

**24. . . . P–QN4 25. RxP RxR 26. QxR QxQ 27. NxQ P–R3 28. N–B3 BxP 29. R–**

Q1 B–B1 (White's pieces are excellently placed, whereas Black's pawns are weak and should fall under the blows of the Rook and Bishop.) **30. N–K4 B–K2 31. B–B5 BxB 32. NxB B–B4** (A confession that his game is hopeless, or a simple blunder? Probably the latter.) **33. NxP R–K1 34. B–B3 N–N6 35. K–N2 B–B7 36. R–Q7 B–B4 37. R–Q1 B–B7 38. R–Q7 B–B4 39. R–Q6 B–K3 40. N–B7 R–K2 41. NxB, Black resigns.**

## Game 39

It almost always makes sense to sacrifice a pawn, sometimes even a piece, to keep the enemy King in the center and attack it with the Queen and Rooks. But one must differentiate between two types of attack: 1) the King is on the first rank, hemmed in by its own pieces or pawns; 2) the King goes to the third or sometimes the fourth rank and seeks shelter on one of the flanks.

The second type is encountered in this game. My opponent utilizes to the utmost the defender's main resource —cool-headedness. At one point I was forced to break off

calculating variations to ask myself who was attacking whom.

During and after the game I was haunted by the feeling that I had a win somewhere. Perhaps a specific variation flashed by, but it has not stayed in my memory. At any rate, I can find no improvement for White; nor could Euwe, Najdorf, or Stahlberg in their annotations of this game. Admittedly, the promising piece sacrifice proved insufficient to win the game. But can a win be found in analysis? At any rate, although I did not get a point, I did get a very lively game.

## Nimzo-Indian Defense

| D. Bronstein | M. Euwe | | |
|---|---|---|---|
| 1. P–Q4 | N–KB3 | 3. N–QB3 | B–N5 |
| 2. P–QB4 | P–K3 | 4. P–K3 | P–B4 |
| | | 5. B–Q3 | P–Q4 |

| 6. | N–B3 | O–O |
|---|---|---|
| 7. | O–O | N–B3 |
| 8. | P–QR3 | BxN |
| 9. | PxB | QPxP |
| 10. | BxP | Q–B2 |

All these opening moves were made almost automatically by both players. White now begins preparations for P–K4.

| 11. | B–Q3 | P–K4 |
|---|---|---|
| 12. | Q–B2 | R–K1 |

This seems stronger to me than 12. . . . Q–K2, as Euwe played against Averbakh in game 176 and later against Botvinnik in the 11th Olympiad. Compare 12. . . . Q–K2 13. PxKP NxP 14. NxN QxN with 12. . . . R–K1 13. PxKP NxP 14. NxN QxN; in the second case Black has an extra tempo. True, 12. . . . Q–K2 would still not allow 13. P–K4, but is that so dangerous?

| 13. | P–K4 | KPxP |
|---|---|---|

Euwe can force the exchange of Queens here and considerably simplify the game by 13. . . . P–B5 14. BxP PxP 15. PxP N–QR4 16. B–Q3 QxQ 17. BxQ NxP, but he accepts the challenge to a complicated struggle abounding in interesting combinations.

| 14. | PxP | B–N5 |
|---|---|---|

14. . . . PxP would be followed by 15. P–K5. Euwe invites White into the variation 15. P–K5 BxN 16. PxN NxP

17. BxPch K–R1 18. PxPch KxP 19. B–N2 QR–Q1, believing he will be in a position to repulse the attack. It was discovered after the game, however, that the resulting complications would soon have turned out in White's favor. My attention was drawn to another, more attractive possibility.

| 15. | QxP | NxKP |
|---|---|---|
| 16. | BxN | RxB |
| 17. | N–N5 | |

White proceeds to attack the King. Of course, 17. P–Q5? BxN 18. PxB R–KR5 19. P–B4 Q–Q2 doesn't work.

Black can now take the QP but declines in view of 17. . . . RxP 18. B–N2 R–Q2 19. Q–B2 P–KN3 20. N–K4. I was a little worried about 17. . . . RxP 18. B–N2 Q–B5, but this Exchange sacrifice was not convincing enough to my opponent.

| 17. | . . . | R–K2 |
|---|---|---|
| 18. | Q–B2 | P–KN3 |
| 19. | N K4 | B–B4 |

Both sides proceed with the continuation involving a piece sacrifice. Black, in order to reserve KB4 for his Bishop, weakened the long diagonal on his previous move by playing P–KN3 instead of the more natural P–B4. White gives up a piece to bring Black's King out to KB3 and K3, figuring to attack it with all his forces. The struggle becomes extremely sharp.

**20. N–B6ch       K–N2**
**21. Q–Q2**

At this point I was very satisfied with my position. In fact, after

**21. . . .        KxN**

Black's King already cannot return to N2 but, stranded in the center, will be subjected to attack by the Queen, both Rooks, the Bishop, and maybe even a few pawns. Nevertheless, my opponent shows no sign of despair—a good example for young players who begin to get nervous in difficult positions, especially when under the threat of a mating attack, and in so doing increase the difficulty of the defense.

**22. P–Q5**

Here I was already considering 22. B–N2 and 22. Q–R6. The text is stronger: both options are retained, and a third, P–Q6, is created.

**22. . . .        R–Q1**

A remarkable move. Black brings his last reserves to the defense and repulses all three of White's threats. 23. Q–R6 would be followed by the calm 23. . . . RxP, and on 23. B–N2ch, as we shall see, Black can resolutely give back the piece. Even so, I was very optimistic about my chances, for I assumed that with material equality the force of White's attack would increase.

**23. B–N2ch       N–K4**
**24. P–B4**

24. QR–Q1 was worth considering, but I saw nothing forcing and decided not to risk too much.

**24. . . .        Q–B4ch**
**25. K–R1**

The QP is lost anyway, so there is no reason to endanger the Bishop by 25. B–Q4, on which Euwe intended 25. . . . RxP 26. BxQ RxQ 27. BxRch KxB 28. PxN, drawing, or 26. PxNch K–K3 27. BxQ RxQ 28. BxR KxB, and Black can draw although he is down the Exchange.

**25. . . .        RxP**
**26. PxNch       K–K3**

His piece regained, White now attacks the exposed King. However, the progress of the attack runs into strategical difficulties: the King is surrounded by pieces that exhibit the overt inclination to counterattack at the first opportunity; also, the King has many escape squares, more in fact than when his castled position was under attack; and furthermore, when White moved his King to R1 he weakened his first rank.

Still, White has one big trump: Bishops of opposite colors, as a rule, favor the attacking side. Perhaps White does not exploit this as he should.

### 27. Q–N5          K–Q2

If 27. . . . Q–B7 Black suddenly falls into a trap, 28. QR–B1, and the threat to take the Bishop turns out to be illusory: 28. . . . QxB? 29. Q–B6ch K–Q2 30. P–K6ch.

### 28. QR–B1

More promising, if not decisive, is 28. P–QR4, exploiting the strategic advantage of his dark-square Bishop, against which the enemy can oppose only a Rook. Practically speaking, in reply to 28. P–QR4 Black has to give up the Exchange, and although he wins another pawn the attack with Queen and two Rooks becomes really menacing; for instance, 28. P–QR4 R–K3 29. B–R3 Q–B5 30. B–Q6 R/3xB 31. PxR RxP 32. QR–Q1 or 28. . . . R/2xP 29. BxR RxB 30. QR–B1.

### 28. . . .          Q–N3
### 29. B–B3          R–K1
### 30. B–N4          R/1xP

White has transferred his Bishop to a stronger diagonal, but compared with 28. P–QR4 the KP was given as a gift.

White can now play 31. RxB PxR 32. Q–N8, but after 32. . . . Q–QB3! perpetual check is the best he has.

### 31. Q–R4          P–QR4

Here the suspicion dawned on me that Black was starting to play for a win. Seeing that 32. QxP PxB 33. QxPch would simply be bad for White, I decided to undertake one more attacking try by transferring the Bishop to KN3 in order to create a threat on QB7.

### 32. B–K1          P–R4
### 33. B–B2          Q–R3
### 34. B–N3          R–K5

One more fact is necessary to complete the picture: neither player has more than two minutes before his flag falls. 35. Q–N5 K–K3 seemed more than obscure, so I decided not to tempt fate.

**35. RxB**

All the commentators gave this move an exclamation point, although there was no other way for White to draw. Nevertheless, I must confess to the reader that I sacrificed the Exchange more through inspiration than calculation. It seemed to me that the variation 35. . . . PxR 36. R–B7ch K–K1 37. R–B8ch was very dangerous for Black; for instance, 37. . . . K–Q2 38. Q–Q8ch K–K3 39. Q–K8ch K–B3 40. Q–R8ch K–K3 41. R–K8ch K–Q2 42. R–Q8ch K–B3 43. Q–R6ch R–K3 44. Q–B1ch R–B4 45. R–B8ch K–Q2 46. RxR. It was discovered later, however, that not all of Black's moves here were compulsory and that with better defense he could draw.

If Euwe took the Rook, in practice he would not necessarily have lost, considering that most of this variation would have taken place after adjournment. He chooses the more natural continuation.

**35. . . .                  RxQ**

For a moment I missed the fact that Black's Queen stood on R3 and had my KB1 under

its control; I almost continued 36. RxRch K–K3 37. R–K5ch?? K–B3 38. R–B1ch. Let the reader not think that grandmasters are without sin: they get in time trouble, fail to calculate variations to the end, make blunders and oversights . . .

**36. RxRch          K–K3**

| 37. R/1–Q1 | Q–B5 |
|---|---|
| 38. R–Q6ch | K–K2 |
| 39. R–Q7ch | K–B3 |

The following seemed too risky: 39. . . . K–B1 40. R–Q8ch K–N2 41. B–K5ch P–B3 42. R/8–Q7ch K–R3 43. BxP, with the threat of B–N7ch, but 43. . . . R–B5 holds everything.

**40. BxRch          QxB**
**41. R–B1ch**

The game was adjourned and Black sealed 41. . . . K–N4, but play was not resumed since after 42. R–Q5ch and 43. Rx QRP the draw is obvious.

# Game 40

In choosing an opening plan one thinks first of all about developing the pieces harmoniously, but sometimes Queen development is overlooked. Yet because the Queen is the most important and valuable piece on the board, the success of the entire operation can depend on how well it plays its role.

In some openings Black's QBP is important not only to attack the enemy pawn center but also to clear a path for the Queen to QB2, QN3, or QR4. This applies especially to systems in which the KB is developed on K2 where it closes the Queen's other diagonal, as in the Orthodox Defense of the Queen's Gambit, the Tchigorin Defense of the Ruy Lopez, and the main variation of the French Defense, for example.

In the Gligoric–Szabo game the development of the Black Queen becomes the main theme of the struggle in the opening and the middlegame, for White maintains a clear advantage as long as Black's Queen is confined to the first rank, and he gets a bad position as soon as its mobility increases.

## Ruy Lopez (Black queen)

**S. Gligoric**     **L. Szabo**

| | |
|---|---|
| 1. P–K4 | P–K4 |
| 2. N–KB3 | N–QB3 |
| 3. B–N5 | P–QR3 |
| 4. B–R4 | N–B3 |
| 5. O–O | NxP |
| 6. P–Q4 | P–QN4 |
| 7. B–N3 | P–Q4 |
| 8. PxP | B–K3 |
| 9. P–B3 | |

The Open Defense of the Ruy Lopez branches out in two variations here: B–K2 and B–QB4. The second seems more natural to me (see game 70, Averbakh–Szabo) because the Bishop is developed actively and the Queen retains possible ways out on the Q1–KR5 diagonal.

| | |
|---|---|
| 9. . . . | B–K2 |
| 10. B–K3 | N–B4 |

Szabo avoids the theoretical continuation 10. . . . O–O 11. QN–Q2 B–KN5 12. NxN PxN 13. Q–Q5 QxQ 14. BxQ PxN 15. BxN PxP 16. KR–K1, which leaves White with the considerably freer game.

| | |
|---|---|
| 11. B–B2 | B–N5 |
| 12. QN–Q2 | N–K3 |

Black cannot take the pawn, for there follows 13. BxN BxB 14. Q–K1, winning a piece, and 13. . . . NxNch 14. PxN B–R6

15. R–K1 is no better. Therefore, Black first retreats the Knight and now really threatens to take the KP. However, Gligoric refutes Black's entire opening setup with a beautiful and original Queen maneuver that frees his Knight from the pin and prevents Black from castling.

**13. Q–N1**

13. . . .           B–R4
14. P–QR4           P–N5

And so, Black's minor pieces are developed well, White's KP is under long-range fire, and by B–N3 Black will be able to castle without having to create a pawn weakness. But there is a significant piece weakness in his position: his Queen is not developed and has no good prospects. White can take advantage of this by 15. P–B4, and whether Black's pawn advances or takes the pawn, White answers 16. B–K4; or if 15. . . . B–N3 White exchanges Bishops and continues 17. R–

Q1. Although Black would face difficult problems, 16. B–K4 hardly decides the fight. 15. . . . P–Q5 16. B–K4 Q–Q2 confronts White with a question: is he willing to give up his good game to win a pawn? After 17. BxN QxB 18. NxP NxN 19. BxN B–N3 I much prefer Black's position.

The positional move in the game does not relinquish the advantage, but it does slow the tempo of play somewhat.

15. P–R5           B–N3
16. N–N3           PxP
17. PxP            Q–N1

Szabo is aware of the basic defect in his position and decides to delay castling in order to get the Queen closer to the battle somehow. The threat was R–Q1 and P–B4.

18. Q–R2           O–O
19. BxB            RPxB
20. QR–N1          Q–N4

The art of the chess master consists not only of finding correct plans but especially of carrying them out accurately, at times with only the best moves. In this case, White's plan directed against the undeveloped Black Queen is strategically correct, but he has chosen an incorrect technical method. 20. KR–N1 was stronger. The difference is that after the move in the game White's QRP, as we shall see, is insufficiently protected. After 20. KR–N1 the answer Q–N4 would obviously be impossible, and 20. . . . Q–Q1, the move recommended by Vukovic, would be pointless since the Queen, as before, would have no outlet for its activity. Even 21. R–Q1 would be possible, and if 21. . . . Q–Q2 then 22. N–B5 NxN 23. RxP, etc., or 21. . . . R–N1 22. QN–Q4 N/KxN 23. NxN NxKP 24. B–B4, or 21. . . . N–R2 22. P–B4.

## 21. Q–B2

Gligoric's desire to win the game only positionally, avoiding all combinative possibilities, leads in the end to his defeat. If 21. QN–Q4 is unsuitable because of 21. . . . QxP, then good is 21. KN–Q4 KNxN 22. NxN QxP and White sacrifices his Queen: 23. NxN QxQ 24. Nx Bch K–R2 25. R–N4 P–N4 26. BxP P–N3 27. R–R4ch K–N2 28. B–B6 mate! Such a finish may be called the consistent completion of a plan. Of course, on 21. KN–Q4 better is 21. . . . QNxN 22. PxN Q–Q2 23. QR–B1, with a minimal advantage.

| 21. . . . | Q–B5 |
| 22. KN–Q2 | Q–KN5 |
| 23. P–KB4 | Q–B4 |
| 24. QxQ | PxQ |

The Black Queen had to go a long distance—Q1–QN1–N4–QB5–KN5–KB4—before it could be exchanged, and now

at last it is the equal of White's Queen. After the exchange the advantage turns out to be Black's because White's QRP is weak and his KBP and KP restrict his Bishop. To summarize the struggle in the opening and middlegame, it may be said that by his strong, consistent play White earned the advantage, which he could have realized by 20. KR–N1; on his 21st move he could have had equal play or, on a blunder by Black, a beautiful combination. Having missed these possibilities, White is now forced to fight in a hard endgame.

| 25. N–B3 | KR–N1 |
| 26. KN–Q4 | QNxN |
| 27. NxN | NxN |
| 28. PxN | |

Taking with the pawn is very unpleasant because the Bishop is still very restricted, but 28. BxN leads to a lost position after 28. . . . R–N4 29. RxR PxR 30. R–R1 R–R3 31. K–B1 K B1.

| 28. . . . | B–N5 |
| 29. R–R1 | R–N4 |
| 30. R–R4 | R/1–N1 |
| 31. R/1–R1 | |

If 31. R–B1 Black simply takes the pawn, and White's attempt to sacrifice the Exchange and then win it back does not work: 31. . . . RxP 32. RxB RxR 33. B–Q2 R/4–N4 34. BxR RxB 35. RxP

RxP, and Black ends up with
two passed pawns.

| 31. | . . . | B–B6 |
| 32. | R–QB1 | R–N8 |
| 33. | RxR | RxRch |
| 34. | K–B2 | R–QR8 |

On 34. . . . R–N4 White replies 35. R–R3 B–N5 36. R–
R4, forcing Black to take the
pawn with his Bishop. To untangle his pieces Black would
have to get his King from KN1
to QN2 or QN3.

| 35. | RxR | BxR |
| 36. | K–K2 | B–B6 |
| 37. | K–Q3 | BxRP |
| 38. | P–R3 | |

Here Gligoric had a chance
to get a beautiful positional
draw despite his missing pawn:
38. B–Q2, and if 38. . . . B–N3
then 39. B–N4, and it would
be very difficult for Black's King
to reach the center, for . . . P–

KB3 is answered by P–K6. The
draw is even clearer in the pawn
ending after 38. . . . BxB 39.
KxB; for example, 39. . . . K–
B1 40. K–B3 K–K2 41. K–N4
K–Q2 42. K–B5.

White would not have had
this chance if Black had
played R–N4 instead of R–
QR8 on his 34th move.

This is yet another example
of the need to notice and exploit even the slightest details in
the endgame and of the value of
knowing endgame studies.

| 38. . . . | B–K8 |

Bishops will not be exchanged
now because Black would answer 39. B–Q2 with B–N6,
winning a tempo for K–B1.

| 39. | P–N4 | P–N3 |
| 40. | K–B2 | K–B1 |
| 41. | K–Q1 | B–N6 |
| | **White resigns** | |

# Game 41

One of the most interesting
games of the tournament. The
basic motif is White's striving
through combinations to open a
path for his QB from QN2 to
the weakened dark squares on
the King's wing. In view of contemporary defensive technique,
however, the exploitation of
only one weakness cannot lead
to a win. White has to accumu-

late other small advantages, all
of which will be needed at the
decisive moment for the concluding combination. Of special
interest in this game is Averbakh's exceptionally stubborn
and ingenious defense. At one
point it looks as though he has
warded off all the threats, but
White finds a way to revive and
beautifully conclude the attack.

## Nimzo-Indian Defense

**M. Taimanov      Y. Averbakh**

| | | |
|---|---|---|
| 1. | P–Q4 | N–KB3 |
| 2. | P–QB4 | P–K3 |
| 3. | N–QB3 | B–N5 |
| 4. | P–K3 | O–O |
| 5. | B–Q3 | P–Q4 |
| 6. | N–B3 | P–QN3 |
| 7. | O–O | B–N2 |
| 8. | P–QR3 | |

In the next round Taimanov was Black in an analogous system against Szabo, who played Q–K2 in this position, and Black could not avoid the exchange of his Bishop; here he can move it to Q3. Averbakh does not want to lose time retreating it and decides to trade it for the Knight in order to exchange on QB5 and open the diagonal for his QB; only then does he counterattack White's center with P–QB4 and with his pieces at long range.

This plan is quite harmless to White, for it leaves his hands free to operate on both flanks.

| | | |
|---|---|---|
| 8. | . . . | BxN |
| 9. | PxB | PxP |
| 10. | BxP | P–B4 |
| 11. | B–Q3 | QN–Q2 |
| 12. | R–K1 | |

White calmly prepares P–K4, which Black can impede only by mechanical means. If he puts his Bishop on K5, there follows B–B1 (which is not possible after 12. Q–K2), and in view of N–Q2 the Bishop will not be able to hold White's pawn on K3 for long.

| | | |
|---|---|---|
| 12. | . . . | N–K5 |
| 13. | B–N2 | R–B1 |
| 14. | P–B4 | N/2–B3 |

A more reasonable defensive setup is R–B2, Q–R1, KR–QB1, and N–B1. On KB1 the Knight would economically defend KR2 and in part KN2. On KB3 it stands far worse as a defensive piece, for it can be easily driven away. The battery QR1 and BN2 would not only control the QR1–K5 diagonal but would also pose a possible threat to White's KNP. Furthermore, by removing his Knight from Q2 Black cedes K4 to his opponent too soon. Later, Averbakh concludes that the Knight must return.

| | | |
|---|---|---|
| 15. | N–K5 | R–B2 |
| 16. | P–QR4 | |

Before continuing operations on the Kingside White creates a favorable pawn tension on the Queenside, and by opening the QR-file he considerably increases the radius of his Rook's activity.

| | | |
|---|---|---|
| 16. | . . . | N–Q3 |
| 17. | P–R5 | N–Q2 |
| 18. | RPxP | RPxP |
| 19. | Q–R5 | |

Black can defend against the direct mating threat in several ways, but of course this threat is not the point; it is rather the positional advantage White obtains on Black's various replies. 19. . . . B–K5 suggests itself, but then there follows 20. KR–Q1 and the opposition of White's Rook on Q1 against Black's Queen on Q8 and the Knights on Q7 and Q6 would be unpleasant for Black. If 19. . . . P–R3 then 20. N–N4 with the strong threat of NxPch at once or after the preliminary P–Q5. 19. . . . P–B4 deprives Black of P–B3 as a possible future defense of his King's position. Averbakh does not want to put his Knight on B3 yet because of 20. Q–R3, and in addition to his having to calculate the threats of N–N4 and PxP, his Knight would be exposed and, as I said, could be easily removed from the defense of KR2. The continuation Averbakh chooses obviously weakens the dark squares, but he has worked out a specific

variation in which a White pawn appears on Black's K4, shutting off every way White's Bishop could have gotten to Black's KB3, KN2, and KR3. In fact, after

| 19. . . . | P–N3 |
| 20. Q–R6 | NxN |
| 21. PxN | N–K5 |

Black will answer any retreat of the Bishop on Q3 with . . . Q–Q7, and in the new position with an immobile White pawn chain, White's Bishops will not be so frightening. But now Taimanov's following brilliant move

**22. BxN**

starts a new phase in this true grandmaster struggle, to which both opponents contribute imagination, calculation, and technique.

| 22. . . . | BxB |
| 23. KR–Q1 | R–Q2 |

Believing that the threats on the Q-file have been parried and that after the exchange of Rooks White will be unable to reach Black's King, Averbakh offered a draw. No doubt he completely overlooked White's obvious next move.

**24. R–Q6**

White controls the Q-file! If Black trades Rooks and defends against the mate by closing the Bishop's diagonal with

P–B3, a Rook bursts into Black's camp via the QR-file, which White had the foresight to open on his 18th move.

**24. . . .      B–N2**
**25. QR–Q1**

There are chess players who think such a move "cannot be bad." But, strange as it seems, this move is a pure loss of a tempo. Actually, after 25. . . . RxR White would not recapture with the Rook, and to recapture with the pawn he does not need the Rook on Q1.

Instead of the text move, Taimanov should choose between 25. P–K4 and 25. P–R4, which do not reduce the swiftness of his attack.

**25. . . .      RxR**

On passive defense White can decisively strengthen his position. One way is to advance P–K4 and then transfer the Rook via Q3 to KR3. Another is to transfer the Bishop via QB1 to KN5 and B6. The plan P–B4–5, to open the Kingside even more, is useful in either case.

**26. PxR      P–B3**

Now White's QR1–KR8 diagonal is closed, and Black has only to play Q–Q2 in order to meet his opponent's main threat.

**27. P–Q7**

A strong move! In going to its certain death the pawn destroys the coordination of Black's pieces. While Black is looking for a way to fight the threatening QP, White's pieces will occupy even more active positions.

Imagine that it is now White's move. Do you see the beautiful combination with a Queen sacrifice?—28. QxRch KxQ 29. BxP. To avoid this threat Black can now move his Rook to B2, attacking the pawn at the same time, but then an echo variation occurs: 28. Q–R3 P–B4 29. Q–R6 RxP 30. Q–N7ch—sacrificing the Queen on the other dark square—30. . . . RxQ 31. RxQch. Black's next move neutralizes the threat 28. QxRch because after 28. . . . KxQ 29. BxP there comes the rejoinder QxP.

**27. . . .      B–B3**

In my opinion, a more radical answer to the problem of defense on the long diagonal, 27. . . . P–K4, is the logical followup to Black's last few moves. For instance:

1) 28. P–R4 R–B2 29. P–R5 RxP 30. RxR QxR 31. PxP PxP 32. QxPch Q–N2;

2) 28. P–B4 R–B2 29. PxP RxP 30. R–KB1 R–Q8;

3) 28. Q–R3 Q–K2, and there is apparently no way for White to prevent the maneuver R–Q1, B–B3, and RxP.

27. . . . B–B3 solves the immediate problem by eliminating White's QP, but that is not enough in such a complicated position. Now Taimanov throws his pawns into the attack with renewed energy and finally breaks through to the Black King.

| 28. P–R4 | BxQP |
| 29. P–R5 | |

The atmosphere is so explosive that combinations flare up everywhere like lightning. If now 29. . . . P–N4, then thanks to the strong pawn that stood on Q7 White can sacrifice 30. BxP, and if Black takes with the Queen White gets a won Rook ending, turning to account the positional capital he

has been accumulating from the start, but if 30. . . . RxB 31. QxNPch K–B2 32. P–R6 P–K4 (32. . . . Q–K2 33. RxB) 33. R–Q6.

| 29. . . . | PxP |
| 30. P–K4 | |

Giving the Rook a green light for the march Q1–Q3–KN3. In reply, Black clears the way for his Bishop to KN5 at least to stop the Rook, but it is not to be.

| 30. . . . | P–K4 |
| 31. P–B4 | |

The King's Gambit as played by Taimanov. A complete success.

| 31. . . . | PxP |

The answer to 31. . . . Q–K2 is 32. PxP PxP 33. R–Q5, and Black cannot defend his KP; however, now the QR1–KR8 diagonal is reopened, and although Black can still hold his pawn on KB3 he cannot avoid defeat.

| 32. R–Q6 | Q–K1 |
| 33. BxP | R–B2 |
| 34. R–Q5 | Black resigns |

# Game 42
## King's Indian Defense

| M. Najdorf | T. Petrosian |
| --- | --- |
| 1. P–Q4 | N–KB3 |
| 2. P–QB4 | P–Q3 |
| 3. N–KB3 | P–KN3 |
| 4. P–KN3 | B–N2 |

| 5. B–N2 | O–O |
| 6. O–O | N–B3 |

One of the ideas peculiar to the King's Indian Defense. Black immediately joins the battle for his Q5, inviting White to win a tempo by advancing his QP. But what would White gain by this? One fianchettoed Bishop would begin to probe the very sensitive points in White's camp, and the other one would be blocked by its own pawn. P–Q5 would make sense if the Knight had to return to N1 or at least advance to K4: after exchanging Knights White could organize a majority pawn attack on the Queenside. But the Knight would go to QR4, where it could not be driven away. For example, 7. P–Q5 N–R4 8. Q–R4 P–B4!, with excellent play.

### 7. N–B3        B–N5

Continuing the fight for Q5. Black soon trades off the White Knight controlling that square.

### 8. P–KR3        BxN
### 9. BxB          N–Q2

Insistently provoking the pawn to advance to Q5. 10. P–K3 is answered by P–K4, and if 11. P–Q5 then not . . .

N–QR4 but . . . N–K2 and . . . P–KB4. But if White continues to fight for his Q4 with 10. P–K3 P–K4 11. N–K2, then 11. . . . PxP 12. PxP Q–B3.

### 10. B–N2

Najdorf, tired of being stubborn, hands over the QP and withdraws his Bishop. Now after P–K3, etc., Black's Queen goes to KB3 without attacking the Bishop at KB3. If you think that White is to some extent forced to trade his QP for Black's QNP, then you have to note a definite strategic success for Black in the opening, for the two pawns are not of equal value.

### 10. . . .        NxP
### 11. BxP          R–N1
### 12. B–N2         P–QB4

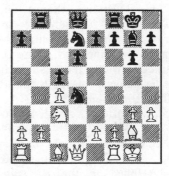

A serious positional mistake, the point of which the reader will appreciate in view of the following considerations. Black has an open file on the Queenside and can soon force White to play P–QN3. Consequently,

Black's further plan is connected with the advance of his
QRP to attack QN6. This attack could succeed if Black were
able to keep his pawn once
it reached R5. But how can he
keep it? He has no light-square
Bishop, and all of his Knight's
legal squares are taken away by
Black's next moves. It is also
clear that the Knight cannot be
maintained on Q5, and that the
light squares on the Queenside
are under the control of White's
KB; so it turns out that neither
of Black's Knights has a good
post. Indeed, from now on they
occupy insignificant positions.

Thus Black has no promising
plan. He can make various
moves, among them probably
some relatively good ones; but
although he will not necessarily
lose, he is already without
a logical guiding thread and
his position is therefore inferior. I recommend that the
reader examine this game in
parallel with the Najdorf–
Geller game in the 28th round.
There Black plays 12. . . . R–
N5!, and after . . . N–K4, provoking White's P–B4 and P–
QN3, he posts a Knight on QB4
and, despite Najdorf's ingenious
counterplay on the Kingside,
consistently carries out the attack on the QNP.

| 13. | P–K3 | N–K3 |
|-----|------|------|
| 14. | Q–B2 | P–QR4 |
| 15. | B–Q2 | N–K4 |

| 16. | P–N3 | Q–Q2 |
|-----|------|------|
| 17. | K–R2 | N–B3 |
| 18. | QR–Q1 | N/K–Q1 |
| 19. | B–K1 | K–R1 |

Black has done everything
he had to do: he provoked P–
N3, he advanced his pawn to
R4—but what now? Unknown.
It is impossible even to suggest
anything except not to create
weaknesses or expose a piece
or a pawn during the battle.
The last moves, N–Q1 and K–
R1, were made according to this
principle. White, meanwhile, is
all ready to improve his position systematically and logically, in general by N–R4, B–
QB3, exchanging Bishops, P–
B4, B–B3, K–N2, P–KR4–5,
R–KR1, etc. This is only an
overview, of course—in actual
play Black will not stand in one
place—but all the chances in
the coming struggle are undoubtedly White's, the more so
because any attempt by Black's
KP to take part in the defense

will cause the irreparable weakening of his QP.

| 20. | N–R4 | Q–B1 |
| 21. | B–QB3 | BxB |
| 22. | NxB | Q–B4 |

Petrosian no doubt realizes that he will lose a pawn after the exchange of Queens, but he is counting on tactical chances to hunt the Rook.

**23. QxQ PxQ 24. R–Q5 N–K3 25. RxKBP N–N5 26. R–R5 N–N2 27. R–R4 N–B4 28. R–B4 P–K3 29. R–Q1 R–N3 30. N–R4 R/3–N1 31. B–K4 N–N2 32. RxQP NxP 33. NxP, Black resigns.**

# Round Seven

## Game 43
### King's Indian Defense

| Y. Averbakh | M. Najdorf |
|---|---|
| 1. P–Q4 | N–KB3 |
| 2. P–QB4 | P–KN3 |
| 3. P–KN3 | B–N2 |
| 4. B–N2 | O–O |
| 5. N–QB3 | P–Q3 |
| 6. N–B3 | P–B4 |
| 7. P–Q5 | N–R3 |

The disposition of forces is very similar to the Bronstein–Najdorf game in the second round. The only difference is that here White's Bishop is on N2; there it was on K2. This circumstance offers Black better chances of success by continuing N–R3–B2 followed by P–QR3 and P–QN4, because White's Bishop is not so active here and White has spent an extra tempo on P–KN3.

| 8. O–O | N–B2 |
|---|---|
| 9. P–K4 | P–QR3 |
| 10. P–QR4 | R–N1 |
| 11. R–K1 | P–QN4 |

The opening struggle is very tense. If White exchanges twice on QN5 his center will look quite pitiful: 12. RPxP PxP 13. PxP NxNP 14. NxN RxN.

Confronted with a flank attack, Averbakh follows classical principles and counters in the center, not stopping even at material sacrifice.

| 12. RPxP | PxP |
|---|---|
| 13. P–K5 | N–N5 |
| 14. KPxP | KPxP |
| 15. B–N5 | N–B3 |
| 16. N–K4 | PxP |
| 17. N/3–Q2 | |

Courage bordering on recklessless. Black cannot take on

104

QN7 or Q4 in view of the terrible threat of N/2xP, when he loses his QP. Come what may, Najdorf must hold on to the point QB5; at the same time he has to keep track of the number of attacks and defenses on his pinned Knight.

**17. . . .        R–N5**
**18. R–QB1      Drawn**

18. Q–B3 is not playable because of the unexpected 18. . . . QNxP, winning for Black.

It is difficult to say who would have won had the game continued, but a draw was the least likely result.

Najdorf offered the draw believing his position to be in danger, and Averbakh accepted perhaps because he could not see exactly how to regain the pawn. Had they changed places maybe they would have continued playing. Najdorf gave the following variation as the basis

for a draw: 18. . . . B–QR3 19. B–B1 P–R3 20. NxNch BxN and further 21. BxRP R–K1 22. RxRch QxR 23. NxP BxN 24. BxB BxP 25. R–B2 or, better for White, 21. BxB QxB 22. N–K4 Q–Q1 23. Q–Q2 K–R2 24. Q–B4 N–K1 25. R–B2, with equal chances.

It seems to me, however, that 18. R–QB1 is not best. The Rook stood well on the QR-file. With the same idea of continuing the attack on the QBP, 18. B–B1 is good, since White's QP does not need the Bishop to defend it anyway. Thus, with almost all of White's pieces actively placed, the strong threat of Q–B3 should win. The serious situation of Black's pinned Knight is emphasized by the general variation 18. B–B1 B–QR3 19. RxB NxR 20. Q–B3, and there is no defense for KB3. Instead of 18. . . . B–QR3, 18. . . . B–B4 is correct.

## Game 44
### Nimzo-Indian Defense

**L. Szabo        M. Taimanov**

1. P–Q4 N–KB3 2. P–QB4 P–K3 3. N–QB3 B–N5 4. P–K3 O–O 5. B–Q3 P–Q4 6. N–B3 P–QN3 7. O–O B–N2 8. Q–K2 QN–Q2 9. P–QR3 BxN 10. PxB P–B4 11. B–N2 QPxP 12. BxP Q–B2 13. B–Q3 B–K5 14. BxB NxB 15. Q–Q3 Q–N2 16. P–B4 QR–B1

Here or on his next move White should do the logical and proper thing by mobilizing his center pawns; for instance, 17. P–Q5 PxP 18. PxP N/2–B3 19. BxN NxB 20. P–K4. His next two moves do not improve his position enough; placing the Rooks a little farther to the right is much more expedient.

17. QR–B1 P–KR3 18. KR–Q1 PxP 19. PxP KR–Q1 20. Q–N3 N–Q3 21. Q–N4 N–N1 22. P–Q5 PxP 23. PxP RxR 24. BxR N–R3

The advance of the pawns has reduced White's advantage, but still he does not stand badly: he has a passed pawn and some attacking chances.

25. Q–KR4 R–K1 26. B–B4 (26. B–N2 is better.) 26. . . . Q–Q2 27. BxN QxB 28. Q–R4 N–B2, Drawn.

## Game 45
### King's Indian Defense

| M. Euwe | S. Gligoric |
|---|---|
| 1. P–Q4 | N–KB3 |
| 2. P–QB4 | P–KN3 |
| 3. P–KN3 | B–N2 |
| 4. B–N2 | O–O |
| 5. N–QB3 | P–Q3 |
| 6. N–B3 | QN–Q2 |
| 7. O–O | P–K4 |
| 8. P–K4 | PxP |
| 9. NxP | N–B4 |
| 10. P–KR3 | R–K1 |
| 11. R–K1 | P–QR4 |
| 12. Q–B2 | P–R5 |
| 13. B–K3 | P–B3 |
| 14. QR–Q1 | KN–Q2 |

This the *the* King's Indian. At the slightest deviation from the "correct" order of moves, the theoreticians promptly brand the culprit with an ominous ± or ∓.

15. P–KN4?!

Suddenly the chief of the theoreticians' guild makes the kind of move capable of puzzling not only his opponent but the reader as well. What is his idea? First, to hinder Black's usual P–KB4 in this opening; second, to transfer a Knight to KN3 and only then to play P–KB4, which is premature if played immediately (according to Tarrasch, P–KB4 is always premature); and third, to play P–KN5 when the opportunity arises.

This is the apparent design of 15. P–KN4, but a more daring one may be guessed: to place a Knight on KN3 and a Bishop on K2, and to start a pawn storm with P–KR4–5 at a convenient moment. It is amazing that a move containing such good ideas should nevertheless turn out badly: the tension exerted by the pieces in the center is too strong for the flank attack to work. White does not succeed even in transferring his Knight to KN3, not to mention the other castles in the air.

| 15. . . . | Q–R4 |
|---|---|
| 16. B–KB1 | |

Defending the QBP in advance, in order to answer . . . N–K4 with P–B4.

| 16. . . . | N–K3 |

Still threatening 17. . . . N–K4, and on 18. P–B4 he answers NxN! and checks with the Knight on KB6.

| 17. | K–N2 | P–R4 |
|-----|------|------|
| 18. | P–B3 | PxP |
| 19. | RPxP | |

The collapse of one hope: P–KR4 will not be played in this game.

| 19. | . . . | N–K4 |
|-----|-------|------|
| 20. | N/3–K2 | NxN |

Gligoric, playing superbly, now turns to direct attack; however, I would prefer not to trade the Knight on K3 for the time being, but to move it to QB4 or KB1, threatening to get in P–Q4 under even more favorable conditions.

| 21. | NxN | P–Q4 |
|-----|-----|------|

Black consistently follows his plan to open the center, which will facilitate his attack on the King after White's KP is eliminated.

| 22. | KPxP | PxP |
|-----|------|-----|

22. . . . NxNP would have been beautifully refuted by 23. PxN BxN 24. BxB RxR 25. B–B3.

| 23. | N–N5 | PxP |
|-----|------|------|
| 24. | N–Q6 | |

This gives rise to a remarkable combination with the sacrifice of two pieces, which would be a fitting conclusion to the game.

| 24. | . . . | B–K3 |
|-----|-------|------|

The combination starts with 24. . . . NxBP and then 25. KxN BxPch 26. KxB Q–R4ch 27. K–N3 B–K4ch 28. K–B2 BxN with the threat R–K4, or 25. NxR NxRch 26. RxN QxR, or 25. BxP NxRch 26. RxN B–K3.

| 25. | NxR | RxN |
|-----|-----|------|
| 26. | Q–B3 | |

Euwe courageously decides to offer the exchange of Queens. It is hard to say whether he figured out all the variations possible after 26. . . . Q–N4 27. B–Q4 B–Q4, but he probably sensed intuitively that he could save himself, at the very least,

with the studylike move 28.
K–N3. Then, if Black's Knight
takes the BP White exchanges
Rooks with check and takes the
Bishop on N7, but if Black
takes with the Bishop White
takes the Knight on K5 and remains a piece up; on 28. . . .
P–B3 White takes on K5 and
then with the Rook on Q5. In
the variation 26. . . . Q–N4 27.
B–Q4 B–Q4 28. K–N3 BxP
29. BxN BxR 30. BxB RxR 31.
QxR KxB 32. QxB QxP, Black
can hope for a draw.

| 26. . . . | QxQ |
| 27. PxQ | N–B3 |
| 28. B–N6 | |

The Bishop has the much
better move B–B5, giving seri-
ous winning chances: 28. . . .
BxBP 29. R–K3 and 30. BxP
or 28. . . . R–QB1 29. R–K3
B–R3 30. RxB PxR 31. BxP
N–Q1 32. B–N4 RxB 33. Rx
Nch.

The Bishop's move to N6
looks strong because it blocks
the pawn, but Euwe seems to
have overlooked Black's 29th
move and he loses the QBP for
nothing.

| 28. . . . | BxBP |
| 29. R–K4 | B–R4 |

Euwe was counting on win-
ning back the QBP, but it turns
out that after the exchange of
Bishops the pawn will be defended by the Knight.

Now White has to switch to a
long, hard struggle. The out-

come of the game will depend
on whether Black can succeed
in connecting two passed pawns.

| 30. BxB | NxB |
| 31. R–K5 | P–N3 |
| 32. R–QN5 | |

White intensifies his efforts to
make the Black pawns work
separately and to keep them
from advancing too far.

| 32. . . . | P–B6 |
| 33. R–B1 | R–QB1 |

**34. R–N4**

Saving the game. White does
not take the harmless QNP but
tries to win the RP. If 34. RxNP
BxRP there would be no
defense against the QBP's advance, its path cleared by the
Bishop and Knight; for example, 35. R–N4 N–N6 36.
R–B2 B–N8, etc.

| 34. . . . | BxRP |
| 35. RxRP | B–Q4 |

If now 35. . . . N–N6 then
36. R–K1 P–B7 37. RxB P–
B8=Q 38. RxQ RxR 39. R–

R8ch K–N2 40. R–N8 with a
draw.

Black's move creates the
threat N–N6.

| 36. | R–N4 | N–N6 |
| 37. | R–B2 | N–R8 |
| 38. | R–B1 | N–N6 |
| 39. | R–B2 | N–Q7 |

Gligoric does not want to repeat moves, but in time pressure he overlooks the loss of a
piece and almost loses the game.
He is saved by his passed pawn.

| 40. | B–K2 | B–N6 |
| 41. | RxN | P–B7 |
| 42. | RxBP | Drawn |

## Game 46

Stahlberg is a pleasant opponent for lovers of the King's
Indian Defense because he
usually adopts not the theoretical continuations but lively,
double-edged ones. However,
he had played so strongly with
White against Boleslavsky in
the first round that I decided
not to repeat the same opening
against him; but I found myself in another system that was
well known to him and in which
he obtained an appreciable advantage.

## Queen's Indian Defense

**G. Stahlberg**     **D. Bronstein**

| 1. | P–Q4 | N–KB3 |
| 2. | P–QB4 | P–K3 |
| 3. | N–KB3 | P–QN3 |
| 4. | P–K3 | B–N2 |
| 5. | B–Q3 | B–K2 |
| 6. | N–B3 | P–Q4 |
| 7. | Q–R4ch |  |

The idea of this check is that
it is unfavorable for Black to
interpose any of the three
pieces. 7. . . . QN–Q2 is followed by 8. PxP PxP 9. N–K5,
and if 7. . . . Q–Q2 then 8. Q–
B2 wins a tempo for N–K5. If
the other Knight interposes,
however, it takes a natural developing square from its
brother. Black must therefore
use the pawn, which temporarily closes the Bishop's diagonal. At that moment Stahlberg exchanges on Q5, forcing
the KP to recapture and thus
foreordaining . . . P–QB4 all
the more.

| 7. . . . | P–B3 |
| 8. PxP | PxP |

9. O–O        O–O
10. Q–B2      P–B4

White was threatening to open the center advantageously with P–K4.

11. P–QN3     N–B3
12. P–QR3     P–KR3

Relieving the King Knight of the need to defend this pawn.

13. B–N2

I would prefer 13. N–K2, making it possible to recapture on Q4 with a Knight, and if 13. . . . R–B1 14. Q–N1.

13. . . .         PxP

Black closes the diagonal of the QB, further exploiting the fact that White is unable to bring his Bishop to KB4 just now. The resulting position is almost symmetrical, but White has an actively developed light-square Bishop.

14. PxP       P–R3
15. KR–K1     P–QN4
16. Q–Q1      R–K1
17. QR–B1     B–Q3

Drawn. Of course, with all the pieces around a lot of play is still possible, but if White offers a draw in this kind of position Black has no right to refuse.

# Game 47
## Ruy Lopez

I. Boleslavsky    S. Reshevsky

1. P–K4 P–K4 2. N–KB3 N–QB3 3. B–N5 P–QR3 4. B–R4 N–B3 5. O–O B–K2 6. R–K1 P–QN4 7. B–N3 P–Q3 8. P–B3 O–O 9. P–KR3 N–QR4 10. B–B2 P–B4 11. P–Q4 BPxP 12. PxP Q–B2 13. QN–Q2 N–B3 14. N–N3 P–QR4 15. B–K3 P–R5 16. QN–Q2 B–R3 17. QR–B1 Q–N2 18. P–R3 B–Q1 19. P–QN4

White forces his opponent to capture en passant; Black's QNP would otherwise be

blocked, and with it his entire Queenside. The opening of the position favors White.

19. . . . PxP e.p. 20. NxNP B–N3 21. N–R4 P–N3 22. B–N1

Drawn, on Black's offer. Boleslavsky agreed to the draw prematurely. He was threatening 23. PxP PxP 24. BxB QxB 25. Q–Q6 or 24. N–QB5, and he should at least have waited to see what his opponent would play.

# Game 48
## Grünfeld Defense

**A. Kotov**           **P. Keres**

| | |
|---|---|
| 1. P–QB4 | N–KB3 |
| 2. P–Q4 | P–KN3 |
| 3. N–QB3 | B–N2 |
| 4. P–KN3 | P–Q4 |

White does not yet want to play P–K4, but, as it turns out, Black can transpose from the King's Indian to the Grünfeld. White's next move is illogical and allows Black to take the QBP, which proves not so easy to win back.

| | |
|---|---|
| 5. B–N2 | PxP |
| 6. Q–R4ch | KN–Q2 |
| 7. P–K3 | |

He should continue still in gambit style: 7. N–B3 QN–B3 8. O–O N–N3 9. Q–B2, or 8. QxBP N–N3 9. Q–Q3 NxP 10. NxN QxN 11. QxQ BxQ 12. N–N5 with lively play, and if 10. . . . BxN, 11. B–R6 is good, keeping Black's King in the center as long as possible.

Kotov wants to win back the pawn even at the cost of two tempos—but it could have cost him the whole game.

| | |
|---|---|
| 7. . . . | O–O |
| 8. QxBP | P–B4 |
| 9. N–B3 | PxP |
| 10. NxP | |

No sweeter is 10. PxP QN–B3 11. P–Q5 N/2–K4 or 11. B–K3 N–N3 12. Q–Q3 B–B4.

| | |
|---|---|
| 10. . . . | N–K4 |
| 11. Q–K2 | QN–B3 |

Black gets the idea of a positional pawn sacrifice. Instead, he can continue to make tactical progress by quick piece development: 11. . . . B–N5 12. Q–B2 QN–B3 13. NxN PxN.

**12. NxN**

**12. . . .            N–Q6ch**

Keres cannot resist giving such a fine check and crowning his deep Knight raid by taking the Queen and the Bishop. The biography of this mustang is very rich: it makes as many as eight of the first fifteen moves of the game; it calls "guardez"; it gives a check; it takes a Queen, a Bishop, and a Knight; and it creates a weak pawn on White's QB3. In another game these exploits would be enough for all the pieces, both White and Black. Fairly good here is 12. . . . PxN 13. O–O Q–N3 14. R–Q1 B–QR3! 15. Q–B2 QR–Q1, with a rather clear positional advantage.

**13. K–Q2**

A cool and precise defense! On any other move, as we shall soon see, his QNP would be undefended after the 16th move and his King would stand much worse.

| 13. . . . | NxB |
|-----------|-----|
| 14. NxQ   | NxQ |
| 15. NxNP  | NxN |
| 16. PxN   | B–K3 |

This type of position is lost for White, despite his extra pawn. His minor pieces are disconnected, his QBP is weak, and his Rooks will be subjected to coordinated attack by Black's active Bishops. Correct for Black here is 16. . . . B–B4! in order to keep White's Rooks from the QN-file and from doubling on the QB-file, at the same time threatening to

give a check on Q1 as soon as he can and push White's King away from his pawns. White would be unable to avoid playing P–K4, shutting out his own Bishop and facilitating his opponent's operations.

After the text move Kotov equalizes with remarkable skill; by keeping his hopelessly sick pawn alive for a long time he brings the game to an approximately even position.

| 17. KR–QB1 | QR–B1  |
|------------|--------|
| 18. R–B2   | R–B2   |
| 19. QR–QB1 | B–B4   |
| 20. R–N2   | R–Q2ch |
| 21. K–K2   | R–B1   |

The QBP is doomed; the only question is whether White can manage to get some kind of compensation for it. He can arrange, for instance, to exchange his Knight for a Bishop or to exchange all the minor pieces. The unusual opening has led to such complicated situations that both players are already in time pressure here on the 22nd move.

| 22. R–N3 | B–N5ch  |
|----------|---------|
| 23. B–B3 | BxBch   |
| 24. KxB  | R/2–B2  |
| 25. P–B4 |         |

A beautiful move. White's idea in giving up the pawn is to exchange only one Rook while the other Rook gains time to attack Black's QRP.

| | |
|---|---|
| 25. . . . | RxP |
| 26. RxR | RxR |
| 27. R–R3 | P–KR4 |
| 28. RxP | |

Everybody takes pawns in time pressure. On 28. P–R4, so as not to allow . . . P–N4, a beautiful variation occurs: 28. . . . R–B2 29. RxP K–R2 30. P–R4 B–B6, and White cannot get out of the pin unless he gives up the pawn, which would lead to an immediate draw.

| | |
|---|---|
| 28. . . . | P–N4 |
| 29. N–R5 | R–B7 |
| 30. N–N3 | P–N5ch |
| 31. K–N2 | P–K3 |
| 32. P–QR4 | B–R3 |
| 33. K–B1 | R–N7 |
| 34. R–N7 | R–N8ch |

| | |
|---|---|
| 35. K–N2 | R–N7 |
| 36. K–B1 | R–N8ch |
| 37. K–N2 | R–N7 |
| 38. N–B5 | |

Fighting spirit triumphs over reason. Kotov spurns a certain draw, only to make an extremely difficult studylike draw

twenty moves later. The art of chess is the winner. Probably because of the severe time pressure, he doesn't see that Black can simply take the KP.

| | |
|---|---|
| 38. . . . | R–B7 |
| 39. N–K4 | BxP |
| 40. K–B1 | B–Q5 |
| 41. R–Q7 | P–K4 |

| | |
|---|---|
| 42. R–Q8ch | K–N2 |
| 43. R–Q6! | |

The beauty of this move shows up in the main variation: 43. . . . P–B4 44. R–Q7ch K–B1 45. N–B6 RxPch 46. K–K1. An exclamation mark is deserved not only by this move but also by the previous one, by which White forced the King to its second rank. Had White played 42. R–Q6 immediately (with Black's King on N1), then Black would have won after 42. . . . P–B4 43. R–Q8ch K–B2. But if now Black tries to get his King to B2 in order to avoid perpetual check, he loses his BP: 43. . . . P–B4 44. R–Q7ch K–N3 45. R–Q6ch

K–B2 46. R–B6ch and RxP. For the practical realization of his conception, White makes good use of the fact that Black's KB2 is occupied by a pawn.

Having safely slipped through the most dangerous ordeals, the rest is no longer so terrible for White; he gives up his QRP, conquers the KRP, and achieves a draw.

43. . . . R–R7 44. P–R5 RxP 45. N–B6 K–B1 46. NxRP K–K2 47. R–QB6 P–B4 48. N–N7 P–K5 49. R–B7ch K–B3 50. N–R5ch K–K4 51. R–B2 R–R8ch 52. K–N2 R–R6 53. N–B4 R–KB6 54. P–R3 PxPch 55. NxP R–R6 56. N–B4 K–B3 57. R–B6ch K–K2 58. R–B4 B–R2, Drawn.

## Game 49
### Nimzo-Indian Defense

| Y. Geller | V. Smyslov |
|-----------|------------|
| 1. P–Q4 | N–KB3 |
| 2. P–QB4 | P–K3 |
| 3. N–QB3 | B–N5 |
| 4. P–K3 | P–B4 |
| 5. B–Q3 | O–O |
| 6. P–QR3 | BxNch |
| 7. PxB | N–B3 |
| 8. N–K2 | P–QN3 |
| 9. O–O | |

Characteristic of the Sämisch Attack against the Nimzo-Indian Defense is that both sides' plans take shape at a more or less early stage. White accepts a doubled pawn on QB4 that becomes weak, not to say doomed, for the sake of rapid seizure of the center with P–K4 and a Kingside attack with P–KB4 and, if possible, P–KB5. Master practice shows that Black can obtain good counterplay if he blocks the Kingside with P–KB4. On his part, White can carry through his attack if he neutralizes Black's Queenside activity and prevents . . . P–KB4.

White must work very energetically to achieve his aims; in this respect, castling is already a loss of time.

| 9. . . . | B–R3 |
|----------|------|
| 10. P–K4 | N–K1 |
| 11. Q–R4 | |

In my opinion this is not the place for the Queen, which should support White's threats on the Kingside. More in the spirit of White's chosen variation is 11. P–B4 P–B4 12. N–N3 with the threat of P–Q5 and P–K5, or immediately 11. N–N3. At any rate, White's play should be developed in that direction and not on the other side, where the Queen is very passive. If Black answers 11. P–B4 with N–R4, attacking the QBP, then after 12. PxP PxP 13. B–K3 White seizes the QN-file and the Q-file and plays P–K5 with a strong game.

**11. . . .          Q–B1**

After considering his move for about an hour, Smyslov finds an excellent plan: he defends QB3 and QR3, indirectly attacks the QBP (after the possible . . . PxP), and on 12. PxP he has the answer N–K4.

| 12. | B–K3 | P–Q3 |
|-----|------|------|
| 13. | QR–Q1 | N–R4 |
| 14. | PxP | |

This trade is not appropriate in the new situation, for Black has been able to play P–Q3 and can recapture with the QP. One would rather expect 14. P–Q5! from Geller, and although he might later lose his QBP this would not be so terrible: a pawn is not the game. White would get fair chances on the Kingside.

| 14. | . . . | QPxP |
|-----|-------|------|
| 15. | P–K5 | Q–B3 |
| 16. | Q–B2 | |

Of course White does not trade Queens; in that case he would lose his QBP without any compensation.

| 16. | . . . | P–B4 |
|-----|-------|------|
| 17. | Q–R2 | |

White buries himself in an obscure defense, after which he is strategically lost. Instead he can play 17. PxP e.p. NxKBP 18. B–N5 BxP 19. BxN BxB 20. RxB RxB 21. P–QB4, keeping the Knight out of B5

and creating strong pressure on the Q-file. Black's win would be far from simple in that case; for instance, 21. . . . QR–KB1 22. P–B3 N–N2 23. KR–Q1, with N–N3–K4 in view.

| 17. | . . . | Q–R5 |
|-----|-------|------|
| 18. | N–B4 | N–B2 |
| 19. | B–B2 | Q–K1 |

The object of this subtle Queen maneuver is to keep White's Knight from KR5 and, by threatening to win the QBP, to force White's Bishop to go to its poorest position, QN3, where it will have absolutely no part in the game. White cannot return the Bishop to Q3.

**20. B–N3          P–KN4**

| 21. | N–R3 | P–R3 |
|-----|------|------|
| 22. | P–B3 | Q–K2 |
| 23. | N–B2 | QR–Q1 |
| 24. | N–Q3 | Q–N2 |
| 25. | P–B4 | R–Q2 |
| 26. | N–B1 | KR–Q1 |
| 27. | RxR | RxR |

On his next move White takes advantage of the tactical opportunity offered by the rather exposed position of Black's King to transfer his Queen to the Kingside.

This cannot substantially affect the course of the struggle. The attack by the Queen alone on Black's King can lead at most to an exchange of Queens and a transition to a hopeless endgame for White.

| 28. | Q–K2 | N–Q4 |
| 29. | B–Q2 | NxKBP |
| 30. | BxN | PxB |
| 31. | RxP | Q–N4 |
| 32. | P–N3 | K–R2 |
| 33. | K–B2 | Q–Q1 |
| 34. | Q–R5 | R–KN2 |
| 35. | Q–K2 | R–Q2 |

The repetition of moves is explained by the severe mutual time shortage.

By skillful defense White still parries Black's direct threats for a while. But his defensive resources gradually dry up.

**36. Q–R5 Q–N4 37. Q–K8 Q–K2 38. QxQch RxQ 39. B–R2 R–Q2 40. K–K2 B–N2 41. B–N1 K–N1 42. P–N4 PxP 43. RxPch R–N2 44. R–R4 R–N8 45. K–Q2 K–N2 46. B–Q3 B–B6 47. R–B4 B–R4 48. N–K2** (Possible here is 48. R–B6, increasing the activity of his pieces a little.) **48. . . . R–N7 49. K–K3 R–N4 50. P–KR4 RxPch 51. K–Q2 N–N6ch 52. K–Q1 R–K6 53. K–B2 P–K4 54. R–B2 P–K5,** White overstepped the time limit.

# Round Eight

## Game 50
### King's Indian Defense

**P. Keres**  **Y. Geller**

1. P-Q4 N-KB3 2. P-QB4
P-KN3 3. N-QB3 B-N2 4. B-
N5 P-Q3 5. P-K3 O-O 6. N-
B3 P-B4 7. B-K2 P-KR3 8.
B-R4 PxP 9. NxP N-B3 10.
O-O B-Q2 11. Q-Q2 P-R3
12. KR-Q1 K-R2

Black shows that his position is impregnable and invites White to attack if he so desires. The possibility is present, of course, but apparently the desire is not.

13. N-N3 B-K3 (Parrying the threat of P-B5.) 14. N-Q5 BxN 15. PxB N-K4 16. P-B4 N/4-Q2 17. B-B3 R-B1 18. QR-B1 RxR 19. RxR Q-N1 20. P-K4 R-B1 21. B-B2 R-B2 22. RxR QxR 23. Q-B1

There is no objective necessity for Keres to hurry with this exchange. Perhaps he is reliving yesterday's draw with Kotov?

23. . . . N-K1 24. QxQ NxQ 25. N-R5 BxP 26. NxP P-B4, Drawn.

## • Game 51
### King's Indian Defense

**S. Reshevsky**  **A. Kotov**

| | |
|---|---|
| 1. P-Q4 | N-KB3 |
| 2. P-QB4 | P-Q3 |
| 3. N-QB3 | QN-Q2 |
| 4. N-B3 | P-KN3 |
| 5. P-K4 | P-K4 |
| 6. B-K2 | B-N2 |
| 7. O-O | O-O |
| 8. R-K1 | P-B3 |
| 9. B-B1 | N-K1 |
| 10. R-N1 | |

White prepares P-QN4 to make the advance of Black's

117

QBP more difficult. He leaves QR3 vacant for the Bishop.

**10. . . .          N–B2**
**11. P–QN4**

On arriving at this position Black became convinced that his planned N–K3 would be met by 12. P–Q5 N–Q5 13. NxN PxN 14. N–K2 P–QB4 15. PxP PxP 16. P–B4, when the terrible pawn avalanche would sweep all obstacles before it. So Kotov decides to carry out his plan by another order of moves and plays P–QB4 first.

**11. . . .          P–QB4**
**12. QPxBP         PxP**
**13. B–R3          N–K3**
**14. PxP           R–K1**

The attempt to retake the QBP with either Knight leads to loss of the Exchange after 15. Q–Q5.

**15. N–QN5         N/2xP**

**16. Q–Q5**

Combining the disagreeable and the useless, Black is forced to transfer his Knight to N3, after which White's QBP becomes mobile.

**16. . . .          N–R5**
**17. R–N3          N–N3**
**18. Q–Q1          B–Q2**
**19. P–B5          N–QB1**
**20. R–Q3**

Black cannot repel all the threats and already has to give up a pawn, but even at that price he cannot coordinate his pieces. White invades the seventh rank and starts an attack on the King.

**20. . . .          N–Q5**
**21. QNxN          PxN**
**22. NxP           Q–R4**
**23. N–N3**

In exchanging his good Bishop for a bad one, White prevents the development of Black's Knight, which on QB1 is killed by White's QBP, on K2 restricted by White's KP. Bad enough that the Knight is without refuge, it is also in the way of the other pieces. The coordination of White's Queen on KB3, Bishop on QB4, and Rook on Q7 promises to decide the game in a few moves.

**23. . . .          QxB**
**24. RxB           N–K2**
**25. RxP           QxRP**
**26. B–N5**

If in such a position one may speak of different roads to victory, much quicker is 26. Q–B3 QR–N1 27. B–B4, and if RxR, mate follows in a few moves. Or 26. . . . KR–N1 27. RxN QxN 28. R–K8ch.

| 26. . . . | KR–Q1 |
|---|---|
| 27. Q–B3 | B–B1 |
| 28. B–B4 | Q–N7 |
| 29. QxPch | K–R1 |
| 30. P–K5 | |

The ensuing developments take place in incredible time pressure, with only a few seconds left for Reshevsky and a few minutes for Kotov. In these circumstances Kotov finds an insidious trap that nearly causes a catastrophe.

| 30. . . . | Q–B6 |
|---|---|
| 31. K–B1 | QR–N1 |
| 32. P–B6 | QR–B1 |
| 33. B–K6 | Q–Q6ch |
| 34. K–N1 | Q–K7 |

How dangerous this move is can be seen in the following variation: 35. R–KB1 R–Q8 36. N–Q2 QxN and White has only 37. B–B4, after which Black plays 37. . . . RxRch 38. BxR Q–N4 and saves himself from the immediate threats.

Reshevsky grabbed his head, glanced anxiously at his flag, which was about to fall at any moment, and at the board . . . and took the Bishop with check.

Then Reshevsky asked how many moves had been made, which is not acceptable among grandmasters, and received an answer from one of the spectators, which is completely against the rules.

**35. QxBch RxQ 36. RxQ RxQBP 37. RxN P–QR4 38. P–R4 P–R5 39. N–Q4 R–B8ch 40. K–R2 R–Q8 41. N–N5 R–QN8 42. N–Q6**

The time control having been passed, Black resigned.

## Game 52
### Nimzo-Indian Defense

**D. Bronstein    I. Boleslavsky**

1. P–Q4 N–KB3 2. P–QB4 P–K3 3. N–QB3 B–N5 4. Q–N3 (An ancient continuation that gives White nothing and is deservedly out of fashion.) 4. ... P–B4 5. PxP N–R3 6. N–B3 O–O 7. B–N5 BxP 8. P–K3 P–QN3 9. B–K2 B–N2 10. O–O B–K2 11. KR–Q1 N–B4 12. Q–B2 KN–K5 13. BxB QxB 14. NxN NxN 15. N–Q4 P–Q4 16. PxP BxP 17. P–B3 KR–B1 18. Q–R4 N–B4 19. Q–R3 B–N2 20. B–B1 P–KR3 21. P–QN4, Drawn.

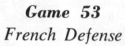

## Game 53
### French Defense

**S. Gligoric    G. Stahlberg**

1. P–K4 P–K3 2. P–Q4 P–Q4 3. N–QB3 B–N5 4. B–Q3 PxP 5. BxP P–QB4 (Inaccurate. First he should bring the Knight to KB3, and on 6. B–Q3 answer P–B4, or if 6. B–B3 prepare P–K4.) 6. N–K2 N–KB3 7. B–B3 PxP 8. QxP QxQ 9. NxQ P–QR3 10. O–O QN–Q2 11. R–K1 O–O 12. B–Q2 R–Q1 13. P–QR3 B–Q3 14. QR–Q1 B–B2 (White's positional advantage grows. Black has no way to develop his Bishop, which shuts in his Rook.) 15. B–N5 P–R3 16. B–R4 P–KN4 17. B–N3 BxB 18. RPxB P–N5 (Now Black's pawn weaknesses are very obvious.) 19. B–K2 N–N3 20. N–N3 B–Q2 21. N–R5 QR–N1 22. R–Q6 N–B1 23. R–Q4 P–K4 24. R–Q2 R–K1 25. N–K4 NxN 26. RxB N–B4 27. R–B7 N–K3 28. RxNP N–Q3 29. R–Q7 R–N3 30. P–N4 N–QN4 31. N–B4 R–B3 32. NxP RxP 33. BxN PxB 34. NxBP K–B1 35. NxP R–K2 36. R–Q5 N–B2 37. R–B5ch K–K1 38. RxRch KxR 39. NxP R–R7 40. R–QB5 K–Q3 41. R–B3, Black resigns.

## Game 54
### Nimzo-Indian Defense

| M. Taimanov | M. Euwe |
|---|---|
| 1. P–Q4 | N–KB3 |
| 2. P–QB4 | P–K3 |
| 3. N–QB3 | B–N5 |
| 4. P–K3 | P–B4 |
| 5. B–Q3 | P–Q4 |
| 6. N–B3 | O–O |
| 7. O–O | N–B3 |

| 8.  | P–QR3 | BxN   |
|-----|-------|-------|
| 9.  | PxB   | QPxP  |
| 10. | BxP   | Q–B2  |
| 11. | B–R2  |       |

One of many possibilities, but maybe not the best. His apparent aim to place his Bishop on QN1 and his Queen on QB2 and to mate Black's King on KR7 is not taken seriously, while his real aim—to move his pawns to QB4 and Q5 in order to open the long diagonal for his Bishop on QN2—is rather fanciful, since these pawns will block the diagonal of the other Bishop.

I think he should choose moves here that contribute to the advance P–K4–5.

| 11. | . . . | P–K4 |
|-----|-------|------|
| 12. | Q–B2  | B–N5 |
| 13. | P–Q5  | N–K2 |
| 14. | P–B4  | BxN  |
| 15. | PxB   | Q–Q2 |

White's position is good if considered only structurally, without regard for the time factor. He should now play K–R1, R–KN1, B–N2, B–N1, etc. The trouble is that Black has completed his opening development before White and is ready to attack; he is already threatening Q–R6 and N–N3–R5. As a result, White has to take extra measures to avoid immediate catastrophe.

**16. B–N1**

White cannot successfully reorganize his ranks by K–R1 and R–KN1; for instance, 16. K–R1 Q–R6 17. Q–K2 P–K5 18. R–KN1 PxP 19. Q–B1 N–N5 20. QxQ NxP mate. He should choose the variation with an Exchange sacrifice: 18. PxP! N–N5 19. P–B4 NxRP 20. Q–KN2 QxQch 21. KxQ NxR, with strong center pawns. But although White defends against the threat of Q–R6, to which he would reply 17. B–N2 QxBP 18. BxP, his position is too passive and his Rooks unconnected.

| 16. | . . . | N–N3 |
|-----|-------|------|
| 17. | Q–B5  | QxQ  |
| 18. | BxQ   | N–R5 |
| 19. | B–K4  |      |

A typical position to illustrate the strength of the two Knights and their advantage over the two Bishops. One Bishop is locked in a cage bound by QR3, QB1, and K3; the other is tied to the KBP. Both are completely harmless, and White has no useful move. The Knights will dominate the Bishops as long as the pawn chain remains immobile; hence White would get better chances by retreating the Bishop to B2 and attempting to open the game.

**19. . . .          NxB**

Euwe yields to the hypnotic Bishop pair and hastens to exchange one of them, even though he has the excellent move 19. . . . QR–K1.

**20. PxN          P–B4**
**21. PxP**

Taimanov easily obtained a passed QP in the opening, but he seems to have forgotten about it. Of course, the passed pawn itself does not worry Black much, but if it sends for help its strength will markedly increase.

Very appropriate is 21. P–B4, and however Black continues, the appearance of the duo K5 and Q5 will be inevitable. White would not have had this chance had Black not rushed to play P–B4. 20. . . . QR–K1 was still possible, and only then P–B4; there was no need to hurry, since White could not have essentially changed the position with one move, and all

of Black's forces would have been fully mobilized.

**21. . . .          P–K5**

A slight inaccuracy that gives White a surprising chance for defense. White's position would be difficult after 21. . . . N–B6ch and only then P–K5. The threats of RxP followed by R–N4ch and R–KR4, and QR–Q1–Q3 would be so strong and dangerous that it is hard to imagine how White could extricate himself.

**22. P–B4**

One of those moves that will be remembered for a long time. Grandmaster Taimanov is a great optimist. He is always satisfied with his position and at times tends not to notice danger approaching from a distance. On the other hand, when disaster is already at the gate his resourcefulness combined with long-range calculation extract from the depths of chess such possibilities as to amaze not only his opponent but all chess lovers.

The plan he now conceives dooms his five central pawns to destruction in order to get a position in which a Rook and two outside pawns successfully hold the defense against a Rook and four pawns.

| 22. . . . | PxP e.p. |
| 23. P–K4 | QR–K1 |
| 24. B–N5 | RxKP |
| 25. BxN | RxB |
| 26. RxP | RxQBP |
| 27. R–K1 | R–N5ch |

A subtle intermediate check, the significance of which becomes clear when compared with what could have happened if Black had put his Rook on Q5 right away. 27. . . . R–Q5 28. R–K7 RxQP 29. RxP R/4x P 30. RxR RxR 31. RxRP with a draw. But now, since White's King goes to the KB-file, his KBP in this variation would be taken with check, and so he is forced to choose something other than RxQNP.

| 28. K–B2 | R–Q5 |
| 29. R–K7 | RxQP |
| 30. P–B6 | |

Very good! Many players can bring an advantage to victory, but it is considerably harder to reduce the opponent's advantage to nought. With 30. P–B6 White wants to separate Black's Kingside pawns, and I am still not sure that Euwe's 30. . . . RxP is the best. It is interesting

to check the variation 30. . . . P–KN3 31. R–N7ch K–R1 32. RxQNP P–B5 33. R–QB7 R–Q3, etc.

| 30. . . . | RxP |
| 31. RxR | PxR |
| 32. RxNP | P–QR4 |
| 33. R–N5 | P–R5 |

Somewhat stronger is 33. . . . R–B5ch 34. K–K3 R–K4ch 35. K–B4 P–B5.

| 34. R–R5 | R–Q5 |
| 35. RxBP | |

It is easier to advise than to play. Here 35. R–R7, seizing the seventh rank, is a more stubborn defense—but to renounce the QBP while two pawns down? This is only possible to advise. Nevertheless, after 35. R–R7 the outcome of the game would still not be entirely clear, despite Black's two extra pawns; Black would have to give up his QRP to free his King. Then White's problem would be to trade his QRP for Black's QBP, and as a last resort to give up his KRP in the bargain. It is sometimes possible to draw an endgame against a RP and a BP.

Although even after 35. Rx BP White gets his Rook to QR7, Black is able to keep his QRP. The main objection to 35. RxBP, however, is that White still does not win a pawn, whereas Black's maneuver R–Q6xP restores a sufficient distance between the two pawn units.

| 35. . . . | R–Q6 |
|-----------|------|
| 36. R–QR5 | RxP |
| 37. R–R7 | R–R8 |
| 38. K–N3 | P–R6 |
| 39. K–N4 | P–R7 |

Black has to move his BP to the sixth rank, after which in even the best position for White—R/QR7, K/KB2; Black R/QR8, K/KR1— Black forces the win by the standard maneuver R–KR8.

| 40. K–R5 | P–B4 |
|----------|------|
| 41. K–R6 | P–B5 |
| **White resigns** | |

The win is obtained by 42. R–R4 P–B6 43. R–R3 P–B7 44. R–N3ch K–R1 45. R–QR3 R–KN8 46. R–R8ch R–N1, and one of Black's pawns becomes a Queen.

## Game 55
### Grünfeld Defense

| M. Najdorf | L. Szabo |
|------------|----------|
| 1. P–Q4 | N–KB3 |
| 2. P–QB4 | P–KN3 |
| 3. N–QB3 | P–Q4 |
| 4. PxP | NxP |
| 5. P–KN3 | B–N2 |
| 6. B–N2 | NxN |

We all know that a basic idea of the Grünfeld Defense is an attack on the pawn center, especially the QP. Why then does Black strengthen White's Q4 and open the QN-file for him without being forced?

There are many reasons, the main one being that the Knight does not have a good retreat square. Furthermore, Black destroys a strong enemy Knight without losing time, and al-

though the QN-file is opened, the QB-file is closed; although White's Q4 is strengthened, his QBP is isolated and his QNP weakened, for in being transferred to QB3 it is torn from its pawn chain. Thus, NxN has its logic.

| 7. PxN | P–QB4 |
|--------|-------|
| 8. P–K3 | O–O |

Of course, it is difficult, not to say impossible, for Black to breach Q5. One of the peculiarities of the pawn tension created in the center is that at the right moment Black can exchange on Q5, while White can practically never do the same on his QB5. At the same time Black's P–QB4, as will be noted again more than once, strengthened his Bishop on KN2.

| 9. | N–K2 | N–B3 |
|---|---|---|
| 10. | O–O | Q–R4 |

Capablanca, who loved clear and effective plans, would have played 10. . . . N–R4, probing White's weakened QB4, and proceeded with unhindered development; for instance, B–Q2, PxP, QR–B1, B–QB3, etc. A strong reply to the text move is 11. P–QR4, intending B–QR3, after which White's position would display all the colors of the rainbow. But B–QR3 would not work right away: after 11. P–QR4 R–Q1 12. B–QR3 B–N5 White would have to close his KB's diagonal by 13. P–B3, for 13. BxP would be met by QxB. Therefore 11. P–QR4 R–Q1 12. Q–N3 would be correct, and then B–QR3.

## 11. Q–N3

In Morphy's day such moves were made to attack the KBP, but now the Queen sets its sights on the QNP.

White seems to have succeeded in his aim to impede the development of Black's QB.

## 11. . . .          B–N5!

Black, like Morphy, is ready to sacrifice a pawn for development; for instance, 12. P–B3 B–K3 and then: 1) 13. P–Q5 P–B5 14. QxP BxQP; 2) 13. QxP B–B5; 3) 13. Q–R3 B–B5 14. QxQ NxQ 15. R–K1 QR–B1 16. B–QR3 P–N3 17. P–B4 KR–Q1—in all cases with equal play for Black.

## 12. N–B4          P–K4

If White's Knight were not on KB4, his QP could pass between Scylla and Charybdis and give Black a lot of trouble. But now the stronghold on Q4 is attacked on four sides, and White's center is split into formless fragments.

| 13. | PxKP | NxP |
|---|---|---|
| 14. | P–KR3 | |

White's game is much worse. His Queen cannot capture on QN7: 14. QxP? QR–N1 15. Q–K7 QxBP and White loses a whole piece; nor can his Bishop for the same reason: 14. BxP QR–N1 15. Q–Q5 B–B6 or 15. . . . RxB, etc., with an irresistible attack.

White's chance to equalize consists of the setup N–Q5 and P–K4, but this idea is not possible right away. 14. N–Q5 B–K7 15. R–K1 N–B6ch 16. BxN BxB and White has a lost position; or 14. P–K4 N–B6ch 15. K–R1 BxP 16. R–QN1 N–Q5 17. QxP QxP. Therefore, Najdorf first plays 14. P–KR3 to clarify the Bishop's intentions.

| 14. | . . . | B–B6 |
|---|---|---|
| 15. | BxB | NxBch |
| 16. | K–N2 | N–K4 |
| 17. | P–K4 | P–QN4 |

The temperamental Szabo spurns the strong positional continuation 17. . . . Q–R3, which is quite logical and incorporates several sound ideas: control of the light squares, which were noticeably weakened after the exchange of White's KB; defense of the QNP; increased scope for the Queen; and interference with the development of White's Knight, for N–Q5 would be answered by Q–K7!.

The strength of Q–R3 is evident not only in abstract ideas but also in concrete variations; for instance, 18. Q–R3 Q–B5, or 18. B–R3 P–N3, or 18. B–K3 P–B5 19. Q–B2 N–Q6. And if 18. P–B3 the weakness of White's second rank would

tell sooner or later (see game 85, Stahlberg–Szabo).

Szabo's choice of the bold P–QN4 almost forces an equal endgame.

| 18. B–K3 | P–B5 |
| 19. Q–B2 | N–Q6 |

Otherwise 20. B–Q4!, and the scales begin to tip in White's favor.

| 20. NxN | PxN |
| 21. QxP | BxP |
| 22. QR–Q1 | QR–B1 |
| 23. Q–Q5 | KR–K1 |
| 24. Q–N3 | R–B5 |
| 25. R–Q5 | P–QR3 |
| 26. QxR | |

Perhaps Szabo overlooked this move; grandmasters do occasionally make oversights. There is nothing substantially better anyway.

| 26. . . . | PxQ |
| 27. RxQ | BxR |
| 28. K–B3 | Drawn |

If his Bishop stood on KN2 Black would have fair winning chances, but now after 28. . . . R–QN1 29. R–B1 P–B6 30. B–Q4 R–N7 31. BxP BxB 32. RxB RxP a clear draw arises.

## Game 56
### Queen's Gambit

| T. Petrosian | Y. Averbakh | 4. P–K3 | B–K2 |
| 1. P–QB4 | N–KB3 | 5. P–Q4 | O–O |
| 2. N–QB3 | P–K3 | 6. B–Q3 | |
| 3. N–B3 | P–Q4 | | |

White calmly prepares to go into the Rubinstein System, in which his other Bishop is developed on the flank. Averbakh finds a good answer, exchanging pawns and transposing into the Queen's Gambit Accepted; he even has an extra tempo, since White will have moved his KB twice: B–Q3 and BxP.

| 6. . . . | PxP |
| 7. BxP | P–B4 |
| 8. O–O | P–QR3 |
| 9. PxP | QxQ |
| 10. RxQ | BxP |
| 11. P–QR3 | P–QN4 |
| 12. B–K2 | B–N2 |
| 13. P–QN4 | B–K2 |

**Drawn**

To understand such short draws, which are found in all tournaments, one must remember that a competition does not last only one day. Various events occur in the course of thirty rounds that affect the players' efficiency. In the present case, Petrosian's peaceful mood, and in part Averbakh's, was probably caused by the unfortunate developments both players had experienced in the previous round. After the extra rest day resulting from his unintended arrangement in this round, Petrosian won three successive games in fine style, which in a tournament like this must be considered an exceptional achievement. Averbakh, too, fought with enthusiasm in the next rounds, although with less success.

In a large tournament one must calculate one's strength not for a single game but for the entire competition. The history of chess competition, as well as that of many other sports, tells of cases in which one participant shoots ahead at the beginning of the tournament but in later rounds loses game after game—and not to the very strongest players—arriving at the finish line far behind the leaders.

# Round Nine

## Game 57
### Queen's Gambit Declined

| L. Szabo | T. Petrosian |
|----------|--------------|
| 1. P–Q4 | N–KB3 |
| 2. P–QB4 | P–K3 |
| 3. N–QB3 | P–Q4 |
| 4. B–N5 | B–K2 |
| 5. P–K3 | O–O |
| 6. N–B3 | P–KR3 |
| 7. B–R4 | P–QN3 |

A straightforward and most natural attempt to solve the problem of the QB. For a long time White obtained the advantage by 8. PxP PxP 9. N–K5; Pillsbury won many such games in his day. This system was revived recently when Bondarevsky and Makogonov had the logical thought that after P–QN3 it was senseless for Black to obstruct his QR1–KR8 diagonal with a pawn, and after 8. PxP they would take back not with the pawn but with the Knight. But if after 8. ... NxP White continued 9. BxB QxB 10. NxN, leaving a pawn on Black's Q4 anyway, Black's

Bishop would show its flexibility and come out to K3 instead of N2. Thus the Bondarevsky-Makogonov defense is completely playable; today White often avoids the main variation, as in this game.

| 8. B–Q3 | B–N2 |
|---------|------|
| 9. O–O | QN–Q2 |
| 10. R–B1 | |

A slight modification compared with the usual 10. Q–K2 N–K5 11. B–N3 NxB 12. BPx N. After the text move Black refrains from 10. ... N–K5 because White no longer withdraws to N3 but exchanges on K7, not fearing 11. ... NxN 12. BxQ NxQ—without check —13. KRxN KRxB 14. PxP PxP 15. RxP. But if 11. ... QxB in this variation, then 12. PxP PxP 13. NxN PxN 14. RxP is possible, and on 14. ... B–B1 15. B–N5 PxN 16. QxP R–N1 17. RxP, White has

128

three pawns for his piece and a strong position.

| 10. . . . | P–B4 |
| 11. Q–K2 | P–R3 |

Although Black has brought out all his minor pieces, his development is still far from complete: it is not easy to find good places for his major pieces, whereas White's Queen and Rooks are excellently developed. The text move prepares 12. . . . QPxP 13. BxP P–QN4, followed by Q–N3 and the development of the Rooks to Q1 and QB1. Nevertheless, Black loses an important tempo. 11. . . . QPxP 12. BxP N–K5 eases the defense.

| 12. BPxP | KPxP |

Taking with the Knight is more in the spirit of the chosen defense, and if 13. BxB then QxB 14. NxN BxN with comfortable play for Black. On 15. P–K4, the Bishop simply retreats to QN2, and if 15. BxRP it is possible to take on QR7, but I would prefer even 15. . . . BxN 16. PxB PxP 17. PxP N–B3, with good prospects thanks to the squares Q4 and KB5 for the Knight.

Petrosian probably did not like 12. . . . NxP because of the simple answer 13. B–N3.

| 13. PxP | PxP |
| 14. KR–Q1 | R–K1 |
| 15. B–B2 | Q–N3 |
| 16. B–QN3 | |

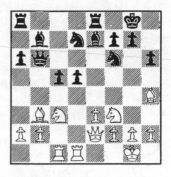

Black's hanging pawns have turned out to be weak. Szabo carried out the typical maneuver B–B2–N3 in order to draw either pawn forward, which makes the other one weaker and gives White an important strong point in the center.

| 16. . . . | P–B5 |
| 17. B–R4 | |

The Rook is in a pin. White threatens either BxKN or BxQN followed by NxP. Petrosian has to agree to exchange one of his QP's defenders, but Szabo should not exchange: an attack on the QP combined with threats to Black's King is much better; and having induced Black's Bishop to QB3 he should withdraw his own to B2 on the next move. After 17. . . . B–B3 18. B–B2! QR–N1 19. N–Q4 B–R1 20. R–N1, Black's game is coming apart at the seams; the threats are B–KN3 and N–B5.

| 17. . . . | B–B3 |
| 18. BxB | QxB |
| 19. P–QN3 | |

The fatal idea crosses Szabo's mind to attack Black's QP from QB4, and with one ill-considered move he weakens an entire group of dark squares in his camp, undermines the support of his QN, and strengthens Black's Bishop by giving it a chance to get to QR6 or QN5.

Correct is either 19. N–Q4 and N–B5 or 19. R–B2 and R/2–Q2. The pawn was perfectly placed on QN2 and should not have been touched.

| 19. . . . | QR–B1 |
|---|---|
| 20. N–R4 | |

Based on some miscalculation, since the Knight immediately returns, but in the meantime the position of Black's Queen is improved and White must already think about defending his Knight on QB3.

| 20. . . . | Q–N4 |
|---|---|
| 21. N–B3 | Q–R4 |
| 22. BxN | NxB |
| 23. PxP | PxP |
| 24. N–Q2 | |

White's position contains so many weaknesses that he should concern himself with making a draw, and with that aim he should let his Rook advance: 24. R–Q4, and if then 24. . . . B–N5 25. RxP BxN 26. R/1xB QxR 27. RxQ RxR 28. P–KR3.

| 24. . . . | R–B3 |
|---|---|
| 25. NxP | |

Extremely dangerous, for now both White Knights will be under Black's direct fire. One manages to get away, but the other . . .

| 25. . . . | Q–B2 |
|---|---|
| 26. N–R4 | |

The more active 26. N–Q5 is no good, since after 26. . . . Nx N 27. RxN B–B3, etc., there is obviously no way out of the pin, but 26. N–N1 is necessary to provide a solid position for at least one Knight. If 26. . . . R–QB1 then 27. N/1–Q2 B–N5 28. R–N1 N–Q4 29. RxB, with fair drawing chances. But now the hanging position of the two Knights gives rise to a combination that wins a piece.

| 26. . . . | R–QB1 |
|---|---|
| 27. R–Q4 | |

Trying to keep his extra pawn, Szabo oversteps the bounds of permissibility and leaves his Rook on QB1 defenseless. 27. N/R–N6 keeps some drawing chances.

The power of the pin, motivated mainly by White's undefended Rook on QB1, is illustrated by the diagram.

**27. . . .          N–K1**

The idea of this beautiful move is to transfer the Knight to Q3 and at the same time to free KB3 for the Bishop; from there it will attack not only the Rook on Q5 but also the Knight if White moves it from R4 to N2. 27. . . . N–Q2 is a mistake in view of 28. R–B2! N–K4— the Knight would block the Bishop's diagonal, giving White time to defend by 29. N/R–N2 and by moving the Rook from QB2 to the Q-file—but if 28. . . . B–B3, deceptive is 29. Rx N? QxR 30. N/R–N6 Q–N2,

instead of the correct 29. R–K4.

| 28. | P–K4 | B–B3 |
| 29. | P–K5 | BxP |
| 30. | R–K4 | N–B3 |

By driving the Rook from the fourth rank, Black wins a piece. If 31. RxB then RxN 32. RxR QxR/B, attacking the Queen and Knight and threatening mate. And in case of 33. Q–Q1 Black calmly "sacrifices" the Queen by QxN, or if 33. QxQ then 33. . . . RxQ.

**31. N/R–N6 RxN/3 32. RxB R–B3 33. R–K7 RxN 34. R–K1 Q–B3 35. P–KR3 R–B8 36. RxR QxRch 37. K–R2 Q–B5 38. Q–B3 QxP 39. R–R7, White resigns.**

## Game 58
### King's Indian Defense

**M. Euwe              M. Najdorf**

| 1. | P–Q4 | N–KB3 |
| 2. | P–QB4 | P–KN3 |
| 3. | P–KN3 | B–N2 |
| 4. | B–N2 | O–O |
| 5. | N–QB3 | P–B4 |
| 6. | P–Q5 | P–K4 |
| 7. | B–N5 | P–KR3 |

An aggressive opening setup. If Black wants to free himself from the pin he must do so at once; else White would put his Queen on Q2 and . . . P–KR3 will be unplayable. If the pin remains, White will push his Bishop to KR6 and without further ado advance his KRP.

This threat is dangerous, but hardly fatal. Therefore, the logical move is of course 7. . . . P–Q3.

| 8. | BxN | QxB |
| 9. | P–Q6 | |

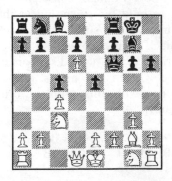

The incursion of the pawn is connected with two strategical ideas: delaying Black's Queenside development and breaking communications between his flanks. In addition, White gains the valuable Q5 for his Bishop and Knight.

Black's development is delayed mainly by his immobile QP, which closes the diagonal QB1–KR6 and thus prevents Black's QB from getting into the game except via QN2 or QR3. But . . . P–N3 cannot be played right away, so the Knight must be brought to B3. My conclusion, therefore, is that Black's next three moves are almost forced: N–B3, P–N3, and B–N2.

Black's Queenside pieces can reach the Kingside only through Q1, which distinctly limits his maneuvering possibilities.

These are the positive aspects of P–Q6, and there is only one negative aspect: the pawn, torn from its base, may be lost. White's problem, consequently, is to hold the pawn and at the same time strive to attack Black's Kingside while it is deprived of the needed support of the Queenside pieces. Euwe copes with this problem brilliantly.

| 9. . . . | N–B3 |
| 10. P–K3 | P–N3 |
| 11. B–Q5 | K–R1 |

With the aim of preparing P–B4. Later, in his notes, Najdorf suggested another plan: B–QR3, R–N1, and P–QN4. However, it seems to me that then White's Kingside attack would develop more quickly and more dangerously.

| 12. N–K4 | Q–Q1 |
| 13. P–KR4! | P–B4 |
| 14. N–N5 | |

I should like to call the reader's attention to this elegant Knight jump. I did not give it an exclamation mark only because I gave one to the previous move.

| 14. . . . | B–N2 |

Of course Black does not think of defending the Exchange, and White wouldn't dream of taking it. If 15. N–B7ch? RxN 16. BxR N–N5, Black gets the initiative.

**15. P–KN4**

White continues methodically to clear the way to the Black King's position. If 15. . . . N–R4 White exchanges Bishops and plays Queen to Q5 with two threats, QxN and N–B7ch; but if 15. . . . Q–B3 White has a choice between 16. N–B7ch, attacking the Queen and winning the Exchange (16. . . . RxN 17. P–N5), or 16. PxP QxBP 17. R–R2.

| 15. . . . | P–K5 |

Opening the KR1–QR8 diagonal not in order to take the

QNP but to give his King shelter on KN2 and perhaps allow him to risk PxN. Now, however, White's Knight gets to KB4.

**16. N–K2          BxP**
**17. N–B4**

In his turn, White sacrifices the Exchange. Shouldn't Black take the Rook? This question cannot properly be answered by giving variations. White would have a multitude of tempting attacking continuations. One of them—17. . . . BxR 18. PxP B–B6ch 19. K–B1—is analogous to the game continuation; White's threats of NxPch, Q–N4, etc., in my opinion could not be met in a practical tournament game. Najdorf apparently shares this opinion, and so he first defends the key square KN3. It should be noted here that the attack would quickly misfire if White limited himself to sacrificing only the Exchange: 18. Qx Bch? Q–B3 19. NxPch K–N2, etc.

**17. . . .          Q–B3**
**18. PxP!          BxR**

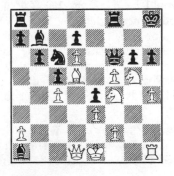

Inasmuch as White will break through anyway to one of the important squares—KN6, KR6, or KR5—Najdorf decides to take the Rook so as to have the later possibility of giving up his Queen for two pieces or for a piece and a pawn. If 18. . . . PxP White continues 19. QR–N1 B–K4 20. Q–R5 with a very strong attack. The next phase of the game recalls the ancient battles among masters of the Italian school.

**19. NxPch          K–N2**
**20. NxP**

As though to confirm that all attacks are conducted by intuition rather than by calculation. Otherwise, why does White need Black's KP? The simple 20. N–B4 is much more attractive, laying the groundwork for such threats as N–R5ch, Q–R5, or R–N1. But Euwe does not play it. Why? The explanation is simple. He does not want to give his opponent any freedom of choice. 20. NxP forces the play and takes QB6 from Black's Queen, eliminating the variation 20. N–B4 Q–B6ch 21. K–B1, although in my opinion this would only benefit White. For example, 21. . . . RxP 22. Q–N4 or 21. . . . PxN 22. PxP RxP 23. R–R7ch.

Euwe received a prize for his beautiful play in this game, but in my opinion the judges were not very strict or sufficiently critical. Every grandmaster has his style, his virtues, his short-comings.

**20. . . .        B–B6ch**

White's position is very strong, but he is still down a whole Rook. Bad is 20. . . . QxBP, when White wins by 21. QxBch KxN 22. R–N1ch. Therefore, Black first withdraws his Bishop with check and only then takes the BP, creating pressure on KB7 and removing the defense from White's Knight on KN6.

**21. K–B1        QxBP**
**22. N–B4**

Black still has to make one or two moves to stabilize his position and keep his extra Rook. But they must be good moves. Thus, on B–K4 White answers 23. N–N3 Q–R2 24. Q–N4ch K–R1 25. N–N6ch; if the Queen goes to K4 White gives a Queen check on N4; if the Bishop retreats to B3, either N–N3 or R–N1ch wins. In my opinion, Black should lose even with the best defense. If White wished to force a draw he could play 22. R–N1, forcing Q–R6ch 23. R–N2 Q–R8ch 24. R–N1 Q–R6ch, etc.

**22. . . .        K–R1!**

This is a good move. White must take the Bishop and allow his opponent a respite, for the consequences of 23. R–N1 are unclear.

**23. NxB        QR–K1**

Instead, 23. . . . N–Q1 is necessary. The Bishop's pressure from Q5 has already been intolerable too long.

After 24. BxB NxB 25. N/3–K2 Q–K5, the variations 1) 26. R–N1 R–KN1 and 2) 26. N–N3 QxPch 27. K–N2 RxN maximize the difficulty of White's task. Nevertheless, it seems to me that instead of the rather timid 25. N/3–K2, the energetic 25. N/3–Q5! would be decisive. The QP no longer needs defense, for its job is done. Yet there is no doubt that Euwe rather slowed the tempo of the attack with 20. NxP and that Najdorf did not take advantage of his good fortune.

**24. N/3–K2        R–KN1**
**25. P–R5        R–N4**
**26. N–N3        RxN**

Disagreeable but necessary. 26. ... Q–N5 is followed by 27. B–B3, and on any other move White has too many advantageous possibilities. At least with RxN Black does not lose his turn to move.

**27. PxR        RxP**

**28. K–B2**

It is not yet the time to give mate. Material is equal, but Black's Bishop on N2 and his Knight on B3, as before, participate poorly in the battle. This last factor allows White to launch a decisive new wave of strong attacks against the Black King's ruined position.

| 28. . . . | R–K1 |
| 29. R–K1 | RxR |
| 30. QxR | K–N2 |
| 31. Q–K8 | |

A poorly shielded King is a good target for attack in the opening, the middlegame, and even the endgame.

**31. . . . Q–B7ch 32. K–N1 Q–Q8ch 33. K–R2 Q–B7ch 34. N–N2 Q–B4 35. Q–N8ch K–B3 36. Q–R8ch K–N4 37. Q–N7ch, Black resigns.** Mate is unavoidable.

## Game 59
### Queen's Indian Defense

**G. Stahlberg        N. Taimanov**

| 1. P–Q4 | N–KB3 |
| 2. P–QB4 | P–K3 |
| 3. N–KB3 | P–QN3 |
| 4. P–KN3 | B–R3 |

A modern opening conception. P–QN3 does not at all mean that Black intends to play B–QN2; he may attack the QBP, and although it can be defended in at least eleven different ways each has its drawbacks. White chooses the best continuation, apparently.

**5. Q–R4**

I would gladly reply to this with P–B4, taking advantage of the fact that White's Queen has gone to one side and that P–Q5 is now unplayable, or if 6. B–N2 B–N2. As the course of the game shows, Taimanov has prepared another destiny for the QBP.

| | |
|---|---|
| 5. . . . | B–K2 |
| 6. B–N2 | O–O |
| 7. N–B3 | P–B3 |
| 8. N–K5 | |

8. B–B4! probably seemed too primitive to White, after which Taimanov would have nothing better than Q–B1 or B–N2 since the complications arising from 8. . . . P–QN4 would end eventually in White's favor.

| | |
|---|---|
| 8. . . . | Q–K1 |
| 9. O–O | P–Q4 |
| 10. R–K1 | |

White has no advantage at all. The text move prepares P–K4, but this will not succeed. Willingly or not, White must continue 10. PxP BPxP 11. QxQ and 12. R–K1 with about equal play.

| | |
|---|---|
| 10. . . . | P–QN4 |

Black seizes the initiative.

| | |
|---|---|
| 11. PxNP | PxP |
| 12. Q–Q1 | P–N5 |
| 13. N–N1 | |

Gripped by the desire to play P–K4 at any price, White takes the Knight God knows where in order to get it to Q2. The Knight would undoubtedly stand better on QR4, with prospects of getting to QB5.

| | |
|---|---|
| 13. . . . | N–B3 |
| 14. NxN | QxN |
| 15. N–Q2 | Q–N3 |
| 16. P–K3 | |

It seems Stahlberg is not in the mood for chess this evening.

16. N–N3 maintains chances to organize a defense.

| | |
|---|---|
| 16. . . . | QR–B1 |
| 17. B–B1 | R–B3 |
| 18. BxB | QxB |
| 19. N–B3 | KR–B1 |
| 20. Q–N3 | N–K5 |
| 21. N–Q2 | R–B7 |

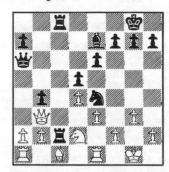

An instructive position in which we see:

1) Why it is recommended, when one Bishop remains, to post one's pawns on squares of the other color. The Bishop must be able to move through the pawn trenches. If White had a light-square Bishop here he would have a fully acceptable game; now his position is hopeless.

2) Why it is clearly favorable to exchange the opponent's fianchettoed Bishop. White's KN2 is very weak, and the usual technical procedure in such cases—Black puts his Queen on KB6 and plays P–KR4–5—soon leads to White's demise.

3) The importance of seizing some part of the seventh rank, even only one square of it.

Black could have won two pieces for a Rook by 21. . . . RxB 22. RxR NxN, but he simply put his Rook on B7. A Rook on the seventh rank ties up the enemy forces and creates possibilities for various combinations, as we shall soon see.

**22. NxN          PxN**
**23. P–QR3**

Black can now decide the game by 23. . . . Q–Q6 24. QxQ PxQ, threatening to win the Bishop, which has not made a single move, and if 25. R–Q1 then R–K7, and the pawn cannot be taken because of the Rook check on K8, winning the ill-fated Bishop. If White does not trade Queens after 23. . . . Q–Q6 but continues 24. Q–R4, the simple P–N6 emphasizes White's utter helplessness; for example, 25. QxRP B–B1 26. P–QR4 R–K7 27. R–B1 R/1–B7 28. P–R5 RxBP 29. RxR Q–Q8ch 30. K–N2 Q–B6ch. But the move played is not bad either.

**23. . . .          P–R4**

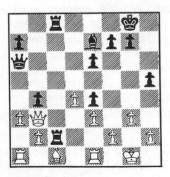

**24. P–Q5          R/1–B5**

White clearly cannot take the KP, since Black's Queen then penetrates through K3–KB3 to KB6, and after P–R5 White would have to lay down his arms. But if he takes the NP after 25. QPxP QxKP, there follows 26. . . . RxB 27. QRxR RxR 28. QxQ RxRch, etc.

**25. R–Q1          KPxP**
**26. B–Q2          Q–KB3**
**27. QR–N1         P–R5**
**28. Q–R4          Q–B4**
**29. QxRP          B–B1**

Giving White a postponement because of a chance to exchange Queens. This possibility would not have existed after 29. . . . B–N4, when White could not have survived P–R6 and Q–B6.

**30. Q–N8          P–N4**
**31. NPxP          KNPxP**
**32. Q–B4          QxQ**
**33. PxQ           P–Q5**
**34. P–N3          R–B3**
**35. PxP           P–B4**

Although Taimanov has dragged out the game a little, White's position is still very bad: he has five isolated pawns, and Black's Rook on B7 combined with the passed pawn assures Black of victory.

**36. P–R3 R–QR3 37. QR–B1 RxR 38. RxR R–R7 39. B–K1 R–N7 40. K–N2 RxP 41. R–B8 R–N8 42. B–Q2 P–K6, White resigns.**

## Game 60
### Sicilian Defense

| I. Boleslavsky | S. Gligoric |
|---|---|
| 1. P–K4 | P–QB4 |
| 2. N–KB3 | N–QB3 |
| 3. P–Q4 | PxP |
| 4. NxP | N–B3 |
| 5. N–QB3 | P–Q3 |
| 6. B–KN5 | P–K3 |
| 7. Q–Q2 | B–K2 |
| 8. O–O–O | NxN |
| 9. QxN | O–O |
| 10. P–B4 | P–KR3 |
| 11. B–R4 | Q–R4 |
| 12. P–K5 | PxP |
| 13. QxKP | P–QN3 |

A curious optical illusion! Theory says that by exchanging Queens White gets the better endgame by force, and that Black's retreat of the Queen to N3 is bad because of 14. N–R4 Q–B3 15. B–QN5 QxP 16. KR–N1. This is all correct, but only in a position with Black's KRP on R2. Then, in fact, after 13. . . . QxQ 14. PxQ N–Q4 15. BxB NxB 16. B–Q3, 16. . . . B–Q2 is impossible because White takes the KRP with check and then plays Rook takes Bishop. Black therefore has to continue 16. . . . N–B3 17. KR–K1 (B–Q2 is still unplayable), etc., with definite pressure for White. In the actual game, however, with the KRP on R3, 16. . . . B–Q2 is quite playable. After 17. B–R7ch KxB 18. RxB N–B3 the ex-

change of Black's QNP for White's KP is not dangerous for Black, but only if White is not too great a lover of endgames; this seems not to apply to Boleslavsky.

Both players fail to notice this, and Gligoric uses an innovation he had prepared for another variation.

| 14. QxQ | PxQ |
|---|---|

Black figures that his doubled isolated pawns will be compensated by active play for his Bishops and Rooks. Nevertheless, White's chances must be rated higher, in my opinion. In the three-against-two pawn setup he has obtained, White does not have to make a passed pawn—he already has one. The QBP's role will become even more meaningful as the endgame approaches.

| 15. B–Q3 | B–N2 |
|---|---|
| 16. KR–N1 | KR–K1 |

Nothing is gained by 16. . . . B–B4 since after KR–K1 the KNP cannot be taken anyway: 17. KR–K1 BxP? 18. BxN PxB 19. R–N1 and White wins two Bishops for a Rook. Gligoric is not attracted by 16. . . . B–B4 17. KR–K1 N–Q4, for any simplification here is of no use to Black, especially after 18. NxN BxN 19. B–K4 BxB 20. RxB, when White stands much better.

## 17. P–KR3

White prepares P–KN4, which does not work at once because of 17. . . . B–B4 and NxP.

| 17. . . . | B–B4 |
| 18. KR–K1 | B–N5 |

As before, taking on KN7 is unfavorable. Perhaps it would have been useful to move the King to R1 on the 16th move, as Boleslavsky himself played in a later tournament.

## 19. P–B5

Not fearing . . . BxN, in which case White gets a passed pawn on the QB-file. Perhaps this remark surprises the reader, for White already has a passed pawn on QB2. Unfortunately for White, this pawn cannot be called passed so long as there are so many pieces on the board, since it cannot take a step without ruining White's King position. But if Black now takes the Knight, then the pawn on QB3, supported by the Bishop pair, will take off down the board while the pawn on QB2, as before, protects the King.

| 19. . . . | P–K4 |

If Black doesn't like the variation 19. . . . PxP, etc., then the only logical continuation is, of course, to work on the pin with 19. . . . N–Q4. Now Black loses his last strong point in the center, which is in no way compensated by the passed KP.

| 20. B–QN5 | R–K2 |
| 21. R–K3 | P–R3 |
| 22. B–R4 | B–B4 |

The White pawn on KN2 is always defended indirectly because Black's King is on the KN-file (BxNP, BxN!; PxB, R–N1; and the Bishop is pinned); if the King now goes to KB1, there can follow 23. P–R3 BxN 24. RxB BxP 25. R–KN3 and 26. R/1–N1, and this time Black will have trouble defending his KNP. However, the text move indicates that Gligoric has not found a plan to improve his position. In the meantime, thanks to Boleslavsky's characteristically well-planned play, White achieves the exchange of minor pieces, seizes control of Q5, and forces Black's KP to advance still farther, which White tries to weaken as much as possible.

| 23. R–K2 | P–K5 |
|---|---|
| 24. B–QN3 | QR–K1 |
| 25. BxN | PxB |
| 26. B–Q5 | P–K6 |
| 27. BxB | RxB |
| 28. R–Q5 | B–N5 |
| 29. R–Q3 | BxN |
| 30. RxB | R/2–K2 |
| 31. R–Q3 | |

White's advantage in the four-Rook ending is obvious. Black's Rooks are anchored like solid steel in defense of the passed pawn, but White's King can move right up next to it, say to KB3. If he wins the KP, White's victory will be a matter of time. Black's King cannot come to help since it is unable to get to White's KBP. White's chances are so clear that if it were now his move, P–QB4 followed by R–QB3 would place Black in a desperate position: his Rook would attack Black's KP and support his own passed pawn. Black's next move is directed against this threat.

| 31. . . . | R–K5 |
|---|---|
| 32. P–B3 | K–N2 |
| 33. K–B2 | R/5–K4 |

| 34. P–KN4 | P–R4 |
|---|---|
| 35. R–Q6 | |

Nailing Black's King to the pawn on B3.

| 35. . . . | PxP |
|---|---|
| 36. PxP | K–R3 |

But Black does not think his King is nailed down at all! He gives up both KB pawns and penetrates to KB6, which, as we shall see, ensures the draw. Could this possibility have been prevented? Yes. The mistake was 34. P–KN4. White transferred the weak link of the chain from KN2 to KN4; i.e., closer to Black's King. He should have played 34. P–KN3 with great winning chances; for instance, 34. P–KN3 RxP 35. R/3xP RxR 36. RxR P–R5 37. P–B4 R–B7ch 38. K–B3 P–R6 39. PxP RxP 40. K–N4. The winning idea in this case consists not of winning Black's KP but of exchanging one pair of Rooks to maximize the strength of the other pieces.

After 34. P–KN4 P–R4, however, White would not have obtained an advantage by either 35. R–Q4 or 35. P–B4. For instance: 35. R–Q4 K–R3 36. K–Q3 K–N4 37. P–B4 PxP 38. PxP K–R5.

| 37. RxPch | K–N4 |
|---|---|
| 38. RxBP | KxP |
| 39. R–Q7 | K–B6 |

Black's King has scored a giddy success, the first to enter the enemy camp.

**40. K–Q3**

It's a good thing he has this move. If White's King could not get to Q3 Black would win.

**40. . . .         RxP**
**41. P–B4       P–R5**
**42. R–Q6**

Drawn, after thorough home analysis.

White must keep his Rook on the Q-file. On 42. P–B5 White even loses, in a very instructive way. The point is that White's King is tied to his Rook on K2 and at the same time defends the pawn on B4. This pawn, in turn, guards the important strong point Q5 for the Rook, which protects the King from checks on the Q-file. 42. P–B5 would give Black the chance to double Rooks on his fourth rank and drive away White's King; for instance, 42. . . . R/1–K4 43. P–B6 R–Q4ch 44. K–B4 R–B4ch 45. K–Q3 R/KB4–Q4ch 46. RxR RxRch 47. K–B4 R–Q7 and Black wins. There are many other combinative possibilities in the ending after 42. P–B5?, all favoring Black, but while his pawn stands on B4, his King on Q3, and his Rook guards the Q-file, White holds the draw.

## Game 61

All chess players love to attack the King, but they do not invariably decide on direct attack, especially if the opponent can counterattack on the other flank. The point is that the objective of a Kingside attack— to mate the enemy King—is more tempting but also much more difficult to achieve than, say, an attack on the Queenside to create some kind of pawn weakness. A Kingside attack by the pieces alone requires great superiority of forces and is generally connected with sacrifices; it is not always possible for the pawns to aid in the attack. The present game is an example of persistent counterplay in various sectors. It is instructive to see how obstinately both players impede the advances P–QB5 for White and P–KB4 for Black. Kotov is the first to attain his goal, and his strong passed pawn, long a key factor, nearly outweighs the entire striking force of Black's pieces.

## King's Indian Defense

| A. Kotov | D. Bronstein |
|---|---|
| 1. P–Q4 | N–KB3 |
| 2. P–QB4 | P–KN3 |
| 3. P–KN3 | B–N2 |
| 4. B–N2 | O–O |
| 5. N–QB3 | P–Q3 |
| 6. N–B3 | QN–Q2 |
| 7. O–O | P–K4 |
| 8. P–K4 | R–K1 |
| 9. P–Q5 | P–QR3 |

Usual is N–QB4—and P–QR4. For this game Black decides to adopt another battle plan, one in which there is no need to move the pawn to QR4 since the Knight is not particularly valuable on B4. The text move first of all guards QN4 and, together with his next move, R–N1, may prove to be useful for the advance of the Queenside pawns.

| 10. N–K1 | R–N1 |
|---|---|
| 11. N–B2 | Q–K2 |
| 12. P–QN4 | R–B1 |
| 13. N–K3 | N–K1 |
| 14. Q–B2 | |

Original play. White has not posted his Knight on Q3, where it would have supported the P–QB5 break, but on K3, where it cooperates with the Queen to maximize the difficulty of Black's P–KB4 break. A protracted maneuvering struggle arises around these strategically important advances.

| 14. . . . | N/2–B3 |
|---|---|
| 15. P–QR4 | P–QR4 |

| 16. PxP | R–R1 |
|---|---|
| 17. B–QR3 | N–Q2 |
| 18. B–R3 | P–R4 |
| 19. N/B–Q1 | RxP |
| 20. N–QN2 | N/1–B3 |
| 21. B–QN4 | R–R3 |
| 22. P–R5 | N–R2 |
| 23. B–N2 | P–R5 |
| 24. N–Q3 | |

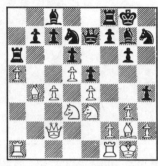

| 24. . . . | N/Q–B3 |
|---|---|

Relying on the QB1–QR3 diagonal for defense (Bishop, pawn, and Rook), Black casts all his pieces to the Kingside. He can inhibit the movement of White's QBP by N–B4, but what a pity it would be to part with this Knight, which is destined to play a definite role in the coming attack. Nevertheless, N–B4 should be played, with a very solid game for Black.

| 25. P–B5 | N–N4 |
|---|---|
| 26. Q–B4 | B–R3 |
| 27. B–Q2 | |

Keeping the option of taking with the KBP in case of . . .

RPxP, and freeing QN4 for the Knight, which induces Black's Rook to retreat from R3 in advance.

| 27. . . . | R–R1 |
|-----------|------|
| 28. KR–B1 | N–R4 |
| 29. BPxP  | BPxP |
| 30. Q–B7  | Q–B3 |
| 31. N–K1  | PxP  |
| 32. RPxP  | N–R6ch |

Black must hurry with his attack, for after the transfer of a White Rook to QN6 Black's position would be in trouble.

| 33. BxN  | BxB |
|----------|-----|
| 34. N–N4 |     |

If White trustingly takes the pawn on N7, Black sacrifices the Knight on N6, breaking in close to the King: 34. QxNP NxP 35. PxN BxNch 36. BxB Q–B8ch, and after 37. K–R2 Black can choose between 37. . . . K–N2, freeing KR1 for the Rook, or 37. . . . QR–N1 38. Q–B6 KR–QB1. Nor does 34. QR–N1 avert the threat of NxP. Kotov's move is the best.

| 34. . . .  | BxN   |
|------------|-------|
| 35. BxB    | KR–B1 |
| 36. QxNP   |       |

| 36. . . . | KR–N1 |
|-----------|-------|

So White was the first to achieve his aim: the weak pawn on N7 has been conquered. But his Bishop finds itself trapped.

| 37. P–R6 | P–N4 |
|----------|------|

Black should give up thoughts of winning the Bishop for now and quickly take the QRP, which grows stronger with each move. 37. . . . RxQ 38. PxR R–N1 39. R–R8 Q–Q1 40. R–B8! RxR/B 41. RxR QxR 42. PxQ=Qch BxQ leads to a clear draw. But now it gets much more complicated.

| 38. QxRch |  |
|-----------|--|

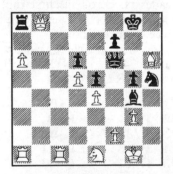

Black's previous error made possible a beautiful, deeply hidden, studylike combination. The quiet 38. KR–N1 is the prelude. The main variation is 38. . . . RxQ 39. PxR R–N1 40. R–R8 Q–Q1 41. BxP P–B3 42. RxR QxR 43. B–K3 B–B1 44. B–R7 QxP 45. RxQ BxR, and now White wins easily by 46. B–N8, attacking Black's pawns from behind. In order to avoid the main variation Black would have to continue 38. . . . R–K1, and after 39. P–R7, as in the game, his King would escape to R2. But White would still have an important tempo, which could be used for Q–B6, attacking both Rooks and threatening to take either, according to Black's reply. The resulting situation would be more favorable than after the game continuation.

| 38. . . . | RxQ |
| 39. P–R7 | R–R1 |
| 40. KR–N1 | K–R2 |

The winning move. The King evades check on his first rank, and Black gets a Queen and a piece for two Rooks.

It is also possible to transpose moves: 40. . . . RxP 41. R–N8ch K–R2.

| 41. R–N8 | RxP |
| 42. RxR | KxB |
| 43. R/8–N7 | K–N3 |
| 44. P–B3 | B–B1 |
| 45. R–B7 | Q–Q1 |

The simplest win of all for Black is to break through to White's King with the Queen. There are two ways to do this: either by the sacrifice of a piece or by the circuitous maneuver Q–QN3. Black takes the second path. 44. . . . NxP was possible one move earlier, but after 45. RxP QxR 46. RxQ KxR 47. PxB NxP 48. N–B2 N–B3 we would have a Knight ending with an extra pawn for Black

but with some drawing chances for White.

| 46. P–N4 | N–B3 |
| 47. K–N2 | B–Q2 |
| 48. N–B2 | BxP |

It can't be done without a sacrifice.

| 49. PxB | NxNP |
| 50. RxP | |

White cannot prevent the Queen from getting to QN3. If the BP is not taken the Queen breaks through via KB3.

| 50. . . . | Q–N3 |
| 51. R–N7ch | K–R4 |
| 52. R–R7ch | N–R3 |

The Knight covers the King, and the Queen proceeds on its decisive trip.

| 53. QR–QB7 | Q–N6 |
| 54. K–B2 | P–N5 |

54. . . . Q–Q6 55. N–K3 Q–Q7ch wins at once, but the game continuation is sufficient to win.

**55. N–K3          Q–Q6**

The penultimate move before the second time control.

Good enough to win is 55. . . . K–N4 56. QR–N7ch K–B5 57. N–N2ch KxP 58. RxN P–N6ch or 58. . . . Q–B6ch.

Black does not give up the Knight in time.

| | | |
|---|---|---|
| **56.** | **N–B5** | **Q–B6ch** |
| **57.** | **K–N1** | **Q–Q8ch** |
| **58.** | **K–N2** | **K–N4** |
| **59.** | **NxN** | **Q–Q7ch** |
| | | **Drawn** |

## Game 62

### Queen's Gambit Declined

| Y. Geller | S. Reshevsky |
|---|---|
| 1. P–Q4 | N–KB3 |
| 2. P–QB4 | P–K3 |
| 3. N–KB3 | P–Q4 |
| 4. N–B3 | P–B4 |
| 5. BPxP | NxP |
| 6. P–K3 | N–QB3 |
| 7. B–Q3 | |

White has a choice between B–Q3 and B–B4. The first, intending quick development and a Kingside attack with the pieces, was in fashion twenty to thirty years ago, until a Botvinnik–Alekhine game in which White used B–B4 and won a beautiful endgame. 7. B–B4 emphasizes that after Black exchanges pawns on his Q5 his Knight on Q4 may feel safe from pawns but not from pieces, and for that reason the Knight's position on Q4 is not very advantageous.

However, in a Kotov–Levenfish game (16th U.S.S.R. Championship, Moscow 1948), an antidote against B–B4 was found. Black withdrew the Knight to N3 at once, and even then he continued to decline the exchange BPxQP so as not to allow White to play KPxQP and open his Bishop's diagonal (a mistake Kotov made in his game with Boleslavsky). So, since White could not play P–QN3 with his Bishop standing on QN3, his Bishop on QB1 was a constant worry. B–Q3 and B–B4 enjoy about equal reputations today.

| 7. . . . | PxP |
|---|---|
| 8. PxP | P–KN3 |

Grandmaster Reshevsky has an affinity for concreteness and plays without preconceptions. Not bothered by the awful weaknesses on his KB3 and KR3, he closes the dangerous KR2–QN8 diagonal in advance and prepares an assault against White's QP. Yet it must be said that not every chess player, nor even every amateur, would permit himself to play this way. But note that despite the draw he obtained in this game,

Reshevsky remained dissatisfied with his opening, for as we will see in the second half of the tournament, in exactly the same position against Szabo he took the Knight on QB6 and developed his Bishop to K2, but after a few moves he played P–KN3 anyway. Reshevsky did not repeat the variation a third time; apparently he disliked his opening the second time even more than the first.

**9. B–KN5        Q–R4**

On 9. . . . B–K2 Geller would no doubt reply 10. P–KR4.

**10. O–O**

The sacrifice of a pawn through an exchange of Knights on QB3 is found in various openings, notably in the well-known Greco Attack in the Giuoco Piano, where it usually delights beginning chess players (1. P–K4 P–K4 2. N–KB3 N–QB3 3. B–B4 B–B4 4. P–B3 N–B3 5. P–Q4 PxP 6. PxP B–N5ch 7. N–B3 NxP 8. O–O, etc.). In the present game, if Black takes the pawn with his Queen, then after B–B6 he will soon find his position hopeless.

**10. . . .        B–N2**
**11. N–K4**

Geller skillfully disguises his plans. N–Q6ch seems to be the threat, but actually the Knight aims for KB6; true, to gain this point he must contend with the Knight on Q4 and the Bishop on N2.

**11. . . .        O–O**
**12. B–QB4      Q–N3**

Reshevsky calmly continues his plan of attack against White's isolated QP. The second idea behind his P–KN3 was to clear a place for the Bishop on KN2. However, I do not know another chess player who would allow White's next two moves. Bravery alone cannot explain such a decision.

**13. BxN        PxB**
**14. N–B6ch     BxN**

Why doesn't the King move out of check? Perhaps because of 15. Q–Q2 or the more forcing 15. NxQP QxNP 16. B–B6. Most likely, Black had already planned BxN and N–R4.

**15. BxB        N–R4**

It is necessary to clarify the Bishop's intentions; leaving it on B6 is very dangerous. There is no time to exchange White's Knight on B3: if 15. . . . B–N5 16. Q–Q2 BxN? 17. Q–R6.

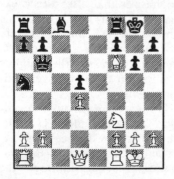

**16. B–K7**

More than a few amateurs can be found who would play Q–Q2 here, forcing Black to go into a somewhat inferior endgame: 16. . . . QxB 17. QxN; but as long as Geller can attack, he attacks. After 16. Q–Q2 the answer 16. . . . R–K1, for example, does not work in view of 17. B–K5 and if 17. . . . N–B5 then 18. Q–R6, and if now NxB or P–B3 White answers N–N5 anyway. I prefer 16. B–N5 in order to transfer the Bishop to R6. A Bishop on that square quite often creates conditions for many unexpected combinations.

**16. . . .          R–K1**
**17. B–B5**

Extremely interesting is 17. R–K1, with the same idea, Q–Q2–R6. If Reshevsky took the NP the beautiful reply would be 18. B–N4, and after RxRch 19. QxR Black would lose his Knight on R4 because of the threat Q–K8ch.

| 17. . . . | QxP |
|---|---|
| 18. R–N1 | Q–B6 |
| 19. R–B1 | Q–N7 |
| 20. R–N1 | Q–B6 |
| 21. R–B1 | Q–N7 |

**Drawn**

Very surprising. Indeed, White would risk nothing by continuing to fight for the initiative. The missing pawn has absolutely no significance, since the Black King's position is extremely insecure.

White has several continuations at his disposal; for instance, I like the move N–K5 at the moment when Black's Queen stands on B6. Simple and good was 21. B–N4 Q–B2 22. BxN! QxB 23. Q–B1 with menacing pressure.

If White wanted to force a draw he could always do it later. In any case he should make Black do a little work for it.

## Game 63
### Queen's Gambit Accepted

| V. Smyslov | P. Keres |
|---|---|
| 1. P–Q4 | P–Q4 |
| 2. P–QB4 | PxP |
| 3. N–KB3 | N–KB3 |
| 4. P–K3 | P–K3 |
| 5. BxP | P–B4 |
| 6. O–O | P–QR3 |

| 7. Q–K2 | P–QN4 |
|---|---|
| 8. B–N3 | B–N2 |
| 9. R–Q1 | QN–Q2 |
| 10. N–B3 | |

A theoretical position often found in tournaments, among them Smyslov–Keres, Budapest

1950. Inasmuch as Black has still not castled, he should have a little more patience and get his Queen away from its unpleasant opposition to White's Rook—to QB2 or QN3. Instead, with B–K2 and P–N5 he brings the game to a well-known variation which theory considers, not without reason, inferior for Black. Keres has often taken the opportunity to refute generally accepted opinions, and he has introduced new ideas into old variations; look at his games even in this tournament with Boleslavsky and Stahlberg. But here he is playing a faulty variation without having prepared any improvement. This mistake immediately places him in a difficult position.*

| 14. . . . | P–K4 |
| 15. PxP | O–O |
| 16. N–Q2 | |

Beginning with this move, Smyslov carries out his idea with iron persistence and logic: his minor pieces will clear the way for the passed pawn; rather than defend the pawn, his Knight and two Bishops attack the squares in front of it. In this connection he considers N–Q2 necessary in order to transfer the Knight to K4 or QB4, preparing to attack the square Q6.

As the course of the game shows, at this point Keres fully appreciated his mistake, and now he displays amazing resourcefulness in doing literally everything possible to make it difficult for White to realize his passed pawn.

| 10. . . . | B–K2 |
| 11. P–K4 | P–N5 |
| 12. P–K5 | |

Of course! The Knight has nowhere to go, and Black is obliged to enter a continuation that leads by force to the formation of a strong White passed pawn.

| 12. . . . | PxN |
| 13. PxN | BxP |
| 14. P–Q5 | |

| 16. . . . | B–K2 |
| 17. N–B4 | P–QR4 |
| 18. NxKP | NxN |
| 19. QxN | B–KB3 |
| 20. Q–N3 | P–B5 |
| 21. B–R4 | Q–K2 |

* In 1959, Smyslov demonstrated a new idea in a game against Petrosian: 10. . . . B–Q3!, and he won brilliantly. —D.B.

Black has achieved something for the sacrificed pawn: it is hard for White to complete the development of his Queenside; any move by White's dark-square Bishop (except, of course, to QN2 or KN5) would be met by Q–R6, winning back the QBP.

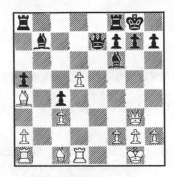

**22. B–B4**

Anyway! A typical Smyslov move, combining consistent realization of an idea with precise tactical calculation. White disregards the QBP in order to force the QP through. The reader's attention is directed to the position of the White Bishops, sweeping the path in front of the pawn.

If 22. . . . Q–R6 White gets a decisive advantage as follows: 23. B–B6 BxB 24. PxB QxBP 25. QxQ BxQ 26. QR–B1 and 27. RxP.

| | |
|---|---|
| **22. . . .** | **KR–Q1** |
| **23. P–Q6** | **Q–K5** |
| **24. R–K1** | **Q–B4** |
| **25. P–Q7** | **P–R4** |
| **26. R–K8ch** | |

Now the Rook attacks the square in front of the pawn.

| | |
|---|---|
| **26. . . .** | **K–R2** |
| **27. P–R4** | **R–R3** |
| **28. B–KN5** | **RxP** |

The battle is lost. Black cannot restrain the charge of the White pieces as they push the pawn through to queen, and he gives up the Exchange. The rest is a matter of simple technique.

**29. BxR QxB/2 30. QR–K1 R–Q3 31. BxB RxB 32. Q–N8 R–B4 33. R–R8ch K–N3 34. R–Q8 Q–N4 35. R–Q6ch K–R2 36. R–Q8 Q–B4 37. R K3 B Q4 38. R–R8ch K–N3 39. Q–Q8 B–B6 40. RxB RxR 41. PxR, Black resigns.**

# Round Ten

## Game 64
### Nimzo-Indian Defense

**S. Reshevsky**    **V. Smyslov**

1. P–Q4 N–KB3 2. P–QB4 P–K3 3. N–QB3 B–N5 4. P–K3 P–B4 5. B–Q3 O–O 6. N–B3 P–QN3 7. O–O B–N2 8. B–Q2 PxP 9. PxP P–Q4 10. PxP BxN

An original decision. Smyslov brings his Queen into play, and his pressure on the long diagonal somewhat hinders his opponent's activity. On 10. . . . NxP it makes no sense for White to win a pawn by 11. Nx N BxB 12. NxP since after 12. . . . QxN 13. QxB BxN 14. PxB N–B3 15. B–K4 KR–Q1 16. BxN QxB Black's game is not at all inferior. But White can continue 11. Q–K2 followed by Q–K4, and Black has nothing better than to put his Knight back on B3.

**11. PxB QxP 12. R–K1**

QN–Q2 13. Q–K2 Q–KR4 14. P–QR4 P–QR3 15. KR–N1 KR–Q1 16. B–K3

Allowing Black to exchange Bishops, after which White's initiative completely evaporates. Nor is anything gained by 16. P–B4 in view of 16. . . . BxN 17. QxB QxQ 18. PxQ N–K4. White could have played P–B4 on his previous move, which would at least have retained the advantage of the two Bishops.

**16. . . . B–K5 17. B–KB4 Q–KB4 18. BxB NxB 19. B–Q2, Drawn.**

One expected more from this game, but the tournament leaders limited themselves only to deep reconnaissance. The main battle was postponed to the second half of the tournament.

# Game 65
## Sicilian Defense

**D. Bronstein**    **Y. Geller**

| | |
|---|---|
| 1. P–K4 | P–QB4 |
| 2. N–KB3 | N–QB3 |
| 3. P–Q4 | PxP |
| 4. NxP | N–B3 |
| 5. N–QB3 | P–Q3 |
| 6. B–KN5 | P–K3 |
| 7. P–KN3 | |

A new idea and not a very good one. Keres often employs the setup Q–Q3, B–K2, QR–Q1, O–O, and later even voluntarily B–QB1. Something similar is obtained in this game, but White spends the extra move P–KN3 to develop his KB. It is instructive to follow how smoothly the mobilization of Black's forces now proceeds. One should not waste time even in the quietest openings, and especially not in the Sicilian Defense.

| | |
|---|---|
| 7. . . . | B–K2 |
| 8. B–N2 | O–O |
| 9. O–O | NxN |
| 10. QxN | P–KR3 |
| 11. B–Q2 | B–Q2 |
| 12. QR–Q1 | Q–B2 |
| 13. Q–Q3 | QR–B1 |
| 14. P–KN4 | |

What is wrong with White's position? His pawn on QB2 is dead and his Knight on QB3 waits to be attacked by Black's QNP; although he has three pawns against two on the Queenside, he cannot advance them but can play only with his Kingside pawns. That is why a system with Queenside castling is attractive against the Sicilian —the pawns stay put, as they should. If White plays passively he will soon find himself in a difficult position, so he sacrifices a pawn for the initiative; for instance, 14. . . . NxNP 15. Q–N3 P–KR4 16. K–R1, and the center of gravity is shifted to the Kingside. It was easy to decide on this variation, but the possibility of a sharp counterattack by Black on the Queenside, like the one in the game, should have been considered.

| | |
|---|---|
| 14. . . . | P–QN4 |

It is interesting to compare this with an analogous move by Geller in his game against Boleslavsky; there, as here, Black had no time for the preliminary P–QR3.

| | |
|---|---|
| 15. P–QR3 | P–QR4 |
| 16. P–N5 | PxP |
| 17. BxP | P–N5 |
| 18. PxP | PxP |
| 19. P–K5 | PxP |
| 20. BxN | BxB |

If Black takes with the pawn White gives perpetual check immediately. Here, and later, White strives insistently to expose Black's King.

| 21. N–K4 | KR–Q1 |
|---|---|
| 22. NxBch | PxN |

White has partly succeeded in his aim and now provokes P–B4 in order to have a Queen check on the KR4–Q8 diagonal; otherwise Black could shelter his King on K2.

| 23. Q–KB3 | P–B4 |
|---|---|

On 23. . . . K–N2 White has a choice between R–K1 and R–Q3, not to mention the simple Q–N4ch followed by QxNP.

| 24. Q–N3ch | K–B1 |
|---|---|
| 25. Q–N5 | |

Here Black accepted the draw offered by White when he played 23. Q–KB3. Possible is 25. . . . B–K1 26. Q–R6ch K–K2 27. Q–R4ch P–B3 28. Qx NPch Q–B4 29. QxQch RxQ

30. RxR KxR, and now R–QB1 would produce a curious position which each player evalu-

ated as unfavorable for himself, and it is hard to say who was right. However, Geller considered it mandatory to play not 25. . . . B–K1 but 25. . . . B–N4, after which a draw by perpetual check would be a certainty.

## Game 66
## Sicilian Defense

| S. Gligoric | A. Kotov |
|---|---|
| 1. P–K4 | P–QB4 |
| 2. N–KB3 | P–Q3 |
| 3. P–Q4 | PxP |
| 4. NxP | N–KB3 |
| 5. N–QB3 | P–QR3 |
| 6. P–KN3 | P–K4 |
| 7. KN–K2 | B–K3 |
| 8. B–N2 | P–QN4 |

When White's Bishop is developed at KN2 and a Black pawn stands on K4 in this opening system, Black plays P–QR3

and P–QN4 not to attack the Queenside—nothing is there to attack—but to make room for two pieces by B–N2, QN–Q2–N3. From this point of view the development of his Bishop to K3 looks illogical. The Bishop later goes to KN5 and then to KR4, as though to reproach Kotov for making it wander aimlessly around the board instead of putting it on the long diagonal right away.

But as for the march P–

QN4–5, this is reasonable when Black's KP is on K3 and White's QN thus has no good retreat. In the present case, after . . . P–N5 the Knight gets the excellent Q5-square, where Black is virtually forced to exchange it, lengthening the diagonal of White's fianchettoed Bishop. Such are the disadvantages of developing the Bishop to K3.

| | | |
|---|---|---|
| 9. | O–O | QN–Q2 |
| 10. | P–QR4 | P–N5 |
| 11. | N–Q5 | NxN |
| 12. | PxN | B–N5 |
| 13. | B–Q2 | |

One of the general rules of chess strategy states that it is useful to isolate or surround a given point before attacking it. 13. P–R5 is good here, but Gligoric is very reluctant to move pawns; he decides to play P–R5 later—nine rounds later, in game 120 against Najdorf.

| | | |
|---|---|---|
| 13. | . . . | P–QR4 |
| 14. | P–QB3 | PxP |
| 15. | BxP | Q–N3 |

White has an extra pawn on the Queenside, but he is far from thinking of creating a passed pawn there. He will do on the Queenside only what he must to allow him to attack on the Kingside. That was the purpose of B–Q2, P–QB3, and BxP. In such circumstances Black must play with extreme circumspection; this he does by postponing castling until move 20, which partially contains his opponent's initiative.

| | | |
|---|---|---|
| 16. | P–R3 | B–R4 |

The further course of the game prompts a legitimate question: isn't it better to take the Knight right away? Probably not. After 16. . . . BxN 17. QxB B–K2 White has no need to undertake Kingside operations, since he already has the advantage of the two Bishops. That would be a good time to remember the pawn on QR4 and to prepare P–QN4 to create a passed QRP.

| | | |
|---|---|---|
| 17. | K–R2 | B–K2 |

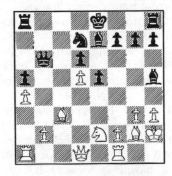

White has achieved a definite advantage, his preparations are complete, and the moment has come to decide a fundamental question: in which way is the game to be won?

Sometimes the so-called natural, normal moves are sufficient: occupy open files with the Rooks, get them to the seventh rank, attack a backward pawn, create a protected passed pawn, promote it to a Queen . . . Many games are won by such unsophisticated means. "White's simple (logical, clear) moves bring his advantage to victory; White's attack develops by itself"—we read such formulae time and again. But in view of today's considerably advanced defensive technique, it is difficult to expect that the game itself, like a rockinghorse, will bring a player happily to the finish line.

To win against an experienced opponent who takes advantage of every defensive resource, a player sometimes has to fight his way through the narrow path of best moves.

Gligoric should use his accumulated advantages for direct attack, starting with 18. P–KN4, first of all driving back the unfortunate Bishop. After 18. . . . B–N3 the move P–B4 would be much stronger. White's threat of P–B5 would force P–B3, on which 20. P–B5 B–B2 21. N–N3 would follow, having in view Q–B3, P–R4, etc. A sharp struggle would be in prospect, though not without risk for White—his exposed King would not be too safe—but the main chances, of course, would be only his. The halfhearted plan White chooses leads his game into a blind alley.

**18. P–B4          BxN**

The Bishop finally switches from words to action and takes White's last Knight out of the game.

**19. QxB          B–B3**
**20. Q–B4**

The plan to create a passed QRP lost much of its strength after P–B4, for Black's constant threat of PxP does not allow White to devote enough attention to the Queenside. A combinative player would certainly play 20. P–KN4 here, with the threat P–N5, Q–N4, and P–B5. If 20. . . . P–R3, then 21. P–R4 would be quite playable, again threatening to advance the KNP and keeping Black's King in the center; it would be unsafe for Black to take the KRP in view of 22. PxP, opening the center. Even the better 22. . . . O–O would leave Black in a difficult position.

White wants to strengthen the position of his pieces before launching a pawn storm, but Kotov, as always, defends excellently.

**20. . . .          O–O**
**21. Q–B6          KR–Q1**

For the second time White tries a technical maneuver to broaden his Bishop's scope, which is limited by the QP. If Queens are exchanged, not only the Bishop but also the pawn get brighter prospects. Naturally, Kotov does not take the Queen.

## 22. QR–K1

A trap. If 22. . . . PxP 23. BxB—ignoring the intermediate check—23. . . . PxPch 24. K–R1 PxB 25. R–K7, with the hard-to-meet threats of RxN or R/1xP.

## 22. . . .          Q–N1

Backing up for a running jump. After a few "natural" moves by Gligoric the initiative passes to Black. White's pawn structure is broken up, and as soon as Black can play PxP and force the exchange of dark-square Bishops all of White's weaknesses will be exposed.

| 23. R–QN1 | R–R2 |
| 24. Q–B4 | R–QB1 |
| 25. Q–K4 | Q–N6 |

The jump. Black threatens to win a pawn by R–B5, as well as to take on White's KB4 and then on QB3. And if White takes the Bishop after 26. . . . PxP, it will then be quite appropriate to give the intermediate check on KN6 first and then take on B3 with the Knight.

| 26. PxP | BxP |
| 27. Q–B5 | R–KB1 |
| 28. Q–KB2 | |

It is because of such one-

move threats that all of White's advantage has evaporated.

| 28. . . . | R/2–R1 |
| 29. Q–KB5 | QxRP |

Were the pawn on R5 it would not have been so easy to take.

## 30. R–B4

Black's position is rock solid. In desperation, White sacrifices the Exchange, counting on a careless oversight by his opponent during the ensuing complications, but they are far more dangerous for White than for Black.

| 30. . . . | BxR |
| 31. PxB | P–N3 |

Courage based on precise calculation.

| 32. Q–N5 | QR–K1 |
| 33. R–KN1 | R–K7 |
| 34. K–R1 | Q–B7 |
| 35. Q–N4 | N–B4 |

The Knight comes into play with decisive effect.

36. Q–R4    N–K5
37. B–Q4    N–B7ch
38. K–R2    N–K5

Time pressure.

39. P–B5    Q–Q6
40. PxP     BPxP
41. B–N6

White adjourned the game and resigned without resuming play. The threat is N–Q7–B6, among others.

## Game 67
### King's Indian Defense

M. Taimanov    I. Boleslavsky

1. P–Q4     N–KB3
2. P–QB4    P–Q3
3. N–KB3    P–KN3
4. N–B3     B–N2
5. P–K4     P–K4
6. B–K2     O–O
7. O–O      N–B3
8. B–K3     N–KN5

Boleslavsky repeats the variation Najdorf used successfully against Taimanov (see game 28 in the 4th round). This time, however, Taimanov refrains from P–Q5 and tries to obtain an advantage by 8. B–K3, but this move is so innocuous that White find himself in the role of defender. The later development of this system has demonstrated that by 8. . . . R–K1 Black can practically force a series of exchanges and completely solve the problems of defense (see game 107, Reshevsky–Najdorf). When this game was played this defensive improvement had not yet been discovered. And on the next move—after 8. . . . N–KN5 9. B–N5—Black can reply 9. . . . B–B3, offering the exchange of dark-square Bishops. Now White can carry out a plan to seize Q5, which should give him a definite advantage. Black's N–KN5 must therefore be considered not fully satisfactory, since he has in mind to follow it with P–B3; N–KN5 is much better in conjunction with 9. . . . B–B3.

9. B–N5     P–B3
10. B–B1    PxP

10. . . . P–B4 is not bad in positions of this type. Boleslavsky nevertheless plays PxP; it is hard to say whether he thinks it is stronger or whether he simply wants to vary his play.

11. NxP     NxN
12. QxN     P–KB4
13. Q–Q5ch

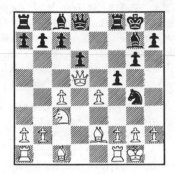

**13. . . .        K-R1**
**14. BxN        PxB**

White removed a Black pawn from the center and in exchange gave his opponent the advantage of the two Bishops. White plans a general strengthening of his position by B-K3, B-Q4, exchanging Bishops, and placing his Rooks on Q1 and QB1 or on Q1 and K1. If all this can be brought about, sooner or later Black will have to move his QBP, after which White can successfully attack the QP.

Black's counterplay is based principally on the two Bishops, which often permit a draw in an endgame a pawn down, and secondly on the weakness of White's KP, for its defender will encounter Black's KNP.

Now let us see what happens when these plans collide.

**15. B-K3        Q-B3**
**16. QR-B1**

White's plan calls for 16. KR-Q1 threatening B-Q4, and on 16. . . . B-K3 17. QxNP

BxP he has 18. QxBP. Black would probably reply 16. . . . Q-B2, and then 17. B-Q4 QxQ 18. NxQ would lead approximately to the above-mentioned position desired by White. 18. BPxQ would also be possible, with strong pressure along the QB-file.

**16. . . .        Q-B2**
**17. P-QN3      QxQ**
**18. NxQ        R-B2**
**19. P-B3**

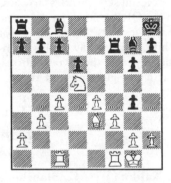

A beautiful tactical stroke. If 19. . . . PxP 20. RxP RxR 21. PxR P-B3 22. N-B7 R-N1 23. BxP, the Rook is lost. The same idea works in the variation 19. . . . P-QR3 20. PxP RxRch 21. RxR P-B3 22. N-B7, etc., and if 21. . . . BxP 22. NxP R-QB1 Black is a pawn down and he still has a weak QP. Therefore, Black hurries to drive the Knight from Q5 while his Rook is guarding QB2; White's hope of taking the imprisoned Rook on QR8 goes up in smoke and his P-B3 proves to be useless.

Although it seems a shame to censure a move that leads almost by force to the gain of a good pawn, the positional 19. KR–Q1 is good here, to exchange Bishops on Q4, maintaining strong pressure.

| 19. . . . | P–B3 |
| 20. N–B4 | PxP |
| 21. PxP | B–Q2 |
| 22. QR–Q1 | B–K4 |
| 23. N–N2 | R–K1 |

Boleslavsky decides to give up his QRP, and in so doing he exchanges his weak QP for White's center pawn; this, considering also the two Bishops, practically guarantees a draw.

24. P–B4 B–B6 25. RxP RxKP 26. BxP B–KN5 27. R–Q3 B–B3 28. R–K3 RxR 29. NxR B–R6 30. R–Q1 B–K2 31. N–N2 K–N1 32. B–K3 R–B1 33. N–K1 B–KN5

White's game is no better at all, despite his extra pawn. White should agree to repeat moves (R–Q3–Q1) after the attack on his Rook, for on leaving the Q-file it gets into a cramped position.

34. R–QB1 R–Q1 35. P–QB5 B–B3 36. K–N2 R–K1 37. B–B2 B–B4 38. K–B3 P–R4 39. P–KR4 B–N5ch 40. K–N3 B–B4 41. N–B3 R–K7, **Drawn.**

## Game 68
## Queen's Gambit
### Declined

| M. Najdorf | G. Stahlberg |
| --- | --- |
| 1. P–Q4 | N–KB3 |
| 2. P–QB4 | P–K3 |
| 3. N–QB3 | P–Q4 |
| 4. B–N5 | B–K2 |
| 5. P–K3 | QN–Q2 |
| 6. N–B3 | O–O |
| 7. R–B1 | P–B3 |
| 8. B–Q3 | PxP |
| 9. BxP | N–Q4 |
| 10. BxB | QxB |

This opening is mainly of historical interest. It was used many times in the Alekhine–Capablanca world championship match, and most of the games with this opening were drawn after positional struggles —anyway, Black did not win a single game. Such defenses without counterchances are completely out of style today. The next move was Alekhine's invention, which Capablanca usually answered by N/4–B3. Stahlberg's immediate P–K4 does not improve Black's defense; rather, it allows White to avoid the exchange of Queens, which is unavoidable after 11. . . . N/4–B3 12. N–N3 Q–N5ch.

| 11. N–K4 | P–K4 |
|---|---|
| 12. O–O | |

Of course White is not tempted to win a pawn by 12. PxP N/2xP 13. BxN NxNch 14. PxN PxB 15. QxP because then Black can bring almost all his pieces quickly into play by attacking White's Queen. 12. Bx N PxB 13. N–B3 does not work because of P–K5 with good play for Black (14. Nx QP? Q–Q3).

| 12. . . . | PxP |
|---|---|
| 13. QxP | N/2–N3 |
| 14. B–N3 | B–N5 |
| 15. N–N3 | BxN |

Here as well as later Stahlberg follows his custom, especially when playing Black, of direct exchanging tactics, figuring that sooner or later this will lead to a draw. Thanks to his experience and tactical ability, he is confident that he can parry any concrete threat that may appear. Nevertheless, if Stahlberg wishes to trade Queens he should keep his Bishop. White's Bishop will be stronger than Black's Knight in the minor-piece ending, although that advantage in itself is of course not enough to win. Inasmuch as Black's Bishop leaves the board in half a move, he should not exchange Queens for the time being. 16. . . . QR–Q1 17. KR–Q1 KR–K1 would be natural: Black is in no particular danger, and in all prob-

ability White would begin to seek the exchange of Queens himself. For instance, 18. N–B5 Q–N4ch 19. Q–N4, and now Black's QxQch would return White's KBP to the file it came from.

| 16. PxB | Q–B3 |
|---|---|
| 17. QxQ | NxQ |
| 18. N–B5 | QR–Q1 |
| 19. KR–Q1 | N–B1 |

It is better to put the other Knight back on Q4, and if P–K4, to occupy KB5.

| 20. K–B1 | KR–K1 |
|---|---|
| 21. K–K2 | K–B1 |
| 22. RxR | RxR |
| 23. R–KN1 | N–K1 |

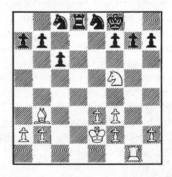

A strange picture. Black has not the slightest desire to play P–KN3, although this would avoid many of his later difficulties. In the next phase of the game he gives himself a number of weaknesses by advancing every pawn except the one he should advance.

**24. R–N4**

It must be said that White has gradually accumulated fairly substantial positional assets: his King has moved nearer the center; his Rook is on the fourth rank, where it can attack the Black pawns; his Bishop controls important points; his Knight is actively posted. Stahlberg, as usual, believes in the intrinsic defensive strength of his position and in his tactical flair to ward off any danger, whereas Najdorf continually and relentlessly strikes right and left to impair Black's position.

**24. . . .　　　N–K2**

Even this exchange of Knights cannot be considered a success for Black. His one remaining Knight cannot create any serious threat to White, whereas a pair of Knights would at least have the power to drive the Bishop from N3 and relieve the pressure on Black's Q4, which grows more significant with each exchange. That is why even now he should play 24. . . . P–KN3.

| 25. NxN | KxN |
|---|---|
| 26. R–K4ch | K–B1 |
| 27. R–QR4 | P–QR3 |
| 28. R–KB4 | P–B3 |

It is amazing how well Stahlberg's rather carefree style works for him. Witness the fact that Black's position is still not completely lost despite a number of inexact and, from a positional point of view, plainly bad moves. True, his choices are already limited—neither 28. . . . R–Q2 nor 28. . . . N–Q3 is good—but after 28. . . . N–B3 he can hold on. As in the game, White would continue to improve his position by P–K4, P–KB4, P–B5, again P–B4, then P–QR4, and, after moving the Bishop, P–N4, gradually gaining more and more space. An important feature of the position is that White's K5 is not weakened after he plays P–KB5 because he has another KBP to prevent Black's Knight from settling there. However, this plan would still encounter many objections by the opponent. But now after 28. . . . P–B3? Black can do nothing about the awful weakness of K3, and he is forced to create a second weakness by . . . P–KR3 (the KN3-square), which considerably facilitates White's task.

| 29. R–KR4 | P–R3 |
|---|---|
| 30. R–R5 | |

A splendid move! Having done its work on the fourth rank, the Rook now crosses to the fifth, condemning Black's pawns to complete passivity. White sets about the further conquest of space by moving his pawns and bringing up his King.

| 30. . . . | N–B2 |
|---|---|
| 31. P–B4 | K–K2 |
| 32. R–QB5 | R–Q3 |
| 33. R–B1 | |

P–B5 suggests itself.

**33. . . .          P–QN3**

Necessary after White's in-accuracy is 33. . . . P–KB4!
34. P–KR4 P–KR4 35. R–KN1 K–B3.

**34. P–B5          P–B4**
**35. P–B4          R–B3**

Black sees that he is on the verge of losing and wants to drive back the Bishop to get some air for his Knight, but this decision comes too late.

**36. P–QR4          P–QN4**
**37. B–B2**

It is not necessary to wait to be driven away. The threat now is B–K4. The variation 37. . . . P–B5 38. B–K4 R–N3 39. P–N3! or 38. . . . R–B4 39. P–N4 is to White's advantage.

**37. . . .          N–K1**
**38. B–K4          R–B2**
**39. B–Q5**

Now the KP's path is free.

**39. . . .          P–B5**
**40. P–K4          N–Q3**
**41. PxP          PxP**
**42. K–K3          R–R2**
**43. R–KN1          K–B1**
**44. K–Q4          R–QB2**
**45. R–QB1**

Najdorf is cautious. The threat was P–N5 and P–B6. For instance, 45. R–QR1 P–N5 46. R–R8ch K–K2 47. R–KN8

P–B6 48. RxPch K–Q1 49. RxR PxP 50. B–R2 KxR.

**45. . . .          N–N2**
**46. R–QR1          N–B4**
**47. R–R8ch          K–K2**
**48. P–K5!**

A precisely calculated final combination.

**48. . . .          N–N6ch**
**49. K–B3          N–B8**

If 49. . . . R–B4 50. R–R7ch K–B1 51. R–B7ch K–K1 52. B–K6 PxP 53. RxP N–Q5 54. K–N4 NxB 55. PxN, with an easily won Rook ending. Black takes the second branch of the combination.

**50. R–KN8          N–K7ch**
**51. K–Q2          NxP**
**52. RxPch          K–Q1**
**53. PxP!          R–Q2**
**54. RxRch          KxR**

**55. B–B6ch!   Black resigns**

An excellently played game by Najdorf.

# Game 69
## Reti Opening

| T. Petrosian | M. Euwe |
|---|---|
| 1. N–KB3 | N–KB3 |
| 2. P–KN3 | P–Q4 |
| 3. B–N2 | B–B4 |
| 4. P–Q3 | P–K3 |
| 5. QN–Q2 | P–KR3 |

A loss of time. In this kind of position it is more appropriate to think of developing the other pieces, leaving the Bishop to its fate. If White exchanges on N6, I think it will only improve Black's position.

| 6. O–O | B–B4 |
| 7. Q–K1! | |

A fine move, directing the Queen's fire against both Black Bishops by the imminent P–K4 or P–QN4. White's system of development is by no means innocuous, as shown also by the Smyslov–Euwe game in the second half of the tournament.

| 7. . . . | O–O |
| 8. P–K4 | PxP |
| 9. NxP | NxN |

Black's last moves seem rather inconsistent to me. He should have formed at least some plan by the 10th move. The first question for Black to decide is whether to keep his QB or allow it to be exchanged. If he wants to trade, he should take on K5 not with the Knight but with the Bishop—for a long time to come he will have no convenient opportunity to trade the Bishop for more than a pawn. But if he does not want to trade, which judging by his 5th move is precisely the case, then on the last move the Bishop should have retreated to R2, maintaining the pawn tension in the center and limiting the mobility of White's QP and KP, and in part even his QBP. If now, after 9. NxP, Black puts his dark-square Bishop on K2, then after 10. N–R4! Black will have to give up one of his Bishops anyway, since 10. . . . B–R2 cannot be played in view of 11. NxNch and BxNP.

| 10. PxN | B–R2 |
| 11. P–QN4 | B–K2 |
| 12. B–N2 | N–R3 |

Black's carelessness has led to difficulties for him, although they are not excessive. He has to develop his Knight from QN1 and find a good square for his Queen. The very best way to solve this problem is by . . . P–QB3, . . . Q–B2, and . . . N–Q2. The transfer of the Knight to QB2 seems artificial, and it is hard even to guess what advantage Dr. Euwe saw in it.

| 13. P–QR3 | P–QB3 |
| 14. R–Q1 | Q–B1 |

| 15. P–B4 | N–B2 |
|----------|------|
| 16. Q–B3 | |

Now White's advantage is clear. All six Black pieces are passive, and the standard exchanges on the Q-file will not ease his situation, since the absence of the hemmed-in Bishop on R2 will be felt all the more as the number of pieces is reduced. The choice of a plan to realize White's advantage is a matter of taste: there are already several possibilities. 16. P–B5 followed by the transfer of the Knight via QB4 to Q6 is not bad.

| 16. . . . | B–B3 |
|-----------|------|
| 17. N–K5 | R–Q1 |
| 18. B–B3 | |

White waits. More active is 18. Q–B1 or still P–B5. Why control an open line if not to use it to invade the enemy camp? White should attempt to place his Knight on Q6 while he is controlling the Q-file.

| 18. . . . | N–K1 |
|-----------|------|
| 19. RxR | QxR |
| 20. R–Q1 | Q–B2 |
| 21. P–B5 | P–QR4 |

Black opens the QR-file—and promptly plays R–Q1. In that case it is better to have the pawn on QR2, keeping the option of a break by P–QN3.

| 22. B–N2 | PxP |
|----------|-----|
| 23. PxP | R–Q1 |
| 24. RxR | QxR |
| 25. Q–B2 | N–B2 |

| 26. B–KB1 | N–N4 |
|-----------|------|
| 27. P–B4 | |

White has not maneuvered very energetically. Black has been able to improve the position of his pieces, but his basic problem remains unsolved: his Bishop on R2 is still out of play. This has made White careless—he has completely stopped worrying about his KP, and now Black has a chance to punish him. With 27. . . . Q–R1, threatening to burst into QR7, Euwe can approximately equalize the chances. Therefore, instead of B–KB1 and P–B4, extending the scope of Black's QB, the more restrained 26. P–B3! would have been correct.

One of the techniques for freeing a hemmed-in Bishop on the Kingside is P–KB3 and P–K4, clearing a path for the Bishop via KN1. This is what Black now intends to do. White is forced to operate actively if he wants to keep his advantage. The immediate threat was . . . N–Q5, attacking the Queen on B2 and breaking the contact between the Bishop on N2 and the Knight on K5; White's reply is directed against this threat. Now Black can effect an exchange of Queens by 27. . . . N–Q5 28. Q–Q1 N–N4. In that case White's Queen could not simultaneously defend the KP and avoid attack by the Knight, so he would continue 29. QxQch BxQ, leading to a somewhat better ending: 30. B–Q3 K–B1 31. K–B2 P–B3 32. N–B4 K–K2 33. K–K3, and Black would be unable to advance his KP; at the same time the unpleasant P–K5 would be imminent. Black therefore prefers to fight with the Queens on.

| 27. . . . | K–B1 |
| 28. K–B2 | BxN |
| 29. BxB | P–B3 |
| 30. B–QN2 | K–K2 |
| 31. B–B4 | B–N3 |
| 32. K–K3 | B–B2 |
| 33. P–N4 | Q–B2 |
| 34. P–K5 | Q–Q1 |
| 35. PxPch | |

Petrosian consistently storms KB7.

The hasty 35. P–B5 leads quickly away from the main idea in view of 35. . . . BPxP (35. . . . KPxP? 36. PxPch PxP 37. QxP) 36. PxP N–Q5, when 37. Q–R7 NxP 38. BxN seems to win; but Black has the unexpected and in time pressure very unpleasant answer 38. . . . Q–Q8, with the unavoidable threat of perpetual check (39. BxB Q–K8ch, and the King cannot go to Q3 because of Q–N8ch!).

| 35. . . . | PxP |
| 36. P–R4 | N–B2 |
| 37. Q–B3 | N–Q4ch |

Q–KR1 is completely hopeless; White can break through either on Q6 or on the Queenside, or he can win the KBP by P–KN5.

| 38. BxN | QxB |
| 39. QxPch | K–K1 |
| 40. Q–R8ch | K–Q2 |
| 41. Q–N7 | |

The adjourned position. The winning idea, based on beautiful symmetrical variations, is to defend against perpetual check with the help of the lone Bishop.

| 41. . . . | K–K1 |
| 42. B–B6 | Q–N6ch |
| 43. B–B3 | Q–Q8 |
| 44. Q–R8ch | K–Q2 |
| 45. Q–QN8 | Q–B8ch |
| 46. B–Q2 | Q–N8ch |
| 47. K–Q3 | Q–B8ch |
| 48. K–B2 | Q–R3 |

On 48. . . . Q–B5ch the King escapes the checks: 49. K–N2 Q–Q5ch 50. B–B3 Q–B7ch 51. K–R3. But now White has time for the important P–R5, fixing Black's KRP on a dark square. Black's Queen starts a series of checks from the other side, but even there the Bishop protects the King.

| 49. P–R5 | Q–R7ch |
| 50. K–Q3 | Q–N8ch |

| | |
|---|---|
| 51. K–K2 | Q–K5ch |
| 52. K–B2 | Q–Q5ch |
| 53. B–K3 | QxNP |
| 54. Q–KB8 | |

White attacks the Bishop and a pawn, forcing Black's Queen to return to KB3, after which White plays the decisive maneu-ver: he exchanges Queens and wins the RP.

54. . . . Q–N7ch 55. K–N3 Q–B3 56. Q–Q6ch K–B1 57. B–Q4 Q–Q1 58. QxQch KxQ 59. B–N7 K–B2 60. BxP P–N3 61. PxPch KxP 62. K–R4, **Black resigns.**

## Game 70

From the 5th move to the end of this tense game, a theoretical duel takes place between two excellently prepared con-noisseurs and lovers of the Open Variation of the Ruy Lopez.

## Ruy Lopez

**Y. Averbakh          L. Szabo**

| | |
|---|---|
| 1. P–K4 | P–K4 |
| 2. N–KB3 | N–QB3 |
| 3. B–N5 | P–QR3 |
| 4. B–R4 | N–B3 |
| 5. O–O | NxP |
| 6. P–Q4 | P–QN4 |
| 7. B–N3 | P–Q4 |
| 8. PxP | B–K3 |
| 9. P–B3 | B–QB4 |

In my opinion this is stronger than B–K2, which Szabo played against Gligoric. And really, are there many opening variations in which Black can develop his minor pieces so actively at such an early stage? The Knight on K5 proves to be the magnetic pole of the ensuing struggle. It is strong now, but if it is driven away Black's entire game will be shaken.

**10. QN–Q2**

On 10. Q–Q3 N–K2 11. B–K3 B–B4! or simply 10. . . . O–O 11. B–K3 P–B4, Black stands well.

| | |
|---|---|
| 10. . . . | O–O |
| 11. B–B2 | P–B4 |

An interesting variation with the sacrifice of a Knight for the KBP flashed by like a meteor and disappeared. Botvinnik played it against Smyslov in the 1943 Moscow Championship; the game became very lively, but so far no one has volunteered to repeat this experiment in a sufficiently crucial game.

## 12. N–N3

12. PxP e.p. is also playable. Black's Knight is then forced to leave the K5 outpost immediately in order to capture on KB3, and White can continue 13. N–N3 B–N3 14. QN–Q4 or 14. N–N5, initiating lively piece play. However, Averbakh hopes to derive a greater advantage by keeping his pawn on K5 and driving the Knight away by P–B3. Moreover, 12. . . . NxP/3 (after 12. PxP e.p.) is not the only move; 12. . . . NxP/7 is still playable.

| 12. . . . | B–R2 |
|---|---|

The Bishop retreats a little farther so as not to allow White to gain a tempo by P–QR4–5.

| 13. KN–Q4 | NxN |
|---|---|
| 14. NxN | BxN |
| 15. QxB | |

Why not the natural 15. Px B? This is an interesting story, the main line of which I will now endeavor to recount.

After the Vienna tournament of 1882 (the game Fleissig–Mackenzie), it was long believed that 15. PxB P–B5 16. P–B3 N–N6 was unquestionably in Black's favor, since

after 17. PxN PxP no way was seen to prevent the Black Queen from getting to KR7. Indeed, on passive defense Black's attack quickly reached menacing proportions; for instance, 18. B–Q3 Q–R5 19. R–K1 Q–R7ch 20. K–B1 B–R6.

Then Grandmaster Boleslavsky's searching investigations forced a reappraisal of the position. In his well-known games with Botvinnik and Ragozin he demonstrated that in the continuation 18. Q–Q3 B–B4 19. QxB RxQ 20. BxR the incursion of the Queen to KR5 was not dangerous, since after 21. B–R3 QxPch 22. K–R1 QxKP 23. B–Q2 a concerted drive by White's pieces against the King diverted the Queen and prevented it from properly aiding the advance of the pawns.

Black then began avoiding this variation, until a Moscow master, Y. Estrin, asked to be heard, and instead of 23. . . . QxP (Botvinnik) or 23. . . . P–B4 (Ragozin), he proposed the immediate P–Q5 and P–Q6. Carrying his analysis to thirty moves, Estrin won a few nice correspondence games and obtained more than he probably expected: the chameleon variation began to be avoided by White as well as Black!

It remains still to be added that on his 18th move it is naive for Black to attempt to block the Queen's way to KR7 by P–KN3 because it can still defend KR2 in time, in this case from KR6.

This, briefly, is why Averbakh takes on Q4 with the Queen and not the pawn. This is how things stand today. What will happen tomorrow? Research continues, and it is White's "turn to move."

Czech players analyzed 17. R–B2 instead of the acceptance of the Knight sacrifice.

Knowing Grandmaster Boleslavsky, I am convinced that sooner or later he will attempt to do battle also against Estrin's weapon.

Let us return to the game.

**15. . . .          P–B4**
**16. Q–Q1          P–KB5**
**17. P–B3          N–N4**

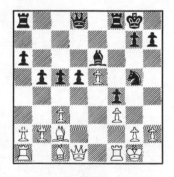

The piece sacrifice 17. . . . N–N6 is clearly fruitless here (18. PxN PxP 19. Q–Q3 B–B4 20. QxB RxQ 21. BxR Q–R5 22. B–R3, and Black does not even have the Queen check on Q5), in view of which the variation right up to 17. . . . N–N4 is considered unfavorable for

Black. Szabo nevertheless makes the move recommended by theory, and later, demonstrating that the Knight does not stand so badly on KN4, he opens if not a new page then a new paragraph in the opening manuals.

**18. P–QR4**

Black wants very much to transfer his Knight to K3, but White does not give him the chance: 18. . . . B–B4 19. BxB RxB 20. PxP PxP 21. RxR QxR 22. Q–Q3, attacking QN5 and KB5.

**18. . . .          P–N5**

Now Black is all ready to fully equalize the game by B–B4; for instance, 19. P–R5 B–B4 20. BxP BxB 21. BxN QxB 22. QxB QxP.

**19. P–R4**

White's QRP and Black's QNP have met and parted, and the crucial point of the entire game almost went unnoticed. To be considered is 19. PxP PxP 20. Q–Q4, but the answer to 19. PxP is 19. . . . P–B5 20. Q–Q4 B–B4, when the undefended KBP could not be taken by the Queen or the Bishop, and the attempt to win the QP would end sadly for White. Here are the variations:

1) 21. BxB RxB 22. BxP N–K3;

2) 21. QxKBP N–R6ch 22.

PxN BxB, with an insecure King position for White;

3) 21. BxB RxB 22. R–Q1 N–K3 23. QxQP Q–N3ch 24. K–R1 R–Q1, and Black wins because his QBP blocks the White Queen's path to QN3.

Szabo's elegant combination is guessed by Averbakh, who does not want to allow Black's Knight to K3 and invites him to sacrifice it, although this entails certain risks for White.

| 19. . . . | N–R6ch |
|-----------|--------|
| 20. PxN | QxP |
| 21. R–B2 | BxP |
| 22. R–KR2 | QR–K1 |
| 23. QxPch | K–R1 |
| 24. B–Q2 | |

Attack and defense at their best. With his KP defended, White threatens to throw back the Black pieces by B–K1. At the last moment Szabo succeeds in announcing perpetual check by sacrificing a Rook. The attempt to sustain the attack by 24. . . . R–K3 would cost the game in view of 25. BxP.

| 24. . . . | RxP |
|-----------|--------|
| 25. QxR | Q–N6ch |
| 26. K–R1 | QxPch |
| 27. K–N1 | Drawn |

Averbakh was excellently prepared, but the Hungarian grandmaster was not caught napping. The two opponents were well matched.

# Round Eleven

## *Game 71*

Even at the height of the middlegame battle a master should always be thinking about the outlines of the coming endgame. Many games, including a number in which the King barely escaped direct threats and utter defeat seemed inevitable, were decided only after deep endgames. A rare but characteristic example is played in the 11th round. Right in the opening Averbakh chooses a plan that entails the creation of a passed pawn on the Queenside. Aware that the value of a passed pawn usually increases as the forces are reduced, Averbakh reconciles himself to the temporary inconvenience of a frontal attack by Euwe. The game is crowned by an elegant Knight sacrifice exactly at the spot where the passed pawn awaits its moment.

## *Nimzo-Indian Defense*

| M. Euwe | Y. Averbakh |
|---------|-------------|
| 1. P–Q4 | N–KB3 |
| 2. P–QB4 | P–K3 |
| 3. N–QB3 | B–N5 |
| 4. P–K3 | O–O |
| 5. B–Q3 | P–Q4 |
| 6. N–B3 | P–B4 |
| 7. O–O | N–B3 |
| 8. P–QR3 | BxN |
| 9. PxB | P–QN3 |
| 10. BPxP | KPxP |
| 11. N–Q2 | B–K3 |
| 12. B–N2 | P–B5 |

By bringing his Bishop to the long diagonal, White has induced his opponent to play P–B5. With White's problem in defending his Q4 thus removed, the advance of his KP will be considerably stronger. Averbakh meets his opponent's challenge willingly, having in

169

mind a swift attack with his Queenside pawn majority.

| 13. B–B2 | P–QN4 |
| 14. P–B3 | P–QR4 |
| 15. R–K1 | |

I would have preferred to advance the pawn to K4 immediately.

| 15. . . . | Q–N3 |
| 16. N–B1 | P–N5 |
| 17. Q–Q2 | P–N6 |

Averbakh thus practically assures himself of an advantage in any type of endgame. Euwe's plan must be considered unusual, at the very least. The point is not that he retreats the Bishop to N1, where it is still on an attacking diagonal, but that on his last move he could have moved his QR to B1. Euwe assumed that Black would not have the power to imprison the Rook on QR1 so he did not want to spend a tempo to move it.

| 18. B–N1 | P–R5 |
| 19. P–K4 | N–K2 |
| 20. N–N3 | K–R1 |
| 21. R–K2 | N/3–N1 |

Averbakh prepares the counterattacking move P–B4 to open a file and exchange several pieces, bringing the endgame closer.

| 22. N–R5 | P–B4 |
| 23. Q–N5 | R–B2 |
| 24. PxBP | |

24. P–K5 looks too risky since it would then be considerably harder to bring the QR into play.

| 24. . . . | BxP |
| 25. BxB | NxB |
| 26. QR–K1 | |

The reserve Rook rushes to the battle site, but it should wait. Stronger is 26. R–K5 first, tying Black to the defense of his QP and considerably impeding his drive toward the endgame.

**26. . . .          Q–Q1!**

Exclamation marks are deserved not only by beautiful sacrifices but also by the crucial links in a consistent strategical plan. The tactical basis of Q–Q1 is that it is dangerous for White to decline the exchange because Black's Queen is threatening to penetrate advantageously to KR5.

| 27. QxQ | RxQ |
| 28. R–K8 | |

Euwe was criticized for this move, and he himself recommended R–K6 here, although his plan for the minor-piece endgame, as we shall see, is to transfer his Knight to QB5 via B4 and K6 and capture the QRP. It must be said that after 28. R–K6 Rooks would be exchanged sooner or later, and the structure of the ending would still be about the same.

| 28. | . . . | RxR |
| 29. | RxR | R–K2 |

The second Rook must be exchanged, else the Bishop perishes.

| 30. | RxR | N/1xR |
| 31. | K–B2 | |

On any other move, not excluding B–B1, Black answers N–K6, winning immediately.

| 31. | . . . | K–N1 |

**32. P–N4?**

Upset by the failure of his plan to transfer his Knight to K6, Euwe insists on having his way and mobilizes his pawns so

as to seize K6 and put his Knight there anyway.

There can be no two opinions about this endgame: it is bad for White. However, the position has a closed character for the moment, and Black has to find a place to break through. It is necessary for White to transfer his Knight to Q2 or QN1, keeping his KNP on KN3. He can accomplish this plan at the very moment that Black completes his preparations for the breakthrough on the Queenside: 32. N–B4 K–B2 (else 33. N–K6) 33. P–N3 N–Q3 34. N–N2 N–N4 35. N–K3 K–K3 36. N–B1 N–B1 37. N–Q2.

| 32. | . . . | N–Q3 |
| 33. | K–K3 | N–N4 |
| 34. | P–B4 | N–B1 |
| 35. | P–B5 | N/1–Q3 |
| 36. | N–B4 | |

Both sides have completed their preparations: White's Knight is ready to go to K6, and Black's . . .

| 36. | . . . | NxRP! |

Averbakh sacrifices a Knight to pave the way for the pawn. His combination is very elegant.

| 37. | BxN | N–N4 |
| 38. | B–B1 | NxBP |
| 39. | N–K2 | N–N8! |

**White resigns**

## Game 72
### King's Indian Defense

| | G. Stahlberg | T. Petrosian |
|---|---|---|
| 1. | P–Q4 | N–KB3 |
| 2. | P–QB4 | P–KN3 |
| 3. | P–KN3 | B–N2 |
| 4. | B–N2 | O–O |
| 5. | N–QB3 | P–Q3 |
| 6. | N–B3 | QN–Q2 |
| 7. | O–O | P–K4 |
| 8. | P–K4 | R–K1 |
| 9. | P–Q5 | P–QR4 |
| 10. | N–K1 | N–B4 |
| 11. | B–N5 | P–R3 |
| 12. | BxN | QxB |
| 13. | P–QR3 | |

The first step on the road to ruin. Having exchanged his dark-square Bishop, White should redouble his attention to the important point Q4. But, strange as it may seem, P–QR3 weakens that point by giving Black's Knight a little bridge from QB4 to N6 and Q5. This is not too serious, however.

| 13. | . . . | P–R5 |
| 14. | R–N1 | B–Q2 |
| 15. | P–R4 | P–R4 |
| 16. | K–R2 | R–KB1 |
| 17. | B–R3 | |

The second and last step. Although the commentators called this oversight incredible, it can

be understood: it is the completion of the plan begun on the 11th move. If White did not lose a pawn after the exchange of Bishops his position would not be too bad. That "if" ruins everything.

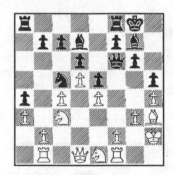

| 17. | . . . | BxB |
| 18. | KxB | NxP |
| 19. | NxN | Q–B4ch |
| 20. | K–R2 | QxN |

It sometimes happens that one extra pawn is not enough to win with the heavy pieces on the board. From now on Stahlberg puts up stubborn though useless resistance against his young opponent.

| 21. | R–B1 | P–N3 |
| 22. | N–N2 | Q–B4 |
| 23. | R–B2 | Q–Q2 |

| 24. | Q–Q3 | KR–K1 |
|---|---|---|
| 25. | R–K1 | QR–N1 |
| 26. | R/2–K2 | P–KB4 |
| 27. | P–B3 | K–R2 |
| 28. | Q–B2 | R–QR1 |
| 29. | Q–Q3 | B–R3 |
| 30. | Q–B2 | Q–B2 |
| 31. | K–R3 | P–B5 |

Black can choose among various plans to realize his advantage. One of them is to make use of the QR-file by R–R4–B4 in conjunction with preparations for P–QN4. Petrosian plans a different scheme of operations. He opens the game on the Kingside and creates isolated KB- and KR-pawns for his opponent; he then localizes an attempt at counterplay on the Queenside, after which two more isolated White pawns appear.

| 32. | PxP | BxP |
|---|---|---|
| 33. | NxB | QxN |
| 34. | R–KN1 | R–KN1 |

If Black takes the KBP counterchances appear for White; for instance, 34. . . . QxBPch 35. R–N3 Q–B4ch 36. QxQ PxQ 37. R–N5 K–R3 38. R/2–N2 or 35. . . . Q–B2 36. R–B2 Q–Q2ch 37. K–R2 R–KN1 38. R–B6.

| 35. | Q–B3 | QR–KB1 |
|---|---|---|
| 36. | R–N3 | R–B3 |
| 37. | R–K4 | Q–R3 |
| 38. | P–B5 | NPxP |
| 39. | RxRP | Q–N2 |

39. . . . P–N4 is met by the interesting retort 40. Q–B2ch K–R1 41. PxP RxNP 42. RxR QxR 43. R–R8ch K–N2 44. Q–N2.

| 40. | R–QB4 | Q–B2 |
|---|---|---|
| 41. | Q–Q3 | R–N1 |
| 42. | P–N4 | PxP |
| 43. | PxP | R–N1 |
| 44. | R–B3 | R–B5 |
| 45. | R–N5 | |

White has lost only one pawn, but, in view of Black's threat of Q–K2, White's game has become too difficult to hold.

45. . . . RxRPch 46. KxR Q–B5ch 47. K–R3 QxR 48. RxPch K–R3 49. R–B2 R–KB1 50. R–KN2 Q–B3 51. Q–K3ch Q–B5 52. R–K2 P–N4 53. QxQ RxQ 54. R–QB2 RxPch 55. K–N2 R–N6 56. R–B6 P–N5 57. RxPch K–N4 58. R–K6 RxP 59. RxPch K–R5 60. K–B2 P–N6ch 61. K–B3 R–N6ch 62. K–K2 R–N7ch 63. K–B1 R–B7ch 64. K–N1 R–Q7, White resigns.

## Game 73
### King's Indian Defense

**I. Boleslavsky      M. Najdorf**

1. P–Q4 N–KB3 2. P–QB4
P–KN3 3. N–QB3 B–N2 4. P–
K4 P–Q3 5. P–B3 O–O 6. B–
K3 P–K4 7. PxP PxP 8. QxQ

White fitted out his ship for
a long voyage but suddenly
turns off into a quiet backwater.
Modern openings, however, permit of such treatment. White
wants a small but definite advantage based on his Q5. It is
interesting to follow how this
square is occupied by a Knight,
a pawn, a Bishop, and a second
Knight, each of them calmly dislodged by Najdorf. As a result,
the game reaches an ending in
which White nevertheless retains an advantage due to his
more active Bishop, but his
hopes are not destined to be
fulfilled.

What can explain why Boleslavsky, who loves complicated
struggles, has chosen such an
innocuous overall plan? It may
be assumed that as a frequent
player of the Black side of the
King's Indian Defense, Boleslavsky did not want to express
his views for White in one of
the main systems.

Soon after the position was
simplified, Najdorf, who had no
objection to a draw, asked his
opponent:

"Did you play this move for
a draw?"

"No."

"Does that mean you played
it to win?"

"Mm . . . partly."

"Maybe you played it to
lose?!"

"I made the move that met
the requirements of the position."

I do not vouch for the absolute accuracy of this conversa-
tion, but I do want to note the
last comment as characteristic
of Boleslavsky's thinking.

8. . . . RxQ 9. N–Q5 NxN
10. BPxN P–QB3 11. B–QB4
PxP 12. BxQP N–B3 13. R–
Q1 N–Q5 14. K–B2 B–K3 15.
BxB NxB 16. N–K2 P–B4 17.
N–B3 P–B5 18. B–B1 B–B1
19. RxR RxR 20. R–Q1 B–
B4ch 21. K–B1 B–Q5 22. N–
Q5

Two Black pawns stand on
the same color as the opponent's
Bishop. Can White exploit this
microscopic advantage?

22. . . . K–B2 23. B–Q2 R–
QB1 24. R–QB1 RxRch 25.
BxR P–KN4 26. K–K2 P–
KR4 27. P–KR3 N–B1 28. P–
QN3 N–N3 29. B–Q2 K–K3
30. B–K1 N–K2 31. NxN KxN
32. K–Q3 P–N4, Drawn.

# Game 74
## Reti Opening

**A. Kotov**  **M. Taimanov**

| | |
|---|---|
| 1. P–QB4 | N–KB3 |
| 2. P–KN3 | P–K3 |
| 3. B–N2 | P–Q4 |
| 4. N–KB3 | P–Q5 |

Such aggression so early is harmless to White. In the Reti Opening Black's P–Q5 is all right after 1. N–KB3 P–Q4 2. P–B4, for example, but in that case Black's KP is still on K2, later moving to K4 in one step.

In this game lively play begins immediately around Black's far-advanced pawn.

**5. P–QN4!**

The idea of P–QN4 as a means of fighting for Q4 is perhaps borrowed from the Evans Gambit: 1. P–K4 P–K4 2. N–KB3 N–QB3 3. B–B4 B–B4 4. P–QN4. In the present position, however, the QNP is untouchable: 5. . . . BxP? 6. Q–R4ch N–B3 7. N–K5 B–K2 8. NxN, and if 8. . . . B–Q2 9. NxQ BxQ 10. NxNP with an extra piece for White.

| | |
|---|---|
| 5. . . . | P–B4 |
| 6. B–N2 | Q–N3 |
| 7. Q–N3 | N–B3 |

Black is worried about the fate of his QP, and so, unconcerned about the loss of a tempo, he provokes P–N5, which lifts the threat to his QBP

and thus simultaneously strengthens his QP.

| | |
|---|---|
| 8. P–N5 | N–QR4 |
| 9. Q–B2 | B–Q3 |
| 10. P–K3 | P–K4 |
| 11. PxP | KPxP |

He should not take with this pawn. Make the move 11. . . . BPxP instead of KPxP and you will see that Black's center is mobile and his dark-square Bishop has a long diagonal. After the text move Black's center pawns are static and his Bishop has much less scope.

| | |
|---|---|
| 12. O–O | O–O |
| 13. P–Q3 | B–Q2 |

It is time to think about bringing the Knight back home by 13. . . . Q–B2 followed by P–QN3 and N–N2.

More than one game has been lost through overestimation of one's position. This is Taimanov's mistake. The chances for both sides are roughly equal here. It is hard to say whether White has any tangible advantage, but at any rate Black has none. For the longest time Black tries to get counterplay on the Queenside. Counterplay —but against what? White completely clears his "herd" of pieces from the area to the left of and below his K1–QR5 diagonal as soon as he can; and after Taimanov exchanges Rooks Black's possession of these squares will not have the slightest significance. But if he does not trade Rooks White will seize the K-file.

| 14. | QN–Q2 | P–KR3 |
|---|---|---|
| 15. | QR–K1 | QR–K1 |
| 16. | B–B1 | RxR |
| 17. | RxR | R–K1 |
| 18. | RxRch | BxR |
| 19. | N–R4! | |

The exclamation mark applies not to one move but to the originality of White's plan. He takes every last one of his pieces away from the Queenside and organizes an attack on the King, exploiting the numerical superiority made possible by the absence of Black's Knight from the battlefield.

| 19. | . . . | P–R3 |
|---|---|---|
| 20. | P–R4 | Q–R2 |
| 21. | N–B5 | B–B1 |

A strategic device characteristic of Taimanov's style. Leaving his King in a strong castle guarded by two Bishops, he determinedly sets about his Queenside operations. His method turns out to be ineffective in this case only because there is absolutely no one and nothing on the Queenside to attack.

| 22. | N–K4 | NxN |
|---|---|---|
| 23. | BxN | |

| 23. | . . . | P–QN3 |
|---|---|---|
| 24. | Q–Q1 | |

Preparing the evacuation of the last troops.

| 24. | . . . | PxP |
|---|---|---|
| 25. | RPxP | B–Q2 |
| 26. | Q–R5 | B–K3 |
| 27. | B–B4 | N–N6 |

Great danger is connected with 27. . . . N–N2; for instance, 28. NxPch PxN 29. BxP BxB 30. QxB, and if now 30. . . . N–Q3 31. B–R7ch K–R1 32. B–B5ch K–N1 33. Q–R7ch K–B1 34. BxB Q–R8ch 35. K–N2 PxB 36. Q–QB7, winning the QNP. Of course 30. . . . N–Q1 is impossible because of 31. Q–N5ch. Bad is 30. . . . Q–R8ch 31. K–N2 N–R4 32. B–R7ch K–R1 33. B–B5ch K–N1 34. BxB PxB 35. QxPch and 36. QxP.

But with the Knight on N6 the sacrifice of a piece on KR6 gives only perpetual check because Black's Queen can defend the King from Q2.

| 28. | Q–Q1 | Q–R7 |
|---|---|---|

Continuing his erroneous plan. Black wants to attack the weak link in White's pawn chain—the QP—from behind; however, he himself has a weak pawn on QN3, which is easily attacked because it is farther from his pieces. It is this, by the way, that forces Black to refrain from exchanging Queens: 28. . . . Q–R8 29. QxQ NxQ 30. B–B7 and Black's pawn chain collapses.

| 29. | P–R4 | N–R8 |
| 30. | P–R5 | N–B7 |
| 31. | B–K5 | Q–N7 |
| 32. | B–B7 | N–R6 |
| 33. | Q–N4 | Q–B8ch |

| 34. | K–N2 | N–N8 |

The concluding stage of the game attests to the complete collapse of Black's plan and the success of White's strategy. The Knight wanders despondently around the corner of the board as though trying to solve the well-known problem of visiting each square once, while White methodically increases his pressure on the King's position.

| 35. | B–B4 | N–Q7? |

An oversight, of course, but Black is lost in any case.

| 36. | Q–K2 | **Black resigns** |

## Game 75
### King's Indian Defense

| Y. Geller | S. Gligoric |
|---|---|
| 1. P–Q4 | N–KB3 |
| 2. P–QB4 | P–KN3 |
| 3. N–QB3 | B–N2 |
| 4. P–K4 | P–Q3 |
| 5. P–B3 | |

The Sämisch System is a dangerous enemy of the King's Indian Defense. White's pieces, enclosed within a pawn fence on KN2, KB3, K4, Q5, and QB4, have full freedom to develop in tranquillity. Black cannot even consider breaking up the center; all of his plans and hopes are based on flank attack. But not all goes smoothly even there, for the main object of the attack —White's King—retires to the Queenside. Black's pawn pressure with P–KB4–5 then loses much of its strength and becomes to some extent meaningless.

In the meantime, White can choose from a variety of strategic plans. With the center locked he can attack on the Kingside by P–KN4, P–KR4, P–R5, etc., or he can conduct a pawn attack in front of his King and look for a breakthrough on the Queenside.

Before deciding on active operations, the two sides engage in an extended trench warfare highly characteristic of many modern grandmaster games. General goals to be pursued in any case are: placing the pieces optimally, limiting the opponent's initiative, exchanging the "bad" Bishop for the opponent's "good" one, and, finally, preparing a breakthrough. In this game, for instance, only one piece and one pawn are exchanged by the 42nd move, at which point the game enters a combinational stage. The reader who has attentively followed the earlier stages will be amply rewarded for his patience: he will see the sacrifice and countersacrifice of a piece,

deceptive feints, an attack on the King—in short, all the attributes of a lively fight.

| 5. . . . | O–O |
| 6. B–K3 | P–K4 |
| 7. P–Q5 | N–R4 |

Not the only plan for Black. Also possible is P–B3 to try to break up the center, or P–QR4 to transfer a Knight to QB4; but in those cases White's Kingside attack develops swiftly, as Makogonov showed in his time. If Black prepares P–KB4 by retreating his Knight to K1, White often continues P–KN4 to be able to meet P–KB4 with NPxP, opening the KN-file for his Rooks.

The move chosen by Black is the result of a long-standing ideological struggle. Since the Knight on KR4 physically prevents White's P–KR5, his P–KR4 would be purposeless now, whereas on P–KN4 the Knight would go immediately to KB5 and stop White's attack. At the same time, N–R4 prepares P–KB4. This is all very logical— but that's all it is.

| 8. Q–Q2 | P–KB4 |
| 9. O–O–O | P–B5 |

Black closes the game in the only sector in which he might have become active. Why? The answer is given by Gligoric's next two moves, but it is hardly a satisfactory answer. Black intends B–B3–R5 to exchange dark-square Bishops, but this does not succeed. In case of 9.

. . . N–Q2, or 9. . . . Q–K1 as Geller himself usually plays for Black, perhaps Gligoric feared 10. PxP PxP 11. P–KN4. There could then follow 11. . . . PxP 12. PxP N–B5. Even though White would get open diagonals they would not be easy to occupy, and chances for Black would appear. A King's Indian player must be ready to encounter dangerous variations. With P–B5 Black condemns himself to less interesting play.

| 10. | B–B2 | B–B3 |
|-----|------|------|
| 11. | KN–K2 | B–R5 |
| 12. | B–N1 | |

With his pawn chain set up entirely on the light squares, Geller of course does not want to be left without his dark-square Bishop. True, his Rook is locked in, but to keep it that way Black must maintain both his Knight on R4 and his Bishop on R5. By the way, note that the possibility of 11. . . . B–R5 was based on the combination 12. P–KN3 PxP 13. PxP RxP.

| 12. | . . . | N–Q2 |
|-----|-------|------|
| 13. | K–N1 | B–K2 |
| 14. | N–B1 | N–B4 |
| 15. | N–Q3 | NxN |
| 16. | BxN | B–Q2 |

Gligoric considers his position solid enough, and he expects to withstand his opponent's siege. Nevertheless, passive Black play will allow White to find a way to break through

sooner or later. 16. . . . P–B4 is worth considering here, in order to restrict White's Bishop on N1 and give his own Bishop a chance to escape via Q1. White would probably take the pawn en passant, getting much the livelier play.

| 17. | B–QB2 | Q–K1 |
|-----|-------|------|

White intended the exchanging maneuver B–R4, analogous to Black's attempt 11. . . . B–R5, but Gligoric does not allow it.

| 18. | B–B2 | P–QR3 |
|-----|------|-------|
| 19. | R–QB1 | K–R1 |
| 20. | B–Q1 | R–B2 |
| 21. | B–QN3 | R–KB1 |

The threat of P–B5 forces Black to move his Rook back to B1 and on his next move to play P–N3. His chance for active play already gone, Black can now only wait and watch as White strengthens his position and prepares a breakthrough. He hopes some kind of fortuitous tactical chance may then appear.

| 22. | N–K2 | P–N3 |
|-----|------|------|
| 23. | N–B3 | N–B3 |
| 24. | Q–Q1 | K–N2 |
| 25. | Q–Q3 | N–R4 |
| 26. | QR–N1 | |

White's following offensive is prophylactic rather than aggressive. Before breaking through on the Queenside White wants to close the Kingside, fearing that if he moves all his pieces away from there Gligoric will be able to carry out P–KN4–5 advantageously. But now the base of White's pawn chain is weakened, and the occasion arises for a breakthrough with the aid of a piece sacrifice.

| 26. . . . | K–R1 |
| 27. P–N4 | N–B3 |
| 28. P–KR4 | K–N2 |
| 29. R–QB1 | P–R3 |
| 30. N–K2 | Q–Q1 |
| 31. QR–N1 | N–R2 |
| 32. B–B2 | B–K1 |
| 33. P–R5 | P–N4 |

Black's dark-square Bishop, unfortunately, is in a state of complete retirement; it does not make another move for the rest of the game.

| 34. Q–Q1 | N–B3 |
| 35. B–QR4 | P–N4 |

Black cannot allow the Bishop to go to B6 and is forced to make an active move. This leads to the first pawn exchange, which opens the QB-file to White's advantage. True, White will no longer be able to break through on QB5, but that is no longer necessary, for his aim of opening a file for attack has been achieved in another way. He switches his attack to the pawns on QB7 and QN5. The QBP will be hard to win because it can be defended effectively by the minor pieces, whereas the QNP will have to be isolated from Black's Bishop on Q2. For this,

N–B1–Q3–N4–B6 is useful, but in order for White to accomplish this, all of his pieces will have to leave the Kingside.

| 36. PxP | PxP |
| 37. B–QN3 | Q–N1 |
| 38. Q–Q2 | Q–N2 |
| 39. R–QB1 | B–Q2 |
| 40. R–B2 | KR–QB1 |
| 41. R–Q1 | R–R3 |
| 42. N–B1 | NxNP! |

The unexpected collapse of White's maneuvering game. Such sacrifices are always hanging in the air around immobile pawn chains. Not only the pawns but also the pieces standing behind them become much more active, so for the time being White must turn to defense.

| 43. PxN | BxP |
| 44. R–R1 | |

Geller would rather give up the Exchange than allow his opponent three connected passed pawns.

| 44. . . . | B–B6 |
| 45. Q–K1 | P–B4 |
| 46. PxP e.p. | R/3xBP |

How pitiful Black's pieces looked when they were huddled tightly together behind the pawn chain, and how his whole position sparkles with the pawns mobilized! If Black is able to capture the last center pawn, White will of course be unable to save the game. Otherwise, the draw will still have to be sought—still, alas, by Gligoric.

| 47. B–Q5 | BxR |
|---|---|
| 48. QxB | Q–Q2 |
| 49. RxR | RxR |
| 50. BxR | QxB |
| 51. N–Q3 | |

Despite all Black's resourcefulness the position remains unclear. Geller has kept the extra piece and a center pawn. If he gets his Knight to Q5 Black will lose. But if Black manages to play P–Q4 and obtain three connected passed pawns, the struggle will flare up anew. White's last move is directed toward the seizure of Q5, but it gives Black a new chance.

However, if 51. Q–B3 Black can play Q–Q2 and P–KN5.

| 51. . . . | Q–B5 |
|---|---|
| 52. Q–B3 | P–Q4 |

| 53. NxKP | Q–KB8ch! |
|---|---|
| 54. K–B2 | PxP |
| 55. QxKP | QxBch |

Black has perpetual check but nothing more, for his King is in a dangerous position.

| 56. K–Q3 | Q–B8ch |
|---|---|
| 57. K–B2 | Q–B7ch |
| 58. K–Q3 | Q–B8ch |
| 59. K–B2 | Q–B7ch |

**Drawn**

## Game 76
### Reti Opening

**V. Smyslov          D. Bronstein**

| 1. P–QB4 | N–KB3 |
|---|---|
| 2. P–KN3 | P–B3 |
| 3. N–KB3 | P–Q4 |
| 4. P–N3 | B–B4 |

If Black wants to obtain absolute equality in the Reti Opening, the formation with P–QB3 and B–B4 (as in the classic Reti–Lasker game) seems best to me. It is true that formerly there were cases when the Bishop turned out to be not well placed on the KR2–QN8 diagonal, but only because

Black's play was stereotyped and not appropriate to the circumstances.

| 5. | B–KN2 | P–K3 |
| 6. | O–O | QN–Q2 |
| 7. | B–N2 | B–K2 |
| 8. | N–B3 | O–O |

After long thought Black decides to do without P–KR3 for the time being, and he castles. Somebody once said, and many now believe, that in closed positions a loss of time does not matter. If this is correct it applies only to permanently closed positions, which the position on the board is not, and it seems to me that 8. . . . P–KR3 would definitely not have been a loss of time.

**9. N–KR4**

Smyslov reacts immediately to Black's "inaccuracy." If he wants to exchange the Bishop on N6 he should begin with PxP and prepare P–K4, which by clearing the pawns from the center would assure White's pieces of much greater activity.

**9. . . .          B–KN5**

A little military ruse: Black conceals his aggressive intentions under the guise of making forced moves.

| 10. | P–KR3 | B–R4 |
| 11. | P–KN4 | |

Somewhat underestimating his opponent's scheme, or simple carelessness. Black's long reflection after 8. N–B3 should have put White on the alert. Smyslov probably thought that Black was only pretending to want to sacrifice a piece. Actually, on 11. . . . BxP 12. PxB NxP 13. N–B3 Black would have no visible threats, but Black's zwischenzug substantially changes the picture.

By the way, in considering his 8th move Black based his calculations precisely on the way events developed, aware that after 11. . . . B–N3 12. NxB RPxN 13. P–K4 White would definitely stand better.

| 11. | . . . | P–Q5 |
| 12. | N–N1 | |

Taking the Bishop is not good in view of 12. . . . PxN 13. QBxP NxP 14. N–B3 B–B3 15. P–Q4 N–B5, or if 12. N–R4 the threat . . . P–QN4 arises at once.

| 12. | . . . | BxP |
| 13. | PxB | NxP |

Of course I could not calculate all the consequences of the

sacrifice, but, judging by a few variations, I believed that Black would get good attacking chances and, often more important, continual improvement of his position. For instance, 14. N–B3 B–Q3 followed by P–KB4, Q–B3, QR–K1 with the constant threat of . . . P–K4–5.

**14. P–K4          NxP**

White mistakenly allowed a tactical stroke that could have decided the game immediately —14. . . . B–R6, with the idea that on 15. QxN Black regains the piece with two extra pawns. If 15. BxB Black obtains a third pawn and an intensified attack: 15. . . . QxN 16. R–K1 QxPch 17. K–R1 Q–R5ch 18. K–N1 and now the quiet . . . P–QB4 is possible, as well as the more energetic . . . P–KB4 and . . . N/2–K4.

Black would have to play without his Rooks for a long time in this variation, and that seemed too great a sacrifice. Fearing that I might not be able to end the game in perpetual check, I decided to insure myself by taking a third pawn for the piece. This was obviously an incorrect evaluation of the position.

**15. RxN          BxN**
**16. R–B3         N–K4**
**17. R–R3         B–N4**

First of all, the retreat to N4 makes it impossible for White's

QP to move, for . . . B–K6ch followed by . . . P–KB4 and . . . N–N5 would ensue; second, it prepares P–Q6; third, it neutralizes the possible thrust Q–R5 because of . . . P–KR3.

**18. N–R3          N–N3**
**19. N–B2          N–B5**
**20. R–R2**

White can give up his Rook for a Knight and a pawn: 20. BxP NxRch 21. BxN B–B3, but then 22. P–K5 will not be playable because of 22. . . . BxP and 23. . . . Q–N4ch.

**20. . . .          P–Q6!**

The decisive maneuver which, together with the following exchange of Bishops, places White in a difficult situation.

**21. N–K3          N–K7ch**
**22. K–R1          P–KB4**

Black refused White's draw offer here, with good reason of course: the three passed pawns now being formed by Black place the White pieces in great danger.

| 23. | PxP | PxP |
| --- | --- | --- |
| 24. | B–KB3 | N–N6ch |
| 25. | K–N1 | B–B3 |

A positional move with the aim of exchanging one of White's few active pieces.

| 26. | BxB | QxB |
| --- | --- | --- |
| 27. | Q–K1 | |

27. . . .          P–B5

A serious mistake. I had written the winning move 27. . . . QR–K1 on my scoresheet and was already about to touch the Rook, but at the last moment I changed my mind. I will always remember with regret the missed opportunity QR–K1.

| 28. | N–N4 | Q–Q5ch |
| --- | --- | --- |
| 29. | K–N2 | QR–K1 |
| 30. | Q–KN1! | Q–N7 |
| 31. | Q–QB1 | Q–Q5 |
| 32. | Q–B3 | |

One must salute Smyslov's fighting qualities—although he

has a somewhat inferior position, he refuses to repeat moves and risks immediate loss. By exchanging Queens here Black would get four passed pawns and all the winning chances. But perhaps Smyslov did not like returning his Queen to KN1 because Black could play not Q–N7 again but Q–Q3.

| 32. | . . . | Q–Q3 |
| --- | --- | --- |
| 33. | P–B5 | Q–N3 |
| 34. | Q–B4ch | K–R1 |
| 35. | R–R3 | P–KR4 |

How adventurous! Black "attacks" the Knight with a pinned pawn.

| 36. | K–R2 | Q–R2 |
| --- | --- | --- |
| 37. | N–B2 | P–KN4 |
| 38. | Q–Q4ch | K–N1 |
| 39. | Q–B4ch | K–R1 |
| 40. | Q–Q4ch | K–N1 |

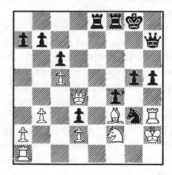

The game was adjourned, and the next day White offered a draw. I saw no way essentially to improve the position of my pieces, and besides, I had virtually agreed to a draw on my 30th move. Since White could give another check on QB4, repeating the position for the third time, I accepted Smyslov's offer. You can imagine my surprise when I found out that the sealed move was 41. R–KN1—Smyslov had again spurned the draw! Whatever his move, however, it seems to me that Black would again get good winning chances by 41. . . . Q–N3, putting his King on R2 in answer to a check, and then playing P–N5 or P–R5. With White's pieces pinned down by Black's pawns, White would have to sacrifice the Exchange to make good the threat created by 41. R–KN1—42. RxN Px Rch 43. RxNP—but Black would get the initiative by 43. . . . P–R5 44. R–R3 R–B5 with strong pressure on the K-file and the KB-file. Meanwhile, Smyslov and his second, V. Simagin, thought that the immediate 41. . . . P–R5 42. N–N4, etc., was mandatory for Black, and it is still difficult to say who was right. When a game is interrupted in a complicated situation, each side usually judges the position in his own favor.

What conclusions can be drawn from this interesting and tense encounter? First, that in appropriate situations one can make sacrifices that do not admit of precise calculation, even in the most crucial games. Second, that having made a mistake or an inaccuracy, one must not think that "all is lost" and get upset, but must quickly adjust to the new situation and find a new plan.

## Game 77

Were the reader to ask me which game in this competition I like best of all, then disregarding my own two encounters with the American former child prodigy, S. Reshevsky, I should settle on this, one of the most remarkable games in the tournament for the depth of its ideas, its beauty, and its complexity. The game was published in chess magazines all over the world and analyzed by dozens of masters and almost every grandmaster, even Botvinnik himself. But it is still not absolutely certain that their analyses have made a final determination. The reader is invited to investigate the possibilities for himself and perhaps make his own contribution to the combined creativity of the world's chess players.

## Nimzo-Indian Defense

| P. Keres | S. Reshevsky |
|----------|--------------|
| 1. P–Q4 | N–KB3 |
| 2. P–QB4 | P–K3 |
| 3. N–QB3 | B–N5 |
| 4. P–K3 | P–B4 |
| 5. B–Q3 | O–O |
| 6. P–QR3 | BxNch |
| 7. PxB | P–QN3 |

7. . . . N–B3 is usually played here, and after 8. N–K2 P–QN3 9. P–K4 N–K1 a position is reached from the well-known games Botvinnik–Reshevsky (Moscow 1948), Bronstein–Najdorf (Budapest 1950), as well as Geller–Smyslov in this tournament. Reshevsky repeats the opening of his game against Euwe, who did not choose the courageous 8. P–K4 as Keres does.

| 8. P–K4 | B–N2 |
|---------|------|
| 9. B–N5 | |

A first-category player from Baku, R. G. Ashurov, points out that White has another possibility at his disposal here: 9. P–K5, and if 9. . . . BxP 10. B–N5 BxR 11. PxN P–N3 12. BxP! RPxB 13. Q–N4 with a powerful attack which Ashurov concludes with mate in many variations. It is true that some of those variations can be improved for Black, but there is no doubt that if Black took the pawn and the Rook he would find himself in a difficult situa-

tion. In reply to 9. P–K5 the Knight would have to retreat, and White could then continue the pressure by 10. Q–R5.

9. . . .          P–KR3

An exciting battle! 9. . . . P–Q3 is possible, and if 10. P–K5 QPxP 11. PxKP, then not 11. . . . BxP, which leads to the quick collapse of Black's game, but 11. . . . B–K5! On 9. . . . P–Q3 White would probably continue 10. P–B4 QN–Q2 11. N–B3 PxP 12. PxP with considerable activity for White; Black therefore prefers to force matters.

10. P–KR4

White continues his development. It is easy to see that if Black takes the Bishop he will have to give the piece right back, for 10. . . . PxB 11. PxP NxP? 12. Q–R5 P–B4 13. P–N6 wins quickly for White.

| 10. . . . | P–Q3 |
|-----------|------|
| 11. P–K5 | QPxP |
| 12. PxKP | B–K5! |

The only move. 12. . . . PxB is answered by 13. PxN QxP 14. B–R7ch K–R1 15. PxP Qx QBPch 16. K–B1 and White wins. But if 12. . . . BxP 13. Bx N PxB 14. Q–N4ch K–R1 15. QxB QxB 16. R–R3, Black loses his QR. Finally, if 12. . . . Q–B2 13. PxN BxP 14. PxP

Q–K4ch 15. K–Q2 R–K1 16. N–B3!, White saves his Rook and remains a piece ahead.

### 13. R–R3!

The only move. The reader will easily convince himself that taking the Knight with the Bishop or the pawn leads to an advantage for Black in the endgame.

| 13. . . . | BxB |
|-----------|-----|
| 14. RxB | Q–B2 |

The best defensive chance in a difficult position. Many players in such circumstances are ready to throw up their hands and give away the game by making the first move that comes to mind, but Reshevsky does not despair.

White can demolish the Black King's pawn shelter in various ways. Keres now conceives an amazing combination, whose main variation goes like this: 15. BxN PxB 16. Q–N4ch K–R1 17. Q–B3 N–Q2 18. O–O–O NxP 19. QxPch K–R2 20. R–Q6 NxP 21. N–R3 NxR 22.

N–N5ch! K–N1 23. QxRP P–B4 24. NxP Q–R2 25. QxQch KxQ 26. NxRch RxN 27. RxN, and the Rook ending is not difficult.

Naturally, there are other possibilities for both sides along the way, but it is not possible for anyone to calculate them all. The length and rare beauty of this conception are characteristic of Keres's versatile talent.

Now let the reader who would admire the combinational patterns with us follow the further analysis on two chess boards (as Nimzovich once recommended): one for the text moves, the other to examine the variations.

### 15. BxN

Good enough here is 15. PxN PxB 16. RPxP, and Najdorf considers the further 16. . . . Q–K4ch 17. K–B1 QxNP 18. PxP R–B1 19. R–N3 Q–B5 20. R–R3 QxQBPch 21. N–K2 N–B3 22. Q–Q2 "interesting and probably winning."

Nedelkovic and Vukovic suggest 19. Q–B3 N–B3 20. Q–R3 in this variation or: 1) 16. . . . PxP 17. PxP Q–K4ch 18. K–B1 QxKBP 19. R–N3ch K–R2 20. Q–R5ch Q–R3 21. Q–B3; 2) 16. . . . Q–R7 17. K–B1 Q–R5 18. R–R3! QxQBPch 19. N–K2 P–K4 20. Q–Q6 Q–K3 21. Q–Q3 P–K5 22. Q–N3 PxP 23. Q–R4. V. Turchuk justly upbraided me for my uncritical attitude in analysis and pointed out that instead of 21. Q–Q3 there is a mate in three: R–R8ch!, QxRch, and QxP. After reexamining the variation critically I found 21. QxRch! KxQ 22. R–R8 mate—one move sooner!

Euwe also thinks the Knight should be taken with the pawn, but after 15. . . . PxB he continues 16. BPxP and not 16. RPxP (that is, he disagrees with Najdorf); for instance: 1) 16. . . . KxP 17. Q–R5 PxP 18. QxRP threatening 19. R–N3ch; 2) 16. . . . Q–K4ch 17. R–K3 QxP 18. R–N3 P–B3 19. N–B3 threatening 20. NxP.

As we see, almost all the commentators agreed that this continuation (15. PxN) was clearer and would have led to a quicker victory. Actually, White had two ways to win, and the one selected was no less forcing nor less beautiful than the one suggested later. It is clear that having conceived a plan good enough to win Keres follows it without being distracted by complicated new variations.

**15. . . .          PxB**
**16. Q–N4ch**

Here White has a remarkably beautiful continuation of the attack—16. P–B4! with the idea of keeping Black's Queen from White's K5. The main variation continues 16. . . . K–R2 17. N–R3 R–N1 18. Q–R5 N–B3 19. PxP R–N3 20. O–O–O R–Q1

21. RxR NxR 22. N–N5ch K–N1 23. RxNch! QxR 24.

QxRch!! PxQ 25. P–B7ch K–R1 26. NxP and the Knight and pawn win against the Queen.

It is not so easy to calculate a combination like this over the board, however, especially if you consider variations like these: 1) 16. P–B4 K–R2 17. N–R3 Q–N2, and the right move for White, 18. R–R2, is hard to find; 2) 16. . . . PxP 17. R–N3ch K–R2 18. Q–N4 P–B4 19. Q–N6ch K–R1 20. QxPch Q–R2 21. QxRch; 3) 16. . . . N–B3 17. R–Q7 Q–N1 18. Q–N4ch K–R1 19. Q–R5.

Grandmaster Botvinnik recommends 16. PxP!, and this is perhaps the most significant thing the reader can learn in these few pages.

**16. . . .          K–R1**
**17. Q–B3**

Keres continues to carry out his idea. 17. R–N3 is insufficient because of 17. . . . QxPch 18.

R–K3 Q–B2 19. R–N3 Q–K4ch; or if 18. K–B1 or 18. N–K2, then 18. . . . P–B4 and Black can defend. Nothing is gained by 17. N–B3 N–Q2! 18. RxN QxR 19. PxP R–KN1 20. Q–R5 Q–Q6! 21. QxPch Q–R2 22. Q–B4 RxP; but 17. O–O–O QxP 18. N–B3 Q–B2 19. R–Q6 N–B3 20. Q–B4 K–N2 21. P–N4 and 22. P–N5 looks very strong, and if 17. . . . N–B3 18. P–B4 PxP 19. R–Q7 Q–B1 20. Q–R5 K–N2 21. P–B5!

**17. . . .                    N–Q2**
**18. O–O–O**

Trifunovic, as well as Reshevsky himself in his later analysis, indicated that in their opinion the winning move was 18. R–Q6. Indeed, White wins on both 18. . . . PxP 19. O–O–O and 18. . . . P–B4 19. Q–B4 K–R2 20. O–O–O, but the defense suggested by the German analyst Rellstab, 18. . . . K–N2, threatening NxP, is good enough to draw; for instance, 19 PxPch NxP 20. O–O–O Q–K2 21. Q–N3ch K–R1 22. Q–B4 K–N2, etc.

**18. . . .                    NxP**
**19. QxPch                    K–R2**
**20. R–Q6                    NxP**

Probably for the first time in this game Reshevsky took an easy breath. Actually, 21. R–Q7 Q–K4 22. RxPch RxR 23. QxRch Q–N2 would not be dangerous now: Black would already be starting to threaten mate, and 24. Q–B3 would be answered by P–N4!

**21. N–B3**

Now Reshevsky can defend himself more successfully by giving up his Queen for both Rooks. 21. N–R3 was more accurate, and if Black then exchanged his Queen for the two Rooks White would continue 23. P–B3, then P–N4 and N–B4 with an unceasing attack despite the reduced forces. After Reshevsky takes the Rook with the Knight, Keres finally comes close to bringing his remarkable combination to its conclusion.

**21. . . .                    NxR**
**22. N–N5ch**

If Black takes the Knight, no power can save him from mate.

**22. . . .                    K–N1**
**23. QxRP**

An examination of the position on the board will reveal that it is the same as the position at move 23 of Keres's combination (note to his 14th move). But at this point Reshevsky deviates from the main line and instead of P–B4 plays which,

**23. . . .    P–B3**

together with Black's next move, is much stronger.

**24. NxP    Q–K2**
**25. RxN**

Keres, getting into severe time trouble and excited by the preceding struggle, does not find the correct maneuver: 25. Q–N6ch K–R1 26. Q–R5ch K–N1 27. R–Q3! N–K5 (27. . . . Q–R2 is followed by 28. QxQch KxQ 29. NxRch and 30. RxN, reaching the position envisaged by Keres at the beginning of his combination) 28. NxR RxN 29. Q–N4ch N–N4 30. R–K3 Q–KN2 31. R–N3 K–R1 32. PxN.

Keres is not to be criticized for this, for many commentators, after lengthy analysis in calmer surroundings, did not find this winning plan either; after 27. . . . N–K5 they suggested 28. Q–N6ch K–R1 29. NxR RxN 30. R–K3, which does not work because instead of 30. . . . P–B4 31. P–B3!, Black plays 30. . . . R–KN1 31. Q–R6ch Q–R2 or 31. RxN RxQ 32. RxQ RxP with a drawn endgame.

**25. . . .    R–B2**
**26. Q–Q2**

A time-pressure move, but there is no longer much choice. 26. Q–N6ch K–R1 27. R–Q5 R–R2 comes to nothing. 26. R–B6 P–B5! 27. K–N2 R–K1 28. P–B4 Q–Q2 29. P–B5 QxR 30. Q–N6ch K–R1 31. QxR QxPch probably leads to a draw. 26. P–KB4 is unclear in view of 26. . . . R–R2 27. Q–N6ch K–R1, and 28. P–B5 is impossible because of R–KN1.

The move recommended by Nedelkovic and Vukovic, 26. P–N4, is not bad.

**26. . . .    R–K1**
**27. P–KB4**

27. P–N4 is better here, to answer 27. . . . P–B4 with P–N5 and 27. . . . Q–N2 with 28. Q–Q3, keeping winning chances for White.

**27. . . .    P–B4**

But now Black has full equality.

**28. Q–Q5    K–R1**

Specifically, Reshevsky could now take the pawn by 28. . . . QxP, and White would have nothing better than to go into a Queen endgame: 29. R–Q8 RxR 30. NxR QxPch 31. K–N2 Q–B2 32. NxR QxN, with winning chances for Black.

**29. Q–K5ch    Q–B3**
**30. K–B2    P–B5**
**31. K–Q2    K–N1**
**32. Q–Q5    QxP**

| 33. QxQBP | Q–B7ch |
|-----------|--------|
| 34. K–B1 | Q–N8ch |
| 35. K–B2 | QxPch |
| 36. K–N3 | P–N4 |

A trap, at the same time seizing QB5, where the exchange of Queens will soon occur.

## 37. Q–Q4

Black's Queen should not be allowed to get to KB8, which can be prevented by 37. Q–Q3.

| 37. . . . | Q–B8 |
|-----------|------|
| 38. K–N4 | Q–B5ch |

Reshevsky had only a few seconds left for three moves, so it remains uncertain whether he rejected or did not see the tempting 38. . . . R–B3. The Rook could not be taken by the Queen because of 39. . . .

Q–B5ch and mate next move. On 39. Q–Q5 Black, naturally, exchanges Queens. But 39. R–Q8 RxN 40. RxRch RxR 41. Q–Q5ch leads to White's salvation.

| 39. QxQ | PxQ |
|---------|-----|
| 40. KxP | R–B1ch |
| 41. K–N5! | |

The game was adjourned here. Both players analyzed all night and all day, not the adjourned position, of course, but the game that had been played. When the time came to resume play, neither Keres nor Reshevsky knew how to continue the game any more than at the moment of adjournment. If either of them did, at least he would not have agreed to a draw without playing it out.

# Round Twelve

## Game 78
### *Sicilian Defense*

| D. Bronstein | P. Keres |
|---|---|
| 1. P–K4 | P–QB4 |
| 2. N–QB3 | P–KN3 |
| 3. P–KN3 | B–N2 |
| 4. P–Q3 | N–QB3 |
| 5. B–N2 | R–N1 |

Perhaps too straightforward, as Black soon agrees. The Rook goes to N1 to support a raid by the QNP. Such an impetuous attack would be reasonable if White's King were in this area, but under the circumstances White hides his King in the right-hand corner.

| 6. P–B4 | P–Q3 |
|---|---|
| 7. N–B3 | P–K3 |
| 8. O–O | KN–K2 |

White is prompted by general considerations to advance his KP. He is not concerned about losing the pawn because he thereby obtains three open lines: the K-file and the diagonals QB1–KR6 and KN2–QB6. Furthermore, a good parking place on K4 is freed for White's QN.

| 9. P–K5 | PxP |
|---|---|

Of course Black could close these lines by 9. . . . P–Q4, after which his backward piece development would not matter so much. That is probably what he should play.

| 10. PxP | NxP |
|---|---|

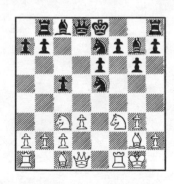

| 11. B–B4 | NxNch |
|---|---|

The Knight takes the opportunity to move with check. Attempting to maintain it on

192

K4 would lead to more trouble for Black's King; for instance, 1) 11. . . . P–B3 12. BxN PxB 13. N–KN5; 2) 11. . . . N/2–B3 12. NxN NxN 13. Q–K2; 3) 11. . . . O–O 12. NxN Q–Q5ch 13. K–R1 BxN 14. N–N5 QxNP 15. QR–N1.

**12. QxN          R–R1**

It is pointless to attack the Bishop by 12. . . . P–K4, for it would be only too happy to leave the KB-file, and best is to take the pawn. After the Rook's retreat to QR1 the Bishop still would not object to leaving B4 for K5, but then Black could castle, taking the opportunity to make "three moves in one." We are so accustomed to castling that we think of it as an ordinary move, but it is not: the Rook, moving from KR1 to KB1, defends KB2, and the King, jumping from K1 to KN1, protects the Bishop on N2.

**13. B–K3**

White has no objection to winning the QBP. 13. B–B7 is rash because of 13. . . . B–Q5ch or 13. . . . Q–Q5ch.

**13. . . .          O–O**
**14. BxP          B–Q5ch**

A symptomatic move. In positions of this type White usually has to make no little effort to force the trade of dark-square Bishops, so that the important points KB6 and KR6,

situated in immediate proximity to Black's King, might then be easily occupied by White's pieces. The fact that Black voluntarily forces the exchange of Bishops indicates that he is not thinking of principles here but only of reducing the number of attacking pieces, which is almost always helpful in defense.

**15. BxB          QxBch**
**16. K–R1          R–N1**

Inasmuch as White has not been able to create concrete mating threats or win material, Black should bring his Bishop quickly into play. The Rook move is for this purpose ( . . . P–N3 and . . . B–N2).

However, time is very precious in chess. On N1 the Rook again turns out to be in an exposed position and is soon struck down by the Queen. Good or bad, he must play 16. . . . N–B3 or immediately 16. . . . P–K4.

**17. N–K4**

The Knight charges irresistibly to KB6. While on K4 it shields the square KB4, through which White's Queen intends to pass on its way to KR6. With the Queen on KR6 a Knight check on B6 would be fatal to Black, so he attacks the Knight at once. Again Keres plays concretely, not overly concerned that he is creating a weak KP that will be vulnerable to frontal attack along the K-file.

**17. . . .            P–B4**
**18. Q–B4         B–Q2**

Black's move can be described by the proverb "better late than never." But in this case "never" would be better.

Strange as it seems, the only possibility of continuing the struggle was 18. . . . R–R1. Black would have serious difficulties, of course, but no forced loss is apparent. You could not purposely think up a game in which Black's Rook swings like a pendulum from QR1 to QN1 and back again, and afterward still somehow keeps its balance.

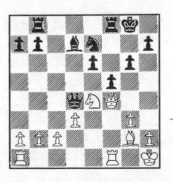

Black loses only a trifle— his turn to move.

**19. P–B3**

The Queen is given the right to choose—straight ahead, left, or right. By going straight ahead to Q6, Black risks losing a piece by 20. N–B5 Q–N4 21. Q–Q6. Going to the left allows White's Knight to get to QB5. So the Queen goes right, keeping control of QB4 and Q3.

However, trouble comes from the other side. Again the cause is the Rook on QN1.

**19. . . .            Q–N3**
**20. N–B6ch       RxN**

The importunate Knight must be eliminated at any price, else it would not only take the Bishop but simultaneously threaten all three of Black's major pieces (20. . . . K–N2? 21. NxB!).

**21. QxRch         B–B1**

The unfortunate Rook has finally perished, leaving a defeated army on the battlefield.

**22. P–Q4          R–B1**
**23. R–B2          N–B3**
**24. Q–B4          B–Q2**
**25. R–K1**

Black has no compensation at all for the lost Exchange, so the rest needs no comment. Let it only be said that White's play in the second part of the game is hardly the best.

25. ... N–Q1 26. P–Q5 N–B2 27. PxP BxP 28. P–N3 B–Q2 29. Q–Q4 B–B3 30. QxQ PxQ 31. BxB PxB 32. R–K6 R–B1 33. R/2–K2 K–B1 34. P–KR4 P–QN4 35. P–R4 PxP 36. PxP R–R1 37. RxBP RxP 38. R–B7 R–R3 39. R–QN2 P–R3 40. P–B4 P–B5 (The game was adjourned here, and play resumed on the appointed day.) 41. P–B5 P–B6 42. K–N1 R–R1 43. R/7–N7 R–R8ch 44. R–N1 R–R3 45. R–Q7 R–R1 46. R–K1 R–R7 47. R–K3 R–R8ch 48. K–B2 R–R7ch 49. KxP R–B7 50. R–B7 P–R4 51. K–K4 N–R3 52. R–R3 R–K7ch 53. K–B4 R–K8 54. R–KR7 K–N1 55. Rx N K–N2 56. P–B6 KxR 57. R–QB3 P–N4ch 58. PxPch, Black resigns.

## Game 79
### Queen's Indian Defense

| S. Gligoric | V. Smyslov |
|---|---|
| 1. P–QB4 | N–KB3 |
| 2. N–QB3 | P–K3 |
| 3. N–B3 | P–B4 |
| 4. P–KN3 | P–QN3 |
| 5. B–N2 | B–N2 |
| 6. O–O | B–K2 |
| 7. P–Q4 | |

A Queen's Indian Defense has been reached by transposition of moves, but the transposition has turned out better for Black. Having played P–QB4 before White played P–Q4, he immediately trades central pawns and does not allow the cramping P–Q5.

| 7. ... | PxP |
|---|---|
| 8. QxP | O–O |
| 9. R–Q1 | N–B3 |
| 10. Q–B4 | Q–N1 |

Completely neutralizing White's efforts to get any opening advantage.

| 11. QxQ | QRxQ |
|---|---|
| 12. B–B4 | QR–B1 |
| 13. B–Q6 | |

Can it be that White chose this variation for the sake of this harmless occupation of Q6? 13. N–K5 is better.

| 13. ... | BxB |
|---|---|
| 14. RxB | N–K2 |
| 15. N–K5 | |

This looks aggressive but in fact it blunders a pawn. However, blunders sometimes have their reason. It is generally not easy to get an advantage in the cautious opening Gligoric has chosen for this game, and, having initiated early simplification, he has arrived at a perfectly drawn position. But now all of a sudden he starts playing for a win. Chess logic does not allow this. If indeed the position is clearly in balance, desire alone cannot tip the scales.

Meanwhile, it is still not too late to defend the QBP: 15. P–N3 N–B4 16. R–Q3 P–Q4 17. PxP NxQP 18. NxN BxN.

| 15. . . . | BxB |
| 16. KxB | N–B4 |

Of course! Black first drives away the Rook and then the Knight, winning the QBP. It's a good thing for White that he has the chance to double Black's pawns by 18. P–K4.

| 17. R–Q2 | P–Q3 |
| 18. P–K4 | NxNP |
| 19. RPxN | PxN |
| 20. P–N3 | |

There is a widespread and therefore dangerous misconception that an extra pawn leads automatically to a win. Black's main advantage in this position, however, is not so much his extra pawn, which is a long way from being exploited, but his control of many squares in the center: Q4, Q5, QB4, KB4, KB5.

White's counterchances lay in his pawn majority on the Queenside and the open Q-file. How many such games end up as draws by accurate play! But Smyslov holds the reins with an iron hand. His plan can be broken down into the following parts:

1) The immediate exchange of one Rook, leaving the other one for the possible fight against White's Queenside pawns and to attack the KP and QBP.

2) The threat to create an outside passed pawn to deflect White's Rook to the KR-file so that his own Rook can take over the Q-file.

3) The advance P–KN5 to undermine White's KBP, the supporter of his KP.

4) An attack on the KP, tying down White's pieces.

5) The dispatch of the King to win the opponent's weak pawns.

As we can see, it is a simple winning plan—simple for Smyslov, of course.

| 20. . . . | KR–Q1 |
| 21. QR–Q1 | RxR |
| 22. RxR | K–B1 |
| 23. P–B3 | K–K2 |

| 24. K–B2 | P–KR4 |
| 25. K–K3 | P–KN4 |

The first part of the plan is completed. White must move away his Rook.

| 26. R–R2 | R–Q1 |
| 27. R–R1 | P–N5 |
| 28. PxP | NxPch |

| 29. | K–K2 | N–B3 |
|-----|------|------|
| 30. | K–K3 | R–Q5 |

Now the KP is attacked twice, and Black intends to continue K–B1–N2–N3–N4–N5.

| 31. | R–KB1 | N–N5ch |
|-----|-------|--------|
| 32. | K–K2  | K–B1   |
| 33. | R–B3  | K–N2   |
| 34. | R–Q3  |        |

White, seeing inevitable loss, decides to take his chances in the Knight ending, but this is possible only at the price of giving Black a passed QP.

| 34. | . . . | K–B3 |
|-----|-------|------|

In view of the altered situation—the possibility of exchanging Rooks—Black's King changes its itinerary. After the automatic 34. . . . K–N3 35. RxR PxR 36. N–N5 P–K4 37. NxRP some hope appears for White.

| 35. | RxR  | PxR  |
|-----|------|------|
| 36. | N–N5 | K–K4 |
| 37. | NxRP | KxP  |
| 38. | N–B8 |      |

At the end, a sly trap: 38. . . . P–K4? 39. N–Q6 mate! But if White plans to continue, 38. N–N5 is better. Now, however, his King is left to fight alone against a King, a Knight, and a strong passed pawn.

| 38. | . . . | P–Q6ch |
|-----|-------|--------|
| 39. | K–Q2  | K–Q5   |
| 40. | P–B5  | PxP    |
| 41. | N–Q6  | N–K4   |

**White resigns**

## Game 80

In examining this interesting game the reader will become acquainted with two strategical ideas. The opening results in Black's QB4–Q3–K4 pawn configuration against White's QB4–Q5–K4, which gives White greater freedom to maneuver in his own camp. He has three ranks at his disposal, Black only two. True, this is an abstract advantage, but it is the task of the master to consider it concretely and find a plan to make use of it. It is instructive to follow how Taimanov almost completely clears his first three ranks of pawns and transfers his forces easily from one flank to the other, while Black's pieces are huddled together on his second and especially his first ranks.

The second idea is that White cannot exploit his doubled Rooks on the QN file because all suitable invasion squares are protected by Black's minor pieces. White organizes play on the other wing, which, though harmless enough in itself, brings about a few exchanges and deflects those minor pieces from the QN-file, thus permitting White's Rooks to break through to QN7 and bring the game to an end within a few moves.

## King's Indian Defense

| M. Taimanov | Y. Geller |
|---|---|
| 1. P–Q4 | N–KB3 |
| 2. P–QB4 | P–KN3 |
| 3. N–QB3 | B–N2 |
| 4. P–K4 | O–O |
| 5. N–B3 | P–Q3 |
| 6. B–K2 | P–K4 |
| 7. O–O | QN–Q2 |
| 8. R–K1 | P–B3 |
| 9. B–B1 | R–K1 |

Geller's 9th move completes the setting up of his forces. He is now ready to become active after the exchange . . . PxP, but Taimanov anticipates Black's intention by advancing his center pawn.

**10. P–Q5**

Offering Black the choice of exchanging on Q4, closing the center, or doing neither. The trade would make sense with White's Bishop on KN2 and Black's Rook on KB1. Maintaining the tension in the center by . . . Q–K2 and . . . P–QR4 is not bad here, having in view . . . N–B4 and later . . . P–KB4. As for Geller's choice of . . . P–B4, this is a matter of taste; it seems to me that a rigid pawn configuration in the King's Indian Defense makes it difficult for Black to find counterplay.

| 10. . . . | P–B4 |
|---|---|
| 11. P–KN3 | |

A farsighted move, whose significance soon becomes clear.

| 11. . . . | N–B1 |
|---|---|
| 12. P–QR3 | N–N5 |
| 13. N–KR4 | P–QR3 |

Black forsakes his preparations for . . . P–KB4 because of 14. PxP PxP 15. B–R3 threatening 16. NxP BxN 17. BxN, and if 15. . . . Q–B3 then 16. N–K4 PxN 17. BxN. So it turns out that 11. P–KN3 was directed against . . . P–KB4: White established a base for his Knight on KR4 and opened the way for his Bishop to KR3. Najdorf's suggested 13. . . . B–B3 14. N–N2 B–N2 is not entirely convincing because 13. . . . B–B3 does not threaten 14. . . . BxN: White can answer 14. P–B3 BxN 15. PxB N–B3 16. B–N5 K–N2 17. Q–Q2.

| 14. B–Q2 | P–KR4 |
|---|---|
| 15. P–R3 | N–B3 |
| 16. P–QN4 | P–N3 |
| 17. PxP | NPxP |
| 18. R–N1 | N/3–Q2 |
| 19. Q–R4 | B–B3 |
| 20. N–B3 | |

White convinces himself that the time for invasion is not yet ripe; for instance, 20. Q–B6 R–R2 21. QxQP? R–B2!! and the Queen is trapped.

| 20. . . . | P–R5 |
|---|---|

An attack on the King with such limited forces can hardly be worthwhile. He should continue to prepare . . . P–KB4 for as long as White has no concrete threats on the Queenside.

| 21. N–Q1 | PxP |
| 22. PxP | N–N1 |

To complete the picture the KB should be "played" to KR1. The diagram shows just what freedom to maneuver means. White can put a Rook on QN3, where it controls the QN-file and simultaneously defends KB3 and KN3. In some lines the Rook on QN1 can go to KR1 and the Knight on Q1 to QB3, K3, or KB2; whereas Black's Rooks and Knights have only one move each, the QN-file is closed to Black's pieces, and his Rooks are in no position to be transferred to the Kingside. However, Black's position is fairly solid, and, as I said, White must still prove his superiority.

| 23. R–K3 | N–R2 |
| 24. R/3–N3 | B–Q2 |

| 25. Q–R5 | Q–B1 |
| 26. N–B2 | B–Q1 |
| 27. Q–B3 | B–R5 |

Geller's exceptionally stubborn and tenacious defense must be noted. He has managed to drive the Queen back and render White's possession of the QN-file useless: if R–N7 there follows simply . . . R–K2, and White's Rook must either retreat or be exchanged. Now White brings his Knight, Bishop, and Queen to the Kingside, forcing Black to withdraw his pieces from the QN-file.

| 28. R/3–N2 | N–Q2 |
| 29. P–R4 | R–R2 |
| 30. B–R3 | Q–B2 |
| 31. N–N5 | NxN |
| 32. BxN/5 | BxB |
| 33. PxB | K–N2 |
| 34. Q–B3! | |

This move deserves an exclamation mark not only for itself but also as the capstone of the entire strategical plan. All the following moves are based on the possibility for White to get his forces quickly from one flank to the other, and this idea includes the threat 35. K–N2! followed by exchanging on Q7, checking on KB6, and, after R–KR1, inevitably giving mate in the vicinity of KR8.

| 34. | . . . | Q–Q1 |
| 35. | R–N7 | RxR |
| 36. | RxR | |

A new threat appears: 37. BxN BxB 38. Q–B6ch, winning the key QP and with it the game.

| 36. | . . . | K–N1 |
| 37. | BxN | BxB |
| 38. | N–N4 | QxP |

On 38. . . . R–K2 there follows 39. N–B6ch, and on any King move 40. Q–R1.

| 39. | RxB | P–B4 |
| 40. | PxP | R–KB1 |

Since White has clearly made it through the time pressure ending to move 40 before his flag fell, Black, naturally, resigned.

## Game 81
### Caro-Kann Defense

**M. Najdorf**          **A. Kotov**

**1. P–K4**

The beginning of a psychological struggle. This was the only time in the whole tournament that Najdorf opened the game with the KP, expecting Kotov, as he explained, to play the "Najdorf Variation" of the Sicilian Defense, for which White had prepared a certain surprise.

**1. . . .          P–QB3**

After long thought Kotov replies . . . P–QB3, unfaithful, also for the only time in this tournament, to the Sicilian Defense. Through diligent and precise play he later achieves full equality, and then he starts

thinking about getting an advantage . . .

| 2. | P–Q4 | P–Q4 |
| 3. | N–QB3 | PxP |
| 4. | NxP | B–B4 |
| 5. | N–N3 | B–N3 |
| 6. | N–B3 | N–Q2 |
| 7. | B–Q3 | KN–B3 |
| 8. | O–O | P–K3 |
| 9. | R–K1 | B–K2 |
| 10. | P–B4 | O–O |
| 11. | BxB | RPxB |
| 12. | B–B4 | R–K1 |

Black, not having played . . . Q–B2 before castling, is now preparing . . . P–QB4, and in view of the possible P–Q5 he makes room for his Bishop on KB1.

| 13. | Q–B2 | P–B4 |
| 14. | QR–Q1 | PxP |

| 15. | NxP | B–N5! |
|-----|-----|-------|

The threat of . . . P–K4 forces the exchange of dark-square Bishops, easing the defense.

| 16. | B–Q2 | BxB |
|-----|------|-----|
| 17. | QxB | P–R3 |
| 18. | P–N4 | Q–B2 |
| 19. | R–QB1 | QR–Q1 |
| 20. | Q–B3 | N–N3 |

White has only the slight advantage of a Queenside pawn majority, whereas Black has more pawns in the center. This means that the chances in the endgame will favor White, but in a complicated fight with Queens Black has fully equal play. With this in mind Kotov should not hurry to exchange Queens, and instead of . . . N–N3 the Knight would stand better on QB3 via QN1.

| 21. | N–B3 | Q–B5 |
|-----|------|------|
| 22. | Q–K3 | QxQ |
| 23. | RxQ | R–QB1 |
| 24. | R/3–B3 | KR–Q1 |
| 25. | K–B1 | K–B1 |
| 26. | K–K2 | |

| 26. | . . . | K–K2 |
|-----|-------|------|
| 27. | P–QR3 | R–B2 |
| 28. | R/3–B2 | R/1–QB1 |
| 29. | K–Q3 | |

It is not clear here whether Najdorf was agreeable to a draw or whether he merely wanted to test his opponent, but in either case, after 29. . . . R–Q1ch White's King would be forced back. True, after 30. K–K2 R/1–QB1 the draw would not be altogether obligatory. White could transfer his Knights to K3 and QN3 and attempt to exploit his advantage on the Queenside. However, Black would maintain strongly supported squares for his Knights in the center, promising a very stubborn fight.

After K–Q3 the game takes an unexpected turn. Kotov, full of his usual optimism and fighting spirit, decides to advance pawns in the center in order to push back White's King and occupy Q6. Even though this plan is fully accomplished, it does not bring Black any advantage, in my opinion. At the same time, the advance of the KP means that the Knight on QN3 cannot go to Q4 if White plays P–B5. On K3 the pawn performs the important duty of guarding Q4.

| 29. | . . . | KN–Q2 |
|-----|-------|-------|
| 30. | N–B1 | P–B4 |
| 31. | N–K3 | P–K4 |

| 32. N–Q2 | P–K5ch | 34. P–B5 | N–Q6 |
|----------|--------|----------|------|
| 33. K–K2 | N–K4 | 35. R–Q1 | N–B5ch |

An oversight leading to a forced loss. However, in case of 35. . . . K–K3 Black's position remains poor because of 36. P–N3 followed by P–B3.

**36. K–B1          K–K3**
**37. NxKP**

After this obvious pseudo-sacrifice, Black's position collapses immediately.

Despite its outward signs of activity, Black's position has worsened: his KP has run past all the squares it should be guarding and his Knights have no bases in the center. After White's next move, the unpleasant N–Q5ch is threatened.

**37. . . .          N–Q2**

If he takes the Knight, the Rook checks on Q6.

| 38. N–Q6 | R–KR1 |
|----------|-------|
| 39. P–N3 | N–R6 |
| 40. N–Q5 | R–B3 |
| 41. R–K2ch | **Black resigns** |

## Game 82
### *English Opening*

**T. Petrosian     I. Boleslavsky**

1. P–QB4 P–K4 2. N–QB3 P–Q3 3. P–KN3 N–QB3 4. B–N2 P–KN3 5. P–Q3 B–N2 6. B–Q2 KN–K2 7. N–B3 O–O 8. O–O B–Q2 9. R–N1 Q–B1 10. P–QN4 B–R6 11. P–N5 N–Q5 12. P–R4 BxB 13. KxB Q–Q2 14. N–Q5 P–QB3 (White logically attacks the Queenside, and now Black commits an inaccuracy. If he wants

to trade Knights, it is better to do it on Q4; if he does not want to trade, he should move it to KB4 and then play . . . P–QB3.) 15. NxNch QxN 16. NxN PxN 17. R–K1 Q–Q2 18. PxP PxP 19. Q–N3 KR–B1 20. Q–N7 Q–B4 21. Q–R6 P–R4, drawn on White's offer, although he has the advantage. Possible is 22. R–N7 P–R5 23. KR–QN1, etc.

## Game 83
### French Defense

Y. Averbakh     G. Stahlberg

1. P–K4 P–K3 2. P–Q4 P–Q4 3. N–Q2 P–QB4 4. KPxP QxP 5. KN–B3 PxP 6. B–B4 Q–Q3 7. O–O N–KB3 8. N–N3 N–B3 9. R–K1 P–QR3 10. P–QR4 B–K2 11. QNxP NxN 12. QxN B–Q2 13. B–B4 QxQ 14. NxQ QR–B1 15. B–QN3 N–R4 16. B–K3 O–O 17. N–B3 B–B4 18. N–K5 N–B3 19. QR–Q1 B–K1 20. BxB RxB 21. P–QB3 B–B3 22. P–B3 R–N1 23. R–Q4 B–K1 24. P–R4 K–B1 25. P–KB4 P–QR4 26. N–Q3 R/4–B1 27. P–B5 (White deviates from the "scientific" tracts on the endgame and rather adventurously tries for advantage. He does not succeed and is left with the inferior position.) 27. . . . PxP 28. R–K5 R–Q1 29. RxBP RxR 30. PxR P–QN3 31. R–B4 R–Q1 (Black takes the initiative.) 32. N–K5 N–R4 33. R–B3 RxP 34. BxP N–B3 35. BxB KxB 36. R–QN3 R–K5 37. N–B3 N–Q2 38. N–N5 RxKRP 39. R–K3ch K–B1 (Facilitating White's defense. It is better to get the King to QN1; for instance, 39. . . . K–Q1 40. N–K6ch K–B1 41. R–B3ch K–N1

42. R–B7 R–Q5!) 40. N–K6ch K–N1 41. N–N5 K–B1 42. N–K6ch K–B2 43. N–Q8ch K–N1! 44. R–K7 N–B1 45. R–N7 R–R3 46. N–B7 R–K3 47. N–N5 R–Q3 48. R–N8 P–R3 49. N–K4 R–Q8ch 50. K–R2 R–Q5 51. N–B3 R–R5ch 52. K–N1 R–QN5 53. N–Q5 RxNP 54. RxP (A mistake before the second time control. It is necessary to take the pawn with the Knight.) 54. . . . R–R7 55. N–B3 R–QB7 56. N–Q5 R–B5 57. R–R6 RxP 58. N–K7ch K–R2 59. N–B6 R–R8ch 60. K–R2 P–R5 61. N–Q4 N–Q2 62. R–R7 N–B4 63. N–B5 K–N3 64. P–N4 N–K3 65. R–R6 K–B2 66. N–Q6ch K–B3 67. N–B4 K–K2 68. R–R7ch K–Q1 69. N–K5 N–B2 70. N–B7ch K–Q2 71. N–K5ch K–B1 72. N–B6 P–R6 73. N–K7ch K–Q1 74. N–B6ch K–Q2 75. N–Q4 K–B1 76. K–N3 R–Q8 77. N–B2 N–N4 78. R–R5 R–QB8 79. NxP R–B6ch 80. K–R4 P–N4ch! 81. K–R5 R–R6ch 82. K–N6 NxN 83. K–N7 N–N8! 84. R–R6 N–Q7 85. RxP RxR 86. KxR N–B6 (The Knight is just in time.), **White resigns.**

## Game 84
### Queen's Indian Defense

**L. Szabo**                    **M. Euwe**

| | | |
|---|---|---|
| 1. | P–Q4 | N–KB3 |
| 2. | P–QB4 | P–K3 |
| 3. | N–KB3 | P–QN3 |
| 4. | N–B3 | B–N2 |
| 5. | P–K3 | B–K2 |
| 6. | B–Q3 | P–B4 |
| 7. | O–O | |

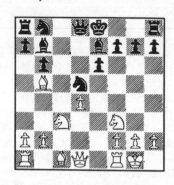

Before starting active play in the center White decides to remove his King, but Black has other ideas and immediately undertakes a typical maneuver in this variation: . . . PxP and . . . P–Q4. Szabo probably thought that Black could not play this before castling because of the check on White's QR4–K8 diagonal, but Euwe takes the chance and equalizes the game anyway.

| | | |
|---|---|---|
| 7. | . . . | PxP |
| 8. | PxP | P–Q4 |
| 9. | PxP | NxP |

Only a chess player with very strong nerves can play this way in the opening.

**10. B–N5ch**

| | | |
|---|---|---|
| 10. | . . . | B–B3 |
| 11. | BxBch | |

Szabo is too quick to exchange Bishops. It is necessary to put pressure on the diagonal with 11. Q–R4; the main variation is 11. . . . BxB 12. QxBch Q–Q2 13. NxN! PxN 14. Q–N3 or 14. Q–K2, and White keeps an advantage in development.

| | | |
|---|---|---|
| 11. | . . . | NxB |
| 12. | Q–R4 | Q–Q2 |

But now Black's calculations have been justified. White cannot increase the pressure. He does make one more attempt, but after

**13. NxN**

Black recaptures not with the pawn, of course, but . . .

13. . . .          QxN
14. B–K3           O–O
15. KR–QB1         P–QN4

Clearly signifying a draw,

which is now recorded by repetition of moves: 16. Q–R6 N–N5 17. Q–R5 N–Q6 18. R–B2 N–N5 19. R/2–B1 N–Q6, **Drawn.**

# Round Thirteen

## Game 85
### Grünfeld Defense

| G. Stahlberg | L. Szabo |
|---|---|
| 1. P–Q4 | N–KB3 |
| 2. P–QB4 | P–KN3 |
| 3. N–QB3 | P–Q4 |
| 4. N–B3 | B–N2 |
| 5. Q–N3 | |

White's opening system is directed against Black's need to play P–QB4. With his pressure on the QP White wants to force Black either to play P–QB3 (meaning, of course, not P–QB4!) or to take on QB5. The various attempts to counter White's formation were unsuccessful until Smyslov worked out the plan used by Black in this game.

| 5. . . . | PxP |
|---|---|
| 6. QxBP | O–O |
| 7. P–K4 | B–N5 |

This move and the next initiate Smyslov's system of defense in the Grünfeld.

**8. B–K3   KN–Q2**

Superficially this move seems illogical, but it has its sense and its history. When this system was first used, 8. . . . N–B3 was played here so that if 9. P–Q5 BxN, and for instance, 10. PxN P–QN4! or 10. PxB N–K4 11. Q–K2 P–B3!. White gradually managed to discover the drawbacks of that setup, and then Smyslov and others, without discarding the idea entirely, made the appropriate corrections. In the process of examining this vigorous system the move 8. . . . KN–Q2 was born, bound up with two ideas: maintaining the possibility of P–QB4 and creating pressure against the QP. For instance, now the threat is . . . N–N3, and if the Queen gives up its support of the QP then . . . BxN and . . . BxP.

Among the continuations that have been tried in this position are 9. N–Q2 and 9. B–K2 N–N3 10. Q–Q3 followed by castling long, which lead to equal play. 9. P–K5 and 9. R–Q1 N–N3 10. Q–N3 used to be

206

played until it was found that the Queen does better to make a prophylactic retreat to N3 rather than wait to be chased by the Knight. In reply to this, Szabo goes into an extremely complex variation with the immediate . . . P–QB4.

9. Q–N3      P–B4
10. P–Q5

If the Queen takes the NP, Black first exchanges his Bishop at N5 for White's Knight and after 11. PxB plays 11. . . . PxP, leaving his QR undefended. Then 12. QxR PxN 13. QxP PxP 14. QR–N1 N–QB3 is possible, and Black gets a strong attack on the King for the Exchange. The text move gives the Bishop on N5 an unpleasant choice: to take on B6, which strengthens White's center, or to stay put and face great danger after N–Q2.

10. . . .      N–R3
11. N–Q2      P–K3

Black voluntarily locks his Bishop in a cage with no apparent escape. This move is not made thoughtlessly; it is the result of an analysis that Szabo had earlier verified in a tournament game. For instance, 12. P–KR3 PxP threatening . . . P–Q5, and if 13. PxP B–B4 14. P–N4 P–B5, freeing QB4 so that the N/Q2 can go there with tempo and allow the Bishop to retreat, and if 15.

QxBP then N–K4 frees the Bishop.

12. P–Q6

White's pawn is torn from its roots and is soon surrounded by the enemy. A bitter struggle over this pawn now begins, and it is possible to foresee that the advantage will be taken over by Black, since all his pieces are developed and he has castled.

12. . . .      B–Q5

The possibility of this move is based on the continuation 13. P–KR3 (winning the Bishop?!) BxB 14. BPxB Q–R5ch—and mate! But even if White traded Bishops immediately and played N–N5, then 14. . . . N/2–B4 and . . . P–K4 would be unpleasant, for Black's passed QP would be defended and therefore much stronger than its White counterpart, and Black's pieces would be better placed.

13. BxN

Securing QB4 for the Knight and gaining a tempo for castling. On the other hand, the QN-file is opened.

| 13. . . . | PxB |
| 14. N–B4 | R–N1 |
| 15. Q–B2 | P–K4 |
| 16. N–Q5 | Q–R5 |
| 17. O–O | B–K3 |
| 18. P–KN3 | |

This is characteristic of Stahlberg's carefree attitude toward the position of his King. He is an excellent tactician and a stubborn defender, and he has squirmed out of so many difficult positions that he pays no attention to such trifles. But P–KN3 will be followed by P–B3, opening the second rank from the QB-file to the KR-file, along which a very dangerous draft will threaten the White King's health.

By playing QR–K1 here, or first N–K7ch and then QR–K1, White would be far from lost, but now the defense becomes very difficult.

| 18. . . . | Q–R4 |
| 19. P–B3 | BxN |
| 20. PxB | N–N3 |
| 21. BxB | KPxB |

White was forced into these exchanges giving Black a passed pawn, since he had no way to defend his Bishop: 21. QR–K1 would have been followed by 21. . . . NxN 22. QxN RxP threatening mate on KR2. The weakness of the second rank is already evident.

| 22. NxN | RxN! |

22. . . . PxN is playable, but Black does not want to close the QN-file, thinking it will be useful for attack. 23. QxP is impossible because of . . . Rx NP, again threatening mate.

| 23. QR–B1 | RxQP |
| 24. QxP | RxP |
| 25. QxRP | P–Q6 |
| 26. Q–K3 | |

It is instructive to see how at every step White is threatened with direct attack along his second rank. He cannot even think of taking the QRP because of . . . R–K1, with a quick finish.

| 26. . . . | P–Q7 |
| 27. QR–Q1 | KR–Q1 |
| 28. P–KN4 | Q–R5 |
| 29. R–B2 | R–Q6 |
| 30. Q–B4 | Q–K2 |
| 31. Q–R4 | Q–B3 |
| 32. Q–N4 | Q–KN4 |
| 33. K–N2 | R/6–Q5 |
| 34. Q–N3 | P–KR4 |

The purpose of this maneuver is to take control of KN6, which becomes accessible after White's forced reply.

| 35. | P–KR3 | P–R5 |
| 36. | P–B4 | Q–K2 |

Of course White could not allow . . . Q–B5, but now comes the decisive . . . Q–K2,

threatening . . . R–Q6 followed by . . . Q–K6 or . . . Q–K8 according to White's reply.

| 37. | R–B3 | R–Q6 |
| 38. | RxR | Q–K7ch |
| 39. | K–N1 | RxR |
| 40. | Q–N8ch | K–R2 |
| | **White resigns** | |

## Game 86
### Queen's Gambit

**I. Boleslavsky      Y. Averbakh**

| 1. | P–QB4 | N–KB3 |
| 2. | N–QB3 | P–K3 |
| 3. | N–B3 | P–Q4 |
| 4. | P–Q4 | B–N5 |
| 5. | PxP | PxP |
| 6. | B–N5 | P–KR3 |
| 7. | BxN | QxB |
| 8. | Q–R4ch | N–B3 |
| 9. | P–K3 | O–O |
| 10. | B–K2 | P–R3 |

Black wants to safeguard his Bishop from the foray N–N5 after its planned retreat to Q3. But if White wants to force the exchange of the Bishop for his Knight on QB3, P–QR3 is good enough, for in connection with his inevitable P–QN4 and his strong pressure on the QN- and QB-files he will have much the better game. That is why this variation cannot be recommended for Black.

| 11. | O–O | B–K3 |
| 12. | QR–B1 | B–Q3 |
| 13. | Q–B2 | KR–Q1 |
| 14. | N–QR4 | N–K2 |

Black's last moves were made to connect his pawn chain and free his pieces from the defense of the QP and QBP.

| 15. | N–B5 | B–B1 |

Black is ready to make the last move to consolidate his position, but the following sudden blow introduces a combinational element that completely changes the situation. The KP's move from the third rank to the fifth brings about a few simplifications favorable to White.

| 16. | P–K4 | |

When the opponent is developed well, a move like this is usually not even considered because of the irreparable "weakness" of the QP. And Black?—what can threaten him when he has no weaknesses? Ideas about weaknesses have changed in our time, however. Not only a pawn formation but even the poor position of a single piece can be a weakness.

**16. . . .                Q–N3**

On 16. . . . B–B5 there follows 17. P–K5 Q–B3 18. N–Q2! and Black cannot well play 18. . . . P–QN3 because of 19. N–Q3 QxQ 20. RxQ BxN 21. RxB, reaching an ending similar to the game, but with a much weaker Black QBP.

But if 16. . . . PxP, the disadvantage of the Black Queen's position becomes evident, and the active piece play turns out clearly in White's favor, as the following example illustrates: 17. NxKP Q–N3 18. B–Q3 B–KB4 19. N–R4 Q–R4 20. NxB/5 NxN 21. NxB NxN 22. QxP.

**17. P–K5**

Continuing the piece play against the Queen by 17. B–Q3 seems more logical. For instance, 17. . . . BxN 18. QxB or 17. . . . PxP 18. BxKP B–B4 19. BxB and after the exchange on KB5 White wins the QNP. That is probably what

Boleslavsky was planning, but, finding that Black would have a good defense in 17. . . . B–B5, he changes his original plan.

**17. . . .                QxQ**
**18. RxQ                BxN**
**19. RxB                P–QB3**

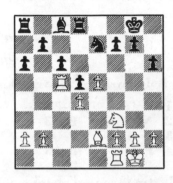

A very interesting position has arisen. White's natural plan —the "minority pawn attack" P–QR4, P–QN4, P–N5—will conflict with Black's possibility for active counterplay, which should be to exploit the weakness of White's QP by . . . P–QN3 and . . . P–QB4. In this effort it will be worthwhile for Black to play P–KB3 with the support of his Rook. If he proceeds passively on both flanks, he will undoubtedly find himself in difficulties. Black is now threatening B–N5 to exchange White's Knight and make it more difficult for him to defend his QP; White's next move is directed against this threat.

**20. N–Q2      P–QR4**

Here Black should first disturb White's QP with 20. . . . N–B4 21. N–N3, and then . . . P–QR4 would be more appropriate. Should White answer this with 22. P–QR4, then 22. . . . B–Q2 would probe White's new weakness, but if 22. R–Q1 then 22. . . . P–R5 23. N–B1 P–KN4! with the possibilities of . . . P–B3 and . . . N–N2–K3.

Averbakh's move inhibits White's P–QN4 followed by N–N3–B5, but it seems to me that this could have been done in a more active way.

**21. R–B3**

The Rook got to QB5 only by chance and withdraws to free that square for the Knight.

**21. . . .      R–B1**
**22. R–K1      P–KN3**

Black's previous move has evidently not succeeded in preparing . . . P–B3 with the idea of recapturing on B3 with the Rook, for now . . . P–B3 would be answered by P–K6! and White's pawn would be very strong. Therefore, Black reluctantly goes completely over to defense.

**23. B–Q3      B–B4**
**24. B–B1      P–R5**
**25. P–KR3     B–Q2**
**26. P–B4      P–R4**

It is impossible to avoid mentioning Boleslavsky's skill in having forced so great a connoisseur of the endgame as Averbakh to put all of his pawns on squares the same color as his Bishop.

**27. N–B3      K–N2**
**28. K–B2      R–R1**
**29. P–KN3     K–B1**
**30. K–N2      N–B4**
**31. B–Q3      N–N2**
**32. N–N5      B–K3**

Forestalling the possible break 33. P–K6; White's idea was then to answer 33. . . . BxP by taking the KNP with his Bishop.

**33. B–B2      K–K2**
**34. R–R3      N–B4**

Black wants very much to avoid playing P–N4, and he sends up a trial balloon, allowing White to play BxN and thus keep a Knight against Black's bad Bishop. But White achieves maximum results by the calm retreat of his Knight to B3. The

QNP is pulled after the QRP like thread from a spool, and as a result the QBP suffers.

| 35. | N–B3 | P–QN4 |
| 36. | R–B3 | QR–QB1 |
| 37. | BxN | BxB |
| 38. | KR–QB1 | B–Q2 |

The logical conclusion of this well-conducted endgame would be 39. P–K6!, and however Black captured, White's Knight would invade K5 with strong pressure on both flanks. Boleslavsky is in no hurry; apparently the variation 39. . . . KxP 40. N–K5 B–K1 41. Nx QBP K–Q3 42. N–K5 RxR 43. RxR P–B3 44. N–Q3 B–Q2 did not seem good enough.

| 39. | N–K1 | R–QN1 |
| 40. | N–Q3 | |

At last White has all he has been striving for: as soon as White's Knight gets to QB5 Black's game will be practically hopeless, for in fact White has an extra pawn on the Kingside which he should gradually be able to exploit. But the text move gives Averbakh a study-like chance to save the game!

| 40. | . . . | P–N5 |
| 41. | R–B5 | |

The Rook again occupies QB5 against its will; that is where the Knight belongs.

| 41. | . . . | B–B4 |
| 42. | N–B2 | |

Hoping the Knight will help to get in P–N4, forcing the Bishop to retreat, but . . .

| 42. | . . . | P–N6 |

Averbakh finds a brilliant maneuver in a difficult situation and sets up a drawn position. If 43. PxP RxP 44. RxBP RxP 45. R–B7ch K–B1, White cannot win. On 43. RxBP there follows, of course, 43. . . . PxP or 43. . . . P–R6!, and the winner, unexpectedly, is Black.

| 43. | P–R3 | B–B7 |

The picture has suddenly changed—Black's weak QNP is as strong as steel and the "bad" Bishop stands well. It is pointless for White to take the QBP: 44. RxBP KR–QB1 45. RxR RxR threatening . . . R–B5, and if White defends the QP with his King—46. K–B3 —then 46. . . . B–K5ch wins for Black; but if White's King were on, say, KB1, he would win by bringing it to K3 via K2. The ability to notice and turn to account such tiny details can sometimes decide the game.

The following maneuvers cannot change the drawn outcome. The question arises: Could White have won, and, if so, where did he go wrong?

Instead of N–Q3 on his 40th move he should have played R–B5!, not allowing Black the two tempos for . . . P–N5 and . . . B–B4. Then he could have replied to 40. . . . P–N5 with

41. R–R5, or if 40. . . . KR–QB1 41. N–Q3 and if then 41. . . . B–B4 42. N–N4, or if 41. . . . P–N5 42. R–R5 threatening 43. N–B5.

It seems to me that in spite of all his inventiveness Black could not have saved the game.

**44. K–B3 K–Q2 45. K–K3 R–R1 46. P–R4 R–QR3 47. N–R3 R–QN1 48. N–N5 K–K2, Drawn.**

## Game 87

I wish to call the reader's attention in this game to Black's QP; though doubled, isolated, and surrounded by enemy pieces, it turns out to be exceptionally tenacious. Such pawns, which did not exist in the games of Morphy, Steinitz, Lasker, Capablanca, or Alekhine, made their appearance in the games of contemporary grandmasters and have enriched the treasury of chess ideas.

We see such pawns not only in the King's Indian Defense, but also in the Sicilian after 1. P–K4 P–QB4 2. N–KB3 N–QB3

3. P–Q4 PxP 4. NxP P–KN3 5. P–QB4 B–N2 6. B–K3 N–B3 7. QN–B3 N–KN5 8. QxN NxN 9. Q–Q1 P–K4! 10. B–Q3 O–O 11. O–O P–Q3 12. N–K2 B–K3 13. NxN PxN, and in a few other openings.

The viability of the QP depends above all on the Bishop at KN2, without which the pawn would be a one-day butterfly, and also on how effectively Black can make use of the open files adjacent to it. The fight between Kotov and Petrosian takes place along these lines.

## Old Indian Defense

| A. Kotov | T. Petrosian |
|---|---|
| 1. P–Q4 | N–KB3 |
| 2. P–QB4 | P–Q3 |
| 3. N–QB3 | QN–Q2 |
| 4. P–K4 | P–K4 |
| 5. N–B3 | B–K2 |
| 6. P–KN3 | |

Correct strategy. White is aware that in an analogous position from Philidor's Defense the Bishop stands on QB4 and plays first violin in the attack on the King, but there White's QBP is on QB2.

On K2 or Q3 the Bishop would only hamper the Rooks' operations along the open files, but on KN2 it has an excellent future, for Black will be forced sooner or later to cede his Q5 to White, whereupon White's KP will become mobile.

| 6. . . . | O–O |
| 7. B–N2 | P–B3 |
| 8. O–O | P–QR3 |
| 9. P–QN3 | |

A rather vague idea. White seems to be protecting his QBP in anticipation of . . . P–QN4, but later he transfers a Knight to Q2 so that he can recapture with it on QB4. However, with the Knight on QB3 the QB will not be effectively developed on QN2. P–KR3 should be played here without delay, safeguarding K3 for the Bishop and thus reinforcing Q4.

| 9. . . . | R–K1 |
| 10. B–N2 | B–B1 |
| 11. Q–Q3 | |

More natural is Q–B2 and QR–Q1. Why expose the Queen to the Black Knights at K4 or QB4?

| 11. . . . | P–QN4 |
| 12. N–Q2 | |

Kotov never stops halfway in implementing a plan, even when he begins to suspect that his chosen plan is not very

good. He figures that after 12. . . . KPxP 13. QxP the move 13. . . . P–B4 would be bad for Black because White's Knight would get Q5 permanently. At the same time he prepares an opportune P–B4. However, Black finds a deep forcing maneuver that leads to his seizure of Q5 and the appearance of that tenacious pawn.

| 12. . . . | B–N2 |

Q–N3 is playable here, after which White would seem to have nothing better than N–K2, but then the question arises: Wouldn't it have been quicker to put the Knights on Q2 and K2 in the first place?

### 13. K–R1

White wants to play P–B4, but he cannot do it right away because if 13. P–B4? PxQP 14. QxP P–Q4! threatening . . . B–B4. Retreating the King is no impediment to Black's ability to carry out this maneuver. Therefore, some kind of developing move, R–K1 for instance, is better.

| 13. . . . | KPxP |
| 14. QxP | P–B4 |

Seizing Q5 with a Knight would be to White's benefit if the Knight could be firmly established there or if its exchange on that square would offer some tangible advantage.

Neither would occur in this case, so Petrosian is not worried about the weakness of his Q4. White's Queen is gradually forced back to its own camp, pursued by Black's Knight.

**15. Q–Q3**

If it goes to K3, possible is . . . P–Q4.

| 15. . . . | N–K4 |
| 16. Q–B2 | N–B3 |
| 17. N–Q5 | N–Q5 |

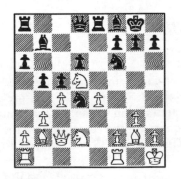

Black is trying to get a positional advantage in a combinative way, his next move, . . . P–N3, playing an important role.

Petrosian had to see all this when he played 13. . . . KPxP, for otherwise his position would now be very alarming.

| 18. Q–Q3 | P–N3 |
| 19. BxN | |

Kotov does not trust his opponent completely, and so, in the hope of eventually capturing the QP, he exchanges Knights. The quieter 19. N–KB3 leads to a slight advantage for Black: 19. . . . PxP 20. PxP BxN! 21. BPxB NxN 22. KBxN B–N2 or 21. KPxB NxN 22. QxN B–N2 23. BxN BxB.

| 19. . . . | PxB |
| 20. NxNch | QxN |
| 21. K–N1 | Q–K4 |
| 22. R–K1 | B–N2 |
| 23. QR–B1 | |

White needs only to put a Rook on Q1 in order to win the QP, but Black exerts such pressure on White's QBP and KP that both Rooks are needed for defense. The plan to win that tenacious pawn does not succeed, and White's game hangs by a thread; but Kotov defends calmly and repulses the onslaught.

| 23. . . . | R–K2 |
| 24. N–B3 | Q–QB4 |
| 25. B–B1 | P–R3 |
| 26. PxP | QxP |
| 27. Q–Q1 | Q–N3 |
| 28. N–Q2 | QR–K1 |
| 29. B–Q3 | |

The tenacious pawn defies its enemies! Not one piece can attack it and all of them together are blockading it. White's game looks suspicious now, in view of the impending 29. . . . P–Q4, but Kotov thinks up a bold pawn sacrifice . . .

| 29. . . . | P–Q4 |
| 30. P–K5 | RxP |
| 31. RxR | RxR |
| 32. N–B3 | |

Now the Bishop on QN2 is solidly bricked up, and the two pawns on the Q-file are as weak as one. Black would gladly agree to have either of them taken off the board.

| 32. . . . | R–K5 |

Petrosian makes a last attempt and offers the Exchange, but of course Kotov does not accept.

| 33. Q–Q2 | Drawn |

It is difficult for Black to activate his Bishops, and White has counterchances in his potential passed pawn and control of the QB-file.

Black's position at the 29th move was so good that a question involuntarily arises: Was it not possible to find a win?

## Game 88
## Sicilian Defense

(57–?)

| Y. Geller | M. Najdorf |
| 1. P–K4 | P–QB4 |
| 2. N–KB3 | P–Q3 |
| 3. P–Q4 | PxP |
| 4. NxP | N–KB3 |
| 5. N–QB3 | P–QR3 |
| 6. B–K2 | P–K4 |
| 7. N–N3 | B–K3 |
| 8. O–O | QN–Q2 |
| 9. P–B4 | Q–B2 |
| 10. P–B5 | B–B5 |
| 11. P–QR4! | |

Against the frequently used Najdorf System Geller has prepared a plan to capture the light squares in the center and on the Kingside. P–B5 was played to drive the Bishop to QB5 where it is to be exchanged. P–QR4 is played to restrict Black's play on the Queenside.

| 11. . . . | R–B1 |
| 12. B–K3 | B–K2 |

In the spirit of this variation is 12. ... P–Q4 13. PxP B–N5 or 13. NxP NxN 14. PxN BxN 15. PxB B–B4.

**13. P–R5        P–R4** ✓

Najdorf's temperament does not allow him to defend passively without counterplay. Seeing that his pieces on the Queenside are cramped, he undertakes a diversion on the Kingside directed mainly against the possibility of White's P–KN4. In one of his later games he castled here and kept the balance—not because his game was so good but rather because of his tactical skill.

| | |
|---|---|
| **14. BxB** | **QxB** ✓ |
| **15. R–R4** | **Q–B2** ✓ |
| **16. P–R3** | **P–R5** ✓ |
| **17. R–B2** ✓ | |

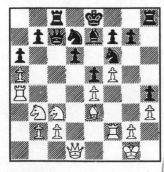

**17. ...        P–QN4** ✓

Najdorf, true to himself, decides to sacrifice a pawn for the initiative. Indeed, Najdorf would have a promising position after the 18th move—if Geller took

the QRP. But as we shall soon see, Geller finds a calm solution to his problem; he refuses material gain and by a series of fine moves obtains a great positional advantage. Although Najdorf attaches an exclamation point to this move in his annotations, 17. ... Q–B3 may be better.

| | |
|---|---|
| **18. PxP e.p.** ✓ | **NxNP** ✓ |
| **19. BxN** ✓ | |

This exchange is directed toward gaining control of the light squares, particularly Q5. White removes one of the pieces defending that square, and the next links in the chain are: to transfer the Rook from KB2 to QR1; to attack the QRP with the heavy pieces, tying down Black's Rooks and Queen; then to transfer the Knight from QN3 to K3; and, finally, to post a Knight at Q5. The first part of this plan continues to the 24th move, the second part from moves 25 to 27, and the third part is completed on the 31st move.

| | |
|---|---|
| **19. ...** | **QxB** ✓ |
| **20. Q–K2** | **R–R1** ✓ |
| **21. K–R2** | **O–O** ✓ |
| **22. R–B1** | **R–R2** ✓ |
| **23. KR–QR1** ✓ | **KR–R1** ✓ |
| **24. R/1–R2** ✓ | |

Geller's play is emphatically orthodox and undeviating. This move defends the QNP in order to free the Knight on N3, al-

though White could also play
Q–Q3 and then N–Q2 (the
QNP cannot be taken because
of R–QN1). The second part
of his plan now begins.

| 24. | . . . | B–Q1 |
|-----|-------|------|
| 25. | N–R5 | R–B1 |
| 26. | N–B4 | Q–B3 |
| 27. | N–K3 | P–R4 |
| 28. | R–B4 | Q–R3 |
| 29. | P–QN3 | B–N3 |
| 30. | RxRch | QxR |
| 31. | N/K–Q5 | NxN |
| 32. | NxN | |

The apotheosis of White's
strategy. The key to the fortress
is now in Geller's hands.

| 32. | . . . | Q–B4 |
|-----|-------|------|
| 33. | R–R1 | |

Attentiveness is always necessary: the threat was . . . Q–N8
mate.

| 33. | . . . | Q–B7 |
|-----|-------|------|

There is a chance in 33. . . .
P–R5 34. PxP RxP, but White
replies 34. Q–N4 and wins as
follows: 1) 34. . . . PxP 35. P–

B6 P–N3 36. QxRP; 2) 34. . . .
Q–B7 35. P–B6 Q–N6ch 36.
QxQ PxQch 37. KxP RPxP 38.
RxR BxR 39. QBPxP.

**34. QxQ**

Quicker is 34. Q–N4 B–Q1
35. P–N4 P–R5, with variations similar to those in the previous note, or even 35. R–R4
followed by R–B4 or P–QN4.
However, Geller deliberately
avoids both, regardless of their
advantage to him, preferring to
win this game in positional
style.

| 34. | . . . | BxQ |
|-----|-------|------|
| 35. | R–KB1 | B–Q5 |

If the Bishop checks it will
never get out of N6.

| 36. | P–B3 | B–B4 |
|-----|------|------|
| 37. | P–KN4 | PxP e.p.ch |
| 38. | KxP | R–N2 |
| 39. | R–QN1 | P–B3 |

A classical endgame of in-
structional value. The pawns
are posted on the same color as
the Bishop, the Knight has a
strong position in the center of
the board, and the light squares
are accessible to White's King.
All that remains is to form a
distant passed pawn.

| 40. | K–B3 | K–B2 |
|-----|------|------|
| 41. | K–K2 | R–N1 |
| 42. | P–N4 | P–N3 |
| 43. | K–Q3 | |

Geller goes too far in his unwillingness to play combina-

tively. 43. PxPch wins in a few moves: 43. . . . KxP 44. PxB RxR 45. P–B6 R–N1 46. P–B7 R–QR1 47. P–B8=Q RxQ 48. N–K7ch.

43. . . . NPxP 44. KPxP PxP 45. PxP B–Q5 46. R–

QB1 K–N2 47. R–B7ch K–R3 48. K–K4 K–N4 49. R–KR7 B–B7 50. R–N7ch K–R5 51. K–B3 B–K8 52. K–N2 R–KB1 53. P–N5 B–R4 54. P–N6 BxP 55. NxB R–QN1 56. R–N4ch K–R4 57. N–Q5, Black resigns.

## Game 89
### Sicilian Defense

**V. Smyslov          M. Taimanov**

1. P–K4 P–QB4 2. N–QB3 N–QB3 3. P–KN3 P–KN3 4. B–N2 B–N2 5. P–Q3 N–B3 6. KN–K2 O–O 7. O–O P–Q3 8. R–N1 R–N1 9. P–QR3 P–QN4 10. P–QN4 PxP 11. PxP (There were years when Smyslov brought home many points with the closed variation.) 11. . . . B–Q2 12. N–B4 P–K3 13. B–

Q2 Q–B2 14. QN–K2 KR–K1 15. N–B1 P–QR4 16. PxP Nx RP 17. N–N3 N–N2 18. P–QB3 P–K4 19. N–K2, Drawn.

The opponents' pieces are so peaceably inclined that not a single one has crossed from the fourth to the fifth rank. Smyslov is taking a time-out after a series of wins in the previous rounds.

## Game 90
### Sicilian Defense

**P. Keres          S. Gligoric**

1. P–K4 P–QB4 2. N–K2 N–KB3 3. QN–B3 P–Q3 4. P–KN3 N–B3 5. B–N2 P–KN3 6. P–Q4 PxP 7. NxP NxN 8. QxN B–N2 9. O–O O–O 10. Q–Q3 B–K3 11. B–Q2 Q–B2 12. P–N3 P–QR3 13. QR–B1 KR–Q1 (Planning to reply to

the maneuver N–Q1–K3 with the immediate . . . P–Q4!) 14. N–Q5 NxN 15. PxN B–B4 16. B–K4 BxB 17. QxB B–N7 18. QR–K1 B–B3 19. P–QB4 QR–B1 20. R–B1 Q–Q2 21. B–R5 R–K1 22. B–N6 P–K4 23. PxP e.p. RxKP 24. Q–Q3 QR–K1 25. B–K3 Q–K2 26. QR–Q1 B–N7 27. B–Q2 Q–B2

**28. KR–K1 B–R6** (Playing with fire. The Bishop has no right to leave its post on the long diagonal.) **29. RxR RxR 30. R–K1** (Instead, 30. B–B3! is strong.) **30. . . . B–B4 31.** RxR PxR **32. P–QN4 B–N3 33. B–B4 P–K4 34. B–Q2 B–Q5 35. B–K3 BxB 36. PxB Q–B3 37. K–B2 P–QN4 38. PxP PxP 39. P–K4 K–B2, Drawn.**

## Game 91

This encounter influenced the position of the leaders, since I was behind Reshevsky by one and a half points and a win for me would reduce the difference to half a point. But should Reshevsky win and remain undefeated, he would catch up with Smyslov. A draw would obviously satisfy none of the three.

Thoughts like these cross one's mind onstage before play begins.

The opening is the well-known King's Indian, in which both sides try for the initiative. The second phase, up to the 23rd move, has a maneuvering character, and it ends with a Black pawn on QR6 and a White one on K5.

In the next phase White tries to convert his initiative in the center and on the Kingside to a mating attack, and he conceives a remarkable combination with the sacrifice of a pawn, a Rook, and the Exchange; but Black ruins this plan by trading an enemy Knight. This is followed by several exchanges, whereupon Reshevsky's impetuous pawn-pushing enterprise begins to display certain shortcomings.

Struggles between Queens with opposite-color Bishops on the board are usually very sharp; in the final phase of this game Black maintains a mating threat to the last move, refusing to exchange Queens unless it should occur on QN7, in which case White would get a hopeless game.

Finally, it seems that Black will not get the win after all, but he finds a problemlike maneuver with his Queen, Bishop, and a pawn that puts White's pieces in complete zugzwang.

## King's Indian Defense

| S. Reshevsky | D. Bronstein | | |
|---|---|---|---|
| 1. P–Q4 | N–KB3 | 4. B–N2 | O–O |
| 2. P–QB4 | P–KN3 | 5. N–QB3 | P–Q3 |
| 3. P–KN3 | B–N2 | 6. N–B3 | QN–Q2 |
| | | 7. O–O | P–K4 |

| | | | | |
|---|---|---|---|---|
| 8. | P–K4 | R–K1 | 26. B–R4 | NxN |
| 9. | P–KR3 | PxP | 27. RxN | Q–B4 |
| 10. | NxP | N–B4 | | |
| 11. | R–K1 | P–QR4 | | |
| 12. | Q–B2 | P–B3 | | |
| 13. | B–K3 | KN–Q2 | | |
| 14. | QR–Q1 | P–R5 | | |
| 15. | N/4–K2 | Q–R4 | | |

The move on which Black's entire strategy in this phase is mainly based. It is very important not to allow White's Knight to get to KB6. The KP cannot be taken by the Bishop because White answers 28. RxB and then takes the Rook on Q8; but now White must think seriously about the defense of his KP.

White is attacking the QP, but Black's reply convinces him that the pawn would be advantageously won back by 16. ... N–K4; 17. P–N3 would only make things worse because of the surprise stroke 17. ... BxP, and the Bishop's capture would be followed by a check on B3, etc.

| | | |
|---|---|---|
| 28. | R/4–K4 | B–R3 |
| 29. | K–R1 | B–K3 |
| 30. | P–N5 | |

| | | |
|---|---|---|
| 16. | B–KB1 | N–K4 |
| 17. | N–Q4 | P–R6 |
| 18. | P–B4 | |

Beginning his combination. Reshevsky makes KB4 available for a Rook, which in turn gives its place to the Knight.

After making this active move Reshevsky offered a draw, although, all things considered, he must have been in a fighting mood and would have been upset had I accepted. His question, "Are you playing for a win?," seems more a type of reconnaissance that he uses when he wants to provoke a rash step.

| | | |
|---|---|---|
| 30. | ... | B–N2 |
| 31. | R–B4 | B–B4 |
| 32. | N–K4 | |

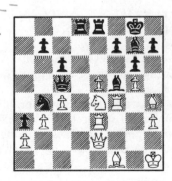

| | | |
|---|---|---|
| 18. | ... | N/K–Q2 |
| 19. | P–N3 | N–R3 |
| 20. | B–B2 | N/2–B4 |
| 21. | R–K3 | N–N5 |
| 22. | Q–K2 | B–Q2 |
| 23. | P–K5 | PxP |
| 24. | PxP | QR–Q1 |
| 25. | P–N4 | N–K3 |

White offers the sacrifice of his KP. It is tempting to take it and on the obvious Knight check to sacrifice the Queen for Rook, Knight, and pawn, with great activity for Black's pieces and good prospects of reinforcing his position later.

Reshevsky had a diabolical combination ready in case the pawn was accepted: 32. . . . QxKP? 33. RxB and: 1) 33. . . . QxR 34. N–B6ch BxN 35. RxRch RxR 36. QxRch K–N2 37. PxBch; 2) 33. . . . PxR 34. N–B6ch BxN 35. PxB!! QxR 36. Q–N2ch and mate.

The beauty of the combination is revealed in the second variation, in which White, already a Rook down, does not take the Queen on his 35th move but plays pawn takes Bishop to create an irresistible mating threat.

**32. . . .**      **BxN**

White's effort comes to nought.

**33. R/4xB**      **N–R3**
**34. P–K6**      **PxP**

Here Reshevsky again offered a draw, and this time I think he was serious.

Black's position is preferable due to his strong QRP, the exposed position of White's King, and the superiority of Black's Knight over White's bad Bishop.

**35. RxP**      **R–KB1!**
**36. R–K7**      **B–Q5**
**37. R/3–Q6**      **Q–B4**

**38. R–K8**      **N–B4**
**39. RxQR**      **NxR**
**40. RxRch**      **KxR**
**41. B–N3**

Reshevsky thought for a long time in adjourning and decided to give up the doomed pawn right away, believing that its capture by the Queen would lead to an opposite-color-Bishop endgame, and by the Knight to perpetual check: 41. . . . NxP 42. B–Q6ch K–N2 43. Q–K7ch.

**41. . . .**      **QxP**
**42. QxN**      **QxB**
**43. Q–B8ch**      **K–K2**

**44. Q–N4**

White wants very much to take the QNP, but surprisingly this would lead to immediate loss—a rare case of a King pushing back a Queen: 44. Qx Pch? K–Q1 45. Q–R8ch K–B2 46. Q–R5ch B–N3, hitting the Queen and threatening mate on N8.

Nevertheless, White's last check was useful. It forced the King to K2, and now Black's Queen cannot go to KB7 because of 45. Q–K2ch with exchange of Queens and an obvious draw.

| 44. . . . | Q–QB6 |
| 45. K–N2 | Q–N7ch |
| 46. Q–K2ch | K–Q3 |
| 47. K–B3 | B–B4 |
| 48. K–K4 | Q–Q5ch |
| 49. K–B3 | Q–B3ch |
| 50. K–N2 | K–B2 |
| 51. Q–B3 | Q–N7ch |
| 52. Q–K2 | Q–Q5 |
| 53. K–B3 | |

Neither player can display any initiative to trade Queens. If White takes on QN2 Black wins merely by creating another passed pawn on the Kingside. If Black takes on K7 the best he can do in the long run is to win the QRP, but that would not be enough to win the game because just then White's King would station itself on QB2 and prevent its enemy from getting out.

| 53. . . . | P–R4 |

The last reserves are called up into battle.

| 54. K–N2 | P–KN4 |
| 55. K–N3 | Q–B5ch |
| 56. K–N2 | P–N5 |
| 57. PxP | PxP |
| 58. K–R1 | |

If the pawn now advances to N6, then 59. B–R3 and there is no way for Black to visibly improve his position. The winning idea is based on zugzwang.

| 58. . . . | K–N3 |
| 59. K–N2 | K–B2 |
| 60. K–R1 | B–Q3 |
| 61. K–N1 | K–N3 |
| 62. Q–KN2 | B–B4ch |
| 63. K–R1 | Q–R3ch |
| 64. Q–R2 | Q–K6 |
| 65. P–N4 | B–Q5 |

Zugzwang is complete. Seeing no salvation, Reshevsky allowed his flag to fall, and he was credited with a loss.

# Round Fourteen

## Game 92

More than twenty theoretical moves are made in this game, the players adding little of their own to the opening books. The game may be rather boring for the reader, but it is enlivened on the 29th move by Gligoric's offer of his Queen for a Rook and Bishop. Although Black's pieces would be more valuable arithmetically, Reshevsky does not accept the sacrifice.

### Ruy Lopez

S. Gligoric     S. Reshevsky

1. P-K4 P-K4 2. N-KB3 N-QB3 3. B-N5 P-QR3 4. B-R4 N-B3 5. O-O B-K2 6. R-K1 P-QN4 7. B-N3 P-Q3 8. P-B3 O-O 9. P-KR3 N-QR4 10. B-B2 P-B4 11. P-Q4 Q-B2 12. QN-Q2 B-Q2 13. N-B1 KR-K1 14. PxKP PxP 15. N/3-R2 P-N3 16. N-K3 B-K3 17. N/2-N4 NxN 18. PxN QR-Q1 19. Q-B3 N-B5 20. N-Q5 BxN 21. PxB N-N3 22. B-K4 P-B5 23. B-Q2 R-Q3 24. QR-Q1 KR-Q1 (The opponents maneuver their pieces unhurriedly, which of course cannot disturb the balance.) 25. B-K3 N-R5 26. R-Q2 P-QR4 27. P-R3 N-B4 28. P-N5 P-B4 29. PxP e.p. RxBP 30. BxN QxB

If Black takes the Queen, there follows 31. BxB QxB 32. BxR, and now there is no minor

224

piece for the necessary blockade of White's passed QP. The Rook would have to attach itself to the pawn, and in the meantime White's Rooks would lay siege to the isolated KP. Black could achieve no more than a draw in that case.

**31. Q–K3 Q–B2 32. B–B3 B–Q3 33. Q–R6 Q–KN2 34. QxQch KxQ, Drawn.**

## Game 93
### Queen's Gambit

| M. Taimanov | P. Keres |
|---|---|
| 1. P–Q4 | N–KB3 |
| 2. P–QB4 | P–K3 |
| 3. N–QB3 | P–Q4 |
| 4. B–N5 | P–B4 |

Keres puts aside his favorite King's Indian and Nimzo-Indian defenses. For this tournament he has prepared a system with . . . P–QB4 at an early stage of the Queen's Gambit. He plays it with success against Stahlberg, Geller, and, in the last round, against Najdorf after 4. N–B3.

**5. P–K3**

A practical game is not a theoretical dispute. Taimanov undoubtedly knows that after 5. BPxP theory gives White the advantage in all the numerous ramifications from "a" to "z." In fact he won against Prins with this very variation in Stockholm 1952. Although it is true that Taimanov has studied the variation 5. BPxP well, he knows too that the last word has not been said, and he therefore chooses another way.

Do variations like the following actually confirm that 4. . . . P–B4 is contrary to chess logic?

1) 5. BPxP BPxP 6. QxP B–K2 7. P–K4 N–B3 8. Q–K3 NxQP 9. PxN BxB 10. P–B4 N–N5 11. O–O–O B–K2 12. PxP Q–B2 13. PxPch KxP 14. N–B3 NxPch; or

2) 5. BPxP BPxP 6. QxP B–K2 7. P–K4 N–B3 8. Q–Q2 PxP 9. BxN BxB 10. PxP N–K4 11. B–N5ch, etc.; or

3) 5. BPxP BPxP 6. QxP B–K2 7. P–K4 N–B3 8. Q–Q2 NxKP 9. NxN PxP 10. BxB QxB 11. QxP O–O 12. P–B3 N–N5 13. Q–KN5, etc.

It remains to be added that after 5. BPxP Black may even play the so-called Peruvian Variation, 5. . . . Q–N3 6. BxN QxNP, etc.

The most exact knowledge of opening theory is no insurance against the unexpected over the board. That is why grandmasters often avoid the "best" continuations, preferring their own systems even if they have not been accepted by theory.

| 5. . . . | BPxP |
|---|---|
| 6. KPxP | B–K2 |

**7. N–B3          0–0**
**8. R–B1**

A loss of time, delaying the development of his Kingside pieces. The position has a semiopen character, and until his King is hidden away White must be careful. The natural move here is 8. B–Q3.

**8. . . .          P–QN3!**
**9. B–Q3          N–B3**
**10. 0–0          N–QN5**
**11. PxP!**

A positional trap. If Black is tempted to take the Bishop by 11. . . . NxB 12. QxN PxP White will have a clear advantage after 13. N–K5: the Knight on K5 will be stronger than either Bishop. White can set a tactical trap by 11. N–K5 and, if Black takes the Bishop, 12. N–B6. The variation 12. . . . Q–Q2 13. NxBch QxN 14. QxN B–R3 15. P–QN3 leads to active play with about even chances. But the trap consists of Black's opportunity to win a pawn along the way: instead of 12. . . . Q–Q2, 12. . . . NxNP 13. Q–K2 Q–Q2 14. NxBch QxN 15. QxN B–R3.

On the 15th move, however, White does not take the Knight on N2 but the doubly defended pawn (15. NxP), after which Black's position falls apart.

Black would have to settle for the main variation (11. N–K5 NxB 12. QxN B–N2), since the immediate 11. . . . B–N2 12.

B–N1 would leave White with good prospects of attacking KN7 and KR7.

**11. . . .          N/3xP**
**12. BxB          QxB**
**13. B–K4          B–N2**
**14. R–K1          QR–B1**
**15. Q–Q2          P–KR3**

A prophylactic waiting move. An exchange of minor pieces is coming, and White wants to provoke . . . NxN in order to retake on QB3 with the pawn and strengthen his QP; but Black has no objection to this, for the pawn group as a whole will not be strengthened. Still, Black is in no hurry to trade; he can do that after White's P–QR3.

**16. P–QR3          NxN**
**17. BxB          QxB**
**18. NPxN          N–B3**
**19. Q–Q3          KR–Q1**

A classic position for the launching of an offensive against the QBP and QP. White must consider his opponent's specific threats and the ways to meet them. If White plays passively Black will have several ways to attack:

1) N–R4–B5, blockading the QBP and pressing the QRP;

2) maneuvering the Rooks along the QB- and Q-files;

3) undermining the QP by P–QN4, P–QR4, and P–N5.

Black's final plan will depend mainly on whether White goes into a deep defense, chooses play in the center by P–QB4 and P–Q5, or attacks Black's King. Taimanov postpones his decision for one move while he opens a little window for his King.

| 20. P–R3 | R–B2 |
|---|---|
| 21. R–K4 | |

A courageous idea. Perhaps 21. P–QB4 is objectively stronger, but Taimanov does not hope to defend his hanging pawns against Keres. He decides to hold the defense at QB3 and simultaneously prepare a Kingside attack.

| 21. . . . | N–R4 |
|---|---|
| 22. N–Q2 | |

Advancing the Knight to K5 is attractive, of course, but it leads to loss of the Exchange.

| 22. . . . | Q–Q4 |
|---|---|

Keres insistently invites his opponent to play P–QB4 in view of the threatened invasion of QR7. Taimanov, however, does not deviate from his plan, even though just now P–QB4 is imperative.

**23. R–N4**

White probes Black's vulnerable KNP. He plans to attack it twice; the Rook in front, the Queen behind, fully in accord with the laws of chess science. Meanwhile he threatens RxPch followed by Q–N3ch and QxR, as well as 24. N–K4.

How unsafe Black's situation can be if he is unwilling to weaken his pawn structure is seen in the variation 23. . . . N–B5 24. N–K4 N–K4 25. Q–N3 NxR 26. QxR. In this line the Rook sacrifice on N7 boomerangs: 25. RxPch KxR 26. Q–N3ch N–N3! 27. QxR QxN! 28. QxR N–B5 with unavoidable mate.

| 23. . . . | P–B4 |
|---|---|
| 24. R–N3 | R/1–QB1 |

Black cannot break through to QB6 without the participation of the pawns, for which the Rook move is useless. 25. . . .

P–K4, torpedoing the QP, would be the fitting conclusion of Black's strategy. Close examination of the variations arising from 25. QxP PxP has convinced me that they are all advantageous for Black. But now the Rook on KN3 returns to the K-file, fixing Black's new weakness on K3. The Rook's journey—K1–K4–KN4–KN3–K3—proves to have been justified.

### 25. R–K3        N–B5

Black is too anxious to simplify the game and obtain a win purely by technical means. If Keres wants to continue playing for a win he has to put White to the test with Q–Q3 or Q–R7.

### 26. NxN        RxN
### 27. Q–Q2

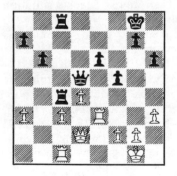

27. . . .        Q–B3

It is hard for Black to keep his KP, for White is not only attacking it directly but also constantly threatening to break through by R–K5 and P–Q5; so Keres decides to trade his KP for White's QBP. But he chooses the wrong moment; R/1–B3 is better first, and then to retreat the Queen to Q2 or even Q3.

For a broader evaluation of such positions, it is useful for the reader to know that if Black's pawn were on KB2 instead of KB4 White would have much greater difficulty in view of Black's P–QN4, P–QR4, and P–N5.

### 28. R/1–K1        RxBP
### 29. RxP          Q–B5
### 30. Q–B4         R–B8

White's pieces have developed great activity, and it is hard for Black to foresee and neutralize all of White's possible plans. For instance, the threat here was R–K8ch. So first of all Black reduces the number of pieces on the board.

### 31. QxBP        QxP
### 32. RxR         RxRch
### 33. K–R2

In a battle of Queens and heavy pieces, the feasibility of concealing the King must be considered first, for the initiative in such endings belongs to the side that can combine the advance of his pawns with threats to the enemy King. White's advantage in the present situation is nothing more than the presence of his KBP and KRP.

Especially important is the KBP, which protects the King from checks on the KR2–QN8 diagonal. The difference in the situations of the Kings is clearly seen in the diagram.

**33. . . .          Q–Q2**
**34. Q–K4**

**34. . . .          R–B1**

Keres is forced to go into a difficult defense, which he handles very skillfully.

**35. P–B4          R–B1**
**36. Q–K5**

Inviting his opponent into a Rook endgame a pawn down: 36. . . . RxP 37. R–K7 Q–Q5 38. RxPch K–R1 39. QxQ RxQ 40. RxP. Black can probably exchange the Queenside pawns, which would lead to a draw, but Keres does not want to take that chance. He has in mind a more simple method of repulsing White's attack; as so often happens, alas, it turns out to be more complicated.

**36. . . .          Q–Q7**

Keres assumes that the KBP is indefensible—for example, 37. K–N3 Q–Q6ch—but he fails to see that the advance of this pawn secures KN6 for White and offers him a new opportunity to attack the KNP. It is better to attack the KBP from the other side—36. . . . Q–KB2, also attacking the square KB4, and if 37. P–N3 Q–B4.

**37. P–B5          Q–R4**

In serious time pressure, Keres does not risk 37. . . . R–B2 38. R–K8ch K–R2 39. Q–N8 RxP, and for the sake of exchanging Queens he allows his Queenside pawns to be doubled. This might have led to his defeat.

**38. QxQ          PxQ**
**39. P–N4**

Taimanov again defends his KBP, but for a moment he lets the initiative slip from his hands and exposes his King. This last circumstance allows Keres to create threats to the QRP and force a draw. With the more active 39. R–K5 Taimanov would retain an extra pawn and real winning chances in all variations.

**39. . . .          R–N1**

The Rook swims out to open waters, and, since the pawns are even, White has no advantage at all. Drawn.

## Game 94
### Nimzo-Indian Defense

M. Najdorf        V. Smyslov

1. P–Q4 N–KB3 2. P–QB4 P–K3 3. N–QB3 B–N5 4. P–K3 P–B4 5. B–Q3 O–O 6. N–B3 P–QN3 7. O–O B–N2 8. P–QR3 (B–Q2 is better here.) 8. ... BxN 9. PxB B–K5 10. B–K2 N–B3 11. N–Q2 B–N3 12. N–N3 (12. P–B3 is more in the spirit of the position.) 12. ... N–K5 13. Q–K1 N–Q3 14. Q–Q1, Drawn.

## Game 95
### Queen's Indian Defense

T. Petrosian        Y. Geller

1. P–QB4 N–KB3 2. N–QB3 P–K3 3. N–B3 P–B4 4. P–KN3 P–QN3 5. B–N2 B–N2 6. O–O B–K2 7. P–Q4 PxP 8. QxP (8. NxP promises greater chances to maintain the advantage, but the Queen's Indian Defense is generally reputed to be a drawish opening.) 8. ... O–O 9. R–Q1 N–B3 10. Q–B4 Q–N1 11. P–QN3 R–Q1 12. QxQ QRxQ 13. B–N2 P–QR3 14. N–Q2, Drawn.

## Game 96

This, the most beautiful game in the Zurich tournament, called forth an enthusiastic reaction from the entire chess world. "Once in a hundred years," "unique in chess literature," "a splendid Queen sacrifice"— thus did the commentators of various countries express their opinions; and the spectators in the tournament hall reacted to the Queen sacrifice even more loudly. I can add only that the Averbakh–Kotov game will enter the golden treasury of chess art.

### Old Indian Defense

Y. Averbakh        A. Kotov

| | |
|---|---|
| 1. P–Q4 | N–KB3 |
| 2. P–QB4 | P–Q3 |
| 3. N–KB3 | QN–Q2 |
| 4. N–B3 | P–K4 |
| 5. P–K4 | B–K2 |
| 6. B–K2 | |

In the previous round Petrosian got a good game as Black in an analogous defense against

Kotov. In this tournament Kotov usually replied to 1. P–Q4 with 1. . . . P–Q4 or played the King's Indian Defense with . . . P–KN3, but in this game he takes up Petrosian's idea and without warning plays it against Averbakh.

In the above-mentioned game White continued 6. P–KN3 and fianchettoed his Bishop, but here Averbakh chooses to develop differently with B–K2. This would make sense in connection with the later advance of the Queenside pawns, but he does not carry his plan to its logical conclusion.

| 6. . . . | O–O |
| 7. O–O | P–B3 |
| 8. Q–B2 | R–K1 |
| 9. R–Q1 | B–B1 |
| 10. R–N1 | P–QR4 |
| 11. P–Q5! | |

P–QR3 is not good at this point because Black exchanges in the center, exposing the KP, and then advances his QRP to impede White's P–QN4.

| 11. . . . | N–B4 |
| 12. B–K3 | Q–B2 |
| 13. P–KR3 | B–Q2 |
| 14. QR–B1 | P–KN3 |
| 15. N–Q2 | QR–N1 |

The position is now dynamically balanced, and great skill is demanded on both sides. Black can prepare a diversion either on the Queenside by KR–QB1, PxP, and P–QN4, or on the Kingside by K–R1, N–N1,

and P–KB4. Neither, in itself, is of mortal danger to White if he takes precautions. The only danger is that while occupied with threats on one side he will miss the critical moment on the other.

| 16. N–N3 | NxN |
| 17. QxN | P–B4 |

This is a loud declaration that Black has chosen the Kingside as his main theater of operations. White should now prepare P–QR3 and P–QN4 without losing a minute; for instance, 18. Q–B2 K–R1 19. P–R3 N–N1 20. B–N4, and if 20. . . . N–B3 he takes the Bishop and opens the QN-file.

| 18. K–R2 | K–R1 |
| 19. Q–B2 | N–N1 |
| 20. B–N4 | N–R3 |
| 21. BxB | |

White declines the opportunity to repeat the position (21. B–K2 N–N1), apparently believing that his chances are not inferior. He would be right if he played P–R3, R–QN1, and P–QN4. But he is not right, for he has a completely different continuation in mind.

| 21. . . . | QxB |
| 22. Q–Q2 | N–N1 |
| 23. P–KN4 | |

Averbakh goes to put out the fire with gasoline. Now . . . P–B4 will be twice as strong because Black will be able to take either of two pawns whereas

White can take the KBP with neither.

| 23. | . . . | P–B4 |
|-----|-------|------|
| 24. | P–B3 | B–K2 |
| 25. | R–KN1 | R–KB1 |
| 26. | QR–KB1 | R–B2 |
| 27. | NPxP | |

This move, which was questioned by many commentators, cannot be considered an error; it is a continuation of the plan begun much earlier. Averbakh, having made up his mind to attack on the KN-file, is opening it. This is entirely logical. But the KRP should be on R2.

| 27. | . . . | PxP |
|-----|-------|-----|
| 28. | R–N2 | P–B5 |
| 29. | B–B2 | R–B3 |
| 30. | N–K2 | |

It is usually thought that the prerequisites of chess creativity are logic, accurate calculation of variations, and technique, the latter including theoretical knowledge. There is a fourth component, however, perhaps the most attractive, although it is often forgotten. I have in mind intuition, or, if you like, imagination.

Sometimes positions occur that cannot be evaluated on the basis of such general principles as pawn weaknesses, open lines, better development, etc., for these positions are unequal in many areas and cannot be measured precisely. Similarly, a calculation of the variations cannot always be attempted. Suppose that White has six or seven different continuations and that Black has five or six replies to any of them. It is not difficult to understand that even a genius cannot carry his calculations as far as the fourth move. It is then that intuition, imagination, is called into play, which brings to the art of chess its most beautiful combinations and which permits chess players to experience the genuine joy of creation.

It is not true that imaginative games were played only in the time of Morphy, Anderssen, and Tchigorin, and that today everything is based on positional principles and calculation. I am convinced that the games that received beauty prizes in this very tournament were not calculated to the end in all variations. Imagination was and remains one of the foundations of chess creativity, a vivid demonstration of which we are about to see.

**30. . . .          QxPch**

Here is where the weakness of the KRP shows up. The idea of Kotov's remarkable combination, which was prepared by all his previous play, consists of dragging White's King to its KB5, where it will be defenseless against Black's two Rooks, Knight, and Bishop, while five White pieces remain deep in the rear and can only watch from a distance.

| 31. | KxQ | R–R3ch |
| 32. | K–N4 | N–B3ch |
| 33. | K–B5 | |

Like a rabbit hypnotized by a boa constrictor, the King moves unwillingly to its place of death. To understand the next stage of the game it should be kept in mind that Kotov has very little time left and, naturally, does not want to ruin such a beautiful and unusual game with a careless move. He therefore decides to give a few checks and bring the game to the 40th move and adjournment. That there are mating chances in this position is unquestionable, and Kotov probably saw them in outline at his 30th move.

| 33. | . . . | N–Q2 |

And here is confirmation. Had the Queen sacrifice been "accurately calculated," Kotov would have preferred Stahlberg's later suggestion . . . N–

N5, and there is no R–N5. After 33. . . . N–N5 White would have had to sustain colossal losses to avoid mate.

**34. R–N5**

The only defense to the threatened mate in three: R–KB1, R–KN1, R–B3.

| 34. | . . . | R–B1ch |
| 35. | K–N4 | N–B3ch |
| 36. | K–B5 | N–N1ch |
| 37. | K–N4 | N B3ch |

The position having been repeated twice, Black takes a pawn and the count starts anew.

| 38. | K–B5 | NxQPch |
| 39. | K–N4 | N–B3ch |
| 40. | K–B5 | N–N1ch |
| 41. | K–N4 | N–B3ch |
| 42. | K–B5 | N–N1ch |
| 43. | K–N4 | BxR |

Black threatens 44. . . . B–K2 and 45. . . . N–B3ch 46. K–B5 N–Q2ch 47. K–N4 R–N1ch with mate next move. White has two tempos in which to organize a defense, but he cannot make use of them because all communication between the upper and lower halves of the board is cut off by pawn barriers or by the fire of Black's pieces. Relatively "best" is 44. B–K3 B–K2 45. BxKBP PxB 46. NxP R–R5ch 47. K–N3 RxN, but even the best is quite hopeless for White.

**44. KxB**

**44. . . .        R–B2**

Threatening mate in two: R–N2ch and R–B3; there is no escape by 45. NxP R–N2ch 46. N–N6ch R/2xNch 47. K–B5 N–K2 mate. White is forced to give up yet another piece.

**45. B–R4        R–N3ch**
**46. K–R5        R/2–N2**

**47. B–N5        RxBch**
**48. K–R4        N–B3**
**49. N–N3**

Carrying out sorties to rescue the surrounded King, the White detachments die out one by one.

**49. . . .        RxN**
**50. QxQP        R/6–N3**
**51. Q–N8ch**

White gives his first check in reply to Black's thirteen, and after

**51. . . .        R–N1**
**White resigns**

A magnificent game, the deserving recipient of the first prize for beauty.

## Game 97
### French Defense

**L. Szabo        I. Boleslavsky**

1. P–K4 P–K3 2. P–Q4 P–Q4 3. N–Q2 P–QB4 4. KPxP KPxP 5. B–N5ch B–Q2 6. Q–K2ch B–K2 7. PxP N–KB3 8. BxBch (The logical continuation of White's opening plan is to hold the pawn by 8. N–N3 O–O 9. B–K3. But now Black is better developed and the BP will soon be recaptured.) 8. . . . QNxB 9. N–N3 O–O 10. N–R3 (An unfortunate

idea: the Knight does not succeed in getting to KB4.) 10. . . . R–K1 11. O–O BxP 12. Q–Q1 B–N3 13. P–B3 P–KR3 14. B–B4 N–K4 15. BxN RxB 16. R–K1 RxRch 17. QxR Q–Q3 18. R–Q1, Drawn.

Black has the advantage. The following curious combination is a possibility here: 18. . . . R–K1 19. Q–Q2 N–K5 20. QxP? NxKBP!! 21. QxQ NxRch 22. QxB R–K8 mate.

## Game 98
### King's Indian Defense

| M. Euwe | G. Stahlberg |
|---------|-------------|
| 1. P–Q4 | N–KB3 |
| 2. P–QB4 | P–KN3 |
| 3. P–KN3 | P–B3 |

In reply to the fianchetto of the Bishop, Black advances his QBP and prepares P–Q4 in order to set up a symmetrical position with an immobile pawn structure. Stahlberg thus issues a challenge to Euwe the opening theoretician: it will be very difficult in that situation for White to obtain an advantage.

Euwe does not attempt to refute the opening, which is impossible, but to destroy the strategic balance and obtain more active play, believing that the first move must then count. Stahlberg willingly agrees to Euwe's proposal, and the two players produce something rather like an adventure story.

| 4. P–Q4 | PxP |
| 5. PxP | P–Q3 |

There are insufficient grounds for Black's sortie 5. . . . Q–R4ch 6. N–B3 N–K5, which is prettily refuted by 7. Q–Q4 NxN 8. B–Q2 QxQP 9. QxN!

| 6. B–N2 | B–N2 |
| 7. N–QB3 | O–O |
| 8. N–B3 | QN–Q2 |

It is not quite clear where this Knight is headed. No good path beyond Q2 can be seen for it. The Bishop should be brought out first by 8. . . . B–N5 9. N–Q4 Q–B1!

| 9. O–O | N–N3 |
| 10. P–QR4 | |

Euwe, like Tarrasch in his time, cannot sit still while an enemy Knight stands on N3. The Knight stands badly enough, however, and there is no need to disturb it. The quiet 10. N–Q4 and 11. P–QN3 would emphasize the Knight's limited mobility, while the fianchetto of the second Bishop would complement the harmoniousness of White's ensemble.

Euwe intends to develop the Bishop to K3. That, no doubt, is by way of avoiding the temptation to move the KP.

| 10. . . . | B–N5 |
| 11. N–Q4 | P–QR3 |

Stahlberg probably wanted to play 11. . . . Q–B1 here, but he did not like 12. P–R5 N–B5 13. P–R6, and White's Knight seizes the important QB6-square.

| 12. P–R3 | B–B1 |
| 13. P–N3 | B–Q2 |

Stahlberg avoided the immediate retreat to Q2 in fear of 13. Q–N3, and Black's attempt to win the QP would have ended sadly: after 12. . . . B–Q2 13. Q–N3 KNxP 14. NxN BxN 15. B–R6 Black would have had to cede the exchange, for otherwise White's threats to the Knight on QN6 combined with his mate threat on KN7 would have been extremely unpleasant. If Black did not take the QP after 13. Q–N3 but continued 13. . . . Q–B2, then after 14. B–K3 N–B5 15. KR–B1 a disagreeable pin would have appeared on the QB-file.

Thus Black's Bishop cannot find a point of support, and unable to apply its power it wanders sadly along the QB1–KR6 diagonal. Three moves were spent to shift it from QB1 to Q2! This is reason enough for White to assume the offensive. 14. P–R5 would push Black's Knight back to QB1, where it would break the coordination of his Rooks and would end up having to wander around in the corner.

| 14. | B–K3 | R–B1 |
| 15. | Q–Q2 | R–B4 |

The conflict begins.

Stahlberg is probably attracted not so much by the prospect of winning the QP as by the piquant position of the Rook on B4, where it seems in danger but is in fact unassailable. It's a pity he does not trade the Rook

for a Knight and pawn at once by 15. . . . RxN 16. QxR QNxQP, for he can hardly expect to do better in his cramped position. This trade remains a possibility for the next two moves, but Stahlberg obstinately keeps his Rook on B4.

**16. N–B6**

A bold invasion! The Knight can be taken by the Rook, the Bishop, or the pawn. Which is best? Stahlberg takes the line of greatest resistance and gets two minor pieces for the Rook instead of one, but his opponent forms an extremely dangerous passed pawn. Possible is 16. . . . BxN 17. PxB RxN 18. QxR N–Q4 19. P–B7 or 16. . . . KNxP 17. NxQ BxN, etc. White retains the advantage in either case.

| 16. . . . | | PxN |
| 17. | BxR | PxB |
| 18. | PxP | B–K3 |
| 19. | QxQ | RxQ |
| 20. | QR–Q1 | R–QB1 |

The Rook must not be exchanged under any circum-

stances, but QB1 should be reserved for the Knight; the Rook
should go to K1.

| 21. | P–R5 | N–R1 |
|---|---|---|
| 22. | N–R4 | |

Another pretty combination.
Euwe offers his QNP, but taking
it would be answered by 23.
N–N6 and White wins a piece
or queens a pawn. Black avoids
this continuation, of course, but
he loses his QBP.

| 22. | . . . | N–B2 |
|---|---|---|
| 23. | NxP | N/3–Q4 |

Black sees that it is necessary
to bring the reserves, which are
sleeping on the Kingside, into
the fight as soon as possible,
and with this in mind he gives
up one more pawn. However,
the situation does not yet require such drastic methods.
Better is . . . N–K1, with . . .
N–Q3 and . . . B–B3 in view.

| 24. | NxP | NxN |
|---|---|---|
| 25. | BxN | BxP |

It is already tempting to exchange Bishops and take the
QBP, but this would lead to a
rapid finish: one White Rook
would invade the eighth rank
and the other would support the
advance of the QNP.

| 26. | B–N2 | B–K3 |
|---|---|---|

The exchange of Bishops is
not playable here either, for
the same reason.

| 27. | R–N1 | B–B6 |
|---|---|---|

First he should find out
where Black's Rook goes after
27. . . . B–B4—it has no great
choice. Stahlberg seems worried that White will agree to a
draw by repeating moves, and
it would be a pity to abandon a
game that promises to be so
very interesting.

| 28. | KR–Q1 | B–QN5 |
|---|---|---|
| 29. | R–Q4 | B–KB4 |
| 30. | QR–Q1 | B–Q3 |
| 31. | R–QB4 | B–K3 |
| 32. | B–Q5 | BxB |
| 33. | RxB | |

Black's overly innocuous
maneuvers have allowed White
to improve the position of his
pieces. One of Black's drawing
chances lay in not trading his
light-square Bishop, making it
possible to give up two pieces
for a Rook and pawn and keeping opposite-color Bishops. It
would have been better, therefore, to put the Bishop on K3
after the preliminary . . . N–B2.

| 33. | . . . | R–N1 |
|---|---|---|
| 34. | P–QN4 | |

Three connected passed pawns display awesome strength when they advance, sweeping all before them. In certain cases such pawns win against two Rooks and even against a Queen and Rook. Stahlberg is therefore forced to take the QNP. He cannot take it with his Rook, since after exchanging Rooks White plays R–QN5–N6 and queens his RP. Taking it with the Bishop is not good because of 35. P–B7. Luckily, Stahlberg is still able to extricate himself from his difficult situation by giving back two pieces for a Rook and pawn, leading to a slightly inferior Rook ending.

| | |
|---|---|
| 34. . . . | NxP |
| 35. RxB | PxR |
| 36. P–B7 | R–QB1 |
| 37. RxN | RxP |
| 38. R–QR4 | |

The game enters its third and most interesting stage. The history of chess competition provides a wealth of material on the theory and practice of Rook endgames; the present endgame, conducted by both opponents on a high creative plane, belongs among the best. Black has a difficult problem in that he must struggle against an outside passed pawn, but he has his counterchances: the possibility of creating a similar pawn on the KR-file, as well as

the fact that there is little material on the board. This latter circumstance sometimes allows the exchange of all but one pawn, giving up the Rook for the opponent's last pawn, and then forcing the opponent to repay the debt in full.

In the comments that follow I have made considerable use of analysis by Euwe.

| | |
|---|---|
| 38. . . . | K–B1 |

He wants to get his King to K4 via N2–B3, but he cannot: 38. . . . K–N2 39. K–N2 K–B3 40. K–B3 K–K4 41. P–R6 R–R2 42. R–R5ch P–Q4 43. P–K4 and White wins a pawn. The reason this turns out favorably for White is that his Rook is stationed behind his far-advanced pawn and has free mobility; this cannot be said of Black's Rook, which stands in front of the passed pawn and whose squares diminish as the enemy pawn advances. This is generally a characteristic factor in evaluating Rook endings, and here it is the main theme of the struggle.

| | |
|---|---|
| 39. K–N2 | K–K2 |
| 40. K–B3 | K–Q2 |

**41. K–K4          R–R2**
**42. K–Q5**

If Black can create a passed pawn on the KR-file his situation will not be so bad.

**42. . . .          P–R4**
**43. P–B4**

Euwe already foresees Black's planned P–B3, P–N4, and P–R4, and he wants to be sure of establishing an outpost on KB5, which after the mutual liquidation of passed pawns will leave him with winning chances.

**43. . . .          R–R3**

Here, according to Euwe's analysis, it is best to set about creating a passed pawn immediately by . . . P–B3, and then:

1) 44. P–R6 P–N4 45. P–B5 P–R5 46. PxP PxP—

a) 47. RxP RxP 48. R–R7ch K–K1 49. K–K6 P–Q4ch 50. KxP R–R4ch with a draw;

b) 47. K–K4 K–B3 48. K–B4 K–N4 49. R–R3 RxP 50. RxRch KxR 51. K–N4 K–N4 52. KxP K–B4 and the pawn ending is drawn because Black's King can get back to defend the BP.

2) 44. R–R3 P–N4 45. P–B5 P–R5 46. PxP PxP 47. K–K4 P–R6 48. K–B3 P–Q4 49. K–N3 K–Q3 50. KxP K–K4 with a draw.

3) 44. P–K4 R–R3, with the same idea as in the game, but with an extra move for Black.

**44. P–K4**

The King should not be deprived of this square, which is important in the following variation: 44. R–R2 P–B3 45. R–R3 P–N4 46. P–B5 P–R5 47. PxP PxP 48. K–K4 P–R6 49. K–B3 P–R7 50. K–N2 K–B3 51. KxP K–N4 52. K–N3 RxP 53. RxRch KxR 54. K–R4 and White takes the BP and can queen one move before Black. The same thing happens in 48. . . . K–B3 49. K–B4 K–N4 50. K–N4 RxP 51. RxRch, etc. But now that the pawn is keeping White's King out, Black can enter this variation, which he does.

**44. . . .          P–B3**
**45. R–R2          P–N4**
**46. P–B5          P–R5**
**47. PxP           PxP**
**48. K–B4          R–R1**

The crisis of this remarkable ending and also of the entire game. Stahlberg is counting on the opportunity to support his KRP and does not seem to realize that it is precisely the illogical 48. . . . R–R2 that would hold the draw, as shown in Euwe's analysis: 49. P–R6 K–B3 and now:

1) 50. R–R3 P–R6 51. RxP RxP 52. R–R6 K–Q2 53. R–R7ch K–K1 54. K–Q5 R–R4ch 55. KxP R–K4, with a draw;

2) 50. K–Q4 P–R6 51. R–R3 P–R7 52. R–R1 K–Q2 53. K–Q5 P–R8=Q 54. RxQ RxP 55. R–R7ch K–K1 56. K–K6 P–Q4ch 57. KxP R–R4ch 58. K–Q4 R–K4 with a draw.

With Black's Rook on R1, the White pawn gets to R7 and then, as in variation 2, White checks on R7 after trading pawns, winning the Rook.

**49. P–R6        K–B3**
**50. P–R7        P–R6**

The attempt to trade passed pawns by 50. . . . K–N2 51. R–R2 RxP 52. RxP leads to

Black's defeat, for his King has no time to defend the pawn— 52. . . . K–B3 53. R–R6 R–KB2 54. R–R8 R–K2 55. K–Q4 R–KB2 56. R–KN8 and Black is in zugzwang.

**51. K–Q4        K–B2**

If Black advances his pawn to the seventh rank, White does not take it at once but gives a preliminary Rook check on QB2, forcing the King back to the QN-file, and wins easily.

**52. K–Q5        K–Q2**
**53. R–R3        P–R7**
**54. R–R1**

Underscoring all the minuses of Black's position, which now cannot be improved; for example, on 54. . . . P–R8=Q 55. RxQ RxP 56. R–R7ch White wins the Rook. If Black first puts his King on the first rank, White places his King in opposition, creating the threat of mate after the trade of the KRP. If 54. . . . K–K2, then obviously 55. K–B6 and K–N7. Black still plays awhile a pawn down, but this is clearly hopeless.

**54. . . .        R–K1**
**55. R–R1        R–K4ch**
**56. K–Q4        R–R4**
**57. RxP         K–B3**
**58. R–R7        R–R5ch**

Stahlberg can give his opponent the chance to finish the game with an elegant combination involving two successive Queen sacrifices: 58. . . . P–Q4

59. P–K5 R–R5ch 60. K–B3 PxP 61. P–B6 K–Q3 62. P–B7 K–K2 63. P–B8=Qch KxQ 64. P–R8=Qch RxQ 65. R–R8ch. He prefers to lose in a more prosaic manner.

59. K–K3 R–R6ch 60. K–B4 R–R8 61. R–KB7 K–B4 62. RxP RxP 63. R–K6 R–R8 64. P–B6 K–B3 65. K–B5 K–Q2 66. R–K7ch K–Q1 67. K–K6, Black resigns.

# Round Fifteen

## Game 99
### Sicilian Defense

| I. Boleslavsky | M. Euwe |
|---|---|
| 1. P–K4 | P–QB4 |
| 2. N–KB3 | N–QB3 |
| 3. P–Q4 | PxP |
| 4. NxP | N–B3 |
| 5. N–QB3 | P–Q3 |
| 6. B–K2 | P–K4 |

Euwe plays the Boleslavsky System against its inventor—a psychological ploy that is often successful. The ex-champion of the world adds a little science to his psychological preparation and improves the well-known variation on the 14th move.

Boleslavsky conducts the game quietly, at times even timidly, and Euwe is able to equalize completely.

| 7. N–N3 | B–K2 |
|---|---|
| 8. O–O | O–O |
| 9. B–K3 | B–K3 |
| 10. B–B3 | N–QR4 |
| 11. NxN | QxN |
| 12. Q–Q2 | KR–B1 |
| 13. KR–Q1 | Q–N5 |
| 14. QR–N1 | P–KR3 |

The players are on a well-traveled road; this whole variation was encountered several times in the Stockholm tournament in 1952. Black continued 14. . . . P–QR3, but after 15. P–QR3 Q–B5 White could pin the Knight by 16. B–N5.

Black's move, anticipating the Bishop's attack, preserves the Knight's freedom of action; for example, . . . N–KR2 intending . . . B–N4, or . . . N–Q2–B4. In the Stockholm games Black had to take the time to defend the Bishop by . . . Q–B2 in order to break the pin, then retreated the Knight to K1.

| 15. P–QR3 | Q–B5 |
|---|---|
| 16. QR–B1 | P–R3 |

| 17. | B–K2 | Q–B2 |
|---|---|---|
| 18. | P–B3 | N–Q2 |

A surprise. Shouldn't Black be controlling Q4 with two pieces so that when White occupies this square he will be forced after the trades to retake with a pawn and relinquish his attack on Black's QP? But now Black consents to give up his "good" Bishop for White's Knight, and White will apparently be able to penetrate to Q5 with a piece. However, Euwe mobilizes his Queenside pawns, occupies QB4 with a Knight, and parries White's attempt to get a Bishop to Q5.

| 19. | B–B1 | P–QN4 |
|---|---|---|
| 20. | P–QR4 | |

Boleslavsky joins the battle for his Q4. He disturbs the Black pawn in order to provoke Black to exchange on QR5 or play P–N5 so that White will be able to play B–QB4.

| 20. | . . . | P–N5 |
|---|---|---|
| 21. | N–Q5 | BxN |
| 22. | QxB | N–B4 |
| 23. | P–QN3 | B–N4 |

Black takes the opportunity presented by the previous moves to exchange White's good Bishop, undisturbed by the fact that his QP is left apparently defenseless.

| 24. | BxB | PxB |
|---|---|---|
| 25. | K–R1 | |

Indirect defense is a common technical device, either as one of the elements in a combination or as a link in a chain of maneuvers. In the diagram position the QP is indirectly defended, since if 25. QxQP QxQ 26. RxQ Black unexpectedly takes the QNP, now safely protected by the Queen and the QBP. The endgame after 26. . . . NxNP 27. R–N1 N–Q5 28. RxNP NxQBP 29. R–N7 N–K6 or 28. BxP RxP 29. RxP N–K7ch would not exactly be a win for White; still, that is what he should play because Black would not have an easy defense.

| 25. | . . . | P–R4 |
|---|---|---|
| 26. | P–R3 | QR–N1 |
| 27. | B–N5 | R–Q1 |
| 28. | P–B3 | |

Creating a passed pawn is a logical plan, but the pawn will be difficult to advance: White's Bishop, which should support it, will itself have no point of support.

| 28. | . . . | PxP |
| 29. | RxP | Q–K2 |
| 30. | Q–B4 | P–N3 |
| 31. | P–QN4 | PxP |
| 32. | QxP | K–N2 |
| 33. | Q–B4 | Q–R2 |
| 34. | R–B2 | N–K3 |
| 35. | Q–B3 | N–Q5 |

Euwe has accomplished one of the main ideas of the Boleslavsky System, the occupation of Q5 by a Knight. The QRP and the QP are roughly equal, but Black's pieces are better posted and White already has to fight for a draw.

| 36. | R–N2 | KR–QB1 |
| 37. | Q–Q2 | K–B3 ! |
| 38. | R–QB1 | RxRch |
| 39. | QxR | Q–B4 |
| 40. | Q–Q2 | R–QB1 |
| 41. | K–R2 | Q–R6 |

The sealed move. After analysis the players agreed to a draw without resuming play. Black is actively placed, but Euwe believes the QRP gives White sufficient counterchances.

## Game 100

Castling on opposite wings usually portends pawn attacks against the respective Kings. The distinctive positions arising from the Sämisch System in the King's Indian Defense are exceptions to this rule; there the players, castled on opposite wings, frequently mobilize the pawns in front of their own King. The present game is an example of this kind of play. With the center closed and the pawn chains immobilized, Black castles on the Kingside and organizes a breakthrough on KN5, for which he plays P–KB4–5, P–KN4, P–KR4, and P–KN5; White, at the same time, even does his opponent the favor of opening the QN-file in front of his own King. The original play by both sides results in breakthroughs on opposite flanks, devious piece maneuvers, and sharp mutual attacks.

The unusual strategic ideas, the players' courageous and resourceful play, the beautiful final combination—all this makes for an especially interesting game.

# King's Indian Defense

| A. Kotov | L. Szabo |
|----------|----------|
| 1. P–Q4 | N–KB3 |
| 2. P–QB4 | P–KN3 |
| 3. N–QB3 | B–N2 |
| 4. P–K4 | P–Q3 |
| 5. P–B3 | O–O |
| 6. B–K3 | P–K4 |
| 7. P–Q5 | N–R4 |
| 8. Q–Q2 | P–KB4 |
| 9. O–O–O | QN–Q2 |

A significant improvement on the Geller–Gligoric game, where Black closed the game with P–B5. Szabo maintains the central tension while keeping the possibility of posting a Knight on KB5.

**10. B–Q3     N–B4**

This is the right moment to turn that possibility into reality by 10. . . . N–B5!, and if the Bishop retreats to QB2, then not . . . N–B4 but . . . N–N3, forcing P–QN3 by playing on the weakness of White's QBP.

**11. B–QB2     P–B5**

Szabo takes the same thorny path that Gligoric took in the above-mentioned game with Geller, and now he too is condemned to a long, difficult defense. Meanwhile, Kotov has a clear plan, one that was carried out successfully several times by Makogonov in similar positions: the King goes to N1; the Knight goes from KN1 to Q3, driving Black's Knight from QB4 or forcing Black to play the weakening . . . P–N3; and the Rooks occupy the QB- and Q-files. White gradually prepares the breakthrough P–B5 with his King guarded by two pawns, whereas Black has to completely deprive his King of its pawn protection in the attempt to break through on the Kingside.

The struggle in this game follows that general scenario, though not so smoothly as I have described it, and soon the scales begin to tip in White's favor. Therefore, Black should not close the game here; better is 11. . . . N–B3, exerting pressure on K5 and tactically impeding White's KN–K2, which would be followed by 12. . . . PxP 13. PxP N–N5 or 13. BxN PxP.

**12. B–B2     P–QR3**
**13. KN–K2     P–R4**

Szabo is at the crossroads. He sees that the projected . . . P–

QN4 does not work because of the reply P–QN4 and P–B5, so he decides at least to safeguard his Knight's position. He plays the next part of the game rather uncertainly, as though still wondering about how to find some plan against White's growing initiative; but after the 20th move he decides to throw caution to the winds and attacks with the pawns in front of his King.

| 14. | K–N1 | B–Q2 |
|-----|------|------|
| 15. | N–B1 | R–B2 |
| 16. | N–Q3 | P–N3 |
| 17. | R–QB1 | B–KB3 |
| 18. | KR–B1 | B–KR5 |

Szabo's desire to exchange dark-square Bishops is so great that he does not notice White's simple reply. He should decide on 18. . . . P–R5 at least to prevent the exchange of light-square Bishops and to take QN3 from the White pieces.

**19. BxN**

Black now has to recapture with the NP because on leaving KB3 his Bishop deprived his KP of defense. The open QN-file becomes a communications link not for Black's pieces, paradoxically, but in fact for White's. The strategy and tactics of chess still conceal many mysteries.

| 19. . . . | NPxB |
|-----------|------|
| 20. B–R4 | |

This maneuver has the same goals as Black's B–KB3–R5 but is more successful. Black cannot avoid the exchange of his "good" Bishop. Retreating it to QB1 would shut it out, and after 21. B–B6 R–R3 22. N–N5 he would be forced to seek exchanges himself.

| 20. . . . | BxB |
|-----------|------|
| 21. NxB | Q–Q2 |
| 22. N–B3 | P–N4 |

A real danger of loss hangs over Black's game. The threat is N–N5, R–B3, and R–R3, and it is not clear how to defend the QRP, the more so because White can even bring his other Knight up to QN3. Knights are very strong when the position has an immobile pawn skeleton. Szabo decides to make use of his mobilized forces where they stand—i.e., on the Kingside—and immediately the character of the game changes sharply. The leisurely maneuvering struggle is replaced by a hand-to-hand fight that requires coolness, resourcefulness, and accuracy.

**23. P–KR3        N–B3**

This is necessary to prepare the breakthrough P–N5, which is not accomplished by 23. . . . N–N6 in view of 24. KR–Q1 P–R4 25. N–B2!, and both Black pieces are sealed up.

| 24. N–N5 | P–R4 |
|----------|------|
| 25. R–R1 | |

Finding the right plan is not nearly so difficult as carrying it out accurately, at times even perfectly, all the while countering the opponent's plans. Kotov's play here and later is beyond praise. He leaves one Rook to parry Black's assault, attacking and defending at the same time.

| 25. . . . | R–KR2 |
| 26. R–B3 | P–N5 |
| 27. RPxP | PxP |
| 28. R–QR3 | B–N6 |
| 29. RxR | QxR |

Black indirectly defends his RP by threatening to check on KR8, undermining White's KNP, the anchor–support of his pawn chain.

### 30. N–B1          Q–R8!

Black's Queen, by means of the circuitous maneuver Q–Q2–KR2–KR8, is the first to penetrate the enemy camp—leaving not only his QBP and his Rook but also his King to their fate. Black has no choice, since otherwise he would lose his RP

without compensation. However, White's last move underlined his clear advantage, which is defined, first of all, by the safer position of his King; second, by the fact that White's Knight is far more dangerous in the attack on the King than Black's Bishop is; and finally, by the fact that in the carrying out of his onslaught White takes a pawn while gaining a tempo by attacking the Rook. These all create conditions for various combinations. The art of the master lies in finding the best ones, the decisive ones.

| 31. NxBP | PxP |
| 32. PxP | R–R2 |
| 33. N–K6 | |

The Knight occupies such a threatening position that Black's King is in danger of being lost to the first Queen check.

| 33. . . . | B–K8 |
| 34. Q–Q1 | R–R2 |
| 35. R–Q3 | |

Parrying Black's threat of R–R7 and B–Q7 in advance.

| 35. . . . | R–R7 |
| 36. P–R3 | |

36. Q–N3 is not so clear in view of . . . Q–N7, when Q–N8ch gives White nothing because Black's KN2 is defended by his Queen.

| 36. . . . | N–Q2 |
| 37. Q–R4 | Q–N7 |
| 38. R–N3 | |

Kotov defends against the mate threat at QN2, and now threatens simply to take the Knight.

**38. . . .          B–B6**

Szabo sets a trap for his opponent. The Bishop, of course, cannot be taken either by the Rook or the pawn. But if White takes the Knight, there follows a combination well known as the "mill": 39. QxN? QxPch! 40. RxQ RxRch 41. K–R1 and now Black can give discovered check by withdrawing his Rook to any of twelve squares, which is usually good for at least a draw but which in this case even wins after 41. . . . R–N2ch 42. K–R2 RxQ.

**39. N–K2**

The beautiful concluding move of a superbly conducted game. White attacks the Bishop and cuts off his second rank. If Black's Queen takes the Knight, he leaves his KN2 unprotected and White then ends the game with mate after sacrificing his Rook: 39. . . . QxN 40. R–N8ch! NxR 41. Q–K8ch and mate in three. Black resigned.

## Game 101
### Sicilian Defense

| Y. Geller | Y. Averbakh |
|-----------|-------------|
| 1. P–K4   | P–QB4       |
| 2. N–KB3  | N–QB3       |
| 3. P–Q4   | PxP         |
| 4. NxP    | N–B3        |
| 5. N–QB3  | P–Q3        |
| 6. B–QB4  | B–Q2        |
| 7. B–KN5  | Q–R4        |

The last two moves by each side conceal quite a few opening subtleties. In the Rauzer System against the Sicilian Defense, which consists of 6. B–KN5, 7. Q–Q2, and 8. O–O–O, White is usually unable to develop his light-square Bishop at an early stage; in the Scheveningen System White brings out both Bishops but to the modest positions K2 and K3. In this game Geller intends to develop both Bishops actively and apparently plans to castle long. If he is able to do this he will stand extremely well. His plan started with 6. B–QB4 to prevent transposition to the

Dragon Variation, among other things. The reply to 6. . . . P–KN3 would have been 7. NxN PxN 8. P–K5!, and the KP obviously cannot be taken because 9. BxPch wins the Queen. Black would have had to play 8. . . . N–KN5, whereupon the pawn would have advanced still farther: 9. P–K6 P–B4 10. O–O with active play for White, as exemplified by an old Schlechter–Lasker game from their 1910 world championship match.

Averbakh's answer, 6. . . . B–Q2, prepared to transpose to the Dragon. White could simply have castled; after something like 7. . . . P–KN3 8. P–KR3 B–N2 9. B–K3 O–O 10. B–N3 he would have had fairly good play. But he stubbornly carried out his idea, B–KN5.

Averbakh counters this with a bold and original plan, forcing White to take his Knight (otherwise White cannot defend both his Bishop and his KP). Then, leaving his King in place, he starts a headlong attack on the Kingside right in the opening. Ordinarily, such a strategy is at variance with the principles of chess, but in this case it turns out that Black has an open KN-file on which to develop two major pieces, and a mighty pawn center as well. It is just this unusual combination of factors that makes this original plan feasible.

But Geller considers Black's attack a mere adventure; he demonstratively castles short and advances his Kingside pawns as though daring his opponent to attack. Black's attack of course does not present a mortal threat to the White King, but some prophylactic measures should still be taken; in particular, 9. B–Q5 is much better than 9. N–N3, not allowing Black's Queen to get to the Kingside and preserving the threat of N–N3.

| 8. | BxN | NPxB |
| 9. | N–N3 | Q–KN4! |
| 10. | O–O | R–KN1! |

While trying subtly and cleverly to weaken the King's pawn cover, one cannot miss the chance to threaten mate.

| 11. | P–N3 | P–KR4 |
| 12. | N–Q5 | R–B1 |

Black definitely renounces castling. Such valor is uncalled for. True, Black's King is comfortable behind the fence Q3, K2, KB2, and KB3 with his pieces nearby; but Black's central pawns are not at full strength here, and his KB does not soon join in the play. The battle cannot be won without them.

12. . . . O–O–O, with the intention of opening the center by P–K3 and P–Q4, is obviously good for Black and offers serious winning chances.

| 13. | P–B4 | Q–N2 |
|-----|------|------|
| 14. | Q–Q2 | P–R5 |
| 15. | R–B3 | Q–R3 |
| 16. | B–B1 | PxP |
| 17. | RxP | R–N3 |
| 18. | R–K1 | P–B4 |

Black begins to cut a swath for his Bishops. The last White pawn is removed from the center.

| 19. | PxP | BxP |
|-----|-----|-----|
| 20. | P–B3 | B–K3 |
| 21. | B–N2 | |

A serious error. White's Knight is stronger than Black's Bishop and he should not allow it to be exchanged; withdrawing it to K3 is better. With so many pieces around White's King, Averbakh could hardly have created decisive threats.

| 21. | . . . | BxN |
|-----|-------|-----|
| 22. | BxB | P–K3 |
| 23. | N–Q4 | |

White's little tactical threat, BxN followed by N–B5 and NxQP, is easily parried. 23. Q–N2 is better.

23. . . .        B–K2

The Bishop takes its first step and White's position immediately darkens. K–Q2 is not bad.

24. B–N2        RxR

The attempt to win the Exchange would be a gross blunder: 24. . . . B–R5? 25. N–B5!

25. PxR        NxN
26. QxN

If White takes with the pawn it will be difficult to defend the two weaknesses Q4 and KN3, all the weaker without his dark-square Bishop.

26. . . .        P–Q4
27. P–QN4

White's situation is difficult, but the text move immediately makes it hopeless. He can resist with 27. K–B1 B–B4 28. Q–Q3 Q–R7 29. Q–B3 and White retains drawing chances, especially with the Rooks exchanged.

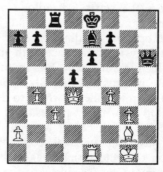

| 27. | . . . | R–B5 |
|-----|-------|------|
| 28. | Q–K5 | Q–B3 |

Why? He should continue the concerted Kingside attack with Queen, Rook, and Bishop. Clearly winning is 28. . . . B–Q1 29. BxP B–B2 30. Q–N5 QxQ 31. PxQ RxBP or 30. Q–K2 RxQBP 31. Q–KN2 Q–N3 32. K–R2 R–B7 33. R–K2 Q–R4ch. But now Black's advantage is merely academic.

**29. QxQ BxQ 30. BxP Rx QBP 31. BxNP RxPch 32. K– R2 R–N5 33. R–K4 K–K2 34. P–B5, Drawn.**

## Game 102
### Nimzo-Indian Defense

**V. Smyslov      T. Petrosian**

| | |
|---|---|
| 1. P–Q4 | N–KB3 |
| 2. P–QB4 | P–K3 |
| 3. N–QB3 | B–N5 |
| 4. P–K3 | O–O |
| 5. B–Q3 | P–Q4 |
| 6. N–B3 | P–B4 |
| 7. O–O | N–B3 |
| 8. P–QR3 | BxN |
| 9. PxB | |

Again the basic position of the Nimzo-Indian Defense, which was seen so often in this tournament that the suggestion was made to begin play from this position.

| | |
|---|---|
| 9. . . . | P–QN3 |
| 10. BPxP | KPxP |
| 11. B–N2 | P–B5 |
| 12. B–B2 | B–N5 |
| 13. Q–K1 | N–K5 |
| 14. N–Q2 | NxN |
| 15. QxN | B–R4 |
| 16. P–B3 | B–N3 |
| 17. P–K4 | Q–Q2 |
| 18. QR–K1 | P–B4 |

Up to and including the 18th move, this is a repetition of the Reshevsky–Petrosian game in the second round, in which White had an appreciable positional advantage, although by subtle defense Petrosian was able to draw. Now, instead of the 18. . . . KR–K1 that he played in that game, Petrosian makes a more active move, but I think the price for this activity —a strong center pawn and the two Bishops—is too high.

| | |
|---|---|
| 19. PxQP | QxP |
| 20. P–QR4 | KR–K1 |

Black plans a series of exchanges, assuming that he will have more pieces to fight for his Q4; however, the play is not only around that square but all over the board, and White is left with Queen and two Bishops, a formidable force.

| | |
|---|---|
| 21. Q–N5 | Q–B2 |
| 22. B–R3 | P–KR3 |
| 23. Q–N3 | RxR |
| 24. RxR | R–K1 |
| 25. RxRch | QxR |
| 26. K–B2 | |

Black's strategy is a fiasco. White's advantage is indisputable: his QRP, QP, and QBP are better than Black's QRP, QNP, and QBP. White already has a passed pawn, whereas Black's QRP can become passed only over the dead body of White's Bishop on QR3. Black undertakes to transfer his Knight to QN6 in the faint hope of diverting White's attention from the center and forcing the exchange of even one White Bishop, but the Knight will be much too far from the action. It is not surprising that it cannot get back in time to hold up the QP's advance to the queening square.

26. . . .         N–R4
27. Q–B4         N–N6

Black goes bravely into the variation 28. P–Q5 QxP 29. P–Q6 QxB 30. P–Q7 Q–B1 31. Q–B7, apparently intending to turn off in time with 29. . . . Q–B3. However, the simple 30. BxP would be just as strong as in the game.

28. BxP          BxB
29. QxB          QxP

White's QP grows stronger with every exchange, its advance combined with the attack against Black's King by the Queen and Bishop. Smyslov's next moves, up to and including the 40th, are made so as not to alter the position before adjournment, when he can find the surest road to victory. The real play begins at move 41, and only a miracle can save Black's game.

30. Q–KB8ch      K–R2
31. Q–B5ch       K–N1
32. Q–K6ch       K–R2
33. Q–K4ch       K–N1
34. Q–R8ch       K–R2

Smyslov checks each time on a different square so as not to repeat the position a third time.

35. Q–K4ch       K–N1
36. Q–Q5ch       K–R2
37. B–K7         N–B8
38. Q–B5ch       K–N1
39. Q–KB8ch      K–R2
40. Q–B5ch       K–N1
41. P–Q5

Having concluded that this move is necessary, Smyslov plays it before adjournment in order to make his opponent think before sealing his move, and so that the adjourned position will not be too easy for his opponent to analyze.

41. . . .        Q–R7ch

Q–K4ch QxQ 49. PxQ N–B5ch Black even wins.

| 45. . . . | K–R2 |
|---|---|
| 46. P–Q7 | Q–K4! |

Chess miracles, as distinct from other miracles, nevertheless do happen sometimes, thanks to the imagination of chess players and the inexhaustible possibilities of chess. Though apparently in an absolutely lost position, Petrosian has composed a draw study and at resumption of play shows Smyslov the solution.

| 42. K–N3 | Q–Q7 |
|---|---|
| 43. P–Q6 | |

If 43. Q–K6ch, in order to avert a check on his K1, then 43. . . . K–R1 44. P–Q6 N–K7ch 45. K–N4 Q–B5ch 46. K–R5 QxRPch with a perpetual. But if 46. K–R3 White is even mated.

| 43. . . . | Q–K8ch |
|---|---|
| 44. K–N4 | N–Q6 |
| 45. Q–Q5ch | |

If White advances his pawn at once—45. P–Q7—the draw is obtained by the studylike 45. . . . P–R4ch! 46. KxP QxB 47. Q–Q5ch K–R2 48. P–Q8=Q N–B5ch, or if 48.

A move of rare beauty. If White queens his pawn he gets mated in two moves; if he trades Queens he loses his QP; if he retreats his Queen to Q4 there follows . . . QxP with unavoidable perpetual check.

Convinced that an authentic miracle has taken place on the board, Smyslov reconciles himself to the fact that the game cannot be won, and he forces the draw by a temporary Queen sacrifice.

| 47. QxNch | PxQ |
|---|---|
| 48. P–Q8=Q | Drawn |

An attempt by Black in his turn to play for a win is easily parried: 48. . . . Q–K7 49. K–R3 P–Q7 50. Q–Q7 P–Q8=Q 51. Q–B5ch.

But it happens at times that chess miracles are mere optical illusions. The studylike 46. . . . Q–K4 could have been refuted by the studylike 47. Q–Q6—

White defends his RP through Black's Queen. 47. . . . N–B7ch is followed by 48. K–R4 P–N4ch 49. K–R5. On other Black moves (after 47. Q–Q6) White simply makes a second Queen, and his King hides easily from the checks.

Curiously, neither the players, the tournament participants, nor the spectators noticed this possibility for White. The move 47. Q–Q6 was discovered a few months after the end of the tournament by a Swedish amateur.

# Game 103
## Sicilian Defense

| P. Keres | M. Najdorf |
|---|---|
| 1. P–K4 | P–QB4 |
| 2. N–K2 | N–KB3 |
| 3. QN–B3 | P–Q3 |
| 4. P–KN3 | N–B3 |
| 5. B–N2 | P–KN3 |
| 6. P–Q3 | B–N2 |

One of the quiet systems in the Sicilian Defense. As we can see, the position is practically symmetrical, the only difference being that Black's pawns are in charge of the Queenside, White's of the center, and this, it seems to me, is what determines the players' further plans. This leisurely maneuvering system is used relatively rarely by Keres, who commits a few inaccuracies later that allow his opponent first to equalize the game and then to gain the advantage.

| 7. B–K3 | O–O |
| 8. P–KR3 | |

Smyslov, who is the leading expert on closed systems and a virtuoso in this opening, prefers 8. Q–B1 here, intending to exchange dark-square Bishops, and if Black avoids this by 8. . . . R–K1 9. B–R6 B–R1, only then 10. P–KR3. Moving the Queen to B1, not to Q2, is to allow White to answer . . . N–KN5 with B–Q2.

| 8. . . . | N–K1 |

Black clearly intends to post a Knight on Q5. This was his last chance to play . . . P–Q4; omitting it leaves his opponent with an advantage in space.

| 9. Q–Q2 | N–Q5 |
| 10. N–Q1 | R–N1 |

Black is already preparing the advance of his QNP and White hasn't even castled yet. White's next maneuver is aimed at driving Black's Knight from Q5 and then playing P–Q4, but Keres does not achieve this aim. Best is simply to take the Knight and play B–R6, at least to deprive Black's advanced pawn of the Bishop's support.

| 11. N–B4 | N–B2 |
| 12. P–QB3 | P–K4! |

A good example of the use of a tactical stroke to refute the opponent's strategical plan. If Black's Knight retreats White plays P–Q4 and stands well, but now it is White's Knight that must retreat, and he will not achieve P–Q4 in this game. Furthermore, Black immediately gets in P–Q4 and P–KB4 and takes full possession of the center.

**13. N–K2**

Nothing is gained by 13. PxN, for Black then seizes important central points.

**13. . . .      NxN**
**14. QxN       P–N3**

White has lost the first battle. His pieces stand poorly and his Knight does not have a single move.

**15. O–O       P–Q4**
**16. P–QB4     PxBP**
**17. PxP**

**17. . . .      P–B4**

Najdorf gives his opponent no respite! The pawn has to be taken in view of the threat . . . P–B5. If he blocks its path by P–B4 there follows . . . N–K3 and the Knight comes very powerfully into play. After the pawn exchange it suddenly becomes clear that Black is threatening B–Q6, with the result that White's Knight, for whose liberation White played P–QB4, does not get to QB3.

**18. PxP       BxP**
**19. R–K1      B–Q6**
**20. B–N5      Q–Q5**

A triumph of centralization.

**21. Q–K3      BxP**
**22. R–QB1**

White has a lost game and no compensating advantage at all for the pawn. The continuation 22. N–B3 N–K3 23. QR–Q1 QxQ 24. BxQ N–Q5 holds no prospects for White, and he therefore searches for some way to alter the normal course of the struggle. He offers Black a choice: to win still another pawn by BxP or to sacrifice the Exchange himself. Either would be in Black's favor:

1) 22. . . . BxP 23. P–N3 N–K3 24. QxQ NxQ 25. B–Q5ch K–R1 26. R–K3 P–K5! with an easy win;

2) 22. . . . B–B2 23. QxQ KPxQ! 24. B–B4 QR–B1 25. B–N7 N–Q4! 26. BxR NxB 27. PxN RxB with a winning position, or if 26. B–Q6 instead of

BxR, then 26. . . . N–N5, and if 27. B–R6 instead of PxN, then 27. . . . P–Q6 is good.

Najdorf refuses either to gain or to sacrifice material, believing that the win will be a matter of elementary technique after the exchange of Queens. However, the exchange noticeably improves White's position, mainly by bringing his Knight into play, and soon Black even allows a Rook to get to his second rank.

| 22. | . . . | QxQ |
|-----|-------|-----|
| 23. | NxQ | BxP |
| 24. | R–R1 | B–N6 |
| 25. | R–R3 | B–K3 |
| 26. | RxP | N–N4 |
| 27. | R–K7 | N–Q5 |
| 28. | N–N4 | BxN |
| 29. | PxB | N–B6ch |
| 30. | BxN | RxB |
| 31. | R–Q1 | |

Black has simplified the game and retained the pawn, but the quality of his position has been so reduced as to place his winning chances in doubt.

**31. . . .        R–B2**

31. . . . B–B1 has its advantages, for after 32. R–R7 R–B2 33. RxR KxR 34. R–Q7ch the King can be moved to the center. It is true that Black must take the loss of a pawn into consideration in the variation 32. RxKP B–N2 33. R–K2 R–N6, but even so the chances remain on his side.

| 32. | RxR | KxR |
|-----|------|------|
| 33. | R–Q7ch | K–N1 |
| 34. | P–N3 | P–N4 |

Black provoked P–N3 by threatening P–B5 and P–K5. Now he can set about creating a passed pawn. He has to employ the following typical method: P–B5, and after White plays PxP he does not take the pawn but advances directly to queen by P–N5–6. Why does Black have to play this way? Because taking the pawn on B5 would allow White's Rook to go to QB7, after which Black would have to defend his pawn from the side and could therefore advance it no farther. White's King would approach and take it.

After the inevitable . . . P–B5 and . . . P–N5 a dangerous situation is created for White. Black's pawn can reach the eighth rank in three moves, so it is absolutely necessary to block its progress beyond N7. The correct plan in this situation is 35. K–B1 P–B5 36. PxP P–N5 37. B–B1 P–N6 38. R–Q2 (also possible is 38. P–B5 P–N7 39. BxP and 40. P–B6) and 39. B–N2, and the pawn is stopped, or 37. . . . R–QB1 38. R–N7 RxP 39. B–Q2 B–B1 40. P–N5 and Black is hardly likely to win.

White's next move, R–QB7, puts his Rook in the path of his own pawn and gives up the chance to play R–Q2. Now the indicated variation is unplayable, and White will have to give up a piece for the pawn.

| 35. | R–QB7 | P–B5 |
|-----|-------|------|
| 36. | PxP   | P–N5 |
| 37. | B–B1  | P–K5 |
| 38. | P–B5  | P–N6 |
| 39. | P–B6  | P–N7 |

| 40. | BxP | RxB |
|-----|-----|-----|

The 40th move! Taking on N7 with the Bishop makes the play difficult for Black but he probably wins the endgame anyway: 40. . . . BxB 41. R–Q7 R–QB1 42. P–B7 B–B3 43. K–B1 K–B1, then . . . B–K2 and . . . K–K1. And if 44. RxP B–N2.

**41. R–Q7       Drawn**

Despite his extra piece, Black cannot win. After 41. . . . R–B7 42. P–B7 Black's only reasonable move would be B–B1; the Bishop then could not move because of the threatened check on Q8, the King could not go to its second rank, and the Rook could move only along the QB-file. Memorize this position!

## Game 104
### Nimzo-Indian Defense

**S. Reshevsky       M. Taimanov**

| 1. | P–Q4  | N–KB3 |
|----|-------|-------|
| 2. | P–QB4 | P–K3  |
| 3. | N–QB3 | B–N5  |
| 4. | P–K3  | O–O   |
| 5. | N–K2  | P–Q4  |
| 6. | P–QR3 |       |

White is trying to squeeze the most out of the opening: he wants the advantage of the two Bishops without getting the usual doubled pawns on the QB-file.

| 6. | . . . | B–K2 |
|----|-------|------|
| 7. | PxP   | PxP  |
| 8. | N–N3  |      |

Reshevsky likes this opening position, although theory, claiming that Black equalizes with . . . P–QB4, disapproves. Reshevsky apparently has his own thoughts about that, for he is always willing to go into the variation N–K2–N3, and he handles it superbly.

His opponents in the present tournament—Taimanov and in the 18th round Averbakh—decline to play 8. . . . P–B4 and employ their own systems, which, though more complicated, cannot be said to be better. I think . . . P–QB4 is the simplest solution to the problems.

| | |
|---|---|
| **8. . . .** | **R–K1** |
| **9. P–N4** | **P–B3** |
| **10. B–Q3** | **P–QN4** |

No higher education in chess is required to brand this move antipositional and to put a plump question mark after it, as almost all commentators have done; its bad points are obvious. But the move is made by an international grandmaster, who must have seen something worthwhile in it; the idea is that Black fixes the White QNP and prepares the break P–QR4 with the aim of isolating one of White's Queenside pawns. As regards the weakness of his QBP, Black is counting on the maneuver QN–Q2–N3–B5 for his Knight to occupy a strong position and close the QB-file.

Perhaps Taimanov would have been criticized less if it had been remembered that the reckless . . . P–QN4 had been played by Reshevsky himself in the same position against Gligoric in a match game, New York 1951.

## 11. B–Q2

As played by Gligoric against Reshevsky. The modest Bishop move is exceptionally strong and destroys both of Black's hopes. Now . . . P–QR4 would be risky in view of 12. PxP RxP 13. P–QR4! P–N5 14. N–R2

N–R3 15. BxN. Therefore, Taimanov first tries to get his Knight to QB5.

| | |
|---|---|
| **11. . . .** | **QN–Q2** |
| **12. P–QR4** | |

White would have played P–QR4 even on 11. . . . P–QR3, and although Black would have held QN4 by 12. . . . B–N2, he still would have been unable to get his Knight to QB5 after 13. Q–N3 QN–Q2 14. P–R5.

| | |
|---|---|
| **12. . . .** | **BxP** |
| **13. PxP** | **P–B4** |
| **14. O–O** | **P–B5** |

White has the freer game. In this particular case it is important that White's QNP exerts strong pressure on the opponent's position, that Black's QP requires defense by a piece, and that Black also has to watch out for the invasion of his KB4 by White's Knight. 14. . . . PxP would only open a path for White's Bishop on Q2, without essentially changing the position. Taimanov, treating the position optimistically, creates a protected passed pawn, but he gives White other trumps. First of all, in releasing the tension in the center he frees his opponent from worrying about his QP and unties his hands for active play with his minor pieces. As for the passed pawn, its defender itself requires defense and keeps Black very busy.

I prefer the waiting move 14. . . . N–N3.

| 15. | B–B2 | P–QR4 |
|-----|------|-------|
| 16. | PxP e.p. | RxRP |
| 17. | RxR | BxR |
| 18. | Q–R1 | |

The beginning of a strong strategical maneuver aimed at the occupation of the QR- and QN-files by the major pieces; the concluding move, 21. R–N2, is particularly fine and refutes Black's defense.

| 18. | . . . | N–N1 |
|-----|-------|------|
| 19. | Q–R4 | B–KB1 |
| 20. | R–N1 | R–K3 |

**21. R–N2**

Black was about to play R–N3 and seize the QN-file, but now this move would achieve nothing, for the reply 22. Q–R5 would force the Rook back to Q3 (22. . . . QN–Q2 23. N–R4 R–N1 24. QxB), and in the end the QN-file would be occupied by White after 23. N–R4. Such extremely subtle moves are often important in combinations and can have decisive influence on the outcome of a game.

Black's position is clearly inferior. White's further plan is to increase his pressure on the QP. Black does not think the White Knight can be allowed to stay on KB4 and he exchanges it.

| 21. | . . . | P–N3 |
|-----|-------|------|
| 22. | KN–K2 | B–Q3 |
| 23. | N–B4 | BxN |
| 24. | PxB | |

Apparently unconcerned about the weakness of his QP, White agreed to the exchange, and he now strives for complete domination of the dark squares. Making use of Black's forced P–N3, White's pawn majority on the Kingside, and the growing strength of his two Bishops, Reshevsky proceeds to storm the enemy King's position with great vigor.

Black can only try to reduce the forces on the board and to parry direct tactical threats.

| 24. | . . . | QN–Q2 |
|-----|-------|------|
| 25. | P–R3 | R–N3 |
| 26. | Q–R5 | Q–N1 |

Black did not have this possibility before, since QN1 was occupied by his Knight. In this connection, it should be noted that on his 18th move Black did not have to return the Knight to its original position; the Bishop on R3 would have been defended better by 18. . . . Q–R1.

| 27. | RxR | QxR |
|-----|-----|-----|

White can now win a pawn by 28. NxP QxQ 29. NxNch NxN 30. BxQ. However, White's position is strong enough; he has no need to divert his attention to the calculation of the endgame after 30. . . . N–Q4.

**28. Q–R3**

| | |
|---|---|
| **28. . . .** | **N–B1** |
| **29. B–K3** | **B–B1** |

Black defends against P–B5, but after 30. P–N4 he has to go back to defending the QP due to the threat P–N5. The loss of time is not significant here, since Black cannot essentially improve the position of his pieces. As usual, Taimanov defends very resourcefully, and his play bears no hint of fatalism. He endeavors at all times to present his opponent with various problems, and although they are not all that complex, they do consume time, and little of that remains!

| | |
|---|---|
| **30. P–N4** | **B–N2** |
| **31. P–B5** | **P–N4** |

| | |
|---|---|
| **32. Q–K7** | **P–R3** |
| **33. N–R4** | **Q–B3** |
| **34. N–B5** | **B–B1** |
| **35. Q–Q8** | **K–N2** |

The time trouble is becoming extreme. Reshevsky has only seconds left for five moves, and as for Taimanov—he has a whole minute!

**36. B–Q2**

Reshevsky destroys the fruits of his skillful play; momentarily leaving the two Bishops on the second rank he gives Taimanov the chance to relieve his Queen of the defense of his Bishop. Instead, 36. B–R4 Q–R1 37. K–N2 would place Black in complete zugzwang.

| | |
|---|---|
| **36. . . .** | **Q–N4** |

**37. QxB**

In time trouble Reshevsky contemplates giving mate, and for this reason he gives up his Bishop on B2 and keeps his dark-square one. However, Taimanov refutes this idea perfectly, and at adjournment Reshevsky has to think seriously about the danger of losing the game.

37. B–B3 is objectively better, not allowing the Queen to get to N7. On . . . Q–Q1 White can even exchange Queens, retaining a big advantage despite Black's protected passed pawn.

| 37. . . . | Q–N7 |
| 38. K–N2 | QxB |
| 39. B–N4 | N–K5! |

Counterattack is the best defense in such positions.

| 40. NxN | QxNch |
| 41. K–N3 | |

This was Reshevsky's strong sealed move. The game was not resumed, for the two players agreed to a draw in view of the following main variation: 41. . . . N–R2 42. B–Q6 QxQP 43. Q–B7 N–B3 44. B–K5 Q–Q6ch 45. K–N2 Q–K5ch and perpetual check.

## Game 105

If you have castled and see that your opponent is closing the center to prepare for a direct pawn storm, it is useful to open a file in advance in the area where the enemy King is or will be. Acting on this principle, Gligoric starts interesting play on the Queenside as early as the 9th move and creates a strong counterinitiative.

### King's Indian Defense

**D. Bronstein**     **S. Gligoric**

| 1. P–Q4 | N–KB3 |
| 2. P–QB4 | P–KN3 |
| 3. N–QB3 | B–N2 |
| 4. P–K4 | P–Q3 |
| 5. P–KR3 | O–O |
| 6. B–K3 | |

A variation of the Sämisch Attack, with P–KR3 instead of P–KB3. The phases of this system: the two dark-square diagonals are not weakened; the Q1–KR5 diagonal remains open, as does the KB3-square; and it will be difficult for Black to establish a Knight on KR4, for it can always be driven away by B–K2. The system has disadvantages, the most important of which is that K4 is not defended by a pawn, a situation which Gligoric skillfully exploits later.

| 6. . . . | P–K4 |
| 7. P–Q5 | QN–Q2 |
| 8. P–KN4 | N–B4 |
| 9. Q–B2 | P–B3 |

White is all ready to castle long and then storm the enemy King's position. Gligoric immediately reminds him that because of the open QB-file

White's King will not feel completely out of danger either.

| 10. | KN–K2 | PxP |
|-----|-------|-----|
| 11. | BPxP | Q–R4 |

Black makes use of the open QB-file to indirectly attack the KP, as in the illustrative variation 12. QR–N1 QNxP 13. P–N4 Q–B2.

| 12. | N–N3 | B–Q2 |
|-----|------|------|
| 13. | B–Q2 |      |

Now Black must consider White's P–N4; the pawn would have to be taken and the Queen could get entangled among the White pieces.

| 13. | . . . | KR–B1 |
|-----|-------|-------|

Returning the compliment. Black invites the execution of the threat P–N4, but White declines the invitation because after 14. P–N4 QxNP 15. N–N5 Black is not obliged to continue 15. . . . Q–R5 16. QxQ NxQ 17. NxQP, which would leave him in a rather inferior ending, but can sacrifice his Queen: 15. . . . QxN 16. BxQ BxB and White's King is in a bad way.

| 14. | QR–N1 | Q–Q1 |
|-----|-------|------|
| 15. | Q–Q1  |      |

The Queens return home, soon to continue their duel on the other side.

| 15. | . . . | P–QR4 |
|-----|-------|-------|
| 16. | Q–B3  | QR–N1 |

| 17. | P–N5  | N–K1 |
|-----|-------|------|
| 18. | P–KR4 |      |

Black's initiative on the Queenside threatens to become a full-scale attack. White hurries to divert his opponent's attention, with partial success.

| 18. | . . . | P–B3 |
|-----|-------|------|
| 19. | B–K2  | N–B2 |
| 20. | K–B1  | Q–K2 |
| 21. | PxP   | QxP  |
| 22. | QxQ   | BxQ  |
| 23. | P–R5  |      |

This might have been an attacking move, but, thanks to Black's foresight, it is played after the exchange of Queens and now has only one aim—to get rid of a weakness that might have been serious after . . . P–KR4.

| 23. | . . .  | R–B1   |
|-----|--------|--------|
| 24. | PxP    | PxP    |
| 25. | K–N2   | B–N2   |
| 26. | B–K3   | P–QN4  |
| 27. | QR–QB1 | N/2–R3 |
| 28. | N–Q1   | KR–B1  |
| 29. | N–B3   | P–R5   |
| 30. | QR–Q1  | P–N5   |

Both adversaries are fighting to win in an approximately even position. While White maneuvers his pieces, Black moves his pawns in an effort to break through to the QNP. He frees QN4 in order to exchange his KB there and give his Knight access to Q6. However, Black's achievements are of a temporary nature, his minuses permanent. The Knight, which now retreats to the first rank, is bound for QB5.

| | |
|---|---|
| 31. N–N1 | B–N4 |
| 32. BxB | RxB |
| 33. K–B3 | R–N2 |
| 34. K–K2 | |

Having run away from the center at a time of danger, the King returns to cover Q3. The drawbacks of the King's Indian Defense begin to show up: if the dark-square Bishop plays no role in the middlegame it usually has little activity in the endgame.

| | |
|---|---|
| 34. . . . | R/2–QB2 |
| 35. R–QB1 | N–Q2 |
| 36. RxR | RxR |
| 37. R–QB1 | |

Clearing a path to the Queenside for the White King.

| | |
|---|---|
| 37. . . . | RxR |
| 38. BxR | N/3–B4 |
| 39. B–K3 | K–B2 |
| 40. N–Q2 | N–N3 |

White had to seal his move and could not resist 41. BxN, which gives him a protected passed pawn and creates a blockaded weakness on the opponent's QB4 that facilitates the passage of White's King to QN5. All the same, it is not the best move; though it does not let the win escape, it considerably complicates it. The Bishop is good and this is not the time to trade it. Correct is 41. N/3–B1, moving up a Knight that hasn't made a single move in the last thirty and maintaining all the threats. The difference is that the Bishop on K3 does not allow Black's King to get to KN4, and in the meantime White could quietly strengthen his position by transferring the Knight, say, to KN4 via KR2, and then BxN and K–Q3 would lead to an easy win.

| | |
|---|---|
| 41. BxN | PxB |
| 42. K–Q3 | K–B3 |
| 43. N–B4 | N–Q2 |
| 44. N–B1 | K–N4 |
| 45. K–K3 | B–R3 |
| 46. N–R2 | K–B3ch |

46. . . . K–R5ch would be followed not by 47. K–B3 B–B5, with great drawing chances, but by 47. K–K2!, leaving B3 for the decisive transfer of the Knight to Q3.

| | |
|---|---|
| 47. K–K2 | B–B5 |
| 48. N–N4ch | K–K2 |

An attempt by Black's King to counterattack would not succeed. White would answer 48. . . . K–N4 with P–B3.

| 49. | K–Q3 | K–Q1 |
|-----|------|------|
| 50. | N–Q6 | K–B2 |

**51. N–B7          P–R6**

Gligoric tires of passive defense and attempts to break through, which leads, however, to a quick loss. If Black stood firm, White would play P–B3, transfer his Knight to Q3, and then break up Black's pawn front with P–R3, etc., according to all the laws of endgame science. Black's impatient move speeds things up considerably.

**52. PxP PxP 53. K–B4 K–N3 54. K–N3 K–R4 55. N–Q6 B–B8 56. N–B4ch K–N4 57. N/NxP, Black resigns.**

# Round Sixteen

## Game 106
### Queen's Indian Defense

This round begins the second half of the tournament. After an interval of three days the grandmasters resume the struggle.

**D. Bronstein    M. Taimanov**

1. P–Q4 N–KB3 2. P–QB4 P–K3 3. N–KB3 P–QN3 4. P–KN3 B–R3 5. QN–Q2 P–B4 6. B–N2 N–B3 7. PxP KBxP 8. O–O O–O 9. P–QR3 B–N2

The attack by Black's Bishop at QR3 has forced a slight slackening of the usual pace of White's development in the Queen's Indian. But Black's achievement was temporary; one Bishop has already returned to its proper place, and the advance of White's QNP forces the other one to retreat.

10. P–QN4 B–K2 11. B–N2 R–B1 12. Q–N3 R–B2 13. QR–B1 Q–R1 14. Q–Q3 P–KR3 15. KR–Q1 R–Q1 16. P–K4 P–Q3

White has not allowed . . . P–Q4, and if his Knight stood on QB3 he could strengthen his

position even more. With the Knight on Q2 I found no promising plan at the board or in analysis. Black's pieces, though cramped, are harmoniously developed and with the pawns form a very solid position. It seems to me that in general the best way to fight the Queen's Indian Defense is not to allow it. Of the fifteen Queen's Indians in this tournament, White won two and Black six. An unenviable result. True, this is not typical. It would be more typical had all fifteen been drawn.

17. Q–K2 P–QR4 18. R–R1 PxP 19. PxP Q–B1 20. B–B3 N–Q2 21. N–Q4 NxN 22. BxN B–KB3 23. BxB NxB 24. Q–K3 P–Q4, Drawn.

265

## Game 107
### King's Indian Defense

**S. Reshevsky**     **M. Najdorf**

| | |
|---|---|
| 1. P–Q4 | N–KB3 |
| 2. P–QB4 | P–KN3 |
| 3. N–QB3 | B–N2 |
| 4. P–K4 | P–Q3 |
| 5. B–K2 | O–O |
| 6. N–B3 | P–K4 |
| 7. O–O | N–B3 |
| 8. B–K3 | |

Najdorf's next two moves, used for the first time in this game, must be considered an important theoretical achievement, for Black almost forces a draw.

**8. . . .     R–K1**

Najdorf seems to have arrived at this move after analyzing the King's Indians played in a big match between these two opponents not long before this tournament. In two of those games Najdorf defended unsuccessfully with 8. . . . N–KN5. Nevertheless, the question whether 8. . . . R–K1 or 8. . . . N–KN5 is better must remain open.

**9. P–Q5**

Apparently gaining a tempo, but the Knight unexpectedly goes forward, not backward.

| | |
|---|---|
| 9. . . . | N–Q5 |
| 10. NxN | PxN |
| 11. BxP | NxKP |
| 12. BxB | KxB |
| 13. NxN | RxN |

**14. Q–B2     R–K1**

Drawn. Perhaps Black has a slight advantage. His King can reach a good position for the endgame via the dark squares. If the attempt by some theoreticians to demonstrate an advantage for White after 8. PxP is not crowned with success, it will apparently be necessary to go back to 8. P–Q5 after all.

## Game 108
### King's Indian Defense

**P. Keres**     **T. Petrosian**

| | |
|---|---|
| 1. P–Q4 | N–KB3 |
| 2. P–QB4 | P–KN3 |
| 3. N–QB3 | B–N2 |
| 4. N–B3 | P–Q3 |
| 5. B–B4 | |

A quiet system that is particularly unpleasant for players who seek sharp combinative play for both sides in the King's Indian Defense. It differs from the more frequent Smyslov System (see games 13 and 184) in that here White's QBP stands on B4, there on B3.

Theoreticians consider it difficult for Black to play P–K4 in this variation, and usually . . . P–QB4 is preferred, followed by advancing the Queenside pawns. Petrosian accomplishes only the first part of this plan. Later both sides maneuver for a long time, probing their opponent's weak points.

Still, it seems to me that Black has no reason to renounce P–K4. In any case, his next move, 5. . . . QN–Q2, fails to carry out Black's plan even for this game; 5. . . . O–O is better, for 6. P–K3 would allow him to get in 6. . . . P–B4 and . . . N–B3!

| 5. . . . | QN–Q2 |
| 6. P–KR3 | P–B4 |
| 7. P–K3 | O–O |
| 8. B–K2 | P–N3 |
| 9. O–O | B–N2 |
| 10. P–Q5! | P–QR3 |

After a few opening inaccuracies, Black has come imperceptibly under positional pressure.

| 11. P–QR4 | N–K1 |
| 12. Q–Q2 | N–K4 |

| 13. N–KR2 | P–K3 |
| 14. QR–Q1 | Q–K2 |
| 15. Q–B2 | R–Q1 |
| 16. Q–N3 | |

An interesting psychological element may be observed in the course of the struggle. Keres, making only "natural" and "necessary" moves, wants to suggest to his opponent that he intends to strengthen his position gradually. Meanwhile, his mind is on something else entirely. Keres wants to organize an attack, believe it or not, on the KR-file. With this in mind, he keeps his Knight on KR2 for a long time, waiting to play it to KN4 at a moment when Black will be forced to take it; in the meantime he conventionally "exerts pressure" on QN6, K6, etc.

| 16. . . . | Q–B2 |
| 17. R–Q2 | PxP |
| 18. NxP | BxN |
| 19. RxB | N–KB3 |
| 20. R/5–Q1 | N–R3 |
| 21. B–B3 | KR–K1 |

And here is a slight inaccuracy (21. . . . N–QN5 is necessary), answered by

**22. N–N4**

Now 22. . . . P–KR4 23. NxNch BxN 24. BxN QxB 25. R–Q5 is bad for Black. There remains a choice only between

22. . . . N–N5 23. B–N5 and
22. . . . NxN. Petrosian chooses
the latter, believing that his position will then be relatively solid.

| 22. . . . | NxN |
|-----------|-----|
| 23. PxN | N–N5 |
| 24. R–Q2 | Q–K2 |
| 25. R/1–Q1 | B–K4 |
| 26. P–N5 | P–QR4 |
| 27. P–N3 | Q–K3 |
| 28. K–N2 | Q–K2 |
| 29. R–KR1 | Q–K3 |

Petrosian has nothing better
than to move back and forth
and wait for Keres to start a new
wave of attacks.

| 30. R–R4 | R–KB1 |
|----------|-------|
| 31. Q–Q1 | BxB |
| 32. KPxB | P–B3 |
| 33. R–K2 | Q–B2 |
| 34. PxP | QxKBP |

Black had to expose his
King's position a little in order
to defend his KRP.

| 35. Q–K1 | R–Q2 |
|----------|------|
| 36. R–K6 | QxNP |
| 37. R–K7 | RxR |
| 38. QxR | Q–N2 |
| 39. QxP | Q–B3 |
| 40. Q–Q7 | Q–B2 |
| 41. Q–Q6 | Q–B3 |
| 42. Q–B7 | R–B2 |
| 43. Q–B8ch | R–B1 |
| 44. Q–Q7 | Q–B2 |

This was the position after
Black's 40th move.

| 45. Q–Q2 | Q–K3 |
|----------|------|
| 46. R–R1 | QxP |
| 47. Q–Q6 | |

| 47. . . . | Q–Q5 |
|-----------|------|
| 48. Q–K6ch | K–R1 |

An amusing move here was
pointed out by Boleslavsky—
48. . . . R–B2 looks bad because of 49. RxP, but then 49.
. . . Q–B3 forces the exchange
of Queens and, against all logic,
reaches a draw! A rare case.

True, on the problem-move
. . . R–B2 White has the no less
original 49. B–K2, but this
chance was worth taking anyway. As we will see, the "more
stubborn" . . . K–R1 leads to
the immediate loss of Black's
extra pawn without achieving
the exchange of Queens.

49. QxKNP Q–N2 50. Q–
K4 N–R7 51. Q–B4 N–N5 52.
B–K4 RxP 53. Q–K6 RxB 54.
QxR Q–Q2 55. Q–K5ch K–N1
56. R–R5, Black resigns.

# Game 109
## Queen's Gambit

| V. Smyslov | Y. Averbakh |
|---|---|
| 1. P–QB4 | N–KB3 |
| 2. N–KB3 | P–K3 |
| 3. N–B3 | P–Q4 |
| 4. P–Q4 | B–N5 |
| 5. PxP | PxP |
| 6. B–N5 | P–KR3 |
| 7. BxN | QxB |
| 8. Q–N3 | Q–Q3 |
| 9. P–QR3 | BxNch |
| 10. QxB | O–O |

The minority attack is not only an opening idea—used mostly in the Exchange Variation (and in the Carlsbad Variation) of the Queen's Gambit—but a general strategic idea which in favorable circumstances can be carried out at any stage of the game, and not only on the Queenside. The idea of this attack is to create weaknesses for the opponent in an area where he possesses a numerical pawn advantage and then to attack the weak pawns with the pieces.

There could be no better circumstances than these for a minority attack by White on the Queenside. To equalize, Black usually prepares a piece attack on the Kingside.

| 11. R–B1 | P–QB3 |
|---|---|
| 12. P–K3 | B–B4 |
| 13. B–K2 | N–Q2 |
| 14. O–O | |

Why is White delaying P–QN4? Black would answer 14. ... B–K5, and 15. N–Q2 would be impossible because of the hanging KNP. And White does not want to give up his Knight for Black's Bishop because the Bishop is restricted by Black's own pawns. However, Black's next move stops the advance of White's QNP for a long time.

**14. ...          P–QR4**

In order to impede the minority attack, the pawn tears itself from its base and itself becomes an object of attack. Such a pawn draws other pawns after it, like a needle pulling thread, but for the moment Averbakh is not worried about its defense. While White is busying himself regrouping for his new plan (a piece attack on the QRP), Black will be able to create the first threats on the Kingside.

| 15. N–K1 | N–B3 |
|----------|------|
| 16. N–Q3 | BxN |

The Knight is felled by the Bishop anyway. The attempt to transfer the Knight to QB5 via N3, avoiding the QN1–KB5 diagonal, would not have worked because Black would have answered 15. N–Q2 with 15. . . . P–R5.

| 17. QxB | KR–K1 |
|---------|-------|
| 18. B–B3 | N–K5 |
| 19. BxN | RxB |
| 20. Q–N3 | Q–Q2 |
| 21. R–B5 | R–N5 |

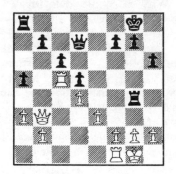

The transfer of the Rook to KN5 is a good illustration of Black's counterchances in such positions. White usually leaves his King completely unprotected by pieces or leaves one minor piece on guard during his minority attack. It is not easy, however, for Black to break through with a pawn storm. Therefore, the most prevalent method is direct frontal attack, the more so because White's KN2 and KR2 are excellent targets for the pieces. Only if White is forced to advance his KNP or KRP can Black enlist the aid of his pawns. The success of such an operation depends on the specific situation, but Smyslov does not wish to accept the risk in this instance, and, abandoning his attempt to win the QRP, he decides to force a draw. It is a moral victory for Black.

**22. P–R3 R–N3 23. K–R1 P–R5 24. Q–N4 R–B3 25. K–N1, Drawn.**

## Game 110
### Nimzo-Indian Defense

**Y. Geller**          **L. Szabo**

| 1. P–Q4 | N–KB3 |
|---------|-------|
| 2. P–QB4 | P–K3 |
| 3. N–QB3 | B–N5 |
| 4. P–K3 | O–O |
| 5. B–Q3 | P–Q4 |
| 6. N–B3 | P–QN3 |
| 7. O–O | P–B4 |

Although the QBP is attacking White's center, its presence on QB4 has its unfavorable aspect: it cuts off the Bishop's retreat. The restrained 7. . . . B–N2 seems more appropriate to me.

| 8. Q–K2 | QN–Q2 |
|---------|-------|
| 9. BPxP | KPxP |

10. P–QR3     B–R4
11. P–QN4

Black's Bishop is spared, but it soon turns out that White's Knight is worth more. White starts an offensive against QB7 and Q6 which seems at first to have a realistic basis: the dark-square Bishop is out of play. As a rule, the opening of lines in such cases favors the better developed side. The sacrificed pawn is the bait.

11. . . .     PxNP
12. N–QN5     P–QR3
13. N–Q6     N–N1
14. NxB     QxN
15. B–Q2     P–N6

The quality of a chess position does not always depend on the number of pawns. In this case, Black has enough weaknesses to clearly define White's advantage. A thematic variation here is 15. . . . PxP 16. BxB PxB 17. KR–B1, and White can expect a fair harvest—not only the three QRPs but also the QP. Szabo does not like this variation, of course, so he decides to return the sacrifice, if only to "paint over" the QR- and QN-files.

16. QR–N1     N–B3
17. RxP     BxB
18. QxB     P–QN4
19. R–B1     Q–Q2
20. R/3–B3     KR–B1
21. N–K5

Geller gives his opponent no breathing spell. After the forced exchange on K4, new worries arise for Szabo, one of which is where to put the Knight on KB3. The jump to K5 looks rash but is actually the best practical chance. If the Knight retreats, the flock of pawns on the K- and KB-files will burst unhindered into the Black King's fortress.

21. . . .     NxN
22. PxN     RxR
23. QxR     N–K5
24. Q–Q4

White is thinking about trapping the Knight, but this is hardly necessary. Seizing all the key points by 24. Q–B7 is simple and good. However, White's position is very good and is difficult to spoil with one move.

24. . . .     Q–N2
25. P–KR4     P–R3
26. R–B2     R–QB1
27. RxRch     QxR
28. QxP     N–B6
29. Q–Q6

The Knight escaped but the QP was lost. Black, of course, cannot wait while the KP and KBP advance, and first he undertakes a desperate attempt to form a passed pawn on the Queenside. The game unexpectedly enters combinational channels and, even more unexpectedly, Szabo appears to have real chances for salvation.

29. . . .     P–QR4
30. P–B4     P–R4

**31. P–B5      N–Q8**
**32. P–K6      NxP**

In spite of everything.

**33. K–B2**

The intended 33. P–K7 is refuted by the invasion of the Queen to the rear of White's position: 33. . . . Q–B8ch, etc. A good idea by Szabo in a brutal mutual time shortage.

**33. . . .      N–N5ch**
**34. K–B3      Q–B8**
**35. PxPch**

A Queen check on the eighth rank does not give the desired result. Sensing that the win is slipping away, Geller first of all makes sure he can get perpetual check.

**35. . . . KxP 36. Q–Q7ch K–B1 37. Q–Q8ch K–B2 38. Q–Q7ch K–B1 39. Q–Q6ch K–B2 40. Q–K6ch K–B1 41. Q–Q6ch K–B2 42. Q–K6ch K–B1**

**43. BxP**

A rash decision. The game was adjourned in this position. White does not have the slightest advantage, and Black's Queen and Knight are dangerously close to his King. Szabo, apparently not wanting to analyze the position at home, called the referee and pointed out that the game was a draw since the same position had been reached three times. Neither player had been keeping score in time pressure, but Geller, with great difficulty, was able to prove that Szabo was wrong, and he was given permission to continue the game.

His sealed move is poor, and at resumption of play he is forced to exert the greatest effort to convince Szabo that the position is a draw after all. In the heat of the tournament struggle it is not difficult for one to over-estimate his own or his opponent's chances.

**43. . . .      QxPch**

Black would create greater winning chances here by playing 43. . . . Q–B6ch instead of taking the RP. The alluring endgame for which Szabo is striving seems to be a draw despite the rules.

**44. K–K4 Q–K6ch 45. K–Q5 N–B3ch 46. K–B6 QxQch 47. PxQ K–K2 48. B–B4 N–K5 49. K–N6 P–R5 50. K–R5 N–Q3** (The position graphically illustrates the advantage of a

Bishop over a Knight; despite his outside passed pawn, Black cannot win.) **51. B–Q5 N–B4 52. KxP NxP 53. K–N3 N–B4 54. K–B3 K–Q3 55. B–B3 P–R5 56. K–Q3 KxP 57. K–K4 K–B3 58. B–N4 N–R3 59. B–Q7 K–N4 60. K–B3 N–B2 61. B–B8 N–K4ch 62. K–K4 N–B5** (Szabo refuses to believe that the position is not a win, and later he tries to succeed by advancing his KNP, but White ignores it.) **63. K–B3 N–K4ch 64. K–K4 K–B3 65. K–B4 P–N3 66. K–K4 P–N4 67. K–K3 K–N3 68. K–K4 N–B5 69. K–B3 N–Q7ch 70. K–K3 N–B8ch** (Even checks don't help!) **71. K–B2 N–N6 72. K–B3 K–B3 73. K–N4 N–B8 74. B–R6 N–K6ch 75. K–R3 N–B4 76. B–Q3 N–N6 77. K–N4 N–R8 78. B–B2, Drawn.**

# Game 111
## Reti Opening

| A. Kotov | M. Euwe |
|---|---|
| 1. P–QB4 | N–KB3 |
| 2. P–KN3 | P–K3 |
| 3. B–N2 | P–Q4 |
| 4. N–KB3 | PxP |
| 5. O–O | P–QR3 |

In his theoretical works Euwe does not recommend playing to keep the pawn but advises 5. . . . QN–Q2 6. N–R3 N–N3 7. NxP NxN 8. Q–R4ch B–Q2 9. QxN B–B3 10. P–N3 B–Q3 with approximately equal play. With 5. . . . P–QR3 he hopes to do better.

| 6. Q–B2 | P–QN4 |
|---|---|
| 7. N–K5 | N–Q4 |
| 8. P–Q3 | |

The decision of an experienced fighter. Kotov does not even try to win back the pawn but strives above all for active piece play.

| 8. . . . | PxP |
|---|---|
| 9. NxQP | B–N2 |
| 10. R–Q1 | Q–B1 |
| 11. P–QR4 | N–Q2 |
| 12. PxP | PxP |
| 13. RxR | BxR |
| 14. N–R3 | BxN |

Black does not want to concern himself with the defense of the QNP and is quite satisfied to part with his KB. However, the exchange of the Bishop grants Kotov too many dark squares. More prudent is 14. . . . Q–N1, although after 15. Q–N3 P–QB3 16. P–K4 N/4–N3 17. B–B4 White stands better.

| 15. PxB | O–O |
|---|---|
| 16. N–B5 | |

It will not be easy to get the Knight out of here, of course, and it is not good for Black to exchange it. White, as before, does not snatch a pawn, for the strong position of his pieces is worth even more.

| 16. . . . | N/2–N3 |
| 17. P–K4 | N–K2 |
| 18. B–B1 | B–B3 |
| 19. P–B3 | |

By letting Black exchange the second pair of Rooks White immediately gives up his advantage. Correct is 19. B–QN2, when 19. . . . R–Q1 is bad because of 20. Q–B3 P–B3 21. RxRch QxR 22. NxP. The variation 19. . . . N–R5 20. NxN PxN 21. Q–B5 R–K1 22. B–R3, threatening Q–K5, is also in White's favor.

19. . . . R–Q1 20. B–N5 RxR 21. QxR N–N3 22. Q–Q8ch B–K1 23. QxQ NxQ 24. B–Q8 P–QB3 (White's positional advantage still fully counterbalances Black's extra pawn, but no more than that.) 25. P–B4 P–K4 26. P–B5 N–B1 27. K–B2 N–Q2 28. N–N7 P–B3 29. K–K3 K–B1 30. P–R3 B–B2 (Black cannot be too active, for White's two Bishops are not to be discounted.) 31. B–R5 K–K1 32. P–N4 N/2–N3 33. B–N4 B–B5 34. B–N2 B–R7 35. B–B1 B–B5 36. B–N2, **Drawn.** An unexciting game.

## Game 112
### French Defense

**I. Boleslavsky    G. Stahlberg**

| 1. P–K4 | P–K3 |
| 2. P–Q4 | P–Q4 |
| 3. N–QB3 | B–N5 |

Stahlberg does not want to play his usual defense, 3. . . . N–KB3, apparently fearing that Boleslavsky has some prepared variation. But with 3. . . . B–N5 he jumps from the frying pan into the fire. The point is that the Winawer Variation is precisely the worst choice against Boleslavsky, for he has played this variation many times himself and is very familiar with the most vulnerable points in Black's setup. True, Stahlberg somewhat modifies the usual defensive scenario, but he falls into a difficult situation just the same.

| 4. P–K5 | P–QB4 |
| 5. P–QR3 | BxNch |
| 6. PxB | N–K2 |
| 7. P–QR4 | |

A flexible move. Depending on Black's answer, White intends to continue 8. B–R3, 8. Q–Q2, 8. Q–N4, or, as in the game, 8. N–B3.

| 7. . . . | QN–B3 |
| 8. N–B3 | B–Q2 |
| 9. B–K2 | QR–B1 |
| 10. O–O | O–O |
| 11. B–R3 | P–QN3 |
| 12. B–R6 | R–B2 |

| 13. | B–Q3 | P–KR3 |
|-----|------|-------|
| 14. | R–K1 | N–R4 |
| 15. | B–QB1 | P–B5 |

Black skillfully disguises his plans so as not to permit White to select a concrete plan of attack. Black is mistakenly tempted by the opportunity to open the KB-file here. It will bring him no advantage at all, whereas after a few defensive moves White will assume the offensive. He should stick to waiting tactics and act in accordance with his opponent's intentions.

| 16. | B–B1 | N–N3 |
|-----|------|------|
| 17. | P–N3 | P–B3 |
| 18. | PxP | QxP |
| 19. | B–KN2 | R/2–B1 |
| 20. | Q–K2 | R–KB2 |
| 21. | P–R4 | |

The signal for the storm. The dark squares are hopelessly weak, and Boleslavsky begins methodically to increase his pressure. The Bishop on QB1 returns to its proper attacking diagonal, QR3–KB8, the Rooks are concentrated on the KB-file,

the Knight invades K5, and the pawns, supported by the Bishop at KR3, proceed to the decisive breakthrough. What can Black do against this? Very little. He can only defend passively.

| 21. | . . . | N–B3 |
|-----|-------|------|
| 22. | P–KR5 | N–B1 |
| 23. | N–R2 | N–R2 |
| 24. | P–B4 | R–K1 |
| 25. | N–B3 | Q–Q1 |
| 26. | N–R4 | N–B1 |
| 27. | R–KB1 | N–K2 |
| 28. | N–B3 | N–B3 |
| 29. | B–QR3 | B–B1 |
| 30. | R–B2 | N–Q2 |
| 31. | QR–KB1 | N–K2 |
| 32. | B–R3 | N–KB4 |
| 33. | K–R2 | N–B3 |
| 34. | P–N4 | N–Q3 |
| 35. | N–K5 | R–B2 |

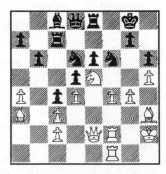

**36. B–KN2**

Having obtained a winning position, White is indecisive. 36. P–N5 is called for here, either at once or after the preliminary 36. BxN. The KN-file would be opened in either case, and, thanks to his marked superiority in maneuverability, White would be able to organize a decisive attack. Now Black can move his Knight from KB3, and P–N5 will no longer gain a tempo.

| 36. . . . | N/Q–K5 |
| 37. R–B3 | N–Q2 |
| 38. N–N6 | |

He can bother the Knight with R–K3, but White, to his misfortune, is quite heedless of the proper time to open the KB-file.

| 38. . . . | N/2–B3 |
| 39. N–K5 | N–Q2 |
| 40. K–N1 | NxN |
| 41. BPxN | N–N4 |

Black is able to entrench himself just where the breakthrough seemed inevitable. The position acquires a closed character, and White's Bishops lose a certain part of their strength. White should now be satisfied with an immediate draw, but he cannot resist winning the Queen.

| 42. R–B8ch | RxR |

Of course, after 42. . . . K–R2 43. RxR QxR 44. R–B8 White would maintain a strong attack. But now the winning chances can only be Black's.

However, Stahlberg finds adjournment playoffs tiresome, and after analyzing the adjourned position he offered a draw, which Boleslavsky accepted.

# Round Seventeen

## Game 113
### King's Indian Defense

| G. Stahlberg | A. Kotov |
|---|---|
| 1. P–Q4 | N–KB3 |
| 2. P–QB4 | P–Q3 |
| 3. N–KB3 | QN–Q2 |
| 4. N–B3 | P–K4 |
| 5. P–K4 | P–B3 |
| 6. B–K2 | B–K2 |

The King's Indian Bishop belongs on KN2, where it is subsequently reassigned.

| | |
|---|---|
| 7. O–O | O–O |
| 8. Q–B2 | R–K1 |
| 9. P–QN3 | |

Nor is White developing his Bishop on the best square. It is more active to put the Rook on Q1 first and then to prepare the Bishop's way to K3 by P–KR3.

| | |
|---|---|
| 9. ... | B–B1 |
| 10. B–N2 | N–R4 |
| 11. P–N3 | P–KN3 |
| 12. QR–Q1 | N/4–B3 |
| 13. P–Q5 | |

The position begins to assume the outlines of the "normal"

King's Indian. White does not want to allow the opening of the center by 13. .... KPxP, so he advances the pawn and the maneuvering continues.

| | |
|---|---|
| 13. ... | P–B4 |
| 14. N–KR4 | B–N2 |
| 15. P–QR3 | N–N3 |
| 16. B–B3 | R–B1 |
| 17. N–K2 | B–Q2 |
| 18. B–B3 | N–K1 |
| 19. B–QR5 | Q–K2 |
| 20. QR–K1 | R–B1 |
| 21. B–Q2 | Q–Q1 |
| 22. Q–B1 | B–KB3 |
| 23. N–N2 | B–K2 |
| 24. B–R6 | N–N2 |

It must be admitted that Kotov has been more successful with his last ten moves and has rebuilt his forces very harmoniously. Now the pawns join the battle.

| | |
|---|---|
| 25. P–KR4 | P–B4 |
| 26. PxP | PxP |
| 27. N–B3 | B–K1 |
| 28. B–Q1 | N–Q2 |

277

| 29. BxN | KxB |
|---------|-----|
| 30. Q-K3 | B-B3 |
| 31. B-B2 | B-N3 |
| 32. Q-K2 | P-K5 |

The players soon turn to reciprocal threats, and the reader will be compensated for the rather boring prelude, for there is a fascinating combination and a subtle endgame in store.

The pawn advances to take control of KB6, which is where Black's Knight is headed. Since Black also happens to be threatening the Knight on QB6, one's first impression is that . . . N–K4–B6 cannot be prevented. Stahlberg dispels this illusion with a long forcing variation.

| 33. N-B4 | R-K1 |
|----------|------|
| 34. N-K6ch | RxN |
| 35. PxR | BxN |
| 36. PxN | QxQP |

So White has won the Exchange, although that was not the reason he checked on K6. If Black can play P–KR4, White's initiative will immediately be blown away. Therefore:

| 37. P-R5 | BxR |
|----------|-----|
| 38. PxB | B-B6 |
| 39. PxP | R-KR1 |

An innocent move concealing an insidious trap. The game is now approximately equal, and after 40. K–N2 and R–KR1 the draw would be obvious. Stahlberg's next moves are made in time pressure, however, and he attacks the Bishop apparently in the certain belief that Black has nothing better than the undesirable 40. . . . B–B3.

**40. Q-K3          K-N3!**

The King solves three problems with one move: it defends KN4, opens the way for the Queen to KR2, and, very important, avoids a check in case of QxB. Not only are the idea and the cleverness of the combination unforgettable, but so is the way Black implements it. White's King finds itself quite unexpectedly in danger.

| 41. R-Q1 | B-Q5 |
|----------|------|
| 42. Q-B4 | QxP |
| 43. K-B1 | Q-R8ch |
| 44. K-K2 | Q-R4ch! |

Kotov plays the second part with rare energy and inventiveness. White is waiting for a chance to play P–KN4, and Black gives him the chance to play it with tempo.

| 45. | P–KN4 | QxPch |
| 46. | QxQch | PxQ |
| 47. | BxPch | K–N4 |

Here is how things have turned out. Despite the opposite-color Bishops, White's position is lost. The reasons:

1) Black's Bishop stands well on Q5 and has a base, which cannot be said of White's Bishop on K4.

2) Black's King is far more active than its colleague and is in direct control of the battle.

3) White's KBP and Black's KNP are not equal in value:

the KBP is weak and defenseless, but the KNP is ready to assist the pieces in the attack on KB7.

All these pluses would carry no weight if White could exchange Rooks, but he cannot. The last part of the game is instructive.

| 48. | R–KR1 | R–K1 |
| 49. | P–B3 | P–N4 |
| 50. | K–B1 | QNPxP |
| 51. | NPxP | P–N6 |
| 52. | R–R7 | R–QN1 |
| 53. | B–N7 | |

Stahlberg tries everything. Above all, he bars the Rook from entering his camp. If Black did not have a passed KNP, this might have saved the game.

| 53. | ... | B–K4 |
| 54. | K–N2 | K–B5 |
| 55. | R–B7ch | K–K6 |

The invasion by Black's King is decisive.

| 56. | P–B4 | BxP |
| 57. | R–K7ch | B–K4 |
| 58. | R–KB7 | P–R4 |
| 59. | P–R4 | K–Q5 |
| 60. | B–Q5 | R–N7ch |
| 61. | K–B1 | R–QR7 |

White resigns

# Game 114
## King's Indian Defense

| M. Euwe | Y. Geller |
|---|---|

1. P–Q4 N–KB3 2. P–QB4 P–KN3 3. P–KN3 B–N2 4. B– N2 O–O 5. N–KB3 P–Q3 6. O–O QN–Q2 7. Q–B2 P–K4 8. R–Q1 R–K1 9. N–B3 P–

B3 10. PxP PxP 11. N–KN5
Q–K2 12. N/5–K4 N–B4 13.
N–Q6 R–Q1 14. NxB RxRch
15. NxR RxN 16. B–Q2 KN–
Q2 17. B–QB3 P–B4 18. N–
K3 N–K3 19. P–QN4 N–Q5

20. Q–N2 Q–B2 21. P–QR4
R–B1 (Euwe's passive play has
permitted Geller to set up a
good attacking position. Sooner
or later White's Bishop will
have to take the Knight on Q4,
which will give Black new advantages.) 22. P–R5 P–B5 23.
PxP QxKBP 24. R–KB1 N–
B3 25. P–B5 N–K5 (Black's
Knights are intolerable, but
. . .) 26. KBxN QxB 27. BxN
PxB (The advantage of the
two Bishops makes itself felt:
in two moves they have an-
nihilated two beautiful Knights.)
28. N–N2 P–QR3 29. Q–N3ch
K–R1 30. Q–Q3 Q–K4 31. P–
B4 (Euwe tries to set up an
impenetrable position.)

31. . . . Q–K3 32. R–B3
R–K1 33. K–B2 R–KB1 34.
K–B1 K–N1 35. K–B2 R–B2
36. K–B1 R–B4 37. K–B2 B–
B3 38. K–N1 R–Q4 39. K–B2
K–N2 40. K–B1 R–R4 41. K–
N1 R–Q4 42. P–R3 K–B2 43.
K–B2 K–K2 44. K–B1 K–Q1
45. N–K1 K–B2 46. N–B2 K–
N1 (An important element in
Black's plan. Having concluded
that White's position is not to be
breached by ordinary means,
Black moves his King to the
other side so that it will not be
in danger during the coming
storm. White's Knight sets out
in pursuit and remains on guard
to remind Black's King of the
possibility of a fatal check on
his first rank.) 47. N–R3 B–Q1
48. N–B4 B–B2 49. N–N6 R–
Q1 50. P–B5 PxP (Euwe's loss
of patience facilitates Black's
task.) 51. QxBP Q–R3 52. Q–
B7 Q–B8ch 53. K–B2 B–R7!
(Black finds the White King's
Achilles' heel—KN1.) 54. Q–
N7 B–B5 55. K–N2 B–K6 56.
R–B1 (White dies without a

murmur. He should take his chances on 56. R–B7, after which Black would have to find the complicated variation 56. ... Q–N8ch 57. K–B3 Q–B8ch 58. K–N3 B–B5ch! 59. K–R4 Q–B7ch 60. K–N4 P–R4ch.

Now things are much simpler.) **56. ... Q–Q7 57. R–B7 Qx Pch 58. K–N3 Q–K8ch 59. K– B3 Q–R8ch 60. K–N3 Q– N8ch 61. K–B3 Q–B7ch 62. K–K4 R–K1ch 63. R–K7 Q– R5ch, White resigns.**

## Game 115
### Queen's Gambit

| L. Szabo | V. Smyslov |
|---|---|
| 1. P–Q4 | P–Q4 |
| 2. P–QB4 | P–QB3 |
| 3. N–KB3 | N–KB3 |
| 4. N–B3 | PxP |
| 5. P–QR4 | B–B4 |
| 6. P–K3 | P–K3 |
| 7. BxP | B–QN5 |
| 8. O–O | QN–Q2 |
| 9. Q–K2 | O–O |
| 10. P–K4 | B–N3 |
| 11. B–Q3 | |

A repetition of the opening of game 34, Boleslavsky–Smyslov, but Szabo's 11. B–Q3 is stronger than Boleslavsky's 11. P–K5, from which White got nothing.

**11. ...          Q–R4**

This does not succeed. In game 128, two rounds later, Smyslov played 11. ... P–KR3 against Stahlberg and soon fully equalized, and in a match against Geller he succeeded with 11. ... B–KR4. Since White gets nothing in this variation, one cannot help asking whether his 10th move, P–K4, and may-

be even his 5th, P–QR4, cannot be improved upon.

| 12. N–R2 | B–K2 |
|---|---|
| 13. B–Q2 | Q–R4 |
| 14. N–B3 | KR–Q1 |
| 15. B–KB4 | P–B4 |
| 16. P–Q5 | |

A typical breakthrough in such positions. White starts by denying Q4 to Black's Knight, then drives the Knight away with P–K5, after which he takes the QP and ends up with his Knight in a strong position in the center.

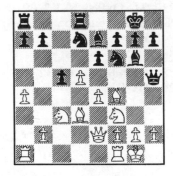

| 16. ... | PxP |
|---|---|
| 17. P–K5 | BxB |
| 18. QxB | N–K1 |

| 19. NxP | B–B1 |
| 20. Q–N3 | Q–N3 |
| 21. P–R5 | |

White nails down the QNP. It cannot be taken for the moment because of "perpetual check" to the Queen by QR–N1–B1. His next move reinforces the threat to the QNP.

| 21. . . . | P–KR3 |
| 22. N–K3 | P–N3 |
| 23. KR–Q1 | N–B2 |
| 24. B–N3 | |

Black must try to find a defense against 25. B–R4. Szabo is playing with great élan and Black's position is critical.

| 24. . . . | P–N4 |
| 25. B–R4 | P–B5 |
| 26. Q–B3 | P–B3 |
| 27. NxP | |

White wins a pawn but complicates the win. Black would have a more difficult defense after 27. P–QN3 NxP 28. NxN RxRch 29. RxR PxN 30. PxP PxP 31. QxPch N–K3 32. N–N4. Best would be 30. . . . P–N5.

| 27. . . . | PxN |
| 28. QxPch | Q–B2 |
| 29. QxN | NxP |

| 30. QxQch | NxQ |
| 31. B–N3 | P–R3 |
| 32. K–B1 | QR–B1 |
| 33. KR–B1 | B–N5 |

Drawn on White's offer. Szabo would have fair winning chances in the endgame after, for instance, 34. RxR RxR 35. R–R4. Black's attempt to win back the QNP would not work: 35. . . . R–R8ch 36. K–K2 R–B7ch 37. K–Q1 RxNP 38. K–B1 R–N6 39. K–B2 R–R6ch 40. K–N2 R–R5 41. K–N3. So the Bishop would have to retreat by 35. . . . B–B1, which would be followed by 36. K–K1, and White would gradually improve the position of his pieces, with chances to realize his extra pawn.

## Game 116
### Ruy Lopez

Y. Averbakh          P. Keres

1. P–K4 P–K4 2. N–KB3 N–QB3 3. B–N5 P–QR3 4. B–R4 N–B3 5. O–O B–K2 6. R–K1 P–QN4 7. B–N3 O–O 8. P–B3 P–Q3 9. P–KR3 N–QR4

10. B–B2 P–B4 11. P–Q4 Q–B2 12. QN–Q2 B–N2 13. P–Q5 (White closes the center in order to start a Kingside storm.) 13. ... B–B1 14. N–B1 B–Q2 15. P–QN3 P–N3 16. B–R6 KR–N1 17. P–KN4 (White makes his first attacking move and stops. Averbakh hints that he will continue aggressively only if Keres starts advancing his Queenside pawns.) 17. ... B–KB1 18. Q–Q2 K–R1 19. N–N5 K–N1 20. N–B3 K–R1 21. N–N5 K–N1 22. N–B3, Drawn.

Black cannot refuse to repeat moves, for after N–B3 White threatens BxB and Q–R6 and then again N–N5. So Black puts his King on R1 in order to answer Q–R6 with N–N1. But White is not absolutely required to repeat moves, of course ...

## Game 117
### Reti Opening

| T. Petrosian | S. Reshevsky |
|---|---|
| 1. N–KB3 | N–KB3 |
| 2. P–KN3 | P–KN3 |
| 3. B–N2 | B–N2 |
| 4. O–O | O–O |
| 5. P–Q3 | P–Q4 |
| 6. QN–Q2 | P–B4 |
| 7. P–K4 | |

The opponents are playing a King's Indian Defense with colors reversed and, consequently, with an extra tempo for White. This setup, often used by Soviet masters of late, demands a certain amount of caution on Black's part. Those plans which are good for White in the normal King's Indian Defense can turn out to be very dangerous when played by Black a move behind. The exchange of pawns Reshevsky initiates in the center is analogous to White's QPxKP in the King's Indian Defense, which usually leads to equality. But here White is able to prepare and then carry out the advance of his KP and KBP beyond the fifth rank.

| 7. ... | PxP |
|---|---|
| 8. PxP | N–B3 |
| 9. P–B3 | P–KR3 |
| 10. Q–K2 | B–K3 |
| 11. N–K1 | Q–N3 |
| 12. P–KR3 | QR–Q1 |
| 13. K–R2 | N–R2 |
| 14. P–KB4 | |

White already stands somewhat better thanks to his space advantage. His next task is to regroup his pieces now arranged on the first and second ranks to support the advance of the KP and KBP. It is very important here that his opponent does not have active play and that for the next seven moves Black's pieces actually lie idle, if we do not count the transfer of the Bishop to its other main diagonal, a maneuver that could have been made earlier without wasting time on B–K3–Q2–B3.

| | |
|---|---|
| 14. . . . | N–R4 |
| 15. N/1–B3 | B–Q2 |
| 16. R–K1 | Q–B2 |
| 17. N–B1 | P–N3 |
| 18. N–K3 | B–QB3 |
| 19. N–N4 | N–B3 |
| 20. N–B2 | B–N2 |
| 21. P–K5 | N–R2 |
| 22. P–KR4 | |

White has achieved a strategic victory in having driven the enemy pieces back to the last two ranks. White's natural plan here is to advance his KBP and KNP for a breakthrough on the Kingside. Petrosian decides

on a rather different action: he threatens P–R5xP, etc., which provokes the blockading move . . . P–KR4, and then he sacrifices a pawn by P–B5!. If Black accepts the sacrifice, White's Knight on B2 will be favorably transferred to KB4. A good idea.

| | |
|---|---|
| 22. . . . | P–R4 |
| 23. P–B5 | Q–Q2 |

Reshevsky declines the sacrifice, of course, but now the KP enters the fight. Black is able to ward off White's attack, but his KP and KRP become isolated.

| | |
|---|---|
| 24. P–K6 | Q–Q4 |
| 25. PxPch | QxP |
| 26. PxP | QxNP |
| 27. N–N5 | BxB |
| 28. KxB | P–K4 |
| 29. Q–K4 | R–B4 |
| 30. NxN | KxN |

Drawn. White's position is much better, of course. If Queens are exchanged, Black's weak pawns will be good targets. But if Queens are not exchanged, Black will have to pay attention to the security of his exposed King, which will bind him hand and foot.

## Game 118
### Nimzo-Indian Defense

| M. Najdorf | D. Bronstein | 3. N–QB3 | B–N5 |
|---|---|---|---|
| 1. P–Q4 | N–KB3 | 4. P–K3 | P–B4 |
| 2. P–QB4 | P–K3 | 5. B–Q3 | P–QN3 |

| 6. | N–B3 | B–N2 |
|---|---|---|
| 7. | O–O | O–O |
| 8. | B–Q2 | P–Q3 |
| 9. | Q–B2 | QN–Q2 |

Black rejects the tempting 9. . . . BxKN, thinking he will be unable to exploit White's weak King protection; for instance, 9. . . . BxKN 10. PxB PxP 11. PxP N–B3 12. B–K3, and the King is quite safe. This is what Black should play, however, with the idea of attacking not White's King but his center. The play would be interesting after 12. . . . BxN 13. QxB P–Q4 or 13. . . . P–K4. But now White's advantage stands out clearly, and Black has to be very careful.

| 10. | P–QR3 | BxQN |
|---|---|---|
| 11. | BxB | R–B1 |
| 12. | N–Q2 | P–KR3 |
| 13. | QR–B1 | P–Q4 |
| 14. | P–QN3 | QPxP |
| 15. | NPxP | Q–B2 |

Black's main concern is to prohibit P–Q5. He also has to see that White's Knight does not establish itself on K5, that White is not permitted to set up the battery B/N1–Q/B2, and, even should this occur, that he always has a Knight ready to go to KB1. As we see, the problems are considerable.

But it is boring to think always of defense. Black's 14. . . . QPxP harbored the hope of making use of the active position of his Bishop on N2 and

perhaps the relative weakness of White's QP and QBP. Black wants very much for one of them to advance. Now, incidentally, White has to consider Black's threat of N–N5.

**16. KR–Q1**

White posts his Rooks incorrectly; they should occupy the K- and Q-files.

| 16. | . . . | KR–K1 |
|---|---|---|
| 17. | N–B1 | PxP |
| 18. | PxP | Q–B5 |
| 19. | N–N3 | P–KR4 |

Black must hurry, else White will play 20. R–K1 and try to transfer his Rook to KN3, after which his Knight goes to K4. The combination of a Rook on KN3 and a Bishop on QB3 can detonate on KN7.

| 20. | P–R3 | P–R5 |
|---|---|---|
| 21. | N–B1 | N–K5 |

Drawn. The Knight must be taken, and after 22. BxN BxB White's advantage disappears.

## Game 119

The sacrifice of a pawn for the initiative is one of the most complex problems of chess strategy and, perhaps, of chess psychology. So varied are the positions that arise as the result of sacrifices that it is impossible to make any generalizations. Some grandmasters who are able to calculate variations quickly often give up a pawn or two for the sake of changing the character of the position and upsetting the balance, even though this may not be to their own benefit. I do not think this manner of play has a great future. The author of this book has sacrificed more than a few dozen pawns all told, but still I believe that a master should have some idea of the value of the initiative he will get for his pawn, and the character the struggle will acquire, even if only in general outline.

Sometimes one is obliged, willing or not, to give up a pawn, or even the Exchange or a piece; this is reasonable if he sees that the normal, logical progress of the struggle will lead to a difficult position. Taimanov, with the White pieces, sacrifices a pawn in the opening but gets no greater initiative than if pawns were equal. White endeavors mightily throughout the whole game to win his pawn back, but he does not succeed and Black's extra pawn becomes a Queen.

## Sicilian Defense

**M. Taimanov**     **S. Gligoric**

| 1. | P–K4 | P–QB4 |
|----|------|-------|
| 2. | N–KB3 | P–Q3 |
| 3. | B–N5ch | |

The exchange of light-square Bishops on the 4th move is bound up with a long-range strategical idea. Black has put his pawns on the dark squares, and Taimanov thinks it will be difficult for Black to maintain positional equality without his light-square Bishop. Of course, Black can gradually shift his center pawns to K3 and Q4, but this will take time.

| 3. | . . . | B–Q2 |
|----|-------|------|
| 4. | BxBch | QxB |
| 5. | O–O | N–QB3 |
| 6. | R–K1 | |

I think it is more appropriate, now that the Bishops have been exchanged, to put a pawn on the light square Q3 and the Knight on QB3, where it controls Q5, and then, when Black plays P–K3 or P–KN3, to prepare P–KB4–5. Taimanov illogically chooses a plan that helps Black clear his cluttered KB1–QB4 diagonal of Black pawns.

**6. . . .          N–B3**
**7. P–Q4        PxP**
**8. B–N5**

White refuses to take the QP and makes a sharp move he has prepared earlier, counting on 8. . . . P–K4 9. BxN PxB 10. P–B3!, or 8. . . . P–KN3 9. BxN PxB 10. NxP, or 8. . . . N–KN5 9. NxP P–KR3 10. B–B1. Gligoric finds an excellent plan, however, eliminating the last White pawn in the center and ensuring active positions for his own pieces.

**8. . . .          P–Q4**
**9. BxN**

There is little choice. Black answers 9. P–K5 with 9. . . . N–K5.

**9. . . .          NPxB**
**10. PxP         QxP**
**11. N–B3        Q–Q2**
**12. N–K4        O–O–O**

**13. P–B3**

Taimanov realizes, of course, that his strategical plans have collapsed: Black has an extra pawn and prospects of creating a strong center, and White's Knights have no points of support. Grandmaster Taimanov is distinguished by the exceptional objectivity of his evaluations, a highly enviable quality that one should strive to emulate. White's only chance here is to complicate the game, and Taimanov is prepared to answer 13. . . . PxP with 14. Q–N3, even giving up the QNP. Gligoric, however, not only refuses further acquisitions but even returns the extra pawn temporarily and advances his pawns to KB5 and K5, firmly holding on to his advantage.

**13. . . .         P–B4**
**14. N–B5        Q–Q4**

The interesting complications after 14. . . . Q–B2 turn out in Black's favor, but still they are complications, and that's just what Taimanov is looking for; therefore, Gligoric settles for the strong Q–Q4, centralizing his Queen.

On 14. . . . Q–B2 White answers 15. PxP P–K4 16. R–QB1 P–K5 17. N–K5 RxP 18. Q–N3, but Black has the better possibility 17. . . . NxN! 18. N–K6 PxN 19. RxQch KxR 20. Q–N3 N–B3 21. QxP NxP 22. Q–K5ch B–Q3.

**15. PxP         P–K4**
**16. R–QB1      PxP**

Taimanov's stubborn play for complications bears fruit: Black makes an inaccurate move. Correct is 16. . . . P–K5, when 17. N–K5 loses a piece and 17. N–KR4 is followed by 17. . . . B–K2 18. Q–R5 BxN/5 19. QxB QxQP 20. Q–R5 Q–B3. But now Black's pawn will play no role in the battle because it's blockaded, and his isolated pawns on the Kingside are weak.

**17. N–Q3    B–Q3**

**18. N/B–K5**

White is looking for chances where they are hard to find; nothing can be gained from the pin on the Knight. He should attack the KBP by 18. N–R4 and 19. Q–R5.

| 18. . . . | KR–K1 |
| 19. NxN | RxRch |
| 20. NxR | PxN |
| 21. Q–Q3 | |

What has White accomplished? The QP is no longer isolated and the blockading Knight has been replaced by the Queen.

| 21. . . . | K–N2 |
| 22. P–QN4 | |

Too venturesome. Taimanov should remember his third move, B–N5ch, and that his opponent has no light-square Bishop and should try to keep Black's pawns on dark squares. Best for this purpose is to play P–QN3 and then bring the Knight to QB4.

| 22. . . . | B–B5 |
| 23. R–Q1 | B–B2 |
| 24. P–QR3 | B–N3 |
| 25. N–B3 | Q–K5 |
| 26. N–N5 | QxQ |
| 27. RxQ | P–QR4! |

A fine move, deciding the game. Black returns his extra pawn at just the right moment and in a few moves takes the QNP, after which the two connected passed pawns bring victory.

| 28. | NxBP | R–Q4 |
|-----|------|------|
| 29. | K–B1 | PxP  |
| 30. | PxP  | K–R3 |
| 31. | P–B4 | K–N4 |
| 32. | N–K5 | B–B2 |
| 33. | R–Q1 | B–Q3 |

A gross blunder would be 33. . . . BxN 34. PxB KxP in view of 35. P–K6!, and the threat to support the advance of the passed pawn with the Rook would make Black the one to look for a draw.

34. K–K2 BxN 35. PxB RxPch 36. K–Q3 KxP 37. R–QB1 K–N4 38. KxP R–Q4ch 39. K–K3 P–B4 40. R–N1ch K–R5 41. R–N7 P–R4 42. K–B4 P–B5 43. K–N5 P–B6 44. KxP R–Q7 45. P–N3 RxPch 46. K–N5 R–KB7, White resigns.

# Round Eighteen

## Game 120
### Sicilian Defense

| S. Gligoric | M. Najdorf |    | 11. PxN | B–B4 |
|---|---|---|---|---|
| 1. P–K4 | P–QB4 |    | 12. O–O | N–Q2 |
| 2. N–KB3 | P–Q3 |    | 13. B–Q2 | QR–N1 |
| 3. P–Q4 | PxP |    | 14. P–KB4 | B–N3 |
| 4. NxP | N–KB3 |    | 15. P–R3 | P–B3 |
| 5. N–QB3 | P–QR3 |    | 16. K–R2 | B–K2 |
| 6. P–KN3 | P–K4 |    | 17. P–R5 | Q–B2 |
| 7. N/4–K2 | B–K3 |    | 18. P–B3 | P–N6 |
| 8. B–N2 | P–QN4 |    | 19. P–B5 | B–B2 |

Najdorf repeats the move Kotov played against Gligoric (game 66). This time Gligoric begins operations on the Queenside immediately. As one of the spectators at the tournament pointed out, however, the sharper 9. N–B4 is playable, and if Black accepts the sacrifice, 10. P–K5 simultaneously attacks QR8 and KB6; if he does not, the Knight triumphantly enters Q5.

An interesting moment: a Rook takes possession of an open line in the middlegame—not a file, as is usually the case, but the fourth rank, completely free of Black and White men. Najdorf could have prevented this with 16. . . . P–QR4, but of course it did not occur to him that with all the pieces around in the middlegame his opponent would open the fourth rank and occupy it with a Rook.

| 9. P–QR4 | P–N5 |
|---|---|
| 10. N–Q5 | NxN |

20. R–R4

On making this original move Gligoric offered a draw; Najdorf declined, although his position does not merit so optimistic an evaluation, as he realized later himself. For instance, after 20. . . . O–O 21. N–B1 N–B4 22. R–QN4! QxP 23. NxP White has good play.

| 20. . . . | N–B4 |
| 21. R–KN4 | P–N3 |
| 22. R–QN4 | |

Unexpected and too courageous. White abandons his KBP for the sake of trying to get the QNP. Gligoric's austere style is unrecognizable in this game.

| 22. . . . | PxP |
| 23. B–K3 | O–O |
| 24. N–B1 | B–N3 |
| 25. NxP | RxR |
| 26. PxR | N–K5 |
| 27. Q–K2 | Q–N2 |
| 28. N–Q2 | Drawn |

But now Najdorf offered the draw, which White accepted although he still has the better position. It is not good for Black to take the QNP in view of 28. . . . QxNP 29. NxN PxN 30. B–R6 R–N1 31. R–B2 threatening P–KR4–5, and possible is 30. QxP QxNP 31. Q–N6 when Black loses if he trades Queens.

Perhaps Black can extricate himself from his difficult position by sacrificing a piece: 28. . . . NxNP 29. KxN P–B5ch 30. BxP PxBch 31. RxP P–B4. Najdorf's analysis continues to the 51st move. It goes without saying that the variations are interesting, but even more interesting variations would have arisen had the game continued.

## Game 121
### King's Indian Defense

**D. Bronstein**    **T. Petrosian**

| 1. P–Q4 | N–KB3 |
| 2. P–QB4 | P–Q3 |
| 3. N–QB3 | QN–Q2 |
| 4. B–N5 | P–KR3 |
| 5. B–R4 | P–KN4 |

One of those moves that abruptly changes the course of the struggle and forces the opponents to rethink every detail of the position. The mechanism of . . . P–KN4 is simple: Black will exchange his Knight for White's Bishop on KN6 and this will favor his KB. However, "pawns do not move backward," and the dislocation of the pawn from KN2 to KN4 determines the pawn structure on this flank prematurely and makes it easier for White to formulate specific plans.

|      |         |      |
|------|---------|------|
| 6.   | B–N3    | N–R4 |
| 7.   | P–K3    | NxB  |
| 8.   | RPxN    | B–N2 |
| 9.   | B–Q3    | N–B3 |
| 10.  | Q–Q2    | P–B3 |
| 11.  | O–O–O   | Q–R4 |

White's last three "attacking" moves were utterly harmless. He has chosen the wrong area for his offensive. The shortcomings of Petrosian's defense could have been exposed on the 9th move by P–B4, taking aim at Black's KNP.

|      |         |       |
|------|---------|-------|
| 12.  | K–N1    | B–Q2  |
| 13.  | KN–K2   | P–K3  |
| 14.  | N–B1    | O–O–O |
| 15.  | N–N3    | Q–B2  |
| 16.  | Q–K2    | KR–K1 |
| 17.  | P–K4    |       |

White has spent a lot of time preparing this advance, which pushes against Black's excellent defensive lines.

|      |         |       |
|------|---------|-------|
| 17.  | . . .   | P–B4  |
| 18.  | P–K5    | QPxP  |
| 19.  | PxKP    | N–N1  |
| 20.  | P–B4    |       |

Now, ten moves late, this is inappropriate and allows Black to open the position advantageously.

|      |         |       |
|------|---------|-------|
| 20.  | . . .   | PxP   |
| 21.  | PxP     | P–B3  |
| 22.  | N–N5    | BxN   |
| 23.  | PxB     | K–N1  |
| 24.  | R–QB1   | P–N3  |
| 25.  | B–N6    | R–KB1 |
| 26.  | KR–K1   |       |

White's pawn offer is a mistake. His idea to lure Black's Rook to K4 cannot be approved, since he does not have the means to exploit the KR1–QR8 diagonal or the open Q-file in view of the unfortunate position of his Knight on QN3. Thus have Tarrasch's "dogmas" been forgotten! (See Preface.)

|      |         |       |
|------|---------|-------|
| 26.  | . . .   | PxP   |
| 27.  | PxP     | R–Q4  |
| 28.  | B–K4    | RxP   |
| 29.  | Q–QB2   | R–Q1  |
| 30.  | KR–Q1   | RxR   |
| 31.  | RxR     | N–K2  |
| 32.  | N–Q2    | Drawn |

White's position would not be bad if he could establish his Knight on QB4. However,

Black can prevent this by 32. . . . P–B5!; e.g., 33. NxP RxP or 33. QxP QxQ 34. NxQ RxB.

But White should not take the pawn. Better is 33. P–R4 and the retreat of the Bishop to

B3 in an attempt to create counterthreats to the Black King. Petrosian, who was in time pressure, did not see 32. . . . P–B5 and accepted the draw offer immediately.

## Game 122
### Nimzo-Indian Defense

| S. Reshevsky | Y. Averbakh |
|---|---|
| 1. P–Q4 | N–KB3 |
| 2. P–QB4 | P–K3 |
| 3. N–QB3 | B–N5 |
| 4. P–K3 | O–O |
| 5. N–K2 | P–Q4 |
| 6. P–QR3 | B–K2 |
| 7. PxP | PxP |
| 8. N–N3 | B–K3 |

Inasmuch as White has not prevented . . . P–QB4, Black should take advantage of this to develop more freely; in particular, the QN can go to QB3 instead of Q2. Averbakh chooses a solid but passive setup in which Black does not have sufficient counterchances and can hope only to draw. With P–QB4 Black would have removed White's QP from the center, opened the QB-file, and freed K4 for a piece.

| 9. B–Q3 | QN–Q2 |
|---|---|
| 10. O–O | P–B3 |
| 11. B–Q2 | R–K1 |

Black believes he has solved his basic problem in the Nimzo-Indian Defense: he has kept

White from playing P–K4 for a long time. White begins leisurely to prepare the advance of his KP, while Black, as before, plays as though under siege, his sortie P–QR4–5 having rather a symbolic character. Because of such tactics, Black's situation noticeably worsens in the next ten to twelve moves: marking time with his Bishop by B–K3–Q2–B1–K3 is connected with no strategical plan and has no purpose but to demonstrate the inaccessibility of Black's position. Meanwhile, White gathers his strength for the decisive blow.

| 12. Q–B2 | P–QR4 |
|---|---|
| 13. QN–K2 | N–N3 |
| 14. N–B4 | B–Q2 |
| 15. KR–K1 | B–KB1 |
| 16. P–B3 | B–B1 |

Black still does not allow White's P–K4, but Reshevsky nevertheless carries out his plan.

| 17. QR–B1 | P–N3 |
|---|---|
| 18. N/4–K2 | B–N2 |
| 19. P–R3 | P–R5 |

| 20. P–K4 | PxP |
|----------|-----|
| 21. PxP  | B–K3 |
| 22. B–K3 | B–N6 |
| 23. Q–Q2 | |

White has established a strong center. The next stage of his plan is an attack on the King, but it is not yet the time for the pieces to enter the battle; he must begin with the advance of the KRP to breach the castle wall.

This game is very characteristic of Reshevsky's artistry. Far from throwing himself headlong into the attack, he consistently accumulates advantages and tries to avoid giving his opponent counterchances. Averbakh is led astray by the slowness of White's attack and mistakes prudence for indecision. The position requires him to take energetic action on the Queenside.

| 23. . . . | KN–Q2 |
|-----------|-------|
| 24. B–KN5! | P–B3 |

An unpleasant weakening of the Kingside. With the pawn on B2 White's standard maneuver P–KR4–5 loses much of its strength, since Black can always recapture with the BP if White plays RPxNP. Of course, 24. . . . B–B3 is bad because White takes the Bishop, brings his Rook to the KB-file, and pushes his pawn to K5. Retreating to QB2 is unfavorable: the Queen would be rather uncomfortable there.

Averbakh's only hope is to counterattack White's center (30. . . . P–QB4).

| 25. B–K3 | N–KB1 |
|----------|-------|
| 26. P–R4 | B–B2 |

The RP can be stopped by 26. . . . P–R4. Therefore, 26. B–R6! and only then 27. P–R4 would have been more accurate.

| 27. P–R5 | N–K3 |
|----------|------|

By N–K3, B–B1, and N–Q2 the defenders of the castle gird for battle, ready to sell their lives dearly. Black is incidentally preparing P–QB4.

| 28. R–B1 | B–B1 |
|----------|------|
| 29. R–KB2 | N–Q2 |
| 30. QR–B1 | P–QB4 |

At last! But wouldn't it have been better to do this on the 8th move?

| 31. P–Q5 | N–B2 |
|----------|------|
| 32. PxP  | PxP |

Black's acquisition of K4 for his pieces does not compensate at all for White's growing power on the KR-file. The only question is how quickly White will double or build up his pieces on it.

| 33. R–B4 | P–QN4 |
|----------|-------|
| 34. R–R4 | N–K4 |
| 35. K–R1 | Q–Q2? |

Black's situation is unenviable, of course, but a grandmaster should not go down so submissively, giving up a pawn and the key point of his position for nothing. White could have begun the conquest of KR6 and KN7 on his 35th move by 35. B–R6! His waiting move, K–R1, was not particularly necessary since White's King was not threatened where it stood. Clearly, Reshevsky had still not finally decided to enforce his attack, and since he was in his usual time pressure he wanted to make a few noncommittal moves to reach the time control. In just these circumstances, Averbakh has to play 35. . . . P–N5 to start some kind of complications. A possibility in time pressure is,

for instance, 36. B–R6 NxB 37. BxB KxB 38. QxN, and Black somehow holds on. But if White still delays B–R6 and answers, say, 36. PxP, then 36. . . . P–R6 gives Black serious counterchances. After Averbakh's carelessness White's task is easier.

| 36. RxP | N–N5 |
|---------|------|
| 37. B–N5! | B–N2 |

Accepting the Exchange sacrifice leads to a quick mate; for instance, 37. . . . NxR? 38. BxN B–N2 39. BxB KxB, then the Queen checks on QB3 with decisive threats. The game would have taken a similar course had Black played 36. . . . B–K2 instead of 36. . . . N–N5.

| 38. R–B4 | N–K4 |
|----------|------|
| 39. B–B6 | BxB |
| 40. RxB | K–N2 |
| 41. Q–N5 | R–R1 |
| 42. N–B5ch | QxN |
| 43. RxQ | RxRch |
| 44. K–N1 | Black resigns |

This game is a good example of how to gradually loosen the foundations of a solid position. Reshevsky considers it his best game in the Zurich tournament.

## Game 123
### Sicilian Defense

| P. Keres | L. Szabo | 3. P–Q4 | PxP |
|----------|----------|---------|-----|
| 1. P–K4 | P–QB4 | 4. NxP | N–KB3 |
| 2. N–KB3 | P–Q3 | 5. N–QB3 | P–QR3 |

| 6. | B–K2 | P–K4 |
| 7. | N–N3 | B–K2 |
| 8. | B–K3 | B–K3 |
| 9. | O–O | QN–Q2 |
| 10. | P–B4 | |

The various systems of development in this opening are distinguished above all by the placement of the KBP and the QRP. Against Najdorf in game 88, Grandmaster Geller played P–KB3 and P–QR4; White's position was active but rather unstable in the center. Against Kotov in game 36, Grandmaster Smyslov advanced both pawns only one square. In the present game Keres plays P–KB3 but for the time being leaves the QRP in place. I prefer the setup P–QR4 and P–KB3.

The creative styles of the masters are revealed right in the opening. The reader should take a critical attitude toward annotations of the type "P–QR4 is better" or "P–KB3 is quieter." There are many roads at the beginning of the game, and more than one leads to Rome.

| 10. | . . . | QR–B1 |
| 11. | K–R1 | B–B5 |

In spite of positional principles, Szabo offers to trade away his good Bishop, and he is right. First, this Bishop is in constant terror of the advance of White's KBP, so it is not all that good. Second, Szabo wants

to make use of the instability of White's KP to fight for Q4 and to make his other Bishop a "good" one.

| 12. | N–Q2 | BxB |
| 13. | NxB | O–O |
| 14. | N–KN3 | P–Q4 |
| 15. | BPxP | N/2xP |

15. . . . N/3xP is no good because of 16. N/2xN PxN 17. B–Q4.

## 16. B–Q4

Keres starts interesting complications, in which, however, Black has sufficient counterchances. The most pleasant variations for White would arise after 16. . . . N–B3 or 16. . . . N–N3; for example: 1) 16. . . . N–B3 17. BxN BxB 18. PxP QxP 19. N/2–K4; 2) 16. . . . N–N3 17. P–K5 N–Q2 18. N–B3, or, as in the first variation, 17. BxN, etc.

Szabo takes the most active continuation, as usual.

| 16. | . . . | N/3–N5 |
| 17. | R–B4 | |

White gets two Knights for a Rook and two pawns after this. As far as 17. P–KR3 is concerned, this is no threat: Black answers B–B4, as in the game, and if PxN he always has a Queen check on R5.

| 17. . . . | B–B4 |
| 18. BxB | RxB |
| 19. RxN | NxR |
| 20. QxN | RxP |
| 21. N–B3 | PxP |
| 22. QxP | RxQNP |
| 23. P–KR3 | R–K1 |
| 24. Q–QR4 | |

In game 186, Kotov–Najdorf, we will again recall the relative strengths of the Queen, the Rook, and the Knight. The Knight and Queen complement each other; the Knight is strong in the center and where there are enemy pawns; the Rook is strong at the end of the game, when it has plenty of room for its straightforward motion. Based on these considerations, White should use his Knights on the Kingside, he should not exchange Queens, and he should

try to find a continuation like: 24. Q–KN4 Q–B3 25. R–KB1 Q–KN3 26. N–N5 Q–B7 27. Q–B3 or 24. Q–KN4 Q–B1 25. N–B5 Q–B6 26. N/3–Q4.

| 24. . . . | Q–B1 |
| 25. N–B5 | Q–B3 |
| 26. Q–Q4 | |

Even now 26. Q–KN4 Q–B3 (26. . . . Q–KN3? 27. N–K7ch!) 27. R–Q1 is not bad. However, the exchange of Queens to get permanent use of KB5 for the Knights was very tempting; it was difficult to foresee that fate would take them all the way to the other side.

| 26. . . . | Q–B3 |
| 27. QxQ | PxQ |
| 28. P–QR4 | R–N5 |
| 29. P–R5 | |

The Knight's active position on KB5 should be used for attacking KB7. For this the Rook must be transferred from QR1 to Q7. The QRP is nothing to worry about since the pawn would be immediately regained: 29. R–Q1 RxP 30. R–Q7 with the double threat of 31. N–R6ch or 31. RxNP. White's seemingly good move makes the ending difficult for him in a surprising way.

| 29. . . . | R–KB5 |
| 30. N–Q6 | R–N1 |
| 31. R–QN1 | R–QR5 |
| 32. RxP | RxR |
| 33. NxR | |

Sometimes a Knight supported by a pawn in the middle

of the board is as strong as a Rook. But at the edge of the board the Knight cannot function at full power, and here a single Rook successfully contends with two Knights. Black's plan to bring up his King and drive away the Knights or force the trade of both of them for his Rook looks very dangerous. Keres's following maneuver—to set up an unassailable defensive position by using only two Knights and a pawn without the King—is of the greatest beauty.

33. . . .              K–B1
34. N–Q2              K–K2
35. N–N3              R–QN5
36. N/3–B5

A remarkable position! All by themselves the two Knights prevent the enemy's approach. Black pushes his pawn to KB4 in order to clear a path for his King via KB3–K4–Q5.

36. . . .              P–B4
37. K–N1              R–N4

Otherwise the Knight forks as soon as the King gets to K4.

38. K–B2              K–B3
39. N–Q7ch            K–K3
40. N–N6

The Knights regroup and again cannot be approached. Black's Rook now tries to enter from the side.

40. . . .              K–K4
41. K–N3              R–N6ch

Here Black has the interesting possibility 41. . . . P–B5ch, intending to answer 42. K–R4 with an attempt to win the KNP by R–N6–KN6. White, meanwhile, would probably be able to take the QRP. This would hardly have changed the outcome of the game.

42. K–R4              R–QB6
43. N–B5!             RxN

Black must take the Knight whether he wants to or not, and although Black gets an ending with an extra pawn he does not get the win.

44. N–Q7ch            K–Q3
45. NxR               KxN
46. K–N5!

Characteristic of pawn endings. The King, of course, goes after the KRP; if Black does not move his King to N4 but to Q4, then White reserves the option of taking the BP/4 first.

| 46. | . . . | K–N4 |
| 47. | K–R6 | KxP |
| 48. | KxP | K–N5 |
| 49. | P–R4 | P–R4 |
| 50. | P–R5 | P–R5 |
| 51. | P–R6 | P–R6 |
| 52. | K–N8 | P–R7 |

| 53. | P–R7 | P–R8=Q |
| 54. | P–R8=Q | |

Black is only one move short of a win.

| 54. | . . . | Q–R1ch |
| 55. | K–R7 | QxP |

55. . . . QxQch 56. KxQ K–B6 57. K–N7 also leads to a draw.

| 56. | Q–Q4ch | K–N6 |
| 57. | Q–Q3ch | Drawn |

# Game 124

The sacrifice of a pawn to seize open lines in the center is one of the oldest strategical ideas and can be found in the classic games of Greco, Morphy, Anderssen, Tchigorin, Spielmann, Alekhine. Sometimes pawns are given up in order to obtain lines for the Bishops; the most striking example is the Danish Gambit: 1. P–K4 P–K4 2. P–Q4 PxP 3. P–QB3 PxP 4. B–QB4 PxP 5. BxP. But sacrifices that open lines for the Rooks, especially in connection with direct attack on the King, are considered the most promising. For this purpose one may at times give up not only pawns but pieces. In addition to the usual gambits, our ancestors knew the "double" (and doubly wild) Muzio Gambit: 1. P–K4 P–K4 2. P–KB4 PxP 3. N–KB3 P–KN4 4. B–B4 P–N5 5. O–O PxN 6. BxPch KxB 7. QxP. This gambit is even seen today once in a while. True, a master or grandmaster views such play rather skeptically, but one can find many players of medium strength who like it. For example, this gambit was a most dreaded weapon in the school and university competitions of Volodya Smirnov, a Moscow first-category player who died prematurely. He had worked out his own analysis; for example, V. Smirnov–V. Tikhonov, Moscow 1954: 1. P–K4 P–K4 2. P–KB4 PxP 3. N–KB3 P–KN4 4. B–B4 P–N5 5. O–O PxN 6. QxP Q–B3 7. P–K5 QxP 8. BxPch KxB 9. P–Q4 QxPch 10. B–K3 Q–B3 11. BxBP B–N2 12. N–B3 N–K2 13. N–Q5 NxN 14. QxNch Q–K3 15. B–Q2ch K–N1 16. QR–K1!! QxQ 17. R–K8ch B–B1 18. B–R6!!, Black resigned.

But whereas formerly a pawn was sacrificed on the second or third move, today such early skirmishes in the center are avoided. Not due to the fear of risk—far from it. Frankly, the King's Indian Defense is a riskier undertaking for Black than the King's Gambit is for White; yet we are not afraid to play the King's Indian, whereas lovers of the King's Gambit are diminishing, as are those of the Scotch Opening, the Giuoco Piano, the Vienna Game. The reason is that in all of these openings the brief skirmish in the center leads to a fixed pawn structure and several exchanges, and the ensuing struggle is too barren and empty. We know how to sacrifice pawns and pieces in our time no less than Morphy and Anderssen did in theirs, but it is typical of modern games that sacrifices are postponed to a later stage while thoughts of combinations lie hidden behind the mask of positional play.

The Smyslov–Euwe game is saturated with combinational ideas that stem organically from the position, and it is one of the best models of chess creativity.

## Reti Opening

| V. Smyslov | M. Euwe |
|---|---|
| 1. N–KB3 | N–KB3 |
| 2. P–KN3 | P–Q4 |
| 3. B–N2 | B–B4 |
| 4. O–O | QN–Q2 |
| 5. P–Q3 | P–B3 |
| 6. QN–Q2 | P–KR3 |

Having reinforced the QP by 5. . . . P–B3, more appropriate is to occupy the center with the KP by 6. . . . P–K4. The problem with the text move is that with his KB still blocked by his own pawns Black will not soon be able to castle short. Smyslov exploits this circumstance by 7. P–K4!, rather later than Morphy played it but with no less effect.

| 7. P–K4 | PxP |
|---|---|
| 8. PxP | NxP |
| 9. N–Q4 | NxN |

Can it be fear of losing the two Bishops that keeps former World Champion Euwe from playing 9. . . . N–Q3 and prompts him to develop another of his opponent's pieces? After 9. . . . N–Q3 10. NxB NxN 11. R–K1 P–KN3 12. N–K4 or 11. . . . P–K3 12. B–R3 N–Q3 13. Q–R5, White would still have to demonstrate the soundness of his pawn sacrifice.

| 10. BxN | B–R2 |
|---|---|

## 11. B–QB3

I have no doubt that in those chess days of long ago, before the subtle methods of modern positional play had been fully worked out and when it was considered bad form to have an extra pawn or piece, White would have sacrificed his Knight on QB6 without much hesitation and forced open the precarious sanctuary of the Black King. The strategic premise for the sacrifice is the complete isolation of Black's Bishops and Rooks. The specific variations: 1) 11. NxP PxN 12. BxP R–B1 13. B–R5!; 2) 11. NxP PxN 12. BxP B–B4 13. Q–B3 R–B1 14. B–R4.

White then posts a Rook on Q1 and obtains a setup in which, very like the well-known game Morphy vs. the Duke of Braunschweig and Count Isouard, Black cannot extricate himself.

That famous game was played at the Paris Opera in 1858, during a performance of *The Barber of Seville*. Morphy announced a beautiful mate to his distinguished opponents: 1. P–K4 P–K4 2. N–KB3 P–Q3 3. P–Q4 B–N5 4. PxP BxN 5. QxB PxP 6. B–QB4 N–KB3 7. Q–QN3 Q–K2 8. N–B3 P–B3 9. B–KN5 P–QN4 10. NxP PxN 11. BxNPch QN–Q2 12. O–O–O R–Q1 13. RxN RxR 14. R–Q1 Q–K3 15. BxRch! NxB 16. Q–N8ch!! NxQ 17. R–Q8 mate.

The indecisive text move takes the game in another direction for a while and forces Smyslov later to show great inventiveness to create new combinative attacking chances.

| 11. | . . . | Q–B2 |
| 12. | Q–B3 | P–K4 |
| 13. | KR–K1 | O–O–O |
| 14. | N–N3 | P–B3 |

Euwe sets up a pawn chain on the dark squares, totally unconcerned about how to protect the light squares. Smyslov soon exploits this circumstance perfectly. 14. . . . P–KB4 should be played at once.

## 15. B–R5    N–N3

Black overestimates his position and too inflexibly refuses to make any concession. He should play 15. . . . P–QN3 16. B–B3 N–B4. Although White would get some chances after 17. NxN BxN 18. P–QR4 B–Q5 19. P–R5, etc., the risks would be reciprocal; now there is no danger for White.

| | |
|---|---|
| 16. P–B4 | R–Q6 |

| | |
|---|---|
| 17. Q–R5 | Q–K2 |
| 18. B–B1 | P–N3 |

It is unpleasant to block one's own Bishop, but after the Rook's only retreat, to Q2, Black would have to play P–KB4 in view of White's B–R3.

| | |
|---|---|
| 19. Q–K2 | R–Q2 |
| 20. Q–K3 | K–N1 |
| 21. QR–Q1 | N–B1 |

Clouds are gathering over the Black King's position. The move recommended by Euwe and Stahlberg, 21. . . . B–N1, could not essentially change the situation; for instance, 22. BxN PxB 23. QxNP, threatening N–R5.

**22. B–R3**

As a consequence of 14. . . . P–B3? instead of the immediate . . . P–KB4, Black's QB1–KR6 diagonal is very weak. He is now forced to move his pawn to KB4, but this is only of partial help.

| | |
|---|---|
| 22. . . . | RxR |
| 23. RxR | P–KB4 |
| 24. B–QN4! | |

Beginning a series of combinational blows. With this move White first exposes Black's insufficiently protected KP and second his weak KRP: 24. . . . Q–QB2 25. BxB RxB 26. QxRP.

| | |
|---|---|
| 24. . . . | Q–B3 |
| 25. B–B3 | B–N2 |

Yet another concession by Black. The Bishop relinquishes control of QB4.

| | |
|---|---|
| 26. N–B5 | K–R1 |

On . . . N–N3 there follows 27. R–Q7!, but now the denouement comes swiftly.

| | |
|---|---|
| 27. NxP | KxN |
| 28. R–Q7ch | K–R1 |
| 29. Q–B5 | |

Enough to win the game, but every chess player—from beginner to grandmaster—would get more pleasure from 29. B–N2 R–K1 30. BxP RxB 31.

QxR! QxQ 32. BxPch K–N1 33. R–N7ch K–R1 34. R moves anywhere on the QN-file with mate. The prosaic 30. RxB QxR 31. BxPch and BxR would therefore not be so strong.

| 29. . . . | N–N3 |
| 30. RxB | QxR |
| 31. BxKP | Q–Q2 |
| 32. BxR | |

An extra pawn with the two Bishops foretells the outcome of the game. The next phase is not particularly interesting; Smyslov could play more accurately in places, and, in particular, he should not allow the exchange of Queens.

32. . . . K–N2 33. B–Q4 Q–K3 34. B–B1 B–N1 35. P–N3 P–B5 36. P–QR4 PxP 37. RPxP B–B2 38. P–R5 N–B1 39. B–KN2 (Immediately decisive is 39. P–R6ch KxP 40. Q–N4. Now the game is rather prolonged.) 39. . . . Q–Q3 40. P–R6ch KxP 41. BxP QxQ 42. BxQ N–N3 43. K–B1 B–K3 44. K–K2 N–Q2 45. B–Q4 K–R4 46. B–B3ch K–N3 47. B–K4 P–N4 48. B–Q4ch K–R4 49. BxP K–N5 50. B–B2 K–B6 (Black has not stood so well for quite a while, but this is small comfort—he is still two pawns down.) 51. B–Q1 N–K4 52. K–K3 N–B3 53. B–N6 P–N5 54. B–B4 P–R4 55. B–K3 N–R4 56. K–K5 B–B1 57. P–B5 NxP 58. B–K2 N–R4 59. B–QN5 N–B5ch 60. K–B4 NxB 61. PxN K–N5 62. B–K8 P–R5 63. PxP KxP 64. P–R5 P–N6 65. KxP K–Q4 66. P–R6 B–B4 67. K–B4 B–R2 68. K–N5, Black resigns.

## Game 125
### French Defense

| Y. Geller | G. Stahlberg |
| --- | --- |
| 1. P–K4 | P–K3 |
| 2. P–Q4 | P–Q4 |
| 3. N–Q2 | P–QB4 |
| 4. KPxP | KPxP |
| 5. KN–B3 | N–KB3 |
| 6. B–N5ch | B–Q2 |
| 7. BxBch | QNxB |
| 8. O–O | B–K2 |
| 9. PxP | NxP |
| 10. N–Q4 | |

White has created an isolated enemy pawn on Q4, but his next plan is not connected with an attack on it. White's play is based on the fact that the square in front of the QP is entirely at White's disposal and offers a good base for his pieces. A piece on this square will exert strong pressure on both flanks. This idea is rather nebulous, though: controlling even the very best squares on the board cannot win the game if there is nothing to attack. Specific objects of attack are defined with particular clarity in this game after . . . P–KN3 and . . . P–KB4, but Stahlberg finds sufficient defensive resources, one of which is the centralization of a Knight on K5.

| 10. . . . | O–O |
|---|---|
| 11. N–B5 | R–K1 |
| 12. N–QN3 | N–K3 |
| 13. B–K3 | Q–B2 |
| 14. P–QB3 | QR–Q1 |
| 15. Q–B3 | |

The QRP obviously cannot be taken.

| 15. . . . | N–K5 |
|---|---|
| 16. NxBch | RxN |
| 17. KR–Q1 | P–QR3 |
| 18. N–Q4 | P–KN3 |

Such moves are not to everyone's taste. Stahlberg, however, always plays without prejudice. The weaknesses of his dark squares do not worry him.

| 19. P–KR4 | N–N2 |
|---|---|
| 20. P–KN3 | P–B4 |
| 21. K–N2 | Q–K4 |
| 22. R–Q3 | Q–B3 |
| 23. QR–Q1 | R/2–Q2 |
| 24. N–K2 | Q–B3 |
| 25. B–Q4 | |

White has succeeded in setting up a strong position. His Queen can penetrate the Kingside, he can create threats on

the dark squares, and, to begin with, he can undermine the Kingside pawns by P–R5. Granted, the results of any of these continuations may not be entirely clear; nevertheless White should not agree to the exchange of Queens, which he does in a few moves. Geller apparently hopes to win the endgame by technique alone, but Stahlberg displays his usual defensive stubbornness and sets up an inaccessible position.

| 25. . . . | N–K3 |
|---|---|
| 26. N–B4 | NxN |
| 27. QxN | R–K1 |
| 28. R–K3 | |

If 28. P–R5 instead, then 28. . . . Q–Q3 29. QxQ RxQ 30. PxP PxP 31. P–B3 N–N4 and White gets nothing, but perhaps it is worth driving away the Knight first and then playing P–R5.

28. . . . Q–Q3 29. QxQ Nx Q 30. RxRch NxR 31. B–K5 K–B2 32. P–B3 N–B3 33. K–B2 K–K3 34. B–Q4 N–N1 35. K–K3 N–K2 36. K–Q3 N–B3 37. R–K1ch K–B2 38. P–R4 R–K2 39. RxRch KxR 40. K–K3 K–K3 41. B–R8 P–QR4, **Drawn.**

White's piece cannot penetrate the enemy camp anywhere.

## Game 126
### King's Indian Defense

A. Kotov        I. Boleslavsky

| | |
|---|---|
| 1. P–QB4 | N–KB3 |
| 2. N–QB3 | P–KN3 |
| 3. P–KN3 | B–N2 |
| 4. B–N2 | P–Q3 |
| 5. N–B3 | O–O |
| 6. O–O | P–B4 |
| 7. P–Q4 | N–B3 |
| 8. P–Q5 | |

8. PxP is the most disagreeable move against players who as Black like to look for complicated struggles in this variation of the King's Indian Defense, but in this game both players are in a fighting mood.

| | |
|---|---|
| 8. . . . | N–QR4 |
| 9. Q–Q3 | P–QR3 |
| 10. N–Q2 | R–N1 |
| 11. P–N3 | P–QN4 |

Black has developed his forces harmoniously and is already threatening 12. . . . P–N5 and . . . NxQP. It seems that White's system of development is not the strongest.

| | |
|---|---|
| 12. R–N1 | PxP |
| 13. NxP | NxN |
| 14. QxN | |

Kotov makes no concessions, but it is time to think about equalizing by means of 14. PxN RxR 15. QxR B–Q2 16. B–Q2 Q–B2 17. Q–B2 R–N1 18. R–N1. After the text move

Black's initiative increases and an object for attack appears—the QP has been deprived of pawn support.

| | |
|---|---|
| 14. . . . | N–K1 |
| 15. B–N2 | N–B2 |
| 16. N–Q1 | R–N5 |
| 17. Q–B2 | BxB |
| 18. NxB | B–B4 |

Black provokes P–K4 to shorten the diagonal of White's KB. Then he switches to attacking the KP.

| | |
|---|---|
| 19. P–K4 | B–Q2 |
| 20. N–Q3 | R–Q5 |
| 21. KR–K1 | P–K4 |

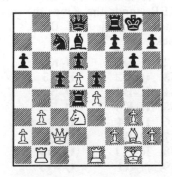

22. PxP e.p.

If White does not take en passant, he will never be able to drive Black's Rook from Q5.

| | |
|---|---|
| 22. . . . | NxP |
| 23. QR–Q1 | B–N4 |
| 24. N–B1 | Q–R4 |

| 25. B–B1 | R–K1 |
| 26. BxB | PxB |

A fleeting glance is enough to notice how Black's pieces hang over White's position like clouds. But how is Black's advantage to be realized? Boleslavsky wants the key to the gate of White's fortress—the KP.

| 27. N–K2 | RxR |
| 28. RxR | N–N4 |
| 29. K–N2 | NxP |
| 30. P–B3 | N–N4 |
| 31. RxP | Q–R1 |

Kotov has won the pawn back, but Boleslavsky relentlessly switches to a diagonal attack against the KBP. What would happen if this pawn were lost or if it moved? Behind the KBP stands the King, the next and final object of Black's attack.

| 32. R–Q3 | N–K3 |
| 33. Q–Q2 | P–N5 |
| 34. K–B2 | Q–N1 |
| 35. R–K3 | Q–R2 |
| 36. P–B4 | R–Q1 |
| 37. Q–B2 | Q–Q2 |
| 38. K–K1 | Q–Q4 |
| 39. N–N1 | Q–Q5 |

By his beautiful maneuvering Black has created irresistible threats—the Rook cannot leave and must be defended. If 40. K–K2 R–K1! threatening . . . NxPch, and on 41. Q–Q3 R–R1 42. Q–N1 P–B5!

**40. Q–K2**

Better is 40. K–B2 R–K1 41. N–B3 QxRch 42. KxQ N–Q5ch 43. Q–K4 or 40. . . . R–R1 41. N–B3 Q–R8 42. R–K2 N–Q5 43. NxN PxN 44. Q–B6!

| 40. . . . | Q–R8ch |
| 41. K–B2 | R–R1 |
| 42. Q–Q3 | |

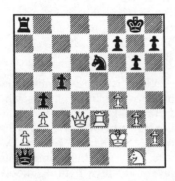

**42. . . .        RxPch**

Taking a pawn with check is not always the best move. Now, as they say, "worth considering" is 42. . . . N–Q5 43. N–K2 RxP, and, in connection with the threat of . . . Q–KR8, Black would probably not have had to play an additional twenty-five moves.

**43. N–K2        Q–Q5**

Now 43. . . . Q–R8 does not work in view of 44. RxN, but 43. . . . N–Q5 is immediately decisive.

**44. K–B3 QxQ 45. RxQ K–B1 46. R–K3 K–K2 47. P–N4 P–B4 48. PxP PxP 49. N–N3 K–B3 50. R–K5 N–Q5ch 51.**

K–K3 R–QB7 52. N–R5ch K–N3 53. N–N3 P–R4 54. P–R4 R–B6ch 55. K–B2 R–B6ch 56. K–N2 RxBP 57. RxQBP RxP 58. R–B4 R–N5 59. K–R3 NxP 60. R–B8 N–Q5 61. R–N8ch K–R3 62. R–R8ch K–N4 63. R–N8ch K–B5 64. NxPch K–B6 65. R–N8 N–K3 66. R–N5 N–N4ch 67. K–R2 R–R5ch 68. K–N1 N–R6ch, White resigns.

# Round Nineteen

## Game 127

The chess struggle takes one of its sharpest forms in the fight for tempos in attacking castled positions on opposite wings. It is important here not to be too hasty in the attack and at the same time not to be excessively concerned with de-fending the King. In this game between two masters of the ag-gressive style we see a har-monious combination of attack and defense, based on experi-ence, knowledge, and imagina-tion.

### Sicilian Defense

**I. Boleslavsky      Y. Geller**

| | |
|---|---|
| 1. P–K4 | P–QB4 |
| 2. N–KB3 | N–QB3 |
| 3. P–Q4 | PxP |
| 4. NxP | N–B3 |
| 5. N–QB3 | P–Q3 |
| 6. P–KN3 | B–N5 |
| 7. P–B3 | B–Q2 |
| 8. B–K3 | P–KN3 |
| 9. Q–Q2 | B–N2 |
| 10. O–O–O | O–O |
| 11. P–KN4 | |

By playing B–N5 on the 6th move, Geller forced White to advance his KBP to B3. Making a virtue of necessity, however, Boleslavsky chose the Rauzer

Attack, in which White plays P–KB3 voluntarily against the Dragon Variation.

| | |
|---|---|
| 11. . . . | R–B1 |
| 12. K–N1 | N–K4 |
| 13. P–KR4 | |

308

An exceptionally interesting position for the theory and practice of the middlegame.

White's strong Knight in the center is a good counterfoil to Black's QB and is ready to repel a Queen sortie to QR4 by going to QN3. White has started a pawn storm and has already been able to play P–KN4 and P–KR4, and there are no weaknesses in his King's position, whereas Black's KNP is like a ring for the White troops to catch hold of.

Black does not start to advance his pawns until later, but he already has an open file against the enemy King. His Knight in the center is very strong, too: it attacks the only supporter—a rather shaky one, at that—of the White pawn chain.

Black controls and will soon take possession of the important QB5-square, which has about the same significance as White's KB5, whereas White does not possess a single point near the Black King. Finally, Black's strong Bishop on KN2 will provide opportunities for dangerous combinations on the long diagonal.

As we see, the position is complicated, and at the moment it is in dynamic balance. It takes great skill to manage an entire army of pieces and pawns and at the same time counteract the opponent's operations. Let us follow this battle move by move.

**13. . . .        P–QN4**

Black replies blow for blow. He prepares not only P–N5 but also N–B5, on which BxN would open the QN-file, which would be more dangerous to White than the open QB-file.

**14. B–R6**

It would be madness to take the QNP, of course. P–R5 is also ineffective so long as Black's KR1 and KR2 are solidly defended by pieces, so White wants to trade off one of Black's most important pieces first.

**14. . . .        BxB**

In such positions the Bishop may sometimes go to R1: the Rook is less valuable here than the Bishop. The crowded long diagonal can be quickly cleared of pieces, given the opportunity; for instance, 14. . . . B–R1 15. BxR RxN 16. PxR NxBP 17. NxN NxKP. Of course this variation is not forced—in this case it is clearly unfavorable for Black—but it is only to illustrate the ideas that arise during the course of the struggle.

**15. QxB        RxN**

Now the threat was P–R5, so the exchange of Rook for

Knight, destroying the King's cover, is almost forced.

**16. PxR**

**16. . . .**          **Q–R4**

The natural continuation of the attack.

**17. Q–K3**

White's King is in an uncomfortable situation, and the Queen is forced to return for defense. The equilibrium has not been disturbed, however, for White has the Exchange as compensation.

**17. . . .**          **Q–R6**

17. . . . N–B5 18. BxN PxB 19. K–R1 R–N1 20. R–QN1 offers Black nothing. Now he threatens P–N5.

**18. P–R5**          **P–N5**
**19. Q–B1**          **QxP**
**20. Q–N2**          **R–B1**

Black refrains from 20. . . . Q–K6 which after 21. Q–B1 Q–B6 can lead to repetition of moves. Black has no advantage,

and after the exchange of Queens he even stands slightly worse.

**21. PxP**

Forcing Black to exchange Queens, since 21. . . . RPxP can be answered by Q–B1 threatening Q–R6.

**21. . . .**          **QxQch**
**22. KxQ**          **RPxP**
**23. P–R3**

An inaccuracy, which together with the oversight on his next move is Boleslavsky's only blunder in his last fifteen years of tournament practice.

Correct is 23. B–Q3 or 23. B–K2, and only on the following move P–R3. White would have winning chances in that case.

**23. . . .**          **PxPch**
**24. KxP**

Even now nothing terrible would happen after 24. K–R2, but Boleslavsky goes fearlessly into his calculated variation: 24. . . . NxBP 25. NxN R–B6ch 26. R–Q3!??! As Boleslavsky explained, he saw of course that Black's Knight could take the KBP and that then the Rook could go to QB6, attacking King and Knight, but he supposed that R–Q3 would defend both attacked pieces, including the King!

**24. . . .**          **NxBP**
**25. NxN**          **R–B6ch**

| 26. | K–N2 | RxN |
|---|---|---|
| 27. | P–K5 | NxP |

With its foundation demolished, the entire edifice is shaken.

| 28. | B–K2 | R–B7 |
|---|---|---|
| 29. | BxN | BxB |
| 30. | QR–KB1 | RxR |
| 31. | RxR | PxP |

It is beyond the power of a Rook to fight against a Bishop and four pawns. Were it not for the QRP, perhaps it might have some chance, but it has to spend a couple of moves to capture that pawn, and in the meantime Black's pawns are able to advance. . . .

32. P–B4 K–B1 33. R–QR1 B–B6 34. P–B5 P–N4 35. Rx P P–N5 36. R–R3 K–K1 37. K–B1 P–B4 38. K–Q2 P–B5 39. R–R6 P–N6 40. K–K1 B–N5, White resigns.

## Game 128
### Queen's Gambit Declined

| | G. Stahlberg | V. Smyslov |
|---|---|---|
| 1. | P–Q4 | P–Q4 |
| 2. | P–QB4 | P–QB3 |
| 3. | N–KB3 | N–B3 |
| 4. | N–B3 | PxP |
| 5. | P–QR4 | B–B4 |
| 6. | P–K3 | P–K3 |
| 7. | BxP | B–QN5 |
| 8. | O–O | QN–Q2 |
| 9. | Q–K2 | B–N3 |
| 10. | P–K4 | O–O |
| 11. | B–Q3 | P–KR3 |

It is often necessary, because of one's standing in the tournament or before an impending decisive game, to draw with the Black pieces. Smyslov employs the Slav Defense when he wishes to draw at such times, and neither Boleslavsky, Szabo, nor in this case Stahlberg were able to succeed against it.

It is true that Szabo, having found the interesting 11. B–Q3, obtained a certain advantage after 11. . . . Q–R4?; but now, two rounds later, Smyslov strengthens the defense for Black with 11. . . . P–KR3, and, in connection with his later maneuver N–N1–B3, he achieves full equality.

| 12. | R–Q1 | Q–K2 |
| 13. | P–R3 | QR–Q1 |
| 14. | P–K5 | N–Q4 |
| 15. | NxN | BPxN |
| 16. | BxB | |

Rather than hurry to exchange, he should play the developing move 16. B–Q2 first.

| 16. | . . . | PxB |
| 17. | B–Q2 | N–N1! |
| 18. | BxB | QxB |
| 19. | P–R5 | R–B1 |
| 20. | Q–Q3 | P–KN4 |
| 21. | Q–N6 | |

| 21. | . . . | Q–K2 |
| 22. | KR–QB1 | P–R3 |
| 23. | R–B3 | N–B3 |
| 24. | QR–QB1 | Q–Q2 |
| 25. | Q–B2 | Q–KB2 |
| 26. | Q–Q2 | Q–B4 |
| 27. | P–QN4 | **Drawn** |

But it is not so simple as the reader may think. In view of the threat 28. P–N5 PxP 29. P–R6, Black must now play 27. . . . QR–K1!, intending to answer 28. P–N5 PxP 29. P–R6 with 29. . . . N–R4! The Exchange sacrifice 28. RxN PxR 29. RxP would not work because of 29. . . . R–B1! 30. RxRP R–B7 or 30. Q–B3 RxR 31. QxR P–R4! Therefore, 28. R–K3 and then 29. P–N5 PxP 30. P–R6 would be relatively better for White. Draws agreed upon by grandmasters sometimes conceal many beautiful continuations.

## Game 129
### Grünfeld Defense

| **M. Euwe** | **P. Keres** |
| 1. P–Q4 | N–KB3 |
| 2. P–QB4 | P–KN3 |
| 3. P–KN3 | B–N2 |
| 4. B–N2 | P–Q4 |
| 5. PxP | NxP |
| 6. P–K4 | N–N3 |

| 7. | N–K2 | P–QB4 |
| 8. | P–Q5 | P–K3 |

Why has Black voluntarily created a hole in his position, inviting the QP to advance? The answer must be sought in Keres's very first moves. Black's entire system of play is aimed at luring White's pawn to Q6, where it will be attacked and destroyed. For the present, White prudently castles, but later he decides to take advantage of the breach in the pawn wall and pushes the pawn to Q6 anyway. It seems to me that the pleasure of attacking the surrounded pawn is too expensive, and the further course of the game corroborates this.

**9. O–O          O–O**
**10. N/2–B3**

We have already seen a similar maneuver in game 19, Euwe–Smyslov: the QN stays in place so that, according to circumstances, it may go to QR3 or Q2 or replace the Knight at QB3 when it leaves.

**10. . . .          PxP**
**11. PxP           QN–Q2**
**12. N–K4**

Now White's advantage is obvious. It is defined by his very mobile QP and the clear weakness of Black's QBP.

White also has more room to maneuver.

**12. . . .          N–B3**
**13. QN–B3         QN–Q2**
**14. P–Q6**

The advance of the pawn sharpens the fight appreciably.

The trade of pawns (QP for QBP) would not have been advantageous for Black; for instance, 13. . . . NxN 14. NxN! NxP 15. NxP, and it is clear that Black cannot hold QN2 and Q4 without positional or material loss.

**14. . . .          R–N1**
**15. B–N5          P–KR3**
**16. BxN           BxB**

A rather sad necessity, for without his dark-square Bishop it will be quite difficult for Black to fight against the passed pawn.

Black's opening plan has been a fiasco.

**17. NxBch         NxN**
**18. R–K1          B–K3**
**19. Q–B3          P–QN4**
**20. Q–B4          K–R2**
**21. QR–Q1         R–N3**

## 22. P–QR3

Each positional achievement —in this case the pawn on Q6 that attracts the attention of Black's pieces—is important not only in itself but also in interconnection with other combinational or positional motifs. In the diagramed position, these motifs are—

For White:

1) Black's unprotected QBP;

2) Black's weak King shelter;

3) the constant possibility of P–Q7;

4) his control of QB7 and K7, and in this connection his striving to seize either the K-file or the QB-file.

For Black:

1) the possibility of surrounding the QP on three sides;

2) a Queenside majority attack;

3) the possibility of . . . N–R4, which would force White's Queen to leave its strong position on KB4.

Comparison and evaluation of the respective chances lead masters usually to more or less objective conclusions, which is called "position judgment." If there were quantitative indexes of such positional values, chess could be played by machines.

It is already clear that White, by virtue of his more active position, should set about probing his opponent's weak points while not forgetting about his own basic threats. Euwe can do this in two ways. He can play 22. P–N3 to impede Black's P–N5, P–B5, and P–B6, but then it will not be easy to break through Black's position, mainly because of the Bishop on Black's K3. So 22. RxB suggests itself, to liquidate the only Black piece that has freedom of action, to completely open the door to the King's shelter on his second rank, and to turn Black's three good pawns on KB2, KN3, and KR3 into two weak ones on K3 and KN3. White's attack could develop like this: 22. . . . PxR 23. Q–K5 Q–Q2 24. B–R3 or 23. . . . R–K1 24. QxBP.

At any rate, the text move has little justification. It does not aid the realization of White's plan and unnecessarily weakens QN3. Keres exploits this skillfully.

**22. . . .          R–K1**

An excellent defensive maneuver. The Bishop threatens to go to N6, and it is clear that the Rook on Q1 is overloaded in defending the QP and the KR.

**23. N–K4          NxN**
**24. RxN          Q–Q2**

Completing the encirclement of the QP, and, most important, blockading it. Having lost its mobility, it is not quite so fearsome. Euwe, meanwhile, having failed to pick up the QBP, does not wait for it to advance but quickly trades his QP for it.

| 25. | Q–K5 | R–Q1 |
| --- | --- | --- |
| 26. | QxP | RxP |

The objects of contention having disappeared, there is no further argument, and a draw is the natural conclusion of a struggle whose fires have gone out.

## Game 130
### Queen's Gambit

| L. Szabo | S. Reshevsky |
| --- | --- |
| 1. P–Q4 | N–KB3 |
| 2. P–QB4 | P–K3 |
| 3. N–KB3 | P–Q4 |
| 4. N–B3 | P–B4 |
| 5. BPxP | NxP |
| 6. P–K3 | N–QB3 |
| 7. B–Q3 | NxN |

If Black wants to trade on QB6, 7. . . . PxP is better first.

| 8. | PxN | B–K2 |
| --- | --- | --- |
| 9. | Q–B2 | P–KN3 |

Black gets ready to castle. In view of the threat of BxRP, one or another weakness is almost inevitable, and it is hard to say whether Reshevsky would have less trouble after . . . P–KR3: Szabo would try to transpose his Bishop on Q3 with his Queen as quickly as possible, and what could be advised then? The further weakening of the pawn barrier by . . . P–KN3 or . . . P–KB4 would be ruinous, and the Knight obviously could not be gotten to KB1. However, N–B1 would be not

only his sole chance but also his only hope. I must therefore conclude that the combination of 6. . . . N–QB3 and 7. . . . NxN does not work well. The text move weakens a whole group of squares and gives White all he needs for a successful attack.

| 10. | P–KR4 | P–KR4 |
| --- | --- | --- |
| 11. | QR–N1 | QR–N1 |
| 12. | B–K4 | |

The first result of Black's carelessness. On 12. . . . B–Q2 White sacrifices a piece: 13. BxP PxB 14. QxPch K–B1 15. P–K4 with the threat B–R6ch.

| 12. | . . . | Q–B2 |
| --- | --- | --- |
| 13. | O–O | B–Q2 |
| 14. | P–Q5 | PxP |
| 15. | BxQP | B–B3 |
| 16. | N–N5 | N–Q1 |
| 17. | P–QB4 | B–B3 |
| 18. | N–K4 | |

Szabo has obtained a superb attacking position, whereas Black's pieces are passive and his King has still not castled.

| 18. | . . . | B–N2 |
| 19. | B–N2 | O–O |
| 20. | N–B6ch | BxN? |

**21. QBxB**

A unique case in many years of tournament experience: neither grandmaster sees the mate in two by 21. QxPch B–N2 22. QxB mate. Black's only move was 20. . . . K–R1, on which White would have continued the attack by 21. P–B4 followed by P–B5 or P–K4–5, with a relatively easy win. To lovers of beautiful ideas one may suggest 21. Q–B3 threatening N–K8, and if 21. . . . BxB 22. NxB.

| 21. | . . . | BxB |
| 22. | PxB | Q–Q3 |
| 23. | Q–B3 | QxP |
| 24. | KR–Q1 | Q–B4 |
| 25. | P–K4 | Q–K3 |
| 26. | B–N7 | P–N3 |

White's position is so strong that despite the unprecedented blunder on the 20th move he still has more than enough to win. This time the main threat is mate on KN7. All he needs is to put his Bishop on the KR-file, 27. B–R6, and on the only reply, 27. . . . P–B3, White wins at least a Rook by 28. Q–KN3.

Szabo plays differently:

**27. BxR?          KxB**

and just now noticing his error, Szabo became so upset that he used up almost all his time just sitting there. He then accepted the draw offered by Reshevsky nearly half an hour earlier, when White played BxR. After such a shock Szabo was not himself for a long time, which of course affected his performance in his later games in the tournament.

## Game 131
### King's Indian Defense

**Y. Averbakh**    **D. Bronstein**

1. P–Q4 N–KB3 2. P–QB4
P–KN3 3. P–KN3 B–N2 4. B–
N2 O–O 5. N–QB3 P–Q3 6.
N–B3 QN–Q2 7. O–O P–K4
8. P–K4 R–K1 9. P–KR3 PxP
10. NxP N–B4 11. R–K1 P–
QR4 12. Q–B2 N–N5 13. R–
Q1 N–K4 14. N/3–K2 P–QB3
15. B–K3 Q–K2 (The threat
was NxP and BxN.) 16. P–N3
P–R4 17. N–QB3 N/K–Q2
18. R–K1 Q–Q1 19. QR–N1

N–B1 20. KR–Q1 Q–K2
(Neither player puts much life
into this well-known and
thoroughly analyzed variation.
White maneuvers deep behind
the lines and Black follows suit.
Though at times one can find
excuses for excessive pacifism,
such a strategy has little to com-
mend it in this case.) 21. P–R3
N/1–K3 22. P–KR4 N–Q2 23.
NxN QxN 24. N–R4 B–B1 25.
P–B5 PxP 26. NxP NxN 27.
BxN, Drawn.

## Game 132
### King's Indian Defense

**T. Petrosian**    **S. Gligoric**

| | |
|---|---|
| 1. P–Q4 | N–KB3 |
| 2. P–QB4 | P–KN3 |
| 3. N–QB3 | B–N2 |
| 4. P–K4 | P–Q3 |
| 5. P–B3 | O–O |
| 6. B–K3 | P–K4 |
| 7. P–Q5 | |

White does not have to close
the center; he can continue 7.
KN–K2 PxP 8. NxP P–B3 9.
N–B2 R–K1 10. Q–Q2 P–Q4
11. O–O–O, winning the QP
in the end but handing the
initiative to Black.

7. . . .      N–R4

Also not obligatory, but for
some reason many believe that
in the King's Indian Defense

the KBP should be moved to
KB4 as soon as possible. I don't
think this is entirely correct.
Certainly the attack . . . P–KB4
or . . . P–KB4–5 is good if
some real advantage is gained
thereby. But if not, then it is
better to delay . . . P KB4 until
it will be most effective. Therefore, 7. . . . QN–Q2 or 7. . . .
P–QR4 is not at all worse than
the text move.

| | |
|---|---|
| 8. Q–Q2 | P–KB4 |
| 9. O–O–O | P–B5 |
| 10. B–B2 | B–B3 |
| 11. KN–K2 | B–R5 |
| 12. B–N1 | P–KN4! |

A new move in comparison
with game 75, Geller–Gligoric,

where Black played 12. . . . N–Q2 and then brought his Bishop back to K2. Since Black had to defend passively for a long time in that game, Gligoric decides to open the KN-file without delay in order to get counterchances on the Kingside. In reply, Petrosian takes advantage of the absence of Black's Knight from Q2 and breaks through on the left side.

**13. P–B5!       P–N5**
**14. K–N1       NPxP**
**15. NPxP       N–R3**

Since Black seemed to be getting ready for a long struggle by blockading part of the board with . . . P–B5, there is no reason to hurry now. The calm 15. . . . K–R1 anticipates White's following threat and creates the possibility of . . . R–KN1, . . . B–K2, and . . . P–QR4, etc.

**16. P–B6**

An energetic move, securing the advantage for White. If 16. . . . P–N3 then after 17. P–QR3 and P–QN4 every square is taken from Black's Knight and his QB; and if 16. . . . PxP 17. PxP, then White's QR2–KN8 diagonal is opened and his pieces seize Q5; for instance, 17. . . . Q–K1 18. N–B1 QxP? 19. B–N5 Q–N2 20. BxN QxB 21. Q–Q5ch.

**16. . . .        N–B3**
**17. PxP         BxP**
**18. N–N3**

A transparent sacrifice that only retards the tempo of the attack. White figures that in view of the threat of N–B5 Black must go into the unfavorable variation 18. . . . PxN 19. PxP BxNP 20. Q–N5ch K–R1 21. QxB, but Gligoric's quiet reply forces the Knight to go back and take another route.

**18. . . .        B–B1**
**19. N–K2       N–B4**

Allowing White to exchange Bishop for Knight and to completely disarrange Black's pawn formation, which brings Black a more or less lost position. Black can exploit his opponent's loss of time by 19. . . . N–Q2 and only then . . . N/3–B4 and . . . P–QR4.

**20. BxN!**

White take immediate advantage of his opponent's error.

**20. . . .        PxB**
**21. N–B1       Q–K2**
**22. N–N3       B–Q2**

Directed against the threats N–R4 and Q–QB2. However, even in this position Petrosian finds an original Queen maneuver to win the QBP.

**23. Q–N2ch!   K–R1**
**24. Q–N1       N–K1**
**25. QxP        N–Q3**
**26. R–B1**

Petrosian correctly refuses the second pawn. After 26. QxBP KR–QB1 27. Q–R5 B–B7!,

Black gets serious counter-chances.

| 26. | . . . | B–K1 |
|-----|-------|------|
| 27. | B–R3 | P–QR4 |

Black's only hope is to attack the King. He gives up still another pawn in order to open the lines and remove one of the pieces protecting the King.

| 28. | NxP | B–B7 |
|-----|-----|------|
| 29. | QxB | RxN |
| 30. | KR–N1 | B–N3 |
| 31. | B–B1 | R–QN1 |
| 32. | R–B2 | N–B2 |
| 33. | P–KR4 | N–Q3 |
| 34. | B–Q3 | R–N5 |

White's rather slow play in time pressure, KR–N1–QB1 and B–B1–Q3–B1, does not let the win escape, but it does let his opponent improve the position of his pieces. The idea of transferring a Rook to the seventh rank is a very good one, but it does not reach its logical conclusion.

| 35. | KR–QB1 | R–Q5 |
|-----|--------|------|
| 36. | B–B1 | Q–Q1 |
| 37. | N–K2 | |

37. . . .        R/5–R5

During the last fifteen moves Black has tried everything to complicate the game, but Petrosian's solid preventive moves have been effective: Gligoric believes he can no longer save himself, and just now, when he has an unexpected—I should say unbelievable—chance to complicate and muddy the play, he misses it. The idea 37. . . . RxKP, giving up a Rook for "only" two pawns, seemed too audacious to him; when sacrificing, however, one does not count up the pawns but calculates the advantages and the specific variations.

If Gligoric had not lost heart, had he found the strength to sacrifice the Rook, the continuation would have been very interesting and Petrosian would have regretted his negligence.

The first argument is of a general order. After 38. PxR NxP White's only reasonable answer is 39. Q–K1 to defend against the suddenly impending threat 39. . . . N–Q7ch 40. K–R1 RxPch 41. KxR Q–R1 mate. But that's not all. Only now does Black take with the Queen on Q4, and, as we plainly see, White's King finds itself quite unexpectedly in a mating net.

For only one Rook of little use Black has cleared the entire pawn obstruction from the center, and as compensation has obtained not only three pawns but also two diagonals, one rank, and a mighty Knight right in the middle of the board. White's material advantage would probably allow him to save his King from direct danger, but the solution of that problem would present no little difficulty.

For lovers of complex and beautiful variations, we give a short analysis which to a certain extent illustrates the possibilities for both sides in this mind-boggling position. (Besides my own variations, I have made use of material from correspondence on this question between Soviet Grandmaster Tigran Petrosian and the regular annotator for the magazine *Chess Voice*, Yugoslavian Master Vukovic.)

1) 40. P–N3 N–Q7ch 41. K–N2 RxPch 42. KxR QxPch and mate in two, or 41. K–R1 Nx Pch 42. K–N2 NxR.

2) 40. P–N4 N–Q7ch 41. K–R1 N–N6ch 42. K–N1 RxP 43. KxR (43. NxP N–Q7ch 44. QxN Q–N6 mate!) 43. . . . NxRch 44. K–R1 Q–R1ch 45. K–N1 Q–R7ch!

3) 40. P–R3 N–Q7ch 41. K–R1 N–N6ch 42. K–N1 NxR 43. NxN R–B4 44. B–Q3 BxB 45.

NxB QxN 46. Q–K2 QxQ 47. RxQ K–N2 48. P–N4 R–Q4, or a) 43. KxN BxR 44. KxB Q–K5ch, b) 43. QxN Q–N6 44. Q–Q2 R–Q4 45. Q–B1 QxRch 46. QxQ R–Q8ch.

4) 40. QxR QxQ 41. K–R1 P–B6 42. N–B3 N–N6 43. R–KB2 P–K5.

It is easy to understand that because Gligoric could not calculate the variations to the end in time pressure he decided not to take the chance of giving up a Rook; but the Rook was not worth sparing, considering that he was to give up the game in four more moves.

**38. N–B3          R–Q5**
**39. P–N3**

Whether intuitively or consciously, Petrosian does not permit such a nice possibility as . . . RxKP a second time. In chess as in life, opportunity knocks but once.

**39. . . .          Q–QN1**
**40. P–R5          BxRP**
**41. Q–R4          Black resigns**

On 41. . . . B–N3 42. Q–B6ch and QxKP Black's entire pawn chain is destroyed, and 41. . . . Q–K1 is answered by B–R3–K6 and the Rook goes to KN2.

## Game 133
### Nimzo-Indian Defense

**M. Najdorf**     **M. Taimanov**

1. P-Q4 N-KB3 2. P-QB4 P-K3 3. N-QB3 B-N5 4. P-K3 O-O 5. B-Q3 P-Q4 6. N-B3 P-QN3 7. O-O B-N2 8. B-Q2 PxP 9. BxP QN-Q2 10. Q-K2 P-B4 11. KR-Q1 PxP 12. NxP Q-K2 (As a result of White's sluggish opening play, Black has completed his development.) 13. QR-B1 P-QR3 14. P-QR3 B-B4 15. B-K1 P-QN4 16. B-R2 QR-B1 17. P-B3 N-K4 18. B-B2 N/3-Q2 19. B-N1 B-R2 20. P-B4

It is a mistake for White to weaken the KR1-QR8 diagonal. Such strong measures are not needed to drive away the Knight. In only two moves Najdorf has to give up a pawn to exchange Queens, but, thanks to the Bishop pair, he reestablishes approximate equality.

20. . . . N-KN3 21. P-KN3 BxN!

This is just the point! If the Rook recaptures on Q4, Black is quite able to bring his main reserves—the KP—into battle and to create a sudden assault on White's King with 22. . . . P-K4 23. R/4-Q1 RxN! 24. RxR PxP. It is enough to set up this continuation on the board to understand why White hastens to take with the pawn and then plays P-Q5 to close the diagonal of the Bishop on QN7.

22. PxB N-B3 23. P-Q5 NxQP (It is tempting for Black to play 23. . . . B-R1 and with . . . Q-N2 to set up a battery that would be lethal to White's King.) 24. NxN PxN 25. QxQ NxQ 26. B-QB5 KR-K1 27. B-R2 P-R3 28. K-B2 R-B2 29. B-N4 RxR 30. RxR N-B3 31. B-Q2 N-Q5 (Black's extra pawn has no meaning at all. Therefore, the game is an obvious draw. Stubbornly continuing to search for a win, Taimanov gets an inferior position. After a little suffering, all ends happily.) 32. B-K3 N-B4 33. B-R7 R-QB1 34. B-B5 R-B2 35. R-B3 P-KR4 36. B-N1 N-R3 37. P-KR4 B-B1 38. B-Q4 R-B5 39. B-Q3 RxR 40. BxR B-B4 41. B-K2 P-N3 42. P-R4 PxP 43. Bx QRP B-B7 44. B-B8 K-B1 45. B-N4ch, Drawn.

# Round Twenty

## Game 134

One of the most beautiful games in the tournament; White successfully breaches the enemy's position purely by combinational means without resorting to a pawn storm.

The reader will notice that this is not the first game I have called one of the most beautiful. There are indeed very many beautiful works in this tournament. Genuine beauty in chess is possible only through the creativity of both players, for if one is at a significantly different level of mastery than the other, the product of their art conveys less than full esthetic enjoyment.

In all, three beauty prizes were established for the Switzerland tournament, but had there been ten times that number the jury would have had no difficulty awarding them.

## Nimzo-Indian Defense

| M. Taimanov | T. Petrosian |
|---|---|
| 1. P–Q4 | N–KB3 |
| 2. P–QB4 | P–K3 |
| 3. N–QB3 | B–N5 |
| 4. P–K3 | P–B4 |
| 5. B–Q3 | O–O |
| 6. N–B3 | P–Q4 |
| 7. O–O | N–B3 |
| 8. P–QR3 | BxN |
| 9. PxB | P–QN3 |
| 10. BPxP | KPxP |

This system of defense was used many times in this tournament, for example in games 12, 102, 71, and 160. In every case Black found sufficient counterchances due to his extra pawn on the Queenside.

In the present game, Taimanov spends two moves to exchange Knights on QB6, and, not fearing the pressure on his QP, he plays P–KB3 and P–K4 as soon as possible.

| | |
|---|---|
| 11. N–K5 | Q–B2 |
| 12. NxN | QxN |

322

| 13. | P–B3 | B–K3 |
|-----|------|------|
| 14. | Q–K1 | N–Q2 |
| 15. | P–K4 | |

In other games in which the Nimzo-Indian Defense was played, White was not able so quickly and effectively to play P–K4, which immediately opens both Bishops' diagonals. The slightest hesitation on Black's part will subject his King to the danger of a strong attack, and Q–R4 is already threatened.

**15. . . .          P–B5**

Petrosian goes into a deep defense based on the support of K3. He is not forced to make this decision, but can use his temporary advantage in development and the pawn tension in the center to initiate sharp play with 15. . . . P–B4; for instance:

1) 16. PxQP QxP 17. B–K3 N–K4, or as well . . . P–B5 or . . . PxP.

2) On 16. P–K5 Black keeps QB5 for a Knight and answers 16. . . . P–QN4 threatening N–N3–B5.

3) Petrosian may not have liked the continuation 16. P–QB4 BPxKP 17. PxKP PxBP 18. P–Q5, but even this is not dangerous for Black after 18. . . . Q–Q3: a) 19. BxP N–K4 20. B–K2 B–N5 21. B–N2 BxB 22. QxB QR–K1 and White's pawns are blockaded; b) 19. PxB QxB 20. PxN RxRch 21. QxR Q–Q5ch; c) Black gets a very strong attack after 19. Rx Rch RxR 20. PxB N–K4, and the Bishop can go neither to N1 nor to K2 because of . . . Q–Q5ch. If it goes to B1 or B2, 21. . . . N–N5 follows, and there is clearly no way to prevent the threats 22. . . . QxP mate and 22. . . . Q–Q5ch.

| 16. | B–B2 | P–B4 |
|-----|------|------|
| 17. | P–K5 | R–B2 |
| 18. | P–QR4 | P–QR4 |
| 19. | P–B4 | P–QN4 |

White has a clear plan of attack—P–R3, K–R2, R–N1, P–N4, and Q–N3 or Q–R4—and Black can offer no Kingside resistance against this strategy. Petrosian, understandably, is trying to distract his opponent with his extra Queenside pawn; however, this creates a breach in his fortress through which the enemy Bishops attack Black's position on the flank, while the Queen and one of the Rooks continue the frontal attack.

| 20. | PxP | QxP |
|-----|-----|-----|
| 21. | B–R3 | N–N3 |
| 22. | Q–R4 | Q–K1 |

| 23. R–B3 | N–B1 |
|---|---|
| 24. B–R4 | |

White's pieces are very harmonious. Obviously, the Bishop cannot be taken because of mate, and on 24. . . . B–Q2 there follows 25. P–K6 QxP 26. Q–Q8ch.

| 24. . . . | R–Q2 |
|---|---|
| 25. R–N1 | |

White does not take the Exchange, which would seem to give Black the chance to untangle himself.

| 25. . . . | Q–Q1 |
|---|---|
| 26. BxR | |

If Black takes the Queen, then after 26. . . . QxQ 27. Bx Bch K–R1 28. BxQP R–R2 he will be powerless against the White pawn phalanx, not to mention that White can even win the Knight: 29. R–N8 Q–Q1 30. P–K6 or 30. B–K6.

| 26. . . . | QxB |
|---|---|
| 27. R–KN3 | |

Taimanov conducts the at-

tack in classical style and very soon creates irresistible mating threats. However, good enough to win is 27. R–R3 P–R3 28. R–KN3 K–R2 29. B–B8, or if 27. . . . P–N3 28. R–N7! with unavoidable mate.

| 27. . . . | N–R2 |
|---|---|
| 28. B–K7 | B–B2 |
| 29. Q–N5 | B–N3 |
| 30. P–R4 | N–B3 |
| 31. B–R3 | N–Q1 |
| 32. P–R5 | N–K3 |
| 33. Q–R4 | B–B2 |
| 34. P–R6 | P–N3 |
| 35. Q–B6 | Q–Q1 |
| 36. B–K7 | Q–B2 |

**37. RxPch**

The concluding combinational stroke. If 37. . . . BxR 38. QxNch B–B2 39. Q–KB6.

| 37. . . . | PxR |
|---|---|
| 38. P–R7ch | |

A rather crude finish. More precise is 38. K–B2 and mate

in no more than four moves,
even after 38. . . . QxB or 38.
. . . K–R2.

| 38. . . . | KxP |
| 39. QxBch | N–N2 |
| 40. K–B2 | **Black resigns** |

## Game 135
### Sicilian Defense

| S. Gligoric | Y. Averbakh |
| --- | --- |
| 1. P–K4 | P–QB4 |
| 2. N–KB3 | N–QB3 |
| 3. P–Q4 | PxP |
| 4. NxP | N–KB3 |
| 5. N–QB3 | P–Q3 |
| 6. B–KN5 | P–K3 |
| 7. Q–Q2 | P–QR3 |
| 8. O–O–O | B–Q2 |

The starting position of much
theoretical elaboration. The
latest analyses give White preference, perhaps without sufficient foundation. The point of
Black's 7. . . . P–QR3 and 8.
. . . B–Q2 is that, due to the
position of White's Queen on
Q2 and his Bishop on KN5,
Black always has the thrust . . .
NxP in reserve.

**9. P–B4**

It is difficult to create an attack in the Sicilian Defense
without this move, but now the
game enters the main variation
of Black's defense.

| 9. . . . | P–R3 |
| 10. B–R4 | NxP |
| 11. Q–K1 | |

This move was not found
until fifteen years ago. It had
been thought that 11. BxQ
NxQ, etc., was obligatory, but
in that case Black had an excellent endgame. Retreating the
Queen to K1 opened new possibilities for White.

| 11. . . . | N–B3 |
| 12. N–B5 | Q–R4 |

In olden times pawns were
given less attention than they
are today. They were not
counted at every move and
were willingly sacrificed to get
various advantages, some of
them problematic and debat-
able. However, they were not
thrown away for nothing. Steinitz, for example, who was quite
willing to suffer if he could keep
and then promote a single extra
pawn, would probably not have
parted with the QP so easily.

But it is understandable why Averbakh refrains from 12. . . . Q–B2. After 13. BxN PxB 14. N–Q5 the Queen must lose a tempo and return to Q1. Though such a prospect is quite unappealing, there are positions that may be solved by just such methods. Is this one of those positions? In any case, no immediate danger to Black is visible after 14. . . . Q–Q1, and to get out of the pin on the K-file there is the interesting move . . . N–K4!

| 13. NxQPch | BxN |
|---|---|
| 14. RxB | O–O–O |
| 15. Q–Q2 | |

The game immediately loses its theoretical interest and takes the tortuous course of maneuvering play, neither player wishing to undertake active operations.

Very interesting here is 15. BxN PxB 16. Q–R4, but the very strongest, in my opinion, is simply to retreat the Rook from Q6 to Q2. White should decide only after Black's reply whether to weaken Black's pawns by BxN or to save this Bishop for attacking the squares around Black's King. This has become one of the most popular variations recently.

15. . . . N–K2 16. B–Q3 B–B3 17. RxRch RxR 18. R–Q1 Q–R4 19. P–KN3 N–B4 20. BxN/6 PxB 21. Q–B2 N–Q5 22. B–K4 Q–QB4 23. K–N1 P–B4 24. BxB QxB 25. P–QR3 Q–B6 26. Q–N1

Does he really expect to win the game with such moves? Gligoric is true to himself and makes no unnecessary pawn moves; but such play at times bears the stamp of excessive caution. It is not surprising that the game soon ends in a draw.

26. . . . N–B3 27. RxRch KxR 28. K–B1 K–B2 29. K–Q2 P–KR4 30. Q–K3 QxQch 31. KxQ K–Q3 32. N–Q1 P–B3 33. K–Q3 N–K2 34. P–B4 P–R5 35. P–QN4 PxP 36. PxP P–N3 37. N–K3 N–B3 38. N–B2 P–R4 39. K–B3 PxPch 40. PxP N–N1 41. N–Q4 N–R3 42. K–N3 N–B2, Drawn.

## Game 136
### Nimzo-Indian Defense

| D. Bronstein | L. Szabo |
|---|---|
| 1. P–Q4 | N–KB3 |
| 2. P–QB4 | P–K3 |
| 3. N–QB3 | B–N5 |
| 4. N–B3 | P–B4 |

| 5. P–K3 | O–O |
|---|---|
| 6. B–K2 | |

Inasmuch as in the main variation, 6. B–Q3, etc., neither the P–K4 break nor a mating attack on the QN1–KR7 diagonal succeeds for White, he leaves the Q-file free.

| 6. | ... | P–Q4 |
|----|-----|------|
| 7. | O–O | N–B3 |
| 8. | BPxP | |

This exchange discloses White's plan:

1) 8. ... KNxP 9. NxN PxN 10. P–QR3 B–R4 11. PxP;

2) 8. ... KNxP 9. NxN QxN 10. P–QR3 B–R4 11. PxP QxP 12. P–QN4.

Black therefore has to accept an isolated pawn, which after 8. ... KPxP 9. PxP BxP 10. P–QR3 or 10. P–QN3 gives White a slight but solid advantage. This idea of the author's was later taken up and successfully used by Gligoric in his game against Euwe.

| 8. | ... | BPxP |
|----|-----|------|
| 9. | PxN | PxN |
| 10. | Q–N3 | |

It is well known from the chess ABCs that possession of a long diagonal is extremely important, so neither player wants to take the QNP. White is a move ahead, however, and although Szabo is unwilling, in the end he must submit.

| 10. | ... | Q–K2 |
|-----|-----|------|

It is better to sacrifice the pawn and continue with the symmetrical 10. ... Q–N3. Now White obtains a serious

advantage by an interesting Knight maneuver.

| 11. | N–K5 | B–Q3 |
|-----|------|------|
| 12. | N–B4 | PxNP |
| 13. | BxP | B–B4 |

Black does not even consider trading his active Bishop for the Knight, since the position would assume an open character.

| 14. | B–KB3 | N–Q4 |
|-----|-------|------|
| 15. | N–K5 | PxP |

**16. P–K4**

White should take with the Knight on QB6, when Black's Queen has no good square: 16. NxQBP Q–Q3 17. P–K4 or 16. ... Q–B2 17. BxN PxB 18. Q–B3. I did not notice that on 16. ... Q–N4, 17. P–KR4 wins.

| 16. | ... | N–B3 |
|-----|-----|------|
| 17. | KR–B1 | B–Q2 |
| 18. | Q–B3 | B–N5 |
| 19. | NxQBP | BxN |
| 20. | QxB/6 | |

After a series of exchanges, White has retained the advan-

tage of the two Bishops on an
open board.

| | |
|---|---|
| 20. . . . | QR–Q1 |
| 21. R–B4 | R–Q7 |
| 22. B–B1 | R–Q2 |
| 23. B–K3 | B–Q3 |
| 24. Q–R6 | KR–Q1 |
| 25. R–N1 | N–K1 |
| 26. P–N3 | B–K4 |
| 27. K–N2 | P–R3 |

The maneuvering will not
continue indefinitely. While
there is time, each side improves
his King's position.

| | |
|---|---|
| 28. R/4–N4 | K–R2 |
| 29. R–N7 | N–Q3 |

The only way to save the
QRP. But the Knight gets into
a double pin on the Q-file.

| | |
|---|---|
| 30. RxR | RxR |
| 31. B–B5 | R–B2 |
| 32. B–R3 | |

Again White is not up to the
mark. The pin on the Knight
can be strengthened by 32. Q–
R3.

| | |
|---|---|
| 32. . . . | Q–Q2 |
| 33. R–QB1 | RxR |
| 34. BxR | B–Q5 |
| 35. P–K5 | |

A pawn sacrifice for the sake
of maintaining the initiative.
The only vulnerable point in
Black's position is his QRP, so
White wants to divert Black's
Bishop from its QN1–KR7 di-
agonal at any price.

| | |
|---|---|
| 35. . . . | BxKP |
| 36. B–K3 | N–B1 |
| 37. P–QR4 | |

It is very important for White
to move the pawn up to R5 to
deny Black's QN3 to his pieces.
Black posts his Bishop on QN1
to free his Knight from QB1,
but this makes no difference.

| | |
|---|---|
| 37. . . . | B–N1 |

After 38. . . . N–K2 39. B–
N7 the QRP is lost, but now
the Knight gets pinned again.

| | |
|---|---|
| 38. P–R5 | N–Q3 |
| 39. B–B4 | P–B3 |
| 40. Q–Q3ch | K–N1 |
| 41. P–R6 | |

Nailing down the QRP. Now
the outcome of the game will
be decided by whether or not
White has sufficient means to
prevent . . . P–K4.

| | |
|---|---|
| 41. . . . | K–R1 |
| 42. Q–N3 | |

The start of an uninterrupted
attack by the Queen and the
light-square Bishop. White definitely wants to force . . . P–B4.
Szabo, on the contrary, strives
for . . . P–K4.

| | |
|---|---|
| 42. . . . | Q–K1 |
| 43. B–R5 | |

A combination on the theme
of the overloaded Queen. One
of Black's pawns is unavoidably
lost.

| 43. . . . | Q–N1 |
|-----------|------|
| 44. B–B7  |      |

| 44. . . .   | QxB          |
|-------------|--------------|
| 45. QxBch   | N–K1         |
| 46. Q–N7    |              |

This is where the pawn on QR6 comes in handy. It is amusing how White's Bishop slipped behind Black's pawns.

| 46. . . .  | Q–R4         |
|------------|--------------|
| 47. P–R3   | K–R2         |
| 48. QxP    | P–K4         |
| 49. B–K3   | P–K5         |
| 50. Q–K7   | Black resigns |

## Game 137

Against Averbakh in game 17, Reshevsky was unable to solve his defensive problems in the opening, and he decided he would use a similar White system himself. He had to wait quite a while—from the 3rd round to the 20th—for no one was interested in playing the main variation of the Nimzo-Indian Defense against him.

### Nimzo-Indian Defense

| S. Reshevsky | M. Euwe |
|--------------|---------|
| 1. P–Q4      | N–KB3   |
| 2. P–QB4     | P–K3    |
| 3. N–QB3     | B–N5    |
| 4. P–K3      | P–B4    |
| 5. B–Q3      | P–Q4    |
| 6. N–B3      | O–O     |
| 7. O–O       | N–B3    |
| 8. P–QR3     | BxN     |
| 9. PxB       | QPxP    |
| 10. BxP      | Q–B2    |
| 11. R–K1     | P–K4    |

Against Averbakh Reshevsky played 11. . . . R–Q1 here to prevent P–Q5, but Euwe does not consider that advance dangerous, and he may be right.

| 12. P–Q5 | P–K5 |
|----------|------|

Euwe has prepared an energetic counterstroke, but it was not necessary. Simply retreating the Knight to QR4 places the QP, torn from its camp, in a difficult situation. For instance, 12. . . . N–QR4 13. P–Q6 Q–B3 14. NxP Q–K5, and the pawn is won back with good play. Another possibility, pointed out later by Euwe, is 13. . . . Q–N3 14. NxP NxB 15. NxN Q–R3.

| 13. PxN | PxN |
| 14. QxP | B–N5 |
| 15. Q–N3 | QxP |

As usual in this variation, White has a slight positional advantage—his extra pawn on the Kingside can drive the Knight from KB6, after which the Bishop pair will get attacking prospects against the King. As for Black's extra pawn on the Queenside, that will have to wait for the endgame.

| 16. P–K4 | B–R4 |
| 17. P–K5 | N–Q4 |
| 18. P–QR4 | P–QR3 |

Euwe started the resolute maneuver B–R4–N3 in order to protect his King's position and forestall the impending attack, but he does not complete it and begins another plan: P–QR3 and P–QN4. The unsupervised Bishop provokes an interesting maneuver by White.

It is better to complete one plan, playing . . . B–N3 at once or after . . . N–B2, and then to start the other one.

| 19. P–R5 | P–QN4 |
| 20. PxP e.p. | NxNP |
| 21. RxP | RxR |
| 22. BxR | |

Not every player would have taken this pawn. After . . . P–B5, threatening . . . N–Q4 or . . . R–R1, it looks as if the Bishop will be lost.

But if Reshevsky sees a chance to win, he is willing to think for two hours and twenty-five minutes in order to make use of his chance and obtain victory.

| 22. . . . | P–B5 |
| 23. Q–R4 | |

Reshevsky thus exploits the insecure position of Black's Bishop. Now . . . B–N3 would be answered by 24. B–K3 with dangerous threats to Black, so Euwe forces matters.

| 23. . . . | R–R1 |
| 24. B–K3 | P–R3 |
| 25. QxB | RxB |
| 26. B–Q4 | N–Q4 |

The game enters a new phase, in which Black has fair drawing chances despite his missing pawn, especially if Queens are exchanged. The point is that

White's one remaining Bishop is not the better of the two, since his pawns are on dark squares; furthermore, White's QBP is weak and Black has the more active Rook.

White, in his turn, has a technical way to lengthen his Bishop's diagonal, for which purpose he must advance his KP to K6. This advance will be stronger if in the meantime his KBP gets to B5.

The ensuing struggle is concerned with these themes.

| 27. | Q–N4 | Q–K3 |
|---|---|---|
| 28. | Q–B3 | N–K2 |
| 29. | P–R3 | |

Rather slow. The immediate invasion of N7 by the Queen is very promising.

| 29. | . . . | Q–Q4 |
|---|---|---|

Now White is forced to trade, since the threat is . . . R–KN3. The exchange of Queens considerably simplifies Black's problems.

| 30. | QxQ | NxQ |
|---|---|---|
| 31. | P–N3 | N–B2 |

Destroying the fruits of his stubborn defense. The obvious 31. . . . R–R6 offers great drawing chances. Euwe gives the variation 31. . . . R–R6 32. P–K6 PxP 33. RxP NxP 34. R–K7 K–B1! 35. B–B5! R–R4! 36. R–QB7ch K–N1 37. B–N4 R–R8ch 38. K–N2 N–Q4, which assures Black of a draw.

**32. R–N1**

The Rook's roundabout maneuver to penetrate to the seventh rank soon decides the game.

| 32. | . . . | N–K3 |
|---|---|---|
| 33. | R–N8ch | K–R2 |
| 34. | R–QB8 | R–R5 |
| 35. | B–K3 | N–N4 |
| 36. | K–N2 | N–K5 |
| 37. | B–Q4 | N–Q7 |
| 38. | P–K6 | |

This break, carried out at the proper moment, creates unavoidable mating threats.

| 38. | . . . | PxP |
|---|---|---|
| 39. | R–B7 | K–N3 |
| 40. | P–N4 | Black resigns |

### Game 138
### Queen's Gambit

| P. Keres | G. Stahlberg |
|---|---|
| 1. P–Q4 | N–KB3 |
| 2. P–QB4 | P–K3 |
| 3. N–QB3 | P–Q4 |
| 4. B–N5 | B–K2 |
| 5. P–K3 | QN–Q2 |

| 6. N–B3 | O–O |
|---|---|
| 7. Q–B2 | P–B3 |
| 8. R–Q1 | R–K1 |
| 9. P–QR3 | PxP |
| 10. BxP | N–Q4 |
| 11. BxB | QxB |
| 12. O–O | NxN |

**13. QxN          P–QN3**
**14. N–K5**

Black has simplified the position by exchanging a Bishop and a Knight, and now by preparing P–QB4 he wants to solve Black's basic problem in the Orthodox Defense, the Queen Bishop. White can play in various ways here. Not bad is to put a Rook on K1 and prepare the advance P–K4 in order to meet . . . P–QB4 with P–Q5. He can retreat the Bishop to R2 and switch a Rook to the QB-file. Keres likes to have a Knight on a central square, and he is frequently able to carry out an attack based on its advantageous position.

The exchange of Knights on K4 may seem tempting for Black. Indeed, if all the pieces were removed from the board, the pawn endgame would be much better for him, perhaps even winning, thanks to his three pawns against White's two on the Queenside. But nobody knows how to remove all the pieces. After 14. . . . NxN 15. PxN B–N2 16. R–Q6 White seizes Q6 as well as the Q-file. The exchange of Rooks can then take place only on Q6, where White recaptures with the pawn and gets a strong passed pawn.

Therefore, Black develops the Bishop first and threatens to take the Knight; for example, 14. . . . B–N2 15. B–R2 NxN

16. PxN QR–Q1!, and the Q-file becomes an arena for exchanges.

**14. . . .          B–N2**
**15. P–B4          NxN**
**16. BPxN          P–QB4**

Black has conducted the opening successfully and has fully equalized the game; he is now prepared to enter an evenly matched and quite interesting struggle, despite the relatively limited forces. He can operate on two open lines, the QB-file and the Q-file, whereas White has only the KB-file at his disposal.

Open lines are valuable when there are objects of attack on them or when they serve as transfer points for the pieces, usually Rooks, to the main battlefields. The KB-file satisfies both of these conditions here, and, more important, it lies close to the King, and this makes Stahlberg uneasy.

The Swedish grandmaster decides to transfer his Bishop via K5 to the defense of his Kingside and then calmly to attack the QP and use the QB-file for indirect operations against White's King. Such a plan is possible, of course, but it seems to me that Black can get more out of the position by exchanging on Q5 as soon as he can and then trying to penetrate to the seventh rank with a Rook. The threat to KN7 would inhibit the activity of White's Rooks.

| 17. Q–K1 | B–K5 |
|----------|------|
| 18. R–B4 | B–N3 |
| 19. P–KR4 | PxP |
| 20. PxP | QR–B1 |
| 21. Q–K2 | R–B2 |

Of course, it makes no sense for Black to exchange his Bishop by 21. . . . B–R4 22. QxB RxB, for it was brought here especially to guard the King. By continuing 23. R–Q3, White would leave his opponent behind in the attack.

**22. QR–KB1**

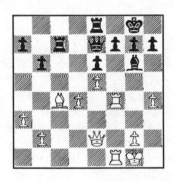

| 22. . . . | P–KR4 |
|-----------|-------|

Such a move should be made only when there is no other way to defend the King. In this case Black has at his disposal the quite satisfactory and less drastic remedy 22. . . . KR–QB1 23. B–R6 R–B7 24. Q–B3 R–B1, and if 25. P–R5 B–B4 26. P–KN4 Q–R5.

| 23. R/1–B3 | R/1–QB1 |
|------------|---------|
| 24. B–Q3 | BxB |
| 25. RxB | P–N3 |

Black's pawn on KR4 drags the KNP behind it, and White's pieces are already threatening to penetrate to the weakened squares KR6, KN5, and KB6.

| 26. R–KN3 | K–R2 |
|-----------|------|

The play is now becoming forced—the threat was QxP, and on his next move White threatens RxRPch.

| 27. R–N5 | Q–B1 |
|----------|------|
| 28. Q–K4 | Q–R3 |
| 29. P–Q5 | |

Keres hastens to crown the attack by his heavy pieces with a pawn breakthrough, but he gives his opponent counterchances. Correct is 29. R–B6, completing the blockade of the Kingside, after which there would no longer be a defense against 30. Q–B4 and 31. P–Q5!

| 29. . . . | PxP |
|-----------|-----|
| 30. QxP | Q–B1 |
| 31. P–K6 | |

| 31. . . . | Q–B4ch |
|-----------|--------|

It is psychologically under-standable that Black immediately makes use of his chance to exchange Queens and escape the mating threats, but he gets a hopeless endgame. Instead, 31. . . . P–B4 gives good drawing chances. In order to keep up his attack, Keres would probably want to sacrifice a Rook on KB5, but after 32. R/4xP PxR 33. RxPch K–N3 34. R–N5ch K–R3 White has no better move than 35. Q–B3, and by answering with the attack 35. . . . R– B8ch 36. K–R2 Q–Q3ch 37. P–N3 Q–Q7ch Black forces an approximately equal ending: 38. K–R3 QxR 39. PxQch KxP (40. P–K7 R–R1ch 41. K–N2 R–B7ch 42. K–N1 R–B8ch, etc.).

**32. QxQ PxQ 33. PxP K– N2 34. P–B8=Qch RxQ 35. RxR KxR 36. RxNP P–B5 37. R–N5 R–QN2 38. RxP RxP 39. R–B5 R–QB7 40. K–R2 K–K2 41. P–R5 P–B6 42. R– B4, Black resigns.**

## Game 139
### King's Indian Defense

**V. Smyslov     I. Boleslavsky**

**1. P–Q4 N–KB3 2. N–KB3 P–KN3 3. B–B4 B–N2 4. QN– Q2 P–Q3 5. P–KR3 O–O 6. P–K3**

An original system against the King's Indian Defense that is used by Smyslov when he does not want to give Black the slightest chance to get the initiative. White firmly reinforces his QP and thrice controls K5, not allowing Black's traditional King's Indian advance P–K4. The move P–KR3 is included to save his Bishop on KB4 from exchange, otherwise possible by . . . N–KR4.

In the present game Bole-slavsky demonstrates the best method of fighting this solid but rather slow system: he advances . . . P–QB4, occupies the QB-file, and sets up a pawn barricade against the dark-square Bishop. If he does not do this, he might get into a cramped position.

**6. . . . P–B4 7. B–K2 N–B3 8. B–R2** (Nobody chased it. More in the spirit of the system is 8. P–B3, to retake on Q4 with the BP.) **8. . . . PxP 9. PxP B–Q2 10. O–O R–B1 11. R– K1 P–QR3 12. B–B1 P–QN4 13. P–B3 N–QR4 14. N–N5 R–K1 15. N/5–K4 NxN 16. NxN N–B5 17. R–N1, Drawn.**

# Game 140
## Nimzo-Indian Defense

| Y. Geller | A. Kotov |
|-----------|----------|
| 1. P-Q4 | N-KB3 |
| 2. P-QB4 | P-K3 |
| 3. N-QB3 | B-N5 |
| 4. P-K3 | P-B4 |
| 5. B-Q3 | O-O |
| 6. N-B3 | P-Q4 |
| 7. O-O | N-B3 |
| 8. P-QR3 | BxN |
| 9. PxB | QPxP |
| 10. BxP | Q-B2 |
| 11. Q-B2 | P-K4 |
| 12. B-R2 | B-N5 |
| 13. NxP | |

Geller repeats the opening of game 54, Taimanov Euwe, but having learned from White's unsuccessful experience with 13. P-Q5, he employs another continuation, with P-K4 in view.

| 13. . . . | NxN |
|-----------|-----|
| 14. PxN | QxP |
| 15. P-K4 | |

An original and sharp idea: exploiting the fact that the Bishop happens to be on his KN4, White advances the pawn to K4 without the support of his minor pieces. White could safely celebrate a strategic victory if the move of the KP were followed by the advance of the KBP two squares. But inasmuch as he has to hold P-KB3 in reserve to avoid the loss of his KP, White's only central pawn is insecure. This is demonstrated, for instance, by the fact that on Black's next move, 15. . . . KR-K1, White cannot make the natural reply 16. R-K1 in view of 16. . . . NxP! 17. P-B3 QxP 18. QxQ NxQ 19. RxRch RxR 20. PxB R-K8ch 21. K-B2 R-K7ch 22. K-B3 RxB. The move recommended by some commentators in this variation, 20. . . . NxB, does not work because White does not take the Knight but plays 21. B-Q2!, and the Knight perishes.

| 15. . . . | KR-K1 |
|-----------|-------|
| 16. B-N1 | |

This would make sense if it somehow prepared P-KB4.

| 16. . . . | QR-Q1 |
|-----------|-------|
| 17. P-B3 | B-Q2 |
| 18. B-N2 | B-B3 |

| 19. | B–R2 | N–R4 |
| 20. | QR–Q1 | N–B5 |
| 21. | R–Q2 | |

While White was spending time shifting his Bishops, Black was able to get his Knight to a strong position. The laws of chess permit a Knight to be driven away by a pawn, but in this position the laws of strategy categorically prohibit a move like P–N3, since it weakens the second rank too much. Now it is necessary to take care that equality is maintained by 21. B–B1, since, fortunately for White, 21. . . . B–N4 does not yet work.

Geller refuses to believe that he does not have the better game; in searching for an advantage on the Q-file he allows Kotov to make a beautiful combination based on the themes of Queen diversion and the interaction of the Queen and Knight. I have noted earlier that Queen and Knight are often stronger than Queen and Bishop and sometimes no worse than Queen and Rook. This is easily understood when you observe that the Bishop duplicates the Queen whereas the Knight complements it.

| 21. . . . | B–R5 |

The introduction. The Queen is now forced into a dark cage where it cannot attack Black's Knight on Q3 or K2.

| 22. | Q–B1 | Q–N4 |

The threat is now 23. . . . RxR and 24. . . . N–R6ch, and if 23. K–R1 then 23. . . . N–Q6 and White must give up the Exchange.

| 23. | B–Q5 | NxB |

Black has the better position and now wins a pawn. He can try to use the active position of his pieces in another way: 23. . . . RxB 24. PxR R–K7, etc.

| 24. | PxN | RxP |
| 25. | RxR | QxR |

| 26. | P–QB4 | Q–Q6 |
| 27. | R–K1 | P–B3 |
| 28. | RxRch | BxR |
| 29. | Q–B3 | Q–K7 |

| 30. | B–B1 | B–B2 |
|-----|------|------|
| 31. | Q–Q2 | Q–K2 |

Black does not agree to the exchange of Queens because of 31. . . . QxQ 32. BxQ BxP 33. B–K3, provoking . . . P–QN3, when White's Bishop will attack Black's pawns from behind. Still, it is possible to exchange Queens, but instead of taking the QBP at once he can continue 32. . . . K–B1 33. B–K3 P–QN3 34. B–B4 K–K2 35. B–N8 K–Q2, and if the Bishop takes the pawn, then 36. . . . K–B2 and the Bishop is trapped!

| 32. | Q–K3 | K–B1 |
|-----|------|------|
| 33. | P–KR4 | QxQch |

| 34. | BxQ | P–QN3 |
|-----|-----|-------|
| 35. | P–R4 | |

On 35. B–B4 Black returns once more to the theme of the trapped Bishop—35. . . . K–K2.

| 35. | . . . | K–K2 |
|-----|-------|------|
| 36. | P–QR5 | BxP |
| 37. | PxP | PxP |
| 38. | K–B2 | K–Q3 |
| 39. | B–B4ch | K–B3 |
| 40. | K–K3 | B–B2 |
| 41. | P–N4 | P–QN4 |

White is powerless against the two connected passed pawns.

| 42. | P–R5 | P–N5 |
|-----|------|------|
|     | **White resigns** | |

# Round Twenty-One

· *Game 141*
*English Opening*

A. Kotov          V. Smyslov

1. P–QB4 P–K3 2. N–KB3 P–Q4 3. P–K3 N–KB3 4. P–QN3 P–KN3 5. B–N2 B–N2 6. P–Q4 O–O 7. B–Q3 P–B4 8. O–O BPxP 9. NxP (Better is 9. KPxP, keeping an important pawn in the center.) 9. . . . . P–K4 10. N–N5 P–QR3 11. N/5–B3 PxP 12. BxBP P–QN4 13. B–K2 B–N2 14. N–Q2 P–K5

Black has successfully solved his opening problems; it remains only to develop his QN, which will then take part in the fight for the QB- and Q-files. White, looking for complications, plays the double-edged P–QN4 with the intention of transferring a Knight to QB5, but this gives Black the chance to occupy his own QB5. The following play is built on these themes: control and possession of the respective QB5-squares, opposition of the Bishops on the long diagonal, and possession of the open files.

15. P–QN4 Q–K2 16. P–QR3 R–Q1 17. Q–B2 QN–Q2 18. N–N3 QR–B1 19. KR–Q1 N–Q4

Does Smyslov really think he is winning White's pinned Knight?! Kotov, not believing his eyes, spent 40 minutes before taking the Knight with his Rook.

## 20. RxN BxN

Smyslov does not realize that he is losing two pieces for a

338

Rook. The Knight has to be eliminated in another way: 20. . . . RxN (21. BxR BxR). Then it is bad for White to play 21. RxN RxQ 22. RxQ RxQB 23. RxB RxN since the game would very soon turn in Black's favor. After 20. . . . RxN 21. BxR BxR, best for White is 22. BxB KxB 23. R–QB1, retaining a slight advantage.

**21. RxN! RxR**

Smyslov saw the blow 21. RxN, of course, but he probably did not notice that 21. . . . BxB would be answered by 22. RxRch.

**22. BxB B–Q4 23. N–B5 R–Q3 24. B–N2 P–B3 25. B–Q4 Q–KB2 26. P–R3 R–K1 27. R–QB1 P–KR4 28. P–QR4 P–B4 29. B–N2 K–R2 30. Q–B3 B–B5 31. BxB PxB 32. QxP R–Q8ch 33. K–R2 QxQ 34. RxQ R–Q7 35. B–B6 RxP 36. R–Q4 P–B5 37. R–Q7ch K–R3 38. P–R4 P–N4 39. BxPch K–N3 40. BxP, Black resigns.**

## Game 142
### Ruy Lopez

| I. Boleslavsky | P. Keres |
|---|---|
| 1. P–K4 | P–K4 |
| 2. N–KB3 | N–QB3 |
| 3. B–N5 | P–QR3 |
| 4. B–R4 | N–B3 |
| 5. O–O | B–K2 |
| 6. R–K1 | P–QN4 |
| 7. B–N3 | O–O |
| 8. P–B3 | P–Q3 |
| 9. P–KR3 | N–QR4 |
| 10. B–B2 | P–B4 |
| 11. P–Q4 | Q–B2 |
| 12. QN–Q2 | R–Q1 |

The beginning of a variation that Keres has prepared especially for this game. The idea is that on 12. . . . B–N2 White usually locks the center by P–Q5 and Black's Bishop has nothing better than to go back to QB1; or if 12. . . . R–K1, possible is 13. PxKP PxP, and

Black's Rook subsequently goes to the Q-file. After the text move P–Q5 makes no sense for White, since Black's Bishop is on QB1; nor does PxKP, since Black's Rook is already on the Q-file. White therefore continues with the Knight's traditional journey from QN1 via Q2–B1 to KN3 or K3.

**13. N–B1    P–Q4!**

And this is Keres's prepared novelty. The possibilities thus created on the board are inexhaustible. On each move three or four distinct continuations are possible, none worse than the others. To calculate to the fifth move one must therefore verify about twenty thousand variations, judging along the way whether the intermediate positions favor oneself or the opponent. Only a computer is capable of such calculations, but computers are not possessed of intuition.

In attempting to evaluate the position on the basis of general considerations, I conclude that White has good attacking chances: both Bishops, both Knights, and his Queen can be quickly brought to the battlefield (his Rook prevents the Black King from escaping). I can discern only two tactical counterchances for Black: his Queen attacks the Bishop on QB2, and, given the opportunity, his Rook threatens the White Queen.

In the course of play, therefore, White should be able to find continuations that will allow him to realize his chances. Why then does . . . R–Q1 and the whole variation deserve an exclamation mark? Because of Keres's sound psychological preparation. He knew in advance what variation he would play, and he presented Boleslavsky with extremely difficult

problems to solve over the board. In such circumstances, Keres has only slight chances of losing, but real chances of winning.

**14. PxQP**

Master Vasiukov later offered this clever solution: 14. PxKP PxP 15. N/1–Q2! PxN 16. PxN BxBP 17. QxP B–K3 18. N–K4 B–K2 19. Q–R5 or 14. . . . NxP 15. N–K3! B–K3 16. Q–K2.

| 14. | . . . | KPxP |
| 15. | PxP | NxP |
| 16. | Q–K2 | B–N2 |
| 17. | N–N3 | PxP |
| 18. | NxP | |

Many annotators considered this move a loss of time and suggested 18. N–B5, but after 18. . . . B–N5 it is not clear how White is to continue the attack, not just for the sake of attacking but for the sake of winning. The loss of time was not here but on the 16th move: Q–K2 instead of the correct 16. N–N5.

**18. . . .                    P–N3**

Simple and good. White was threatening to invade KB5 or KR5 with a Knight and to bring in his Queen to help. With one modest move, denying KR5 and KB5 to White's pieces, Keres immediately solves many defensive problems. White's advantage must be considered temporary; if he does not exploit it in two or three moves, Black will bring up his reserves—the Knight on QR4—and reinforce his King's position. After Black's strong move, Boleslavsky has, in my opinion, only one continuation of the attack left—19. N/4–B5!—and if Black takes the Knight:

1) the KN-file is opened;

2) White's QN1–KR7 diagonal is opened;

3) White's Queen is allowed to get to KR5; and

4) most important, a White Knight will still occupy KB5!

If Black can defend himself in this case—well, what can you do? But it would not be easy for Keres. Now White's game deteriorates with each move.

| 19. | B–R6 | B–KB3 |
|---|---|---|
| 20. | N–N3 | N–QB5 |
| 21. | N–K4 | BxP |
| 22. | N/3–B5 | |

White decides to give up the Exchange, since on R–N1 or R–Q1 Black's pressure on the Queenside would be intolerable.

22. ... BxR 23. RxB P–B4 24. NxB QxN 25. N–B5 Q–B3 26. N–Q3 N–B6 27. Q–K1 Q–B3 28. P–B4 N–K5 29. K–R2 Q–B6 30. Q–QN1 N/B–Q7 31. Q–QB1 RxN 32. BxR Qx B 33. Q–B7 N–B6ch!, White resigns.

## Game 143

Even among the strongest masters today there are those who play much better with White than with Black. As Black these players think about a draw from the very first move. Though roused to flights of imagination and a will to win at any price when playing White, they are bored and think only of how to "equalize" in similar positions as Black.

In Reshevsky this quality stands out in bold relief, as the reader can see for himself in his games. I note only numerical results, but in this tournament Reshevsky as White won seven games, lost only one, and made six draws, and as Black he won only one game, lost three, and drew ten! In the present game Reshevsky plays listlessly and does not even attempt to realize the counterchances inherent in the King's Indian Defense.

### King's Indian Defense

**G. Stahlberg        S. Reshevsky**

1. P–Q4 N–KB3 2. P–QB4 P–KN3 3. P–KN3 B–N2 4. B–N2 O–O 5. N–QB3 P–Q3 6. N–B3 QN–Q2 7. O–O P–K4 8. P–K4 PxP 9. NxP R–K1

**10. P–KR3 N–B4 11. R–K1 P–QR4 12. Q–B2 N–N5** (All theory so far. In game 131, Averbakh–Bronstein, White continued 13. R–Q1 at this point. In answer to the text move, 13. N–N3, Reshevsky can start a sharp fight by means of 13. . . . N–K4.) **13. N–N3 NxN 14. PxN N–K4 15. B–K3 N–B3 16. QR–Q1 N–N5 17. Q–B1** (Much more active here is 17. Q–Q2, having in mind the transfer of the Queen to KB2 after P–B4.) **17. . . . B–Q2 18. K–R2 Q–K2 19. P–B4 B–QB3 20. Q–Q2 Q–B1 21. Q–KB2 P–B4 22. B–Q4 BxB 23. RxB Q–B3 24. R–Q2 R–K2 25. PxP RxR 26. QxR R–K1 27. R–K2 RxR 28. QxR QxP 29. BxB PxB 30. Q–K7 Q–B2 31. Q–K3 Q–B4 32. Q–K7 Q–B2 33. Q–K3 Q–B4 34. Q–K7, Drawn.**

## Game 144
## Dutch Defense

| M. Euwe | D. Bronstein |
|---|---|
| 1. P–Q4 | P–K3 |
| 2. P–QB4 | P–KB4 |

How can one not play . . . P–KB4 against the Dutch Champion? It comes as no surprise to him, however, and after a few introductory moves the game assumes the character of a theoretical debate.

| 3. P–KN3 | N–KB3 |
|---|---|
| 4. B–N2 | B–K2 |
| 5. N–KB3 | O–O |
| 6. O–O | P–Q3 |
| 7. N–B3 | Q–K1 |
| 8. R–K1 | |

This old continuation is re-appearing on the chess horizon due to the possibility of a later Rook sacrifice on White's K4.

| 8. . . . | Q–N3 |
|---|---|
| 9. P–K4 | |

Some theoreticians think this move opens the K-file. Practical chess players know that it opens two files: the K-file for White and the KB-file for Black. The initiative will be seized by the player who is quickest to take practical advantage of "his" file.

| 9. . . . | NxP |
|---|---|
| 10. NxN | PxN |
| 11. RxP | |

**11. . . .        P-K4**

Black does not take the Rook, of course, since if 11. . . . QxR? 12. N-R4!; but in the interest of quickest development he sacrifices a pawn. The correctness of the sacrifice would be tested not by accepting the gift but by quietly retreating the Rook by 12. R-K1. However, White plays differently.

**12. Q-K2        B-B4**
**13. N-R4**

Euwe probably underestimated the intrinsic strength of Black's position. White's desire to exchange one of Black's Bishops is entirely understandable, but the Rook will stand badly on R4.

**13. . . .        BxN**
**14. RxB        N-B3**

White's situation is becoming a little uncomfortable. If he gives up his KB for the Knight he weakens the light squares, but how else is Q4 to be rein-

forced? The simplest solution seems to be 15. B-K3, but after 15. . . . B-Q6 16. B-Q5ch K-R1 the initiative is in Black's hands. White decides to trade pawns.

**15. PxP        PxP**

Having gotten off to a sharp start, Black switches to the positional track at the wrong time. It is better to take with the Knight on K4 and to continue . . . QR-K1.

**16. B-K3        QR-Q1**
**17. B-B5        KR-K1**
**18. B-Q5ch**

White's Bishops take a suitable opportunity to show their strength.

**18. . . .        K-R1**
**19. Q-R5**

The prelude to interesting complications.

**19. . . .        QxQ**
**20. RxQ        P-KN3**
**21. RxB!        PxR**
**22. B-B7**

Black is confronted with a difficult choice: which of White's Bishops is more important? After long consideration he decides to take the dark-square one, mainly because of the possibility of invading Q7 with his Rook.

| 22. . . . | R–K2 |
| 23. BxR | NxB |
| 24. B–R5 | |

The only chance. Now 24. . . . R–Q7 is parried by 25. R–Q1, and if 25. . . . RxNP 26. R–Q7. The whole question is whether Black can play P–K5 and bring his King to the center by the convenient route N2–B3–K4. He now sets about the execution of this plan with great expectations, but it meets with a clever retort.

| 24. . . . | N–B3 |
| 25. R–Q1 | N–Q5 |
| 26. R–K1 | P–K5 |

It would be a pity to agree to a draw by repeating moves— 26. . . . N–B3 27. R–Q1 N–Q5 28. R–K1. Euwe elegantly demonstrates that even the bold pawn move cannot change the outcome of the battle.

| 27. P–B3 | N–B7 |
| 28. R–QB1 | Drawn |

The intrusion of the Knight to QB7 was careless on my part, of course. Time trouble was not the cause, but I should not have thought that by playing P–B3 Euwe was conceding the game. After 27. . . . N–B7, putting the Rook on K2 would in fact be bad because of . . . R–Q8ch, but I should have paid more attention to R–QB1. Instead, I superficially calculated two variations—28. R–QB1 R–Q7 29. PxP PxP and 28. R–QB1 P–K6 29. RxN R–Q8ch 30. K–N2 R–Q7ch. Both seemed advantageous to me, and I planned to make the final decision after White's reply.

However, the choice turned out to be a difficult one. In the first variation, White would have the better ending after 30. R–Q1!; and in the second, after 31. RxR PxR the QP would by no means become a Queen, as Black had expected, because of the simple 32. P–B4, and White would have a Bishop while Black would not have his Knight. Therefore, 28. . . . N–N5 would have been correct, but then White could have gone over to the attack. Evidently, Euwe was in a peaceful mood that day, and all's well that ends well.

## Game 145

To say "the modern way of playing the opening" still does not explain how an opening was played. Sometimes it begins sharply, and the first mistake influences the outcome of the game. In such cases the opponents reveal their plans right away: one conducts the attack on, say, the Kingside, the other on the Queenside. This is one of the most common situations nowadays, as it was in the past. In the present game we come across a new way, one that appeared in tournaments comparatively recently and was aptly called by A. M. Konstantinopolsky the "clash of openings." Each side deploys his forces and makes his plans without coming in contact with his opponent for the time being, and in most cases without crossing the line of demarcation between the fourth and fifth ranks.

But such slowness is often the precursor of interesting play, as in this game.

## English Opening

| L. Szabo | S. Gligoric |
|---|---|
| 1. P–QB4 | N–KB3 |
| 2. P–KN3 | P–KN3 |
| 3. B–N2 | B–N2 |
| 4. P–K4 | P–Q3 |
| 5. N–K2 | O–O |
| 6. O–O | P–B4 |
| 7. QN–B3 | N–B3 |
| 8. P–Q3 | B–Q2 |
| 9. P–KR3 | N–K1 |
| 10. P–KN4 | N–B2 |
| 11. P–B4 | R–N1 |

The resulting position resembles the closed variation of the Sicilian Defense, with the insignificant difference that White's QBP has moved to B4. White's pawns are advantageously arrayed and are ready for a menacing attack on the King. As soon as Szabo plays P–B5 Black responds immediately with . . . P–QN4 and the battle is on!

| 12. P–B5 | P–QN4 |
|---|---|
| 13. NxP | NxN |
| 14. PxN | RxP |
| 15. N–B3 | R–N1 |
| 16. P–N5 | N–K4 |

On Q5 this Knight would block the base of White's pawn chain and take control of more important squares. In particular, it would render White's next move unplayable, and Szabo would have to decide what to do about his KBP.

| | |
|---|---|
| 17. N–Q5 | P–K3 |
| 18. P–B6 | PxN |
| 19. PxB | |

The reader who is well acquainted with opening theory will have no trouble recalling a predecessor of White's "little combination"—the game Milner-Barry vs. Capablanca. In a similar position Black took on KN2, but Moscow players later demonstrated that . . . R–K1 was stronger. Perhaps that is the best move here, too. On 20. P–Q4 BPxP 21. QxP, then, instead of 21. . . . Q–N3, 21. . . . PxP is good, with definite counterplay.

19. . . .          KxP

20. P–Q4

An energetic move in Szabo's style, leading to an endgame in White's favor.

| | |
|---|---|
| 20. . . . | BPxP |
| 21. QxP | Q–N3 |

Exchanging Queens is Black's best defense, but not on QN3; there is nothing wrong with 21. . . . Q–B1 (threatening . . . BxP) and after 22. K–R2 Q–B5. Black would thus win an important tempo.

| | |
|---|---|
| 22. QxQ | RxQ |
| 23. PxP | B–B4 |
| 24. P–N3 | P–B3 |
| 25. B–K3 | R–N2 |
| 26. PxPch | KxP |
| 27. QR–B1 | |

On White's positional ledger he can list the open QB-file, the two Bishops, an extra pawn on the Queenside; on Black's, a strong Knight in the center and an extra pawn on the Kingside. White will more easily realize his chances because in such positions:

1) the two Bishops are more useful than even a centralized Knight and Bishop;

2) White's potential passed pawn on the QR- or QN-file is more dangerous than Black's passed pawn, which is easily stopped by White's King;

3) no small role is played by the comparatively weak Black pawns on QR2 and Q3.

| | |
|---|---|
| 27. . . . | R–K1 |
| 28. R–QB3 | R/2–K2 |

| 29. B–Q4 | K–N4 |
|----------|------|
| 30. R–N3ch | K–B3 |
| 31. B–K4 | R–KB2 |

A picturesque position. Black's pieces are pinned, but White can derive nothing from these pins because his pawns are not where they belong—on the KB- and KN-files.

| 32. R–QB3 | K–N2 |
|-----------|------|
| 33. B–N2 | |

The two Bishops are to be prized but not spared. After 33. BxB! PxB 34. R–B6 it is not clear how Black can satisfactorily defend his weak QRP, QP, and KBP. For instance, 34. ... R–Q1 35. RxQP RxR 36. BxNch or 34. ... R–Q2 35. RxBP. On 34. ... R–B3 good enough is 35. R–R6 or 35. R–B7ch. Exchanging Rooks in the variation 33. ... RxB 34. RxR PxR is also bad for Black, if only because of 35. BxP.

| 33. ... | K–B1 |
|---------|------|
| 34. P–N4 | R–N1 |
| 35. P–R3 | R–N4 |

| 36. R–Q1 | R–K2 |
|----------|------|
| 37. R–K3 | K–B2 |
| 38. R/1–K1 | R–Q2 |
| 39. R–QB1 | |

Szabo again refuses to win a pawn—39. BxN PxB 40. RxP, and if 40. ... P–QR4, then 41. B–B1 simply repulses all attempts to create complications. However, he returns to this idea in a few moves.

| 39. ... | N–Q6 |
|---------|------|
| 40. R–B1 | N–K4 |
| 41. R–B1 | N–Q6 |
| 42. R–B8 | N–K4 |
| 43. BxN | |

But here I would not take the pawn: 43. B–B1 R/4–N2 44. R/3–QB3 is far more convincing.

| 43. ... | PxB |
|---------|------|
| 44. RxP | K–B3 |
| 45. R–K3 | K–N4 |
| 46. R–B5 | R–N1 |
| 47. K–B2 | P–KR4 |
| 48. R–N3ch | K–R3 |
| 49. P–KR4 | R–KB1 |
| 50. R–KB3 | R/1–B2 |
| 51. R–R5 | R–B2 |
| 52. K–N3 | R–B5 |
| 53. B–R3 | |

Carelessness. Szabo has allowed Black's Rook onto the QB-file and permitted it to attack the passed pawn from behind, which rather complicates White's task.

| 53. ... | R–KN2 |
|---------|-------|
| 54. P–Q6 | R–Q5 |

| 55. BxB | PxBch |
|---|---|
| 56. K–B2 | P–B5! |

White seems to have forgotten about this possibility. Now his King will be forced back to the first rank, and his material advantage becomes practically meaningless.

| 57. R–R6 | K–N3! |
|---|---|
| 58. P–Q7ch | K–B4 |
| 59. RxP | R–Q7ch |
| 60. K–K1 | |

| 60. . . . | R/2–N7 |
|---|---|

60. . . . RxP is probably playable, but the text move is more convincing. Now White has to give up his proud QP, since the threat is R–QR7 or KR–K7ch and R–KR7.

| 61. P–Q8=Q | RxQ |
|---|---|
| 62. R–B7ch | K–K4 |
| 63. R/3xP | R–QR7 |
| 64. R–B3 | R/1–Q7 |

The last difficult move in this ending, virtually assuring the draw.

65. R–B2 RxR 66. RxR RxP 67. R–KN2 R–R8ch 68. K–B2 R–R7ch 69. K–N1 R–R8ch 70. K–B2 R–R7ch 71. K–N1 R–R8ch 72. K–R2 R–QN8 73. R–N5ch K–B5 74. P–N5 K–B6, Drawn.

## Game 146
### Sicilian Defense

| Y. Averbakh | M. Taimanov |
|---|---|
| 1. P–K4 | P–QB4 |
| 2. N–KB3 | N–QB3 |
| 3. P–Q4 | PxP |
| 4. NxP | N–B3 |
| 5. N–QB3 | P–Q3 |
| 6. B–QB4 | |

White gives notice of his intention to breach his opponent's impregnable "Sicilian position" in the center by direct attack— one of the strategical ideas of B–B4. At the same time, it must

not be forgotten that the players are human: Grandmaster Averbakh wants very much to avenge his loss against Grandmaster Taimanov in the first half of the tournament.

| 6. . . . | P–K3 |
|---|---|
| 7. O–O | P–QR3 |
| 8. B–K3 | Q–B2 |
| 9. B–N3 | |

White has his reasons for spending two moves to develop a Bishop which Black can easily exchange by N–R4xB. The exchanging operation will take no little time, after which White will retain a strong Knight on Q4, while for the moment Black's Bishops will have no great scope.

| 9. . . . | B–K2 |
| 10. P–B4 | N–QR4 |
| 11. Q–B3 | P–QN4 |

This is not Taimanov's first experience with this opening. He played all this against Lipnitsky in the 20th U.S.S.R. Championship in 1952, when White continued 12. P–K5 and achieved nothing.

**12. P–K5!**

The exclamation mark is not for the quality of the move but for Averbakh's courage. Taimanov, in his notes to the above-mentioned game with Lipnitsky, pointed out the best method of play for Black and wrote that White's entire variation could safely be discarded. Averbakh plans to find a more appropriate use for it.

| 12. . . . | B–N2 |
| 13. Q–N3 | PxP |
| 14. PxP | N–R4 |
| 15. Q–R3 | |

On 15. Q–B2 Black sacrifices a piece by 15. . . . O–O! 16. P–N4 NxB 17. RPxN QxP 18. PxN QxRP with a very strong attack.

| 15. . . . | QxP |

Just what Averbakh was waiting for! It is clear from what follows that 15. . . . NxB 16. NxN QxP is correct, and after 17. N–R5, neither 17. . . . B–Q4 nor 17. . . . N–B3 is very good, but a highly interesting struggle follows 17. . . . P–N5! 18. N–B4 Q–B2! 19. QxN O–O 20. N–N6 PxN 21. NxR BxN.

**16. BxP!**      **PxB**

Beautiful sacrifices like this are sometimes apt to be refuted simply by castling. But in this case 16. . . . O–O would be followed by 17. R–B5 N–KB5 18. RxQ NxQch and the Bishop takes on KR3.

**17. NxKP**      **B–QB1**

Black parries the threat 18. B–Q4, but there is another threat . . .

| 18. QxNch | QxQ |
| 19. NxPch | |

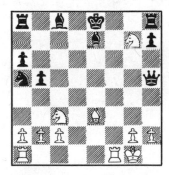

| 19. . . . | K–Q2 |
| 20. NxQ | |

Of course, two extra pawns are enough for White to win,

but he even keeps his attack on the King.

**20. . . . N–B5 21. B–Q4 KR–N1 22. N–Q5 R–N4 23. N/R–B6ch BxN 24. NxBch K–B3 25. NxP R–N3 26. QR–K1 P–N5 27. P–QN3 N–R6 28. R–K5 N–N4 29. B–K3 N–B6 30. N–B8** (The White

pieces get closer and closer to the Black King.) **30. . . . R–N2 31. R–B6ch K–B2 32. B–R6 R–N5 33. R–K7ch K–Q1 34. R–KR7 QR–N1 35. N–K6ch! BxN 36. R–B8 mate.**

In this tournament Averbakh and Taimanov have created two beautiful examples of chess art.

# Game 147
## Queen's Indian Defense

**T. Petrosian        M. Najdorf**

**1. P–Q4 N–KB3 2. P–QB4 P–K3 3. N–KB3 P–QN3 4. N–B3 B–N2 5. P–K3 B–K2 6. B–Q3 P–Q4** (In game 84, Szabo–Euwe, which also ended in a quick draw, Black played 6. . . . P–B4 here; 6. . . . P–Q4 leads to a variation of the Queen's Gambit in which White gets no particular advantage.) **7. O–O O–O 8. Q–K2 QN–Q2 9. P–QN3 P–QR3** (Black wants to

get his Bishop to a more active position, and he safeguards it from the thrust N–QN5.) **10. B–N2 B–Q3 11. QR–Q1 N–K5 12. PxP PxP 13. N–K5 Q–K2 14. N/5xN QxN 15. N–N1!, Drawn.**

One of those positions in which almost any pawn advance creates a weakness, and in which it is not possible to obtain an advantage with the pieces alone.

# Round Twenty-Two

## Game 148

The middlegame and the endgame are inseparable. In the middlegame, and sometimes even in the opening, the grandmaster already sees the outlines of possible endgames. Averbakh, a great connoisseur and lover of the endgame, is very consistent and logical. He envisions a Knight-against-Bishop endgame as early as the 12th to 15th moves, and he does all he can to see that his Knight has optimal working conditions for its struggle against the Bishop. The Knight is known to be strong when the pawn structure is immobile, when the Knight has points of support, and when the enemy's pawns and Bishop are on the same color squares. By subtle maneuvering Averbakh succeeds in obtaining all of this, and he places Najdorf in complete zugzwang.

### Queen's Indian Defense

| M. Najdorf | Y. Averbakh |
|---|---|
| 1. P–QB4 | N–KB3 |
| 2. N–KB3 | P–K3 |
| 3. P–KN3 | P–QN3 |
| 4. B–N2 | B–N2 |
| 5. 0–0 | B–K2 |
| 6. P–Q4 | 0–0 |
| 7. N–B3 | N–K5 |
| 8. Q–B2 | NxN |
| 9. PxN | |

It is said that this move weakens the pawn on QB4 and that the usual 9. QxN is therefore better. I do not think a weakness like this has any vital significance in the overall pawn mass, but the situation of this pawn (QB4) must be taken into consideration in future planning, and Black must not be allowed to attack it freely. Black's Knight is now headed for QR4 through QB3, and White's Knight should be ready to meet it at QN3. The game

351

might take the following course:
9. . . . N–B3 10. N–Q2 N–R4
11. BxB NxB 12. N–N3;
White's immediate intention of
P–QR4–5 would force Black
to play . . . P–QR4, taking this
square from his Knight. Should
Black's Knight go to Q3 it
would be attacked by the pawn
advance P–B5.

| | |
|---|---|
| 9. . . . | N–B3 |
| 10. N–K5 | N–R4 |
| 11. BxB | NxB |
| 12. Q–R4 | |

Of course, this position is not
nearly so attractive for White
as the one in the previous variation. The role of pawn-protector
is generally not befitting a
Queen, and besides, the Queen
might be exchanged.

| | |
|---|---|
| 12. . . . | P–Q3 |
| 13. N–Q3 | N–R4 |
| 14. P–B5 | Q–K1 |
| 15. QxQ | KRxQ |
| 16. R–N1 | KR–QB1 |
| 17. P–KR4 | P–Q4 |
| 18. B–B4 | P–KB3 |

| | |
|---|---|
| 19. N–N4 | P–QR3 |
| 20. PxP | PxP |
| 21. B–Q2 | |

White has an unenviable
position. What's wrong with it?

1) First of all, his pawns on
QR2 and QB3 are clearly
weaker than their counterparts
on QR6 and QN6, and his QBP
is in constant need of defense.

2) There is a gaping hole at
White's QB4, which Black exploits excellently with his
Knight and, given the opportunity, his Rook.

3) His dark-square Bishop,
unlike Black's, occupies a passive position.

White's only hope is to attack the weak QNP, but this is
a mirage since the pawn can
always be moved to QN4; moreover, it can be defended by a
Knight at QB5.

It is true that Black will not
keep all of his advantages, but
he does not need all of them to
win.

White soon gets rid of his
weakness on QB3, but he there-

by enters the endgame desired by Averbakh. He would get a sounder position by 21. N–Q3 N–B5 22. KR–B1 R–B3 23. K–B1.

| 21. . . . | N–B5 |
| 22. B–K1 | BxN |
| 23. PxB | |

This position must be considered lost for White. Black's pieces gain admittance to the enemy camp: his Rook, which soon takes up a position on QB7, and his Knight on QB5 will completely dominate the surrounding squares.

| 23. . . . | N–R6 |
| 24. R–N3 | N–N4 |
| 25. P–K3 | R–B7 |
| 26. P–R4 | N–Q3 |
| 27. P–QR5 | P–QN4 |

White has nothing better than to offer to exchange the first pair of Rooks, for otherwise . . . R/1–QB1 would follow.

| 28. R–B3 | R–QB1 |
| 29. RxRch | NxR |
| 30. P–B3 | N–K2 |
| 31. B–B2 | |

Hoping Black will be tempted by a pawn—31. . . . R–N7 32. R–B1—but Averbakh simply brings up his King.

| 31. . . . | K–B2 |
| 32. R–N1 | N–B4 |

| 33. K–B1 | N–Q3 |
| 34. R–N3 | N–B5 |
| 35. K–N2 | P–B4 |

White is in complete zugzwang. If 36. P–B4 N–Q7 and . . . N–K5; if 36. P–K4 BPxP 37. PxP N–Q7 and . . . NxP. The King cannot move because of . . . N–Q7 and . . . NxP; if the Rook goes to Q3, then . . . R–N7 and . . . RxP. After White's next move Black takes an important center pawn with impunity and the game is virtually over.

| 36. R–N1 | NxPch |
| 37. K–N1 | P–B5 |
| 38. PxP | N–B4 |
| 39. K–B1 | P–N3 |
| 40. R–N3 | K–K2 |
| 41. R–N1 | K–Q2 |

White resigns. After the obvious 42. . . . R–B5, one of the pawns on the fourth rank dies, and then the others.

# Game 149
## Dutch Defense

| M. Taimanov | L. Szabo |
|---|---|
| 1. P–Q4 | P–K3 |
| 2. P–QB4 | P–KB4 |
| 3. N–QB3 | N–KB3 |
| 4. P–K3 | P–Q4 |
| 5. B–Q3 | P–B3 |
| 6. P–B4 | B–K2 |
| 7. N–B3 | O–O |
| 8. O–O | |

A peculiar, rarely encountered position known as the "double stonewall," which at one time was very prevalent. The locked pawn position in the obstructed center leads to a complex maneuvering game, to which sharpness is added by the stationing of Knights on the respective K5-squares and by the possibility (not fulfilled in this game) of either side's suddenly playing P–KN4. The position is not quite symmetrical—White's QBP presages a certain White initiative on the Queenside, whereas Black usually gathers his forces on the Kingside.

Each side has a "bad" QB and would gladly exchange it for "only" a Knight, or gradually bring it out on the Kingside. These are the factors on which the struggle for the next eight to ten moves is based.

| 8. . . . | P–QN3 |
|---|---|
| 9. B–Q2 | B–R3 |

This move would be expedient if Black could trade light-squared Bishops. But the exchange on QB5 entails a concession in the center, as soon becomes clear.

**10. Q–K2**

Inasmuch as on 10. . . . BxP 11. BxB PxB 12. QxP the weaknesses on K3 and QB3 would be too serious, Black's Bishop goes right back to N2.

| 10. . . . | B–N2 |
|---|---|
| 11. PxP | |

It is often advantageous in such positions for White to trade on Q5 when Black cannot take back with his KP. This is one of those times, and Taimanov seizes the QB-file.

| 11. . . . | BPxP |
|---|---|
| 12. KR–B1 | |

Taking the file with the other Rook is more accurate.

| 12. . . . | P–QR3 |
|---|---|
| 13. N–QR4 | N–K5 |
| 14. N–K5 | B–Q3 |
| 15. P–QN4 | BxN |

The exchange is more or less forced, for otherwise it will be difficult for Black to complete the development of his Queenside. On 15. . . . N–Q2 there could follow 16. N–B6 BxN 17.

RxB, attacking the Bishop on Q6 and threatening the QRP and, incidentally, also threatening finally to consolidate the open file with R/1–QB1.

| | | |
|---|---|---|
| 16. BPxB | B–B3 |
| 17. N–N2 | |

An inappropriate place for the Knight. It should return to QB3 and take the Knight on K4 at the first opportunity.

| | |
|---|---|
| 17. . . . | B–K1 |
| 18. R–B2 | N–Q2 |

Szabo wants to break out of his impending positional cramp. If 19. BxP then 19. . . . Q–N4 with the threat B–R4 or 19. . . . NxB. Should the Bishop then leave QR6, Black's Rook could penetrate to White's QR3. Taimanov therefore does not take the pawn.

| | |
|---|---|
| 19. P–QR4 | Q–N4 |
| 20. R–KB1 | |

Clearly, the Rook should not have left here on the 12th move. Thus Taimanov pays back his opponent's loss of a tempo at the very beginning (9. . . . B–R3 and 10. . . . B–N2).

| | |
|---|---|
| 20. . . . | P–N4 |

Szabo cleverly and persistently seeks the initiative, again offering a pawn sacrifice: 21. PxP PxP 22. BxP R–R6! with good chances; e.g., 23. B–Q3 B–R4 24. Q–K1 KR–R1.

So, after a brief maneuvering phase, more and more combinational ideas make their appearance.

| | |
|---|---|
| 21. P–R5 | B–R4 |
| 22. Q–K1 | KR–Q1 |
| 23. R–B6 | N–B1 |
| 24. B–N1 | KR–B1 |
| 25. RxR | RxR |
| 26. N–Q3 | N–Q2 |

Black's active play has brought him a considerable advantage: his "bad" light-square Bishop is better developed than his opponent's passive dark-square Bishop, he has won back the QB-file, and White's threat of N–QB5 is not dangerous: 27. N–B5 N/5xN 28. NPxN Q–K2 and then . . . N–N1–B3.

| | |
|---|---|
| 27. N–B4 | B–B2 |
| 28. BxN | BPxB |
| 29. Q–N1 | R–B5 |

| 30. R–B1 | Q–B4 |
|---|---|
| 31. N–K2 | B–N3 |
| 32. R–B1 | Q–N4 |
| 33. N–B4 | B–B4 |
| 34. B–K1 | N–N1 |
| 35. Q–N2 | N–B3 |

Black has finished regrouping and stands better: he is attacking the QNP, he controls the QB-file, his Queen is actively placed. White is saved only by the rather insecure position of the Bishop on KB5, for after the next move White threatens NxQP followed by QxB.

### 36. Q–KB2

White wins a pawn due to the threat of NxKP, but his position remains inferior. I shall explain why when the shooting is over.

| 36. . . . | P–R3 |
|---|---|
| 37. NxQP | PxN |
| 38. QxB | QxKPch |
| 39. B–B2 | Q–N4 |
| 40. Q–K6ch | K–R2 |
| 41. QxP | |

| 41. . . . | Q–N3 |
|---|---|

Black does not yet advance his KP so as not to open a way for White's Queen to get to the Kingside. The threats are now . . . NxNP, . . . R–B7, and . . . P–K6, in this or another order. The strength of Black's position is that his pieces are ready to attack the King and his KP is worth a piece. White's pawn merely moves forward, supporting nothing and needing support itself.

However, all this is general; the specific play here demands great accuracy and long-range calculation. The next moves by both sides are the very best (from each player's point of view), inasmuch as the game was adjourned here and resumed after thorough analysis.

| 42. P–K6 | NxNP |
|---|---|
| 43. Q–Q6 | |

This is stronger than Q–Q7, on which 43. . . . P–K6 follows, and if 44. BxP Q–K5 or if 44. B–N3 P–K7 45. R–K1 Q–N5. Black wins in either case, as proved by detailed analysis. The variations reach the 53rd move; I give only one: 44. B–N3 P–K7 45. R–K1 Q–N5 46. Q–KB7 QxPch 47. K–R1 Q–Q4 48. RxP R–B7 49. Q–B1 Q–Q6 50. R–K1 QxQch 51. RxQ R–K7 52. R–K1 RxRch 53. BxR N–Q4 and wins.

| 43. . . . | N–Q6 |
|---|---|
| 44. P–R3 | R–B7 |
| 45. B–N3 | P–K6 |

| 46. P–K7 | Q–K5 |
|---|---|
| 47. R–B3 | P–K7 |
| 48. Q–Q7 | |

Having analyzed the adjourned position, Taimanov should have recognized the seriousness of Szabo's counterchances and tried to end the argument peaceably. This was a good time to do it. After 48. P–K8=Q! QxQ 49. RxN P–K8=Qch 50. BxQ QxBch 51. K–R2 the game would be a forced draw. The text move not only does not increase White's chances, it could even lead to his defeat.

| 48. . . . | P–K8=Qch |
|---|---|

At the last moment Szabo's nerves fail him—perhaps there was not enough time—and he does not see the beautiful thematic move 48. . . . N–B5, after which even with two Queens White cannot avoid mate. For example: 49. P–K8=Q P–K8=Qch 50. BxQ RxPch 51. K–R1 QxR or 49. B–K1 R–B8 50. P–K8=Q RxBch 51. K–R2 R–R8ch 52. KxR P–K8=Qch 53. K–R2 QxQ or 49. Q–B5ch QxQ 50. P–K8=Q P–K8=Qch 51. BxQ RxPch 52. K–B1 R–KR7 53. Q–K5 Q–B7.

| 49. BxQ | RxPch |
|---|---|
| 50. KxR | NxBch |
| 51. K–B2 | Drawn |

In view of perpetual check. A beautiful and complicated game.

## Game 150

The "basic position" of the Nimzo-Indian Defense—1. P–Q4 N–KB3 2. P–QB4 P–K3 3. N–QB3 B–N5 4. P–K3 P–B4 5. B–Q3 P–Q4 6. N–B3 N–B3 7. O–O O–O—was seen in the tournament in Switzerland eleven times before the 22nd round; six of the games were drawn, and Black had a slight advantage in the others.

Gligoric is not among the adherents of the main variation, as are predominantly Reshevsky, Euwe, and Averbakh. In this game Gligoric comes close to the main variation for the first time in the tournament, but he treats it more like a Queen's Gambit: he puts a Bishop on K2, exchanges central pawns, and gives Black an isolated pawn on Q4.

The game's interest lies in the continuing positional struggle around this pawn. The fight between the heavy pieces around an isolated pawn is one of the most important elements of positional play. It is not at all a matter of White's attacking it twice, Black's defending it twice, reaching a draw. The themes of the struggle are the pin on the isolated pawn when the heavy pieces are defending it from behind, the sudden shift to an attack on the King, and the attempt to seize the seventh rank just when the enemy pieces are busy defending the isolated pawn. Endgames with isolated pawns were played with virtuosity by the classical artists of chess—Lasker, Capablanca, Rubinstein. Gligoric and Euwe come to this game armed with the knowledge inherited from the old masters. The reader who investigates the fine points of the struggle, studies the technical maneuvers, and familiarizes himself with the basic ideas of this type of endgame will take a great step forward in positional play.

Also, the concluding part of the game—a four-pawns-against-three Rook ending—is of great theoretical interest.

## Nimzo-Indian Defense

| S. Gligoric | M. Euwe |
|---|---|
| 1. P–Q4 | N–KB3 |
| 2. P–QB4 | P–K3 |
| 3. N–QB3 | B–N5 |
| 4. P–K3 | P–B4 |
| 5. N–B3 | P–Q4 |
| 6. B–K2 | O–O |
| 7. O–O | N–B3 |
| 8. BPxP | KPxP |
| 9. PxP | BxP |
| 10. P–QR3 | |

Black's task is to get rid of his weak pawn—i.e., to move it to Q5 and exchange it—but this cannot be done immediately because of N–QR4. The natural preparation for Black's P–Q5 is P–QR3 and B–R2. White's task is to make use of these two tempos to bring another piece to control Q4, having in mind the occupation of this square later with a Knight. The most logical way to accomplish this plan is considered to be 10. P–QN3! P–QR3 11. N–QR4 B–R2 12. B–N2, and if 12. . . . P–QN4 13. R–B1! and then N–B5. The square Q4 would remain in White's power, and this would be no small strategical success.

| 10. . . . | P–QR3 |
|---|---|
| 11. P–QN4 | B–Q3 |

In his detailed annotations to this game in a Yugoslav maga-

zine, Gligoric's second, Grandmaster Trifunovic, pointed out
that Black should play 11. . . .
B–R2 here, and if 12. B–N2
then P–Q5. If 12. P–N5 (in
reply to 11. . . . B–R2), Trifunovic gives the pretty variation 12. . . . P–Q5 13. PxN
PxN 14. Q–N3 Q–B2 15. Qx
BP B–Q2 16. N–K5 N–Q4. But
even here, after 17. Q–N2 Bx
BP 18. NxB QxN 19. B–B3
White retains a certain advantage due to his two Bishops, his
open lines, and his extra pawn
in the center.

| 12. B–N2 | B–N5 |
| 13. R–B1 | B–B2 |
| 14. N–QR4 | |

Gligoric has accomplished the
first part of his plan: the QP has
been nailed down. Euwe is hoping to start play on the Kingside,
but White easily repulses Black's
threats and by gradually exchanging the minor pieces nears
his projected goal—the battle of
heavy pieces against the isolated
pawn.

| 14. . . . | Q–Q3 |

| 15. P–N3 | N–K5 |
| 16. N–B5 | |

It is necessary above all to
eliminate Black's centralized
Knight. 16. N–Q4 is poor because of 16. . . . B–R6 17. R–
K1 Q–B3.

| 16. . . . | NxN |
| 17. RxN | QR–Q1 |
| 18. N–Q4 | |

White is now in firm control
of Q4; as for Black's attack, it
cannot amount to anything in
view of the paucity of material
that will remain on the board.

| 18. . . . | BxB |
| 19. QxB | NxN |
| 20. BxN | B–N3 |
| 21. R–Q1! | |

White's entire plan hangs by
this tactical move. Were the
Rook to retreat from B5, an
isolated White pawn would appear after the exchange of
Bishops and White could not
even dream of winning.

| 21. . . . | BxR |
| 22. BxB | Q–K4 |
| 23. BxR | KxB |
| 24. R–Q4 | P–KN3 |
| 25. P–N5 | |

To understand the events that
follow it must be kept in mind
that, as a rule, a Rook endgame
with four pawns against three
on the same side is not a win.
Therefore, if the Queenside

pawns disappear Black risks little even if he loses his isolated pawn. From this standpoint, the exchanging move P–N5 is unfortunate; more consistent is 25. Q–Q2, threatening P–K4 and thus forcing . . . P–B4. Attacking the isolated pawn along the file with the threat of P–K4 is a typical technique in such endings.

| 25. . . . | PxP |
|---|---|
| 26. QxP | Q–B2 |
| 27. Q–N2 | K–N1 |
| 28. Q–Q2 | Q–B4 |

Euwe is defending superbly. The threat was 29. P–K4; if 28. . . . R–R1 29. RxP RxP White continues 30. R–Q8ch K–N2 31. Q–Q4ch K–R3 32. R–KN8. By provoking White's QRP to advance farther and farther, Black increases the likelihood of exchanging it in the hope of bringing the game to a drawn ending.

| 29. P–QR4 | Q–R6 |
|---|---|
| 30. P–R5 | R–QB1 |

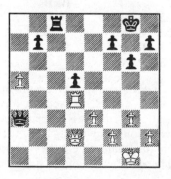

There is no use defending the pawn, so Black gives it up, intending to prepare the exchange of Queens.

**31. RxP**

Gligoric, who has been conducting the game consistently and strongly, commits an imperceptible but very characteristic inaccuracy. Having done everything to get Black to give up his QP, White should not yet take it, for now Euwe gets the chance to bring his Rook to a favorable position. Correct is 31. K–N2 and on the reply 31. . . . Q–B8 he should not yet trade Queens but go to N4. An important point is that Black cannot go into the variation 31. . . . Q–B8 32. Q–N4 R–B7 33. RxP QxP in view of 34. R–Q8ch, 35. Q–B8ch, and 36. R–Q6ch.

| 31. . . . | Q–B8ch |
|---|---|
| 32. QxQ | RxQch |
| 33. K–N2 | R–N8 |

With this Rook maneuver Black guarantees the exchange of the last pawns on the Queenside. Though elementary, it is very important that White accomplishes nothing by attacking QNP from behind: 34. R–Q8ch K–N2 35. R–N8 R–N4 and White does not have the move P–R6.

So, in a few moves there unavoidably arises a theoretically drawn endgame—four against three. Gligoric wishes to test the validity of the theory to its conclusion and plays on, risking nothing; in the meantime he puts his pawns in more active positions.

| 34. | P–N4 | K–N2 |
|-----|------|------|
| 35. | P–R4 | P–N3 |
| 36. | P–R5 | QNPxP |
| 37. | RxP | R–N2 |
| 38. | P–N5 | |

Opinions concerning this move vary. Euwe appends an exclamation mark—"A fine pawn sacrifice giving [White] good prospects"—while Trifunovic considers it an important mistake that allows Black to exchange two pawns. Instead of P–N5, he recommends preparing the advance of the NP by K–N3, P–B3, P–K4, K–B4, and R–R6. I think neither is completely right: with or without P–N5, Black should not lose.

The move P–N5 is interesting psychologically. It was played just before the time control, and Euwe had to decide whether to reply 38. . . . PxP, which could lead to a weakening of his pawn position; "but who could suppose," he wrote, "that in the resulting endgame—three pawns against two!—this would play such a significant role?" He could play 38. . . . P–R3 instead, which after the exchange of two pawns would lead to a clearer draw.

**38. . . .     PxP**

**39. R–R6**

Excellently played! Now, of course, . . . P–R3 is impossible, and at the same time White threatens to put his pawn on K4 and bring his King to KB5 and his Rook to KR6. White would win the endgame by taking the RP/4 and nailing down the BP and RP.

**39. . . .     R–N6**

Euwe had no time to think, or he figured that he could draw at his pleasure, but in any case he underestimated his opponent's scheme. He must transfer his Rook to K3, and if Rooks are exchanged Black can draw the pawn ending in time: 39. . . . R–K2 40. K–N3 R–K3 41. RxR PxR 42. K–R4 K–N3 43. P–B4 P–R3. And if White does not take on K6, there follows 41. . . . P–R3. Finally, if on 39. . . . R–K2 White replies 40. R–R6, then 40. . . . R–K4 41. RxP K–N3. It is interesting that the transfer of the Rook to K3 is possible only through K2; Euwe's recommended 39. . . . R–N5 40. P–B4 R–K5 41. K–B3 R–K3, etc., is refuted by 40. P–B3: White covers the points KN4 and K4 and does not allow the Rook to use its fifth rank, at the same time threatening 41. R–R6.

| 40. R–R6 | R–R6 |
| 41. K–N3 | R–R8 |

Black parries the threat RxP by . . . K–N3.

| 42. P–K4 | R–N8ch |
| 43. K–B4 | R–KR8 |
| 44. P–K5 | P–R5 |

Euwe could have adjourned the game immediately after the 40th move, but he continued until move 44 and was able to make his last blunder. The advance of this pawn gives White's King the square KN4 and inhibits the maneuvers of Black's Rook, and it gives White sufficient basis to fight realistically for a win. I believe it would not be possible to win with Black's pawn on his KR4. For example, if White sets up the position K–KB5, R–QN7, pawns on KB4, K5, and KN5, with the threat P–K6, Black places his Rook on the K-file and the pawn cannot advance, and White's King has not a single move.

| 45. K–N4 | R–N8ch |
| 46. K–B5 |

White avoids the pitfall 46. KxP R–R8ch, when after the exchange of Rooks Black obtains a drawn pawn endgame: 47. K–N4 RxR 48. PxRch KxP 49. K–B5 K–N2 50. P–B3 P–R3 51. P–B4 P–R4 52. K–N5 P–B3ch 53. PxPch K–B2, etc.

| 46. . . . | R–KR8 |
| 47. K–N4 | R–N8ch |
| 48. K–B5 | R–KR8 |

This position will enter every textbook on the endgame. Gligoric's discovery over the board of a beautiful and consistent winning method constitutes a valuable contribution to theory.

In order to bring about the final position, White must have his Rook on the seventh rank when he advances P–K6, but this cannot be accomplished immediately. Gligoric's plan is divided into the following parts:

1) To provoke the advance of Black's RP/5 and to win it.

2) To transfer his Rook to Q1 and drive the enemy Rook away from the K-file.

3) To carry out the final maneuver—the advances P–B5 and P–K6 with the support of his King and Rook.

**49. P–B4          P–R6**

In the first edition of this book it was pointed out that Black advanced his pawn to R6 because of the threat 50. K–N4, for with White's pawn now on B4, White can take the RP with his King: 50. K–N4 R–N8ch 51. KxP R–R8ch 52. K–N4 RxR 53. PxRch KxP 54. P–

B5 with a won ending for White.

A Leningrad amateur, G. Orlov, pointed out that this was incorrect. This endgame turns out to be a draw! Black continues 54. . . . K–N2 55. K–N5 P–B3ch 56. PxPch K–B2. He noted that the text move 49. . . . P–R6 was necessary for another reason: otherwise, after 50. K–N4 R–N8ch 51. K–R3! R–R8ch 52. K–N2 the pawn is lost.

| 50. | K–N4 | R–N8ch |
|-----|------|--------|
| 51. | K–B3 | R–B8ch |
| 52. | K–N3 | R–N8ch |
| 53. | K–B2 | R–KR8 |
| 54. | R–KB6 | |

A beautiful move which aims to use zugzwang either to push back the Black King or to force his Rook to leave, after which White's King will attack and win the RP. His Rook goes no farther than KB6 in order to defend the BP.

An interesting variation is 54. . . . K–N1 55. K–N3 K–N2 56. K–N4 K–N1 57. R–KR6 and the pawn is lost, for in case Rooks are exchanged by 57. . . . R–N8ch 58. KxP R–R8ch 59. K–N4 RxR 60. PxR Black's King, having been driven back to N1, is unable to take the RP.

| 54. | . . . | R–R8 |
|-----|-------|------|
| 55. | K–N3 | R–R8 |
| 56. | K–N4 | K–N1 |
| 57. | R–KR6 | |

Now White threatens RxP/3, and if 57. . . . R–N8ch then 58.

KxP is possible, with the same idea as discussed above.

| 57. | . . . | P–R7 |
|-----|-------|------|

In Orlov's opinion, this move is Black's decisive mistake, letting the draw escape. He claims the pawn ending is drawn by 57. . . . R–N8ch 58. KxP R–R8ch 59. K–N4 RxR 60. PxR P–B3 61. PxP K–B2 62. K–B5 K–B1 63. K–K6 K–K1 64. P–B7ch K–B1.

Just as I was about to take issue with the talented Leningrad analyst, I was anticipated by the well-known connoisseur of pawn endgames, I. L. Maizelis. He pointed out that in the position at which Orlov ended his analysis believing it to be a clear draw, White wins by the studylike maneuver 65. K–Q6!! KxP 66. K–Q7 K–B1 67. K–K6, etc. In Orlov's above-mentioned variation, if instead of 62. . . . K–B1 Black plays 62. . . . K–K1, then 63. K–K6 K–B1 64. K–Q7 K–B2 65. K–Q8 K–B1 66. P–B7 KxP 67. K–Q7 K–B3 68. K–K8, and White's

King approaches Black's last pawn, wins it, and escorts his own pawn to R8.

Moreover, Master G. Friedstein pointed out that in Orlov's variation the move 57. . . . R–N8ch instead of 57. . . . P–R7 does not compel White to go into a pawn endgame, but allows him to win the pawn in another way: 58. K–B3 R–B8ch 59. K–N3 R–N8ch 60. K–B2 R–KR8 61. R–R4. It remains for me to thank Comrades Orlov, Maizelis, and Friedstein for their interesting and valuable contributions.

| 58. | K–N3 | R–N8ch |
|-----|------|--------|
| 59. | KxP  | R–N5   |

White has completed the first part of his plan, but the win is not easy: his King has been pushed back and his BP needs protection.

Indeed, can't White's King be kept on the KR-file indefinitely? No, it cannot. After 60. R–KB6 K–N2 61. K–R3 R–N8 62. R–QR6 threatening to play P–K6 (by getting his King to R5 and his Rook to QR7), Black's Rook will be forced to leave the KN-file.

| 60. | R–KB6 | K–N2   |
|-----|-------|--------|
| 61. | K–R3  | R–N8   |
| 62. | K–R4  | R–R8ch |
| 63. | K–N4  | R–N8ch |
| 64. | K–B5  | R–KB8  |

Black chooses to defend by tying White's King to his BP. Attacking the pawn from be-

hind assures Black's King of relative freedom to maneuver (K–N2–B1–N2) and at the same time does not allow White's King to occupy his KB6, which with White's Rook on the seventh rank would decide the game immediately. As soon as the King leaves the KB-file, Black begins checking on the files. However, by skillful maneuvering Gligoric succeeds in forcing the Rook off the KB-file and secures the win. Another possible plan is 64. . . . R–QR8, as pointed out by Euwe, which also does not save Black: 65. R–B6 R–R5 66. R–B7 K–B1 67. K–N4 R–R8 68. P–B5, and now comes a series of checks from which the King escapes to QB8: 68. . . . R–N8ch 69. K–B4 R–B8ch 70. K–K4 R–K8ch 71. K–Q5 R–Q8ch 72. K–B6 R–B8ch 73. K–Q7 R–Q8ch 74. K–B8 R–Q4 75. P–B6 RxP 76. K–Q7, and White, forcing the exchange of Rooks, goes into a won pawn endgame: 76. . . . R–Q4ch 77. K–B6 R–Q1 78. R–Q7. If 74. . . . R–KN8 75. P–B6 RxP 76. K–Q7, etc.

| 65. | R–B6 | K–B1 |
|-----|------|------|

Had Black not played 64. . . . R–KB8 in time, the simple invasion of KB6 by White's King would now be decisive. If here 66. R–B4 Black's King returns immediately to N2, of course.

| 66. | R–B8ch | K–N2 |
|-----|--------|------|
| 67. | R–Q8   |      |

Zugzwang again. What can Black do?

1) 67. . . . P–R3 68. PxPch KxP 69. R–KN8 and with Black's King cut off White wins easily.

2) 67. . . . R–QR8 68. R–Q7 with the threat 69. P–K6, and Black loses because of: a) 68. . . . R–R4 69. K–N4 K–B1 70. R–Q8ch K–N2 71. P–B5 RxP 72. P–B6ch and mate; b) 68. . . . K–N1 69. K–B6 R–R3ch 70. R–Q6!, etc.; c) 68. . . . R–R3 69. K–N4 P–R3 70. P–B5 K–N1 71. R–Q8ch K–R2 72. P–N6ch PxP 73. P–B6. There remains the move in the game.

**67. . . .          R–B7**

But after White's reply . . .

**68. R–Q1**

Black no longer has any checks, and his Rook cannot go back to KB8. Thus Black has completed the second part of his plan and is ready to drive the Rook from the KB-file and advance his pawns to B5 and K6.

But if the Rook does not leave, Black will have to move his King to N1 or B1, where it will be in an extremely dangerous situation after P–B5–6; e.g., 68. . . . K–B1 69. K–N4 R–K7 70. K–B3 R–QR7 71. P–B5.

**68. . . .          R–B6**
**69. K–K4          R–B7**
**70. K–K3          R–QR7**
**71. P–B5!**

The final stage—the White pawns advance.

**71. . . .          R–KN7**

On 71. . . . R–R2 there follows 72. K–K4, then R–Q8 and P–K6 or P–B6ch.

**72. R–Q7**

There is even another road to victory here: 72. P–N6 RPxP 73. P–B6ch.

**72. . . .          RxP**

White wins prettily on 72. . . . K–B1 73. P–B6 K–K1 74. R–K7ch K–B1 75. R–N7 K–K1 76. R–N8ch K–Q2 77. R–KB8 K–K3 78. R–K8ch K–B4 79. P–K6!

**73. K–B4          R–N8**
**74. P–K6          R–B8ch**
**75. K–K5          R–K8ch**
**76. K–Q6          P–R4**
**77. RxPch          K–N1**
**78. K–K7          Black resigns**

On 78. . . . P–R5 there would follow 79. K–B6 P–R6 80. R–N7ch K–R1 81. R–N3.

The ending deserves careful study.

## Game 151
### Queen's Gambit

| D. Bronstein | G. Stahlberg |
|---|---|
| 1. P–Q4 | P–Q4 |
| 2. P–QB4 | P–K3 |
| 3. N–KB3 | N–KB3 |
| 4. N–B3 | QN–Q2 |
| 5. PxP | PxP |
| 6. B–N5 | B–K2 |
| 7. P–K3 | P–B3 |
| 8. Q–B2 | N–B1 |
| 9. B–Q3 | N–K3 |
| 10. P–KR4 | |

In my preparations for my game with Stahlberg I placed great hopes on this flank attack. It seemed to me that this was the way to refute Black's plan of transferring a Knight to K3. If 10. . . . P–KN3 very strong is 11. BxN BxB 12. P–R5. On 10. . . . P–KR3 I intended 11. BxN BxB 12. P–KN4, then to castle long and proceed with P–N5, assuming that such an attack must succeed. Stahlberg nevertheless answers

| 10. . . . | P–KR3 |
|---|---|

after which I immediately realized my mistake.

| 11. BxN | BxB |
|---|---|
| 12. O–O–O | |

A pity. In case of 12. P–KN4 N–B2! White lacks one tempo to continue his pawn storm. White should play 12. P–KN4 anyway, but after 12. . . . N–B2 he should forget about his crushing attack for the time being and turn to the accumulation of positional advantages by 13. B–B5. White's absolute desire to intensify the play soon forces him to defend himself.

| 12. . . . | N–B2 |
|---|---|
| 13. P–R5 | B–N5 |
| 14. K–N1 | O–O |

The decision of a great master. Not everyone would risk castling when the opponent has already advanced a pawn to KR5. Stahlberg has precisely calculated that the QB-file will be opened even before a White pawn gets to KN5.

| 15. N–K2 | N–N4 |
|---|---|
| 16. N–K5 | B/3xN |
| 17. PxB | Q–N3 |

More logical is 17. . . . P–R3. Then if 18. BxN RPxB, opening the QR-file; this, in connection with the possibility of a pawn storm, would cause White no little trouble.

| 18. | BxN | QxB |
|-----|-----|-----|
| 19. | P–B3 | B–B4 |
| 20. | QxB | QxN |
| 21. | KR–K1 | |

Offering Black's Queen a choice: to leave and allow White's KNP to join in the attack or to remain in a designated battle zone.

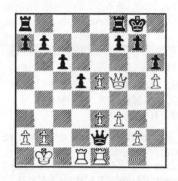

| 21. | . . . | Q–B7 |
|-----|-------|------|

Black's decision depended on his evaluation of 22. Q–N4 P–KB4 23. PxP e.p. RxP 24. P–B4, when it seems the capture of his Queen is unavoidable. However, Black can get out of trouble by using a pin: 24. . . . R–K1 25. R–K2 RxBP.

**22. Q–N4**

The same move that introduced the above-mentioned variation but with the more modest aim of creating a passed KP. It is scarcely White's faith in the omnipotence of this pawn that is his undoing, but, in the final analysis, it doesn't help him either. Another plan, involving

22. P–KN4, is possible, leading to sharp play; but by move 20 White's attacking ardor had already cooled considerably.

| 22. | . . . | P–KB4 |
|-----|-------|-------|
| 23. | Q–R3 | QR–Q1 |
| 24. | P–B4 | P–Q5 |

Returning the Queen to active duty.

| 25. | PxP | QxBP |
|-----|-----|------|
| 26. | Q–N3ch | R–B2 |
| 27. | P–Q5 | PxP |
| 28. | P–K6 | |

The future course of events is determined to a considerable extent by this advance. If the Rook simply takes the QP, then in the variation 28. . . . RxR 29. Qx R Q–KR5 White has to remove his Rook from the K-file. 28. P–K6 is therefore played to free K5 for White's Queen. The conception as a whole is correct, but White completely forgets that his KRP can be defended by 31. Q–Q1.

| 28. | . . . | R K2 |
|-----|-------|------|
| 29. | RxP | RxR |
| 30. | QxR | Q–KR5 |
| 31. | Q–K5 | QxP |
| 32. | Q–N8ch | K–R2 |
| 33. | Q–Q6 | |

But not 33. Q–KB8 RxP!

| 33. | . . . | Q–N4 |
|-----|-------|------|
| 34. | P–KN3 | Q–B3 |
| 35. | P–R3 | P–KR4 |
| 36. | K–R2 | P–KN4 |
| 37. | Q–Q5 | K–N3 |
| 38. | Q–Q8 | |

White does not sense the danger, so strong is his faith in the amulet on K6. While White's Queen marks time, Black forms a passed pawn of his own and things sharply worsen for White. It goes without saying that the KP badly hampers the activity of Black's pieces, but then, White's pieces are stuck to it themselves. White's advantage is his Rook's greater mobility. Therefore, so long as Black is not able to reorganize his forces, White should rush his King to the pawn's rescue, the more so since the King's path QN3–QB4–Q5 is perfectly safe even though it is completely in the open. A King march to the center in the presence of Queens and Rooks is no laughing matter, however; White is afraid to make this decision immediately, but there is nothing to fear.

**38. . . .**          **K–N2**
**39. Q–Q6**          **K–N3**
**40. Q–Q8**          **K–R3**

Black's King, unlike White's, cannot be too active. In the time scramble he resolves not to leave his camp.

**41. Q–Q5**          **P–B5**

Now Black's two pawns will far outweigh White's one pawn.

**42. PxP**          **QxBP**
**43. R–K5**          **Q–B3**
**44. Q–K4**          **P–N4!**

Somewhat forestalling White's reinforcing P–R4, and creating a threat to exchange Queens on QB5. White is therefore compelled to move his QRP anyway, but then Black will have two extra pawns.

**45. Q–K2**          **P–R3**
**46. P–R4**          **PxP**
**47. Q–K3**          **P–R5**

In case of 47. . . . Q–B5 White attacks the Rook by Q–B5. Had White not dislodged Black's pawn from QN5 in time, Black would now win easily by 47. . . . Q–B5 48. Q–B5 Q–B5ch.

**48. R–K4**          **K–N3**
**49. Q–K2**          **P–KR6**
**50. R–K3**

Retreating along the entire front. In addition to worrying about his KP, he is concerned about Black's KNP and KRP.

**50. . . .**          **K–N2**
**51. Q–R2**          **R–N2**
**52. Q–K2**          **R–K2**
**53. Q–R2**          **P–R6**

White is coming to the end of his defensive resources. Black decides to return one of his two extra pawns, since 54. PxP would completely expose White's King, and taking with the King would not be without danger to White in view of the possible checks along his QR3–KB8 diagonal or from his QR4 and QR5. White's King has no choice, however, and this time he takes the plunge without a second thought. On Black's previous move (instead of 52. . . . R–K2) he could have put White in zugzwang: 52. . . . K–B1! (53. R–KB3 RxPch!), but such moves are often overlooked in the midst of play.

| 54. | KxP | RxP |
| 55. | Q–B7ch | Q–B2 |
| 56. | Q–B3ch | |

This maneuver, which Black probably underestimated, saves the game for White. With his King in an exposed position, Black cannot exploit the advantage of his extra pawn on N4.

| 56. | . . . | R–B3 |
| 57. | RxP | Q–K2ch |
| 58. | K–R2 | Q–K3ch |
| 59. | K–R1 | K–N1 |
| 60. | R–R1 | Q–B3 |
| 61. | Q–KR3 | |

White's Queen and Rook have again found freedom of action, and Black thinks the time has come to formalize the peace treaty by perpetual check.

| 61. | . . . | Q–R5ch |
| 62. | K–N1 | Q–K5ch |
| 63. | K–R1 | Drawn |

## Game 152

Chess is infinite, and chess players, in order not to lose their way in its vastness, are guided in the evaluation of positions and the choosing of plans by certain signposts, such as weak pawns, open lines, advantage in development, good and bad Bishops, poor King position, and others. It must be said, however, that such signposts are not found in every game, so we cannot always compare the pros and cons of a position as the basis for choosing the correct plan. On the one hand, chess theory has not yet discovered all the signposts, which if it had would mean the exhaustion of diversity in chess; and on the other, the signposts are difficult to apply in positions in which there are certain imbalances. In any case, there are many games whose course must be based solely on intuition and on calculation over the board, and these are the most difficult games, even for grandmasters.

## King's Indian Defense

**S. Reshevsky    I. Boleslavsky**

| | |
|---|---|
| 1. P–Q4 | N–KB3 |
| 2. P–QB4 | P–KN3 |
| 3. P–KN3 | B–N2 |
| 4. B–N2 | O–O |
| 5. N–QB3 | P–Q3 |
| 6. N–B3 | P–B4 |
| 7. P–Q5 | N–R3 |

This move is not in classical style, of course. The piece is developed to one side and immediately moves a second time, as a result finding itself on QB2, which is not considered a particularly good place for a Knight. However, such ideas are often employed in modern games, and they are dangerous because they seem to be illogical whereas actually they have specific purposes.

The idea behind the maneuver N–R3–B2 in connection with QR–N1 is that Black wishes to prepare P–QN4 without resorting to P–QR3. Why is P–QN4 necessary? Can't White simply reply P–N3? It proves to be not that simple. First, in order to play P–N3 he must be able to remove two pieces from the long diagonal; second, Black will exchange on QB5 and then put his Bishop on QR3 and his Rook on QN5, and it will be extremely difficult for White to defend his QBP. This is the reason—to reserve QR3 for his Bishop—that Black does not want to play P–QR3.

| | |
|---|---|
| 8. O–O | N–B2 |
| 9. N–Q2 | R–N1 |
| 10. P–QR4 | P–K3 |

Black now sneaks up on the QBP from the other side. Not wanting to play P–K4, which would block the diagonal of his Bishop, White exchanges on K6, and after

| | |
|---|---|
| 11. PxP | BxP |

he is faced with a choice: to tie his Knight down to the defense of the QBP or . . .

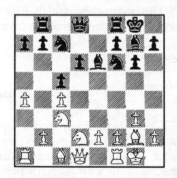

**12. N/2–K4!**

From this point until about move 23 the game follows a long and complex tactical calculation for which no general rules have yet been found. The two players are well matched in their ability to calculate complex combinations; at the time this tournament took place they,

along with Geller and Taimanov, were the best calculative players in the world, which
of course is not to disparage
their qualities as positional
players.

Let me point out some of the
themes of the combination that
will arise during the further
course of the game. Black's
Rook has left QR1 and defends
the QNP, but at this moment
his Knight and Rook stand on
the same diagonal and are vulnerable to flank attack. White's
QNP will be unprotected after
his QB moves, and Black's KB
can take it with tempo; after
White's Knight takes the QP,
Black's Rooks will be deprived
of K1 and QB1, and all White's
Bishop has to do to win the Exchange is to go to K7 and attack
the Rook on KB8, etc. This is
hardly everything, of course; it
is only a fraction of the considerations that rush through a
chess player's brain when he has
a choice of continuations.

| 12. . . . | NxN |
| 13. NxN | BxBP |
| 14. B–N5 | Q–Q2 |

Boleslavsky temptingly invites
his opponent's forces into his
fortress, but Reshevsky staunch-
ly resists the temptation. There
is plainly no great satisfaction
for White in 15. N–B6ch BxN
16. BxB Q–K3, while a loss
would be in the offing. If Black
played 14. . . . P–B3, White

could answer 15. B–B4 P–KN4
16. NxQP.

| 15. QxP | QxQ |
| 16. NxQ | BxKP |
| 17. KR–K1 | B–Q6 |
| 18. B–K7 | |

The likelihood of giving up a
Rook for the dark-square
Bishop and a couple of pawns
seems not to have bothered
Black in the least. But Reshevsky has noticed an important
feature of the coming endgame:
the possibility of concerted action by his two Rooks against
the Bishop and the two pawns.
He is a little troubled only by
the presence of Black's two
powerful Bishops.

| 18. . . . | BxP |
| 19. R–R2 | B–N2 |

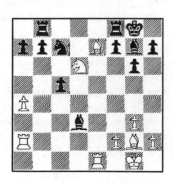

**20. B–B1**

The beautiful concluding
move of the game's combinational phase. Black's reliance on
his two Bishops is broken. His
Rook on KB1 has nowhere to
go, and his Bishop on Q6 can-

not avoid being exchanged. Now White will be able to exploit his advantage in development and his favorably placed Rooks. Black's position is by no means lost, by the way; his undoing comes later, when he overestimates his chances.

| 20. . . . | BxB |
|-----------|-----|
| 21. KxB | N–Q4 |

A Knight is doubly strong when it is defended by a pawn. Boleslavsky would get a safe position by playing 21 . . . N–K3 here. White's attempt to win a pawn on the Queenside would be prevented by the Knight's moving to Q5.

| 22. BxR | BxB |
|---------|-----|
| 23. R/2–K2! | |

Beautiful play! White threatens to exchange the Black Rook and attack the pawns from behind. If Black's Knight stood on K3, this combination would obviously be impossible. That is why it was important to close the K-file with the Knight. Black is now forced to capture, for 23. . . . K–N2 would be followed by 24. N–K8ch and 25. R–K5.

| 23. . . . | BxN |
|-----------|-----|
| 24. R–Q2 | B–B1 |

If Black is tempted by the KNP, he loses after 24. . . . BxP 25. RPxB N–B2 26. R–K7 N–K3 27. R/2–Q7. It is hard to believe, however, that with two pawns for the Exchange Black can think of no more active move than B–B1. For example, he can dare to go for a third pawn by 24. . . . N–N3. However, if the author of this book had been playing Black and lost after 24. . . . N–N3, then Boleslavsky could have written in his annotations that moving the Bishop from Q3 to KB1 should have been tried, and very likely he would have been right.

| 25. RxN | P–B5 |
|---------|------|

Black plans to advance his pawn to B6 and defend it with his Bishop. If 25. . . . P–QR3, Euwe advises 26. R/5–K5 P–QN4 27. P–R5 with the intention of winning the QRP. In my opinion, 26. P–R5 would be more comfortable for White.

**26. R–K4**

Frustrating Black's idea. On 26. R–B1 R–B1 Black would have nothing to fear after . . . P–B6 and . . . B–N2. But now 26. . . . R–B1 would be followed by 27. R/5–Q4 P–B6 28. R–QB4, and after the exchange of Rooks the pawn is lost: 28. . . . RxR 29. RxR B–N2? 30. R–B8ch. The same thing would happen after 26. . . . P–B6 27. R–QB4 B–N2 28. R/5–QB5!, and after the inevitable exchange of Black's Rook, White wins easily by bringing his King to Q3 while his liberated Rook begins the extermination of Black's undefended QRP and QNP.

**26. . . .      P–QR3**

Boleslavsky has one chance left—to exchange White's QRP and to advance a little farther the one pawn he has for the Exchange.

**27. RxP        P–QN4**
**28. PxP        PxP**
**29. R–B7       P–N5**
**30. R/5–Q7     R–R1**

Further pawn advances are not possible for the time being because of 30. . . . P–N6? 31. R–N7.

**31. K–N2       R–R7**
**32. RxP        P–N6**
**33. R–N7       B–B4**

To understand the following very curious events, it is necessary to keep in mind that they occurred not only in a brutal time shortage for Reshevsky but also late at night. Round 22 was played on a Saturday. For religious reasons, Reshevsky begins his Saturday games only after sundown, a few hours later than the usual time, and on Fridays he plays in the daytime in order to finish playing before sundown.

Fearing that anything might happen in time pressure, Reshevsky plans the maneuver R–B3–Q3–Q7–KB7 in advance, which is playable with Black's pawn on QN6 but which gives Black a chance to be saved by the pawn on QN7.

**34. R–B3       P–N7**
**35. R–Q3       B–B1**

Good enough to win is 36. R–Q8, but Reshevsky sticks to his "plan."

**36. R/3–Q7**

Now Black can save the game by the sly retreat of his Rook to R2. Boleslavsky still had a few minutes left, and in the daylight he would undoubtedly have seen and played that move, but at 2:30 in the morning, after a tense and fatiguing struggle, he automatically played

**36. . . .      B–B4?**

and after

**37. R–Q8ch     B–B1**
**38. R/7–N8     Black resigns**

# Game 153
## Catalan System

| P. Keres | A. Kotov |
|----------|----------|
| 1. P–Q4 | N–KB3 |
| 2. P–QB4 | P–K3 |
| 3. P–KN3 | P–Q4 |
| 4. B–N2 | B–K2 |
| 5. N–KB3 | O–O |
| 6. O–O | P–B3 |

After this Keres transposes to the classical Reti setup, in which Black does not particularly need P–QB3. Kotov could have chosen the perhaps more accurate order of moves 6. . . . QN–Q2 and if 7. P–N3 then 7. . . . P–B4 immediately.

| 7. P–N3 | QN–Q2 |
|---------|-------|
| 8. B–N2 | P–QN3 |
| 9. QN–Q2 | B–N2 |
| 10. R–B1 | R–B1 |
| 11. P–K3 | P–B4 |

There is hardly any noticeable difference between the White and Black positions. But what is "hardly"? White's Bishop stands on KN2, Black's on K2. What effect will this have on the future play?—Keres asked himself—and the answer: White's Queen has the K2-square, whereas Black's corresponding K2 is occupied by a Bishop, and Black's Queen will be uncomfortable on an open file. So White's plan starts with P–K3, Q–K2, and KR–Q1, but that is just the beginning.

| 12. Q–K2 | BPxP |
|----------|------|
| 13. NxP | N–B4 |
| 14. KR–Q1 | Q–Q2 |

Black must make room for a Rook on Q1 and then get his Queen off the Q-file. He spends two moves to do this, but even on K1 his Queen will be inferior to White's on K2.

| 15. N/2–B3 | KR–Q1 |
|------------|-------|
| 16. N–K5 | Q–K1 |
| 17. PxP | |

Keres begins an unusual, complicated combination with many variations, which is based on possible pins along the QB-file, on the activity of his Bishop at KN2 and, in one variation, even on the threat of mate at KN7!

17. . . .                    BxP

## 18. N/4–B6

A brilliant and completely un-expected move. The Knight is hit three times and defended only once—by the Knight on K5—but it soon turns out that QB6 is controlled by the Bishop on KN2 through the Bishop on Q5 and by the Rook on QB1 through the Knight on B5!

If now 18. . . . BxN 19. RxR BxR 20. NxB RxN 21. BxR QxB 22. P–QN4, the Knight finds itself pinned and White wins the Exchange for a pawn. If 18. . . . BxB 19. NxR B–R1 20. N/8xBP.

| 18. . . . | RxN |
| 19. NxR | QxN |

If 19. . . . BxN the game transposes to the variation in the previous note.

## 20. BxB

So White wins the Exchange for a pawn, a disproportionately small result for such a grand combination. White gets much more on 20. BxN B/2xB 21. P–K4 BxKP 22. RxRch BxR 23. BxB QxB 24. QxQ NxQ 25. R–B8 or 20. . . . BxKB 21. BxB R–K1 22. BxN B–B6 23. BxP BxQ 24. RxQ BxR 25. BxP, and White remains two pawns up.

| 20. . . . | PxB |
| 21. P–QN4 | N/3–K5 |
| 22. PxN | PxP |
| 23. Q–N4 | |

| 23. . . . | P–N3 |
| 24. P–KR4 | Q–K3 |
| 25. QxQ | PxQ |

White's position is better but Black has great counterchances. In order to win the game, it will be necessary to start afresh and overcome Kotov's inexhaustible resourcefulness; after the work and imagination expended by Keres in the preceding phase, this will not be so easy.

| 26. B–K5 | P–B5 |
| 27. R–B2 | |

B–Q4 is better here, not al-lowing the Knight to QB4 or Q6.

| 27. . . . | N–B4 |
| 28. R–N1 | K–B2 |
| 29. B–Q4 | R–Q2 |
| 30. R/2–N2 | |

It is necessary not to allow . . . P–K4; K–B1 should be played. But one cannot always foresee everything.

| 30. . . . | P–K4 |

Having been able by com-binative means to advance this

pawn and bring up his King, he is no longer worried about the fate of the game.

| 31. BxN | BxB |
| 32. R–B2 | R–B2 |
| 33. P–K4 | |

Keres tries to win anyway, but perhaps it is already too late. Now that . . . P–Q5 is prevented, he wants to get a Rook back to QB1 and take the QBP.

| 33. . . . | K–K3 |
| 34. K–B1 | B–Q5 |
| 35. P–B3 | P–B6 |
| 36. K–K2 | R–B2 |

Reminding his opponent that Black has a Rook, too.

| 37. R–KB1 | K–Q3 |
| 38. K–Q3 | K–B4 |
| 39. R–K2 | R–QN2 |
| 40. P–B4 | PxPch |
| 41. RxP | |

If 41. KxP K–B5 42. PxP, then 42. . . . BxP.

| 41. . . . | R–Q2 |
| 42. K–B2 | K–Q4 |
| 43. R/1–K1 | R–QN2 |

**44. K–B1**

In case of 44. PxP, Black gets not only drawing chances but even winning chances, although he cannot restrain the passed pawn: 44. . . . R–N7ch 45. K–B1 RxP 46. P–K6 K–B5 47. K–N1 R–N7ch 48. K–R1 K–N6. White can improve his play by 47. R/1–K2, but Black can choose the variation 45. . . . B–B7 46. R/1–K2 B–B4 instead of 45. . . . RxP.

**44. . . .          R–N7**

With the same threats, after which the heat of battle cannot help but subside, and after one more attempt, by now harmless, the game ends in a draw.

**45. R/4–K2 P–K5 46. RxP RxP 47. P–N4 R–KN7 48. P–B5 PxP 49. PxP R–B7 50. R–K7 K–B5 51. R/1–K4 K–Q6 52. RxBch KxR 53. RxKRP P–R4 54. R–Q7ch K–K4 55. P–R5 RxP 56. P–R6 R–R4, Drawn.**

## • *Game 154*

One of the postulates of opening theory says that at the start of the game White should strive for the advantage and Black should try to equalize. I do not know for sure what Geller's opinion is, but, judging by his games, he believes that the advantage in the opening belongs to the side he is playing. His remarkable ability to get the most out of the opening and his readiness at any moment to switch suddenly from positional themes to open combinative play, and vice versa, are characteristic traits of Geller's artistry.

### King's Indian Defense

| V. Smyslov | Y. Geller |
|---|---|
| 1. P–Q4 | N–KB3 |
| 2. P–QB4 | P–KN3 |
| 3. N–QB3 | B–N2 |
| 4. P–K4 | P–Q3 |
| 5. N–B3 | O–O |
| 6. B–K2 | P–K4 |
| 7. O–O | P–B3 |
| 8. R–K1 | PxP |
| 9. NxP | R–K1 |
| 10. B–B1 | N–N5 |

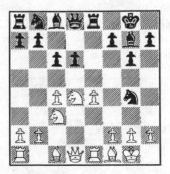

Having set up the White pieces harmoniously, Smyslov was planning to devote himself to a systematic siege of Black's camp without creating any weakness for himself. He was intending to breach the fortress wall at Q6, but the unexpected Knight thrust with its unequivocal threat of . . . Q–R5 compels him to revise his plans.

**11. P–KR3       Q–B3**

This turns out the same as 11. . . . Q–N3 12. PxN QxN would, but 12. . . . BxN would be inferior because of 13. Q–Q2, threatening 14. N–R4 and forcing Black to retreat along the entire front.

**12. PxN           QxN**
**13. P–N5**

A splendid idea! Smyslov sets up a patrol right next to enemy headquarters. This audacious pawn, though torn from its chain, directly or indirectly keeps three enemy pawns under pressure, and of particular importance is that it prevents . . .

P–KB4, Black's thematic advance in the King's Indian.

| 13. . . . | N–Q2 |
| 14. B–B4 | QxQ |
| 15. QRxQ | B–K4 |
| 16. B–K3 | N–B4 |

Now that Queens have been exchanged, Black is ready to trade his Bishop even for White's Knight if he gets a pawn in the bargain; for instance, 17. P–B4 BxN 18. PxB NxP. White therefore limits himself to the calmer P–B3, waiting for the right moment to drive the Bishop from K5 and take the QP. A dynamically balanced position having been established, Black advances his Queenside pawns but at the same time keeps a proper eye on the distribution of forces in the center.

| 17. P–B3 | B–K3 |
| 18. R–B1 | P–QR4 |
| 19. R–B2 | P–R5 |
| 20. P–R3 | KR–N1 |

White defended his QNP with his previous move so that he could transfer his Knight to Q4 via K2. Geller intends to meet this maneuver with the aggressive variation 21. N–K2 N–Q6 22. R–N1 P–N4 23. PxP B–R7 24. R–R1 B–QN6 with interesting complications. If Geller were in a peaceful mood, he would play 20. . . . P–B3 here, and after 21. PxP BxKBP the game would soon end in a draw.

**21. R–N1    P–R3**

Geller decides to liquidate the unpleasant pawn on his KN4 just when White's Rooks are on the same diagonal, as though they were asking to be attacked by a Bishop at Black's KB4. However, Smyslov's accurately calculated counterattack refutes Black's idea.

| 22. PxP | P–B4 |
| 23. P–B4 | |

Geller evidently overlooked that 23. . . . BxN would be followed by 24. BxN PxB 25. RxB PxP 26. R–K3 B–B4 27. B–K2 R–K1 28. R–Q1 with a winning position.

| 23. . . . | B–B3 |
|---|---|
| 24. P–K5 | B–K2 |
| 25. PxP | BxQP |
| 26. R–Q1 | B–KB1 |
| 27. N–Q5 | |

A beautiful stroke, characteristic of Smyslov, that leads to complications advantageous for White. If Black takes the Knight with his pawn he gets into a hopeless position: 27. . . . PxN 28. PxP N–K5 29. PxB BxKRP 30. R–B7 or 28. . . . BxQP 29. RxB N–K5 30. R–B7 intending B–B4, etc.

| 27. . . . | R–Q1 |
|---|---|
| 28. N–B6ch | K–B2 |

Much stronger is 28. . . . K–R1 and on the natural reply 29. B–Q4 to sacrifice the Exchange and go after the Knight: 29. . . . RxB 30. RxR B–K2. White must have had a way to save his Knight after . . . K–R1. It seems this could be done by 29. R–K1 B–K2 30. B–B2; White's position would still be a little better but Black would have defending chances for the time being.

| 29. RxR | RxR |
|---|---|
| 30. N–R7 | N–K5 |
| 31. N–N5ch | K–B3 |
| 32. P–KN4 | R–Q8 |
| 33. NxNch | PxN |
| 34. P–N5ch | |

Now White's passed pawn is solidly protected and his victory is not in doubt.

34. . . . K–B2 35. K–B2 R–Q2 36. R–Q2 RxR 37. BxR B–B4ch 38. B–K3 B–Q3 39. B–Q4 K–N1 40. K–K3 B–KB4 41. P–B5 B–B2 42. B–K2 B–R4 43. B–Q1 B–Q1 44. BxP, Black resigns.

# Round Twenty-Three

## Game 155
### Queen's Gambit

| Y. Geller | P. Keres |
|-----------|----------|
| 1. P–Q4 | N–KB3 |
| 2. P–QB4 | P–K3 |
| 3. N–QB3 | P–Q4 |
| 4. N–B3 | P–B4 |
| 5. BPxP | BPxP |
| 6. QxP | PxP |
| 7. P–K4 | |

Keres repeats the new defense he prepared especially for the tournament in Switzerland and used successfully against Stahlberg (game 33). Geller's choice of an attacking plan with P–K4 takes us from the realm of positional themes in the Queen's Gambit to the brink of the open games of the Italian school. On 7. . . . PxP White trades Queens and plays N–KN5, aiming at the pawns on KB7 and K4.

| 7. . . . | N–B3 |
|----------|------|
| 8. B–QN5 | NxP |
| 9. O–O | |

Geller conducts the game in classical style. Having sacrificed a pawn, he does not rush to win it back but brings up his pieces to attack the King.

| 9. . . . | N–B3 |
|----------|------|

Black's problem is to get his King out of the center at any cost; otherwise, neither an extra pawn nor even an extra piece will save him from a terrific attack. Exchanging Knights on QB6 by 9. . . . NxN 10. QxN does not solve the problem, since with his KNP still under attack by White's Queen he cannot bring out his dark-squared Bishop and this prevents him from castling.

| 10. R–K1ch | B–K2 |
|------------|------|
| 11. Q–K5 | |

The player of open variations must not only search for and invent various attacks and combinations but must also keep a wary eye on his opponent and not forget that he too may find some complicated maneuver. Geller's move seems very strong, for the pin on the Bishop keeps Black from castling, and if 11. . . . B–K3 then 12. N–Q4 is extremely unpleasant.

Keres, however, finds a beautiful combinative solution: although he "cannot" castle, he castles! And White is in an almost hopeless situation—he has no attack and is a pawn down. Thus, Geller's strategically correct conception is embodied in incorrect tactics.

Geller can keep the King in the center for a long time by 11. BxNch PxB 12. Q–K5, after which the threats of N–Q4 as well as P–QN3 and B–R3 would force Black to play K–B1 immediately.

**11. . . .          O–O**

Black's Knight suddenly comes to life: 12. BxN B–Q3! and then 13. . . . PxB.

| 12. | Q–K2 | R–K1 |
| 13. | B–N5 | B–KN5 |
| 14. | QR–Q1 | P–KR3 |
| 15. | B–KR4 | |

Instead White could win back the pawn: 15. BxKN BxB 16. QxRch QxQ 17. RxQch RxR 18. RxP, but he would hardly be able to save himself in the endgame. White's Knights would have no points of support and would be confined to their posts, whereas Black's Bishops would be absolute masters of the board; White's QRP and QNP would have to fall sooner or later.

**15. . . .          N–K5**

Another little combination: on 16. BxB the position is simplified—16. . . . NxN 17. BxQ NxQch 18. RxN RxR 19. BxR RxB, and with a pawn more Black should gradually win. But if first 16. BxN, then 16. . . .

PxB, strengthening the QP. On 16. RxP there follows 16. . . . NxN, and again Black simplifies favorably or even wins the Exchange.

| 16. | B–N3 | NxN |
|-----|------|-----|
| 17. | PxN | B–B3 |
| 18. | QxRch | QxQ |
| 19. | RxQch | RxR |
| 20. | RxP | R–QB1 |
| 21. | R–Q3 | |

This is followed by the third and last of the "little combina-tions," which in sum are fully equivalent to one "big" one. Although condemned by the commentators, R–Q3 does not change but merely accelerates the outcome of the game. After 21. R–QB5 B–K2 22. R–B4 B–K3 23. R–QR4 P–R3 Black wins easily.

**21. . . . N–N5 22. R–K3 NxP 23. P–R3 BxN 24. PxB NxP 25. B–Q7 R–Q1 26. B–B5 P–KN3 27. B–Q3 N–Q8, White resigns.**

# Game 156
## Queen's Indian Defense

| A. Kotov | S. Reshevsky |
|----------|--------------|
| 1. P–Q4 | N–KB3 |
| 2. P–QB4 | P–K3 |
| 3. N–KB3 | P–QN3 |
| 4. P–K3 | B–N2 |
| 5. B–Q3 | B–K2 |
| 6. O–O | O–O |
| 7. N–B3 | P–Q4 |
| 8. Q–K2 | QN–Q2 |
| 9. P–QN3 | P–QR3 |

Too quiet. White is preparing to open the center with P–K4, and one would rather expect from Reshevsky 9. . . . B–N5 10. B–N2 BxN 11. BxB PxP 12. PxP P–B4 or 12. . . . B–K5.

| 10. | B–N2 | B–Q3 |
|-----|------|------|
| 11. | P–K4 | PxKP |
| 12. | NxP | NxN |
| 13. | BxN | BxB |
| 14. | QxB | |

White has the freer position and controls more important lines for regrouping. Since the dark-square Bishop is on the QR1–KR8 diagonal, it is extremely tempting to bring a Rook to KN3, but it is necessary at the same time to counteract Black's attempts to give his pieces more scope by . . . P–QB4 or . . . P–K4.

| 14. . . . | Q–K2 |
|-----------|------|
| 15. QR–K1 | KR–K1 |
| 16. R–K2 | P–QR4 |
| 17. KR–K1 | B–N5 |
| 18. R–Q1 | QR–Q1 |
| 19. R–Q3 | P–KB3 |
| 20. R/3–K3 | Q–B2 |
| 21. P–N3 | B–Q3 |
| 22. Q–B6 | N–N1 |
| 23. Q–N5 | N–Q2 |
| 24. K–N2 | B–B1 |

| 25. P–QR3 | R–B1 |
|---|---|
| 26. Q–B6 | N–N1 |
| 27. Q–N7 | Q–Q2 |
| 28. Q–K4 | Q–B2 |

The lengthy maneuvering within each player's own territory has led to no essential change in the position. The following careless move by White allows Reshevsky to seize the initiative.

| 29. Q–N4 | P–R4! |
|---|---|
| 30. Q–K4 | P–QB4! |

Well played. Black now removes White's QP from the center and gets fully equal play.

| 31. R–Q3 | N–B3 |
|---|---|
| 32. R/2–Q2? | |

White loses his head and puts his Rook in a bad position. He should take the QBP first.

| 32. . . . | PxP |
|---|---|
| 33. NxP | N–K4 |
| 34. R–QB3 | QR–Q1 |

**35. P–B4**

An extremely risky decision. He should continue with a plan to gain the Q-file by, say, 35. R–B1 and 36. R/1–Q1. The adventurous advance of the KBP might have cost the game. It decisively weakens both of White's vitally important diagonals, KN1–QB5 and KR1–QR8.

**35. . . .          N–N5**

Of course. Immediately a multitude of combinative threats appears for Black. Now, by the way, the threat is . . . P–K4, so the Knight has to leave Q4.

| 36. N–B3 | RxRch |
|---|---|
| 37. NxR | R–Q1 |

Returning the mistake. Reshevsky thinks that without Rooks it will be difficult for White to defend his QRP and QNP, but Kotov keeps the balance.

I would choose the more obvious 37. . . . P–B4, especially since the Rook is already on the K-file. After 38. Q–B3 P–K4 39. P–R3 P–K5 or 39. PxP NxKP 40. Q–Q5 B–B4, Black's pieces are excellently posted. Meanwhile, White seems to have no useful move. His best after 37. . . . P–B4 is 38. Q–B6.

| 38. R–Q3 | RxR |
|---|---|
| 39. QxR | Q–N2ch |
| 40. Q–K4 | Q–Q2 |
| 41. N–B3 | B–B4 |
| 42. B–Q4 | BxB |
| 43. NxB | K–B2 |
| 44. P–R3 | P–B4 |

**45. Q–Q3          N–B3**
**46. N–B3          QxQ**

46. . . . Q–K2, taking aim at the QRP, retains somewhat better chances for success. As the further course of the game shows, Reshevsky overestimated his chances during his home analysis. However, neither you nor I will regret this. The Knight ending is very interesting.

**47. N–K5ch        K–K2**
**48. NxQ           N–K5**
**49. P–QN4         K–Q3**
**50. N–K5          P–QR5**

50. . . . PxP might have drawn. Black, however, wants to keep his QRP and eliminate his opponent's. There is no denying Reshevsky's logic, but Kotov finds an amazing defense.

**51. K–B3          P–KN4**

Black exerts maximum effort. Kotov's position seems critical in view of the threat 52. . . . N–Q7ch 53. K–K3 N–N8 54. K–Q3 P–R5 or 52. . . . P–N5ch 53. PxP RPxPch 54. NxP N–Q7ch 55. K–K2 NxBP, etc. However, by an abrupt turn to the left his King leaves the danger area.

**52. K–K3**

A very beautiful move. And here are the variations, the first of which resembles a short story:

1) 52. . . . N–B6—going for the QRP—53. K–Q3 N–N8 54. K–B2 NxPch 55. K–N2. The Knight perishes but the breakthrough comes on the other side. 55. . . . P–R5 56. KxN RPxP, and if the Knight on K5 rushes to help—57. N–B3?—then 57. . . . PxP and the pawn formation K3, KB4, KB5, and KN6 is free to advance to the eighth rank. But the Knight can jump in devious ways—57. N–B7ch! and after 58. NxP and N–B3 the KNP is stopped at the threshold.

2) 52. ... NxP 53. N–B7ch K–K2 54. NxP and again Black's Knight is in a quagmire.

Reshevsky nevertheless finds a way to break through the QRP.

| 52. ... | P–N5 |
| 53. PxP | RPxP |
| 54. NxP | N–B6 |
| 55. N–K5 | N–N8 |
| 56. K–Q3 | NxP |
| 57. P–N5 | |

Allowing Black to sacrifice his Knight for two pawns and obtain serious drawing chances. Isn't the simple 57. K–B3 better? Apparently not. By 57. ... P–N4 Black reaches a draw at once: 58. P–B5ch K–Q4 59. P–B6 K–Q3 60. K–N2 N–B5ch.

57. ... NxNP 58. PxN K–B4 59. N–B3 KxP 60. N–Q4ch K–N5 61. K–B2 P–K4 62. PxP K–B4 63. P–K6 K–Q3 64. K–B3 P–N4 65. K–N4 K–K2 66. K–B5 P–R6 67. K–Q5, **Black resigns.**

# Game 157
## English Opening

**I. Boleslavsky    D. Bronstein**

1. P–QB4 P–K4 2. N–QB3 P–Q3 3. N–B3 P–KB4 4. P–Q4 P–K5 5. N–Q2 P–B3

Black's manner of play, with pawns only, is not likely to find imitators. It is not surprising that Black soon finds himself in a difficult position.

6. P–K3 N–B3 7. B–K2 P–KN3 8. O–O B–R3 9. P–QN4 O–O 10. P–N5 R–K1 11. N–N3 QN–Q2 12. Q–B2 Q–B2 13. B–Q2 P–B4

In order at least to avoid the opening of the QN-file.

14. PxP PxP 15. N–Q5 Q–Q3 16. QR–Q1 P–N3 17. P–B4 NxN 18. PxN N–B3

19. B–QB3 B–QN2 20. Q–N2

White's positional advantage is obvious. The transfer of the Knight by N–Q2–B4 suggests itself here. Black could hardly take the QP, since the opening of the Q-file and of White's QR2–KN8 diagonal would be fatal for Black. Missing this opportunity, White hands his opponent the initiative.

20. . . . N–N5 21. Q–B1 B–N2 22. P–KR3 BxB 23. QxB N–B3 24. B–B4 QR–Q1 25. R–Q2 P–KR3 26. N–B1 K–R2 27. N–K2 Q–B1 28. KR–Q1 R–Q3 29. Q–N3 R/1–Q1 30. N–B3 Q–K2 31. R–KB2 B–B1 32. N–K2 B–K3 33. N–B3 B–B2 34. P–QR4

White's position is becoming alarming, but he opens the QR-file for operations by his major pieces just in time.

34. . . . N–K1 35. P–R5 Q–B3 36. R–R2 P–N4 37. R–KB1 Q–N3 38. RPxP RPxP 39. R–R7 R/1–Q2 40. R–R8 N–B3 41. Q–N2 P–N5

42. PxP QxP 43. R–Q1 Q–R4

Now it is Black who misses his chance. He should try 43. . . . Q–N6. In view of the threat . . . N–N5 the defensive move 43. Q–KB2 would be necessary, but after 44. . . . QxQch 45. KxQ NxP 46. NxN BxN 47. BxB RxB 48. RxR Black would have an extra pawn in the Rook ending. However, I don't think the ending could be won.

44. Q–KB2 Q–N3 45. R–QB8 N–N5 46. Q–K1 R–R2 47. R–B6 R–R6 48. R–B1 Q–B3 49. B–K2, Drawn.

# Game 158
## King's Indian Defense

| G. Stahlberg | S. Gligoric |
|---|---|
| 1. N–KB3 | N–KB3 |
| 2. P–B4 | P–KN3 |
| 3. P–KN3 | B–N2 |
| 4. B–N2 | O–O |
| 5. O–O | P–Q3 |
| 6. P–Q4 | P–B4 |
| 7. P–KR3 | |

White may sometimes permit himself to lose a tempo in the opening, especially since this move is generally of some use.

Stahlberg wants to develop his Bishop to K3 without worrying about the threat . . . N–KN5.

| 7. . . . | N–B3 |
| 8. N–B3 | B–Q2 |

Gligoric avoids exchanges here and later, wishing to give the game a complicated character. Good enough is 8. . . . PxP 9. NxP NxN 10. QxN B–K3, and if 11. BxP BxRP.

| 9. PxP | PxP |

Perhaps White should have made this exchange on the 7th move.

| 10. B–K3 | Q–B1 |
| 11. K–R2 | R–Q1 |
| 12. Q–B1 | |

On 12. BxP BxP 13. BxB RxQ 14. BxQ RxQR 15. RxR RxB the ending soon turns out in Black's favor.

| 12. . . . | N–Q5 |
| 13. R–Q1 | B–B3 |
| 14. N–K1 | |

White has played the opening rather listlessly, and now, unnecessarily removing an important piece from the center, he finds himself in a difficult position. A few exchanges here would be more to the point: 14. NxN PxN 15. RxP RxR 16. BxR BxB 17. KxB QxP 18. P–K3 or 15. BxP N–N5ch 16. PxN RxB 17. RxR BxR 18. P–K3.

| 14. . . . | P–N3 |
| 15. B–N5 | BxB |
| 16. NxB | Q–K3 ! |

This move and the next constitute a very fine maneuver that leads to the win of a pawn. Its subtlety is illustrated by the following variation: 17. Q–K3 QxP 18. QxP R–Q2 19. Q–K3 R–K1 and White has a hopeless position, or 17. N–K3 N–K5 and Black threatens to trap the Bishop.

| 17. N–K3 | N–K5 |
| 18. NxN | QxN |
| 19. N–Q5 | |

The bravery of despair. White's pieces are in very bad positions: his Rooks have no scope, his Queen is so blocked that it is hardly visible, every single one of his pawns is passive. Even his Bishop finds itself stranded among the Black pieces. The Swedish grandmaster's desire to give the Knight its freedom is understandable.

| 19. . . . | QxP |
| 20. Q–K3 | |

Checking on K7 leads to even more serious trouble: 20. Nx Pch K–B1 21. Q–K3 QxQ 22. PxQ N–B6ch or 21. NxPch RPxN 22. BxR QxPch.

| 20. | . . . | QxQ |
| 21. | BxQ | P–K3 |
| 22. | BxN | BxB |
| 23. | N–K7ch | K–B1 |
| 24. | N–B6 | R–Q3 |
| 25. | NxB | RxN |
| 26. | RxR | PxR |
| 27. | R–Q1 | P–K4 |

A protected passed pawn in the center and the prospect of two connected passed pawns are more than enough to win. The ensuing phase is a matter of simple technique. Black moves his King up to the center, forms a second passed pawn, and advances his pawns with the support of his Rook, forcing his opponent to lay down his arms.

| 28. | K–N2 | K–K2 |
| 29. | P–B4 | P–B3 |
| 30. | K–B3 | K–K3 |
| 31. | R–QB1 | R–Q1 |
| 32. | PxP | PxP |
| 33. | K–K4 | |

Stahlberg makes it as difficult as possible for his opponent. The pawns are blockaded for the time being, and Black's win will be possible only by getting his Rook to the rear, but White is threatening to push his QBP in that case. In the end, White's undoing is the undefended position of his Rook and Black's threats to get his Rook to the sixth or seventh rank and give mate on K6.

33. . . . R–QB1 34. P–R3 P–QR4 35. P–N3 R–B1 36. P–B5 R–B1 (Removing the last hope: 37. PxP RxR!) 37. P–QN4 NPxP 38. R–B4 K–Q3 39. P–N5 R–QN1 40. P–QR4 R–QB1 41. R–B1 R–B2 42. R–QN1 P–B5, White resigns.

## Game 159
### Nimzo-Indian Defense

| M. Euwe | M. Taimanov | |
| --- | --- | --- |
| 1. P–Q4 | N–KB3 | |
| 2. P–QB4 | P–K3 | |

| 3. N–QB3 | B–N5 |
| 4. Q–B2 | P–B4 |
| 5. PxP | O–O |
| 6. B–B4 | |

One of Euwe's many opening novelties, which does not pretend to gain any particular advantage but serves to introduce some variety into this well-known variation.

| | | |
|---|---|---|
| 6. | . . . | BxP |
| 7. | P–K3 | N–B3 |
| 8. | N–B3 | P–Q4 |
| 9. | P–QR3 | Q–K2 |
| 10. | B–N5 | R–Q1 |
| 11. | R–Q1 | PxP |
| 12. | RxRch | QxR |
| 13. | BxP | B–K2 |
| 14. | O–O | B–Q2 |
| 15. | R–Q1 | Q–K1 |

Since Black was forced to lose a few moves on the Queen maneuver Q–K2–Q1–K1, White has gained some advantage in development.

**16. BxN        BxB**

White has eliminated one of the main defenders of Black's KR2. Euwe thinks that the thrust N–QN5, aiming at QB7, was worth considering after Black took on KB3 with his Bishop instead of his pawn, and if . . . R–Q1 then N–Q6. But on 17. N–QN5 Q–K2! 18. N–Q6 B–K1 White's advantage evaporates.

**17. N–K4        B–K2**
**18. N/3–N5**

As the opening leads into the middlegame, White has the better chances. His advantage is in his more active piece position and his control of the open Q-file. White undertakes an interesting combination, which, however, does not achieve its purpose. It is much better to move the other Knight to N5, without trying to be so clever. After 18. N/4–N5 Black has nothing better than 18. . . . P–KN3. After 19. P–KR4 and later P–R5, Black's King could find itself in great danger in view of White's constant threat to sacrifice a piece on K6 and burst in at KN6 with his Queen. Furthermore, after 18. N/4–N5 P–KN3 Black's weak KB3 is sensitive, and bringing his Bishop to KN2 does not work: 19. P–KR4 B–B3 20. N–K4 B–N2 21. N–Q6 Q–N1 22. NxBP.

**18. . . .        P–KR3**

Taimanov goes bravely to meet his opponent's idea, having more correctly evaluated the endgame that perforce arises.

| 19. N–Q6 | BxN/3 |
|----------|-------|
| 20. Q–R7ch | K–B1 |
| 21. RxB | PxN |

By destroying the threatening Knights, Black, of course, completely avoids any kind of surprise.

| 22. RxB | QxR |
|---------|-----|
| 23. Q–R8ch | K–K2 |
| 24. QxR | Q–Q8ch |

White's Queen is temporarily out of play, and Black hurries to attack White's defenseless pawns.

| 25. B–B1 | Q–N6 |
|----------|------|
| 26. P–R3 | |

White is too calm. Obligatory is 26. Q–R8 and then P–KR4 at once. Euwe evidently plans to close the QN-file by B–N5, in which case the Queen's place is of course QR8.

| 26. . . . | QxNP |
|-----------|------|
| 27. P–QR4 | Q–N3 |
| 28. Q–R8 | |

White is still a pawn down, but his active Queen on the eighth rank is some compensation.

| 28. . . . | K–B3 |
|-----------|------|

Would you believe that White's humble little pawn on KR3 will become a Queen in a few moves? Necessary is 28. . . . P–N3 29. P–R4 PxP 30. QxPch K–Q2 31. Q–B6 N–Q1 32. B–N5ch K–B1, retaining the extra pawn with a safe King position.

| 29. P–R4 | Q–B4 |
|----------|------|

Suspecting nothing.

**30. P–KR5**

And now what? How is Black to defend against the threat of P–R6–7–8=Q?

| 30. . . . | P–N5 |
|-----------|------|
| 31. P–R6 | Q–KN4 |
| 32. P–R7 | |

Black's King takes a sudden turn for the worse. A catastrophe is about to occur. However, the ambulance, P–N5–6, arrives just in time to save his majesty's life.

| 32. . . . | P–N6 |
|-----------|------|

In view of the threat 33. . . .
PxPch 34. KxP Q–R5ch,
White's Queen cannot leave the
KRP.

**33. Q–KN8    PxPch**
**34. KxP      N–K2**
**35. P–R8=Q**

The outside pawn has had a
brilliant career. Now White even
wins a piece.

**35. . . .     NxQ**
**36. QxN      Q–R5ch**

A draw was agreed, since
White's material advantage cannot be realized. Taimanov's resourceful play neutralized his
error on the 28th move.

## Game 160
### Nimzo-Indian Defense

| L. Szabo | M. Najdorf |
|----------|-----------|
| 1. P–Q4 | N–KB3 |
| 2. P–QB4 | P–K3 |
| 3. N–QB3 | B N5 |
| 4. P–K3 | O–O |
| 5. N–B3 | P–Q4 |
| 6. P–QR3 | BxNch |
| 7. PxB | P–QN3 |
| 8. PxP | PxP |
| 9. B–Q3 | P–B4 |
| 10. O–O | N–B3 |
| 11. P–QR4 | |

Black has maintained the
pawn tension in the center and
has not allowed his opponent to
advance P–K4, so Szabo seeks
a way out for his Bishop on the

QR3–KB8 diagonal. No sooner
is P–QR4 played than Najdorf
immediately closes the center
and plays his Knight to K5, inviting White either to exchange
his Bishop or worry about the
defense of his QBP. The game
is significant for opening theory
because Najdorf's 12th move is
an improvement on the game
Taimanov–Botvinnik from the
20th U.S.S.R. Championship.

**11. . . .     P–B5**
**12. B–B2     N–K5**

Botvinnik played his Bishop
to N5 here, but his opponent

ignored the threat to double his
pawns and replied 13. Q–K1!

**13. Q–K1**

After this Black is able to
take firm possession of K5.
More in the spirit of the position is 13. BxN PxB 14. N–Q2,
and then P–B3 in order to open
the KB-file for his Rook and a
path to KN3 for his Queen.

| | |
|---|---|
| **13. . . .** | **R–K1** |
| **14. B–N2** | **B–B4** |
| **15. N–Q2** | **Q–N4** |

Black's pieces are much more
active. If he succeeds in his fight
for the strategic point K5 the
advantage will clearly be his.

| | |
|---|---|
| **16. NxN** | **BxN** |

To solve his basic problem he
should recapture on K5 with the
pawn, exploiting the fact that
because K6 is attacked twice
White cannot play P–B3. After
16. . . . PxN both of White's
Bishops would be blocked for
some time, and Black would be
able to create threats to White's
King; e.g., 17. Q–Q2 B–N5
(threatening . . . B–B6) 18. K–
R1 R–K3 19. B–Q1 R–R3 20.
BxB QxB 21. P–B3 Q–N6 22.
P–R3 PxP 23. RxP RxPch.

| | |
|---|---|
| **17. BxB** | **RxB** |
| **18. B–R3** | **R–N5** |

| | |
|---|---|
| **19. P–N3** | **R–K5** |
| **20. R–N1** | **R/1–K1** |
| **21. R–N5** | **Q–Q1** |
| **22. Q–K2** | **P–QR3** |
| **23. R–N2** | **N–R4** |
| **24. R/1–N1** | **R/5–K3** |

Also possible is 24. . . . N–
N6, on which White would
probably answer 25. RxN PxR
26. QxRP, and with a couple of
pawns for the Exchange he
would be all right. Black therefore postpones N–N6 until
White's Queen stops threatening
the QRP.

| | |
|---|---|
| **25. K–N2** | **P–R3** |
| **26. Q–R5** | **N–N6** |
| **27. R–K2** | **Q–Q2** |
| **28. B–N2** | **K–R2** |
| **29. P–R3** | **P–N3** |
| **30. Q–B3** | **R–K5** |
| **31. P–N4** | |

**31. . . .          P–B4**

The only weak link in Black's position is his KBP. Why not the simple 31. . . . K–N2, at the same time defending KB3? White's QRP would then be easily won and Black's victory would be quite simple.

| 32. | PxP   | PxP    |
|-----|-------|--------|
| 33. | R–N1  | R–N1ch |
| 34. | K–R1  | RxRch  |
| 35. | KxR   | R–K2   |
| 36. | K–R1  | Q–K3   |
| 37. | Q–B4  | R–KN2  |

Najdorf wants to decide the game forcibly and seizes the KN-file. Exchanging Queens and advancing the Queenside pawns is safer.

**38. K–R2          Q–N3**

White's position seems hopeless.

| 39. | Q–N3 | Q–R4 |
|-----|------|------|
| 40. | Q–B4 |      |

A happy idea: White leaves his Rook without protection, utilizing the fact that Black's King cannot escape perpetual check.

| 40. | . . . | Q–N3 |
|-----|-------|------|
| 41. | Q–N3  | Q–K3 |
| 42. | Q–B4  | Q–K5 |
| 43. | P–B3  | Q–Q6 |

Drawn. Actually, White replied 44. R–N2. After exchanging Rooks Black would win the Bishop—but not the game, because of perpetual check. Nothing would have been gained by 43. . . . Q–N8, instead of the text move, for the same reason; but Black could have tried 43. . . . QxQch 44. PxQ K–N1, and 45. R–K5 would not have worked because of 45. . . . N–Q7! threatening mate in two. By rushing his King to the

Queenside, he would have obtained real winning chances, for he would have been in effect a pawn up. Black's position was so strong that even two mistakes did not spoil it completely.

## Game 161
### Sicilian Defense

**Y. Averbakh        T. Petrosian**

1. P–K4 P–QB4 2. N–KB3 P–Q3 3. P–Q4 PxP 4. NxP N–KB3 5. N–QB3 P–KN3 6. B–K2 B–N2 7. B–K3 O–O 8. O–O N–B3 9. Q–Q2 P–Q4

By this all-purpose advance of the QP, Black provokes a series of exchanges to simplify the defense, but this entails some risk in view of the possibility 10. NxN PxN 11. P–K5 N–Q2 12. P–B4 P–K3 13. N–R4 with advantage for White. And after 11. . . . N–N5 12. BxN BxB 13. P–B4 the threat of B–B5 would place Black in a ticklish situation. Averbakh takes another path.

10. PxP NxP 11. N/3xN NxN 12. P–QB4

More interesting than the obvious 12. BxN QxN 13. QR–Q1, etc., and giving Black a problem—whether to keep the Knight on Q5 or be tempted by the Bishop on K7. If 12. . . . NxBch 13. QxN P–K3, then the calm 14. N–B3, and although Black would keep the

Bishop pair White would have the better chances due to his extra pawn on the Queenside and his control of a number of central squares. Black finds the best move.

12. . . . P–K4 13. P–B4 B–K3 14. PxP NxBch 15. QxN BxN

16. QR–Q1 BxBP 17. QxB Q–B1

This seems the time to let the reader in on a secret: up to and including Black's 17th move the opponents have reproduced a game from the tournament at Shchavno-Zdruj (Poland) in 1950, in which Averbakh played

Black. Geller continued 18. Q–Q5 and after 18. . . . Q–K3 19. QxQ PxQ 20. R–Q7 achieved not the slightest advantage. Here Averbakh is playing White and has prepared an improvement, which, however, also does not lead to anything serious.

**18. QxQ QRxQ 19. R–Q7 BxP 20. RxNP R–N1 21. RxR RxR 22. P–QN3, Drawn.**

# Round Twenty-Four

## Game 162
### English Opening

| T. Petrosian | L. Szabo |
|---|---|
| 1. P–QB4 | N–KB3 |
| 2. N–QB3 | P–B4 |
| 3. N–B3 | P–Q4 |
| 4. PxP | NxP |
| 5. P–KN3 | NxN |
| 6. NPxN | P–KN3 |
| 7. Q–R4ch | N–Q2 |
| 8. P–R4 | P–KR3 |
| 9. QR–N1 | B–N2 |
| 10. B–KN2 | |

The opening is quite characteristic of modern strategy. The energetic moves Q–R4ch, P–KR4, and QR–N1 are only means to create a somewhat more favorable position from which to start the middlegame struggle.

| 10. . . . | O–O |
|---|---|
| 11. P–B4 | P–K4 |
| 12. P–Q3 | N–N3 |
| 13. Q–B2 | B–Q2 |

For a few moves each side maneuvers quietly in his own camp.

| 14. B–K3 | Q–K2 |
|---|---|
| 15. N–Q2 | P–B4 |
| 16. N–N3 | QR–B1 |
| 17. BxNP | R–B2 |
| 18. B–N2 | P–B5 |

| 19. B–QB1 | B–QB3 |
|---|---|
| 20. BxB | RxB |
| 21. N–Q2 | PxP |

At the cost of a pawn Black has been able to keep White's King in the center. Far more important in this case, however, is the opening of the KB-file—it would have been unsafe for White to castle anyway (the

396

pawn cover KB2, KN3, KR4 is weak). Petrosian later conducts the game quite resourcefully; he successfully repulses his opponent's threats and retains his material advantage.

| | |
|---|---|
| 22. PxP | N-B1 |
| 23. R-N8 | N-Q3 |

Of course, the consequences of P-K5 were difficult to calculate accurately, but the resulting positions would be quite intricate and not without chances for Black; and that, after all, was what Szabo was looking for when he sacrificed a pawn.

| | |
|---|---|
| 24. RxRch | QxR |
| 25. P-K4 | |

Black's Bishop is now completely stifled, the result of Black's decision not to play P-K5.

| | |
|---|---|
| 25. . . . | Q-B1 |
| 26. N-B1 | P-KR4 |
| 27. N-K3 | R-R3 |
| 28. N-Q5 | Q-N5 |
| 29. Q-KN2 | NxKP |

White has fortified his position well, and there is nothing left for Black but to try to breach the wall.

| | |
|---|---|
| 30. PxN | RxP |
| 31. QxR | QxKPch |

| | |
|---|---|
| 32. Q-K2 | QxRch |
| 33. Q-B1 | Q-R7 |
| 34. B-K3 | QxPch |

Black has been able to exhaust White's pawn reserves completely. If only Black's Bishop could help his Queen a little! Guessing that the time has finally come to break out of its dungeon, the Bishop prompts the pawn to advance, but alas, it is already too late.

White's pieces turn to counterattack, and, thanks to their numerical superiority, they sweep everything from their path.

35. Q-B2 Q-R6 36. K-Q2 P-K5 37. N-B6ch K-R1 38. NxKP Q-K3 39. K-Q3 Q-Q2ch 40. K-K2 Q-K3 41. N-Q2, Black resigns.

# Game 163
## Nimzo-Indian Defense

**M. Najdorf**      **M. Euwe**

| | |
|---|---|
| 1. P–Q4 | N–KB3 |
| 2. P–QB4 | P–K3 |
| 3. N–QB3 | B–N5 |
| 4. P–K3 | P–B4 |
| 5. B–Q3 | P–QN3 |
| 6. N–B3 | B–N2 |
| 7. O–O | O–O |
| 8. N–QR4 | |

For some reason, masters readily employ the defensive system with the fianchetto of the QB against Najdorf (see, for instance, games 94 and 118). In this game Najdorf chooses one of the best continuations, forcing Black to exchange pawns under the most unfavorable conditions.

| | |
|---|---|
| 8. . . . | PxP |
| 9. PxP | Q–B2 |
| 10. P–QR3 | B–K2 |
| 11. N–B3 | |

White turns off the main road, and the theoreticians can learn nothing more from this game. 11. P–QN4! is more logical, in order to use the Knight's position to support the possible P–B5. It is true that 11. P–QN4 can be answered by 11. . . . N–N5, forcing 12. P–N3, but this is not so terrible. Now, however, Black gets in P–Q4.

| | |
|---|---|
| 11. . . . | P–Q4 |
| 12. PxP | NxN |

| | |
|---|---|
| 13. NxN | BxN |
| 14. N–K5 | Q–N2 |
| 15. R–K1 | N–B3 |
| 16. Q–R5 | P–B4 |
| 17. NxN | QxN |

Each player has the Bishop pair and an approximately equivalent weakness, on Q4 and K3 respectively, which balance the chances for attack and defense.

| | |
|---|---|
| 18. B–KB4 | B–B3 |
| 19. QR–B1 | Q–R5 |
| 20. B–K5 | BxB |
| 21. PxB | QR–B1 |
| 22. Q–K2 | Q–KB5 |

Black's Queen occupies a square that rightfully belongs to White's Queen, and it creates the threat to seize the QB-file.

23. Q–K3

A fine reply, with the idea of controlling the light squares in the center with his Bishop and the dark squares with his pawns after the exchange of Queens. Despite the doubling and isolation of White's pawns after the Queen exchange, they will not be weak, since Black's Rooks will be unable to approach them.

| 23. . . . | QxQ |
| 24. PxQ | KR–Q1 |
| 25. B–R6 | RxR |
| 26. RxR | B–K5 |

Black was forced to give up the QB-file, but he seized an adjacent file and will be the first to break through to the seventh rank. The two sides' chances gradually equalize, and the game concludes with perpetual check.

**27. B–B8 R–Q7 28. BxPch K–B1 29. R–B7 RxPch 30. K–B1 RxNP 31. R–B7ch K–K1 32. RxRP**

**32. . . . R–N8ch 33. K–B2 R–N7ch**

White's whole problem is that his King cannot go to N3 because of 34. . . . R–N7ch 35. K–R4 R–N5ch 36. K–R5 B–B6 or 35. K–R3 R–N5. In either case Black wins by the threat of mate.

**34. K–B1 R–N8ch 35. K–K2 R–N7ch 36. K–K1 R–N8ch 37. K–Q2 R–N7ch 38. K–B3 R–B7ch 39. K–Q4 R–Q7ch 40. K–B4 R–B7ch 41. K–Q4, Drawn.**

The King finds no shelter on the other side either: 41. K–N5 R–B4ch and Black takes the KP; or 41. K–N3 R–B4 42. B–Q7ch K–Q1 43. P–K6 R–R4 forcing a draw.

# Game 164
## Reti Opening

| M. Taimanov | G. Stahlberg |
|---|---|
| 1. P–QB4 | P–K3 |
| 2. P–KN3 | N–KB3 |
| 3. B–N2 | P–Q4 |
| 4. N–KB3 | PxP |
| 5. Q–R4ch | QN–Q2 |
| 6. QxBP | P–QR3 |
| 7. O–O | B–Q3 |

The moves . . . B–Q3 and then . . . Q–K2 should prepare . . . P–K4. That being the case, . . . P–QR3 was a pointless waste of time.

| 8. P–Q4 | O–O |
| 9. R–Q1 | Q–K2 |
| 10. Q–B2 | R–N1 |

Again inconsistent. The QNP's advance leaves the QBP far behind and it soon perishes —on Q3, it is true, but this is a mere detail.

He should play 10. . . . P–K4 immediately, and if 11. PxP NxP 12. NxN, he should take on K4 not with the Queen but with the Bishop.

| 11. N–B3 | P–QN4 |
| 12. P–K4 | P–N5 |
| 13. N–QR4 | P–K4 |
| 14. PxP | N/2xP |
| 15. NxN | QxN |
| 16. B–B4 | Q–QR4 |
| 17. RxB | |

When there are two equivalent ways to win a pawn, it is difficult to resist a little joke.

Black's Queen could not go back to K2 because of 17. P–K5.

| 17. . . . | PxR |
| 18. BxP | B–K3 |
| 19. BxKR | RxB |
| 20. P–N3 | R–B1 |
| 21. Q–Q2 | B–Q2 |

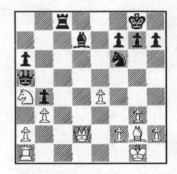

| 22. N–N2 | B–K3 |
| 23. N–Q3 | BxP |
| 24. QxP | QxQ |
| 25. NxQ | B–B5 |
| 26. P–K5 | N–Q2 |
| 27. P–B4 | |

Clearing a path for the King to Q4. As regards the KP, it does not require defense, as a variation like this illustrates: 27. R–QB1 NxP? 28. N–B6! NxN 29. RxB N–K2 30. RxRch NxR 31. B–N7 N–N3 32. BxP.

| 27. . . . | P–N3 |
| 28. R–Q1 | N–N3 |
| 29. R–Q6 | |

White stubbornly refuses to take a second pawn by B–N7. In agreeing to the exchange of QRPs, Taimanov drags out the game excessively and has to seek victory in a long Knight ending.

| | |
|---|---|
| 29. . . . | N–R5 |
| 30. P–QR3 | R–N1 |
| 31. B–Q5 | BxB |
| 32. RxB | |

32. NxB is better.

| | |
|---|---|
| 32. . . . | N–N3 |
| 33. R–R5 | |

33. R–B5 would restrict the activity of Black's Knight.

| | |
|---|---|
| 33. . . . | N–B5 |
| 34. RxP | NxP |
| 35. N–Q5 | N–B7 |
| 36. R–R4 | K–N2 |
| 37. R–B4 | R–Q1 |
| 38. N–B6 | N–K6 |
| 39. R–B3 | N–B4 |
| 40. R–B7 | P–R4 |

Black is doomed to passive defense. Stahlberg's last move solidified his Knight's position on B4 somewhat and simplified shifting it back and forth between B4 and R3.

| | |
|---|---|
| 41. N–K4 | R–K1 |
| 42. K–B2 | R–K2 |

White's perpetual threat to the BP forces Stahlberg to consent to the exchange of Rooks, thus extinguishing his still flickering hope of reaching the well-known "three pawns against four" drawn Rook ending. As for the "four against three" Knight ending, that, as we shall see, is a win.

| | |
|---|---|
| 43. RxR | NxR |
| 44. K–B3 | K–B1 |
| 45. N–Q6 | N–B3 |
| 46. K–K4 | K–K2 |
| 47. P–B5 | N–N5 |

| | |
|---|---|
| 48. P–B6ch | K–B1 |

The King is forced to retreat to the first rank; if 48. . . . K–K3 49. N–N7, threatening N–Q8ch or N–B5 mate.

| | |
|---|---|
| 49. N–N7 | N–R3 |
| 50. K–Q5 | N–B2ch |

| 51. K–Q6 | N–N4ch |
|---|---|
| 52. K–Q7 | |

It seems it is not so easy to get away from even a single Knight.

| 52. . . . | N–Q5 |
|---|---|
| 53. N–B5 | N–B4 |
| 54. K–Q8 | |

There is nowhere to go beyond the eighth rank. The author wishes to take the opportunity to dispel an erroneous idea that is floating around among some groups of beginning players: that according to the rules of chess "if the King reaches the last rank one of its lost pawns is returned." More than one King reached the last rank in this tournament, but no pawn was put back on the board, as the reader can verify. This "rule" is an incorrect fabrication and not in accordance with chess logic, the laws of which have been proved by many years' experience.

| 54. . . . | N–Q5 |
|---|---|
| 55. N–Q7ch | |

In the next stage of the struggle White pushes back the Black King and begins to move to the right.

| 55. . . . | K–N1 |
|---|---|
| 56. K–K8 | N–K3 |
| 57. K–K7 | P–N4 |

Zugzwang: the King is chained to his BP while his Knight tries to block the KP—but Black's defensive resources are by now exhausted.

| 58. K–K8 | N–B2ch |
|---|---|
| 59. K–Q8 | N–K3ch |
| 60. K–K7 | N–Q5 |
| 61. N–B5 | |

Now everything is ready for the decisive P–K6.

| 61. . . . | N–B3ch |
|---|---|
| 62. K–Q6 | N–R4 |
| 63. P–K6 | PxP |
| 64. K–K7 | |

This would seem to be it; but Stahlberg, as always, resourcefully looks for the tiniest chance.

| 64. . . . | N–B3ch |
|---|---|
| 65. K–K8 | N–K4 |
| 66. NxP | N–B2 |

Black occupies the last line of defense; beyond it, defeat.

| 67. K–K7 | P–N5 |
|---|---|
| 68. N–N7 | N–R3 |
| 69. NxP | N–B4ch |

If a contest were organized among chess Knights to find the one that gave the most checks, Stahlberg's would set the record.

| 70. K–K8 | N–Q3ch |
|---|---|
| 71. K–Q7 | N–B4 |
| 72. N–N7! | N–R3 |

The pawn ending is not altogether to his liking.

| 73. K–K7 | N–B2 |
|---|---|
| 74. N–B5 | **Black resigns** |

## Game 165
### Queen's Gambit

**S. Gligoric**     **I. Boleslavsky**

1. P–K4 P–QB4 2. N–KB3 P–Q3 3. P–Q4 PxP 4. NxP N–KB3 5. N–QB3 P–QR3 6. P–KN3 P–K3

Inasmuch as Gligoric is willing to play this system as White, Boleslavsky refrains from 6. . . . P–K4; he had to consider that Gligoric might have prepared an improvement over his game against Najdorf in the 18th round.

7. B–N2 B–K2 8. O–O O–O 9. P–N3 Q–B2 10. B–N2 N–B3 11. N/3–K2 B–Q2 12. P–QB4

White wants to seize control of Q5, and against this Black starts removing all his pieces and pawns from the long diagonal, somewhat reducing the activity of the Bishop on KN2, and then he undermines White's QBP, achieving fully equal chances.

12. . . . QR–B1 13. R–B1 Q–N1 14. B–QR3 KR–Q1 15. Q–Q2 P–QN4 16. PxP PxP 17. B–N2 NxN 18. NxN Q–N3 19. P–QR3, Drawn.

## Game 166
### Queen's Indian Defense

**D. Bronstein**     **A. Kotov**

| | |
|---|---|
| 1. P–QB4 | N–KB3 |
| 2. N–KB3 | P–QN3 |
| 3. P–KN3 | B–N2 |
| 4. B–N2 | P–B4 |
| 5. O–O | P–K3 |
| 6. N–B3 | B–K2 |
| 7. P–Q4 | PxP |
| 8. NxP | BxB |
| 9. KxB | |

In the Queen's Indian Defense there often appears a fianchettoed . . . King. What prompted White to bring his Bishop to KN2 and then exchange it? Surely KN2 is not a very good place for the King. The positional struggle in the Queen's Indian Defense concerns the advance P–Q4 for Black: if White is able to prevent it he will have the better game, but if Black gets in P–Q4 the play will be equalized. White therefore trades Bishops in order to neutralize the Black QB's support of the advance of the QP, and thus the King finds itself on KN2.

In other variations, White plays N–K1 and recaptures on KN2 with the Knight.

9. . . .         Q–B1

This is also a characteristic maneuver in such positions. Taking advantage of White's undefended QBP and the position of White's King, Black gets his Queen onto the long diagonal without loss of time.

| 10. Q–Q3 | N–B3 |
|----------|------|
| 11. P–N3 | O–O |
| 12. B–N2 | R–Q1 |

An unhurried move, underlining the strength of Black's position. White no longer has the means to keep Black's QP in place.

| 13. QR–B1 | NxN |
|-----------|------|
| 14. QxN | B–B4 |
| 15. Q–B4 | Q–N2ch |
| 16. K–N1 | P–Q4 |
| 17. PxP | Drawn |

White's means of fighting for an advantage were too cautious and were therefore harmless.

## Game 167
### Nimzo-Indian Defense

| S. Reshevsky | Y. Geller |
|--------------|-----------|
| 1. P–Q4 | N–KB3 |
| 2. P–QB4 | P–K3 |
| 3. N–QB3 | B–N5 |
| 4. Q–B2 | P–Q4 |
| 5. PxP | PxP |
| 6. B–N5 | P–KR3 |
| 7. BxN | QxB |
| 8. P–QR3 | BxNch |
| 9. QxB | |

Why has Reshevsky brought the opening to this position? Is it not symmetrical? Does White have any advantage at all?

The position is symmetrical, but not completely. Geller's pawns are posted on light squares; consequently, the squares in front of the pawns are dark, and on those squares White can solidly establish a Knight which Geller's light-square Bishop will not be able to drive away. Furthermore, after the inevitable . . . P–QB3 there will appear in Black's camp a convenient hook for the attacking White pawns. White therefore has prospects for further improving his position. Black must of necessity work on the Kingside, but it is unclear what his plan for these operations will be.

| 9. . . . | O–O |
|----------|------|
| 10. P–K3 | P–B3 |
| 11. N–K2 | B–B4 |
| 12. N–B4 | N–Q2 |
| 13. B–K2 | KR–K1 |
| 14. O–O | N–B1 |
| 15. P–QN4 | N–K3 |
| 16. N–R5 | |

The opposite side of the standard minority attack shows up if White ingenuously exchanges Knights: 16. NxN RxN 17. P–N5 Q–N4 18. PxP RxBP 19. Q–N3 B–R6 20. B–B3 Bx

P!, and Black's Queenside remains whereas White's Kingside is already smashed. The combining of attack and defense is a precious and essential quality for every chess master. Enthusiasm only for one's own ideas generally leads to underestimation of the opponent's activities. Reshevsky, transgressing against this truth, ends up losing half a point.

| 16. | . . . | Q–N3 |
| 17. | N–N3 | QR–B1 |
| 18. | QR–B1 | N–N4 |

It always makes sense here for Black to start with . . . P–QR3 in order to provoke P–QR4 so that White's further "minority" advance will involve an exchange of pawns. The more pawns Black can exchange on the Queenside, the fewer weaknesses he will have there.

**19. P–N5**

The breakthrough is based on the fact that however Black replies after 19. . . . PxP 20. Q–N3 White will not only regain his pawn but win another.

| 19. | . . . | N–K5 |
| 20. | Q–R5 | |

The Queen attacks the QRP. If Black had in due course put it on QR3, he would now be in much less danger.

| 20. | . . . | P–B4! |

Geller does not lose his resourcefulness or presence of mind in difficult situations. Seeing that with "normal" moves Black must gradually lose the battle, he sacrifices a pawn, allowing White two connected passed pawns but creating interesting counterchances in view of his own far-advanced pawn on the QB-file. If now, for example, 21. QxRP, then 21. . . . P–B5.

| 21. | NxB | QxN |
| 22. | PxP | P–QN3! |
| 23. | QxRP | |

Of course not 23. PxP?? RxR 24. RxR QxPch.

| 23. | . . . | PxP |
| 24. | B–Q3 | P–B5 |
| 25. | BxN | QxB |
| 26. | KR–Q1 | P–B6 |
| 27. | Q–Q4 | |

Geller's tactics are vindicated. Fearing the speedy advance of the QBP followed by that of the QP, Reshevsky hurries to exchange Queens, after which serious drawing chances appear. Black's problems would be more difficult after 27. P–N6 or 27. R–Q4; for instance, 27. P–N6 P–B7 28. R–B1, but not 28. R–K1 P–Q5!

| 27. | . . . | R–B5 |
| 28. | QxQP | P–B7 |
| 29. | R–Q2 | QxQ |
| 30. | RxQ | R–R1 |
| 31. | P–N6 | R–N1 |

One of the rare cases in Geller's practice of his overlooking the chance for a saving combination, this one based on the White King's having no "luft." 31. ... RxP 32. P–N7 R–QN5 33. R–Q8ch K–R2 34. P–N8= Q RxQ 35. RxR R–Q6 36. R–B1 R–B6!, and White has nothing better than to go into a "four pawns against three" Rook endgame, which theory considers drawn. (A related ending is game 150, Gligoric–Euwe.)

| 32. | R–Q6 | R–QR5 |
|-----|------|-------|
| 33. | RxBP | RxRP |
| 34. | P–R3 | R–N6 |
| 35. | R/2–B6 | R–N7 |
| 36. | P–K4 | P–R4 |
| 37. | P–K5 | P–R5 |
| 38. | R–Q4 | |

It already seems that nothing will save Black here. All the same, I would not exchange the QNP for the outside KRP. Can't White shift his Rooks to the seventh rank? 38. P–K6 P–B3 39. R–B7 R/7xNP 40. R/6–Q7 would appear to work for White. By the way, a very similar sudden attack on KN7 was used by Reshevsky earlier in this tournament, against Euwe.

| 38. | ... | R/7xNP |
|-----|-----|--------|
| 39. | RxR | RxR |
| 40. | RxP | |

To understand the following stage it is necessary to keep in mind that there are Rook endings in which two extra pawns do not always win. For instance, the ending of Rook, KBP, and KRP against Rook sometimes cannot be won, and the same goes for the ending of Rook and two connected passed pawns against Rook, if the pawns can be blockaded. Geller hopes to bring the game to one of those endings.

| 40. | ... | R–N8ch |
|-----|-----|--------|
| 41. | K–R2 | R–K8 |
| 42. | P–B4 | R–K6 |
| 43. | R–N4 | K–R2 |
| 44. | R–N3 | R–K7 |
| 45. | P–R4 | R–K5 |
| 46. | R–KB3 | P–B3 |
| 47. | PxP | PxP |
| 48. | K–N3 | |

Thinking that he can win as he pleases, Reshevsky is playing carelessly. He should continue 48. P–N4. Now Black is able to make the important blockading move P–B4.

| 48. | ... | K–N3 |
|-----|-----|------|
| 49. | R–R3 | P–B4 |

Black has accomplished a great deal: his Rook and King

are active and White's pawns are awkward. Still, if White now played 50. R–R8, his two extra pawns would easily give him the point.

**50. R–R6ch    K–R4**

**51. R–KB6**

This second inaccuracy, surprisingly, finally lets the win escape. 51. R–R8 is still correct. True, now Black's King is restricted—too much so.

| 51. . . . | R–K6ch |
|-----------|--------|
| 52. K–B2  | R–QR6  |
| 53. P–N3  |        |

After 53. RxPch KxP one of those drawn positions arises, despite White's two extra pawns.

**53. . . .    R–B6ch!**

After 54. KxR or 54. K–N2 RxPch 55. KxR, it is stalemate! The King retreats to the K-file, but even this does not change the result. With White's Rook on QR8 there would be no stalemate in this variation and White would win.

**54. K–K2 RxNP 55. RxPch KxP 56. K–B2 R–QR6 57. R–KN5 R–QN6 58. R–N1 K–R4 59. K–K2 R–QR6 60. P–B5 R–R4, Drawn.**

## Game 168

On the eve of the 24th round Keres was half a point behind Smyslov, and on the next day Keres would be free. In the event of a draw with Smyslov he would remain half a point or even a full point behind, depending on Smyslov's result against Reshevsky in the 25th round. In these psychological circumstances, Keres had the idea of taking his chances on a sharp and unusual Kingside attack using two Rooks and no pawns.

Keres could not or would not make himself prepare his attack methodically and consistently. As early as the 19th move he offers the sacrifice of a Rook "for nothing," as they say in English. To me, the concept of a sacrifice is usually connected with some resounding check—BxPch or RxPch—whereupon the opponent must willy-nilly take the piece. The subtlest sacrifices, however, have a different look—a Rook is attacked and it is not touched . . .

## English Opening

| P. Keres | V. Smyslov |
|----------|------------|
| 1. P–QB4 | N–KB3 |
| 2. N–QB3 | P–K3 |
| 3. N–B3 | P–B4 |
| 4. P–K3 | B–K2 |
| 5. P–QN3 | O–O |
| 6. B–N2 | P–QN3 |
| 7. P–Q4 | PxP |
| 8. PxP | P–Q4 |
| 9. B–Q3 | N–B3 |
| 10. O–O | B–N2 |
| 11. R–B1 | |

If 11. Q–K2 Black can try to win a pawn without great risk: 11. . . . N–QN5 12. B–N1 PxP 13. PxP BxN and 14. . . . QxP.

| 11. . . . | R–B1 |
|-----------|------|
| 12. R–K1 | N–QN5 |
| 13. B–B1 | N–K5 |
| 14. P–QR3 | NxN |
| 15. RxN | |

White is halfway along his original plan to transfer his Rooks to the Kingside. However, 15. BxN is obviously unplayable because of . . . N–R7.

| 15. . . . | N–B3 |
|-----------|------|
| 16. N–K5 | NxN |
| 17. RxN | |

Both Rooks are ready to spring.

| 17. . . . | B–KB3 |
|-----------|-------|
| 18. R–R5 | P–N3 |

It is not inappropriate to mention that White already had some threats; namely, 19. Rx RP KxR 20. Q–R5ch K–N1 21. R–R3 B–R5 22. RxB P–B4 23. Q–R7ch with an irresistible attack.

**19. R/3–R3**

"I thought for a long time," Smyslov said afterward. "I wanted very much to take the Rook, the more so because I did not see how White could win here. . . ." Indeed, to take a whole Rook for nothing! His main worry was this: if he did not take it and then did not win the game—how annoying that would be! And after the next move the Rook will already have taken the KRP—try to catch it then! And so, since there was no question of his calculating all the variations over the board, it remained only to examine the main continuations and to have self-confidence.

**19. . . .       PxP**

Smyslov's intuition does not disappoint him: he makes the best move, as later analysis demonstrated. But how did he find it? What is the mechanism, if it can be so called, of a grandmaster's intuition? Did Smyslov reason it out, or did he simply guess it like a lucky number in a lottery? The text move occurred to him as a result, of course, of his deep understanding of the position. First of all, Black opens the diagonal for his Bishop, which may now be transferred to KB4 or KN3 via K5. Secondly, he opens the Q-file, and the possibility arises of putting the Queen on Q4 when the opportunity is presented and attacking KN7 on the long diagonal, or of simply taking the QP with the Queen. Thirdly, the passed pawn now on the QB-file can

advance to B6 and close the diagonal of the dangerous White Bishop. Meanwhile, White's Rook is under attack and is now really endangered by the threat of PxR. If 20. PxP, for instance, then 20. . . . PxR 21. QxP B–K5.

One is curious, nevertheless: What would happen if Black took the Rook right away? Wouldn't he be saved after 19. . . . PxR 20. QxP R–K1, opening an escape hatch for the King? It appears that White would cut him off by the hidden maneuver 21. P–R4!!, threatening B–R3. Examples:

1) 21. . . . PxP 22. QxRPch K–B1 23. B–R3ch R–K2 24. R–N3.

2) 21. . . . Q–Q3 22. P–B5 and further: a) 22. . . . PxP 23. Q–R6 B–N2 24. QxRPch K–B1 25. PxP; b) 22. . . . Q–Q1 23. P–B6 RxP 24. B–R3 R–Q3 25. Q–R6 BxP 26. B–Q3; c) 22. . . . Q–B5 23. QxRPch K–B1 24. B–R3 PxP 25. BxPch R–K2 26. R–N3 K–K1 27. B–N5ch.

**20. RxP**

Keres could still draw here by means of 20. Q–N4 P–B6 21. BxP RxB 22. RxR QxP 23. QxQ BxQ 24. R–B7 PxR 25. RxB, but he did not launch his attack for the sake of drawing.

**20. . . .       P–B6**

The Bishop can neither take the pawn—21. BxP RxB—nor

leave it—21. B–B1 QxP. Keres finds the best chance.

**21. Q–B1          QxP**

Taking the Bishop would be rash: 21. . . . PxB 22. Q–R6 QxP 23. R–R8ch BxR 24. Q–R7 mate.

| 22. | Q–R6 | KR–Q1 |
|-----|------|-------|
| 23. | B–B1 | B–N2 |
| 24. | Q–N5 | Q–B3 |
| 25. | Q–N4 | P–B7 |
| 26. | B–K2 | R–Q5 |

Accurate to the end. Black provokes P–B4 in order to open a diagonal for checks.

| 27. | P–B4 | R–Q8ch |
|-----|------|--------|
| 28. | BxR  | Q–Q5ch |
|     | **White resigns** | |

# Round Twenty-Five

## Game 169

In his struggle for the right to play a match for the world championship, Smyslov had to endure a heated encounter with Keres in the previous round, and in the 25th round Reshevsky, his other rival, was in a similarly aggressive mood.

At this point Reshevsky was half a point behind Smyslov and had played one more game. Strictly speaking, Reshevsky would not outdistance the leaders even by winning, but clearly he would not do it by drawing. The American grandmaster set himself the task of winning, whatever the cost.

## Reti Opening

| V. Smyslov | S. Reshevsky |
|---|---|
| 1. P–QB4 | N–KB3 |
| 2. N–QB3 | P–K3 |
| 3. N–B3 | B–N5 |
| 4. P–KN3 | P–QN3 |
| 5. B–N2 | B–N2 |
| 6. O–O | O–O |
| 7. Q–N3 | KBxN |

| | |
|---|---|
| 8. QxB | P–Q3 |
| 9. P–N3 | Q–K2 |
| 10. B–N2 | P–B4 |
| 11. P–Q4 | QN–Q2 |
| 12. QR–Q1 | B–K5 |

The rather unusual ... B–N5 and the ensuing exchange on QB6 were evidently planned earlier by Reshevsky. He wants to create a position far removed from theory and to do battle with Knights against Bishops.

The correct move, characteristic of the Queen's Indian Defense. With the Bishop now outside his pawn chain, he is no longer worried about P–Q5. The Bishop would be condemned to a passive role if it remained on QN2, but now it is worthy of its opponent on KN2.

411

| 13. PxP | NxP |
| 14. Q–K3 | |

A strong move, combining the tactical threat 15. BxN and 16. P–QN4 with the positional idea of either pushing the Bishop back or provoking the KP to advance to K4.

| 14. . . . | P–K4 |

Black has more or less neutralized the activity of both Bishops. The Black Bishop at K5 stands guard over one of them, and the other is restricted by Black pawns. True, Black's QP requires attention, but this is not very dangerous, and at present Black's position has no other weaknesses. White's further maneuvers are aimed at exchanging Black's Bishop for a Knight.

| 15. B–KR3 | P–QR4 |
| 16. N–R4 | KR–K1 |
| 17. P–B3 | |

Perhaps his purpose could be achieved without this move, for after 17. N–B5 Black would have to trade his Bishop; but Smyslov leaves himself the option of taking the Bishop on KN6 later, when it is more convenient.

| 17. . . . | B–N3 |
| 18. R–Q2 | QR–Q1 |
| 19. KR–Q1 | Q–B2 |
| 20. NxB | RPxN |
| 21. B–N2 | |

It cannot be said even now that the Bishop pair gives White any advantage. Positional equality has been established, which in this case promises not a draw but an interesting fight. In the next ten to twelve moves the players maneuver pieces, each keeping his plans hidden from the other and waiting for the distribution of forces to offer the chance for decisive action.

| 21. . . . | N–R4 |
| 22. Q–B3 | |

| 22. . . . | N–B3 |

The activity of White's Bishops is still limited, but the dark-square one can be transferred to K3, the intersection of two important diagonals. Black should avoid this and attempt to seize the initiative on the Kingside by playing 22. . . . P–B4!

It is possible to believe that Reshevsky deliberately refrained from this continuation here in order to play it after White's P–K4 so as to attempt to muddy the waters when the time control is nearer. Such tactics, however, do not work against Smyslov's logical and clear play.

| 23. | P-K4 | N-R4 |
|-----|------|------|
| 24. | Q-K3 | N-B3 |
| 25. | B-KR3 | N-R2 |
| 26. | R-K2 | N-B3 |
| 27. | R-KB1 | N-R4 |
| 28. | B-N2 | Q-K2 |
| 29. | B-B1 | Q-B2 |
| 30. | R-Q1 | K-R2 |
| 31. | Q-B2 | N-B3 |
| 32. | B-K3 | N-R4 |
| 33. | R-B2!! | |

I give this move two exclamation marks in order not to give one to each of Smyslov's moves. He emerges the victor in this game both as chess player and psychologist. Reshevsky has not divined the intricate pattern of his moves. Smyslov was only making it appear that he was preparing P-B4, while actually he was setting up a battery along the KN1-QR7 diagonal. Already the threat is P-QR3 and P-QN4 to drive the Knight away and attack the QP. R-B2 is played so that Black cannot reply to 34. P-QR3 with . . . NxQNP, and in order to support P-B5 in some variations. As for Black's pieces, their positions differ from those of eleven moves earlier only in that his King has moved from KN1 to KR2, and even this single change is of no use to Black.

33. . . .          P-B4

Reshevsky carries out the long-considered thrust when essentially he no longer has any great choice. The following events take place at a swift pace, in sharp contrast to the leisurely maneuvering of the previous stages.

| 34. | PxP | PxP |
|-----|-----|-----|
| 35. | P-KN4 | N-B5 |

In pursuit of his aim to complicate the game at any price, Reshevsky sacrifices a pawn.

| 36. | BxN | PxB |
|-----|-----|-----|
| 37. | Q-R4ch | K-N1 |

| 38. | PxP | P-Q4 |
|-----|-----|-----|

After the first pawn sacrifice comes a second, for the sake of getting a position in which the pawn count will temporarily have no significance. If by calm, accurate play White comes through this stage, his two extra pawns must count. And again Smyslov rises to the occasion, despite all his adversary's tactical skill.

39. PxP

If 39. RxP RxR 40. PxR Q–K4 with the threats . . . Q–R8ch, . . . N–Q6, or simply . . . QxBP.

**39. . . .** **Q–K4**
**40. R/2–Q2**

40. R–B4 is a mistake: 40. . . . Q–K6ch 41. K–R1 N–Q6.

**40. . . .** **R–Q3**
**41. R–Q4** **Q–K6ch**

Stronger is 41. . . . QxBP 42. QxP QxQ 43. RxQ R–K7. That position is reached in three moves, but White keeps his P/B5. But if on 41. . . . QxBP White replies 42. RxP, then 42. . . . Q–B7 43. R–K1 RxRch 44. QxR N–Q6 with complications.

**42. K–R1** **R–K4**
**43. QxP** **QxQ**
**44. RxQ** **R–K7**
**45. R–KN4**

The threat is P–B6 and P–Q6. White's pawns are ready to advance, and they now stand six to three!

**45. . . . K–B1 46. R–N6 N–N2 47. R–K6 RxRP 48. P–B4 R–QN7 49. R/1–K1 RxR 50. QPxR N–Q3 51. P–K7ch K–B2 52. B–Q5ch K–K1 53. B–B6ch K–B2 54. P–K8=Qch NxQ 55. BxNch K–B3 56. B–N6, Black resigns.**

In this game (as well as in the next one) the fate of the first prize was in fact decided. Smyslov revealed all his best qualities, whereas my conduct of the important game with Geller was beneath criticism.

## Game 170
### Queen's Gambit

**Y. Geller** **D. Bronstein**

**1. P–Q4 P–K3 2. N–KB3 N–KB3**

More appropriate for playing to win is 2. . . . P–KB4; Black is in a peaceful mood, however.

**3. P–B4 P–Q4 4. PxP PxP 5. N–B3 P–B3 6. Q–B2 B–KN5 7. B–N5 QN–Q2 8. P–K3 B–Q3 9. B–Q3 Q–B2 10.**

O–O–O P–KR3 11. B–R4 B–
N5 12. K–N1 BxQN 13. QxB
O–O

The invasion of K5 by the
Knight should not be delayed.
After 13. . . . N–K5 14. Q–B2
B–B4 White must consider the
possibility 15. . . . P–KN4.

14. P–KR3 B–R4 15. Q–B2
N–K5 16. BxN PxB 17. P–
KN4 B–N3 18. N–Q2

On 18. B–N3 a Queen sacrifice can be considered: 18. . . .
QxB 19. PxQ PxN 20. P–K4
N–B3. A Bishop and Knight
and the pawn on B6 would be
sufficient compensation.

18. . . . N–N3 19. N–B4 N–
Q4 20. B–N3 Q–Q2 21. N–K5
Q–K3 22. Q–N3 B–R2 23. R–
QB1

Black has gone too far, it
seems, in his unwillingness to
undertake active operations.
White has successfully exploited
his opponent's timid play and
has created some pressure
against Black's Queenside, although no real threats are yet
visible. Therefore, it was not
necessary to make the following pawn offer.

23. . . . P–QR4

24. QxP

Of course! I completely overlooked that my QN1 was controlled by White's Bishop. Now
Black's game goes rapidly
downhill.

24. . . . N–N5 25. N–B4 P–
QB4 26. PxP N–Q6 27. P–B6
P–B4 28. PxP BxP 29. KR–
N1 B–N3 30. R–B2 QR–B1
31. B–Q6 KR–K1 32. Q–Q7
Q–B3 33. P–B7 B–B4 34. Q–
N5 BxP 35. B–N3 B–K3 36.
N–Q6 N–N5 37. NxKR BxPch
38. K–B1 Q–K2 39. N–Q6
N–Q6ch 40. K–Q2 RxP 41.
Q–K8ch QxQ 42. NxQ R–Q2
43. R–B7, Black resigns.

## Game 171

The blockade in chess is not
only an important technical device but also one of the elements
of a strategical plan. The fight
against a piece may take the
following forms, arranged in
descending order: capture (destruction), exchange, attack,

blockade. An attacked piece can be defended in various ways: simplest of all is to retreat it, but it may be protected or the attacking piece may be captured. The purpose of a blockade is to deprive the target of its mobility and then to attack it.

A blockade, in the broad meaning of the term, can be applied to any piece, including even the King; but in practice, the blockade refers mainly to pawns. They are the easiest to blockade, and they are dangerous when mobile.

Which pieces are best able to fulfill the role of blockader? The Knight belongs in first place, of course, for not only does it block the pawn's way, it even attacks the squares behind it.

The Bishop also serves this purpose well, since it can single-handedly bar the advance of not only one pawn but several. A pawn may be blockaded by a pawn, but that is a double-edged sword, since the blockading pawn is itself blockaded.

These are the simplest blockading techniques, but reality in chess is far more complex. In Kotov's game with Gligoric, Black is able to set up a blockade along a large segment of the pawn chain and to severely inhibit the advance of not only pawns but even pieces. True, Gligoric is not given this success free of charge: he has to display great ingenuity, and, what is more, he has to sacrifice a couple of pawns.

## King's Indian Defense

| A. Kotov | S. Gligoric |
|----------|-------------|
| 1. P–Q4 | N–KB3 |
| 2. P–QB4 | P–KN3 |
| 3. N–QB3 | B–N2 |
| 4. P–K4 | P–Q3 |
| 5. P–B3 | O–O |
| 6. B–K3 | P–K4 |
| 7. P–Q5 | P–B4 |

Having experienced great difficulties in his games against Geller and Petrosian in connection with the constant threat of the breakthrough P–B5, Gligoric closes the center. Although he takes QB4 away from his own Knight, on the other hand he will retain firm control of Q5, even after his pawn on K4 leaves its post. Kotov's next move, 8. B–Q3, is the natural reaction for White. Its purpose is to create threats along the QN1–KR7 diagonal in the event of . . . P–KB4.

| 8. B–Q3 | N–R4 |
|---------|------|
| 9. KN–K2 | P–B4 |
| 10. PxP | PxP |
| 11. Q–B2 | P–K5! |

The first step in Black's blockading conception: he lures a White pawn to K4, where it will remain until the end of the game and prevent White from attempting to show any initiative along the diagonal on which he so threateningly stationed his Queen and Bishop. At the same time, he frees K4 for his pieces and clears an important diagonal for the operation of his "Indian" Bishop, in anticipation of White's Queenside castling. For all these advantages Black gives up one pawn, which at this stage is irrelevant.

**12. PxP      P–B5**
**13. B–B2      N–Q2**

Black's Knight is headed for K4, and White should get it out of there at any price: this explains the White Knight's following retreat to its original position.

The variation 14. P–K5 NxP 15. BxPch K–R1 holds no attraction for White because, although he would have an extra pawn and the appearance of an

attack on the King, his position would be utterly hopeless in view of the threats . . . NxBP, . . . P–B6, . . . Q–N4.

**14. N–KN1      Q–N4**
**15. B–B1      N–K4**

Black has won the first battle in having driven back the enemy forces, but he has not yet won the entire campaign. After regrouping, White's pieces will return to more active positions.

**16. N–B3      Q–K2**
**17. NxN      QxN**
**18. O–O–O      N–B3**
**19. P–KR3      B–Q2**

Gligoric likes to prepare his breakthroughs well. A more impatient player would not refrain from 19. . . . P–QR3 20. B–Q3 P–N4 21. PxP PxP 22. BxNP B–QR3 with a terrific attack along the QR- and QN-files and the long diagonal.

**20. B–Q3      P–QR3**
**21. N–N1**

Splendid! Now after . . . P–N4 White does not take the pawn but replies N–Q2, threatening one way or another to banish the Queen from the main blockading square.

**21. . . .      P–B6!!**

Beautifully played. The maneuver N–Q2–B3 might have led to the collapse of Black's entire blockading position. Gligoric reveals himself to be a

true chess artist; he gives up a
second pawn in order to deny
KB3 to White's Knight and ex-
tend the range of the blockade.

| 22. | PxP | N–R4 |
|-----|-----|------|
| 23. | N–Q2 | N–B5 |

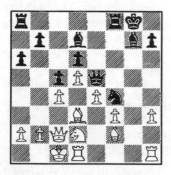

A classical model of the
blockaded position. The four
White pawns appear to be the
direct objects, but the blockade has far deeper influence;
White's light-square Bishop has
been transformed into a pawn,
his own pawns take away
his Knight's most important
squares, and furthermore, even
so mobile a piece as the Queen
is almost completely blockaded!
The threat now is no more or
less than mate in two, and after
the best defending move, there
follows, finally, the well-
prepared breakthrough.

One can only be astonished
at the defensive strength of
White's position and at the
mastery of Kotov, who despite
great difficulties nevertheless
maintains his equilibrium.

| 24. | B–B1 | P–N4 |
|-----|------|------|
| 25. | P–KR4 | K–R1 |
| 26. | R–N1 | B–KB3 |
| 27. | N–N3 | QR–N1 |

At this critical moment Black
does not display the appropriate
decisiveness. It is necessary to
work out the variations and advance one of the pawns. 27. . . .
P–QR4 28. PxP P–R5 29. N–
Q2 P–R6 30. N–B4 PxPch 31.
K–N1 Q–K2 does not work because then 32. P–K5 destroys
the blockade, but very strong
is 27. . . . P–N5 28. N–R5 B–
R5 29. P–N3, and Black has at
least perpetual check; but he can
move the Bishop back to Q2
and continue the attack.

| 28. | B–K1 | P–N5 |
|-----|------|------|
| 29. | K–N1 | R–R1 |

Black's Rook returns, but
White has markedly improved
his position: QB1 has become
available for his Knight, and
from there it can go to Q3 in
order to loosen the grip of the
blockade.

| 30. | B–N3 | R–KN1 |
|-----|------|-------|
| 31. | Q–R2 | |

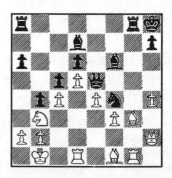

**31. . . .          RxB**

An exchanging combination on the theme "interference and distraction." If White's KBP and KP become mobile Black's game will collapse.

**32. RxR          N–K7**
**33. QxN          QxR**
**34. N–B1          P–QR4**
**35. N–Q3          B–Q5**

The Bishop has to be stationed near the center in view of the threat P–K5.

**36. P–R5          Q–R5**
**37. B–N2          R–KN1**
**38. R–R1          Q–N6**
**39. B–B1          P–R5**

The last moves before the time control were played in time pressure. Black could have advanced his QRP instead of maneuvering his Queen. Nor is White's next King move necessary.

**40. K–B2**

**40. . . .          P–R6**

Gligoric would retain some winning chances after 40. . . . P–N6ch 41. PxP PxPch 42. Kx P Q–N2 43. P–R6 B–R5ch 44. KxB Q–N2 or 43. K–B2 R– QN1 44. Q–N2 B–R5ch 45. K– B1 Q–N2.

**41. P–N3          Drawn**

After thorough analysis, the players came to the conclusion that Black could not win.

## Game 172

Is the first move really an advantage? This question, which every chess player asks himself, is not easy to answer.

In this regard, one cannot help recalling Vsevolod Rauzer —a most remarkable master and theoretician who proclaimed the formula, "1. P–K4! and White wins." This was probably said in jest, but in every

jest there is a grain of truth. Rauzer's conviction that opening with the King pawn gave White the advantage whereas P–Q4 led only to a draw inspired him to work out amazingly deep and powerful attacking systems in various openings—Sicilian, French, Ruy Lopez, Caro-Kann, and others. Granted, it was not the strength of P–K4 that had decisive importance in Master Rauzer's numerous victories, as it turned out, but his original talent, his unusually logical thought, his accuracy in calculation. Rauzer attacks and Rauzer variations are still alive and remain in use up to the present time, but Black can successfully defend against them. The working out of forced variations as a method of fighting the opening battle, which was a fearsome weapon in the hands of players like Morphy, Tchigorin, Pillsbury, Alekhine, Fine, and Botvinnik, can be used by Black as well as White. A prepared forced variation may run into a forced refutation, as occurred in several games in this tournament. There were and are no infallible chess players, and this applies both to over-the-board play and to analytical homework. This means, as a rule, that this is not the way to obtain an opening advantage.

There is, therefore, another interpretation of opening strategy, which can be formulated thus: it is not necessary to make best moves, but merely good ones.

This was the creative attitude of, for example, Lasker, Capablanca, Smyslov. The opening advantage here is considered to be the right of the player who has White to choose the system of development that best suits his taste, giving his individual creative ability its fullest scope.

Statistics—a reliable method for the study of mass phenomena—prove that an opening advantage for White actually exists. In every outstanding tournament for which calculations were performed, in several historical periods, White's advantage was invariably demonstrated in terms of the number of games won. This advantage for White should be considered a tendency, which, though manifested in tens or hundreds of games, should not influence the result of any given game. It would be extremely interesting to investigate this tendency in historical cross-section: has the percentage of White wins in our time, compared with, say, twenty, fifty, a hundred years ago, increased or decreased? I can mention one peculiarity: the stronger the composition of a tournament, the less the right of the first move influences the results of the games. This can be demonstrated, for instance, in the 1948 match-tournament for the world championship and in the 1951 world championship match, in which White won four games and Black six, and in several other contests. Does this mean that in the future the right of the first move will give no advantage whatever? Time will tell.

In this game the reader will

encounter a model by Boleslavsky of a well-prepared and accurately calculated opening, then an organic transition to a combinational middlegame, and from that to an interesting winning endgame for White. And finally, a resourceful counter-combination by Taimanov . . .

## Queen's Indian Defense

**I. Boleslavsky   M. Taimanov**

| 1. | P–Q4 | N–KB3 |
|----|------|-------|
| 2. | P–QB4 | P–K3 |
| 3. | N–KB3 | |

White's first "merely good" move. "Best" by unanimous consent is 3. N–QB3.

| 3. | . . . | P–QN3 |
|----|-------|-------|
| 4. | P–KN3 | B–N2 |
| 5. | B–N2 | B–K2 |
| 6. | O–O | O–O |
| 7. | N–B3 | N–K5 |

Unlike the King's Indian Defense, in which Black is obliged to observe his K5-square vigilantly, here he is indifferent toward the position of White's KP. The explanation is simple: in the King's Indian Black places his central pawns on Q3 and K4, and his QB remains on the marvelous working diagonal QB1–KR6. But here Black's Bishop is developed on QN2 and its working diagonal is QR1–KR8. Consequently, the fewer pawns cluttering the road from QN2 to KB6, the richer Black's prospects. The next phase of the game is the familiar struggle for and against White's P–K4, and Boleslavsky proves to be in charge; unlike Tai-

manov, he does not forget about another possibility—shutting out the QB by P–Q5.

| 8. | Q–B2 | NxN |
|----|------|-----|
| 9. | QxN | |

The second and third "merely good" moves. The advantage has been restlessly sought through the moves 8. B–Q2 and 9. PxN. The latter move, in fact, is strongly met by the retort 9. . . . N–B3. (See the Najdorf-Averbakh game.)

| 9. | . . . | P–KB4 |
|----|-------|-------|

Opinions concerning this fashionable move differ greatly. It suffices to say that some consider it defensive, others aggressive.

The author is a modest expert on the Queen's Indian, and, although the continuation 9. . . . P–KB4 was seen in the third and last meeting between the former and the present world champions (Amsterdam 1938, games A. Alekhine–M. Botvinnik), it seems to me that Keres, who prefers the unhurried transfer of the Bishop to a better position by 9. . . . B–K5, is more correct. The KBP belongs on KB2 in this opening. The pawns on Q3, K3, and KB4 overload the QB1–KR6 diagonal.

**10. P–N3        B–KB3**
**11. B–N2        N–B3**

Black realizes, of course, that QB3 is not the place for the Knight; he is using QB3 as a springboard for its transfer to the Kingside. However, Black thus loses yet another move and accelerates White's growing advantage. White, making use of his advantage in time, methodically prepares and carries out the important advance P–Q5, severely restricting the activity of Black's light-square Bishop.

**12. QR–Q1       Q–K1**
**13. Q–B2        N–Q1**
**14. P–Q5**

Black could no longer prevent this attack. The same 14. P–Q5 would have followed 13. . . . N–K2; the variation 14. . . . BxB 15. QxB PxP 16. N–N5 Q–N3 17. N–R3 is in White's favor.

**14. . . .        BxB**
**15. QxB         PxP**

Black must dislodge the White pawn from his Q4 at any price. If Black plays inactively there follows the very powerful 16. N–Q4, and the opening of the center by P–K4 will be unavoidable.

**16. PxP         P–B4**
**17. PxP e.p.    PxP**
**18. N–K5!       R–B3**

Black's position is undeniably bad. We see that it is not necessary to make gross blunders to lose a game of chess; it is enough to play the opening superficially. But from this moment Taimanov begins to play at full strength and demonstrates his usual resourcefulness and inventiveness.

**19. P–B4**

Boleslavsky's combinational style is notable for one characteristic in particular: strict logic interlaced with tactical strokes. The style of Smyslov or V. Makogonov would probably be to play the more restrained 19. R–Q2 and later KR–Q1, and if 19. . . . R–K3 then the temporary retreat 20. N–Q3.

**19. . . .        N–B2**
**20. R–Q7**

Forcing a series of exchanges.

**20. . . .        NxN**
**21. PxN         QxR**
**22. PxR**

The position of the KBP, behind Black's, is very unusual.

| 22. ... | R–KB1 |
|---|---|
| 23. PxP | QxP |
| 24. QxQch | KxQ |
| 25. P–K4! | PxP |
| 26. RxR | KxR |
| 27. BxP | |

Is that all?, the reader asks. Yes, and it is not so little. It is well known that as the number of pieces on the board decreases the significance of one or another weakness increases.

But White has at least three advantages here:

1) White's Bishop is active, Black's is not;

2) White can create a passed pawn, on the KR- or KN-file, before Black;

3) White's King also gets to the center of the battlefield sooner.

These advantages are quite enough to win.

| 27. ... | P–KR3 |
|---|---|
| 28. K–B2 | K–K2 |
| 29. K–B3 | P–QR4 |
| 30. K–N4 | B–B1ch |

Correct—Black sacrifices a pawn but activates his Bishop. On the passive 30. ... K–B3 31. K–R5 K–N2 32. P–KN4 and P–N5 Black loses without a struggle.

| 31. K–R5 | P–B4 |
|---|---|
| 32. KxP | K–B3! |

Black defends excellently. White's King is pinned to the KR-file and thus his KRP is impeded.

| 33. B–B3 | P–R5 |
|---|---|

A trial balloon. White must decide whether Black's threat of P–R6 followed by B–B4–N8xP or B–K3xP is dangerous.

**34. PxP**

Boleslavsky conceives an interesting combination, but Taimanov will find an unexpected refutation. The immediate P–KN4 is better, and White will queen on N8 before Black can organize a breakthrough on the other side.

| 34. ... | P–B5 |
|---|---|
| 35. P–N4 | P–B6 |
| 36. P–N5ch | K–K4 |
| 37. B–Q1 | B–N5 |
| 38. B–B2 | B–B4 |
| 39. P–N6! | BxB |
| 40. P–N7 | |

Not doubting that after 40. ... B–N6 41. PxB P–B7 42. P–N8=Q P–B8=Q 43. Q–N5ch and the compulsory exchange of Queens, White's KRP will advance to queen.

**40. . . .        B–R2**

Taimanov's correction. Black is able to avoid the exchange of Queens, for White's King has to move away from KN5.

**41. KxB        P–B7**
**42. P–N8=Q    P–B8=Q**
**43. Q–N8ch**

The Queen ending also promises Black little joy, but all the same it is a Queen ending with all its characteristic drawing chances. White is unsettled by the unexpected turn in a game that seemed already over. Boleslavsky's further play is planless, and in the end he himself overlooks a drawing Queen exchange.

**43. . . .        K–Q4**
**44. Q–N7ch    K–K4**
**45. Q–N7ch**

He should simply devour the NP.

**45. . . .        K–Q4**
**46. Q–B7ch    K–K4**
**47. P–R4       Q–B7ch**
**48. K–N7       QxP/5**
**49. Q–B6ch    K–K5**
**50. Q–K6ch**

And now he should advance his pawn to queen. It is a mistake for White to push the Black King nearer the KRP.

**50. . . .        K–B5**
**51. P–R5       K–N4**
**52. Q–K5ch    K–N5**
**53. P–R6       Q–Q2ch**
**54. K–B6       Q–Q1ch**
**55. K–B7       Q–Q2ch**
**56. Q–K7       Q–Q6**
**57. Q–K6ch    K–R4**
**58. K–K8       P–N4**

The advance of this pawn would seem to be inoffensive to White: what difference does it make whether it is on N6 or N4? White uncaringly repeats moves.

**59. K–K7       P–N5**
**60. K–K8       Q–N3ch!**

Draw agreed. After 61. Qx Qch KxQ 62. K–Q7 KxP 63. K–B6 K–N3 64. K–N5 K–B2 65. KxP K–K1 66. K–N5 K–Q1 67. K–N6, Black's King manages to get to QB1 just in time. The exchange of Queens was unplayable while Black's pawn was situated on N3 (or N4), since White's King could have occupied QN7, ensuring the march P–R4–5 . . . 8=Q.

## Game 173
### King's Indian Defense

| G. Stahlberg | M. Najdorf |
|---|---|
| 1. P–Q4 | N–KB3 |
| 2. P–QB4 | P–KN3 |
| 3. P–KN3 | B–N2 |
| 4. B–N2 | O–O |
| 5. N–QB3 | P–B4 |
| 6. P–Q5 | P–K4 |

A defense used by Najdorf more than once before the tournament in Switzerland and refuted by Euwe in game 58. After a respectable interval, Najdorf uses it again, no longer worried about Euwe's 7. B–N5, on which he plans to reply 7. . . . P–Q3 8. N–K4 Q–R4ch or 8. Q–Q2 P–QR3.

| 7. N–B3 | P–Q3 |
| 8. O–O | QN–Q2 |
| 9. Q–B2 | Q–K2 |
| 10. P–K4 | P–QR3 |
| 11. P–QR4 | N–R4 |
| 12. B–Q2 | K–R1 |

Black is preparing the freeing and counterattacking advance P–B4 and for this purpose has conceived the maneuver N/2–B3–N1. The immediate 12. . . . P–B4 is no good in view of 13. N–KN5 N/2–B3 14. PxP BxP 15. N/5–K4, and the pin is not dangerous because the Knight on K4 is amply defended. Interesting in this variation is 14. N–K6?! so as to open his KB's diagonal after . . . BxN.

### 13. P–R5

While Black is occupied with his complicated maneuver on the Kingside, White threatens to blockade the Queenside and with 14. N–QR4 and P–QN4 to beat his opponent to the attack. Therefore, Najdorf's following sharp move is in a sense the only one to retain the possibility of a struggle with mutual chances.

| 13. . . . | P–QN4 |
| 14. PxP | |

Stahlberg decides to give up a Rook for a Bishop and a pawn on the QR-file. He later concluded that keeping his positional advantage with the simple PxP e.p. would have been preferable. His self-criticism is laudable, but I don't think Stahlberg's text move is any worse than 14. PxP e.p.

| 14. . . . | PxP |
| 15. NxNP | B–QR3 |
| 16. N–R3 | |

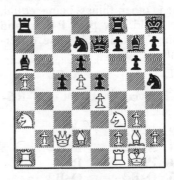

If White were afraid of losing he could play 16. N–B7 BxR 17. BxB QR–B1 18. N–N5 and Black would have nothing better than to return his Rook to QR1. Stahlberg is fighting for a win.

| 16. . . . | BxR |
| 17. RxB | |

Having given up the Exchange, White must advance his passed pawn as rapidly as possible, and for this purpose it is better to leave the Rook on

QR1 and put the Bishop on KB1. If Black is able to blockade the QRP, the advantage will most likely be his.

| 17. . . . | N/4–B3 |
|-----------|--------|
| 18. N–B4  | N–K1   |
| 19. B–R3  | R–R2   |
| 20. B–K3  | R–N2   |

White was threatening $\overline{P-}$QN4.

**21. R–R1**

Rather disappointed, Stahlberg puts the Rook back on QR1. If only he had taken with the Bishop on his 17th move, then, other things being equal, he could now play P–R6, and things would look quite different.

| 21. . . . | N–B2 |
|-----------|------|

Parrying the threat of P–R6–7 just in time.

| 22. Q–R4  | N–N1  |
|-----------|-------|
| 23. N–N6  | P–B4  |
| 24. PxP   | PxP   |
| 25. Q–R4  | Q–B2  |
| 26. B–R6  | N/1–R3|
| 27. N–B4  | N–N4  |
| 28. N–K3  | P–KB5 |

Having blockaded the QRP, Black goes over to attack on the other flank.

| 29. BxBch | QxB   |
|-----------|-------|
| 30. N–B5  | Q–N3  |
| 31. Q–N4  | QxQ   |
| 32. BxQ   | R–R2  |
| 33. N–Q2  | N–N5  |
| 34. N–B4  | R–B3  |
| 35. R–Q1  | K–N1  |

The exchange of Queens initiated a difficult ending in which the chances are clearly Black's, but the play is very complicated, since eight pieces roam the board and a surprise from any of them may be expected.

It is instructive to follow how the players endeavor to limit the activity of the enemy pieces by keeping them chained to the defense of weaknesses. Thus, a Black Rook and Knight are attached to his QP, while a White Knight, Bishop, and Rook defend his QRP, his QP, and his Knight at B5. The Black King approaches the battlefield.

| 36. B–R3  | K–B1     |
|-----------|----------|
| 37. K–N2  | R/2–KB2  |
| 38. N–R4  | PxP      |
| 39. BPxP  | N–Q5     |
| 40. B–K6  |          |

An interesting but insufficient chance, seeming again to complicate a by now simplified position. If 40. . . . NxB 41. PxN RxP 42. NxQP R–Q2 43. R–B1ch, etc. Najdorf finds a particularly interesting refutation.

| 40. . . . | R–B7ch |
|---|---|
| 41. K–R3 | R–B8 |

The game was adjourned here, and after analysis Black confidently brought his advantage to victory.

White has a choice—which Rook should he take? If Stahlberg plays 42. BxR there follows 42. . . . RxR 43. B–R5 R–QR8 44. NxQP NxP 45. N–N7 P–K5 46. NxP P–K6 47. N–N2 P–K7 48. N–Q3 N–KB3 49. B–N4 P–R4 50. B–B8 N–B6 and Black wins a piece. This variation, given by Najdorf, is testi-

mony that he did not waste his time between playing sessions.

42. RxR RxR 43. NxQP NxB 44. PxN K–K2 45. N–K4 KxP 46. NxPch K–Q4 47. N–R4 P–K5 48. K–N2 R–QR8 49. N–B3ch K–K4 50. P–N4 RxP 51. N–B5 N–Q4 52. N–Q1 R–R8 53. N–B2 N–B5ch 54. K–N3 R–N8ch 55. K–R4 R–N7 56. N–Q1 RxRPch 57. K–N3 R–R6ch 58. K–B2 R–B6ch 59. K–K1 P–R4 60. N/1–K3 P–R5 61. P–N5 P–R6, White resigns.

## Game 174
### Old Indian Defense

| M. Euwe | T. Petrosian |
|---|---|

1. P–Q4 N–KB3 2. P–QB4 P–Q3 3. N–QB3 P–K4 4. N–B3 QN–Q2 5. B–N5 B–K2 6. P–K3 O–O 7. Q B2 P–B3 8. B–Q3 PxP 9. PxP R–K1 10. O–O P–KR3 11. B–Q2 N–B1 12. P–KR3 N–K3 13. QR–K1 P–Q4 14. PxP PxP 15. Q–N3 B–B1 16. R–K2 Q–Q3 17. B–B1 (The fatigued players display no willingness to fight.) 17. . . . P–R3 18. KR–K1 P–QN4 19. B–B5 B–Q2 20. P–R3 QR–B1 21. Q–Q1 N–B2 22. BxB NxB 23. N–K5, Drawn.

## Game 175

A curious game in which Szabo twice overlooks simple "little combinations" on the very same Q4-square, but he is

nevertheless able to set up a drawn position after inaccuracies by Averbakh.

## Sicilian Defense

| L. Szabo | Y. Averbakh |
|---|---|
| 1. P–K4 | P–QB4 |
| 2. N–KB3 | N–QB3 |
| 3. B–N5 | P–KN3 |
| 4. O–O | B–N2 |
| 5. N–B3 | P–Q3 |
| 6. P–Q3 | |

A comparatively rare and not very active system in the Sicilian. White is in no hurry to play P–Q4, and since his pawns are posted on light squares he makes no secret of his intention to exchange his light-square Bishop.

| 6. . . . | B–Q2 |
|---|---|
| 7. N–Q5 | P–K3 |
| 8. N–K3 | KN–K2 |
| 9. P–B3 | O–O |
| 10. P–Q4 | NxP |

A technical maneuver for getting out of a pin: the pinned piece attacks one of the opponent's pieces and simultaneously attacks the pinning piece. Such tricks are often possible; for instance, with Black's Queen on Q1 and his Knight on KB3 and with White's Bishop on KN5 and his Queen on QB3, Black plays N–K5, attacking the Queen with his Knight and the Bishop with his Queen.

This "little combination" does not entail material loss for White in this case, but it gives Black free play.

| 11. NxN | PxN |
|---|---|
| 12. BxB | PxN |
| 13. QxP | |

He has to go into this rather risky continuation in order not to be a pawn down.

| 13. . . . | PxPch |
|---|---|
| 14. RxP | N–B3 |
| 15. B–B4 | Q–N3 |
| 16. R–Q1 | |

It was time for the unpretentious capture on QB6 and playing the Bishop to N5.

| 16. . . . | QR–Q1 |
|---|---|
| 17. Q–B7 | B–Q5 |

Again in the same place! Black cuts off the White Rook's active file and deprives the B/Q7 of its protection. After this he quickly doubles Rooks and wins the QP. A very elegant combination.

| 18. PxB | QxQ |
|---|---|
| 19. BxQ | RxB |
| 20. B–N3 | P–B4 |

No doubt Averbakh thinks he will always be able to take the pawn. He does not want to take it immediately because of some complications: 20. . . . RxP 21. RxR NxR 22. B–K5 N–B3 23. B–B6 or 22. . . . R–Q1 23. B–B6 R–Q2 24. K–B1 N–B3 25. R–B2. On 20. . . . R/1–Q1 there may follow 21. R/1–KB1 NxP 22. B–R4 R–QB1 23. B–B6. In both cases Black's win would be unclear despite his extra pawn. Black wants to create the best working conditions for his Knight and to avoid the possibility of the cramping B–B6 in the above variation.

**21. P–Q5!**

Black counted on provoking either the trade or the advance of the KP, after which the position of his Knight on QB3 would become stronger; for example, 21. PxP RxBP 22. RxR NPxR 23. B–B2 R–Q4! and P–K4. But Szabo has found a witty countercombination: if 21. . . . BPxP 22. RxRch KxR 23. R–B1ch and 24. PxN. Black therefore has to take on Q4, and an equal ending arises.

**21. . . . KPxP 22. RxQP R/2–KB2 23. PxP RxP 24. R/2xR RxR 25. R–Q7 R–B2 26. R–Q6 K–B1 27. P–QR3, Drawn.**

# Round Twenty-Six

## Game 176
### Nimzo-Indian Defense

| Y. Averbakh | M. Euwe |
|---|---|
| 1. P–Q4 | N–KB3 |
| 2. P–QB4 | P–K3 |
| 3. N–QB3 | B–N5 |
| 4. P–K3 | P–B4 |
| 5. N–B3 | O–O |
| 6. B–Q3 | P–Q4 |
| 7. O–O | N–B3 |
| 8. P–QR3 | BxN |
| 9. PxB | QPxP |
| 10. BxP | Q–B2 |
| 11. B–Q3 | P–K4 |
| 12. Q–B2 | Q–K2 |

By the end of the tournament the grandmasters' inventiveness in the opening is running a little low. Averbakh repeats the opening of game 39, Bronstein–Euwe, in which White got excellent chances. In that game Euwe played 12. . . . R–K1 with the idea of restraining White's P–K4 for as long as possible, but that move turns out to be playable anyway, since after 13. . . . KPxP 14. PxP PxP the opposition of the Queens allows 15. NxP. In this sense, 12. . . . Q–K2 is more effective. After the Zurich tournament everyone was playing 12. . . . R–K1! hoping for 13. P–K4 P–B5!

| 13. PxKP | NxP |
|---|---|
| 14. NxN | QxN |
| 15. R–K1 | B–Q2 |

Thus ends the opening. The theme of the struggle in the next stage is White's P–K4, but to this are added many secondary themes. In particular, White's QB is blocked by pawns, and later Black keeps it locked in at the cost of a pawn. Another point is that White has been deprived of his Knight at KB3, a staunch defender of the Kingside; this gives Euwe the idea of undertaking a sharp attack against White's King. It should be acknowledged that in general Black has solved the problems of the opening successfully, but his last move, B–Q2, is part of a tactical trap and has no place in his overall scheme. If 16. P–K4 B–R5! 17. QxB? QxBP. Instead, he could considerably strengthen his attack on the King with 15. . . . R–K1, so as to answer 16. P–K4 with 16. . . . N–N5 17. P–KB4 Q–R4 18. P–R3 P–B5 with the better game, or, as played, if 16. B–N2 P–B5.

## 16. B–N2        P–B5

A beautiful, courageous move: the QBP perishes to prevent White from playing P–QB4, without which his Bishop on QN2 will be trapped and lifeless. There is also a tactical element here: Averbakh will have to keep a watchful eye on his KN1–QB5 diagonal, since by jumping to QB4 Black's Queen will also attack the Bishop on QB5, which may be very unpleasant for White.

## 17. BxP         N–N5
## 18. P–B4

On 18. P–N3 Black carries out an invasion of the light squares in accordance with a well-known technique that should be part of every player's equipment: 18. . . . Q–KR4 19. P–KR4 N–K4 20. B–K2 B–N5.

## 18. . . .        Q–QB4

Put Black's Bishop back on QB1 and his KR on K1 and you will see that on 15. . . . R–K1 the move 16. B–N2 would have been simply bad.

## 19. Q–Q3        QR–Q1
## 20. QR–Q1

In connection with his last move, this is a bold and original idea that identifies Averbakh as a genuine artist. I'm not even referring to the long calculation that was necessary. Many would be enticed here by Najdorf's recommended 20. Q–Q4, but this leads to immediate collapse: 20. . . . Q–KR4 21. P–R3 B–B3! 22. PxN QxP, and Black wins the Queen for a Rook and a piece.

20. B–Q5 was tempting, but then some symmetrical Bishop move (K3–B3, B4–N4) in connection with the threat . . . NxKP would probably give Black the possibility of a comfortable endgame, if not an advantage. Now, however, White keeps his extra pawn in spite of a superb defense by Euwe.

**20. . . .      Q–N3**

Black defends his Rook, renewing the threat of B–R5, and at the same time he attacks the Bishop.

**21. Q–K2**

White removes his Queen from a dangerous spot, defends his Bishop on N2, and attacks the Knight, bringing matters to a head.

**21. . . .      NxKP**
**22. QxN      QxB**
**23. R–K2      Q–N3!**

Attack and defense at their best. Black offers to trade Queens as though he doesn't see White's threat to double on the Q-file and win a piece. The exchange of Queens, however, is Black's only chance to hold the game, and his Bishop will not be lost because he can attack White's Bishop with his Rook and thus free himself from the pin (25. R/2–Q2 R–B1).

**24. QxQ      PxQ**
**25. R–K7**

**25. . . .      B–K3**
**26. RxR      RxR**
**27. BxB      PxB**
**28. RxNP      R–QB1**
**29. RxP      RxP**
**30. R–R6      K–B2**

Thus we get an ending in which White has an extra, outside pawn that can be attacked from behind by Black's Rook. This type of ending is usually considered drawn. The pawn cannot be promoted without the help of the King, and while the King is getting to the QR-file Black's Rook or King can take a couple of pawns on the Kingside, after which as a last resort the Rook can be given up for the passed pawn.

**31. K–B2      P–R4**
**32. P–QR4      R–QR6**
**33. P–R4      K–B3**
**34. R–R5      P–N3**
**35. K–K2      R–KN6?**

The draw is easily achieved by the rudimentary 35. . . . R–R7ch.

**36. R–KN5!**

Now White's Rook defends both pawns, and his King is free to approach the passed QRP.

36. ... R–QR6 37. P–R5

K–B2 38. K–Q2 K–K2 39. K–B2 K–Q2 40. K–N2 R–R5 41. P–N3 K–B3 42. K–N3 R–R8 43. K–N4 R–N8ch 44. K–B4 R–QR8 45. K–B3, Black resigns.

## Game 177

This entire game is an outstanding example of Petrosian's artistry. The game's original positional design, its logic, its consistency create an integrated work of art.

It is interesting that annotators of this game, Stahlberg among them, found no noticeable mistake by Black! The nuances of modern chess are so subtle that mistakes are difficult to discern even in analysis, let alone in over-the-board play.

### Sicilian Defense

| T. Petrosian | G. Stahlberg |
|---|---|
| 1. P–K4 | P–QB4 |
| 2. P–Q3 | N–QB3 |
| 3. N–KB3 | P–KN3 |
| 4. P–KN3 | B–N2 |
| 5. B–N2 | P–Q3 |
| 6. O–O | N–B3 |
| 7. QN–Q2 | O–O |
| 8. P–QR4 | B–Q2 |
| 9. N–B4 | Q–B1 |
| 10. R–K1 | |

No doubt the reader has noticed that Petrosian is playing the King's Indian Defense with the White pieces. Defense against what? The King's Indian is usually played against White's P–Q4, but here Black has not played a corresponding P–Q4; his setup resembles the Dragon

Variation of the Sicilian Defense. This is an example of the clash of openings that characterizes modern play. The forces of both sides are arranged according to definite schemes, but they occupy their own territory and for the time being do not come in contact.

| 10. ... | N–KN5 |
|---|---|
| 11. P–B3 | P–KR3 |
| 12. Q–K2 | K–R2 |
| 13. N/3–Q2 | P–B4 |

Black, fooled by his opponent's outwardly quiet development, starts a skirmish and commits a serious inaccuracy, weakening not only his Kingside but also his central squares. Most appropriate for him is to put his Queen on QB2 instead of QB1, his Rooks on K1 and Q1, and gradually to prepare P–Q4.

| 14. | P–B4 | PxP |
| 15. | PxP | N–B3 |
| 16. | N–B3 | B–N5 |
| 17. | N–K3 | B–R6 |
| 18. | N–R4 | BxB |
| 19. | QxB | P–K3 |
| 20. | Q–QB2 | |

White's position uncoils like a spring. His pieces and pawns turn out to be harmoniously posted for operations in the center and on the right. Black has weak pawns on Q3 and K3. There is danger of a whirlwind's suddenly sweeping all obstacles from White's QN1–KR7 diagonal.

| 20. | . . . | N–K2 |
| 21. | N–B4 | N–K1 |
| 22. | B–Q2 | Q–B3 |
| 23. | R–K2 | R–Q1 |
| 24. | QR–K1 | P–QN4 |

Aware of White's superiority on the Kingside and in the center, Stahlberg takes his chances on the other wing, but White's position is solid enough there too.

| 25. | PxP | QxNP |
| 26. | N–K3 | R–QN1 |
| 27. | B–B1 | B–B3 |
| 28. | N–B3 | P–B5 |
| 29. | K–N2 | |

He is in no hurry, sure of his power.

| 29. | . . . | B–N2 |
| 30. | P–R4 | K–N1 |
| 31. | R–Q1 | R–B1 |
| 32. | P–K5 | |

An elegant breakthrough! Now 32. . . . P–Q4 33. P–R5 would lead to an utterly hopeless position. Taking the pawn looks relatively safe and even appears to give Black counterchances; e.g., 32. . . . PxP 33. NxKP BxN 34. PxB Q–B3ch. But Petrosian's idea is much more subtle.

| 32. | . . . | PxP |
| 33. | Q–K4 | R–QB4 |
| 34. | PxP | Q–B3 |
| 35. | N–B2 | QxQ |
| 36. | RxQ | N–QB3 |
| 37. | N–K3 | N–R4 |

The KP is hanging by a thread, but Black cannot take it here or on his next move. For instance, 37. . . . NxP 38. NxN RxN 39. RxR BxR 40. NxP B–N2 41. B–K3, and White wins the QRP: 41. . . . P–R3 42. R–QR1 N–B2 43. B–N6.

| 38. | N–Q2 | N–B2 |
| 39. | N/3xP | R–Q1 |
| 40. | R/1–K1 | NxN |
| 41. | NxN | N–Q4 |
| 42. | N–Q2 | R–N1 |
| 43. | R–R4 | R–B2 |
| 44. | N–B3 | N–N3 |
| 45. | R–KN4 | K–R2 |
| 46. | N–Q4 | R–K1 |

Black has lost a pawn and his weaknesses remain, so a victory for White is quite natural. A certain accuracy is required, however: the Queenside pawns must be reinforced, and, if absolutely necessary, the KP can be given up in exchange for the QRP in order to form two connected passed pawns more quickly. The following moves are directed toward this end.

| | |
|---|---|
| 47. R/4–K4 | P–R3 |
| 48. R/1–K2 | N–Q2 |
| 49. N–B3 | R–QN1 |
| 50. B–K3 | B–B1 |
| 51. R–R4 | R–B3 |
| 52. B–Q4 | R–N4 |
| 53. P–QN4 | B–N2 |
| 54. R/2–R2 | NxP |
| 55. NxN | BxN |
| 56. BxB | RxB |
| 57. RxP | |

| | |
|---|---|
| 57. . . . | RxR |

If only Black could take the QBP he would be saved, but 57. . . . RxP? 58. R–R7ch K–N1 59. R–R8ch K–B2 60. R/2–R7ch K–B3 61. R–B8—mate!

58. RxR K–N2 59. P–B4 K–B3 60. P–N5 R–K7ch 61. K–B3 R–B7 62. R–B6 R–B6ch 63. K–B4 R–B8 64. P–N6 R–QN8 65. P–N4 K–K2 66. K–K5 R–K8ch 67. K–Q4, Black resigns.

## Game 178
### King's Indian Defense

| M. Najdorf | I. Boleslavsky |
|---|---|
| 1. P–Q4 | N–KB3 |
| 2. P–QB4 | P–KN3 |
| 3. P–KN3 | B–N2 |
| 4. B–N2 | O–O |
| 5. N–KB3 | P–Q3 |
| 6. O–O | P–B4 |
| 7. PxP | PxP |
| 8. N–K5 | |

A valuable innovation by Najdorf. The transfer of the Knight from KB3 to Q3 infuses this seemingly inoffensive variation with new possibilities. It was concluded after the tournament that the best reply here is 8. . . . KN–Q2! 9. N–Q3 N–QB3. Boleslavsky chooses a more natural continuation, but it is just the one that Najdorf's variation was counting on.

| | |
|---|---|
| 8. . . . | Q–B2 |
| 9. N–Q3 | N–B3 |

| 10. | N–B3 | B–B4 |
|-----|------|------|
| 11. | B–B4 | Q–R4 |
| 12. | B–Q2 | |

The persecution of Black's Queen continues. Black must make the important concession of giving up his light-square Bishop. White's Bishop on KN2 will now have no proper opponent, and this will be felt for the rest of the game.

| 12. | . . . | BxN |
|-----|-------|-----|
| 13. | PxB | Q–B2 |
| 14. | B–K3 | KR–Q1 |

A chess player today is guided in the choice of a move not by a position's outward appearance but by concrete evaluation of the several possibilities. Black could occupy Q5 with a Knight, but he has also considered that subsequently he would not have sufficient prospects for strengthening his position, and meanwhile White could play R–QN1, P–QN4, etc. This, in connection with White's working Bishop on the KR1–QR8 diagonal, would pose a serious threat to Black's Queenside. Furthermore, on Q5 the Knight would actually be protecting White's weak QP from direct attack along the Q-file. That is why Black rejects the "strategical" N–Q5 in favor of the combinational KR–Q1, taking aim at the QP.

| 15. | BxP | N–K4 |
|-----|-----|------|
| 16. | P–Q4 | NxP |
| 17. | Q–K2 | N–Q3 |

The position has undergone a number of small changes. White's QB has moved to QB5 and hampers Black's activity. White's QP has advanced one more square but remains isolated, meaning weak. Is it weak? The defects of an isolated pawn are often mentioned but its advantages are often forgotten. One of these is the absence of pawns on the neighboring files, which will favor the side with the isolated pawn if he can put his heavy pieces on them. The absence of pawns on the QB-file and K-file obviously does not favor Black. His Queen, for instance, is very uncomfortable on QB2: the long-range power of White's Bishops is making itself felt. Black makes the only correct decision in the circumstances: he attacks and destroys the QP, the fulcrum of White's center, as soon as he can.

| 18. | P–QR4 | P–K3 |
|-----|-------|------|
| 19. | P–R5 | N–B4 |
| 20. | P–R6 | N–Q4 |

Black wrongly stops halfway. 20. . . . P–N3 would meet both of Black's purposes: the Bishop would be banished from QB5 and the QP would be lost. Moreover, after 20. . . . P–N3 21. BxR Black would have a pleasant choice: which Bishop should White be left with? I would leave him the dark-square Bishop, since after 21. . . . RxB 22. B–R3 NxQP the position would become sharper, but not to White's advantage. However, the zwischenzug 22. N–N5 would strengthen the defense, so it may be advisable to take the other Bishop by 21. . . . PxB, forming a strong passed pawn after 22. B–N2 PxP. In this case Black's pressure along the QN-file and the advance of his QP and KP supported by the Bishop on KN2 would promise him equal chances despite his slight material deficit.

Boleslavsky chooses another, quieter continuation, but White's Bishop on QB5 thereby remains unmolested, and two new weaknesses appear in Black's camp—the QRP and the QP.

| 21. | PxP | QxQNP |
|-----|-----|-------|
| 22. | NxN | PxN |
| 23. | R–R4 | P–QR4 |
| 24. | Q–Q3 | QR–N1 |
| 25. | R–N1 | Q–N6 |

White's pressure is becoming intolerable. Black goes for the exchange of Queens, but this should lead to the loss of a pawn.

| 26. | QxQ | RxQ |
|-----|-----|-----|
| 27. | RxP | |

The main drawback of this exchanging maneuver is that White loses his best piece, the Bishop on QB5. He can keep both Bishops by 27. P–N4, leading to the loss of Black's pawns and a much worse situation for Black: 27. . . . N–R5 28. B–K7 or 27. . . . N–R3 28. P–R3, and

the QP and QRP will not last long.

| 27. | . . . | BxP |
|-----|-------|-----|
| 28. | BxB | NxB |
| 29. | BxP | R–N5 |
| 30. | K–N2 | |

White's task—to queen his QNP—is extremely complicated. It is counteracted by the opponent's pieces set up on the dark squares, which are very difficult to drive away. White's King makes its way to the scene of battle, and Black decides to provoke the exchange of the last minor pieces and completely immobilize the QNP.

| 30. | . . . | N–N6 |
|-----|-------|------|
| 31. | BxN | RxB |
| 32. | R–R3 | R–N5 |

The beginning of an interesting and unquestionably instructive Rook endgame. Ideally, White would like to bring his King to the QNP, exchange one Rook, and also keep Black's King away from the pawn.

| 33. | R–KB3 | R/1–N1 |
|-----|-------|--------|
| 34. | P–N3 | R/1–N2 |

| 35. K–B1 | K–N2 |
| 36. K–K2 | R/5–N3 |
| 37. K–Q2 | R–N1 |
| 38. K–B2 | R–B3ch |

The first part of White's plan has been carried out, but Boleslavsky's clever Rook maneuver pushes White's King back to the Q-file.

| 39. R–B3 | R–K3 |
| 40. R–K3 | R–B3ch |
| 41. K–Q2 | P–N4 |

The purpose of this move is to break up White's pawn structure, and it should obviously be answered by the analogous pawn advance 42. P–KN4. True, by the maneuver R–KR3–KB3–KR3 Black could try to tie one of White's Rooks to the KRP, but if White did not deviate from his fundamental plan—the advance of his QNP—Black's defense, as before, would be very difficult. For example, 42. P–KN4 R–KR3 43. P–R3 R–KB3 44. P–B3 R–KR3 45. P–N4 RxRP 46. P–N5!, and if 46. . . . R–N3 the King goes to attack the Rook.

| 42. R–K4 | R–Q1ch |
| 43. K–K1 | R–KR3 |
| 44. P–R4 | PxP |
| 45. PxP | P–B4 |

Najdorf has rather confidently allowed Black to break up White's Kingside pawns, resulting in the exposure of White's King. Black's Rooks

begin to threaten checks not only along the files but also along the ranks, and he considerably activates his own King. In these circumstances it is difficult for White to pay attention to more than one thing at a time, and so the QNP is unable to advance more than one square.

| 46. R–QB4 | R–K3ch |
| 47. K–B1 | |

The King returns home. And immediately guests come calling: the Black Rooks.

| 47. . . . | R–Q7 |
| 48. P–N4 | R/3–K7 |
| 49. R–B4 | K–B3 |

50. R–N3

By skillful defense Black has managed to greatly activate his forces. The fact that he is not blockading the square in front of the QNP by no means signifies that he intends to let it out of his sight. Two Rooks on the seventh rank are a tremendous force. For instance, 50. P–N5 would be answered by 50. . . . R–N7 and White would not have 51. R/4–QN4 because of 51. . . . RxPch. On the other hand, Black was threatening K–K4 to drive White's Rook away from the intersection of White's KB4–QN4 and KB4–KB2. White's last move parried this threat since 50. . . . K–K4 51. R/3–KB3 would lead to the win of Black's KBP.

| 50. . . . | R–N7 |
| 51. RxR | |

51. R/4–B3 would be answered by 51. . . . RxPch!

| 51. . . . | RxR |
| 52. K–N2 | |

The QNP cannot go far without the King's help. But how can the KBP and KRP be abandoned? For then they would be destroyed by the Black King, and even if White could promote his QNP, Black would achieve a draw by giving up his Rook for the pawn when it got to N8. To accomplish this he would have to remember only to keep his BP or RP in reserve.

52. . . . R–B7 53. R–Q4 K–K4 54. R–Q7 R–B5 55. RxP RxNP 56. P–R5 K–B3 57. K–N3, Drawn.

## Game 179
### Queen's Gambit

| M. Taimanov | A. Kotov |
| --- | --- |
| 1. P–Q4 | N–KB3 |
| 2. P–QB4 | P–K3 |
| 3. N–KB3 | P–Q4 |
| 4. N–B3 | B–N5 |
| 5. PxP | PxP |
| 6. Q–R4ch | N–B3 |
| 7. B–N5 | P–KR3 |
| 8. BxN | QxB |
| 9. P–K3 | O–O |
| 10. B–K2 | B–K3 |
| 11. O–O | P–R3 |

In the Ragozin System the abstract concept of White's advantage in the opening assumes concrete form: the fact that Black's Knight stands in front of his QBP means that the pawn must sooner or later become an object of attack and that Black's QP will in effect be isolated for a long time. In exchange, Black has, as they say, good piece play. It cannot be denied that a backward pawn outweighed active piece play in the eyes of Schlechter, Teichmann, and even Rubinstein, but today the latter is often preferred.

Taimanov's next move is the beginning of a plan to gradually accumulate small positional advantages. In the meantime, he solidifies his possession of the open file.

| 12. KR–B1 | B–Q3 |
| 13. Q–Q1 | N–K2 |
| 14. N–QR4 | |

. . . P–QB4 must not be allowed, and he hopes to provoke . . . P–QN3.

| 14. . . . | P–QN3 |
| 15. N–B3 | |

Having efficiently executed both tasks, the Knight returns.

| 15. . . . | KR–Q1 |
| 16. Q–B1 | |

An interesting positional maneuver. White's threat to the QRP provokes yet another weakening of the pawn skeleton. This maneuver would have been stronger on the last move, instead of 15. N–B3.

| 16. . . . | P–B3 |
| 17. N–QR4 | |

The Bishop would be trapped if it took the QRP.

| 17. . . . | KR–N1 |
| 18. R–B3 | P–QR4 |
| 19. QR–B1 | B–Q2 |
| 20. P–QR3 | |

Inviting Black to "free" himself by 20. . . . P–B4, on which White would reply 21. PxP BxN 22. PxB QxP 23. N–Q4 with an excellent position.

| 20. . . . | N–N3 |
| 21. B–Q3 | Q–K3 |
| 22. Q–Q1 | B–B2 |

| 23. Q–B2 | N–K2 |
| 24. R–K1 | |

Having reached the limit of his pressure on the QBP and convinced that it will nevertheless hold out, White switches to the K-file. The immediate 24. P–K4 does not work because Black's Knight gets to Q4. It is necessary to set up a situation in which after the pawn exchange on K4 White is threatening Black's Queen.

| 24. . . . | P–KB4 |

Yet another positional achievement for White—Black's KBP inhibits the activity of his Queen, while the weakening of Black's KN1–QR7 diagonal will make itself felt later. But Kotov went into this voluntarily; had he feared its consequences he would have played Q–B3 here.

**25. P–QN4**

More or less forced. The attempt to strengthen his position on K4 generally by N–Q2, P–B3, and P–K4 would lead to stronger play for Black's pieces, which have long had their eye on White's Kingside.

The text move conceals an insidious trap: 25. . . . PxP 26. PxP P–B4 27. N–N2 P–QB5 28. NxP! PxN 29. BxQBP N–Q4 30. BxN QxB 31. RxB.

| 25. . . . | PxP |
| 26. PxP | B–Q3 |
| 27. R–N1 | P–QN4 |

Almost forced. Again 27. . . . P-B4 28. P-N5 P-QB5 is unplayable because of 29. RxP! PxR 30. BxQBP N-Q4 31. Q-N3. Taimanov planned to advance his own pawn to QN5.

| 28. | N-B5 | BxN |
|-----|------|-----|
| 29. | RxB | R-R5 |
| 30. | N-K5 | R/1-R1 |
| 31. | Q-K2 | B-K1 |
| 32. | Q-B3 | R-R8 |
| 33. | R/5-B1 | RxR |
| 34. | RxR | P-N3 |

Thus White has obtained all that a positional player might wish for. Black has a light-square Bishop, and five of his pawns stand on light squares; White's Knight occupies an ideal position in the center and cannot be driven away; Black's pieces are chained to the defense of his weak pawns on KN3 and QB3, which are situated on open files. If only White's Rook could occupy the QR-file!

But what plan of attack should White choose? Inasmuch as the opponent's weaknesses are fixed on light squares, it is necessary to attack those squares in accordance with the following general scenario, adapting it, of course, to the opponent's play: P-R3, K-R2, R-N1, and P-N4; it is also possible to bring back the Queen and play P-B3 and P-K4. Taimanov's P-B4 and P-R4 remove the possibility of a breakthrough on the light squares and reduce his chances by three fourths.

| 35. | P-R4 | K-N2 |
|-----|------|------|
| 36. | Q-N3 | Q-Q3 |
| 37. | P-B4 | P-R4 |
| 38. | B-K2 | R-R5?! |

Convinced that there are no threats, Kotov shifts the play from the realm of chess to that of psychology and offers his opponent the KRP in consideration of a variation something like this: 39. BxRP RxP 40. RxR QxR 41. BxP BxB 42. P-R5 Q-Q3 43. K-B1, etc. But even this would hardly give Black an advantage, the more so because White would also have the possibility 39. BxRP RxP 40. R-QB1.

It must be added that the psychological experiment was founded largely on competitive considerations: should he win this game Kotov would significantly improve his standing in the tournament, catching up with Keres and remaining only half a point behind Reshevsky.

**39. B–Q1!!**

A brilliant reply. Before deciding whether or not to take the RP, Taimanov puts the question to the Rook—if it leaves the QR-file, then he will take the RP. The position of White's Bishop and its simultaneous action against QR4 and KR5 is very reminiscent of the King in Russian checkers. Was the Bishop's move borrowed from there?

**39. . . .         RxP**
**40. R–R1**

White's dream has come true; the Rook burrows into the eighth rank and creates utter havoc.

**40. . . .         N–B1**

The might of White's Rook, and the defects of Black's position, show up in a variation like this: 40. . . . B–B2 41. R–R7 R–N8 42. Q–N5—White doesn't need the Bishop any more—42. . . . RxBch 43. K–R2 K–B1 44. Q–R6ch.

**41. R–R8 Q–K3 42. BxP K–B1 43. BxP BxB 44. Nx Bch K–K1 45. N–K5 K–Q1 46. Q–N7 R–R5 47. R–N8 P–N5 48. R–N7, Black resigns.**

## Game 180

The second meeting between these players greatly resembles their first: the identical opening with colors reversed, the same pawn forays, the same kind of difficult and fascinating endgame—only the result is different.

## King's Indian Defense

| S. Gligoric | Y. Geller |
|---|---|
| 1. P–Q4 | N–KB3 |
| 2. P–QB4 | P–KN3 |
| 3. N–QB3 | B–N2 |
| 4. P–K4 | P–Q3 |
| 5. N–B3 | O–O |
| 6. B–K2 | P–K4 |
| 7. O–O | P–B3 |
| 8. P–Q5 | |

Driving a wedge between the flanks, White splits the battlefield into two independent parts. Geller immediately begins activities in the vicinity of the enemy King, while Gligoric intends an indirect maneuver, first breaking through on the Queenside and only then going after the King. The next moves are easy to understand, but the position does not lend itself to precise evaluation. In cases like this the winner will be the one who

invests his plan with the greater
imagination, courage, and logic.

| 8. . . . | P-B4 |
| 9. N-K1 | P-QR3 |
| 10. B-K3 | N-K1 |
| 11. N-Q3 | P-B4 |
| 12. P-B3 | P-B5 |
| 13. B-B2 | P-KN4 |
| 14. P-QN4 | |

By playing P–QN4 here, Gligoric intends to take advantage
of the opening of the QN-file.
The point QB5 cannot be
breached.

| 14. . . . | P-N3 |
| 15. PxP | NPxP |
| 16. R-N1 | R-B3 |

The clumsy Rook makes its
way to KN3 in order to support
the attacking pawns.

| 17. N-R4 | N-Q2 |
| 18. P-N4 | PxP e.p. |
| 19. PxP | R-N3 |
| 20. N-K1 | N/2-B3 |
| 21. N-N6 | R-N1 |
| 22. NxB | RxR |
| 23. QxR | QxN |
| 24. K-N2 | P-N5 |

Both opponents are noticeably nearing their goals: Black
begins insistently to storm KN6;
White's Queen invades QN6.

| 25. N-B2 | PxPch |
| 26. BxP | B-R3 |
| 27. Q-N6 | Q-Q2 |
| 28. QxRP | Q-KN2 |
| 29. R-KR1 | B-B5 |
| 30. R-R3 | P-R4 |

White has reinforced his KN3
as well as he could. Black's KRP
—the last reserve—runs to the
aid of his pieces.

| 31. K-R2 | N-N5ch |
| 32. BxN | PxB |
| 33. R-R5 | B-N4 |
| 34. Q-B8 | |

Which side has the advan-
tage? Each has pluses and minuses: White, for instance, has
an extra pawn, but his Rook
stands badly on KR5. Such positions can be called dynamically
balanced.

| 34. . . . | Q-KB2 |
| 35. K-N1 | R N2 |
| 36. R-R2 | Q-Q2 |

A brilliant decision, based on
an exceptionally profound assessment of the position. Geller
transposes to the endgame, in
which despite Black's missing
pawn Gligoric will have to fight
painstakingly for the draw.

| 37. Q-R8 | Q-Q1 |
| 38. QxQ | BxQ |
| 39. N-K3 | R-QR2 |
| 40. B-K1 | N-B3 |

Emphasizing the weakness of White's pawns on QB4, Q5, and K4. It seems it is not always an advantage to place one's pawns on squares the opposite color of one's Bishop. Although there are other pieces, the pawns will be frequently exposed to danger.

**41. R–QN2**

**41. . . .　　　B–B2**

Despite the limited forces, Black has solved his first problem satisfactorily—the Rook has not been allowed into his camp.

**42. K–B1　　　K–B2**
**43. K–K2　　　NxKP**

Otherwise White's King goes to Q3.

**44. NxP　　　K–N3**
**45. K–Q3　　　N–N4**
**46. N–K3　　　R–R6ch**
**47. K–K2　　　B–Q1**
**48. B–Q2　　　P–K5**
**49. R–N8**

Gligoric has waited too long, and Black has managed to strengthen the position of his pieces to the utmost. Inasmuch as White's passed QRP and KNP are actually inactive, it is not surprising that the initiative is entirely in Black's hands. White wants to make up for his mistake by invading with his Rook, and he almost succeeds.

**49. . . .　　　B–B3**
**50. N–N4　　　N–B6**
**51. NxB　　　KxN**
**52. B–B4　　　N–Q5ch**
**53. K–B1　　　P–K6**

White should not have permitted Black's pawn to get to K6 so easily. He should have played 53. K–B2 instead, because after 53. . . . RxPch 54. K–B1 Black would not have P–K6 and White could successfully attack the pawn from behind by R–K8. It will soon become clear why the KP's advance should have been prevented.

**54. R–K8　　　P–K7ch**
**55. K–B2　　　R–B6ch**
**56. K–N2　　　R–B8**

Gligoric most likely did not fear this position in his preliminary calculations because he was intending simply to take the KP with his Rook, but too late he discovers that this would be answered not by 57. . . . NxR but by 57. . . . RxB.

**57. B–Q2　　　R–Q8**
**58. B–B3　　　R–QB8**
**59. BxNch**

The last mistake. He should not trade his Bishop. White gets rid of the KP but the QP turns out to be even more dangerous. It is not clear how Black can win if the Bishop stays on the K1–QR5 diagonal. For instance, 59. B–Q2 R–Q8 60. B–R5 or 59. . . . RxP 60. K–B2 R–B7 61. B–K1 RxP 62. B–B3.

| 59. . . . | PxB |
| 60. RxP | P–Q6 |
| 61. R–B2ch | K–K4 |

**62. K–B3       K–Q5**

The pawn, supported by the King and Rook, will be worth a Rook in a move or two.

**63. P–N4**

White remembers his passed pawn too late.

**63. . . . K–B6 64. K–K4 R–K8ch 65. K–B5 P–Q7 66. RxP KxR 67. P–N5 K–Q6 68. P–B5 PxP 69. P–Q6 R–K1 70. P–Q7 R–QR1, White resigns.**

An instructive position on the theme Rook against separated passed pawns. White lacks one tempo to achieve a draw: 71. K–K6 P–B5 72. K–K7 P–B6 73. P–Q8=Qch RxQ 74. KxR P–B7 75. P–N6 P–B8=Q 76. P–N7 Q–KN8.

## Game 181
### Ruy Lopez

**D. Bronstein       V. Smyslov**

1. P–K4 P–K4 2. N–KB3 N–QB3 3. B–N5 P–QR3 4. BxN

One of the favorite variations of a former world champion, Dr. Emanuel Lasker. In the Petersburg tournament of 1914 he used this opening to gain a famous victory against José Capablanca. Nowadays Black's defensive plans are worked out in the minutest detail, due to which this variation is rarely employed and is considered drawish.

4. . . . QPxB 5. N–B3 P–B3 6. P–Q4 PxP 7. QxP QxQ 8. NxQ B–Q2 9. B–K3 O–O–O 10. O–O–O N–K2 11. P–KR3

N–N3 12. N–N3 B–QN5 13. N–K2 KR–K1 14. P–R3 B–B1 15. N–B3 B–K3 16. RxRch RxR 17. R–Q1 RxRch 18. KxR N–K4 19. B–B5 B–Q3 20. BxB PxB, Drawn.

## · Game 182
### Nimzo-Indian Defense

S. Reshevsky      P. Keres

1. P–Q4 N–KB3 2. P–QB4 P–K3 3. N–QB3 B–N5 4. P–K3 P–QN3 5. N–K2 B–R3 6. N–N3

White's threat to run his pawn from K3 to K5 cannot be averted by 6. . . . P–Q4 in view of 7. Q–R4ch. Keres makes an interesting decision—to allow the advance of the pawn and counterattack against Q5—but it is not the best.

6. . . . O–O 7. P–K4 P–Q3 8. B–Q2 P–B4 9. P–QR3 B–R4

Wrong. He should simply take on QB6 and play N–B3.

10. P–Q5 PxP 11. BPxP BxB 12. KxB QN–Q2 13. P–KR4 R–K1 14. P–B3, Drawn.

In a position like this, dear reader, White should not agree to a draw, and Black should not offer one. White's position is better. He can attack on either flank with chances for success. Why then did Reshevsky accept the draw? He evidently had his reasons: with three rounds left for him to play, he was out of the running for first place, but he considered second place a sure thing. So perhaps it was not only arithmetic but also psychology that played a role here. But in his last three games he collected all of half a point . . .

# Round Twenty-Seven

## Game 183
### King's Indian Defense

**P. Keres      D. Bronstein**

| | | |
|---|---|---|
| 1. | P–Q4 | N–KB3 |
| 2. | P–QB4 | P–KN3 |
| 3. | N–QB3 | B–N2 |
| 4. | P–K4 | P–Q3 |
| 5. | P–B4 | |

The Four Pawns Variation, which has an interesting history. In its first appearance on the chess scene it struck no little fear into the hearts of adherents of the King's Indian setup. Through the collective efforts of many masters the destructive tendencies of the Four Pawns Attack were neutralized, and Black even started to score wins. The variation disappeared for a long time, making way for the more solid P–KN3, B–N2, etc., or the "riskier" 5. P–B3, B–K3, and Q–Q2.

In recent years the pawn-storm variation seems to have reappeared with new ambitions and renewed energy, enriched by the full range of modern positional ideas.

In this game Black defends with a thirty-year-old prescription of A. Alekhine's. Not surprisingly, the prescription is out of date, and Black is saved only by stopping in time and changing his original plan.

| | | |
|---|---|---|
| 5. | . . . | P–B4 |
| 6. | PxP | |

Formerly the pawn was advanced to Q5, but practice has shown that the variation 6. . . . O–O 7. N–B3 P–K3 8. B–Q3 PxP 9. BPxP P–QN4 is fully acceptable for Black.

| | | |
|---|---|---|
| 6. | . . . | Q–R4 |
| 7. | B–Q3 | QxBP |
| 8. | N–B3 | |

This is how the variation is played today. White has good piece play, and unless prevented he will organize a decisive mating attack without much difficulty.

| | | |
|---|---|---|
| 8. | . . . | O–O |
| 9. | Q–K2 | N–B3 |
| 10. | B–K3 | Q–KR4 |

447

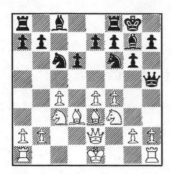

The Queen goes to the King-side to attack White's QB with . . . N–KN5 if White castles. The Bishop then cannot go to Q2 since by 12. . . . N–Q5! Black effects a well-known technical maneuver to divert the Queen and Knight from the defense of KR2.

But White can play more strongly.

**11. P–KR3          N–KN5**
**12. B–Q2!**

Now, to avoid the worst, Black must go back. 12. . . . N–Q5, the logical followup to the aggressive . . . Q–KR4 and . . . N–KN5, would land Black in insoluble difficulties after 13. Q–B1!

Black's defensive system has not been vindicated.

**12. . . .          N–B3**
**13. O–O          N–Q2**

The Knight, having suffered a fiasco on the Kingside, moves over to the Queenside. Black has to be very careful and must continually calculate all varia-

tions starting with P–KB5, for his Queen on KR4 is a very tempting target for White's minor pieces.

**14. QR–Q1          Q–R4**
**15. B–N1          Q–N5**

White has systematically strengthened his position, and it is extremely difficult for Black, who has lost a lot of time with Q–QR4–KR4–QR4, to oppose this with a plan of equal value. The diversion undertaken on the Queenside again places the Queen in a most dangerous position, but it appears to be the only way to keep the balance. 15. . . . Q–N5 is the thread by which his game hangs.

**16. B–K3**

Rapid simplification now follows.

**16. . . . N–N3 17. N–Q5 QxNP 18. QxQ BxQ 19. NxN PxN 20. R–B2, Drawn.**

Lovers of the King's Indian Defense will have to look for a more effective antidote against the Four Pawns Attack.

## Game 184
### King's Indian Defense

**V. Smyslov          S. Gligoric**

1. P-Q4 N-KB3 2. N-KB3 P-KN3 3. B-B4

In the last rounds, Smyslov, separated by two points from his closest rivals, plays sound, quiet systems and does not avoid draws as either Black or White. In this game he repeats the variation he used against Boleslavsky in game 139.

3. . . . B-N2 4. QN-Q2 P-Q3 5. P-KR3 O-O 6. P-K3 P-B4 7. B-K2 N-B3 8. B-R2 P-N3 9. O-O B-N2 10. P-B3 Q-Q2 11. R-K1 KR-Q1 12. Q-B2 QR-B1 13. QR-Q1 Px P 14. NxP P-Q4 15. NxN QxN 16. Q-N3 Q-B4 17. Q-N5

The opponents have set up a type of position in which it is difficult to create any kind of complications.

17. . . . QxQ 18. BxQ N-K1 19. B-Q3 N-Q3 20. P-B3 B-KR3 21. B-KB4, Drawn.

## Game 185

Why aren't all of today's masters willing, as were those of fifty years ago, to undertake energetic combinative attacks with piece sacrifices? The most likely reasons are the very high level that combinative defensive skill has reached by now and the difficulty at times of telling who is attacking whom. It is pleasant, of course, to break down the fortifications of the enemy King move by move, to set up irresistible threats, and to decide the game with a mating attack; but how sad it is to be left a piece down with no attack, to sit and think about how it came to this and about "where did I go wrong?"

This is the overall psychological framework of the Geller-Taimanov game; in the end fortune smiles upon the brave.

### Ruy Lopez

**Y. Geller          M. Taimanov**

| 1. P-K4 | P-K4 |
| 2. N-KB3 | N-QB3 |
| 3. B-N5 | B-N5 |

In the Evans Gambit White sacrifices his QNP to lure Black's Bishop to QN5 so that he can play P-QB3 and P-Q4 with tempo. Here the Bishop goes to QN5 voluntarily, and White can carry out almost the same idea free of charge, so to speak. Geller makes a surprising choice: since he has been spared the necessity of sacrificing a pawn, he decides to take one of his opponent's.

| 4. | O–O | KN–K2 |
|----|-----|-------|
| 5. | P–B3 | B–R4 |
| 6. | BxN | NxB |
| 7. | P–QN4 | B–N3 |
| 8. | P–N5 | N–R4 |
| 9. | NxP | O–O |
| 10. | P–Q4 | P–Q4 |

I would prefer 10. . . . Q–K1 here, intending . . . P–Q3.

| 11. | B–R3 | R–K1 |
|-----|------|------|
| 12. | Q–R5 | |

White is planning an attack with the sacrifice of a piece. The prerequisites are present, of course: Black's QN has been cast off to QR4 and his Bishop is out of play on N3. The coordination of White's Bishop on QR3, his Rooks on the KB-file, and his Queen promises the Black King little pleasure. 12. N–Q2 first is even better, for complete success cannot be achieved without this Knight anyway.

| 12. | . . . | P–KB3 |
|-----|-------|-------|
| 13. | P–KB4 | |

As the further course of the game will show, this move leads by force to a lost game.

| 13. | . . . | PxN |
|-----|-------|-----|
| 14. | BPxP | B–K3 |

The main variation of Geller's combination goes like this: 14. . . . N–B5 15. Q–B7ch K–R1 16. B–B8 with unavoidable mate. It is not his fault that Taimanov's sharp eye has spotted this combination and neutralized it. However, many attacking possibilities for White still remain.

| 15. | N–Q2 | PxP |
|-----|------|-----|
| 16. | NxP | BxPch |

A strong positional move, bringing Black's Bishop into play. The fact that it takes a pawn, and with check, is secondary.

| 17. | K–R1 | |
|-----|------|--|

After 17. PxB QxPch 18. N–B2 N–B5 White's attack comes to a sad and rapid end. But now 17. . . . BxKP would be followed by 18. N–N5, or after 17. . . . B–K6 a Rook would go to the open Q-file with tempo, and limitless possibilities for an attacking player's imagination would appear in connection with 19. R–B3 or 19. R–Q3.

Taimanov again finds the best move.

| 17. | . . . | B–Q4 |
|-----|-------|------|
| 18. | N–B6ch | |

A new sacrifice, but this one is forced since the Knight has no time to retreat.

| 18. | . . . | PxN |
|-----|-------|-----|
| 19. | PxB | Q–Q2 |

Good enough for defense, but bringing up the reserves by 19. . . . N–B5 is better.

| | |
|---|---|
| 20. PxP | Q–B2 |
| 21. R–B5 | |

White is forced to agree to the exchange of Queens and to continue the struggle with two pawns against a piece.

| | |
|---|---|
| 21. . . . | QxQ |
| 22. RxQ | B–B2 |
| 23. R–N5ch | B–N3 |
| 24. B–K7 | K–B2 |
| 25. R–QB1 | QR–B1 |
| 26. P–KR4 | R–KN1 |

Having successfully conducted a complicated defense and obtained a winning position, Taimanov begins to play carelessly. He should restrain the enemy pawn by 26. . . . P–KR4, and if 27. P–N4 then 27. . . . PxP 28. P–R5 R–KR1.

| | |
|---|---|
| 27. R–K5 | P–N3 |
| 28. P–N4 | B–Q6 |
| 29. P–N5 | KR–K1 |

Yet another inaccuracy. Necessary is 29. . . . N–B5 30. R/5–K1 N–Q3.

| | |
|---|---|
| 30. R–B3 | B–B5 |

The last mistake. He could have held on by 30. . . . B–N3.

| | |
|---|---|
| 31. R–KN3 | P–B3 |
| 32. P–R5 | R–KN1 |

| | |
|---|---|
| 33. B–N4 | QR–K1 |
| 34. R/3–K3 | RxR |
| 35. RxR | B–K3 |

| | |
|---|---|
| 36. BxN | PxB |
| 37. PxP | R–Q1 |
| 38. P–B7 | R–QB1 |
| 39. P–Q5 | B–N5 |
| 40. R–K7ch | K–B1 |
| 41. P–N6 | PxP |
| 42. PxP | Black resigns |

The stubbornness and persistence with which Geller sought out chances with two pawns against a piece after his unsuccessful attack is noteworthy. This was Geller's third straight win after his draw with Reshevsky in the 24th round, and in the next round he made it four in a row—the longest winning streak in the tournament. Geller's brilliant finish assured him of a good place in the tournament after his unfortunate start.

## Game 186
### King's Indian Defense

| A. Kotov | M. Najdorf |
|----------|------------|
| 1. P–QB4 | N–KB3 |
| 2. N–QB3 | P–KN3 |
| 3. P–Q4 | B–N2 |
| 4. P–K4 | P–Q3 |
| 5. P–B3 | O–O |
| 6. B–K3 | P–K4 |
| 7. P–Q5 | P–B4 |
| 8. P–KN4 | |

After White's unsuccessful opening with 8. B–Q3 in game 171, Kotov–Gligoric, this time Kotov uses the even more aggressive P–KN4 and P–KR4, intending to break open the Black King's fortress immediately.

| 8. . . . | N–K1 |
|----------|------|
| 9. P–KR4 | P–B4 |
| 10. KPxP | PxP |
| 11. P–N5 | P–K5 |
| 12. P–B4 | |

Advancing the pawn to B4 has the advantage of preventing a Black piece from using K4, but at the same time the move has serious drawbacks: it gives Black a protected passed pawn in the center, it inhibits White's dark-square Bishop, and it takes KB4 from a White Knight. Much better is N–R3–B4, with a perpetual threat to K6 and the possibility of transferring the Knight to KR5.

| 12. . . . | P–N4 |
|-----------|------|
| 13. PxP | P–QR3 |

Najdorf, relying on his advantage in the center, undertakes a decisive diversion on the flank.

| 14. Q–Q2 | PxP |
|----------|-----|
| 15. BxNP | B–QR3 |
| 16. BxB | NxB |
| 17. KN–K2 | |

Black's threat of N–N5–Q6ch compels White to castle short without delay, and this means that White's main strategical plan—to attack on the Kingside—has been a failure. His game looks quite dubious: Black's Queen can approach the exposed King via the light squares KB2–KR4–KN5, White's QP is all alone, and his Bishop has no good prospects. His extra pawn is small consolation in a situation like this.

| 17. . . . | N–N5 |
|-----------|------|
| 18. O–O | N–B2 |
| 19. N–B1 | Q–K1 |
| 20. P–R3 | Q–R4 |

A beautiful maneuver. Threatening Q–N5ch and QxRPch, Najdorf provokes the White Rook to B2. White is willing to give up the KRP without check, but Najdorf has other intentions.

**21. R–B2          Q–B2**

So that's it! Now that the Rook cannot get to Q1, White's QP is left defenseless. And when the outpost at Q5 is destroyed and Black's pawn advances from Q3 to Q5, the game will be over. Kotov does not acquiesce to such a quick and unattractive outcome, and with a characteristically ingenious defense he sacrifices the Exchange for a pawn and takes the game into a sea of interesting complications. Najdorf, who probably thought the win was a matter of technique, now has to begin the struggle anew, and this is sometimes very difficult psychologically.

**22. PxN          RxR**
**23. PxP          PxP**

The first mistake. The win is achieved without much trouble by 23. . . . BxN 24. PxB NxP 25. PxP NxB 26. QxN Q–Q4; but how can one part with the "Indian" Bishop?

**24. BxP          R–Q1**
**25. P–Q6**

**25. . . .          N–K1**

The second mistake, perhaps letting the win escape. After 25. . . . N–K3 26. B–N6 R–Q2 27. R–B1 R–R3 White loses his passed pawn without counterchances. The text move looks stronger but allows Kotov later to find an amazing chance for salvation.

**26. K–N2          B–B1**
**27. N/1–K2          NxP**
**28. Q–Q5          N–N2**
**29. QxQch          KxQ**
**30. BxB          RxB**
**31. N–N3          N–Q3**

If Najdorf had only foreseen White's plan, he would now play 31. . . . K–K3 followed by . . . N–B4–Q6, but, quite certain that the position is an automatic win, he continues to play carelessly . . .

**32. R–Q2          K–K3**
**33. R–Q5          R–QN1**

And so, Najdorf prepares to reap the harvest: he will now knock off the QNP, his Rooks will squeeze the White Knights, and his KP will become a Queen; but, as the oriental saying goes, "if there were no wolves our goat would get to Mecca." And here on the board, in the form of White Knights, appear two ferocious wolves.

Note, by the way, that in the diagram position 34. NxBP NxN 35. R–K5ch K–Q2 36. RxN is not playable in view of 36. . . . RxPch 37. K–N3 R–N6. Black can also take the QNP at once— 34. . . . RxPch 35. K–R3 NxN 36. R–K5ch K–Q2 37. RxN R–R6.

| 34. | RxNch! | KxR |
|-----|--------|-----|
| 35. | NxBPch | K–B3 |
| 36. | NxP | RxPch |
| 37. | K–B3 | R–N5 |
| 38. | N/5–N3 | R/8–R5 |
| 39. | P–R5 | R–R6ch |

Najdorf's main problem is that he doesn't know whether to play for a win or think about how to save the game. One of the Knights could suddenly fork, so he keeps his Rooks at a respectful distance.

| 40. | K–N4 | K–Q2 |
|-----|------|------|

| 41. | P–N6 | PxP |
|-----|------|-----|
| 42. | PxP | K–K2 |
| 43. | N–B5ch | K–K3 |
| 44. | N–N7ch | K–K2 |
| 45. | N–B5ch | K–K3 |
| 46. | P–N7 | R–R1 |
| 47. | N/4–N3 | R–KN1 |
| 48. | N–R5 | RxBPch |

A worthy conclusion to an interesting game! Though Kotov got a Knight and a pawn for each of his Rooks, Najdorf gets only a couple of pawns for his, leaving Kotov with two Knights as interest, so to speak. As we know, however, two Knights cannot mate the lone King; they can only stalemate it.

| 49. | KxR | RxP |
|-----|-----|-----|
| 50. | N/RxRch | Drawn |

The game should be put not in a tournament collection but in the magazine *The World of Adventure*.

## Game 187
### Caro-Kann Defense

**I. Boleslavsky    T. Petrosian**

**1. P–K4 P–QB3 2. N–QB3 P–Q4 3. P–Q4 PxP 4. NxP B–B4**

This is Black's main continuation in this opening, but although theory considers it quite solid I much prefer the audacious 4. . . . N–B3 5. NxNch NPxN. If the reader wishes to take me at my word and asks why I did not play it once in thirty rounds, I will give one reason above all—no one opened against me by pushing his KP two squares.

**5. N–N3 B–N3 6. N–R3 P–K3 7. N–B4 B–Q3 8. P–QB3 N–B3 9. P–KR4 Q–B2**

Now White has a choice: 10. Q–B3, starting interesting double-edged complications like 10. . . . QN–Q2 11. P–R5 B–B7

12. P–R6 P–KN3 13. B–B4 P–K4 14. Q–K2 O–O–O; or 10. P–R5, sacrificing a pawn but creating a permanent weakness for Black on his K3. Boleslavsky makes the latter, better choice.

**10. P–R5 BxN 11. BxB Qx B 12. PxB BPxP 13. Q–Q2**

White makes a curious decision—a pawn down, he offers to trade Queens! Petrosian may have had a glimmer of hope that Boleslavsky would be tempted by the possibility 13. Q–N3, simultaneously attacking QN7 and K6, but the text move dispels his dream (13. Q–N3 N–N5 14. QxPch K–Q1).

**13. . . . QxQch 14. KxQ QN–Q2 15. R–K1 K–B2 16. B–B4 QR–K1 17. B–N3 P–B4**

18. N–K4 NxNch 19. RxN N–B3 20. R–K5 PxP 21. PxP R–K2

Black's pieces are chained to K3; on the other hand, White cannot improve his position,

and, since he is a pawn down, the game is soon concluded with a peace treaty.

22. R/1–K1 R/1–K1 23. K–Q3 P–KR3 24. P–B4, **Drawn.**

## Game 188
### *Queen's Indian Defense*

G. Stahlberg      Y. Averbakh

| | |
|---|---|
| 1. P–Q4 | N–KB3 |
| 2. P–QB4 | P–K3 |
| 3. N–KB3 | P–QN3 |
| 4. P–KN3 | B–N2 |
| 5. B–N2 | B–K2 |
| 6. N–B3 | N–K5 |
| 7. B–Q2 | |

This is not at all weaker than the usual 7. Q–B2. The Bishop move evokes pleasant memories of the chief tournament arbiter, the Czechoslovakian chess veteran, Karel Ivanovich Opocensky, who introduced this variation in practice a long time ago.

| | |
|---|---|
| 7. . . . | P–KB4 |
| 8. O–O | O–O |
| 9. Q–B2 | NxN |
| 10. BxN | B–K5 |
| 11. Q–N3 | P–QR4 |
| 12. N–K1 | |

Beginning the fight for K4.

| | |
|---|---|
| 12. . . . | P–R5 |
| 13. Q–Q1 | BxB |
| 14. NxB | B–B3 |
| 15. Q–Q3 | N–B3 |
| 16. P–K4 | PxP |
| 17. QxP | Q–K1 |

| | |
|---|---|
| 18. QR–Q1 | Q–B2 |
| 19. N–K3 | Q–N3 |

Black's QRP has been torn from its base in vain. Now he agrees to the exchange of Queens in order not to lose the pawn in the heat of battle (19. . . . QR–K1 20. Q–B2).

| | |
|---|---|
| 20. QxQ | PxQ |
| 21. KR–K1 | N–R4 |
| 22. R–K2 | KR–K1 |
| 23. R–B2 | P–Q3 |
| 24. K–N2 | K–B2 |
| 25. R–Q3 | K–K2 |
| 26. P–R4 | K–Q2 |
| 27. P–B4 | N–N2 |
| 28. N–N4 | N–R4 |
| 29. N–K5ch | |

**29. . . .          K–B1**

The Knight cannot be taken:
1) 29. . . . PxN 30. PxPch K–
K2 31. PxBch PxP 32. R/2–Q2
R–Q1 33. BxPch; 2) 29. . . .
BxN 30. QPxB NxP 31. PxP
NxQP 32. BxP, and although
pawns are even, Black has a lost
game, for a White passed pawn
will inevitably appear on the
KR-file.

Averbakh finds the relatively
best defense.

**30. BxN**

The Knight can take the KNP,
but after 30. . . . NxP 31. B–N4
Black sacrifices a piece by 31.
. . . P–R6! 32. RxN PxP 33. R–
N3 RxP, bringing the game to a
complicated position with unclear consequences. Stahlberg
takes the more cautious course.

| | |
|---|---|
| **30. . . .** | **PxN** |
| **31. BPxP** | **RxB** |
| **32. PxB** | **PxP** |
| **33. P–B5** | **PxP** |
| **34. PxP** | **R–Q1** |

A pointless loss of time. After
34. . . . P–K4 Black would have
every reason to expect a draw.
But now a White Rook gets to
K5 by force and completely
blockades the KP and KBP.

**35. R–KB3**

The winning move. Black's
Rooks must take up passive

positions, and in Rook endgames this is most unpleasant.

| | |
|---|---|
| **35. . . .** | **P–B4** |
| **36. R–K3** | **R–K1** |

It is already too late even for
the active defense 36. . . . R–
Q4 37. RxP R/QxP 38. R–
KB2.

**37. R–K5**

| | |
|---|---|
| **37. . . .** | **K–Q1** |
| **38. R/2–K2** | **R–N4** |
| **39. K–B3** | **R–N5** |
| **40. P–B6** | |

40. P–R3 is calmer. Black's
only counterchance is his hope
somehow to take the QRP and
QNP in exchange for his KP and
KNP. Should that occur, it
would be better for White to
have lost the QRP on its third
rank.

**40. . . .          R–K5**

But this is completely useless.
He should attack the pawn by
40. . . . R–N3. The variation

41. RxKP RxR 42. RxR RxNP
43. K–B4 RxP 44. RxP leaves
Black with some chances.

**41. R/2xR PxRch 42. RxP
P–R6 43. R–Q4ch K–B1 44.
R–R4, Black resigns.**

## Game 189
### King's Indian Defense

| M. Euwe | L. Szabo |
|---|---|
| 1. P–Q4 | N–KB3 |
| 2. P–QB4 | P–KN3 |
| 3. P–KN3 | B–N2 |
| 4. B–N2 | O–O |
| 5. N–QB3 | P–B4 |
| 6. P–Q5 | P–Q3 |
| 7. N–B3 | N–R3 |
| 8. N–Q2 | N–B2 |
| 9. Q–B2 | R–N1 |
| 10. P–N3 | P–K3 |

White's temporary weakening of his QR1–KR8 diagonal provokes a quite natural reaction by Black.

| 11. B–N2 | PxP |
| 12. PxP | P–QN4 |
| 13. O–O | R–K1 |

Black played P–QN4 without hindrance and stands quite well. It would therefore be venturesome and inappropriate to try to attack by 13. . . . P–N5 14. N/3–K4 N/2xP 15. KR–Q1, and Black would not keep the extra pawn.

| 14. P–K4 | B–QR3 |
| 15. KR–K1 | N–N5 |
| 16. N–K2 | N–K4 |
| 17. QR–N1 | |

While Black plays on the flanks, White methodically gathers strength in the center.

| 17. . . . | P–N5 |
| 18. N–QB4 | N–N4 |
| 19. P–B4 | |

His position is sufficiently reinforced for White to take this step.

| 19. . . . | NxN |
| 20. PxN | N–Q5 |

Black's pawn on Q5 will be doomed, but on the other hand the QB-file will be opened and White's QBP will also be subject to attack. It was very tempting to put the Knight on QR6, for after 21. BxN PxB the important QN7 would be at Black's mercy. But not for long—by 22. Q–R4 White would attack both the pawn and the Bishop on R6. The Knight therefore takes another route. But as far as "doomed" pawns are concerned, we know from game 87, for instance, that they are inclined to be very tenacious at times. Even in this game, the Black QP survives despite the bloodshed to come.

| 21. NxN | PxN |
| 22. B–KB1 | QR–B1 |
| 23. B–Q3 | |

The Bishop stands well here. It defends the KP and the QBP

and prevents the advance of the enemy pawns. Now it is possible to consider a siege of the QP.

| 23. . . . | Q–N3 |
| 24. Q–N3 | |

Black's last move strengthened his threat to the QBP. Therefore White cannot play 24. Q–R4, since after 24. . . . BxP 25. BxB P–Q6ch 26. K–N2 P–Q7 27. KR–Q1 BxB White's position is smashed.

| 24. . . . | R–K2 |
| 25. K–N2 | Q–B4 |
| 26. Q–R4 | B–N2 |
| 27. P–QR3 | P–QR4 |
| 28. B–QB1 | |

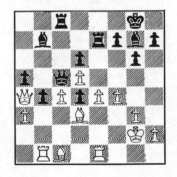

It is hard to believe, looking at the diagram, that White's structure will crack at what seems its most solid point, Q5, which is twice firmly supported and cannot be attacked by pawns.

A combinational theme now makes its appearance: by a series of exchanges Black diverts both White Rooks from the defense of the Bishop at QB1, and the QBP, which shields this Bishop on the file, cannot fulfill its role of defending the QP.

| 28. . . . | P–B4 |
| 29. RPxP | RPxP |
| 30. QxP | QxQ |
| 31. RxQ | PxP |
| 32. RxP | BxP |

White could not prevent this move; had the Bishop taken on K4 it would have been pinned and White would even have risked losing: 32. BxP R/1–K1 33. K–B3 B–QB1 34. B–Q2 P–R4. But now detente sets in.

| 33. PxB | RxR |
| 34. BxR | RxB |
| | **Drawn** |

# Round Twenty-Eight

## *Game 190*
### *Queen's Gambit*

**L. Szabo**        **G. Stahlberg**

1. P–QB4 P–K3 2. N–KB3
N–KB3 3. P–Q4 P–Q4 4. N–
B3 QN–Q2 5. PxP PxP 6. B–
N5 B–K2 7. P–K3 P–B3 8.
Q–B2 N–B1

The Stahlberg Defense, with
which we became familiar in
game 8.

9. B–Q3 N–K3 10. B–R4
P–KN3 11. O–O O–O 12. QR–
N1

The QNP will be assigned the
task of marching to QN5 and
breaking up the opponent's
pawn position.

12. . . . P–QR4 13. P–QR3
N–N2 14. P–QN4 PxP 15.
PxP B–KB4 16. P–N5 BxB
17. QxB N–Q2 18. PxP

The pawns have engaged.
White's QNP thus perishes, but
the bastion on QB6 remains as
before, with the QBP replaced
by its colleague from QN2.
White has been able to give his
opponent a weak pawn on the
open QB-file, but his Rooks
certainly won't take it as long
as the cavalry is guarding it
from behind.

18. . . . PxP 19. BxB QxB
20. Q–B2 N–KB4 21. N–QR4
Q–Q3 22. N–N6 NxN 23. RxN
N–K2

The Knight goes on sentry duty.

**24. P–N3 KR–N1 25. R/1–N1 RxR 26. RxR P–B3**

Keeping the White Knight out of K5 and clearing KB2 for the King.

**27. K–N2 K–B2 28. N–Q2**

R–QN1 29. Q–N2 RxR 30. QxR Q–R6 31. P–R4 Q–Q3, **Drawn.**

Since White's King will have difficulty hiding from the probing checks, Szabo renounces his aggressive pretensions and agrees to end the struggle amicably.

## Game 191
### Dutch Defense

| Y. Averbakh | I. Boleslavsky |
|---|---|
| 1. P–Q4 | P–K3 |
| 2. N–KB3 | P–KB4 |
| 3. P–KN3 | N–KB3 |
| 4. B–N2 | B–K2 |
| 5. O–O | O–O |
| 6. P–B4 | P–Q3 |
| 7. P–N3 | |

The "solidity" of Black's chosen system can be challenged only by the strictly theoretical 7. N–B3, for now Black is immediately relieved of many problems. A tempo in the opening is a nice gift.

| 7. . . . | P–QR4 |
|---|---|
| 8. B–N2 | Q–K1 |
| 9. QN–Q2 | N–B3 |
| 10. P–QR3 | B–Q1 |

It is interesting to examine the regrouping of Black's pieces: the Queen has moved to the King's place, the Bishop to the Queen's. Such arrangements are typical of positions in which Black is preparing P–K4.

| 11. N–K1 | P–K4 |
|---|---|
| 12. P–K3 | B–Q2 |
| 13. N–B2 | PxP |

Averbakh's flaccid play has allowed Black to obtain chances for a successful Kingside attack. Black's intention now is to sacrifice a pawn by 14. PxP P–B5!, opening a diagonal for his Bishop on Q2. White, though tempted to open the K-file for his pieces, considers this variation dangerous to himself and takes on Q4 with the Knight.

| 14. NxP | NxN |
|---|---|
| 15. BxN | B–B3 |

Boleslavsky gains a definite positional victory in bringing his Bishop to an attacking position and then getting his opponent to agree to exchange Bishops. In the Dutch Defense Black's light-square Bishop is considered bad (particularly so in the Stonewall system), whereas the Bishop on KN2 is crucial to White's position. The exchange of these Bishops creates a bleak situation for the White King.

| 16. | N–B3 | B–K5 |
| 17. | N–K1 | P–QN3 |
| 18. | P–QR4 | N–Q2 |
| 19. | N–Q3 | |

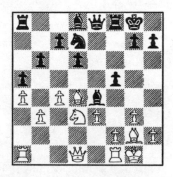

**19. . . .     P–KN4!**

In the Dutch Defense the KNP is an indispensable participant in all attacks on the King, its advance energizing the entire position. B–KB3 on his next move would strengthen his position even more.

| 20. | N–B1 | N–K4 |
| 21. | BxB | PxB |
| 22. | BxN | QxB |
| 23. | Q–Q5ch | QxQ |
| 24. | PxQ | |

Boleslavsky, having absent-mindedly overlooked the obvious Queen check, has fallen from a promising middlegame to a dubious ending. He has to go into a laborious defense.

**24. . . .     R–N1**

In connection with the following pawn advance, this is Black's best chance.

**25. R–Q1 P–N4 26. P–KN4 B–B3 27. R–R2 B–K4 28. K–N2 R–B2 29. PxP RxP 30. R–R4 B–N7 31. RxKP, Drawn,** because of 31. . . . BxN 32. RxB RxQP.

# Game 192
## King's Indian Defense

**T. Petrosian          A. Kotov**

1. P–Q4 N–KB3 2. P–QB4 P–Q3 3. N–KB3 P–KN3 4. N–B3 B–N2 5. P–KN3 O–O 6. B–N2 QN–Q2 7. O–O P–K4 8. Q–B2 P–B3 9. R–Q1 R–K1 10. PxP PxP 11. N–KN5 Q–K2 12. N/5–K4 NxN

Following a tough two-day encounter with Najdorf, Grandmaster Kotov decides to take a little rest, and in this game he undertakes a number of simplifying exchanges. First he liquidates his opponent's horses; then the Rooks disappear, after which the breath of a draw comes over the board. It is necessary to add that Black's activities flow all the more smoothly in that they have Petrosian's full approval and support.

**13.** NxN N–B4 **14.** N–Q6 R–Q1 **15.** NxB RxRch **16.** QxR RxN **17.** B–K3 R–Q1 **18.** Q–B2 P–B4 **19.** R–Q1, Drawn.

## *Game 193*

This game follows the Najdorf–Petrosian game exactly up to the 12th move. Najdorf again trades a central pawn for Black's QNP, thus declining a struggle over one of the main problems in the opening. In the above-mentioned game from the 6th round, Petrosian immediately committed a serious positional error with P–QB4, taking the best square from his Knight; but Geller, who learned a lesson from that game, conducts the attack on the Queenside successfully.

### *King's Indian Defense*

**M. Najdorf**          **Y. Geller**

| | |
|---|---|
| 1. P–Q4 | N–KB3 |
| 2. P–QB4 | P–KN3 |
| 3. P–KN3 | B–N2 |
| 4. B–N2 | O–O |
| 5. N–KB3 | P–Q3 |
| 6. O–O | N–B3 |
| 7. N–B3 | B–N5 |
| 8. P–KR3 | BxN |
| 9. BxB | N–Q2 |
| 10. B–N2 | NxP |
| 11. BxP | R–N1 |
| 12. B–N2 | R–N5 |
| 13. P–K3 | N–K3 |
| 14. Q–K2 | N–K4! |

In some openings—for example, Alekhine's Defense, the Grünfeld Defense—Black stations undefended pieces in the center in order to provoke White to advance his pawns so that the pawns can later be attacked. Geller carries out a similar idea in the middlegame. He wants to get White's pawns to advance to KB4 and QN3, which he soon does. Then he sets up an attack on the QNP, for which he arranges his heavy pieces on the QN-file and puts his Knight on QB4 in order to support the advance P–QR4–5. The reader will recall that Petrosian's similar attack did not succeed only because he had no pieces capable of controlling QR5—his Queen seemed inappropriate for that purpose, and, as stated above, Black's QB4, needed for the Knight, was occupied by a pawn.

| 15. P–B4 | N–Q2 |
| 16. N–Q5 | R–N1 |

Despite the threatening position of White's Knight and Black's relatively modest pawn structure, I think Black's game is preferable. The Knight will not stay on Q5 for long, and the Black pawns are holding their potential power in reserve. White will have difficulty developing his Rooks, and his flank attack on the King has less chance of success than Black's attack on the Queenside.

| 17. Q–QB2 | P–QB3 |
| 18. N–B3 | Q–B2 |
| 19. R–N1 | P–QR4 |
| 20. B–Q2 | N/3–B4 |

| 21. N–K2 | Q–N3 |
| 22. K–R2 | KR–B1 |
| 23. B–QB3 | |

Najdorf is using approximately the same scheme as in his game with Petrosian—he exchanges Bishops to weaken Black's King position and prepares a pawn offensive.

| 23. . . . | BxB |
| 24. NxB | Q–R3 |

The correct strategical idea with an inaccurate tactical execution. The weakening P–N3 would be achieved by 24. . . . Q–N5 with a much more actively placed Queen.

| 25. P–N3 | R–N3 |
| 26. N–K4 | NxN |
| 27. QxN | R–K1 |

Black goes too far in his desire to avoid advancing pawns to the center. This is the right moment to reply to a flank attack with a counterblow in the center, according to classical principles; for instance, 27. . . . P–K3! 28. P–KN4 P–Q4, and White's main attack would be repulsed whereas Black's pawn would inevitably get to QR5.

| 28. P–KB5 | N–K4 |
| 29. P–B6! | Q–R2 |

It is clear now that Black, carried away by his ideas on the Queenside, has not made use of his chances in the center and has handed the initiative to his opponent.

**30. QR–Q1          R–N5**

This could lead to serious difficulties. Necessary is . . . Q–B2, defending the QP.

**31. Q–Q4          P–B4**

Exchanging Queens would repair White's pawn chain, and White would win the QBP and the game.

**32. Q–R4**

32. Q–B4 would be right on target, with the same idea of penetrating to KR6 but without releasing the Queen's pressure on Black's Knight and indirectly on the QP; Black would then have to turn entirely to defense. Now, however, Black is able to complete his plan to break into White's camp via QN6.

**32. . . .          P–R5**
**33. RxP          RPxP**

The difference is that if the Queen stood on KB4 Black's move would be impossible because of 34. QxN.

**34. RPxP RxNP 35. PxP QxP 36. QxQ RxQ 37. B–Q5 RxP 38. R–Q8ch K–N2 39. R–QB8 N–Q6 40. R–QR8 R–K7ch 41. K–N1 R–Q7 42. R/8–R1 N–N5, White resigns.**

## *Game 194*
### *Catalan System*

**M. Taimanov          V. Smyslov**

1. P–Q4 N–KB3 2. P–QB4 P–K3 3. P–KN3 P–Q4 4. B–N2 PxP 5. Q–R4ch B–Q2 6. QxBP B–B3 7. N–KB3 B–Q4 8. Q–R4ch Q–Q2

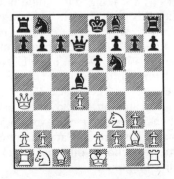

**9. QxQch**

The Queen has no good retreat. If it withdraws, there follows 9. . . . P–B4, and Black's two main problems in the Catalan System are solved: his QB is developed and he is attacking the QP. After the trade of Queens, further simplification occurs and the game ends in a draw. It must be admitted that the Queen's excursion Q–R4–B4–R4 to recover the sacrificed pawn is of absolutely no danger to Black. White gets better prospects by developing the Kingside more quickly with an earlier N–KB3. The pawn on QB4 would not run anywhere, and if Black started to defend it he would create one weakness or another in his camp.

9. . . . N/1xQ 10. O–O P–B4 11. N–B3 B–B3 12. PxP BxP 13. B–B4 O–O 14. QR–Q1 KR–Q1 15. B–Q6 BxB 16. RxB K–B1 17. KR–Q1 K–K2 18. R/6–Q2 N–B4 19. RxR RxR 20. RxR KxR 21. N–K5 BxB 22. KxB, **Drawn.**

## Game 195
### Nimzo-Indian Defense

| S. Gligoric | P. Keres |
|---|---|
| 1. P–Q4 | N–KB3 |
| 2. P–QB4 | P–K3 |
| 3. N–QB3 | B–N5 |
| 4. P–K3 | P–QN3 |
| 5. P–QR3 | BxNch |
| 6. PxB | B–N2 |
| 7. P–B3 | N–B3 |
| 8. P–K4 | |

Five pawn moves in a row. Strictly speaking, one should not play this way, but in this case White's slow pawn crawl is justified by the closed nature of the position. White intends to kill three birds at once: to put pressure on the Black Knights by threatening to advance his pawns, to clear a way to KN5 for his Bishop, and at the same time to choke off the Black QB's diagonal.

But all of White's achievements will pale as soon as Black remembers his chances—above all, an attack on the chronically ill QBP.

As we see, the players enter the middlegame with about equal chances. The question now is who will deploy his pieces better.

| 8. . . . | P–Q3 |
|---|---|
| 9. B–Q3 | N–QR4 |
| 10. N–K2 | |

White refrains from defending his QBP in order more quickly to organize an attack on KB6. Besides, one has to think about developing the pieces once in a while.

| 10. . . . | Q–Q2 |
|---|---|
| 11. O–O | B–R3 |

| 12. | N–N3 | BxP |
| 13. | BxB | NxB |
| 14. | Q–K2 | Q–B3 |
| 15. | B–N5 | P–KR4 |

A strong move. White was planning to take on KB6 with the Bishop and play his Knight to R5. Black has no objection to such a course, but he makes a small structural alteration— 15. . . . P–KR4. Now White's Knight can get to R5 only by taking the KRP. This detail materially changes the situation: after NxRP Black will have not one but two attacking files.

| 16. | B–R4 | O–O–O |
| 17. | P–B4 | QR–N1 |
| 18. | BxN | PxB |
| 19. | NxP | |

**19. . . .          P–B4**

Inviting the Knight to B6, but after 20. N–B6 R–N3 21. P–K5 White would not find the return visit 21. . . . N–K6 to his liking.

**20. N–N3**

The merit of Black's plan is well illustrated by the thematic

variation 20. PxP RxN 21. QxR QxP mate. If Black's KRP were standing on KR2, White's Knight would be inaccessible on KR5. All this was very well done by Keres.

| 20. | . . . | PxP |
| 21. | NxP | R–R6 |
| 22. | N–N3 | R–R3 |
| 23. | R–B3 | R/1–R1 |

The Black Rooks enter the fray probing weak spots.

| 24. | P–R3 | P–B4 |
| 25. | N–B1 | R–N1 |
| 26. | R–N3 | RxR |
| 27. | NxR | P–R4 |
| 28. | P–QR4 | |

White's QRP, long under attack by the Knight, has been limiting the mobility of his QR. Black's pawn was now threatening to go to R5, definitely fixing White's QRP as an object of attack.

| 28. | . . . | R–N3 |
| 29. | K–R2 | K–N2 |
| 30. | R–R2 | P–Q4 |

Gligoric's accurate defense has successfully beaten back the first attack, and his King is now completely safe. But what should be done about his ragged Queenside?

| 31. | Q–R5 | Q–K1 |
| 32. | R–K2 | N–Q3 |
| 33. | R–K5 | |

Usually, K5 is a good place for a Knight. Gligoric's enterprising centralization of the Rook could have led to immediate loss. But to say that White has committed an oversight explains little. It is interesting to ponder the cause of White's mistake. When both players are engaged in lengthy maneuvering, their combinational alertness is often dulled. It seems to me that this was precisely the case here.

**33. . . .          Q–B2**

This is not like Keres. Annotators usually blame time pressure in cases like this. Shutting the Rook in a cage by 33. . . . N–K5 would force White either to play 34. RxN or allow the capture of his Knight, which would be unable to leave KN3 because of the obvious combination 34. . . . RxPch! 35. KxR QxQ.

| | |
|---|---|
| **34. Q–B3** | **Q–Q2** |
| **35. Q–R5** | **Q–B2** |
| **36. Q–B3** | **R–R3** |
| **37. R–K2** | **Q–Q2** |
| **38. R–R2** | **Q–B3** |
| **39. R–R1** | **Q–B5** |

The Queen deviously penetrates behind White's pawns. White is well entrenched, but Black has a permanent advantage, one that manifests itself not only in this or that actively posted piece but in his better pawn configuration. Specifically:

1) All of Black's pawns are bound by a single cord, but White's pawns are divided into three "islands," to use M. M. Botvinnik's expression.

2) Black's QP and KBP ensure his Knight's invasion of K5. If White exchanges Knights on that square a protected passed pawn will appear for Black.

3) If Black manages to win the pawn on QR5, his protected passed QRP will promote to a Queen without hindrance. However, White's "ready-made" passed pawn on KR3 cannot do the same since White's pieces are unable to clear the path in front of it.

These main positional signposts adequately explain why Black is continually attacking and White is passively defending. In such circumstances, White's defense should be overcome sooner or later.

| | |
|---|---|
| **40. K–N1** | **Q–N6** |
| **41. N–K2** | **Q–B7** |

A powerful position for the Queen, where it is aimed at the QRP, QBP, and KNP.

**42. P–N4**

The bravery of despair. White has no fully satisfactory defense to Black's plan of R–N3, N–K5, etc. Keres now forces the win by a series of pretty moves.

| | |
|---|---|
| **42. . . .** | **PxP** |
| **43. PxP** | **R–R5** |
| **44. R–QB1** | **Q–R2** |

| 45. | P–B4 | R–R6 |
|-----|------|------|
| 46. | Q–N2 | Q–Q6 |
| 47. | PxP | N–K5 |
| 48. | PxP | Q–K6ch |
| 49. | K–B1 | R–B6ch |
| | **White resigns** | |

## Game 196
### Ruy Lopez

| | D. Bronstein | S. Reshevsky |
|---|---|---|
| 1. | P–K4 | P–K4 |
| 2. | N–KB3 | N–QB3 |
| 3. | B–N5 | P–QR3 |
| 4. | B–R4 | N–B3 |
| 5. | O–O | B–K2 |
| 6. | R–K1 | P–QN4 |
| 7. | B–N3 | P–Q3 |
| 8. | P–B3 | O–O |
| 9. | P–KR3 | N–QR4 |
| 10. | B–B2 | P–B4 |
| 11. | P–Q4 | Q–B2 |
| 12. | QN–Q2 | N–B3 |
| 13. | PxBP | PxP |
| 14. | N–B1 | R–Q1 |
| 15. | Q–K2 | N–KR4 |
| 16. | P–QR4 | R–N1 |
| 17. | PxP | PxP |
| 18. | P–KN3 | |

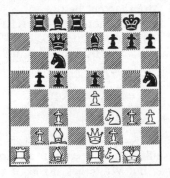

This variation, through the 17th move, is known to theory, which recommends here 18. P–KN4 N–B5 19. BxN PxB 20. P–K5, and White wins a pawn due to the threat Q–K4. Manuals on theory consider the extra pawn sufficient to give the conclusion ±, but this is not enough for a chess player seated at the board. It is very often possible to win a pawn at the cost of a move like P–KN4, but how is it to be converted to a full point?

Is P–KN4 justified in the present case? I think not. After 18. P–KN4 N–B5 19. BxN PxB 20. P–K5 Black can play, for instance, 20. ... B–N2 21. Q–K4 P–N3, and if 22. QxP then 22. ... P–B3. Black would have a clear advantage, with at least a draw always in hand.

Reasoning thus, I gradually came to the conclusion that P–KN4 should not be played, but it is necessary to keep Black's Knight out of KB5. Thus was born P–KN3, which as far as I know had not been encountered in a tournament before.

Black cannot take the KRP, of course, since after 19. N–N5, with Black's Bishop and Knight under fire, White wins in all variations.

18. ...     P–N3
19. K–R2

19. N–K3 BxP 20. N–Q5 is insufficient to keep the advantage, but White has no need to hurry. Q5 has been reserved for the Knight, and it will not run away.

19. ...     B–K3
20. N–K3     P–B5
21. R–Q1

White is worried about the transfer of Black's Knight to Q6 and tries to reduce the number of pieces controlling that square.

21. ...     RxR
22. QxR     R–Q1
23. Q–K2     Q–B1
24. N–Q5

A pawn sacrifice, characteristic of such positions, which Black pays for with his light-square Bishop. Now White will be able to annoy his opponent in various parts of the board.

24. ...     BxN
25. PxB     RxP
26. P–N3

White intends to open the position to the maximum, when his advantage of the two Bishops will be more pronounced. Black, on the contrary, wants to keep the position at least semiclosed.

26. ...     N–B3
27. N–N5

Black was ready to play P–K5 and transfer his Rook to KR4. So far White has not forgotten the golden rule: to combine attack and defense. Unfortunately he forgets it later.

27. ...     N–Q1
28. PxP     QxP
29. QxQ     PxQ
30. R–R4     N–Q2
31. RxP     N–B4

Black has regrouped his forces well, and White's Rook has no way to penetrate. Nevertheless, White has certain advantages: he has created a passed pawn, which, although not advanced, will have potential mobility working with the Bishop pair.

32. N–K4     N/1–K3
33. NxN     NxN
34. R–QN4     N–Q6

The Knight, as White feared, finally lands on Q6. However, White's Rook penetrates to the eighth rank and gives the game's first check.

| 35. | R–N8ch | K–N2 |
|-----|--------|------|
| 36. | B–K3 | P–K5 |
| 37. | R–K8 | B–B3 |
| 38. | R–QB8 | |

In severe time trouble, White refrains from 38. P–QB4 because of 38. . . . R–KB4, not noticing that after 39. RxP NxP 40. R–B4! the Knight could not get out. Correct for Black would be 38. . . . R–K4, and White's minimal advantage could hardly be realized.

**38. . . .           NxP**

Unexpected and beautiful. If White takes the Knight, as he should, Black's Rook gets to the seventh rank and takes one of the Bishops. Striving to win at any price, White rejects this variation and sets a hidden trap, then waits with bated breath for Reshevsky to fall into it.

**39. P–B4           R–QR4**

**40. B–N3           R–R6**

Black wants to attack the two Bishops immediately. Having played this, Reshevsky offered a draw—for the third time in this game, by the way—as I was sealing my move.

**41. B–B5**

Threatening mate by 42. B–B8ch, and the rest is clear: White wins the Exchange and with it the game.

**41. . . .           B–K2**

41. . . . RxB? 42. B–B8ch K–R1 43. B–R6ch B–Q1 44. RxB mate.

| 42. | BxR | BxB |
|-----|-----|-----|
| 43. | P–B5 | |

Black will soon have to give up his Bishop for this pawn.

43. . . . P–K6 44. P–B6 N–K5 45. R–K8 P–B4 46. B–B4 B–Q3 47. P–B7 BxPch 48. K–N2 BxP 49. R–K7ch K–B3 50. RxB P–B5 51. K–B3, Black resigns.

# Round Twenty-Nine

## Game 197
### King's Indian Defense

| S. Reshevsky | S. Gligoric |
|---|---|
| 1. P–Q4 | N–KB3 |
| 2. P–QB4 | P–KN3 |
| 3. P–KN3 | B–N2 |
| 4. B–N2 | O–O |
| 5. N–QB3 | P–Q3 |
| 6. N–B3 | P–B4 |

Credit for the introduction of this move into serious international practice belongs to Yugoslavian chess players. White must now decide whether to put his pawn on Q5 or to let Black's Knight go to QB3 so that it may then be driven immediately to QR4.

In either case the struggle promises to be very interesting. True, White's opening advantage will hardly be neutralized right away, but Black must not worry: even though White is a little more active, Black will retain quite enough chances to exercise his own creative imagination.

Among our chess players, Leningrad grandmaster V. Korchnoi is a virtuoso with this variation.

| 7. P–Q5 | N–R3 |
| 8. N–Q2 | N–B2 |
| 9. Q–B2 | R–N1 |
| 10. P–N3 | |

Reshevsky copies Euwe's play in his game against Szabo. It seems to me that he should not allow Black to play P–QN4 so easily. 9. P–QR4 can be played, which of course weakens QN4 —but what significance does that have and what use can Black make of it? In fact, that is just what Reshevsky played a few days earlier against Boleslavsky, and he got the advantage; here he wants more—and gets nothing!

| 10. . . . | P–QN4 |
| 11. B–N2 | PxP |
| 12. NxP | |

This capture would be justified if the Knight could later penetrate to QB6; but inasmuch as the variation 12. . . . B–QR3

13. N–R5 N/2xP 14. N–B6 N–
QN5 is in Black's favor, it
makes more sense to take on
QB4 with the pawn—QN5 and
Q5 would be firmly defended,
and a Rook on QN1 would
also prove to be very convenient.

| | |
|---|---|
| 12. . . . | B–QR3 |
| 13. N–K3 | R–N5 |
| 14. O–O | Q–Q2 |
| 15. P–KR3 | KR–N1 |
| 16. QR–N1 | Q–B1 |
| 17. K–R2 | N/2–K1 |

Black has obtained a very
good game out of the opening
but seems unable to decide
which is the best side from
which to launch an offensive
against the QP, and he just
shifts his pieces about. This cat-
and-mouse play allows Reshevsky to regroup his pieces quite
successfully and to start making
trouble for his opponent. Gligoric should find a convenient
moment to transfer his Knight
from QB2 to Q5. For some reason or other, he brings it to K1
instead and then puts its back
where it came from.

| | |
|---|---|
| 18. B–R3 | R/5–N2 |
| 19. KR–B1 | Q–Q1 |
| 20. N–R4 | N–Q2 |
| 21. B–K4 | |

White wants to exchange his
restricted Bishop for the one on
QR6. In positions like this I find
the undermining maneuver P–
R3 and P–QN4 attractive.

| | |
|---|---|
| 21. . . . | N–B2 |
| 22. B–QN2 | N–B3 |
| 23. B–Q3 | B–R3 |

Gligoric suddenly loses patience and conceives a rather
dangerous plan to open the
game with P–K3. The K-file
does fall into Black's hands, but
the danger is that the combination of his B–KR3 and P–K3
will leave his KR1–QR8 diagonal and his key KB3-square at
White's mercy. Reshevsky exploits these riches perfectly.

| | |
|---|---|
| 24. P–B4 | Q–Q2 |
| 25. N–B3 | P–K3 |
| 26. N–K4 | |

The refutation of Black's
idea. What is most annoying is
that White's QP, which is attacked three times and not defended at all, cannot be taken.

| | |
|---|---|
| 26. . . . | NxN |

White was threatening to an-
nounce check to the King and
guardez to her highness. The
Knight on K5 must therefore be
destroyed. Other variations turn
out even more favorably for
White; for instance, 26. . . .
N/3–K1 27. Q–B3 B–N2 28.
QxBch NxQ 29. N–B6ch, or
26. . . . N/3xP 27. NxN BxB
28. N/5–B6ch, or finally, 26.
. . . N/3–K1 27. Q–B3 P–K4
28. PxP BxN 29. P–K6.

| | |
|---|---|
| 27. BxN | P–B4 |
| 28. PxP | QxP |
| 29. BxR | RxB |

Taking with the Bishop does not improve Gligoric's situation much, for after 30. Q–B4 N–Q4 31. N–N2 followed by R–Q1 Black's attack comes to a dead end.

**30. Q–B3 N–K1
31. Q–Q2**

In time pressure, Reshevsky decides not to go into the forcing variation, although it is exactly 31. Q–R8ch K–B2 32. QxPch B–N2 33. BxB NxB 34. R–B3 P–Q4 35. N–N2 that would have broken Black's resistance. Now drawing chances appear for Black.

**31. . . . R–K2
32. N–Q5 QxPch
33. QxQ RxQch
34. K–N1 K–B1
35. R–K1 R–Q7
36. R/K–Q1 R–K7
37. N–B6**

**37. . . . B–KN2**

The last mistake, in severe time pressure. He should exchange on KB3, bring the Rook back to K3, and try to transfer his Bishop to K5, after which the struggle might have begun anew. But White would win with 38. RxP, sacrificing two pieces for a Rook but maximizing the activity of his forces: 38. . . . N–K5 39. RxB N–Q7 40. R–QB1 N–B6ch 41. K–B1 RxB 42. RxBP or 38. . . . B–QN2 39. BxN R–N7ch 40. K–B1 RxNP 41. R–Q8ch K–B2 42. B–K5. Still, Black would have had practical drawing chances. Now the game is over.

**38. NxPch K–N1 39. BxB KxB 40. N–N5 R–K6 41. R–K1, Black resigns.**

## Game 198
### Sicilian Defense

| P. Keres | M. Taimanov | | |
|---|---|---|---|
| | | 3. P–Q4 | PxP |
| | | 4. NxP | N–B3 |
| 1. P–K4 | P–QB4 | 5. N–QB3 | P–Q3 |
| 2. N–KB3 | N–QB3 | 6. B–QB4 | |

The sharp Sozin System, which we encountered earlier. The theorctical evaluation of this variation has changed more than once. It was used three times in the Zurich tournament, and today it is a favorite weapon of the young Robert Fischer.

| 6. . . . | P–K3 |
| 7. O–O | P–QR3 |
| 8. B–K3 | Q–B2 |
| 9. B–N3 | N–QR4 |

In game 146 against Averbakh, Taimanov played 9. . . . B–K2 here and lost. This time he reverts to the earlier system with 9. . . . N–QR4 in order to eliminate the poisonous Bishop more quickly. Taimanov later repaired the 9. . . . B–K2 variation and used it successfully in one of his games in the 21st U.S.S.R. Championship.

| 10. P–B4 | P–QN4 |
| 11. P–B5 | |

An old idea in a new setting. In the last round of the 1935 Moscow international tournament, sixty - seven - year - old Emanuel Lasker crushed V. Pirc's position right in the opening with a similarly swift attack and earned a prize for the most beautiful game. Keres carries out an analogous idea, following not Lasker but A. Tolush, who employed 11. P–B5 against Taimanov in the 1953 Leningrad Championship, not long before this tournament.

| 11. . . . | NxB |
| 12. BPxN | B–K2 |

Capturing with a pawn toward the center is a positional rule that has frequently been violated in recent years. The idea is clear in this case—to open the QB-file for the Rooks —but the drawbacks of White's pawn configuration may be felt in the endgame.

Black should exercise some caution, for his development is incomplete. Such moves as 12. . . . P–N5 or 12. . . . P–K4 and then . . . P–N5 might win the KP but would run counter to Black's strategy.

| 13. R–B1 | Q–Q2 |

This is what Taimanov had prepared. In the mentioned Tolush–Taimanov game, 13. . . . Q–N2 14. P–QN4 O–O 15. PxP PxP 16. Q–N3 was played, with some pressure for White, but here Black guards K3 with two pieces and then calmly castles.

| 14. PxP | PxP |
| 15. P–QN4 | O–O |
| 16. Q–N3 | |

An uncommon place for the Queen in the Sicilian. Keres hopes either to provoke . . . P–Q4 or to nail Black's Bishop to QB1. Taimanov finds a third solution: to prepare P–K4.

| 16. . . . | K–R1 |

Black does not want to be prematurely active, considering the dangerous situation of his King. In fact, after 16. . . . N–N5 White has the beautiful stroke 17. N–Q5, placing Black in a difficult position.

**17. P–KR3          P–K4**

Combinations occur not only in attack but also in defense. We see here the beginning of a combination whose ultimate aim is to intercept the opponent's initiative.

**18. N–B5**

18. N–B6? is a mistake in view of 18. . . . QxN 19. N–Q5 Q–K1 20. N–B7 Q–N3 21. NxR BxP.

**18. . . .          B–N2**
**19. NxB**

White is compelled to carry out a series of exchanges, for retreating to N3 would mean switching entirely to defense.

Perhaps Keres was hoping to seize Q5 by means of B–N5 followed by BxN and N–Q5, and

only now realized that 19. B–N5 would lead to the loss of a pawn after 19. . . . NxP 20. NxB NxB or 20. BxB RxN. Therefore, White takes the Bishop on K7 first and only then plays B–N5; next, in order not to find himself unexpectedly in a bad position, he strengthens his KP by a series of exchanges and simultaneously attempts to lay claim to the QP.

**19. . . .          QxN**
**20. B–N5          P–R3**
**21. BxN          RxB**
**22. RxR          QxR**
**23. R–B1          Q–N3**

White has made no visible errors; nonetheless the initiative has gradually passed to Black. This suggests that the attack against the pawn on K6 by transferring the Queen to QN3 takes too much time and does not offer real chances. A more promising plan was chosen by Geller against Taimanov in the 21st U.S.S.R. Championship. Instead of opening the KB-file on the 14th move with PxP he played Q–B3 and continued the attack by P–KN4–5. The fate of Taimanov's defense to the 6. B–QB4 variation will evidently be finally decided somewhere along those lines.

Meanwhile, Keres must think of some simple way to fully neutralize Taimanov's pressure in the forthcoming difficult ending. He decides to give up his KP for Black's QP and to play with the heavy pieces against the passed KP, which is in effect an extra pawn.

**24. Q–Q1     R–QB1**

Black does not fear the White pieces' invasion of his first rank, since after the KP falls White's King will be first to come under a mating attack.

**25. Q–B3     R–B5**
**26. R–Q1     K–R2**
**27. P–R3     BxP**

Keres's accurate play has successfully mended the holes in his position, and Taimanov finds nothing better than to switch to a Queen ending in which White has passive double pawns on the Queenside.

**28. NxB     RxN**
**29. RxP     R–K8ch**
**30. K–B2     QxR**
**31. KxR     Q–KN3**
**32. K–Q2     P–K5**
**33. Q–B2**

After a cursory glance at the position, one would not believe that even Keres, who is well known for his skill in Queen endings, can save the game. There are two peculiarities of the position, however, that ease White's problems somewhat: the weak shelter of Black's King, which creates the permanent danger of perpetual check, and the solid pawn position on the Queenside. It is still three against two! The significance of this latter circumstance will soon become clear.

**33. . . .     Q–N4ch**

33. . . . Q–KB3 is useless, since White boldly exchanges Queens and continues not with 35. P–N4, of course (this would be good if Black played 35. . . . K–N3 36. K–K3 P–B4, but 36. . . . K–N4 refutes it), but with the immediate 35. K–K3!, which now forces the 35. . . . P–B4 variation, when after 36. P–N4 the chances—though slim —are only White's.

**34. K–K2     Q–Q4**
**35. K–K3!**

Saving the game. All of White's pawns seem to be just where they belong. Were it not for White's pawn on QN4, . . . Q–B4ch would win; the pawn on QN2 defends the pawn on QR3, which otherwise would be lost after . . . Q–Q6ch.

**35. . . .     Q–Q6ch**

White was threatening to attack the KP by 36. Q–B2, and 35. . . . K–N3 does not work in view of 36. Q–B2 K–B4 37. Q–B8ch.

| 36. | K–B4 | P–N4ch |
|-----|------|--------|
| 37. | K–K5! | |

Drawn, since Black has no satisfactory defense against perpetual check.

## Game 199
### King's Indian Defense

**V. Smyslov          M. Najdorf**

1. P–Q4 N–KB3 2. N–KB3 P–KN3 3. P–KN3 B–N2 4. B–N2 O–O 5. O–O P–Q3 6. P–N3 P–K4 7. PxP N–N5 8. B–N2 N–QB3 9. P–B4 R–K1 10. N–B3 N/5xKP 11. NxN, Drawn.

By making this quick draw Smyslov assured himself of clear first place in the candidates tournament for the world championship, irrespective of the results of all other games to come in the final rounds.

## Game 200
### Nimzo-Indian Defense

**Y. Geller          T. Petrosian**

| | | |
|-----|--------|--------|
| 1. | P–Q4 | N–KB3 |
| 2. | P–QB4 | P–K3 |
| 3. | N–KB3 | B–N5ch |
| 4. | N–B3 | P–B4 |
| 5. | P–K3 | O–O |
| 6. | B–K2 | P–QN3 |
| 7. | O–O | B–N2 |
| 8. | Q–N3 | PxP |
| 9. | QxB | N–B3 |
| 10. | Q–R3 | PxN |
| 11. | QxBP | N–K5 |
| 12. | Q–B2 | P–B4 |

While White has been spending five moves in pursuit of the two Bishops, Black has developed successfully and has reinforced his Knight in the center.

Petrosian brings his Rook to KR3, blockades White's Queen-side pawns, and achieves an excellent position.

| | | |
|-----|--------|--------|
| 13. | P–QR3 | R–B3 |
| 14. | P–QN4 | R–R3 |
| 15. | B–N2 | P–Q3 |
| 16. | QR–Q1 | Q–K2 |
| 17. | B–Q3 | P–R4! |
| 18. | P–N5 | |

Black, in advancing his outside pawn, makes use of a well-known technique in the fight against pawns on QR3, QN4, and QB4. 18. PxP would be answered by 18. . . . NxRP with an attack on the QBP along the QB-file. Geller's reply weakens his QB5, where a Black Knight wants to settle immediately, and that forces White to exchange it on his next move. This helps only 50 percent, since Black still has another Knight.

But if 18. Q–N3, White's Queen would become tied to the defense of the QNP, and in the meantime Black could launch a Kingside attack. Still, QB5 should not have been weakened.

| 18. | . . . | N–N1 |
| 19. | BxN | BxB |
| 20. | Q–K2 | N–Q2 |
| 21. | N–K1 | P–K4 |
| 22. | P–B3 | B–N2 |
| 23. | Q–KB2 | R–QB1 |
| 24. | R–B1 | Q–K3 |

White has taken the necessary defensive measures on the King-side, in particular protecting Q3 from the possible invasion of Black's Knight via QB5, but he has no convenient defense for his QBP and therefore decides to sacrifice it.

| 25. | P–B4 | P–K5 |
| 26. | N–B2 | N–B4 |

Complications like 26. . . . QxP 27. N–Q4 Q–KB2 28. Q–N3 R–N3 29. RxRch BxR 30. Q–R4 evidently seemed double-edged to Black, so Petrosian declined the offered sacrifice. White is lucky to slip past the dangerous turning point and is assured of arriving at a drawn finish.

| 27. | N–Q4 | Q–B2 |
| 28. | Q–N3 | Drawn |

## Game 201
### Nimzo-Indian Defense

| A. Kotov | Y. Averbakh |
|---|---|
| 1. | P–Q4 | N–KB3 |
| 2. | P–QB4 | P–K3 |
| 3. | N–QB3 | B–N5 |
| 4. | P–K3 | O–O |
| 5. | N–K2 | P–Q4 |
| 6. | P–QR3 | B–K2 |
| 7. | PxP | PxP |
| 8. | N–N3 | R–K1 |
| 9. | B–Q3 | QN–Q2 |
| 10. | O–O | P–QR3 |

Having had no success in his game against Reshevsky, in which for a long time Black stuck to waiting tactics, this time Averbakh employs the more logical system with . . . P–B4 and soon achieves full equality. The prophylactic move 10. . . . P–QR3 is directed against White's possibility of invading QN5 with his pieces.

| 11. | Q–B2 | B–B1 |
| 12. | B–Q2 | P–B4 |
| 13. | PxP | NxP |
| 14. | QR–Q1 | B–N5 |

The immediate 14. . . . B–K3 is more accurate. White's Bishop is stronger on K2 than on Q3.

| 15. | B–K2 | B–K3 |
|---|---|---|
| 16. | N–B5 | R–B1 |
| 17. | N–Q4 | B–Q3 |
| 18. | B–B3 | N/4–K5 |
| 19. | NxB | PxN |
| 20. | Q–N3 | N–B4 |
| 21. | Q–R2 | Q–B2 |
| 22. | P–KN3 | Q–B2 |
| 23. | B–B1 | B–K4 |
| 24. | N–K2 | R–B2 |
| 25. | B–N2 | |

White has no place to show his initiative; he maintains his waiting tactics, seeing to it that Black is not permitted a superiority in any important sector.

25. . . . P–KN3 26. Q–N1 N–N6 27. B–Q2 NxB 28. RxN KR–QB1 29. P–R3 R–B5 30. R–B1 Q–B2 31. RxR QxR 32. P–B4 B–N1 33. N–Q4 Q–QB8ch 34. QxQ RxQch, Drawn.

## Game 202
### English Opening

| I. Boleslavsky | | L. Szabo |
|---|---|---|
| 1. | P–Q4 | N–KB3 |
| 2. | P–QB4 | P–K3 |
| 3. | N–KB3 | P–B4 |
| 4. | N–B3 | PxP |
| 5. | NxP | B–N5 |
| 6. | Q–N3 | N–R3 |
| 7. | P–K3 | |

White intends to sacrifice a pawn in the interest of quicker development. The experiment has little basis in this position: Black is excellently mobilized and his King is safely protected. Interesting complications arise on 7. B–N5; e.g., 7. . . . Q–R4 8. B–Q2 N–B4 9. Q–B2 N/4–K5! 10. NxN NxN 11. N–N3 BxBch 12. NxB P–Q4, and Black is more active.

| 7. | . . . | N–K5 |
|---|---|---|
| 8. | B–K2 | Q–R4 |
| 9. | O–O | N/3–B4 |

Refuting White's idea. If the Bishop takes on QB6 right away, then after 10. PxB QxBP 11. B–N2 White's development fully compensates for the missing pawn. The exchange of Queens on QN3 is not dangerous to White, since in that case his broken QRP and QBP would be united. But now the Queen moves to QB2, and the exchange takes place under unfavorable conditions for White.

| 10. | Q–B2 | BxN |
|---|---|---|
| 11. | PxB | QxBP |
| 12. | QxQ | NxQ |

| | |
|---|---|
| 13. B–B3 | K–K2 |
| 14. N–N3 | |

White's dark-square Bishop cannot show its strength because of the extremely solid Knight on Black's QB4. With his next moves Boleslavsky tries to expel the Knight.

| | |
|---|---|
| 14. . . . | N/6–R5 |
| 15. B–R3 | P–Q3 |
| 16. N–R5 | P–K4 |
| 17. KR–B1 | R–QN1 |
| 18. QR–N1 | B–B4 |
| 19. RxPch | |

His problem has turned out to be not so easy, and White has to resort to drastic measures.

| | |
|---|---|
| 19. . . . | NxR |
| 20. NxN | RxN |
| 21. BxR | R–QN1 |
| 22. B–B6 | |

White's position has improved somewhat and he has succeeded in winning his pawn back; but his pawns are disconnected, and therefore he has a difficult endgame despite his two Bishops.

| | |
|---|---|
| 22. . . . | N–B4 |
| 23. P–B3 | R–N3 |
| 24. BxN | PxB |
| 25. B–Q5 | R–N7 |
| 26. R–B3 | RxP |
| 27. R–N3 | B–Q2 |
| 28. R–N7 | K–Q3! |

Szabo is playing the endgame well. Of course 28. . . . P–B3 docs not work because of 29. B–B6 R–Q7 30. RxP.

29. BxP B–B3 30. R–N1 P–QR4 31. B–Q5 BxB 32. R–Q1 P–R5 33. RxBch K–B3 34. P–R4 R–QB7 35. RxP P–R6 36. R–K6ch K–B2 37. R–K7ch K–N3 38. R–K6ch K–R4 39. R–K8 P–R7 40. R–R8ch K–N5 41. K–R2 K–N6 42. R–N8ch KxP, White resigns.

## Game 203
### Nimzo-Indian Defense

| G. Stahlberg | M. Euwe |
|---|---|

1. P–Q4 N–KB3 2. P–QB4 P–K3 3. N–KB3 P–QN3 4. N–B3 B–N2 5. B–N5 B–N5 6. R–B1

White wants to keep all his

Queenside pawns connected, and he defends the Knight with the Rook in anticipation of . . . BxN. After PxB the QRP would be isolated from the pawn mass.

6. . . . P–KR3 7. BxN QxB 8. P–K3 O–O 9. B–K2 P–Q3 10. O–O BxQN 11. RxB N–Q2 12. N–Q2 P–K4 13. B–B3 BxB 14. NxB, Drawn.

# Round Thirty

## Game 204
### King's Indian Defense

**Y. Averbakh    Y. Geller**

1. P–Q4 N–KB3 2. P–QB4 P–KN3 3. P–KN3 B–N2 4. B–N2 O–O 5. N–KB3 P–Q3 6. O–O QN–Q2 7. N–B3 P–K4 8. P–K4 R–K1 9. P–KR3 PxP 10. NxP N–B4 11. R–K1 P–QR4 12. Q–B2 KN–Q2

The idea of this move is to transfer the Knight to QN5 via K4 and Q6 after White plays B–K3.

13. R–Q1 P–QB3 14. B–K3 P–R5 15. QR–N1 Q–K2 16. R–K1 N–K4 17. P N3 PxP 18. PxP N/K–Q6 19. R–K2 N–N5 20. Q–Q1 Q–B2 21. R–Q2 Q–R4

White is aiming for the QP; to take it he will have to bring a minor piece—a Bishop, for example—to KB4. In the meantime Black will prepare the threat P–KB4.

22. N/4–K2 B–B1 23. P–N4 N–K3 24. N–N3 Q–K4 25. N/B–K2 R–R3 26. N–Q4 Q–QR4

26. . . . N–B5 is unplayable on account of 27. N–B3 Q–B3 28. P–N5.

27. N–B2 NxN 28. RxN Q–N5 29. B–Q2 Q–N3 30. B–K3 Q–N5 31. B–Q2 Q–N3 32. B–K3 Q–N5, Drawn.

## Game 205
### Queen's Gambit

**T. Petrosian    V. Smyslov**

1. P–Q4 P–Q4 2. P–QB4 P–QB3 3. PxP PxP 4. N–QB3 N–KB3 5. N–B3 N–B3

A sort of four Knights game. It is not so inoffensive as it may appear. A symmetrical position is not in itself an indication that the players are renouncing the fight, but possibly that they are postponing it until a later stage. In this case they postpone it until the next tournament.

**6. B–B4 B–B4 7. P–K3 P–K3 8. Q–N3 B–QN5**

A continuation found by Trifunovic. It is considered to equalize fully. Even Botvinnik, as White against Trifunovic in 1947, had to agree to a draw as early as move 13. Petrosian and Smyslov follow that example.

**9. B–QN5 Q–R4 10. BxNch PxB 11. P–QR3 BxNch 12. QxB QxQch 13. PxQ, Drawn.**

## Game 206
### King's Indian Defense

| M. Taimanov | S. Reshevsky |
|---|---|
| 1. P–Q4 | N–KB3 |
| 2. P–QB4 | P–Q3 |
| 3. N–KB3 | P–KN3 |
| 4. N–B3 | B–N2 |
| 5. P–K4 | O–O |
| 6. B–K2 | QN–Q2 |
| 7. O–O | P–K4 |
| 8. R–K1 | PxP |
| 9. NxP | N–B4 |
| 10. B–B1 | R–K1 |
| 11. P–B3 | KN–Q2 |
| 12. B–K3 | P–QB3 |
| 13. Q–Q2 | P–QR4 |
| 14. QR–Q1 | P–R5 |
| 15. N–B2 | |

**15. . . .          B–K4**

A well-known method of defending the weak QP in the King's Indian.

| 16. B–Q4 | N–K3 |
|---|---|
| 17. BxB | |

Self-confidently weakening Q4. Fortunately for Taimanov, this is not very dangerous in view of White's good development.

| 17. . . . | PxB |
|---|---|
| 18. Q–B2 | Q–K2 |
| 19. P–KN3 | N–B3 |

The weakness of White's Q4 can be exploited only in the endgame. Actually, this is a good time to think about exchanging Queens with that aim. The variation 19. . . . Q–B4 20. QxQ N/2xQ seems to meet the requirements of the position, since the Knight on Q2 gets to QB4 while the Knight on K3 threatens to invade Q5, forcing a

White Knight at QB2 to keep permanent watch over that square. Reshevsky avoids the exchange of Queens, however. After 19. . . . Q–B4 20. P–QN4 PxP e.p. 21. PxP QxQch 22. KxQ Black's minimal advantage would not be enough to win.

**20. P–QN4**

This strong move, now threatening P–B4, completely equalizes the chances. Therefore Reshevsky accepted the offer of a draw, although a draw is not what he wanted. It seems to me that the American grandmaster made a mistake even before the game started: he should have chosen a different opening variation, or possibly a different opening. The variation that occurred in the game was too well known to Taimanov.

**Drawn.**

## Game 207
### King's Indian Defense

| M. Euwe | I. Boleslavsky |
|---------|----------------|
| 1. P–Q4 | N–KB3 |
| 2. P–QB4 | P–KN3 |
| 3. P–KN3 | B–N2 |
| 4. B–N2 | O–O |
| 5. N–QB3 | P–Q3 |
| 6. N–B3 | QN–Q2 |
| 7. O–O | P–K4 |
| 8. P–N3 | |

An old continuation now out of fashion. The Bishop never gets to N2.

| 8. . . . | R–K1 |
|----------|------|
| 9. Q–B2 | P–B3 |
| 10. R–Q1 | P–K5 |
| 11. N–K1 | |

On 11. N–Q2 Black can boldly continue 11. . . . P–Q4!. White's attempt to make use of the fork 12. PxP PxP 13. N–N5 is repulsed by 13. . . . R–K3

14. Q–B7 Q–K1. If 11. N–KN5 Black can sacrifice a pawn with good prospects by 11. . . . P–K6. If 12. BxKP then 12. . . . RxB 13. PxR N–N5; or if 12. PxP then 12. . . . N–N5 immediately, with good piece play.

| 11. . . . | Q–K2 |
|-----------|------|
| 12. P–KR3 | P–QR3 |
| 13. P–QR4 | P–Q4 |
| 14. PxP | PxP |
| 15. P–R5 | P–QN4 |
| 16. PxP e.p. | NxP |
| 17. Q–Q2 | B–K3 |
| 18. N–B2 | Q–Q2 |
| 19. K–R2 | P–KR4 |
| 20. N–R4 | NxN |
| 21. RxN | Q–B2 |

Black threatens P–R5, so White's King goes to N1.

| 22. K–N1 | KR–N1 |
|----------|-------|
| 23. N–R1 | K–R2 |

| 24. Q–R2 | R–N3 |
|---|---|
| 25. B–B4 | Q–Q2 |
| 26. K–R2 | N–K1 |
| 27. R–QB1 | N–Q3 |
| 28. BxN | |

Yet another achievement for Black, resulting from the threat of . . . N–B4. The Bishop will be missed very much later on.

| 28. . . . | QxB |
|---|---|
| 29. P–K3 | P–R5 |
| 30. P–N4 | |

Boleslavsky's attack has become very threatening, and Euwe decides to sacrifice a pawn to distract his opponent from his King and to free himself a little.

| 30. . . . | B–R3 |
|---|---|
| 31. R–B3 | RxP |
| 32. N–N3 | RxR |
| 33. QxR | B–Q2 |
| 34. Q–R5 | B–QN4 |

The light-square Bishop, long held in reserve, joins the battle.

| 35. N–B5 | R–QN1 |
|---|---|
| 36. Q–R1 | B–N4 |
| 37. Q–Q1 | PxPch |
| 38. PxP | P–B4 |
| 39. Q–K1 | B–QB5 |
| 40. K–N1 | B–Q1 |

The second Bishop joins the attack. Now it speeds toward QB2 in order to support the Queen's operations on the QN1–KR7 diagonal. Boleslavsky is conducting this part of the game very skillfully.

| 41. R–B2 | B–B2 |
|---|---|
| 42. B–B1 | |

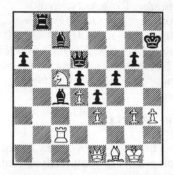

Euwe offers to trade his KNP for Black's QRP and at the same time dreams of exchanging Queens to relieve himself of the mating threats.

If 42. K–R2 Black can offer an elegant Rook ⌐sacrifice:⌐ 42. . . . R–N8 43. QxR QxPch 44. K–N1 Q–R7ch. Apart from the Rook's threat to invade on the QN-file, Black has the even simpler plan of breaking though by P–N4 and P–B5, and therefore White's position is hopeless.

| 42. . . . | BxB |
|---|---|

Black can bring the other Bishop into play here with⌐decisive⌐ effect: 42. . . . B–R4 43. QxB (43. Q–B2 R–N8) 43. . . . QxPch 44. R–N2 QxPch 45. K–R1 R–N8 46. Q–B7ch K–R3 47. N–K6 QxPch!

| 43. KxB | QxP |
|---|---|
| 44. QxQ | BxQ |
| 45. NxRP | R–N6 |
| 46. K–K2 | P–N4 |
| 47. N–B5 | R–N3 |

| 48. | R–R2 | P–B5 |
| 49. | R–R7ch | K–N3 |
| 50. | R–R6 | P–B6ch |
| 51. | K–B1 | RxR |
| 52. | NxR | B–Q3 |

This is why a Bishop is stronger than a Knight.

| 53. | K–B2 | K–B2 |

**White resigns**

## Game 208
### Nimzo-Indian Defense

**S. Gligoric**        **D. Bronstein**

| 1. | P–Q4 | N–KB3 |
| 2. | P–QB4 | P–K3 |
| 3. | N–QB3 | B–N5 |
| 4. | P–K3 | O–O |
| 5. | N–K2 | P–Q4 |
| 6. | P–QR3 | B–K2 |
| 7. | PxP | PxP |
| 8. | N–N3 | P–B4 |

As played by Alekhine against Euwe in the 25th game of their world championship match (1937). Black's counterattack against White's center dislodges the White pawn at Q4 and gives Black chances to take up a convenient position at K4.

| 9. | B–Q3 | N–B3 |
| 10. | O–O | R–K1 |
| 11. | PxP | BxP |
| 12. | P–N4 | B–Q3 |
| 13. | B–N2 | B–K4 |
| 14. | N–QR4 | BxB |

The struggle for White's Q4 is on. This is not an end in itself, however; possession of the square in front of the isolated pawn will be significant only if White can firmly establish a piece there and if there are no vulnerable points in his own camp.

Essentially, Black's further play in this game is to take the White pieces a little farther from his Q4 and create weaknesses in his Queenside pawn formation. Here, for example, the exchange of dark-square Bishops favors White, but Black cannot very well allow White's QB to be the boss on the long diagonal. Moreover, White's Knight lands on a bad spot and will need at least four moves to get to Q4.

| 15. | NxB | B–N5 |
| 16. | B–K2 | |

White's Queen has no good place to go, but now the exchange of the second pair of Bishops is to Black's advantage, not White's.

| 16. | . . . | BxB |
| 17. | NxB | Q–Q3 |
| 18. | N–Q3 | P–QR3 |
| 19. | R–B1 | P–QR4 |

At just the right time. On his last move White could have played 19. P–N5 advantageously (it was important then for Black to secure QB3 for his Knight), Black having played 18. . . . . P–QR3. Now White's QRP is insufficiently defended, and

Black is able to transfer a Knight to K3, where its functions will be quite extensive: it will control KN2, KB5, Q5, and QB4.

| 20. | P–N5 | N–Q1 |
|-----|------|------|
| 21. | P–QR4 | N–K3 |
| 22. | N–N3 | |

| 22. | . . . | Q–R6 |
|-----|-------|------|

The Queen sneaks up on the QRP from behind. White expels it, but it goes to QB6, the Rook attacks it again, and it returns . . .

| 23. | R–R1 | Q–B6 |
|-----|------|------|
| 24. | R–B1 | Q–R6 |
| 25. | R–R1 | Q–B6 |
| | **Drawn** | |

# Game 209
## Nimzo-Indian Defense

**L. Szabo**          **A. Kotov**

| 1. | P–Q4 | N–KB3 |
|----|------|-------|
| 2. | P–QB4 | P–K3 |
| 3. | N–QB3 | B–N5 |
| 4. | P–K3 | O–O |
| 5. | B–Q3 | P–Q4 |
| 6. | N–B3 | P–B4 |
| 7. | O–O | QN–Q2 |
| 8. | Q–K2 | P–QR3 |
| 9. | P–QR3 | BPxP |
| 10. | KPxP | PxP |
| 11. | BxP | B–K2 |
| 12. | B–R2 | |

Black is preparing to develop his Bishop on QN2. White's Bishop goes back so that . . .

P–QN4 can be answered by P–Q5.

| 12. | . . . | N–N3 |
|-----|-------|------|
| 13. | B–N5 | KN–Q4 |

White plans to build a strong attacking position by KR–K1, QR–Q1, B–N1, N–K5, and P–B4, which suggests an exchanging strategy to Black. As a result, the number of pieces decreases and the immediate danger of mating attacks disappears; but White's advantage remains, taking other forms.

| 14. | BxB | NxN |
|-----|-----|-----|
| 15. | PxN | QxB |
| 16. | P–B4 | |

| 16. | . . . | N–R5 |
|---|---|---|
| 17. | B–N3 | B–Q2 |
| 18. | Q–B2 | N–N3 |
| 19. | P–B5 | QR–B1 |
| 20. | N–K5 | KR–Q1 |
| 21. | Q–K4 | |

There is no question about White's positional advantage. He has a choice: to bring his QRP to the fifth rank and fix Black's pawn on QN2 for good, or to rush immediately to attack with P–B4–5, or to bring the Rooks to the Q-file and the K-file. These plans are all good, but they are not specific enough and allow Black the possibility of obstinate defense. Szabo prefers to simplify the position a little and obtain one important advantage—pressure on the QNP along the open QN-file.

| 21. | . . . | N–Q4 |
|---|---|---|
| 22. | BxN | PxB |
| 23. | Q–B4 | P–B3 |
| 24. | NxB | QxN |
| 25. | QR–N1 | R–K1 |
| 26. | P–B3 | R–K2 |
| 27. | R–B2 | QR–K1 |
| 28. | R/2–N2 | R–K8ch |

By exchanging one Rook, Black removes a piece that defends White's K1-square, and he subsequently creates counterplay on the K-file.

| 29. | RxR | RxRch |
|---|---|---|
| 30. | K–B2 | R–K1 |
| 31. | R–N6 | |

White's threats take concrete shape—R–Q6. Kotov organizes a Queen excursion to divert his opponent's attention to the defense of his King.

| 31. | . . . | Q–K2 |
|---|---|---|
| 32. | Q–Q2 | R–Q1 |

The K-file should not be given up under any circumstances, especially if Queens are exchanged. The only possibility to resist White's pressure consists of 32. . . . P–B4; for instance, 33. P–N3 P–B5 34. R–Q6 PxPch 35. PxP R–Q1 or 33. P–R3 Q–R5ch 34. K–B1 P–B5. Although White would retain an advantage, it would not be easy to coordinate the attack on the QNP and the QP with the defense of his King.

By exchanging Queens on the next move, Black finds himself in a difficult Rook ending.

| 33. | Q–K3 | QxQch |
|---|---|---|
| 34. | KxQ | R–Q2 |
| 35. | P–KR4 | |

Black's Rook is tied to the defense of his QNP and QP. White plans to break through with his King to KB5 or K5; Black's next moves impede this, but there arises a new weakness for him—his KBP.

| 35. | . . . | K–B2 |
|-----|-------|------|
| 36. | P–R5 | P–N4 |
| 37. | PxP e.p.ch | KxP |
| 38. | K–B4 | P–KR4 |
| 39. | P–N3 | R–R2 |
| 40. | K–K3 | R–K2ch |
| 41. | K–B4 | R–R2 |

After analyzing the adjourned game Kotov came to the conclusion that his position was hopeless and that his only chance was to activate his Rook.

| 42. | P–R4 | P–R5 |
|-----|------|------|
| 43. | PxP | RxPch |
| 44. | K–K3 | R–R2 |

| 45. | R–Q6 | R–K2ch |
|-----|------|--------|
| 46. | K–Q3 | K–N4 |
| 47. | RxPch | K–B5 |
| 48. | R–Q6 | P–B4 |
| 49. | R–KB6 | R–K8 |
| 50. | R–B7 | R–QN8 |
| 51. | P–R5 | R–N6ch |

Black has made the most of his chances—his King has broken through, he has activated his Rook, and he is twice attacking White's KBP. But all this has come too late—the game will be decided by the passed QP.

52. K–B4 R–N8 53. R–B6 R–KR8 54. R–QN6 R–R2 55. R–N3 R–Q2 56. P–Q5 K–K4 57. P–Q6 P–B5 58. R–N1 R–R2 59. R–K1ch K–B3 60. P–B6 PxP 61. K–B5 R–R7 62. R–Q1, Black resigns.

## *Game 210*
### *Queen's Gambit*

| M. Najdorf | P. Keres | 3. N–QB3 | P–Q4 |
|------------|----------|----------|------|
| 1. P–Q4 | N–KB3 | 4. N–B3 | P–B4 |
| 2. P–QB4 | P–K3 | 5. BPxP | BPxP |

| 6. | QxP | PxP |
|---|---|---|
| 7. | P–K4 | N–B3 |
| 8. | B–QN5 | P–QR3 |

Keres loves to play  all-out,  especially at the finish, if the final result depends on it—and he knows how to do it. Let us not forget that his last-round victories earned him first place at such outstanding tournaments as the 15th, 18th, and 19th U.S.S.R. championships, as well as at the international tournament in Budapest 1952.

For Keres, the word "tournament" probably evokes the image of knights with lances atilt and offering their opponents no draws. And perhaps he saw himself as one of those knights now: in this last round he decided to fight for clear second place and for the third time to use his  double-edged  sword—a new defense, or more correctly a counterattack, in the Queen's Gambit. The risk was very great: even his game against Geller looked dubious, and Najdorf, who is a great lover of forcing variations and a great expert with them, was no doubt excellently prepared here.

The move 8. . . . P–QR3 is an improvement on game 155, Geller–Keres, in which 8. . . . NxP was played.

| 9. | BxNch | PxB |
|---|---|---|
| 10. | N–K5 | |

Better than castling, on which 10. . . . PxP 11. QxQch KxQ 12. N–KN5 K–K1 might follow. The text move forces Black's Bishop into a passive position.

| 10. . . . | | B–N2 |
|---|---|---|
| 11. | PxP | NxP |

Instead of this, 11. . . . B–K2 has been suggested. White can reply 12. P–Q6 QxP 13. QxQ BxQ 14. N–B4 with advantage due to Black's weak pawns on QR3 and QB3. Even so, that is better than 11. . . . NxP, since Black would avoid the danger of direct attack which his King now undergoes.

| 12. | O–O | B–K2 |
|---|---|---|
| 13. | NxQBP | |

A beautiful piece sacrifice with the idea of keeping Black's King in the center and attacking it with Rooks, Queen, and minor pieces. Keres has come up against a worthy opponent for his final duel.

| 13. . . . | BxN |
| 14. QxP | R–KB1 |
| 15. R–K1 | Q–Q3 |

**16. N–K4        Drawn**

Najdorf refrained from 16. NxN because of 16. . . . QxN,

and on any reply Black castles long and plays R–N1, creating very dangerous threats to the White King; for instance, 17. B–R6 O–O–O 18. Q–N4ch P–B4 or 18. RxB R–N1 and White's KN2 is defenseless.

The next day, when the tournament had already ended, Najdorf with his Argentine temperament showed the players that he had a win by 17. B–B4 in order to answer 17. . . . O–O–O with 18. RxB R–N1 19. R–B7ch. But if 16. . . . BxN, then 17. B–N5 B–K3 18. QR–Q1 Q–N5 19. B–R6 with a formidable attack. In reply Keres just smiled . . .

# Table of Results

| | Player | 1 | 2 | 3 | 4 | 5 | 6 | 7 | 8 | 9 | 10 | 11 | 12 | 13 | 14 | 15 | Pts. | Place |
|---|---|---|---|---|---|---|---|---|---|---|---|---|---|---|---|---|---|---|
| 1 | Smyslov | – – | ½ ½ | 1 1 | ½ 1 | ½ ½ | 1 1 | ½ ½ | ½ 0 | ½ ½ | ½ ½ | ½ ½ | ½ ½ | 1 ½ | 1 1 | 1 ½ | 18 | I |
| 2 | Bronstein | ½ ½ | – – | 1 ½ | 1 1 | ½ ½ | ½ 0 | ½ ½ | ½ ½ | 1 ½ | ½ ½ | ½ ½ | 0 1 | 1 ½ | ½ ½ | ½ ½ | 16 | II–IV |
| 3 | Keres | 0 0 | 0 ½ | – – | ½ ½ | ½ 1 | ½ 1 | ½ ½ | ½ ½ | ½ ½ | 0 ½ | 1 1 | 1 ½ | ½ 1 | ½ ½ | 1 1 | 16 | II–IV |
| 4 | Reshevsky | ½ 0 | 0 0 | ½ ½ | – – | ½ ½ | ½ ½ | ½ ½ | 1 0 | ½ ½ | ½ 1 | ½ 1 | 1 ½ | ½ 1 | 1 1 | 1 ½ | 16 | II–IV |
| 5 | Petrosian | ½ ½ | ½ ½ | ½ 0 | ½ ½ | – – | ½ ½ | 0 ½ | ½ ½ | 0 0 | ½ ½ | ½ ½ | 1 1 | ½ 1 | 1 ½ | 1 1 | 15 | V |
| 6 | Geller | 0 0 | ½ 1 | ½ 0 | ½ ½ | ½ ½ | – – | 1 1 | ½ 0 | 0 1 | ½ ½ | 0 1 | 1 ½ | ½ 1 | 0 1 | ½ ½ | 14½ | VI–VII |
| 7 | Najdorf | ½ ½ | ½ ½ | ½ ½ | ½ ½ | 1 ½ | 0 0 | – – | 1 ½ | 1 ½ | ½ 0 | ½ ½ | ½ ½ | ½ ½ | 0 ½ | 1 1 | 14½ | VI–VII |
| 8 | Kotov | ½ 1 | ½ ½ | ½ ½ | 0 1 | ½ ½ | ½ 1 | 0 ½ | – – | 1 0 | 1 ½ | 0 0 | 1 0 | 1 ½ | 0 ½ | 0 1 | 14 | VIII–IX |
| 9 | Taimanov | ½ ½ | 0 ½ | ½ ½ | ½ ½ | 1 1 | 1 0 | 0 ½ | 0 1 | – – | 1 0 | ½ ½ | ½ ½ | ½ 0 | 0 ½ | 1 1 | 14 | VIII–IX |
| 10 | Averbakh | ½ ½ | ½ ½ | 1 ½ | ½ 0 | ½ ½ | ½ ½ | ½ 1 | 0 ½ | 0 1 | – – | ½ ½ | ½ ½ | 0 ½ | 1 1 | 0 0 | 13½ | X–XI |
| 11 | Boleslavsky | ½ ½ | ½ ½ | 0 0 | ½ 0 | ½ ½ | 1 0 | ½ ½ | 1 1 | ½ ½ | ½ ½ | – – | ½ 0 | ½ ½ | ½ 1 | ½ ½ | 13½ | X–XI |
| 12 | Szabo | ½ ½ | 1 0 | 0 ½ | 0 ½ | 0 0 | 0 ½ | ½ ½ | 0 1 | ½ ½ | ½ ½ | ½ 1 | – – | 1 ½ | ½ ½ | 1 ½ | 13 | XII |
| 13 | Gligoric | 0 ½ | 0 ½ | ½ 0 | ½ 0 | ½ 0 | ½ 0 | ½ ½ | 0 ½ | ½ 1 | 1 ½ | ½ ½ | 0 ½ | – – | ½ 1 | 1 1 | 12½ | XIII |
| 14 | Euwe | 0 0 | ½ ½ | ½ ½ | 0 0 | 0 ½ | 1 0 | 1 ½ | 1 ½ | 1 ½ | 0 0 | ½ 0 | ½ ½ | ½ 0 | – – | 1 ½ | 11½ | XIV |
| 15 | Stahlberg | 0 ½ | ½ ½ | 0 0 | 0 ½ | 0 0 | ½ ½ | 0 0 | 1 0 | 0 0 | 1 1 | ½ ½ | 0 ½ | 0 0 | 0 ½ | – – | 8 | XV |

# Index of Games